AICPA Technical Questions and Answers

As of June 1, 2017

22501B-349

 Printed in Canada.

1 2 3 4 5 6 7 8 9 0 PrP 1 9 8 7

ISBN 978-1-94549-882-4

CHANGES SINCE THE LAST EDITION

Section	Title	Status
	ASSETS	
	Inventories	
2140.06	Inventory of Meat Packer	Revised
2140.08	Valuing Precious Metals Inventory Used in Manufacturing Applications	Revised
2140.09	Standard Cost for Inventory Valuation	Revised
	SPECIALIZED INDUSTRY PROBLEMS	
	Investment Companies	
6910.36	Determining Whether Loan Origination Is a Substantive Activity When Assessing Whether an Entity Is an Investment Company	Added
6910.37	Considering the Length of Time It Will Take an Investment Company to Liquidate Its Assets and Satisfy Its Liabilities When Determining If Liquidation Is Imminent	Added
6910.38	Determining If Liquidation Is Imminent When the Only Investor in an Investment Company Redeems Its Interest, and the Investment Company Anticipates Selling All of Its Investments and Settling All of Its Assets and Liabilities	Added
6910.39	Presentation of Stub Period Information by an Investment Company	Added
6910.40	Applying the Financial Statement Reporting Requirements in FASB ASC 946-205-45-1 When an Investment Company Presents a Stub Period	Added
6910.41	Separation of Final-Period Financial Statements Between Going Concern and Liquidation Periods for Certain Investment Companies That Liquidate Over a Short Period of Time	Added
6910.42	Presenting Financial Highlights Under the Liquidation Basis of Accounting for an Investment Company	Added
6910.43	Accrued Income When Using the Liquidation Basis of Accounting	Added

Section	Title	Status
	Financial Statement Reporting and Disclosure-Employee Benefit Plans	
6931.01	Computation of Net Appreciation/Depreciation in Fair Value of Investments	Deleted
6931.03	Should the Sale of Real Estate Investments Held by Employee Benefit Plans Be Treated as Discontinued Operations?	Deleted
6931.08	Types of Investments Subject to FASB ASC 962	Deleted
6931.09	Financial Statement Presentation When a Plan Invests in a Common Collective Trust Fund or in a Master Trust That Holds Fully Benefit-Responsive Investment Contracts	Deleted
6931.10	Financial Statement Disclosure Requirements When a Plan Invests in a Common Collective Trust Fund or in a Master Trust That Holds Fully Benefit-Responsive Investment Contracts	Deleted
6931.11	Fair Value Measurement Disclosures for Master Trusts	Revised
6931.12	Accounting and Disclosure Requirements for Health and Welfare Plans Related to the COBRA Premium Subsidy Included in the American Recovery and Reinvestment Act of 2009	Deleted
6931.13	Health and Welfare Plan Accounting for Reimbursements Received Under the Patient Protection and Affordable Care Act's Early Retiree Reinsurance Program When the Reimbursement Is Not Remitted to the Trust	Deleted
6931.14	Health and Welfare Plan Accounting for Reimbursements Received Under the PPACA's ERRP Described in Q&A Section 6931.13	Deleted
6931.15	Health and Welfare Plan Accounting for Reimbursements Applied for Prior to Year-End but Not Approved Until After Year-End Under the PPACA's ERRP Described in Q&A Section 6931.13	Deleted
6931.16	Accounting for the Effects of the Reimbursement on the Health and Welfare Plan's Postretirement Benefit Obligations Under the PPACA's ERRP Described in Q&A Section 6931.13	Deleted
6931.17	Health and Welfare Plan Disclosures About the PPACA's ERRP Described in Q&A Section 6931.13	Deleted

Section	Title	Status
	ERISA Reporting and Disclosures	
6932.01	Employee Benefit Security Administration Guidance on Insurance Company Demutualizations	Revised
6932.05	How Should Investments in Brokerage Accounts Be Reported in the Financial Statements and Form 5500?	Revised
	AUDIT FIELD WORK **Internal Control**	
8200.17	Obtaining an Understanding of Business Processes Relevant to Financial Reporting and Communication	Added
8200.18	Obtaining an Understanding of Internal Control Relevant to the Audit	Added
8200.19	Obtaining an Understanding of the Controls Relevant to the Audit	Added
8200.20	Control Activities That Are Always Relevant to the Audit	Added
8200.21	Control Activities That May Be Relevant to the Audit	Added
	ATTESTATION ENGAGEMENTS **Attestation Reports**	
9510.03	Reporting on New York State Medicaid Cost Reports	Revised
	Service Organization Controls Reports	
9530.22	Attestation Standards and Interpretive Guidance for Reporting on a Service Organization's Controls Relevant to User Entities and for Reporting on an Entity's Internal Control	Revised

HOW THIS PUBLICATION IS ORGANIZED

Arrangement of Material in *AICPA Technical Questions and Answers*

The material in *AICPA Technical Questions and Answers* is arranged as follows:

Financial Statement Presentation
Assets
Liabilities and Deferred Credits
Capital
Revenue and Expense
Specialized Industry Problems
Specialized Organizational Problems
Audit Field Work
Auditors' Reports
Attestation Engagements

Description of Content

The major divisions are divided into sections, each with its own section number. Each paragraph or equivalent is decimally numbered for reference purposes. With respect to Technical Questions and Answers, within each section, each question and answer is decimally numbered. For example, Q&A section 9100.02 is the second question and answer in Q&A section 9100, *Signing and Dating Reports*. When a question and answer is deleted, its number is reserved. Reserved sections are deleted permanently if no future questions and answers are expected for a particular topic.

Authoritative pronouncements are referenced in the questions and answers, whenever possible, to support the guidance provided. The following list explains the references and cites the publications containing the authoritative literature:

AR	Accounting and Review Services standard or interpretation contained in AICPA *Professional Standards*
AR-C	Clarified Accounting and Review Services standard or interpretation contained in AICPA *Professional Standards*
AT	Attestation standard or interpretation contained in AICPA *Professional Standards*
AU-C[1]	Clarified auditing standard or interpretation contained in AICPA *Professional Standards*
AUD	Statements of Position—Auditing and Attestation contained in AICPA *Professional Standards*
ET	Section from the Code of Professional Conduct of the AICPA contained in AICPA *Professional Standards*
TSP	Trust Services Principles and Criteria of ASEC contained in AICPA *Trust Services Principles and Criteria*

[1] The "AU-C" identifier was established to avoid confusion with references to existing "AU" sections, which have been superseded and deleted from *Professional Standards* as of December 2013. The AU-C identifier was scheduled to revert back to the AU identifier at the end of 2013, by which time the previous AU sections would be superseded for all engagements. However, in response to user requests, the AU-C identifier will be retained indefinitely.

Note: Generally, abbreviations are not used to reference AICPA Audit and Accounting Guides. Each guide is published separately and is also included in the AICPA Audit and Accounting Guides subscription service.

The Q&A Topical Index for Technical Information Service Questions and Answers uses the key word method to facilitate reference to the inquiries. This index is arranged alphabetically by subject, with references to section numbers.

Special Note About FASB *Accounting Standards Codification*®

FASB released the FASB *Accounting Standards Codification* (ASC) on July 1, 2009. On its effective date, FASB ASC became the source of authoritative U.S. accounting and reporting standards for nongovernmental entities, in addition to guidance issued by the SEC. FASB ASC significantly changes the way financial statement preparers, auditors, and academics perform accounting research.

FASB ASC flattens the U.S. generally accepted accounting principles (GAAP) hierarchy to two levels: one that is authoritative (in FASB ASC) and one that is nonauthoritative (not in FASB ASC). Exceptions include all rules and interpretive releases of the SEC under the authority of federal securities laws, which are sources of authoritative U.S. GAAP for SEC registrants, and certain grandfathered guidance having an effective date before March 15, 1992. The codification creates FASB ASC 105, *Generally Accepted Accounting Principles*.

Amendments to FASB ASC are now issued by FASB through Accounting Standards Updates (ASUs) and serve only to update FASB ASC. FASB does not consider the ASUs authoritative in their own right; such amendments become authoritative when they are incorporated into FASB ASC. The ASUs issued include the amendments to the codification and an appendix of FASB ASC update instructions. ASUs also provide background information about the amendments, and explain the basis for FASB's decisions. This method of updating the accounting guidance means that there will no longer be, for example, accounting standards in the form of statements, staff positions, Emerging Issues Task Force (EITF) abstracts, or AICPA Accounting Statements of Position (SOPs). ASUs are issued in the form of ASU No. 20YY-XX, in which "YY" is the last two digits of the year and "XX" is the sequential number for each update. For example, ASU No. 2011-01 is the first update in the year 2011. FASB organizes the contents of each ASU using the same section headings as those used in FASB ASC.

FASB ASC is a major restructuring of accounting and reporting standards designed to simplify user access to all authoritative U.S. GAAP by providing the authoritative literature in a topically organized structure. FASB ASC disassembled thousands of nongovernmental accounting pronouncements (including those of FASB, the EITF, and the AICPA) and reassembled them under approximately 90 topics and included all accounting standards issued by a standard setter within levels A–D of the current U.S. GAAP hierarchy. FASB ASC also includes relevant portions of authoritative content issued by the SEC, as well as selected SEC staff interpretations and administrative guidance issued by the SEC; however, FASB ASC is not the official source of SEC guidance and does not contain the entire population of SEC rules, regulations, interpretive releases, and staff guidance. Moreover, FASB ASC does not include governmental accounting standards. FASB ASC is not intended to change U.S. GAAP or any requirements of the SEC.

FASB ASC uses a topical structure in which guidance is organized into *areas*, *topics*, *subtopics*, *sections*, and *subsections*. These terms are defined as follows:

Areas. The broadest category in FASB ASC and represent a grouping of topics.

Topics. The broadest categorization of related content and correlate with the International Accounting Standards (IASs) and International Financial Reporting Standards (IFRSs).

Subtopics. Represent subsets of a topic and are generally distinguished by type or scope.

Sections. Indicate the nature of the content such as recognition, measurement, or disclosure. The sections' structure correlates with the IASs and IFRSs.

Subsections. Allow further segregation and navigation of content.

Topics, subtopics, and sections are numerically referenced. This effectively organizes the content without regard to the original standard setter or standard from which the content was derived. An example of the numerical referencing is FASB ASC 305-10-05, in which 305 is the *Cash and Cash Equivalents* topic, 10 represents the "Overall" subtopic, and 05 represents the "Overview and Background" section.

FASB ASC represents a major shift in the organization and presentation of U.S. GAAP. Users are encouraged to read the notice to constituents, which explains the scope, structure, and usage of consistent terminology in FASB ASC. This document is available on the FASB website at http://asc.fasb.org. In addition to the notice, this link contains information on the options available for users to access the codification. FASB ASC is offered by FASB at no charge in a Basic View and for an annual fee in a Professional View. FASB ASC and the notice to constituents are also offered by certain third party licensees, including the AICPA.

FASB ASC Effect on AICPA Literature Included in This Publication

As noted previously, FASB ASC disassembled and reassembled thousands of nongovernmental accounting pronouncements (including those of FASB, the EITF, and the AICPA) and codified them under approximately 90 topics. FASB ASC reduces the U.S. GAAP hierarchy to two levels: one that is authoritative (in FASB ASC) and one that is not (not in FASB ASC). Those standards you have come to memorize through FASB Statement Nos., FASB Interpretation Nos., accounting SOPs, and the like now reside in FASB ASC and have a FASB ASC reference for accountants to use. FASB ASC codified all AICPA accounting SOPs and Practice Bulletins and also sections .38–.76 of Q&A section 5100, *Revenue Recognition*.

Levels of Authority

The following tables outline the three levels of authority for auditing, attestation, and compilation and review publications, including levels of authority under Statements on Standards for Accounting and Review Services (SSARS) No. 21, *Statements on Standards for Accounting and Review Services: Clarification and Recodification* (AICPA, *Professional Standards*). Also included are links to authoritative standards and the publications that fall within each category.

Auditing Publications

AU-C section 200, *Overall Objectives of the Independent Auditor and the Conduct of an Audit in Accordance With Generally Accepted Auditing Standards* (AICPA, *Professional Standards*), sets forth the following three types of auditing publications and their authority:

- Auditing Standards: Authoritative per the "Compliance With Standards Rule" of the AICPA Code of Professional Conduct (AICPA, *Professional Standards*, ET sec. 1.310.001 and 2.310.001).
- Interpretive Publications: Issued under the authority of the Auditing Standards Board; if the auditor does not apply the auditing guidance included in an applicable interpretive publication, the auditor should be prepared to explain how he or she complied with the Statements on Auditing Standards (SASs) provisions addressed by such auditing guidance.
- Other Auditing Publications: No authoritative status; however, other auditing publications may help the auditor understand and apply the SASs.

Auditing Standards	*Interpretive Publications*	*Other Auditing Publications*
• AU-C sections (SASs) in *Professional Standards*	• Auditing interpretations (AU-C 9000 sections in *Professional Standards*) • Appendixes to the SASs • Auditing guidance in AICPA Guides • Auditing Statements of Position in *Professional Standards*	• AICPA Alerts • *Audit and Accounting Manual* • Specific sections of *AICPA Technical Questions and Answers* • Checklists and Illustrative Financial Statements • Practice Aids • White papers • Auditing articles in the *Journal of Accountancy* or other professional publications • Auditing articles in the AICPA *CPA Letter Daily* • Continuing professional education programs • Other instruction materials, textbooks, guide books, audit programs, and checklists • Auditing publications from state CPA societies, other organizations, and individuals

Attestation Publications

AT section 50, *SSAE Hierarchy* (AICPA, *Professional Standards*), sets forth the following three types of attestation publications and their authority:

- Attestation Standards: Authoritative per the "Compliance With Standards Rule" of the AICPA Code of Professional Conduct (AICPA, *Professional Standards*, ET sec. 1.310.001 and 2.310.001).
- Interpretive Publications: Issued under the authority of the Auditing Standards Board; if the practitioner does not apply the attestation guidance included in an applicable interpretive publication, the practitioner should be prepared to explain how he or she complied with the Statements on Standards for Attestation Engagements (SSAEs) provisions addressed by such attestation guidance.
- Other Attestation Publications: No authoritative status; however, other attestation publications may help the practitioner understand and apply the SSAEs.

Attestation Standards	*Interpretive Publications*	*Other Attestation Publications*
• AT sections (SSAEs) in *Professional Standards*	• Attestation interpretations (AT 9000 sections in *Professional Standards*) • Appendixes to the SSAEs • Attestation guidance in AICPA Guides • Attestation Statements of Position in *Professional Standards*	• AICPA Alerts • *Audit and Accounting Manual* • Specific sections of *AICPA Technical Questions and Answers* • Checklists and Illustrative Financial Statements • Practice Aids • White papers • Attestation articles in the *Journal of Accountancy* or other professional publications • Attestation articles in the AICPA *CPA Letter Daily* • Continuing professional education programs • Other instruction materials, textbooks, guide books, audit programs, and checklists • Attestation publications from state CPA societies, other organizations, and individuals

Compilation and Review Publications

AR section 60, *Framework for Performing and Reporting on Compilation and Review Engagements* (AICPA, *Professional Standards*), sets forth the following three types of compilation and review publications and their authority:

- Compilation and Review Standards: Authoritative per the "Compliance With Standards Rule" of the AICPA Code of Professional Conduct (AICPA, *Professional Standards*, ET sec. 1.310.001 and 2.310.001).
- Interpretive Publications: Issued under the authority of the Accounting and Review Services Committee; if the accountant does not apply the compilation and review guidance included in an applicable interpretive publication, the accountant should be prepared to explain how he or she complied with the Statements on Standards for Accounting and Review Services (SSARSs) provisions addressed by such compilation and review guidance.
- Other Compilation and Review Publications: No authoritative status; however, other compilation and review publications may help the accountant understand and apply the SSARSs.

Compilation and Review Standards	*Interpretive Publications*	*Other Compilation and Review Publications*
• AR sections (SSARSs) in *Professional Standards*	• Compilation and Review interpretations (AR 9000 sections in *Professional Standards*) • Appendixes to the SSARSs • Compilation and Review guidance in AICPA Guides • Compilation and Review guidance in Statements of Position in *Professional Standards*	• AICPA Alert *Developments in Review, Compilation, and Financial Statement Preparation Engagements* • *Audit and Accounting Manual* • Specific sections of *AICPA Technical Questions and Answers* • Checklists and Illustrative Financial Statements • Practice Aids • White papers • Compilation and Review articles in the *Journal of Accountancy* or other professional publications • Compilation and Review articles in the AICPA *CPA Letter Daily* • Continuing professional education programs • Other instruction materials, textbooks, guide books, audit programs, and checklists • Compilation and Review publications from state CPA societies, other organizations, and individuals

Review, Compilation, and Preparation Publications—For Engagements Conducted Under SSARS No. 21

SSARS No. 21, *Statements on Standards for Accounting and Review Services: Clarification and Recodification* (AICPA, *Professional Standards*), sets forth the following three types of review, compilation, and preparation publications and their authority:

- Compilation and Review Standards: Authoritative per the "Compliance With Standards Rule" of the AICPA Code of Professional Conduct (AICPA, *Professional Standards*, ET sec. 1.310.001 and 2.310.001).
- Interpretive Publications: Issued under the authority of the Accounting and Review Services Committee; if the accountant does not apply the compilation and review guidance included in an applicable interpretive publication, the accountant should be prepared to explain how he or she complied with the Statements on Standards for Accounting and Review Services (SSARSs) provisions addressed by such compilation and review guidance.
- Other Review, Compilation, and Preparation Publications: No authoritative status; however, other compilation and review publications may help the accountant understand and apply the SSARSs.

Review, Compilation, and Preparation Standards	*Interpretive Publications*	*Other Review, Compilation, and Preparation Publications*
• AR-C sections (SSARSs) in *Professional Standards*	• Review, Compilation, and Preparation interpretations, when issued (AR-C 9000 sections in *Professional Standards*) • Review, Compilation, and Preparation guidance in AICPA Guides • Review, Compilation, and Preparation guidance in Statements of Position in *Professional Standards*	• AICPA Alert *Developments in Review, Compilation, and Financial Statement Preparation Engagements* • *Audit and Accounting Manual* • Specific sections of *AICPA Technical Questions and Answers* • Checklists and Illustrative Financial Statements • Practice Aids • White papers • Review, Compilation, and Preparation articles in the *Journal of Accountancy* or other professional publications • Review, Compilation, and Preparation articles in the AICPA *CPA Letter Daily* • Continuing professional education programs • Other instruction materials, textbooks, guide books, audit programs, and checklists • Review, Compilation, and Preparation publications from state CPA societies, other organizations, and individuals

TABLE OF CONTENTS

AICPA Technical Questions and Answers (Nonauthoritative)

Notice to Readers

The questions and answers in *AICPA Technical Questions and Answers* are not sources of established authoritative accounting principles as described in FASB *Accounting Standards Codification* and GASB Statement No. 55, *The Hierarchy of Generally Accepted Accounting Principles for State and Local Governments*, the authoritative sources of generally accepted accounting principles for nongovernmental and governmental entities, respectively. This material is based on selected practice matters identified by the staff of the AICPA's Technical Hotline and various other bodies within the AICPA and has not been approved, disapproved, or otherwise acted upon by any senior committee of the AICPA.

This publication is designed to provide accurate information in regard to the subject matter covered. It is sold with the understanding that the publisher is not engaged in rendering legal, accounting, or other professional service.

AICPA TECHNICAL HOTLINE
The AICPA Technical Hotline answers inquiries about specific audit or accounting problems.
Call Toll Free:
877.242.7212
This service is free to AICPA members.

Q&A Section 1000

FINANCIAL STATEMENT PRESENTATION

TABLE OF CONTENTS

Section

Section

Q&A Section 1100

Statement of Financial Position

[.01] Reserved

[.02] Reserved

.03 Unclassified Balance Sheet for Venture With Limited Life

Inquiry—A corporation has recently been organized with the sole purpose of constructing a shopping center which will take several years to complete, after which the company will be liquidated. The company uses the completed contract method to recognize income, and will have only one operating cycle. Would an unclassified balance sheet be appropriate?

Reply—An unclassified balance sheet would be more appropriate than a classified one in this situation. The sole purpose of the corporation is to construct the shopping center, and the appropriate time frame for reporting purposes, by definition, becomes the time required to complete the project, rather than an arbitrary one-year period.

[.04] Reserved

[.05] Reserved

[.06] Reserved

.07 Comparative Statement Disclosures

Inquiry—When financial statements of the prior period are presented on a comparative basis with financial statements of the current period, should the notes to the comparative financial statements disclose details for the prior year?

Reply—Generally, in practice notes to comparative financial statements are also comparative if they present details of items on the financial statements or are otherwise pertinent. For example, details of notes payable outstanding at the end of each period are normally disclosed, but the future maturities disclosure need only be disclosed for the current year.

[Amended, June 1995.]

.08 Classification of Outstanding Checks

Inquiry—Should the amount of checks that have been issued and are out of the control of the payor but which have not cleared the bank by the balance sheet date be reported as a reduction of cash?

Reply—Yes. A check is out of the payor's control after it has been mailed or delivered to the payee. The balance sheet caption "cash" should represent an amount that is within the control of the reporting enterprise, namely, the amount of cash in banks plus the amount of cash and checks on hand and deposits in transit minus the amount of outstanding checks. Cash is misrepresented if outstanding checks are classified as liabilities rather than a reduction of cash.

[.09] Reserved

[.10] Reserved

[.11] Reserved

[.12] Reserved

[.13] Reserved

.14 Classification of Convertible Debt

Inquiry—A company has debt that is convertible into common stock of the company at the option of the company. The debt by its terms is considered long-term debt in the classified balance sheet. The company intends to call the debt and issue the common stock within one year of the balance sheet date. Should this debt be classified as a current liability?

Reply—No. The expected call of the debt securities will not consume current assets or increase current liabilities, and accordingly should continue to be classified as a long-term obligation.

The general principle underlying the classification of debt in a debtor's principal balance sheet should be based on facts existing at the date of the balance sheet rather than on expectations. According to Financial Accounting Standards Board (FASB) *Accounting Standards Codification* (ASC) glossary, the term *current liabilities* "is used principally to designate obligations whose liquidation is reasonably expected to require the use of existing resources properly classifiable as current assets, or the creation of other current liabilities."

[Revised, June 2009, to reflect conforming changes necessary due to the issuance of FASB ASC.]

.15 Liquidity Restrictions

Inquiry—Entities may invest in assets such as money market funds or other short term investment vehicles from which they generally may withdraw funds at any time without prior notice or penalty, but for which the fund (or its trustee) may restrict the ability of an entity to withdraw its balance in the fund or other short term investment vehicle. In some circumstances, with little or no notice, the fund (or its trustee) may impose such withdrawal restrictions. For example, the fund (or its trustee), in accordance with the terms of the fund, may, with little or no notice, stipulate that up to 20 percent of the fund balance can be withdrawn immediately, an additional 30 percent can be withdrawn in 6 months, and the remaining balance can be withdrawn in 2 years.

What are the potential accounting and auditing implications of such an event for a nongovernmental entity (the event being restrictions on the ability of an entity to withdraw its balance in the money market fund or other short term investment vehicle)?

Reply—The following are examples of potential accounting and auditing issues that may be relevant if such an event exists. Each situation is different and should be evaluated based on its specific facts and circumstances:

Balance Sheet Classification. Such withdrawal restrictions should be considered in determining whether such assets meet the definition of *cash equivalents*. (This technical question and answer does not address whether such assets met the definition of *cash equivalents* prior to the imposition of such withdrawal restrictions.)

Financial Accounting Standards Board (FASB) *Accounting Standards Codification* (ASC) glossary provides a definition of *cash equivalents* for the purposes of applying FASB ASC 230, *Statement of Cash Flows*.

Such withdrawal restrictions should be considered in determining whether such assets meet the definition of *current assets*.

FASB ASC glossary defines *current assets* for balance sheet classification purposes.

For entities that do not prepare a classified balance sheet, such withdrawal restrictions should be considered in determining the sequencing of assets on the balance sheet or disclosures in the notes to financial statements providing relevant information about the liquidity or maturity of assets.

Disclosures. The entity may be required to provide financial statement disclosures about such events. For example, such events may create or lead to risks and uncertainties pertaining to certain significant estimates, such as measurement, liquidity, and violation of debt covenants, and vulnerability from concentrations of investments in volatile markets. Entities should consider whether they should make disclosures in their financial statements (beyond those required or generally made in financial statements) about the risks and uncertainties resulting from such events and existing as of the date of the financial statements. In addition, auditors should consider whether such disclosures include forward-looking statements that are not required by generally accepted accounting principles and therefore may not be audited.

FASB ASC 275, *Risks and Uncertainties*, provides guidance pertaining to disclosures about risks and uncertainties.

Debt Covenants. Such events may result in balance sheet classifications (balance sheet classifications are previously discussed) and other events that may trigger violations of debt covenants. If a covenant violation occurs, issuers of debt should consider whether that covenant violation triggers classification of the debt liability as current (or otherwise affects reported information about liquidity) or cross covenant violations in other arrangements.

FASB ASC glossary defines *current assets* and *current liabilities* for balance sheet classification purposes. FASB ASC 470-10-45-11 clarifies how the debtor should present obligations that are callable by the creditor in a balance sheet in which liabilities are classified as current or noncurrent.

Paragraphs 12A–12B of FASB ASC 470-10-45 provide guidance for the classification of short-term obligations that are expected to be refinanced on a long-term basis.

FASB ASC 470-10-45 and FASB ASC 470-10-55 address the classification of obligations at the balance sheet date that are not callable at the balance sheet date, but that become callable by violation of a debt agreement provision after the balance sheet date but before the financial statements are issued.

FASB ASC 470-10-45-2 and FASB ASC 470-10-50-3 provide guidance pertaining to balance sheet classification in circumstances in which debt agreements include subjective acceleration clauses.

Events Occurring Subsequent to the Balance Sheet Date. Events occurring subsequent to the balance sheet date, but prior to the issuance of the financial statements, such as significant changes in fair value or changes in liquidity leading to violation of debt covenants, may need to be reflected in the financial statements (either through adjustment to or disclosure in the financial statements).

AU-C section 560, *Subsequent Events and Subsequently Discovered Facts* (AICPA, *Professional Standards*), addresses the auditor's responsibilities relating to subsequent events and subsequently discovered facts in an audit of financial statements.

Going Concern. Certain events (some interrelated) could call into question the entity's ability to continue as a going concern. For example:

- The inability to withdraw funds can pose significant challenges to the entity's liquidity.
- As discussed earlier, balance sheet reclassifications or other events may trigger violations of debt covenants.

AU-C section 570A, *The Auditor's Consideration of an Entity's Ability to Continue as a Going Concern* (AICPA, *Professional Standards*), addresses the auditor's responsibilities in an audit of financial statements with respect to evaluating whether there is substantial doubt about the entity's ability to continue as a going concern.

AU-C section 260, *The Auditor's Communication With Those Charged With Governance* (AICPA, *Professional Standards*), addresses the auditor's responsibility to communicate with those charged with governance.

Paragraph .06 of AU-C section 706, *Emphasis-of-Matter Paragraphs and Other-Matter Paragraphs in the Independent Auditor's Report* (AICPA, *Professional Standards*), requires that if the auditor considers it necessary to draw users' attention to a matter appropriately presented or disclosed in the financial statements that, in the auditor's professional judgment, is of such importance that it is fundamental to users' understanding of the financial statements, the auditor should include an emphasis-of-matter paragraph in the auditor's report, provided that the auditor has obtained sufficient appropriate audit evidence that the matter is not materially misstated in the financial statements. For example, the auditor may wish to refer, in the auditor's report, to financial statement disclosures about restrictions on liquidity pertaining to such events.

[Issue Date: October 2008; Revised, June 2009, to reflect conforming changes necessary due to the issuance of FASB ASC; Revised, December 2012, to reflect conforming changes necessary due to the issuance of SAS Nos. 122–126.]

Q&A Section 1200
Income Statement

.01 Disclosure of Revenues of an Agent

Inquiry—Company A is in the business of arranging sales of used cars for which service it receives a commission based on an established fee schedule. Company A receives title to the cars sold but simultaneously transfers title to the car buyer. Company A warrants main engine components for thirty days after date of sale.

The following presentations of revenue in the income statement are being considered:

Commission Earned	$20,000
or	
Sales	$300,000
Cost of Sales	(280,000)
Gross Profit (or Net Commissions)	$20,000

What is the proper presentation of revenue?

Reply—Since Company A is operating as a broker, Company A should report Commissions Earned rather than Sales. However, Company A could disclose above the Commissions Earned figure, without showing a deduction, the amount of sale, as follows:

Sales Arranged	$300,000
Commissions Earned	$20,000
Expenses, etc.	XXX

Company A should also make proper provision for the cost of warranties.

[.02] Reserved

[.03] Reserved

.04 Statement Title When There Is a Net Loss

Inquiry—What title is suggested for the "Statement of Income" when a "net loss" exists in one or more years?

Reply—Companies included in the annual survey entitled *Accounting Trends & Techniques* ("Trends") file with the Securities and Exchange Commission. Accordingly, their annual reports include a three year statement of income. If a current year net loss is shown in the income statement, the "Trends" companies usually describe the statement of income as the "Statement of Operations." They occasionally use the title "Statement of Income (Loss)" and very rarely use the title "Statement of Loss."

Some companies always use "Statement of Operations" since the heading will be the same whether there is a "net loss" or "net income."

.05 Presentation of Reimbursed Payroll Expense

Inquiry—One company of a controlled group, in addition to its own operations, acts as a "paymaster" for the entire group. This company records the entire payroll of all members in the group on its general ledger to facilitate reconciliation with state and federal payroll tax returns. Each member of the group reimburses the "paymaster" for its share of payroll and payroll taxes and records management fee expense while the paymaster records it as management fee income.

Should the reimbursement be classified as other income in the separate income statement of the "paymaster" company?

Reply—No. The reimbursement should be allocated as a reduction of payroll and payroll tax expense because this approach would more accurately present the "paymaster" company's expenses for its own operations.

.06 Note to Q&A Section 1200.07 to 1200.16—Accounting by Noninsurance Enterprises for Property and Casualty Insurance Arrangements That Limit Insurance Risk

Insurance enables a company (the insured) to transfer insurance risk to an insurer for a specified premium. Insurance may be purchased for a number of economic reasons generally with the underlying goal of transferring insurance risk, including property damage, injury to others, and business interruption.

The following series of questions and answers (Sections 1200.07–.16) focus on certain aspects of finite insurance products that are utilized by noninsurance enterprises. Due to the diverse nature of contracts in the marketplace, the guidance in these questions and answers is designed to assist practitioners in identifying the relevant literature to consider in addressing their specific facts and circumstances. The TPAs contain many excerpts of applicable guidance, but readers should be familiar with all the guidance contained in that literature not only the specific paragraphs listed.

GAAP guidance for an insurance enterprise's purchase of reinsurance is more extensive than guidance on accounting by noninsurance enterprises for insurance contracts. The accounting guidance for reinsurance addresses transactions between an insurer (the contract holder) and a reinsurer (the issuer of the contract). Q&A sections 1200.07–.16 address property and casualty insurance contracts between a policyholder and an insurance enterprise, which is similar to the relationship between an insurer and a reinsurer.

.07 Finite Insurance

Inquiry—What are "finite" insurance transactions?

Reply—Finite insurance contracts are contracts that transfer a clearly defined and restricted amount of insurance risk from the policyholder to the insurance company, and the policyholder retains a substantial portion of the related risks under most scenarios. Nevertheless, under certain finite contracts there may be a reasonable possibility that the insurance company will incur a loss on the contract.

.08 Insurance Risk Limiting Features

Inquiry—What types of insurance risk limiting features do finite insurance contracts normally contain?

Reply—Contractual features that serve to limit insurance risk transfer are found in both traditional and finite insurance contracts; however, the degree to which these features limit risk is relatively higher in finite insurance. All contractual provisions that limit risk transfer need to be considered when reviewing insurance contracts. Common features that may limit the transfer of insurance risk include:

- *Sliding scale fees and profit sharing formulae*. These features adjust cash flows between the policyholder and insurance company based on loss experience (for example, increasing payments from the insured enterprise as losses increase and decreasing payments as losses decrease, subject to maximum and minimum limits).
- *Experience refunds*. These arrangements allow the policyholder to share in the favorable experience of the underlying contracts by reference to an "experience account" that typically tracks premiums paid, less fees, less losses incurred, plus interest. Experience provisions also can require the policyholder to share in unfavorable experience by requiring additional payments to the insurer in the event that the experience account is negative.
- *Caps*. Caps are used to limit the insurer's aggregate exposure by imposing a dollar limit, or a limit expressed as a percentage of premiums paid, on the amount of claims to be paid by the insurer. For example, the insurer will not be responsible for losses beyond 150 percent of the premiums paid. While commercial insurance policies usually have limits on the amount of coverage provided, there may be significant risk mitigation for the insurer if the premium paid is a substantial percentage of the maximum coverage provided.
- *Loss Corridors*. This feature, which may exist in various forms, serves to eliminate or limit the risk of loss for a specified percentage or dollar amount of claims within the contract coverage. For example, in a contract providing coverage for a policyholder's first $3,000,000 of losses, the insurer will pay the first million and last million of losses but will exclude the corridor from $1,000,000 to $2,000,000.
- *Dual-triggers*. This feature requires the occurrence of both an insurable event and changes in a separate pre-identified variable to trigger payment of a benefit/claim. An example is a policy entered into by a trucking company that insures costs associated with rerouting trucks over a certain time period if snowfall exceeds a specified level during that time period.
- *Retrospectively-Rated Premiums*. Such premiums are determined after the inception of the policy based on the loss experience under the policy.
- *Reinstatement Premiums*. To the extent the coverage provided by a contract is absorbed by losses incurred, the contract provides for the policyholder to reinstate coverage for the balance of the contract period for a stated additional premium. To the extent reinstatement is required rather than optional, the additional premium may mitigate risk to the insurer.
- *Termination Provisions*. These provisions can be structured to reduce the risk of the insurer, for example, by allowing for termination by the insurer at a discounted amount under certain circumstances.

- *Payment Schedules*. Features that delay timely reimbursement of losses by the insurer prevent the transfer of insurance risk.

There may be other features and provisions, in addition to the list of common insurance risk transfer limiting features above, that exist in a contract. Determining the appropriate accounting requires a full understanding of all of the features and provisions of the contract.

.09 Transfer of Insurance Risk

Inquiry—Why is transfer of insurance risk important under GAAP?

Reply—If a contract does not provide for the indemnification of the insured by the insurer, it is accounted for as a deposit (financing) rather than as insurance as noted in Financial Accounting Standards Board (FASB) *Accounting Standards Codification* (ASC) 720-20-25-1.

[Revised, June 2009, to reflect conforming changes necessary due to the issuance of FASB ASC.]

.10 Accounting Guidance for Transfer of Insurance Risk

Inquiry—What GAAP accounting literature provides guidance related to transfer of insurance risk?

Reply—The assessment of transfer of insurance risk requires significant judgment and a complete understanding of the insurance contract and other related contracts between the parties. The greater the number and/or degree of insurance risk limiting features that exist in a contract, the more difficult it becomes to assess whether or not the insurance risk transferred is sufficient to permit the contract to be accounted for as insurance rather than as a deposit.

Financial Accounting Standards Board (FASB) *Accounting Standards Codification* (ASC) 720-20-25-1 provides the following guidance on insurance contracts that do not provide for indemnification of the insured by the insurer against loss or liability:

> To the extent that an insurance contract or reinsurance contract does not, despite its form, provide for indemnification of the insured or the ceding entity by the insurer or reinsurer against loss or liability, the premium paid less the amount of the premium to be retained by the insurer or reinsurer shall be accounted for as a deposit by the insured or the ceding entity. Those contracts may be structured in various ways, but if, regardless of form, their substance is that all or part of the premium paid by the insured or the ceding entity is a deposit, it shall be accounted for as such.

FASB ASC 944, *Financial Services—Insurance*, establishes the conditions required for a contract between an insurer and a reinsurer to be accounted for as reinsurance and prescribes accounting and reporting standards for those contracts. FASB ASC 944-20-15-41 notes:

> Unless the condition in paragraph 944-20-15-53 is met, indemnification of the ceding entity against loss or liability relating to insurance risk in reinsurance of short-duration contracts exists under paragraph 944-20-15-37(a) only if both of the following conditions are met:
>
> *a.* Significant insurance risk. The reinsurer assumes significant insurance risk under the reinsured portions of the underlying insurance

contracts. Implicit in this condition is the requirement that both the amount and timing of the reinsurer's payments depend on and directly vary with the amount and timing of claims settled under the reinsured contracts.

b. Significant loss. It is reasonably possible that the reinsurer may realize a significant loss from the transaction.

FASB ASC 944 looks to the present value of all cash flows between the parties, however characterized, under reasonably possible outcomes in determining whether it is reasonably possible that the reinsurer may realize a significant loss from the contract.

FASB ASC 720-20-25-2 suggests that noninsurance entities look to the risk transfer guidance in FASB ASC 944 and states, in part:

> Entities may find the conditions in Section 944-20-15 useful in assessing whether an insurance contract transfers risk.

FASB ASC 944-20-25-1 states that a multiple-year retrospectively rated insurance contract must indemnify the insured as required by FASB ASC 944-20-15-36 to be accounted for as insurance. FASB ASC 944-20 also indicates that there may be certain situations in which the guarantee accounting in accordance with FASB ASC 460, *Guarantees*, is applicable.

FASB ASC 815, *Derivatives and Hedging*, addresses scenarios where there are dual-triggers and includes a number of relevant examples.

[Revised, June 2009, to reflect conforming changes necessary due to the issuance of FASB ASC.]

.11 Differences Between Retroactive and Prospective Insurance

Inquiry—What are the differences between retroactive and prospective insurance?

Reply—Financial Accounting Standards Board (FASB) *Accounting Standards Codification* (ASC) 944-605-05-7 states that for property and casualty insurance: The distinction between prospective and retroactive reinsurance contracts is based on whether the contract reinsures future or past insured events covered by the underlying contracts.

[Revised, June 2009, to reflect conforming changes necessary due to the issuance of FASB ASC.]

.12 Accounting for Prospective Insurance

Inquiry—How does a noninsurance enterprise account for prospective insurance contracts that qualify for insurance accounting?

Reply—A noninsurance enterprise amortizes the premiums over the contract period in proportion to the amount of insurance protection provided. If an insured loss occurs, and if it is probable that the policy will provide reimbursement for the loss and the amount of the loss can be reasonably estimated, the noninsurance enterprise records a receivable from the insurance enterprise and a recovery of the incurred loss in the income statement. If it is not probable[1] that the policy will provide reimbursement, then the receivable and recovery are not recorded.

---

[1] According to the Financial Accounting Standards Board (FASB) *Accounting Standards Codification* (ASC) glossary, *probable* means that the future event or events are likely to occur.

[Revised, June 2009, to reflect conforming changes necessary due to the issuance of FASB ASC.]

.13 Accounting for Retroactive Insurance

Inquiry—How does a noninsurance enterprise account for retroactive insurance contracts that qualify for insurance accounting?

Reply—Paragraphs 3–4 of Financial Accounting Standards Board (FASB) *Accounting Standards Codification* (ASC) 720-20-25 state:

> Notwithstanding that Topic 944 applies only to insurance entities, purchased retroactive insurance contracts that indemnify the insured shall be accounted for in a manner similar to the manner in which retroactive reinsurance contracts are accounted for under Subtopic 944-605. The guidance in that Subtopic shall be applied, as appropriate, based on the facts and circumstances of the particular transaction. That is, amounts paid for retroactive insurance shall be expensed immediately. Simultaneously, a receivable shall be established for the expected recoveries related to the underlying insured event.
>
> If the receivable established exceeds the amounts paid for the insurance, the resulting gain is deferred. Immediate gain recognition and liability derecognition are not appropriate because the liability has not been extinguished (the entity is not entirely relieved of its obligation). Additionally, the liability incurred as a result of a past insurable event and amounts receivable under the insurance contract do not meet the criteria for offsetting under paragraph 210-20-45-1.

FASB ASC 720-20-35-2 further states:

> If the amounts and timing of the insurance recoveries can be reasonably estimated, the deferred gain shall be amortized using the interest method over the estimated period over which the entity expects to recover substantially all amounts due under the terms of the insurance contract. If the amounts and timing of the insurance recoveries cannot be reasonably estimated, then the proportion of actual recoveries to total estimated recoveries shall be used to determine the amount of the amortization.

Paragraphs 22–23 of FASB ASC 944-605-25 state:

> Amounts paid for retroactive reinsurance of short-duration contracts that meets the conditions for reinsurance accounting shall be reported as reinsurance receivables to the extent those amounts do not exceed the recorded liabilities relating to the underlying reinsured contracts. If the recorded liabilities exceed the amounts paid, reinsurance receivables shall be increased to reflect the difference and the resulting gain deferred.
>
> If the amounts paid for retroactive reinsurance for short-duration contracts exceed the re-corded liabilities relating to the underlying reinsured short-duration contracts, the ceding entity shall increase the related liabilities or reduce the reinsurance receivable or both at the time the reinsurance

contract is entered into, so that the excess is charged to earnings.

FASB ASC 944-605-35-9 further states:

> Any gain deferred under paragraph 944-605-25-22 shall be amortized over the estimated remaining settlement period. If the amounts and timing of the reinsurance recoveries can be reasonably estimated, the deferred gain shall be amortized using the effective interest rate inherent in the amount paid to the reinsurer and the estimated timing and amounts of recoveries from the reinsurer (the interest method). Otherwise, the proportion of actual recoveries (the recovery method) shall determine the amount of amortization.

[Revised, June 2009, to reflect conforming changes necessary due to the issuance of FASB ASC.]

.14 Accounting for Multiple-Year Retrospectively Rated Insurance

Inquiry—How does a noninsurance enterprise account for a multiple-year retrospectively rated insurance contract?

Reply—As noted in Financial Accounting Standards Board (FASB) *Accounting Standards Codification* (ASC) 720-20-05-10, multiple-year retrospectively rated contracts:

> include a retrospective rating provision that provides for any of the following based on contract experience:
>
> a. Changes in the amount or timing of future contractual cash flows, including premium adjustments, settlement adjustments, or refunds to the noninsurance entity
>
> b. Changes in the contract's future coverage.

FASB ASC 720-20-05-9 also states, in part:

> A critical feature of these contracts is that part or all of the retrospective rating provision is obligatory such that the retrospective rating provision creates for each party to the contract future rights and obligations as a result of past events.

FASB ASC 944-20-25-2 also discusses the accounting for retrospective adjustments and states:

> For a multiple-year retrospectively rated insurance contract accounted for as insurance, the insurer shall both:
>
> a. Recognize an asset to the extent that the insured has an obligation to pay cash (or other consideration) to the insurer that would not have been required absent experience under the contract.
>
> b. Recognize a liability to the extent that any cash (or other consideration) would be payable by the insurer to the insured based on experience to date under the contract.

Paragraphs 3–4 of FASB ASC 944-20-35 further state:

> The amount recognized under paragraph 944-20-25-4 in the current period shall be computed, using a with-and-without method, as the difference between the ceding entity's total contract costs before and after the experience under the contract as of the reporting date, including costs such as premium adjustments, settlement adjustments, and impairments of coverage.
>
> The amount of premium expense related to impairments of coverage shall be measured in relation to the original contract terms. Future experience under the contract (that is, future losses and future premiums that would be paid regardless of past experience) shall not be considered in measuring the amount to be recognized.

FASB ASC 944-20-25-4 also further states:

> For contracts that meet all of the conditions described in paragraph 944-20-15-55:
>
> *a.* The ceding entity shall recognize a liability and the assuming entity shall recognize an asset to the extent that the ceding entity has an obligation to pay cash (or other consideration) to the reinsurer that would not have been required absent experience under the contract (for example, payments that would not have been required if losses had not been experienced).
>
> *b.* The ceding entity shall recognize an asset and the assuming entity shall recognize a liability to the extent that any cash (or other consideration) would be payable from the assuming entity to the ceding entity based on experience to date under the contract.

[Revised, June 2009, to reflect conforming changes necessary due to the issuance of FASB ASC.]

.15 Deposit Accounting

Inquiry—What is deposit accounting?

Reply—Deposit accounting essentially treats the contract as a financing transaction similar to a loan taking into account the time value of money. Financial Accounting Standards Board (FASB) *Accounting Standards Codification* (ASC) 340, *Other Assets and Deferred Costs*, provides guidance on how to account for insurance and reinsurance contracts that do not transfer insurance risk.

[Revised, June 2009, to reflect conforming changes necessary due to the issuance of FASB ASC.]

.16 Identifying Accounting Model for Insurance Transactions

The accompanying chart depicts the basic decision process in identifying the appropriate accounting model for insurance transactions.

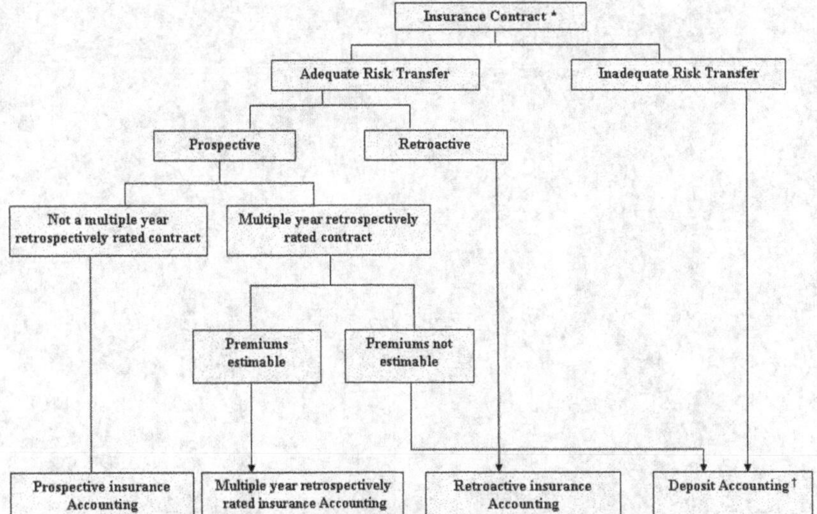

* The insurance model discussed in this series of technical practice aids is based on property and casualty and other short-duration contracts, as defined in Financial Accounting Standards Board (FASB) *Accounting Standards Codification* (ASC) 944, *Financial Services—Insurance*.

† FASB ASC 944-20 should also be considered in determining the accounting for multiple-year retrospectively rated contracts that do not transfer risk.

[Revised, June 2009, to reflect conforming changes necessary due to the issuance of FASB ASC.]

Q&A Section 1300
Statement of Cash Flows

[.01] Reserved

[.02] Reserved

.03 Comparative Statements of Cash Flows

Inquiry—Is it necessary to provide a statement of cash flows for both the current and prior periods if comparative income statements are presented, but only the current balance sheet is presented?

Reply—Financial Accounting Standards Board (FASB) *Accounting Standards Codification* (ASC) 230-10-15-3 states:

> A business entity or not-for-profit entity that provides a set of financial statements that reports both financial position and results of operations shall also provide a statement of cash flows for each period for which results of operations are provided.

Therefore, if a balance sheet is presented, a statement of cash flows should be presented for both current and prior periods if income statements are presented for such periods.

[Revised, June 2009, to reflect conforming changes necessary due to the issuance of FASB ASC.]

[.04] Reserved

.05 Statement of Cash Flows for Annual Report With Balance Sheet Only

Inquiry—When only a statement of financial position is presented, is it necessary that the auditor's opinion be qualified relative to the omission of the statement of cash flows?

Reply—Financial Accounting Standards Board (FASB) *Accounting Standards Codification* (ASC) 230-10-15-3 states:

> A business entity or not-for-profit entity that provides a set of financial statements that reports both financial position and results of operations shall also provide a statement of cash flows for each period for which results of operations are provided.

Therefore, when a statement of financial position is not accompanied by a statement of operations, there is no need for presentation of a statement of cash flows, and no comment on the absence of such a statement is necessary.

[Revised, June 2009, to reflect conforming changes necessary due to the issuance of FASB ASC.]

[.06] Reserved

[.07] Reserved

[.08] Reserved

[.09] Reserved

.10 Special Purpose Frameworks

Inquiry—When an entity prepares its financial statements in accordance with a special purpose framework, is a statement of cash flows required?

Reply—Financial Accounting Standards Board (FASB) *Accounting Standards Codification* (ASC) 230-10-15-3 states:

> A business entity or not-for-profit entity that provides a set of financial statements that reports both financial position and results of operations shall also provide a statement of cash flows for each period for which results of operations are provided.

Paragraph .A17 of AU-C section 800, *Special Considerations—Audits of Financial Statements Prepared in Accordance With Special Purpose Frameworks* (AICPA, *Professional Standards*), states, in part:

> Terms such as *balance sheet*, *statement of financial position*, *statement of income*, *statement of operations*, and *statement of cash flows*, or similar unmodified titles, are generally understood to be applicable only to financial statements that are intended to present financial position, results of operations, or cash flows in accordance with GAAP.

Paragraph .A34 of AU-C section 800 states, in part:

> Special purpose financial statements may not include a statement of cash flows. If a presentation of cash receipts and disbursements is presented in a format similar to a statement of cash flows or if the entity chooses to present such a statement, the statement would either conform to the requirements for a GAAP presentation or communicate their substance. As an example, the statement of cash flows might disclose noncash acquisitions through captions on its face.

[Revised, June 2009, to reflect conforming changes necessary due to the issuance of FASB ASC; Revised, December 2012, to reflect conforming changes necessary due to the issuance of SAS Nos. 122–126.]

.11 The Effect of an Error Correction on the Statement of Cash Flows When Single Period Statements Are Presented

Inquiry—How would an error correction be presented in the statement of cash flows if single period statements are presented?

Reply—Financial Accounting Standards Board (FASB) *Accounting Standards Codification* (ASC) 250-10-45-24 states that "error corrections shall, in single period statements, be reflected as adjustments of the opening balance of retained earnings." A corresponding error correction will normally result in a change in the beginning balance of an asset or liability account. FASB ASC 230-10-50-3 states, in part:

> Information about all investing and financing activities of an entity during a period that affect recognized assets or liabilities but that do not result in cash receipts or cash payments in the period shall be disclosed.

Therefore, the difference in an account between the current balance sheet and that same account in the restated beginning balance sheet (even if not presented) that resulted from the error correction, should be reflected in the related footnote disclosures and clearly referenced to the statement of cash flows.

[Revised, June 2009, to reflect conforming changes necessary due to the issuance of FASB ASC.]

[.12] Reserved

[.13] Reserved

[.14] Reserved

.15 Presentation of Cash Overdraft on Statement of Cash Flows

Inquiry—A company has accounts at three separate banks. One of the bank accounts is in an overdraft position at year end, thus it is shown as a liability on the balance sheet. Does the company show as cash and cash equivalents on the statement of cash flows only the two accounts with the positive balances or does it show the net cash (the three accounts combined) at the end of the year as its cash and cash equivalents?

Reply—The amount that will be shown on the statement of cash flows is the two accounts with the positive balances. Per Financial Accounting Standards Board (FASB) *Accounting Standards Codification* (ASC) ASC 230-10-45-4, "The total amounts of cash and cash equivalents at the beginning and end of the period shall be the same amounts as similarly titled line items or subtotals shown in the statements of financial position . . ." The net change in overdrafts during the period is a financing activity.

[Revised, June 2009, to reflect conforming changes necessary due to the issuance of FASB ASC.]

.16 Purchase of Inventory Through Direct Financing

Inquiry—An automobile dealer purchases its inventory from a manufacturer which finances purchases through a finance subsidiary. The finance subsidiary pays the manufacturer directly on behalf of the dealer. Cash is not disbursed by the dealer until the automobiles are sold.

Under the provisions of Financial Accounting Standards Board (FASB) *Accounting Standards Codification* (ASC) 230, *Statement of Cash Flows*, how should the purchases of inventory be reported by the automobile dealer in the statement of cash flows?

Reply—A statement of cash flows reports an enterprise's cash receipts and cash payments during the period. Transactions that do not involve cash receipts and cash payments should be excluded from the statement of cash flows. Noncash investing and financing transactions should be reported in separate disclosures.

The purchases of inventory described above do not involve a cash flow by the automobile dealer until the automobiles are sold and the dealer pays the finance subsidiary under the financing arrangement. Therefore, only the cash outflows from payments to the finance subsidiary should be included in the body of the statement of cash flows.

Payments made to the finance subsidiary of the manufacturer should be classified as operating cash outflows in accordance with FASB ASC 230-10-45-17, which defines operating cash outflows to include principal payments on accounts and notes payable to suppliers for goods acquired for resale.

[Revised, June 2009, to reflect conforming changes necessary due to the issuance of FASB ASC.]

.17 Omission of Reconciliation of Net Income to Cash Flow From Operations

Inquiry—When an accountant is requested to compile financial statements that omit substantially all of the disclosures required by accounting principles generally accepted in the United States of America in accordance with paragraph .20 of AR section 80, *Compilation of Financial Statements* (AICPA, *Professional Standards*), would the omission of the schedule, "reconciliation of net income to net cash flow from operating activities" required by the direct method of reporting cash flows under FASB ASC 230 be considered a departure from accounting principles generally accepted in the United States of America?

Reply—Yes. Under the direct method of reporting net cash flows from operating activities, the separate schedule reconciling net income to net cash flow from operating activities is a required part of the cash flow statement. If the schedule is omitted, the accountant should modify his compilation report to disclose a departure from accounting principles generally accepted in the United States of America in accordance with paragraphs .27–.29 of AR section 80.

[Revised, June 2009, to reflect conforming changes necessary due to the issuance of FASB ASC; Revised, December 2010, to reflect conforming changes necessary due to the issuance of SSARS No. 19.]

[.18] Reserved

.19 Classification of Payments on Equipment Finance Note

Inquiry—Under the provisions of Financial Accounting Standards Board (FASB) *Accounting Standards Codification* (ASC) 230-10-50-3, noncash investing and financing transactions are to be disclosed in related narrative form or summarized in a schedule. An example of a transaction of this type would be an acquisition of equipment in a transaction in which an enterprise borrows money from a financial institution for the purchase of equipment and the financial institution remits the money directly to the vendor. In a transaction of this nature, should the payments of principal be presented as an outflow in the financing or investing section of the cash flow statement?

Reply—Payments on the aforementioned notes would be recorded as financing outflows per FASB ASC 230-10-45-15(b).

[Revised, June 2009, to reflect conforming changes necessary due to the issuance of FASB ASC.]

.20 Direct vs. Indirect Method for Statement of Cash Flows

Inquiry—A company has decided to present its statement of cash flows using the direct method for the current year although the indirect method was used in the prior year. Would this change require an emphasis-of-matter paragraph noting a lack of consistency in the financial statements?

Reply—No. A change in the presentation for the statement of cash flows from the indirect to direct method (or vice versa) is considered a change in classification rather than a consistency problem. If the statement of cash flows is presented for the prior period, it should be restated using the direct method approach for comparative purposes. In addition, disclosure should be made indicating the prior period restatement.

[Revised, June 2009, to reflect conforming changes necessary due to the issuance of recent authoritative literature; Revised, December 2012, to reflect conforming changes necessary due to the issuance of SAS Nos. 122–126.]

.21 Presentation of Financing Transaction on Statement of Cash Flows

Inquiry—A buyer contracts to purchase real estate. The lender gives the buyer a check made payable to the buyer for a loan to purchase the property. The buyer in turn endorses the check over to the seller. How should this financing transaction be presented on the buyer's statement of cash flows?

Reply—This transaction should be treated as a cash receipt by the buyer since the buyer was named as payee on the check. The amount of the check should be reported on the statement of cash flows even though the buyer did not convert the check to currency or deposit it in his or her bank account. The cash receipt belongs to the payee named on the check. The buyer should present the amount of the check as "Proceeds From Borrowings" as a cash inflow from financing transactions and "Purchase of Real Estate" as a cash outflow from investing activities.

.22 Negative Amortization of Long-Term Debt in Cash Flows Statement

Inquiry—The cash repayments on a long-term loan are less than the interest expense for the period. The amount of the interest expense not paid becomes part of the principal balance (negative amortization). How should the negative amortization be shown on the cash flows statement?

Reply—Financial Accounting Standards Board (FASB) *Accounting Standards Codification* (ASC) 230-10-45-28(a) indicates:

> Adjustments to [reconcile] net income to determine net cash flow from operating activities shall reflect accruals for interest earned but not received and interest incurred but not paid.

The negative amortization should therefore be treated as an adjustment to net income to remove the effect of this noncash expense. Disclosure should also be considered.

[Revised, June 2009, to reflect conforming changes necessary due to the issuance of FASB ASC.]

Q&A Section 1400

Consolidated Financial Statements

[.01] Reserved

.02 Consolidation of Corporation and Proprietorship

Inquiry—How should the financial statements of a corporation and a proprietorship be consolidated?

Reply—This answer assumes that 100 percent of the corporation capital stock is owned by the proprietorship.

As in any consolidation, the stockholders' equity of the subsidiary corporation should be eliminated against the investment of the parent (the proprietorship). Any net earnings of the subsidiary corporation subsequent to its acquisition and not recorded on the books of the parent should be reflected in the consolidated net equity, which, because the parent is a sole proprietorship, will be a single figure. As income taxes are assessed against the owner as an individual rather than against the proprietorship, no provision is made for income taxes beyond those payable by the corporation. However, a footnote should disclose such omission, and if it is anticipated that funds will have to be withdrawn from the proprietorship to meet future taxes on income earned to date, this too should be disclosed, with an estimate of the amount thereof if practicable. Of course, provision should be made for elimination of profits to the extent that they may be reflected in consolidated inventories or in other consolidated assets.

[Revised, April 2010.]

[.03] Reserved

[.04] Reserved

[.05] Reserved

.06 Combined and Separate Financial Statements

Inquiry—Company A and Company B are new car dealers with A selling an American made car and B selling a foreign made car. One individual owns 100 percent of the outstanding stock of both companies.

Both companies A and B are at the same location with separate buildings for sales staffs. Company A maintains the parts and service departments for both companies with the parts inventory, warranty and service receivables of Company B on Company A's books. In return, Company B pays Company A a per car fee for services to be performed on each new car sold by B.

Company A maintains the only used car inventory on the lot adjacent to Company B's building. Each time B receives a used car in trade, it is sold to Company A at the wholesale fair market value.

Although there is a differentiation in sales staffs, management, accounting, secretarial, and other related services are performed by the same staff out of both buildings, and Company B pays a monthly fee for services performed.

Company A has income for the year, but Company B has a loss for the period. Combined financial statements will be prepared, but is it also necessary to provide combining statements for the individual companies?

Reply—Financial Accounting Standards Board (FASB) *Accounting Standards Codification* (ASC) 810-10-55-1B states, in part:

> There are circumstances, however, in which combined financial statements (as distinguished from consolidated statements) of commonly controlled entities are likely to be more meaningful than their separate statements. For example, combined financial statements would be useful if one individual owns a controlling interest in several entities that are related in their operations.

Combined financial statements of the companies would be appropriate, and there is no necessity for presenting separate statements for the companies.

Unfortunately, FASB ASC 810, *Consolidation*, makes no statement as to appropriate presentation of the stockholder's equity section of a combined balance sheet. Appropriate disclosure, therefore, may depend upon the circumstances. Either on the statement of financial position, or in a note, there should be disclosure for each company of their number of shares of stock that are authorized and outstanding, and the par value. While under some circumstances it might not be necessary to disclose the allocation of retained earnings between the two companies, other circumstances may exist under which such disclosure would be required—for example, if the losses of either company have been so severe that an insolvent condition might be anticipated.

[Revised, June 2009, to reflect conforming changes necessary due to the issuance of FASB ASC.]

.07 Reporting on Company Where Option to Acquire Control Exists

Inquiry—Corporation A acquired debentures from Corporation B convertible into common voting stock within ten years at $1 per share. Corporation A also has an option to purchase additional shares at $1 per share upon conversion to bring A's holdings in B up to 51 percent of the total outstanding shares. Corporation A also has the right to appoint a majority of Corporation B's Board of Directors and has done so. Other intercompany transactions are negligible.

May each company issue separate financial statements, or are consolidated statements required? What disclosures would be necessary?

Reply—At present there is no ownership of one company by the other, and consolidation would not be proper. Further, since intercompany transactions (other than interest on the debentures) are negligible, combined statements would probably not be particularly useful.

Corporation A should disclose in its financial statements the terms under which it may obtain controlling stock ownership of Corporation B, the amount of interest received, that no other intercompany transactions are significant, and that it presently has the right to and does appoint a majority to Corporation B's Board of Directors. It should also present summarized information as to the assets, liabilities, and operating results of Corporation B, or include B's financial statements with its report.

Corporation B, in addition to disclosing the interest rate and maturity of the convertible debentures, should disclose Corporation A's conversion and option privileges and should disclose that Corporation A has the right to and has appointed a majority to Corporation B's Board of Directors.

[.08] Reserved

[.09] Reserved

[.10] Reserved

[.11] Reserved

[.12] Reserved

[.13] Reserved

[.14] Reserved

[.15] Reserved

[.16] Reserved

[.17] Reserved

[.18] Reserved

[.19] Reserved

[.20] Reserved

[.21] Reserved

.22 Intervening Intercompany Transactions Between Subsidiary's and Parent's Year-End

Inquiry—A parent company has a December 31 year-end and its wholly owned subsidiary has a November 30 year-end. The two companies generally have substantial intercompany sales and purchases which are recorded by each company as they occur. The parent uses the subsidiary's November 30 year-end statement to prepare the consolidated financial statements.

The intervening intercompany transactions, which occur between December 1 and December 31, create intercompany account balances which do not eliminate upon consolidation due to the difference in year-ends of the parent and its subsidiary. How should these intervening transactions be accounted for in the consolidated financial statements?

Reply—In discussing differences in fiscal periods, Financial Accounting Standards Board (FASB) *Accounting Standards Codification* (ASC) 810-10-45-12 states, "if the difference is not more than about three months, it usually is acceptable to use, for consolidation purposes, the subsidiary's financial statements for its fiscal period; if this is done, recognition should be given by disclosure or otherwise to the effect of intervening events that materially affect the financial position or results of operations."

When a subsidiary's fiscal year differs from that of the parent, intercompany accounts may not agree. Transactions in the interval between the subsidiary's year-end and the parent's year-end must be analyzed and appropriate consolidation entries prepared.

A practical approach to preparing these consolidation entries would be to reverse the intervening intercompany transactions in the parent company's accounts but not in the subsidiary's accounts. A summary of these intervening transactions could then be disclosed in a note to the consolidated financial statements.

[Revised, June 2009, to reflect conforming changes necessary due to the issuance of FASB ASC.]

.23 Conforming Subsidiary's Inventory Pricing Method to Its Parent Company's Method

Inquiry—A parent company uses the first-in, first-out (FIFO) cost assumption to price its inventory, while its subsidiary uses the last-in, first-out (LIFO) cost assumption to price its inventory. Must the subsidiary's inventory method be changed to conform to the FIFO method used by its parent company in consolidated financial statements?

Reply—There is no requirement under generally accepted accounting principles for the subsidiary to conform its inventory pricing method with the parent company's method. Consolidated statements may be presented with the subsidiary using LIFO and the parent using FIFO. Also, separate subsidiary only statements may be presented on the LIFO basis.

[.24] Reserved

.25 Issuance of Parent Company Only Financial Statements

Inquiry—Generally accepted accounting principles preclude preparation of parent company financial statements for issuance to stockholders as the financial statements of the primary reporting entity. Are there any circumstances under which parent company financial statements may still be prepared?

Reply—Yes. Financial Accounting Standards Board (FASB) *Accounting Standards Codification* (ASC) 810-10-45-11 states: "In some cases parent entity statements may be needed, in addition to consolidated statements, to indicate adequately the position of bondholders and other creditors or preferred stockholders of the parent. Consolidating statements, in which one column is used for the parent entity and other columns for particular subsidiaries or groups of subsidiaries often are an effective means of presenting the pertinent information."

[Revised, June 2009, to reflect conforming changes necessary due to the issuance of FASB ASC.]

.26 Consolidated Versus Combined Financial Statements

Inquiry—S Corporation has 2000 common shares and 1000 preferred shares outstanding. The preferred shareholders have the same rights as the common shareholders, except the right to vote. Of the 2000 common shares outstanding, 1000 shares are owned by P Corporation and 1000 shares are owned by I (an individual) who also owns all of the outstanding common shares of P Corporation. The preferred shares of S Corporation are owned by an outside party. Should P Corporation consolidate S Corporation for financial reporting purposes?

Reply—Financial Accounting Standards Board (FASB) *Accounting Standards Codification* (ASC) 810-10-05-6 states that to "justify the preparation of consolidated financial statements, the controlling financial interest shall rest directly or indirectly in one of the entities included in the consolidation." In this situation P does not control S directly or indirectly and therefore consolidation is not appropriate. Combined financial statements could be presented if the circumstances are such that combined financial statements of S Corporation and P Corporation are more meaningful than separate financial statements.

[Revised, June 2009, to reflect conforming changes necessary due to the issuance of FASB ASC.]

.27 Subsidiary Financial Statements

Inquiry—Generally accepted accounting principles indicate that "consolidated rather than parent-company financial statements are the appropriate general-purpose financial statements." May subsidiary-only financial statements be issued without consolidated financial statements?

Reply—Yes. Generally accepted accounting principles do not preclude issuance of subsidiary-only statements. Care should be taken to include all disclosures required by Financial Accounting Standards Board (FASB) *Accounting Standards Codification* (ASC) SC 740-10-50-17, FASB ASC 850, *Related Party Disclosures*, and other relevant pronouncements.

[Revised, June 2009, to reflect conforming changes necessary due to the issuance of FASB ASC.]

[.28] Reserved

.29 Consolidated Versus Combined Financial Statements Under FASB ASC 810, *Consolidation*

Inquiry—If a reporting entity is the primary beneficiary of a variable interest entity (VIE) under Financial Accounting Standards Board (FASB) *Accounting Standards Codification* (ASC) 810, *Consolidation*, would it be appropriate to issue combined financial statements rather than consolidated financial statements?

Reply—No. FASB ASC 810-10-05-6 permits combined financial statements in certain situations in which consolidated financial statements are not required. However, FASB ASC 810-10-25-38 states that "an entity shall consolidate a variable interest entity if that entity has a variable interest (or combination of variable interests) that will absorb a majority of the variable interest entity's expected losses, receive a majority of the variable interest entity's expected residual returns, or both." Furthermore, the starting point for the preparation of combined financial statements is two or more sets of financial statements that are prepared in accordance with GAAP; in the case of a primary beneficiary of a VIE, financial statements prepared in accordance with GAAP would be consolidated financial statements.

[Revised, June 2009, to reflect conforming changes necessary due to the issuance of FASB ASC.]

.30 Stand-Alone Financial Statements of a Variable Interest Entity

Inquiry—Regarding Financial Accounting Standards Board (FASB) *Accounting Standards Codification* (ASC) 810, *Consolidation*, is it appropriate to present stand-alone financial statements of a variable interest entity (VIE)?

Reply—FASB ASC 810 does not specifically address this issue. Subsidiary-only financial statements are appropriate under generally accepted accounting principles. By extension, it may be appropriate to present stand-alone financial statements of a VIE.

[Revised, June 2009, to reflect conforming changes necessary due to the issuance of FASB ASC.]

.31 GAAP Departure for FASB ASC 810

Inquiry—If a reporting entity is the primary beneficiary of a variable interest entity under Financial Accounting Standards Board (FASB) *Accounting Standards Codification* (ASC) 810, *Consolidation*, what are the implications for the auditors' report if the reporting entity does not consolidate the variable interest entity?

Reply—AU-C section 705, *Modifications to the Opinion in the Independent Auditor's Report* (AICPA, *Professional Standards*), addresses the auditor's responsibility to issue an appropriate report in circumstances when, in forming an opinion in accordance with AU-C section 700, *Forming an Opinion and Reporting on Financial Statements* (AICPA, *Professional Standards*), the auditor concludes that a modification to the auditor's opinion on the financial statements is necessary. Paragraph .07*a* of AU-C section 705 states that when the auditor concludes that, based on the audit evidence obtained, the financial statements as a whole are materially misstated, the auditor should modify the opinion in the auditor's report.

As paragraph .02 of AU-C section 705 explains, the decision regarding which type of modified opinion (a qualified opinion, an adverse opinion, and a disclaimer of opinion) is appropriate depends upon the following:

a. The nature of the matter giving rise to the modification (that is, whether the financial statements are materially misstated or, in the case of an inability to obtain sufficient appropriate audit evidence, may be materially misstated)

b. The auditor's professional judgment about the pervasiveness of the effects or possible effects of the matter on the financial statements

If an auditor concludes that a qualified opinion is appropriate, he or she should disclose the GAAP departure in a separate paragraph headed "Basis for Qualified Opinion" preceding the opinion paragraph of the report. Furthermore, the opinion paragraph of the report should include the appropriate qualifying language and a reference to the basis for qualified opinion paragraph. The basis for modification paragraph should include a description and quantification of the financial effects of the misstatement, unless impracticable. If it is not practicable to quantify the financial effects, the auditor should so state in the basis for modification paragraph. If such disclosures are made in a note to the financial statements, the basis for modified opinion paragraph may be shortened by referring to it.

[Revised, June 2009, to reflect conforming changes necessary due to the issuance of FASB ASC; Revised, December 2012, to reflect conforming changes necessary due to the issuance of SAS Nos. 122–126.]

.32 Parent-Only Financial Statements and Relationship to GAAP

Inquiry–Financial Accounting Standards Board (FASB) *Accounting Standards Codification* (ASC) 810, *Consolidation*, addresses parent company financial statements. If consolidation is required under generally accepted accounting principles (GAAP), are there any circumstances in which an entity may prepare parent company-only financial statements without preparing related consolidated financial statements and say that the parent company-only financial statements are in accordance with GAAP?

Reply–No. FASB ASC 810-10-10-1 notes the presumption in GAAP that consolidated financial statements are more meaningful than parent entity-only financial statements. FASB ASC 810-10-15-10 states that all majority-owned subsidiaries shall be consolidated, with few exceptions. FASB ASC 810-10-45-11 adds that parent company financial statements may be needed in addition to consolidated financial statements, but it does not suggest that parent company financial statements may be prepared in place of consolidated financial statements.

For example, if, as a condition of a legal or regulatory agreement, an entity is required to submit "restricted" or "special use" parent-only financial statements without related consolidated financial statements, the restricted or special use parent-only financial statements are not in accordance with GAAP.

[Revised, June 2009, to reflect conforming changes necessary due to the issuance of FASB ASC.]

[.33] Reserved

Q&A Section 1500

Financial Statements Prepared in Accordance With a Special Purpose Framework

For nonauthoritative guidance regarding financial statements prepared in accordance with the cash- or tax-basis of accounting, consult the AICPA publication *Accounting and Financial Reporting Guidelines for Cash- and Tax-Basis Financial Statements*. That practice aid alerts the reader to some of the most frequently-encountered issues faced by accounting professionals in dealing with cash- and tax-basis financial statements and provides suggestions and insight into how these issues are resolved in practice. In addition, the AICPA has published a separate practice aid, *Applying OCBOA in State and Local Government Financial Statements*. To order these publications, call the AICPA at 1.888.777.7077 or visit www.cpa2biz.com.

[.01] Reserved

[.02] Reserved

[.03] Reserved

.04 Terminology for Special Purpose Financial Statements

The Clarification and Convergence project of the AICPA Accounting and Review Services Committee is currently underway. Upon the completion of this project, this Inquiry and Reply will be conformed to include references to the pertinent clarified AICPA Statements on Standards for Accounting and Review Services that are expected to be issued as a result of the project.

Inquiry—(1) If an entity prepares financial statements in accordance with a special purpose framework, may GAAP financial statement titles be used?

(2) What should be the caption for "net income" or "net loss," and may the corporation use "retained earnings"?

Reply—(1) No. Paragraph .A17 of AU-C section 800, *Special Considerations—Audits of Financial Statements Prepared in Accordance With Special Purpose Frameworks* (AICPA, *Professional Standards*), explains that unmodified GAAP financial statement titles are not acceptable for use in special purpose financial statements. The paragraph contains a few examples of appropriate financial statement titles (for example, *Statement of Assets and Liabilities Arising from Cash Transactions* and *Statement of Income—Regulatory Basis*). However, the examples presented in the authoritative literature were not meant to be all-inclusive and are not the only acceptable titles. Equally acceptable titles would be *Balance Sheet—Cash Basis* or *Statement of Operations—Income Tax Basis*. The selection of specific financial statement titles is a matter of judgment; any modified title would fulfill the requirements of AU-C section 800 as long as it is clear that the financial statements are not prepared in accordance with GAAP.

(2) The authoritative literature is silent regarding the captions to be used within special purpose financial statements. Therefore, there is no requirement to modify standard GAAP financial statement captions in special purpose financial statements. If modifications are desired, common examples for cash basis financial statements are *Excess of revenue collected over expenses paid, Excess of expenses paid over revenue collected*, and *Accumulated excess of revenue over expenses paid*. For tax-basis financial statements, acceptable modifications include *Retained earnings—income tax basis* and *Net income—tax basis*.

[Amended, February 1995; Revised, December 2012, to reflect conforming changes necessary due to the issuance of SAS Nos. 122–126.]

[.05] Reserved

[.06] Reserved

.07 Disclosure Concerning Subsequent Events in Special Purpose Financial Statements

Inquiry—FASB *Accounting Standards Codification* (ASC) 855, *Subsequent Events*, sets forth general standards of accounting for and disclosure of events that occur after the balance sheet date but before financial statements are issued or are available to be issued. FASB ASC 855 also requires disclosure of the date through which an entity has evaluated subsequent events and the basis for that date, that is, whether that date represents the date on which the financial statements were issued or were available to be issued. Should full disclosure financial statements prepared in accordance with a special purpose framework contain the disclosures set forth in FASB ASC 855?

Reply—Paragraph .A26 of AR-C section 80, *Compilation Engagements* (AICPA, *Professional Standards*), and paragraph A80 of AR-C section 90, *Review of Financial Statements* (AICPA, *Professional Standards*), state "financial statements prepared when applying a special purpose framework[1] are not considered appropriate in form unless the financial statements include informative disclosures similar to those required by GAAP if the financial statements contain items that are the same as, or are similar to, those in financial statements prepared in accordance with GAAP." Paragraph .A20 of AU-C section 800 states, in part, "when the special purpose financial statements contain items that are the same as, or similar to, those in financial statements prepared in accordance with GAAP, informative disclosures similar to those required by GAAP are necessary to achieve fair presentation."

Therefore, the date through which an entity has evaluated subsequent events and the basis for that date should be disclosed. Furthermore, some nonrecognized subsequent events are of such a nature that disclosure is required to keep the financial statements prepared from being misleading. Such events should be disclosed following the guidance in FASB ASC 855.

[Issue Date: June 2009; Revised, December 2012, to reflect conforming changes necessary due to the issuance of SAS Nos. 122–126; Revised, March 2016, to reflect conforming changes necessary due to the issuance of SSARS No. 21.]

---

[1] [Footnote deleted to reflect conforming changes necessary due to the issuance of SSARS No. 21.]

Q&A Section 1600

Personal Financial Statements

[.01] Reserved

[.02] Reserved

.03 Social Security Benefits—Personal Financial Statements

Inquiry—Do social security benefits to be received based on the future life expectancy of an individual qualify as an asset in personal financial statements?

Reply—No. Financial Accounting Standards Board (FASB) *Accounting Standards Codification* (ASC) 274, *Personal Financial Statements*, indicates that nonforfeitable rights to receive future sums must meet certain criteria to be accounted for as assets. One of these criteria is that the rights must not be contingent on the individual's life expectancy or the occurrence of a particular event, such as disability or death. In this example, because the social security benefits are contingent on the individual's life expectancy, they do not qualify as a recognizable asset for the personal financial statements.

[Revised, June 2009, to reflect conforming changes necessary due to the issuance of FASB ASC.]

.04 Presentation of Assets at Current Values and Liabilities at Current Amounts in Personal Financial Statements

Inquiry—Financial Accounting Standards Board (FASB) *Accounting Standards Codification* (ASC) 274, *Personal Financial Statements*, states that personal financial statements should present assets at their estimated current values and liabilities at their estimated current amounts at the date of the financial statements. FASB ASC 274 also defines estimated current values and current amounts.

Are the definitions of *current values* (assets) and *current amounts* (liabilities) for personal financial statements meant to be the same as *fair value*, as defined in FASB ASC 820, *Fair Value Measurements and Disclosures*?

Reply—No. FASB ASC 820 did not contemplate the reporting of personal financial statements, and FASB did not amend the definitions of estimated current values and current amounts for personal financial statements as part of its codification process.

[Issue Date: June 2009.]

Q&A Section 1700

Prospective Financial Statements

[.01] Reserved

Q&A Section 1800

Notes to Financial Statements

[.01] Reserved

[.02] Reserved

.03 Disclosure of Change in Fiscal Year

Inquiry—What disclosure in the financial statements is necessary when a company changes its fiscal year?

Reply—Generally accepted accounting principles (GAAP) do not specifically require disclosure of a change in the fiscal year. However, disclosure of such a change is generally considered necessary to make the financial statements meaningful to users.

[.04] Reserved

.05 Applicability of Fair Value Disclosure Requirements and Measurement Principles in Financial Accounting Standards Board (FASB) *Accounting Standards Codification* (ASC) 820, *Fair Value Measurements and Disclosures*, to Certain Financial Instruments

Inquiry—Do the fair value measurement principles and disclosure requirements in Financial Accounting Standards Board (FASB) *Accounting Standards Codification* (ASC) 820, *Fair Value Measurements and Disclosures*, apply to financial instruments that are not recognized at fair value in the statement of financial position, but for which fair value is required to be disclosed in the notes to financial statements in accordance with paragraphs 10–19 of FASB ASC 825-10-50?

Reply—The measurement principles of FASB ASC 820 apply when determining for disclosure purposes the fair value of financial instruments that are not recognized at fair value in the statement of financial position. FASB ASC 820-10-15-1, which establishes the scope of FASB ASC 820, provides that "Except as noted below, this Topic applies when another Topic requires or permits fair value measurements or disclosures about fair value measurements (and measurements, such as fair value less costs to sell, based on fair value or disclosures about those measurements)." The exceptions relate to (*a*) share-based payment transactions, (*b*) FASB ASC sections, subtopics, or topics that require or permit measurements that are similar to fair value but that are not intended to measure fair value, and (*c*) certain fair value measurements for purposes of lease classification or measurement in accordance with FASB ASC 840.

In addition, certain disclosure requirements of FASB ASC 820 apply to financial instruments for which fair value is only disclosed. Specifically, FASB ASC 820-10-50-2E provides that for each class of assets and liabilities not measured at fair value in the statement of financial position but for which the fair value is disclosed,

> a reporting entity shall disclose the information required by paragraph 820-10-50-2(b), (bbb), and (h). However, a reporting entity is not required to provide the quantitative disclosures about significant unobservable inputs used in fair value measurements categorized within Level 3 of the fair value hierarchy required by paragraph 820-10-50-2 (bbb). For such assets and liabilities, a reporting entity does not need to provide the other disclosures required by this Topic.

[Issue Date: May 2010; Revised, April 2014, to reflect conforming changes necessary due to revisions to FASB ASC.]

.06 Applicability of Fair Value Disclosure Requirements in FASB ASC 820 to Financial Statements Prepared in Accordance With a Special Purpose Framework

Inquiry—If management prepares an entity's financial statements in accordance with a special purpose framework, and those financial statements include accounts measured at fair value, what is the auditor's responsibility with respect to fair value disclosure requirements in FASB ASC 820-10-50?

Reply—As indicated in paragraph .19 of AR section 80, *Compilation of Financial Statements* (AICPA, *Professional Standards*), and paragraph .32 of AR section 90, *Review of Financial Statements* (AICPA, *Professional Standards*), "financial statements prepared in accordance with an OCBOA[1] are not considered appropriate in form unless the financial statements include informative disclosures similar to those required by GAAP if the financial statements contain items that are the same as, or are similar to, those in financial statements prepared in accordance with GAAP." Additionally, paragraph .A20 of AU-C section 800, *Special Considerations—Audits of Financial Statements Prepared in Accordance With Special Purpose Frameworks* (AICPA, *Professional Standards*), states "when the special purpose financial statements contain items that are the same as, or similar to, those in financial statements prepared in accordance with GAAP, informative disclosures similar to those required by GAAP are necessary to achieve fair presentation."
Therefore, if special purpose financial statements reflect assets or liabilities measured at fair value in accordance with FASB ASC 820, the accountant/auditor should consider whether the financial statements (including the accompanying notes) include the fair value disclosure requirements of FASB ASC 820 as appropriate for the basis of accounting used.

[Issue Date: June 2010; Revised, December 2012, to reflect conforming changes necessary due to the issuance of SAS Nos. 122–126.]

[1] The cash, tax, and regulatory bases of accounting are commonly referred to as *other comprehensive bases of accounting* (OCBOA). [Footnote added, December 2012, to reflect conforming changes necessary due to the issuance of SAS Nos. 122–126.]

Q&A Section 1900

Interim Financial Information

.01 Condensed Interim Financial Reporting by Nonissuers

Inquiry—Financial Accounting Standards Board (FASB) *Accounting Standards Codification* (ASC) 270, *Interim Reporting*, provides accounting and disclosure guidance relating to *recognition and measurement* in interim financial information (including condensed interim financial statements). FASB ASC 270 does not provide a reporting framework for condensed interim financial statements—that is, minimum requirements for the *form and content* of condensed interim financial statements. Article 10 of Securities and Exchange Commission (SEC) Regulation S-X provides guidance on the form and content of condensed interim financial statements of issuers. When preparing condensed interim financial statements, because specific guidance with respect to form and content is absent, may nonissuers apply Article 10 of SEC Regulation S-X in addition to complying with FASB ASC 270 with respect to recognition and measurement?

Reply—Yes. In the absence of established accounting principles for form and content in preparing condensed interim financial statements, nonissuers may analogize to the guidance in Article 10 of SEC Regulation S-X.

Preparers should keep in mind that the purpose of *condensed* interim financial statements is to provide an update to users of the entity's annual financial statements prepared in accordance with generally accepted accounting principles. Article 10 of SEC Regulation S-X also has this premise. Therefore, to avoid being considered misleading,

- such condensed interim financial statements would include a note that the financial information should be read in conjunction with the entity's latest annual financial statements, and
- the entity's latest annual financial statements would either accompany such condensed interim financial statements or be made readily available by the entity. The financial statements are deemed to be readily available if a user can obtain the financial statements without any further action by the entity (for example, financial statements on an entity's Web site may be considered readily available, but being available upon request is not considered readily available).

[Issue Date: January 2009; Revised, June 2009, to reflect conforming changes necessary due to the issuance of FASB ASC.]

Q&A Section 2000

ASSETS

TABLE OF CONTENTS

Section

Section

Section

Q&A Section 2110

Cash

[.01] Reserved

.02 Checks Held at Balance Sheet Date

Inquiry—It is the practice of a company to eliminate its recorded accounts payable balance at the end of each month by writing checks to all of its trade vendors prior to the end of the month. To prevent overdrafts that would result from this practice, the company retains possession of the checks and only mails them to the vendors after the end of the month, when sufficient funds are available to satisfy them.

How should these held checks be accounted for by the company at month end?

Reply—At month end the aggregate dollar amount of held checks should be added back to cash and accounts payable. Checks which have not left the custody of the company should not reduce the company's recorded cash or accounts payable balances because they have not been tendered to the vendor to satisfy the debt.

[.03] Reserved

[.04] Reserved

[.05] Reserved

.06 Disclosure of Cash Balances in Excess of Federally Insured Amounts

Inquiry—Should the existence of cash on deposit with banks in excess of FDIC-insured limits be disclosed in the financial statements?

Reply—The existence of uninsured cash balances should be disclosed if the uninsured balances represent a significant concentration of credit risk. *Credit risk* is defined in Financial Accounting Standards Board (FASB) *Accounting Standards Codification* (ASC) glossary as follows:

> For purposes of a hedged item in a fair value hedge, credit risk is the risk of changes in the hedged item's fair value attributable to both of the following:
>
> a. Changes in the obligor's creditworthiness
>
> b. Changes in the spread over the benchmark interest rate with respect to the hedged item's credit sector at inception of the hedge.
>
> For purposes of a hedged item in a cash flow hedge, credit risk is the risk of changes in the hedged item's cash flows attributable to all of the following:
>
> a. Default
>
> b. Changes in the obligor's creditworthiness
>
> c. Changes in the spread over the benchmark interest rate with respect to the hedged item's credit sector at inception of the hedge.

As a result, bank statement balances in excess of FDIC-insured amounts represent a credit risk.

A concentration of credit risk exists if an entity has exposure with an individual counterparty or groups of counterparties. For example, a material uninsured cash balance with a single bank should generally be disclosed. In contrast, numerous immaterial uninsured cash balances on deposit with several banks may not require disclosure. The threshold for "significance" is a matter of judgment and will vary with individual circumstances.

An example of disclosure for this circumstance might be:

> The Company maintains its cash accounts primarily with banks located in Alabama. The total cash balances are insured by the FDIC up to $100,000 per bank. The Company has cash balances on deposit with two Alabama banks at December 31, 1996 that exceeded the balance insured by the FDIC in the amount of $1,100,000.

[Revised, June 2009, to reflect conforming changes necessary due to the issuance of FASB ASC.]

Q&A Section 2120

Temporary Investments

[.01] Reserved

[.02] Reserved

[.03] Reserved

[.04] Reserved

[.05] Reserved

.06 Accounting for Preferred Dividends Received on Investments in Common Stock

Inquiry—A company received dividends on its investment in common stock of another company in the form of preferred stock. How should the dividend be recorded?

Reply—The assets and related dividend income should be recorded at fair value. Financial Accounting Standards Board (FASB) *Accounting Standards Codification* (ASC) 845-10-30-1 states that in general, accounting for nonmonetary transactions should be based on the fair values of the assets (or services) involved which is the same basis as that used in monetary transactions and that a nonmonetary asset received in a nonreciprocal transfer should be recorded at the fair value of the asset received. (FASB ASC 505, *Equity*, discusses accounting for stock dividends by the recipient; however, the scope of that pronouncement specifically excludes distributions of a different class of shares from that owned.)

[Amended, June 1995; Revised, June 2009, to reflect conforming changes necessary due to the issuance of FASB ASC.]

[.07] Reserved

[.08] Reserved

Q&A Section 2130

Receivables

[.01] Reserved

[.02] Reserved

[.03] Reserved

[.04] Reserved

.05 Out-of-Pocket Costs Incurred by a Law Firm

Inquiry—A law firm incurs certain out-of-pocket costs on behalf of its clients. If the law firm's efforts on behalf of the client are successful, these costs are recovered from the client in addition to the legal fees. If the case is lost, the costs are absorbed by the law firm. How should these costs be treated by the law firm?

Reply—These out-of-pocket costs should be reported as an asset in the financial statements of the law firm (for example, in an account called "client costs receivable"). At each balance sheet date, the law firm should apply the criteria in Financial Accounting Standards Board (FASB) *Accounting Standards Codification* (ASC) 450-20-25-1 to determine whether a loss contingency should be accrued.

If an asset is recorded, an allowance for unrecoverable client disbursements should be established representing the estimated amount of such costs that will not be realized. If these out-of-pocket costs become uncollectible because a case is lost, they should be written off against the allowance.

[Amended, June 1995; Revised, June 2009, to reflect conforming changes necessary due to the issuance of FASB ASC.]

[.06] Reserved

.07 Requirement for Doubtful Accounts Allowance

Inquiry—Do generally accepted accounting principles require an enterprise to establish an allowance for doubtful accounts even though management, based on analysis of the receivables and past charge-off experience, believes that no accounts are uncollectible at the balance sheet date?

Reply—FASB ASC 310-10-35-7 states that "the conditions under which receivables exist usually involve some degree of uncertainty about their collectibility, in which case a contingency exists . . . ." FASB ASC 450-20-25-2 would require an accrual of a loss by a charge to income if both of the following conditions exist:

a. "Information available prior to issuance of the financial statements indicates that it is probable that an asset had been impaired . . . at the date of the financial statements." and

b. "The amount of loss can be reasonably estimated."

If both conditions are not met, an allowance for doubtful accounts would not be required. Further, there is no requirement to disclose the absence of a loss accrual. If the conditions are met, an accrual for the loss should be recognized even though the specific receivables that are uncollectible may not be identifiable.

[Revised, June 2009, to reflect conforming changes necessary due to the issuance of FASB ASC.]

[.08] Reserved

.09 Scope Part I: Application of FASB ASC 310-30 to Debt Securities

Inquiry—Does the scope of FASB ASC 310-30 include debt securities?

Reply—Yes. FASB ASC 310-30 applies to *loans*, as defined in the FASB ASC glossary, as follows:

> Loan: A contractual right to receive money on demand or on fixed or determinable dates that is recognized as an asset in the creditor's statement of financial position. Examples include but are not limited to accounts receivable (with terms exceeding one year) and notes receivable. This definition encompasses loans accounted for as debt securities.
>
> Debt Security: Any security representing a creditor relationship with an entity. The term debt security also includes all of the following:
>
> a. Preferred stock that by its terms either must be redeemed by the issuing entity or is redeem-able at the option of the investor
> b. A collateralized mortgage obligation (or other instrument) that is issued in equity form but is required to be accounted for as a nonequity instrument regardless of how that instrument is classified (that is, whether equity or debt) in the issuer's statement of financial position
> c. U.S. Treasury securities
> d. U.S. government agency securities
> e. Municipal securities
> f. Corporate bonds
> g. Convertible debt
> h. Commercial paper
> i. All securitized debt instruments, such as collateralized mortgage obligations and real estate mortgage investment conduits
> j. Interest-only and principal-only strips.
>
> The term debt security excludes all of the following:
>
> a. Option contracts
> b. Financial futures contracts
> c. Forward contracts
> d. Lease contracts
> e. Receivables that do not meet the definition of security and, so, are not debt securities (unless they have been securitized, in which case they would meet the definition of a security), for example:
>   1. Trade accounts receivable arising from sales on credit by industrial or commercial entities

2. Loans receivable arising from consumer, commercial, and real estate lending activities of financial institutions.

Therefore, the scope of FASB ASC 310-30 includes acquired loans that are accounted for as debt securities.

[Revised, June 2009, to reflect conforming changes necessary due to the issuance of FASB ASC.]

.10 Scope Part II: Instruments Accounted for as Debt Securities Under FASB ASC 310-30

Inquiry—Some types of instruments are measured like debt securities. In accordance with the guidance of FASB ASC 310-30 and considering expected cash flows for instruments measured like debt securities, when does the investor follow the guidance of paragraphs 8–9 of FASB ASC 310-30-35 (loans accounted for as debt securities) or paragraphs 10–11 of FASB ASC 310-30-35 (loans not accounted for as debt securities)?

Reply—FASB ASC 860-20-35-2 provides an example of instruments that are measured like debt securities:

> Financial assets, except for instruments that are within the scope of Subtopic 815-10, that can contractually be prepaid or otherwise settled in such a way that the holder would not recover substantially all of its recorded investment shall be subsequently measured like investments in debt securities classified as available for sale or trading under Topic 320. Examples of such financial assets include, but are not limited to, interest-only strips, other beneficial interests, loans, or other receivables.

For these types of instruments measured like debt securities, investors should follow the impairment guidance in paragraphs 8–9 of FASB ASC 310-30-35 (loans accounted for as debt securities) unless the asset is otherwise excluded according to FASB ASC 310-30-15.

[Revised, June 2009, to reflect conforming changes necessary due to the issuance of FASB ASC; Revised, April 2014, to reflect conforming changes necessary due to revisions to FASB ASC.]

.11 Determining Evidence of Significant Delays and Shortfalls Relative to FASB ASC 310-30

Inquiry—FASB ASC 310-30-15-8 states that "investors shall consider the significance of delays and shortfalls for a loan so FASB ASC 310-30 is not applied in evaluating payment collectability when such delays and shortfalls are insignificant with regard to the contractually required payments." How might that assessment be determined?

Reply—That assessment will likely be based on individual facts and circumstances and should be guided by an accounting policy adopted and applied consistently by the investor. For instance a percentage could be established to indicate an "insignificant" shortfall and for those items that meet the percentage shortfall, the dollar shortfall itself would be evaluated as to whether it is insignificant in the aggregate.

[Revised, June 2009, to reflect conforming changes necessary due to the issuance of FASB ASC.]

.12 Determining Evidence of Deterioration of Credit Quality and Probability of Contractual Payment Deficiency in Accordance With FASB ASC 310-30

Inquiry—In accordance with FASB ASC 310–30, how can an investor identify loans that have evidence of deterioration of credit quality and for which it is probable that the investor will be unable to collect all contractually required payments receivable so that they can identify whether the loans are in the scope of FASB ASC 310-30?

Reply—There are several things to consider when determining whether certain loans are within the scope of FASB ASC 310-30. An investor may set policies, including thresholds based on the type of loan product. Commercial loans are generally classified or graded into risk categories as part of an ongoing credit review process. An investor may identify commercial loans with evidence of deterioration using the previous owner's record of changes in classification and accrual status. Such records may also provide evidence concerning whether it is probable that the investor will be unable to collect all contractually required payments receivable. In contrast, consumer loans are generally not individually reviewed or graded and non-accrual and charge-off policies vary by product. For instance, some types of consumer loans are immediately charged-off when the loan is a certain number of days past due and may never be classified as non-accrual. As a result, indicators of credit quality deterioration for consumer products may vary depending on the product and may include non-accrual classification, past due status, or FICO score and changes therein. For debt securities, investors may establish other criteria to determine when securities should be considered for review for application under FASB ASC 310-30; for example, downgrades in credit grade categories.

[Revised, June 2009, to reflect conforming changes necessary due to the issuance of FASB ASC.]

.13 Non-Accrual Loans Part I: Acquired Non-Accrual Loans Under FASB ASC 310-30

Inquiry—Does an acquired loan (purchased individually or as part of a business combination) that was classified by the seller as non-accrual fall within the scope of FASB ASC 310-30?

Reply—Non-accrual status may be an indicator that a loan that meets the criteria of FASB ASC 310-30. However, the investor should analyze whether the loan meets all the scope criteria in FASB ASC 310-30-15, including evidence of credit deterioration. Classification of a loan as non-accrual by the seller and/or investor does not provide an exemption from FASB ASC 310-30. FASB ASC 310-30 does not prohibit carrying acquired loans on non-accrual status, when appropriate. However, certain disclosures are required for such loans in accordance with FASB ASC 310-30-50-2(a)(4).

[Revised, June 2009, to reflect conforming changes necessary due to the issuance of FASB ASC.]

.14 Non-Accrual Loans Part II: Consumer Loans on Non-Accrual Status Under FASB ASC 310-30

Inquiry—Should FASB ASC 310-30 be applied to non-accrual (for example, 90 days past due) consumer loans that are reported as non-performing loans when such loans may be charged off completely in relatively short order (that is, after 120 days)?

Reply—Yes. FASB ASC 310-30 is applicable to all loans within its scope, including non-accrual loans. The accrual accounting specified in FASB ASC 310-30 should be applied if the investor is able to estimate expected cash flows, including cash flows resulting from foreclosure and other collection efforts. However, when the investor does not have the ability to reasonably estimate cash flows, FASB ASC 310-30 does not prohibit carrying loans on non-accrual. Also, investors should note there are additional disclosure requirements for these circumstances.

[Revised, June 2009, to reflect conforming changes necessary due to the issuance of FASB ASC.]

.15 Loans Held for Sale in Accordance With FASB ASC 310-30

Inquiry—Why are only mortgage loans held for sale and not all loans held for sale excluded from the scope of FASB ASC 310-30?

Reply—Only mortgage loans held for sale that are accounted for under FASB ASC 948, *Financial Services—Mortgage Banking*, are excluded from the scope because FASB ASC 948 had to provide an exception.

[Revised, June 2009, to reflect conforming changes necessary due to the issuance of FASB ASC.]

.16 Treatment of Commercial Revolving Loans Under FASB ASC 310-30

Inquiry—FASB ASC 310-30-15-2(f) excludes revolving credit agreements from its scope specifically noting as examples two types of consumer revolving agreements, credit cards and home equity loans. *Revolving privilege* is defined in the FASB ASC glossary as "a feature in a loan that provides the borrower with the option to make multiple borrowings up to a specified maximum amount, to repay portions of previous borrowings, and then to reborrow under the same loan." Are commercial revolving loans also excluded from the scope of FASB ASC 310-30?

Reply—Commercial revolving loans should be treated the same as consumer revolving loans. Thus, commercial revolving loans are excluded as well, if the borrower has revolving privileges at the acquisition date.

[Revised, June 2009, to reflect conforming changes necessary due to the issuance of FASB ASC.]

.17 Application of FASB ASC 310-30

Inquiry—The scope of FASB ASC 310-30 excludes loans that are retained (transferor's beneficial) interests. How does the scope of FASB ASC 310-30 relate to the scope of FASB ASC 325-40?

Reply—Accounting for retained interests should follow FASB ASC 325-40 and for purchased interests should follow FASB ASC 310-30 if they meet the scope criteria in FASB ASC 310-30-15.

[Revised, June 2009, to reflect conforming changes necessary due to the issuance of FASB ASC.]

.18 Loans Reacquired Under Recourse Under FASB ASC 310-30

Inquiry—If a loan that was transferred with recourse and qualified for accounting as a sale under FASB ASC 860, *Transfers and Servicing*, is subsequently repurchased under the recourse provision, is it within the scope of FASB ASC 310-30?

Reply—Yes, if it meets the criteria in FASB ASC 310-30-15 related to credit quality. Except for purchases triggered by initial representations and warranty deficiencies, it is likely that the repurchased loan would meet the criteria to be included in the scope of FASB ASC 310-30. FASB ASC 310-30 includes guidance on the evidence of credit deterioration. (See Q&A section 2130.11, "Determining Evidence of Significant Delays and Shortfalls Relative to FASB ASC 310-30.")

[Revised, June 2009, to reflect conforming changes necessary due to the issuance of FASB ASC.]

.19 Acquired Loans Where Purchase Price Is Greater Than Fair Value Under FASB ASC 310-30

Inquiry—If the fair value of a purchased loan is less than the purchase price because a loan is repurchased under a recourse provision, does FASB ASC 310-30 permit recording the loan at the purchase price?

Reply—If a loan meets the criteria of FASB ASC 310-30-15 such that it is in the scope of FASB ASC 310-30 and the seller repurchases the asset at a price that is more than fair value, the seller should record the asset at its fair value and record a loss for the difference between the price paid and the fair value, if not already recognized. An allowance for loan losses to offset recording the loan at the purchase price should not be recorded. In most cases, if the loan had previously been transferred with recourse, the seller should already have recognized an associated liability for the recourse obligation in accordance with FASB ASC 450, *Contingencies*, and FASB ASC 860, *Transfers and Servicing*, as well as FASB ASC 460, *Guarantees*.

[Revised, June 2009, to reflect conforming changes necessary due to the issuance of FASB ASC.]

.20 Acquired Loans Where Purchase Price Is Less Than Fair Value Under FASB ASC 310-30

Inquiry—In accordance with FASB ASC 310-30, if the fair value of a purchased loan is more than the purchase price because a loan is acquired (for example, as part of a clean up call) should the seller record a gain?

Reply—No. There may be instances where the seller is required or has an option to re-purchase an asset at a price that is less than fair value. In that situation and if the loan is within the scope of FASB ASC 310-30, the investor should record the asset at the purchase price and the excess of expected cash flows over the initial investment should be recognized as the yield under FASB ASC 310-30.

[Revised, June 2009, to reflect conforming changes necessary due to the issuance of FASB ASC.]

.21 Accounting for Loans With Cash Flow Shortfalls That Are Insignificant Under FASB ASC 310-30

Inquiry—Related to FASB ASC 310-30-15-8, an investor might establish a policy that a shortfall in contractually required payments below a certain amount or percentage is insignificant and thus, certain acquired loans would not be in the scope of FASB ASC 310-30. For loans with shortfalls in payments of less than the established threshold, how should those discounts be accreted into income as a yield adjustment?

Reply—If a loan is not in the scope of FASB ASC 310-30, then FASB ASC 310-20 applies, and FASB ASC 310-20-35-15 requires that the entire discount be accreted to income over the life of the loan.

[Revised, June 2009, to reflect conforming changes necessary due to the issuance of FASB ASC.]

[.22] Reserved

.23 Carrying Over the Allowance for Loan and Lease Losses (ALLL) Under FASB ASC 310-30 (Part II)

Inquiry—Are there any recommendations on calculating allowance ratios relating to loans in the scope of FASB ASC 310-30?

Reply—Although the nonaccretable difference is akin to an ALLL because it represents amounts that are not expected to be collected, it should not be included in the ALLL or ALLL ratios. The only time there is any ALLL for the loans within the scope of FASB ASC 310-30 is when the expected cash flows have decreased after acquisition and a loss is recognized by the investor. In other words, at the purchase date, for loans within the scope of FASB ASC 310-30, the allowance-to-loans ratio is always zero. The investor may wish to disclose in the notes to the financials the amount of the nonaccretable difference so that the readers understand by how much the loans have already been "written down."

[Revised, June 2009, to reflect conforming changes necessary due to the issuance of FASB ASC.]

[.24] Reserved

.25 Income Recognition for Non-Accrual Loans Acquired Under FASB ASC 310-30 (Part I)

Inquiry—What is the accounting for a purchased loan that was classified by the previous owner as non-accrual and for which cash flows cannot be reasonably estimated under FASB ASC 310-30?

Reply—FASB ASC 310-30 does not prohibit placing (or keeping) loans on non-accrual. At inception or thereafter the investor may place a loan on non-accrual, if the conditions in FASB ASC 310-30-35-3 are met. FASB ASC 310-30-50-2(a)(4) requires certain disclosures for purchases of non-accrual loans.

[Revised, June 2009, to reflect conforming changes necessary due to the issuance of FASB ASC.]

.26 Income Recognition for Non-Accrual Loans Acquired Under FASB ASC 310-30 (Part II)

Inquiry—A loan is classified as non-accrual by a seller because the debtor is not meeting its obligations under the loan's contractual terms. That loan is sold to an investor who determines that the loan meets the requirements of FASB ASC 310-30. If the investor can reasonably estimate cash flows, should the investor classify the loan as an accruing loan?

Reply—Yes, if the investor can reasonably estimate cash flows, it should recognize an accretable yield and the loan is an accruing loan as discussed in FASB ASC 310-30-35-3.

[Revised, June 2009, to reflect conforming changes necessary due to the issuance of FASB ASC.]

.27 Income Recognition for Non-Accrual Loans Acquired Under FASB ASC 310-30 (Part III)

Inquiry—Assuming the investor followed the cost recovery method on a loan, and assuming the loan was brought current for a period of time, could the investor return the loan to accrual status and account for the loan as a new loan?

Reply—If the loan was within the scope of FASB ASC 310-30 when it was purchased, it is not accounted for as a new loan but is always under the requirements of FASB ASC 310-30, even if the loan's performance improves. However, as discussed in Q&A section 2130.26, the loan should be accruing income whenever the investor is able to reasonably estimate cash flows. Also, if the currently expected cash flows exceed the originally expected cash flows, the guidance in paragraphs 8–11 of FASB ASC 310-30-35 should be applied, which may result in recognizing income at a higher yield than originally expected.

[Revised, June 2009, to reflect conforming changes necessary due to the issuance of FASB ASC.]

.28 Estimating Cash Flows Under FASB ASC 310-30

Inquiry—In accordance with the guidance in FASB ASC 310-30, how often should an investor reassess the cash flows expected to be collected?

Reply—Investors should reassess expected cash flows at the end of each reporting period. Thus, for entities that prepare quarterly GAAP-basis financial statements, it is expected that cash flows will be re-assessed at least quarterly.

[Revised, June 2009, to reflect conforming changes necessary due to the issuance of FASB ASC.]

.29 Implications of FASB ASC 310-20-35-11 With a Restructured or Refinanced Loan Under FASB ASC 310-30 (Part I)

Inquiry—Can a loan that meets the requirements of FASB ASC 310-20-35-11 be removed from the scope of FASB ASC 310-30? If a loan is within the scope of FASB ASC 310-30 and there are modifications to that loan, should the guidance in FASB ASC 310-20-35-11 apply?

Reply—No. FASB ASC 310-20-35-11 only applies to loans that are not within the scope of FASB ASC 310-30. The point of FASB ASC 310-30-35-13 is that a loan stays in the scope of FASB ASC 310-30, regardless of restructuring or refinancing, except for a troubled debt restructuring.

[Revised, June 2009, to reflect conforming changes necessary due to the issuance of FASB ASC.]

.30 Implications of FASB ASC 310-20-35-11 With a Restructured or Refinanced Loan Under FASB ASC 310-30 (Part II)

Inquiry—Can a loan that has been extinguished in accordance with FASB ASC 310-20-35-11 and given a new loan number, with new terms, but which has not been paid off, be accounted for as a new loan under the guidance in FASB ASC 310-30? What steps could the investor and borrower take to permit the loan to be accounted for as a new loan?

Reply—A loan within the scope of FASB ASC 310-30 can never be accounted for as a new loan, except through a troubled debt restructuring in accordance with FASB ASC 310-40.

[Revised, June 2009, to reflect conforming changes necessary due to the issuance of FASB ASC.]

.31 Variable Rate Loans and Changes in Cash Flows and FASB ASC 310-30

Inquiry—In accordance with the guidance in FASB ASC 310-30, should an investor in variable rate loans determine the cause of a decrease in expected cash flows?

Reply—Yes. To the extent that the investor can directly attribute a decrease in expected cash flows to a decrease in the contractual interest rate, the investor should reduce the yield recognized in income on a prospective basis. However, if the investor is not able to directly attribute the decrease in expected cash flows to a decrease in the contractual interest rate (for example, because the change in the index or rate has no direct effect on the cash flows available to the borrower to service the loan or because the change in the index or rate had no direct effect on expected cash flows that relate to the value of the collateral) the investor should immediately recognize any decrease in expected cash flows as an impairment, not over time as reduced yield.

[Revised, June 2009, to reflect conforming changes necessary due to the issuance of FASB ASC.]

.32 Pool Accounting Under FASB ASC 310-30 (Part I)

Inquiry—In accordance with the guidance in FASB ASC 310-30, if a loan is removed from a pool, how is the specific carrying amount of a loan determined?

Reply—As discussed in FASB ASC 310-30-40-1, once a pool has been assembled the integrity of the pool should be maintained. If the loan is removed under the specific criteria in FASB ASC 310-30-40-1, it should be removed at its carrying amount. In some cases the cash flows of the pool will have been estimated for the pool as a whole such that there is no specific information on the carrying amount and cash flows related to any particular loan. In that case, an allocation of carrying amount to the loan on a pro rata basis is an appropriate way to achieve the goal of not impacting the accounting for the remaining pool. In other cases, the cash flows of the pool may have been built up as the sum of cash flows of individual loans and there is specific information related to the loan being removed. In that case, the carrying amount is allocated on the basis of the specific information for the loan removed. In either case, the goal remains the same—that is, to not have a removal event result in either impairment or an increase in yield for the remaining pool.

[Revised, June 2009, to reflect conforming changes necessary due to the issuance of FASB ASC.]

.33 Pool Accounting Under FASB ASC 310-30 (Part II)

Inquiry—Alternatively, and related to Q&A section 2130.32, should the loan be removed at its initial fair value in accordance with the guidance in FASB ASC 310-30?

Reply—Generally, no. Removing a loan at its initial fair value, unless done very shortly after acquisition of the loan and creation of the pool, would likely result in a change in the effective yield of the remaining pool and the stated intent of FASB ASC 310-30 is that removing a loan from a pool should not result in such a change.

[Revised, June 2009, to reflect conforming changes necessary due to the issuance of FASB ASC.]

.34 Application to Fees Expected to Be Collected Under FASB ASC 310-30

Inquiry—In accordance with the guidance in FASB ASC 310-30, should fees be included in "expected cash flows?" The FASB ASC glossary definition for *cash flows expected at acquisition* includes "principal, interest and other cash flows expected to be collected." Does FASB ASC 310-30 address late fees and other fees?

Reply—"Other cash flows expected to be collected" includes all fees. If late fees are expected to be collected and are contractual, the investor should include them in total contractual cash flows and expected cash flows for purposes of calculating yield and making disclosures. If late fees are contractual but not expected to be collected, the investor should exclude late fees from contractual cash flows and disclose that accounting policy (if it is considered material).

[Revised, June 2009, to reflect conforming changes necessary due to the issuance of FASB ASC.]

.35 Application to Cash Flows From Collateral and Other Sources Under FASB ASC 310-30

Inquiry—In accordance with the guidance in FASB ASC 310-30, should cash expected to be received from the ownership and sale of assets taken in settlement of loans be included in "other cash flows expected to be collected?"

Reply—Cash flows expected at acquisition includes all cash flows directly related to the acquired loan, including those expected from collateral. Although yield is measured on this basis under FASB ASC 310-30 for the loan prior to foreclosure, an asset received by the investor in full or partial settlement of a loan should be accounted for in accordance with paragraphs 2–4 of FASB ASC 310-40-40.

[Revised, June 2009, to reflect conforming changes necessary due to the issuance of FASB ASC.]

.36 Impact on Cash Flows on a Group of Loans Accounted for as a Pool in Accordance With FASB ASC 310-30 if There Is a Confirming Event, and One Loan Is Removed as Expected

Inquiry—FASB ASC 310-30-15-6 states that investors may aggregate loans acquired in the same fiscal quarter that have common risk characteristics and thereby use a composite interest rate and expectation of cash flows expected to be collected for the pool. FASB ASC 310-30-40-1 states that once the pool is assembled, the integrity of the pool should be maintained. What is the impact on the accounting for a group of loans accounted for as a pool, if there is a confirming event, and one loan is removed from the pool as expected?

Reply—The following is an example of the impact on the accounting for a pool of loans, if there is a confirming event, and one loan is removed as expected.

FASB ASC 310-30 Example

Group of Loans

Example 1—Confirming Event, One Loan Is Removed From Pool, as Expected

Facts: The investor purchases 10 loans that individually meet the scope of FASB ASC 310-30 for $800. Based on the aggregation criteria, the investor assembles the loans into a pool. The investor initially expects to collect $929.29 in cash flows (which generates a yield of approximately 5.387 percent over 3 years). The investor recognizes one month of yield income. The investor then receives notification that one obligor has become bankrupt and that it will make no further payments on its loan. The investor concludes that event is in accordance with the original expectation of cash flows. That is, the investor continues to expect that it will collect $929.29 from the pool of loans. The investor removes the contractual cash flows from that loan and an equal amount of nonaccretable difference, in the amount of $117.42, from the pool such that the yield is unaffected. This TPA does not address charge-offs.

	Original Purchase	*Accrue Income*	*Receive Payment*	***Balance***	*Removal of Loan*	***Balance***
Contractual Cash Flows	1,200.00		(25.81)	1,174.19	(117.42)	1,056.77
Nonaccretable Difference	(270.71)			(270.71)	117.42	(153.29)
Expected Cash Flows	929.29		(25.81)	903.48	0.00	903.48
Accretable Yield	(129.29)	6.67		(122.62)	0.00	(122.62)
Recorded Amount	800.00	6.67	(25.81)	780.86	0.00	780.86
Bad Debt Expense/ALLL	0.00			0.00	0.00	0.00
Carrying Amount	800.00	6.67	(25.81)	780.86	0.00	780.86
Yield (computed on carrying amount)*	**5.387%**			**5.384%**		**5.384%**
Principal Balance	1,000.00		(19.14)	980.86	(98.09)	882.77
Delinquent Accrued Interest Rec.	50.00			50.00	(5.00)	45.00
Balance	1,050.00		(19.14)	1,030.86	(103.09)	927.77
Remaining Interest Due Under Contract	150.00		(6.67)	143.33	(14.33)	129.00
Nonaccretable Difference	(270.71)			(270.71)	117.42	(153.29)
Expected Cash Flows	929.29		(25.81)	903.48	0.00	903.48
Accretable Yield	(129.29)	6.67		(122.62)	0.00	(122.62)
Recorded Amount	800.00	6.67	(25.81)	780.86	0.00	780.86
Bad Debt Expense/ALLL	0.00			0.00	0.00	0.00
Carrying Amount	800.00	6.67	(25.81)	780.86	0.00	780.86

* Yield =Accretable yield divided by the carrying amount divided by 36 times 12

[Revised, June 2009, to reflect conforming changes necessary due to the issuance of FASB ASC.]

.37 Impact on Cash Flows on a Group of Loans Accounted for as a Pool in Accordance With FASB ASC 310-30 if There Is a Confirming Event, One Loan Is Removed From the Pool, and the Investor Decreases Its Estimate of Expected Cash Flows

Inquiry—FASB ASC 310-30-15-6 states that investors may aggregate loans acquired in the same fiscal quarter that have common risk characteristics and thereby use a composite interest rate and expectation of cash flows expected to be collected for the pool. FASB ASC 310-30-40-1 states that once the pool is assembled, the integrity of the pool should be maintained. What is the impact on the on the accounting for a group of loans accounted for as a pool, if there is a confirming event, one loan is removed from the pool, and the investor decreases its estimate of expected cash flows?

Reply—The following is an example of the impact on the accounting for a group of loans accounted for as a pool, if there is a confirming event, one loan is removed from the pool, and the investor decreases its estimate of expected cash flows:

FASB ASC 310-30 Example

Group of Loans

Example 2—Confirming Event, One Loan Is Removed From Pool, and Investor Decreases Estimate of Expected Cash Flows From Pool

Facts: The investor purchases 10 loans that individually meet the scope of FASB ASC 310-30 for $800. Based on the aggregation criteria, the investor assembles the loans into a pool. The investor initially expects to collect $929.29 in cash flows (which generates a yield of approximately 5.387 percent over 3 years). The investor recognizes one month of yield income. The investor then receives notification that one that one obligor has become bankrupt and that it will make no further payments on its loan. The investor concludes that the expected cash flows from the pool are decreased by $90.35, which has a present value at 5.387 percent of $78.09. The investor records a provision of $78.09, increasing the loan loss allowance by $78.09. In addition, the investor removes the contractual cash flows from that loan and an equal amount of nonaccretable discount, in the amount of $117.42, from the pool such that the yield is unaffected. This TPA does not address charge-offs.

	Original Purchase	*Accrue Income*	*Receive Payment*	**Balance**	*Decrease in Expected Cash Flows*	**Balance**	*Removal of Loan*	**Balance**
Contractual Cash Flows	1,200.00		(25.81)	1,174.19		1,174.19	(117.42)	1,056.77
Nonaccretable Difference	(270.71)			(270.71)	(12.26)	(282.97)	117.42	(165.55)
Expected Cash Flows	929.29		(25.81)	903.48	(12.26)	891.22	0.00	891.22
Accretable Yield	(129.29)	6.67		(122.62)	12.26	(110.36)	0.00	(110.36)
Recorded Amount	800.00	6.67	(25.81)	780.86	0.00	780.86	0.00	780.86
Bad Debt Expense/ALLL	0.00			0.00	(78.09)	(78.09)		(78.09)
Carrying Amount	800.00	6.67	(25.81)	780.86	(78.09)	702.77	0.00	702.77
Yield (computed on carrying amount)*	5.387%			5.384%		5.384%		5.384%

	Original Purchase	*Accrue Income*	*Receive Payment*	**Balance**	*Decrease in Expected Cash Flows*	**Balance**	*Removal of Loan*	**Balance**
Principal Balance	1,000.00		(19.14)	980.86	0.00	980.86	(98.09)	882.77
Delinquent Accrued Interest Rec.	50.00			50.00	0.00	50.00	(5.00)	45.00
Balance	1,050.00		(19.14)	1,030.86	0.00	1,030.86	(103.09)	927.77
Remaining Interest Due Under Contract	150.00		(6.67)	143.33	0.00	143.33	(14.33)	129.00
Nonaccretable Difference	(270.71)			(270.71)	(12.26)	(282.97)	117.42	(165.55)
Expected Cash Flows	929.29		(25.81)	903.48	(12.26)	891.22	0.00	891.22
Accretable Yield	(129.29)	6.67		(122.62)	12.26	(110.36)	0.00	(110.36)
Recorded Amount	800.00	6.67	(25.81)	780.86	0.00	780.86	0.00	780.86
Bad Debt Expense/ALLL	0.00			0.00	(78.09)	(78.09)	0.00	(78.09)
Carrying Amount	800.00	6.67	(25.81)	780.86	(78.09)	702.77	0.00	702.77

* Yield = Accretable yield divided by the carrying amount divided by 36 times 12

[Revised, June 2009, to reflect conforming changes necessary due to the issuance of FASB ASC.]

.38 Certificates of Deposit and FASB ASC 820, *Fair Value Measurements and Disclosures*

Inquiry—Are certificates of deposit within the scope of the disclosure requirements of FASB ASC 820, *Fair Value Measurements and Disclosures*?

Reply—Generally not. Certificates of deposit that meet the definition of a security in FASB ASC 320, *Investments—Debt and Equity Securities*, are subject to the disclosure requirements of FASB ASC 820-10-50; those that do not meet the definition are not subject to those disclosure requirements. FASB ASC 320-10-20 defines a *security* as:

> A share, participation, or other interest in property or in an entity of the issuer or an obligation of the issuer that has all of the following characteristics:
>
> a. It is either represented by an instrument issued in bearer or registered form or, if not represented by an instrument, is registered in books maintained to record transfers by or on behalf of the issuer.
>
> b. It is of a type commonly dealt in on securities exchanges or markets or, when represented by an instrument, is commonly recognized in any area in which it is issued or dealt in as a medium for investment.
>
> c. It either is one of a class or series or by its terms is divisible into a class or series of shares, participations, interests, or obligations.

Most certificates of deposit would not meet that definition. However, some negotiable certificates of deposit may meet the definition of a security and, therefore, may be subject to the disclosure requirements of FASB ASC 820-10-50 if they are not classified as held to maturity.

[Issue Date: May 2010.]

.39 Balance Sheet Classification of Certificates of Deposit

Inquiry—Where should a certificate of deposit be classified on the balance sheet?

Reply—Certificates of deposit with original maturities of 90 days or less are commonly considered "cash and cash equivalents" under FASB ASC 305. A certificate of deposit with an original maturity greater than 90 days would not be included in cash and cash equivalents. If the certificate of deposit is not a security, as defined in FASB ASC 320, it could be included in "investments—other."

The following is an example of a policies and procedures note disclosure:

> Investments—Other
>
> Certificates of deposit held for investment that are not debt securities are included in "investments—other." Certificates of deposit with original maturities greater than three months and remaining maturities less than one year are classified as "short-term investments—other." Certificates of deposit with remaining maturities greater than one year are classified as "long-term investments—other."

[Issue Date: May 2010.]

.40 Certificates of Deposit and FASB ASC 320

Inquiry—Are certificates of deposit within the scope of FASB ASC 320?

Reply—Generally not. FASB ASC 320-10-20 defines a *security* as:

> A share, participation, or other interest in property or in an entity of the issuer or an obligation of the issuer that has all of the following characteristics:
>
> a. It is either represented by an instrument issued in bearer or registered form or, if not represented by an instrument, is registered in books maintained to record transfers by or on behalf of the issuer.
>
> b. It is of a type commonly dealt in on securities exchanges or markets or, when represented by an instrument, is commonly recognized in any area in which it is issued or dealt in as a medium for investment.
>
> c. It either is one of a class or series or by its terms is divisible into a class or series of shares, participations, interests, or obligations.

Most certificates of deposit would not meet that definition. Certain negotiable certificates of deposit, however, may meet the definition of a security and, therefore, may be subject to FASB ASC 320.

[Issue Date: May 2010.]

Q&A Section 2140
Inventories

.01 Warehousing Included in Cost of Inventory

Inquiry—A client deals in wholesaling and retailing automotive tires for foreign cars. Most of the inventory is imported, and it is valued on the company's records at the actual inventory cost plus freight-in. At year-end, the warehousing costs are prorated over cost of goods sold and ending inventory. The company's auditor believes the warehousing costs should not be capitalized to inventory, but the entire amount should be expensed in the year the costs are incurred. Are warehousing costs considered to be product costs or period costs?

Reply—Financial Accounting Standards Board (FASB) *Accounting Standards Codification* (ASC) 330-10-30-1 states, in part:

> As applied to inventories, cost means in principle the sum of the applicable expenditures and charges directly or indirectly incurred in bringing an article to its existing condition and location.

Kieso and Weygandt, *Intermediate Accounting*, 9th Edition states:

> Product costs are those costs that "attach" to the inventory and are recorded in the inventory accounts. These costs are directly connected with the bringing of goods to the place of business of the buyer and converting such goods to a saleable condition. Such charges would include freight charges on goods purchased, other direct costs of acquisition and labor, and other production costs incurred in processing the goods up to the time of sale. It would seem proper also, to allocate to inventories a share of any buying costs or expenses of a purchasing department, storage costs, and other costs incurred in storing or handling goods before they are sold (i.e., warehousing costs). Because of the practical difficulties involved in allocating such costs and expenses, however these items are not ordinarily included in valuing inventories.

Costs of delivering the goods from the warehouse would be considered a selling expense and should not be allocated to the goods that are still in the warehouse.

[Revised, June 2009, to reflect conforming changes necessary due to the issuance of FASB ASC.]

.02 Obsolete Items in Inventory—I

Inquiry—A client purchased in bulk various inventories of stock material. This material is used to produce various specialized parts used in electronic equipment. The bulk purchase took place some eighteen months ago, and less than ten percent of these inventories have been used. The client claims that there may be some obsolete stock on hand from this bulk purchase, but an eighteen month period is not enough time to effectively determine the complete degree of obsolescence because the highly specialized nature of the product line may not lead to renewed orders until periods beyond one or more operating cycles. Based on the information available to the client, about one-third of the original bulk purchase will be written off because of obsolescence. For the remaining inventories, the client will present a representation letter indicating that he or she believes the remaining inventory not to be obsolete.

There may be more obsolete inventory than the client is willing to admit. The poor turnover of such items is the chief reason for concern. Pricing the inventory at the lower of cost or market will be difficult. The nature of the inventory (many small items at low unit cost) and its poor turnover make obtaining market prices difficult.

What is the responsibility of auditors, not being inventory experts, in determining the extent of obsolescence?

Reply—Paragraphs .11 and .A25 of AU-C section 501, *Audit Evidence—Specific Considerations for Selected Items* (AICPA, *Professional Standards*), address the auditor's responsibility to obtain sufficient appropriate audit evidence regarding the condition of inventory, which includes identifying obsolete, damaged or aging inventory. This audit evidence might include the opinion of other experts, for example an electronics engineer, with respect to the quality of the inventories in this case.

Over the eighteen-month period since the inventories were purchased, less than ten percent have been utilized. Such a usage rate indicates that the client has close to an estimated fifteen year supply of these inventories. This would indicate that little or no value should be assigned to these inventories.

[Revised, May 2007; Revised, December 2012, to reflect conforming changes necessary due to the issuance of SAS Nos. 122–126.]

[.03] Reserved

.04 Airplanes Chartered While Held for Sale

Inquiry—A company purchases airplanes for sale to others. However, until they are sold, the company charters and services the planes. What would be the proper way to report these airplanes in the company's financial statements?

Reply—The primary use of the airplanes should determine their treatment on the balance sheet. Since the airplanes are held primarily for sale, and chartering is only a temporary use, the airplanes should be classified as current assets. However, depreciation would not be appropriate if the planes are considered inventory. Financial Accounting Standards Board (FASB) *Accounting Standards Codification* (ASC) glossary states, in part, that the term inventory "excludes long-term assets subject to depreciation accounting, or goods which, when put into use, will be so classified."

If the use period were to exceed one year, reclassification to fixed assets and recognition of depreciation expense would be appropriate under generally accepted accounting principles (GAAP).

[Revised, June 2009, to reflect conforming changes necessary due to the issuance of FASB ASC.]

[.05] Reserved

.06 Inventory of Meat Packer

Inquiry—A client engaged in the meat packing business uses the "National Provisioner Daily Market Service" quotations in valuing its inventories. The client contends that these quotations, adjusted for freight differentials, reflect an accurate approximation of actual costs and, in lieu of a complete cost accounting system, should be considered as cost for inventory valuation. Is this method of inventory valuation acceptable for meat packers?

Reply—Meat packing companies generally value their work in process and finished goods inventories at market price less cost to bring to market in accordance with Financial Accounting Standards Board (FASB) *Accounting Standards Codification* (ASC) 905, *Agriculture*. Live animals and whole carcasses are carried at the lower of cost and net realizable value for inventories measured using any method other than LIFO or the retail method. Inventories measured using LIFO or the retail inventory method are carried at the lower of cost or market. Many companies use quoted costs such as the National Provisioner quotations which are estimated costs of producing a particular cut of meat adjusted for the fluctuating daily livestock prices and other factors. These quoted prices must be further adjusted by the individual meat packers to take into account individual factors such as freight and storage.

[Revised, May 2017.]

[.07] Reserved

.08 Valuing Precious Metals Inventory Used in Manufacturing Applications

Inquiry—Should inventories of precious metals used in manufacturing applications (for example, diamonds used in drill bits, plutonium or uranium used in steel fabrication, or titanium used in paint manufacturing) be valued at market or at the lower of cost or market?

Reply—These inventories should be valued at either the lower of cost and net realizable value or the lower of cost or market, depending on the cost method, in accordance with Financial Accounting Standards Board (FASB) *Accounting Standards Codification* (ASC) 330-10. The excess of market value over cost may be disclosed.

The exception to "lower of cost or market" that allows precious metals to be recorded at market on the balance sheet does not apply to these industrial applications because the metals will be used in the manufacturing process rather than held for immediate sale and do not meet the other conditions specified in FASB ASC 330-10-35-15, which states:

> Only in exceptional cases may inventories properly be stated above cost. For example, precious metals having a fixed monetary value with no substantial cost of marketing may be stated at such monetary value; any other exceptions must be justifiable by inability to determine appropriate approximate costs, immediate marketability at quoted market price, and the characteristic of unit interchangeability.

FASB ASC 330-10-50-3 further states:

> Where goods are stated above cost, this fact shall be fully disclosed.

[Amended, June 1995; Revised, May 2017.]

.09 Standard Cost for Inventory Valuation

Inquiry—A client uses standard costs for valuing inventory. What disclosure is necessary in the financial statements regarding inventory valuation?

Reply—Ordinarily, standard costs should be adjusted to a figure which approximates lower of cost and net realizable value or the lower of cost or market, depending on the cost method. If this is done, then it is appropriate to use standard costs for financial reporting purposes. This is usually the case where standards are currently and frequently adjusted.

Financial Accounting Standards Board (FASB) *Accounting Standards Codification* (ASC) 330-10-30-12 states:

> Standard costs are acceptable if adjusted at reasonable intervals to reflect current conditions so that at the balance sheet date standard costs reasonably approximate costs computed under one of the recognized bases. In such cases descriptive language shall be used which will express this relationship, as, for instance, "approximate costs determined on the first-in first-out basis," or, if it is desired to mention standard costs, "at standard costs, approximating average costs."

Accordingly, if in this particular case standard costs do in fact approximate the lower of cost and net realizable value or the lower of cost or market, then disclosure along the lines indicated in the above reference is adequate.

On the other hand, if the difference between standard costs and the lower of cost and net realizable value or the lower of cost or market is material, then mere footnote disclosure will not cure the known statement imperfection.

[Revised, May 2017.]

[.10] Reserved

.11 Average Cost Method for Subsidiary

Inquiry—Company A and all of its subsidiaries, except one, determine the cost of inventories by the last-in, first-out method (LIFO). The one subsidiary uses an average cost method. Is the average cost method acceptable for determining the cost of inventory? Is it acceptable for one subsidiary to use the average cost method and Company A and the other subsidiaries to use the LIFO method?

Reply—The average cost method is an acceptable method for determining the cost of inventory. An entity may use more than one method to determine the cost of inventory provided the methods are disclosed.

.12 Classification of Replacement Parts Under a Maintenance Agreement

Inquiry—Company A has entered into a maintenance agreement with Company B, an unrelated party, to provide maintenance and service for specialized computer equipment leased by Company B to third parties. The maintenance contract between A and B requires that A maintain a spare/replacement parts inventory for the equipment. Company A has no use for these parts other than to fulfill the obligation under its contract with Company B. The term of the contract between Company A and Company B is for several years.

Most of the spare parts (i.e., circuit boards) are of a repairable nature, and it is expected that as A replaces a part, A will have the removed part refurbished, at its own cost. The refurbished parts will be available for future use as necessary.

Should Company A classify the refurbished replacement parts as inventory? Should Company A's investment in the parts be amortized?

Reply—Company A should classify the refurbished replacement parts as inventory. Inventory costs should not be amortized; a loss in their utility should be reflected as a charge against revenues of the period in which it occurs, as discussed in Financial Accounting Standards Board (FASB) *Accounting Standards Codification* (ASC) 330-10-35-2.

[Revised, June 2009, to reflect conforming changes necessary due to the issuance of FASB ASC.]

.13 Classification of Slow-Moving Inventory

Inquiry—A client, engaged in an oil field related industry, has slow-moving products that are not considered obsolete. The inventory is properly stated at the lower of cost or market. The client plans to continue selling the inventory on hand but will cease manufacturing the specialized product. Based on current sales estimates and demand for the product, it appears likely that the client will be able to sell all of the items in the inventory over a period of about four years. Is it correct to classify a portion of the slow-moving inventory as a long-term asset in the client's classified balance sheet?

Reply—The portion of the slow-moving inventory not reasonably expected to be realized in cash during the client's normal operating cycle should be classified as a long-term asset in the company's classified balance sheet. Financial Accounting Standards Board (FASB) *Accounting Standards Codification* (ASC) 310-10-45-9 states that the term *current assets* is used to designate cash and other assets or resources commonly identified as those that are reasonably expected to be realized in cash or sold or consumed during the normal operating cycle of the business.

[Revised, June 2009, to reflect conforming changes necessary due to the issuance of FASB ASC.]

.14 Disclosure of LIFO Reserve

Inquiry—Should a company using the last-in, first-out (LIFO) method of inventory valuation be required to disclose the LIFO reserve in its financial statements or in the accompanying footnotes?

Reply—Yes. The Accounting Standards Division Issues Paper, *Identification and Discussion of Certain Financial Accounting and Reporting Issues Concerning LIFO Inventories*, addresses this matter in section 2, paragraphs 24 through 28. Paragraph 28 indicates that the task force voted (9 yes, 0 no) that either the LIFO reserve or replacement cost and its basis for determination should be disclosed. Paragraph 26 states that the Securities and Exchange Commission (SEC) requires companies whose securities trade publicly to disclose this information [Regulation S-X, section 210.5-02.6(c)] and that many nonpublic companies also disclose this information.

[Amended, June 1995; Revised, June 2009, to reflect conforming changes necessary due to the issuance of recent authoritative literature.]

[.15] Reserved

[.16] Reserved

Q&A Section 2210

Fixed Assets

.01 Settlement of Mortgage Installment on Real Estate Between Buyer and Seller

Inquiry—A company purchased an office building subject to the seller's assumable mortgage. The closing of the transaction occurred in the middle of a month which was between payment dates on the mortgage. The closing statement reflected a credit from the seller to the buyer for the interest that accrued on the mortgage from the last payment date until the date of the closing. How should this credit be accounted for by the buyer?

Reply—The buyer would treat the accrued interest credit as a reduction of interest expense for the first month of ownership. When the buyer makes the first interest payment after the closing, the credit will offset the full month's interest paid and thus reduce the buyer's net interest expense to the amount attributable to the period that the property was owned by the buyer.

[Amended, June 1995.]

.02 Broker's Commission Received by Purchaser of Property as Purchase Price Concession

Inquiry—A corporation ("purchaser") is engaged in negotiations to purchase real property. During the negotiations, the purchaser was unwilling to accept the seller's best offer. To induce the purchaser to agree to the sale, the broker agreed to rebate a portion of the seller-paid commission to the purchaser.

Would this rebate be considered income to the purchaser or a reduction of the cost of the property acquired?

Reply—The "rebate" received from the broker should be accounted for as a reduction of the cost of the property rather than as income. Income should not be recognized on a purchase. The receipt of the rebate was part of the acquisition of the real estate and, when netted against the purchase price, reflects the amount the purchaser was willing to pay for the property.

[Amended, June 1995.]

[.03] Reserved

[.04] Reserved

[.05] Reserved

.06 Valuation of Cattle Herd

Inquiry—A client, in the business of raising and selling cattle, has not been in business long enough to develop enough cost information to reliably value the cattle raised by them. Each cow costs $2,000 or more and has an estimated salvage value of about $300 at the end of its productive breeding life. The client has adopted a life of seven years for its breeding herd based on the various ages of the cows.

The client proposes to price the cattle raised as follows:

Purchased calves

When a cow is purchased with a "calf at side," twenty percent of the purchase price is allocated to the calf. An additional $50 is allocated to the calf every six months for the first eighteen months. At eighteen months of age, the cows are considered mature enough for breeding and are then either sold or placed in the breeding herd and depreciated.

Raised calves

Since the mother is maintained principally for breeding and is expected to produce one calf each year, the calf birthed and raised is allocated one year's depreciation of the mother, plus $50 at birth. An additional $50 is allocated every six months for the first eighteen months.

The problem of valuing the cattle is compounded by the fact that cattle purchased for breeding and those purchased for sale are not separated, and any cow may be sold at any time. What improvements could be made in the pricing scheme, and how should the breeding herd and the herd held for sale be shown on the balance sheet?

Reply—Rather than setting an average breeding life of seven years for the breeding herd, it would appear more reasonable to set an estimated age at which a cow should be fully depreciated and to depreciate the cost of each cow over the remaining estimated years of life. Also, instead of allocating twenty percent of the purchase price of the cow to the calf "at side," it would be better to determine the percent applicable to the calf on the basis of the number of expected additional calves for that cow.

In valuing the calves, if the $50 figure is a reasonable estimate of six months of costs, the method seems reasonable. However, instead of allocating one year's depreciation of the mother plus $50 at birth, it might be better to allocate only the depreciation plus the direct expenses of birth such as veterinarian's fees, etc.

Since it is difficult to determine which of the cattle are "inventory" and which are "fixed assets," it might not be appropriate in this case to classify the assets and liabilities as current or long-term in the balance sheet.

.07 Costs of Ski Slopes and Lifts

Inquiry—A company has developed a piece of land into a skiing resort. The company has cut the trees, cleared and graded the land and hills, and constructed ski lifts and platter pulls.

Should the tree cutting, land clearing, and grading costs of constructing the ski slopes be capitalized to land? If so, are these costs amortizable?

Should the clearing and grading costs connected with the construction of the ski lifts and platter pulls be capitalized to this equipment and depreciated?

Reply—All expenditures incurred which are made for the purpose of making the land suitable for its intended use or purpose (whether that use be for the construction of a ski lodge, lifts, slopes, platter pulls, or other facilities) are properly capitalizable as land costs, and land is not subject to depreciation. During the course of clearing the land to make it useful for the purpose acquired, salable timber may be recovered, and since the clearing costs are capital items, amounts realized from the sale of the timber may properly be credited to the land account. Recurring maintenance of right-of-way (i.e., the slope and ski-lift areas) would be properly treated as a period cost.

.08 Restaurant Dishes and Silverware

Inquiry—Should a base stock inventory of silverware and dishes be shown on the balance sheet of a restaurant as a fixed asset? In the base stock method, the base stock is recorded at an unchanging amount and additions to the stock are charged to expenses for the period. Inasmuch as fixed assets are specific items which are subject to depreciation (except land), and the base stock is an approximate figure for many items and is not depreciated, it would seem that the base stock should not be classified as a fixed asset.

Reply—Various publications recommending treatment for large stocks of short-lived, replaceable assets such as silverware and dishes indicate that the assets should be valued on the basis of physical inventories at year-end, with used equipment being valued at 50 percent of current cost, and unused equipment valued at full cost. This, in effect, assigns an average useful life of two years for the equipment. It is recommended that such assets be included in fixed assets.

The classification in the balance sheet should not depend upon the method of valuing the assets. Therefore, regardless of the method of valuation, the assets should be included in fixed assets. If the valuation differs materially from the depreciated cost of individual goods on hand at year-end, the presentation is not in accordance with generally accepted accounting principles.

[.09] Reserved

[.10] Reserved

[.11] Reserved

[.12] Reserved

[.13] Reserved

[.14] Reserved

.15 Capitalization of Cost of Dredging Log Pond

Inquiry—Corporation A operates a log pond and dredged the pond during the year at a cost of $350,000. Thus, the useful life of the log pond was extended several years. Should the dredging cost be expensed or capitalized?

Reply—FASB Concept No. 6, *Elements of Financial Statements—a replacement of FASB Concepts Statement No. 3 (incorporating an amendment of FASB Concepts Statement No. 2)*, paragraph 149 states, in part, "... many assets yield their benefits to an entity over several periods .... Expenses resulting from their use are normally allocated to the periods of their estimated useful lives (the periods over which they are expected to provide benefits) by a 'systematic and rational' allocation procedure, for example, by recognizing depreciation or other amortization."

Since the dredging cost will benefit future periods, Corporation A should capitalize the cost and amortize it in a systematic and rational manner over the estimated period of benefit.

[Revised, June 2009, to reflect conforming changes necessary due to the issuance of FASB ASC.]

[.16] Reserved

[.17] Reserved

.18 Revaluation of Assets

Inquiry—Company A acquired a material amount of treasury stock resulting in a stockholders' equity deficit. Since state law (where Company A is incorporated) prohibits the impairment of legal capital, Company A revalued certain of its assets at fair market value. Should Company A record depreciation for the revalued assets based on historical cost or fair market value?

Reply—An opinion expressed on the financial statements of Company A should be qualified or adverse because the write-up of assets is a departure from generally accepted accounting principles.

[Revised, June 2009, to reflect conforming changes necessary due to the issuance of FASB ASC.]

[.19] Reserved

.20 Compounding Capitalized Interest

Inquiry—Company A is constructing a building for its own use. The company capitalized interest cost on the average amount of accumulated expenditures for the asset during the current year end. The building was completed in the next year. Should the company capitalize interest on the average amount of expenditures for the assets that were made during the current period only or the average amount of accumulated expenditures for the asset during the period including the expenditures made in the prior period, which already includes capitalized interest cost?

Reply—Financial Accounting Standards Board (FASB) *Accounting Standards Codification* (ASC) 835-20-30-3 states, in part:

> The amount capitalized in an accounting period shall be determined by applying the capitalization rate to the average amount of accumulated expenditures for the asset during the period.

FASB ASC 835-20-35-3 further states:

> The compounding of capitalized interest is conceptually consistent with the conclusion that interest on expenditures for the asset is a cost of acquiring the asset.

Accordingly, the rate should be applied to the average of all the accumulated expenditures.

[Revised, June 2009, to reflect conforming changes necessary due to the issuance of FASB ASC.]

[.21] Reserved

[.22] Reserved

[.23] Reserved

[.24] Reserved

.25 Capitalization of Interest Costs Incurred by Subsidiary

Inquiry—A subsidiary with an asset qualifying for interest capitalization under Financial Accounting Standards Board (FASB) *Accounting Standards Codification* (ASC) 835, *Interest*, incurs its entire interest cost from a loan from its parent.

What is the extent of interest that may be appropriately capitalized?

Reply—FASB ASC 835-20-30-3 states, in part: "the amount capitalized in an accounting period shall be determined by applying the capitalization rate to the average amount of accumulated expenditures for the asset during the period." FASB ASC 835-20-30-6 further states

> The total amount of interest cost capitalized in an accounting period shall not exceed the total amount of interest cost

> incurred by the entity in that period. In consolidated financial statements, that limitation shall be applied by reference to the total amount of interest cost incurred by the parent entity and consolidated subsidiaries on a consolidated basis. In any separately issued financial statements of a parent entity or a consolidated subsidiary and in the financial statements (whether separately issued or not) of unconsolidated subsidiaries and other investees accounted for by the equity method, the limitation shall be applied by reference to the total amount of interest cost (including interest on intra-entity borrowings) incurred by the separate entity.

Such financial statements should disclose related party transactions as required by FASB ASC 850, *Related Party Disclosures*.

[Revised, June 2009, to reflect conforming changes necessary due to the issuance of FASB ASC.]

[.26] Reserved

.27 Construction of Asset—Foreign Currency Transaction Gains/ Losses

Inquiry—A company is constructing a building in the United States for its own use. In order to finance the cost of the building, a loan denominated in a foreign currency is obtained from a bank in a foreign country. The company is appropriately capitalizing interest incurred as part of the cost of the building in accordance with Financial Accounting Standards Board (FASB) *Accounting Standards Codification* (ASC) 835, *Interest*. However, the company wants to also capitalize as part of the cost of the building any foreign currency transaction gains or losses it incurs as a result of the loan with the bank in the foreign country. The company's rationale is that the transaction gains or losses relate specifically to the building and therefore should be considered part of the cost of the building. Is this appropriate?

Reply—No. According to FASB ASC glossary, *foreign currency transactions* are transactions whose terms are denominated in a currency other than the entity's functional currency. Foreign currency transactions arise when a reporting entity does any of the following:

> a. Buys or sells on credit goods or services whose prices are denominated in foreign currency
>
> b. Borrows or lends funds and the amounts payable or receivable are denominated in foreign currency
>
> c. Is a party to an unperformed forward exchange contract
>
> d. For other reasons, acquires or disposes of assets, or incurs or settles liabilities denominated in foreign currency.

FASB ASC 830-20-05-2 states:

> Foreign currency transactions may produce receivables or payables that are fixed in terms of the amount of foreign currency that will be received or paid.

FASB ASC 830-20-35-1 further states:

> A change in exchange rates between the functional currency and the currency in which a transaction is denominated increases or decreases the expected amount of functional currency cash flows upon settlement of the transaction. That

> increase or decrease in expected functional currency cash flows is a foreign currency transaction gain or loss that generally shall be included in determining net income for the period in which the exchange rate changes.

Thus, even though the loan was obtained to construct the building, the transaction gains and losses are not part of the cost of the building, but are a result of the change in the exchange rate and are included in income each period in which the exchange rate fluctuates.

[Revised, June 2009, to reflect conforming changes necessary due to the issuance of FASB ASC.]

.28 Accounting for Certain Liquidated Damages

Inquiry—"Liquidated damages" represent contractual payments to a buyer of property, plant, and equipment (PP&E) for the nondelivery or noncompletion of construction of PP&E by a stated completion date. The amount is specified in advance by contract—for example, a stated amount per day of delay—rather than a computation of actual losses of the buyer caused by the delay. Liquidated damages are negotiated to represent compensation for a reasonable estimate of the buyer's costs associated with a delay. Liquidated damages are specified in advance in order to eliminate the need for possibly contentious after-the-fact negotiations about actual costs incurred. How should a buyer of PP&E account for liquidated damages, as defined above?

Reply—Because the buyer does not provide the payer of the damages with an identifiable benefit in exchange for the payment, a buyer typically records liquidated damages as a reduction of the payments it has made to the vendor for the PP&E (that is, a reduction of the cost of the PP&E). Amounts of liquidated damages in excess of the total cost of PP&E would be recognized by the buyer as income.

The basis for this reply is Financial Accounting Standards Board (FASB) *Accounting Standards Codification* (ASC) 605-50. The underlying principle in FASB ASC 605-50 is that unless the customer provides the vendor with an identifiable benefit, the payment received from the vendor is a reduction of the purchase price of the goods purchased from the vendor—that is, a return of amounts paid.

Contracts between a buyer and provider of PP&E could be drafted in two ways—with a realistic completion date and contract price with liquidated damages for late delivery, or with a pessimistic completion date and a bargain contract price with a bonus for early delivery. The accounting for liquidated damages, as noted in this reply, results in the same accounting for the buyer regardless of how the contract is drafted.

[Revised, June 2009, to reflect conforming changes necessary due to the issuance of FASB ASC.]

Q&A Section 2220

Long-Term Investments

.01 Equity Method When Current Direct Ownership Less Than Twenty Percent

Inquiry—Company A purchased a 19 percent stock ownership interest in B. The company also made a loan to B that is convertible into stock of B and is secured by shares of C (B's subsidiary). For as long as the loan is outstanding, Company A will have several seats on B's board. The company also has options to purchase shares of C.

Is the company required to report its investment in B under the equity method?

Reply—Paragraphs 6 and 8 of Financial Accounting Standards Board (FASB) *Accounting Standards Codification* (ASC) 323-10-15 state that the ability to exercise the type of influence contemplated in FASB ASC 323, *Investments—Equity Method and Joint Ventures*, may be indicated in several ways such as representation on the board of directors and investment (direct or indirect) of 20 percent or more in the voting stock of an investee.

The company would own only 19 percent of the outstanding voting stock. Although it is not indicated whether the conversion feature of the loan may result in ownership of 20 percent or more, or whether the board seats would allow A to significantly influence the voting at meetings of B's board of directors, the overall impact of the proposed transaction could demonstrate that the company has the ability to exercise significant influence over the investee. Therefore, the equity method should be followed in accounting for the investment.

[Revised, June 2009, to reflect conforming changes necessary due to the issuance of FASB ASC.]

[.02] Reserved

.03 Equity Method for Investee Following Completed Contract Method

Inquiry—A client, a contractor who follows the percentage of completion method for income recognition, has entered into a joint venture. The joint venture follows the completed contract method in its financial statements. The client accounts for his investment in the joint venture on the equity basis. May the client recognize his share of the venture's income (determined on the percentage of completion method) even though the venture will not recognize income until the contract is completed?

Reply—The FASB ASC glossary defines the terms *earnings or losses of an investee* and *financial position of an investee* as "net income (or net loss) of an investee determined in accordance with U.S. generally accepted accounting principles" and "financial position of an investee determined in accordance with U.S. generally accepted accounting principles," respectively.

Both the completed contract method and the percentage of completion method are generally accepted, and the investor should not change the investee's method of accounting from completed contract to percentage of completion in applying the equity method. If the investee's financial statements are prepared on a comprehensive basis of accounting other than generally accepted accounting principles (GAAP), the investor should eliminate material variances from GAAP in applying the equity method, in accordance with FASB ASC 970-323-35-20.

[Revised, June 2009, to reflect conforming changes necessary due to the issuance of FASB ASC.]

[.04] Reserved

.05 Assuming Pro Rata Share of Venture's Revenues and Expenses

Inquiry—A company has entered into a joint venture with another venturer. Would it be permissible for the company to include in its income its pro rata share of each of the revenue and expense accounts of the venture?

Reply—FASB ASC 323-10-45-1 states:

> Under the equity method, an investment in common stock shall be shown in the balance sheet of an investor as a single amount. Likewise, an investor's share of earnings or losses from its investment shall be shown in its income statement as a single amount except for the extraordinary items as specified in the following paragraph.

However, FASB ASC 810-10-45-14, relating to accounting for investments in unincorporated joint ventures states, in part:

> If the investor-venturer owns an undivided interest in each asset and is proportionately liable for its share of each liability, the provisions of paragraph 323-10-45-1 may not apply in some industries. For example, in certain industries the investor-venturer may account in its financial statements for its *pro rata* share of the assets, liabilities, revenues, and expenses of the venture.

Guidance for transactions of this type relating to real estate can be found in FASB ASC 970-323-25-12 and FASB ASC 970-810-45-1.

[Revised, June 2009, to reflect conforming changes necessary due to the issuance of FASB ASC.]

[.06] Reserved

[.07] Reserved

.08 Acquisition of Subsidiaries by Exchange of Assets With No Book Value

Inquiry—A client, a computer services company, acquired 50 percent of the capital stock of a corporation in exchange for rights to computer programs. The cost of these programs had been expensed by the client. Another party acquired the remaining 50 percent of the stock for $150,000. The client recorded this transaction as a debit to investments in subsidiaries and a credit to earnings of $150,000.

A similar transaction, an exchange of rights to computer programs for capital stock with a stated value of $200,000, occurred later. Investments in subsidiaries was debited and earnings was credited for $200,000.

The subsidiaries are accounted for under the equity method.

Can the earnings recorded on the exchange of expensed computer programs for common stock be reflected in parent company financial statements, or do generally accepted accounting principles require elimination?

Reply—Intra-entity profit eliminations under the equity method is discussed in FASB ASC 323-10-35-8 and states, in part, "All intra-entity transactions are eliminated in consolidation under that Subtopic, but under the equity method intra-entity profits or losses are normally eliminated only on assets still remaining on the books of an investor or an investee."

FASB ASC 323 indicates that the intercompany gain ($150,000 and $200,000) recorded by the investor company would be eliminated under the equity method.

In the second case, measuring the value of the computer programs by the $200,000 stated value of the stock may not be appropriate, and the auditor should try to satisfy himself concerning the estimated values assigned to the tangible and intangible assets contributed by the other stockholders. (See FASB ASC 323, FASB ASC 350, *Intangibles—Goodwill and Other*, and FASB ASC 805, *Business Combinations*.)

[Revised, June 2009, to reflect conforming changes necessary due to the issuance of FASB ASC.]

[.09] Reserved

[.10] Reserved

[.11] Reserved

.12 Investor's Share of Losses in Excess of Its Investment

Inquiry—Company A's share of the losses of a real estate venture exceeds its investment in the venture. How should Company A account for its investment?

Reply—FASB ASC 970-323 recommends that the equity method be used to account for investments in corporate or noncorporate real estate ventures. Paragraphs 19–22 of FASB ASC 323-10-35 state, in part:

> An investor's share of losses of an investee may equal or exceed the carrying amount of an investment accounted for by the equity method plus advances made by the investor. The investor ordinarily shall discontinue applying the equity method if the investment (and net advances) is reduced to zero and shall not provide for additional losses unless the investor has guaranteed obligations of the investee or is otherwise committed to provide further financial support for the investee. An investor shall, however, provide for additional losses if the imminent return to profitable operations by an investee appears to be assured. For example, a material, nonrecurring loss of an isolated nature may reduce an investment below zero even though the underlying profitable operating pattern of an investee is unimpaired. If the investee subsequently reports net income, the investor shall resume applying the equity method only after its share of that net income equals the share of net losses not recognized during the period the equity method was suspended.

Accordingly, the investor should reflect its investment at a zero amount and disclose in a note to the financial statements the amount of its share of investee losses in excess of the zero amount.

If the investor is committed to provide further financial support to the investee, the investor should show the excess of its share of investee losses over its investment and advances as a liability up to the amount of its commitment.

[Revised, June 2009, to reflect conforming changes necessary due to the issuance of FASB ASC.]

.13 A Change in Circumstances Using the Equity Method of Accounting for an Investment

Inquiry—An investor had guaranteed obligations of an investee and the investor's share of losses of this investee have exceeded the carrying amount of the investment on the investor's book in a prior year. This procedure is in accordance with paragraphs 19–22 of FASB ASC 323-10-35. In the current year, the investee fully paid the obligation which was guaranteed by the investor; accordingly, the investor will no longer guarantee the obligations of the investee and, therefore, will not record its share of the investee's losses.

(1) Does this constitute a change of accounting principle?

(2) How should the liability recorded on the investor's books be accounted for?

Reply—(1) This is not a change in accounting principle. According to FASB ASC 250-10-45-1, an "adoption or modification of an accounting principle necessitated by transactions or events that are clearly different in substance from those previously occurring" is not a change in accounting principle. The situation described is a change in circumstances and not a change in accounting principle.

(2) The liability recorded on the investor's books should be reversed in the current year and reported in the income statement with appropriate footnote disclosure.

[Revised, June 2009, to reflect conforming changes necessary due to the issuance of FASB ASC.]

[.14] Reserved

.15 Accounting for Distribution From Joint Venture

Inquiry—A corporation invests in a joint venture which is involved in real estate. The joint venture is a corporation and it is not controlled by the corporate investor. It accounts for this investment in accordance with FASB ASC 323. The joint venture incurred losses over the next few years. That resulted in the investment account on the corporation's books to decline to zero. At this point, the joint venture paid the corporation a cash distribution. How should the corporation account for this distribution?

Reply—FASB ASC 323 states that the investor ordinarily shall discontinue applying the equity method when the investment (and net advances) is reduced to zero and shall not provide for additional losses unless the investor has guaranteed obligations of the investee or is otherwise committed to provide financial support for the investee.

In this situation, the corporate investor in the joint venture should account for the cash distributions received as income if the distribution is not refundable by agreement or by law and the investor is not liable for the obligations of the joint venture and is not otherwise committed to provide financial support to the joint venture.

[Revised, June 2009, to reflect conforming changes necessary due to the issuance of FASB ASC.]

[.16] Reserved

.17 Tax Basis Accounting—Use of Equity Method

Inquiry—Can an investor who prepares its financial statements in accordance with U.S. GAAP use the equity method of accounting for an investment in the common stock of an investee that presents its financial statements on the income tax basis of accounting if the investment would otherwise qualify for the equity method?

Reply—FASB ASC 323-10-35-4 states, in part:

> Under the equity method, an investor shall recognize its share of the earnings or losses of an investee in the periods for which they are reported by the investee in its financial statements.

The FASB ASC glossary defines the term *earnings or losses of an investee* as the "net income (or net loss) of an investee determined in accordance with U.S. generally accepted accounting principles."

If the investment qualifies for equity method accounting, the investor must adjust the investee's tax basis financial statements to GAAP basis to determine its share of earnings or losses. If the adjustment cannot be determined, and the amounts are material, it would be considered a GAAP exception.

[Revised, June 2009, to reflect conforming changes necessary due to the issuance of FASB ASC.]

Sections 2220.18–.27 are intended to assist reporting entities when implementing the provisions of FASB ASC 820, *Fair Value Measurements and Disclosures*, to estimate the fair value of their investments in certain entities that calculate net asset value. Sections 2220.18–.27 apply to investments that are required to be measured and reported at fair value and are within the scope of paragraphs 4–5 of FASB ASC 820-10-15.

.18 Applicability of Practical Expedient

Inquiry—Which investments are permitted, as a practical expedient, to be measured at fair value on the basis of the net asset value (NAV)?

Reply—FASB ASC 820-10-35-59 permits reporting entities, as a practical expedient, to estimate the fair value of their investments in certain entities that calculate NAV per share (or its equivalent) by using NAV. Such investments, which are often referred to as alternative investments, include interests in hedge funds, private equity funds, real estate funds, venture capital funds, commodity funds, offshore fund vehicles, and funds of funds, as well as some bank common/collective trust funds and other similar funds. Companies in various industries, including investment companies, broker-dealers, banks, insurance companies, employee benefit plans, healthcare organizations, and not-for-profit organizations, often invest in alternative investments.

[Issue Date: December 2009]

.19 Unit of Account

Inquiry—According to the FASB ASC glossary, the *unit of account* is "[t]he level at which an asset or a liability is aggregated or disaggregated in a Topic for recognition purposes." How should the unit of account be identified for an interest in an alternative investment?

Reply—For interests in alternative investments, the appropriate unit of account is the interest in the investee fund itself, not the underlying investments within the investee fund; this is because the reporting entity owns an undivided interest in the whole of the investee fund portfolio and typically lacks the ability to dispose of individual assets and liabilities in the investee fund portfolio. However, as discussed in FASB ASC 820-10-35-61, if it is probable at the measurement date that a reporting entity will sell a portion of an investment at an amount different from NAV, and the criteria described in FASB ASC 820-10-35-62 are met, the portion that the reporting entity intends to sell is valued in accordance with other provisions of FASB ASC 820. The remaining portion of the interest that is not probable of being sold may be valued by using NAV as a practical expedient in accordance with FASB ASC 820-10-35-59.

[Issue Date: December 2009; Revised, May 2016, to reflect conforming changes necessary due to the issuance of FASB ASU No. 2011-04.]

.20 Determining Whether NAV Is Calculated Consistent With FASB ASC 946, *Financial Services—Investment Companies*

Inquiry—FASB ASC 820-10-35-59 states:

> A reporting entity is permitted, as a practical expedient, to estimate the fair value of an investment within the scope of paragraphs 820-10-15-4 through 15-5 using the net asset value per share (or its equivalent, such as member units or an ownership interest in partners' capital to which a proportionate share of net assets is attributed) of the investment, if the net asset value per share of the investment (or its equivalent) is calculated in a manner consistent with the measurement principles of Topic 946 as of the reporting entity's measurement date.

How does a reporting entity conclude that the NAV, as most recently reported by the manager of the alternative investment (reported NAV), has been calculated in a manner consistent with the measurement principles of FASB ASC 946, *Financial Services—Investment Companies*?

Reply—A reporting entity's management is responsible for the valuation assertions in its financial statements. Determining that reported NAV is calculated consistently with FASB ASC 946, including measurement of all or substantially all of the underlying investments of the investee in accordance with FASB ASC 820, requires a reporting entity to independently evaluate the fair value measurement process utilized by the investee fund manager to calculate the NAV. Such an evaluation is a matter of professional judgment and includes determining that the investee fund manager has an effective process and related internal controls in place to estimate the fair value of its investments that are included in the calculation of NAV. The reporting entity's controls used to evaluate the process of the investee fund manager may include the following:

- *Initial due diligence* (procedures performed before the initial investment)
- *Ongoing monitoring* (procedures performed after the initial investment)
- *Financial reporting controls* (procedures related to the accounting for, and reporting of, the investment) (Refer to the AICPA Audit

Guide *Special Considerations in Auditing Financial Instruments* for examples of these controls.[1])

Before concluding that the reported NAV is calculated in a manner consistent with the measurement principles of FASB ASC 946, the reporting entity might evaluate the evidence that is gathered via the initial due diligence and ongoing monitoring of the investee fund. Only after considering all relevant factors can the reporting entity reach a conclusion about whether the reported NAV is calculated in a manner consistent with the measurement principles of FASB ASC 946. For example, the reporting entity might consider the following key factors relating to the valuation received from the investee fund manager:

- The investee fund's fair value estimation processes and control environment, and any changes to those processes or the control environment[2]
- The investee fund's policies and procedures for estimating fair value of underlying investments, and any changes to those policies or procedures[3]
- The use of independent third party valuation experts to augment and validate the investee fund's procedures for estimating fair value
- The portion of the underlying securities held by the investee fund that are traded on active markets
- The professional reputation and standing of the investee fund's auditor (this is not intended to suggest that the auditor is an element of the investee fund's internal control system, but as a general risk factor in evaluating the integrity of the data obtained from the investee fund manager)
- Qualifications, if any, of the auditor's report on the investee fund's financial statements
- Whether there is a history of significant adjustments to the NAV reported by the investee fund manager as a result of the annual financial statement audit or otherwise
- Findings in the investee fund's adviser or administrator's type 1 or type 2 service auditor's report prepared under AT section 801, *Reporting on Controls at a Service Organization* (AICPA, *Professional Standards*), if any.[4] (a type 1 report is a report on management's description of a service organization's system and the

[1] The AICPA also has a project to develop guidance which addresses the challenges associated with auditing an entity's investments in alternative investment funds that calculate net asset value per share, or its equivalent (NAV) and the reporting entity uses NAV as a practical expedient. Please be alert to further developments. [Footnote revised, May 2016, to reflect removal of the nonauthoritative practice aid *Alternative Investments—Audit Considerations* from the AICPA's website and the project to address auditing the NAV practical expedient.]

[2] For further guidance, see AU-C section 501, *Audit Evidence—Specific Considerations for Selected Items* (AICPA, *Professional Standards*). Also see footnote 1. [Footnote revised, December 2012, to reflect conforming changes necessary due to the issuance of SAS Nos. 122–126. Footnote revised, May 2016, to reflect removal of the nonauthoritative practice aid *Alternative Investments—Audit Considerations* from the AICPA's website.]

[3] See footnote 2.

[4] AT section 801, *Reporting on Controls at a Service Organization* (AICPA, *Professional Standards*), establishes the requirements and application guidance for a service auditor reporting on controls at a service organization relevant to user entities' internal control over financial reporting. AU-C section 402, *Audit Considerations Relating to an Entity Using a Service Organization* (AICPA,

(continued)

suitability of the design of controls; a type 2 report is a report on management's description of a service organization's system and the suitability of the design and operating effectiveness of controls)

- Whether NAV has been appropriately adjusted for items such as carried interest and clawbacks (more fully described in section 6910.29, "Allocation of Unrealized Gain (Loss), Recognition of Carried Interest, and Clawback Obligations")
- Comparison of historical realizations to last reported fair value

If the last reported NAV is not as of the reporting entity's measurement date, refer to section 2220.22 for further considerations.

In cases when the reporting entity invests in a fund of funds (the investee fund invests in other funds that do not have readily determinable fair values), the reporting entity might conclude that the NAV reported by the fund of funds manager is calculated in a manner consistent with FASB ASC 946 by assessing whether the fund of funds manager has a process that considers the previously listed items in the calculation of the NAV reported by the fund of funds, and that the fund of funds manager has obtained or estimated NAV from underlying fund managers in a manner consistent with paragraphs 59–62 of FASB ASC 820-10-35 as of the measurement date. The reporting entity is not required to look through the fund of funds interest to underlying fund investments if the reporting entity has concluded that the fund of funds manager reports NAV consistent with FASB ASC 946 for the fund of funds interest.

[Issue Date: December 2009; Revised, June and August 2011, to reflect conforming changes necessary due to the issuance of SSAE No. 16; Revised, December 2012, to reflect conforming changes necessary due to the issuance of SAS Nos. 122–126; Revised, May 2016, to reflect removal of the nonauthoritative practice aid *Alternative Investments—Audit Considerations* from the AICPA's website and the project to address auditing the NAV practical expedient.]

.21 Determining Whether an Adjustment to NAV Is Necessary

Inquiry—FASB ASC 820-10-35-59 allows the reporting entity, as a practical expedient, to estimate the fair value of an investment within the scope of paragraphs 4 and 5 of FASB ASC 820-10-15 using the NAV as reported by the investee when the reporting entity has satisfied itself that (*a*) the investee has calculated NAV consistent with FASB ASC 946 (see section 2220.20), and (*b*) the NAV has been calculated as of the reporting entity's financial reporting (measurement) date.

(footnote continued)

Professional Standards), contains the requirements and application guidance for an auditor auditing the financial statements of an entity that uses a service organization.

In April 2016, the AICPA Auditing Standards Board issued SSAE No. 18, *Attestation Standards: Clarification and Recodification*, which, among other things, supersedes AT section 801. As a result of this, AT section 801 will be superseded by AT-C Section 320, *Reporting on an Examination of Controls at a Service Organization Relevant to User Entities' Internal Control Over Financial Reporting* (AICPA, *Professional Standards*), which is effective for service auditors' reports dated on or after May 1, 2017. SSAE No. 18 is available at www.aicpa.org/Research/Standards/AuditAttest/DownloadableDocuments/SSAE_No_18.pdf. [Footnote revised, August 2011, to reflect conforming changes necessary due to the issuance of SSAE No. 16. Footnote revised, December 2012, to reflect conforming changes necessary due to the issuance of SAS Nos. 122–126. Footnote revised, May 2016, to reflect conforming changes necessary due to the issuance of SSAE No. 18.]

FASB ASC 820-10-35-60 further states:

> If the net asset value per share of the investment obtained from the investee is not as of the reporting entity's measurement date or is not calculated in a manner consistent with the measurement principles of Topic 946, the reporting entity shall consider whether an adjustment to the most recent net asset value per share is necessary. The objective of any adjustment is to estimate a net asset value per share for the investment that is calculated in a manner consistent with the measurement principles of Topic 946 as of the reporting entity's measurement date.

How does a reporting entity determine whether an adjustment to the last reported NAV is necessary?

Reply—Examples of when an adjustment to the last reported NAV may be necessary include, but are not limited to the following:

- NAV is not as of the reporting entity's measurement date
- NAV is not calculated in a manner consistent with the measurement principles of FASB ASC 946 (which requires, among other things, measurement of all or substantially all of the underlying investments of the investee in accordance with FASB ASC 820)
- Both

The existence of either of these factors may lead the reporting entity to conclude that an adjustment to the last reported NAV may be necessary. Practically, it is difficult to assess whether an adjustment is necessary unless an estimate of the adjustment is calculated.

[Issue Date: December 2009]

.22 Adjusting NAV When It Is Not as of the Reporting Entity's Measurement Date

Inquiry—If the reporting entity concludes that the reported NAV is calculated consistently with FASB ASC 946, but an adjustment is necessary because the NAV is not as of the reporting entity's measurement date, how should the reporting entity estimate the adjustment? (Refer to the inquiry in section 2220.21 for applicable FASB literature.)

Reply—FASB ASC 820-10-35-60 states that "The objective of any adjustment is to estimate a net asset value per share for the investment that is calculated in a manner consistent with the measurement principles of Topic 946 as of the reporting entity's measurement date." If the last reported NAV is calculated consistently with FASB ASC 946 but is not as of the reporting entity's measurement date, the reporting entity may either request the investee fund manager to provide a supplemental NAV calculation consistent with the measurement principles of FASB ASC 946 as of the reporting entity's measurement date, or it may be necessary to adjust or roll forward (or roll back)[5] the reported NAV for factors that might cause it to differ from the NAV at the measurement date. For example, the following factors might necessitate an adjustment to the

[5] When the reporting entity's measurement date is prior to the net asset value (NAV) calculation date, it may be more appropriate to use that NAV and perform a roll back rather than using a reported NAV calculated prior to the entity's measurement date.

reported NAV when it is not calculated as of the reporting entity's measurement date:

- The reporting entity has made an additional investment(s) (capital contributions) since the calculation date of the reported NAV and prior to the reporting entity's measurement date
- The reporting entity has received a distribution(s) or partial redemption since the calculation date of the reported NAV
- The reporting entity has become aware (through inquiry of the investment manager or communication by the investment manager to the reporting entity) of changes in the value of underlying investments since the calculation date of the reported NAV
- Market changes or other economic conditions have changed to affect (favorably or unfavorably) the value of the investee's portfolio after the calculation date of the reported NAV
- Changes have occurred in the composition of the underlying investment portfolio of the investee fund after the NAV calculation date

The roll forward NAV might be calculated as follows:

i.	Last Reported NAV (calculated consistently with FASB ASC 946)	$ X,XXX
ii.	Add capital contributions/subscriptions	C,CCC
iii.	Subtract distributions/redemptions/withdrawals	(D,DDD)
iv.	Adjust for changes in valuations[(a)]	V,VVV
Roll forward NAV (as of the reporting entity's measurement date)		$ R,RRR

[(a)] Market changes refer to market fluctuations between the date of the reported NAV and the reporting entity's measurement date. Examples of other economic conditions for which it may be necessary to adjust a reported NAV include, but are not limited to, a portfolio company being acquired, going public, or declaring bankruptcy between the date of the reported NAV and the reporting entity's measurement date, or changes in the value of underlying investments caused by company performance or market conditions, or both.

[Issue Date: December 2009]

.23 Adjusting NAV When It Is Not Calculated Consistent With FASB ASC 946

Inquiry—If the reporting entity concludes that an adjustment is necessary because a reported NAV is not calculated consistently with the measurement principles of FASB ASC 946, how does a reporting entity estimate the adjustment? (Refer to the inquiry in section 2220.21 for applicable FASB literature.)

Reply—Although it is not possible to state all the reasons why a reported NAV may not be consistent with the measurement principles of FASB ASC 946 (that is, it is not fair value based), the reporting entity would need to consider and understand the following:

- The reasons why NAV has not been based upon fair value. In some cases investees may appear to function similarly to investment companies, but do not meet the assessment described in paragraphs 4–9 of FASB ASC 946-10-15 to be an *investment company* and it is not industry practice for the investee to issue financial statements using the measurement principles in FASB ASC 946. (In those cases, the practical expedient is unavailable and the entity should be valued using the general measurement principles of FASB ASC 820.)

- Whether a fair value based NAV can be obtained from the investee manager.
- Whether the specific data needed to adjust the reported NAV can be obtained and properly utilized to estimate a fair value based NAV.

Examples of circumstances in which the reporting entity may be able to obtain data to estimate an adjustment include, but are not be limited to the following:

- Reported NAV is on a cash basis. The reporting entity could estimate the fair value of each underlying investment as of the measurement date by obtaining additional information from the investee manager.
- Reported NAV utilizes blockage discounts taken on securities valued using level 1 inputs, which is not consistent with FASB ASC 820. The reporting entity could estimate the adjustment to reported NAV required to remove the blockage discount based on additional information from the financial statements or from the investee manager.
- Reported NAV has not been adjusted for the impact of unrealized carried interest or incentive fees. The reporting entity could estimate the impact of carried interest or incentive fees and adjust reported NAV.

If the reporting entity finds that it is not practicable to calculate an adjusted NAV (for example, because sufficient information is not available or it is not in a position to reasonably evaluate the information available and estimate values consistent with FASB ASC 946), then the practical expedient is not available. The reporting entity may also elect not to utilize the practical expedient. In those instances, the reporting entity should apply the general measurement principles of FASB ASC 820 instead (see section 2220.27).

[Issue Date: December 2009; Revised, May 2016, to reflect conforming changes necessary due to the issuance of FASB ASU No. 2013-08.]

.24 Disclosures—Ability to Redeem Versus Actual Redemption Request

Note: Section 2220.24 is superseded by FASB ASU No. 2015-07, *Fair Value Measurement (Topic 820): Disclosures for Investments in Certain Entities That Calculate Net Asset Value per Share (or Its Equivalent)*, which removed the requirement to categorize within the fair value hierarchy all investments for which fair value is measured using the net asset value per share practical expedient. Consistent with the effective date of FASB ASU No. 2015-07, section 2220.24 is superseded as follows:

- For public business entities—for fiscal years beginning after December 15, 2015, and interim periods within those fiscal years.

- For all other entities—for fiscal years beginning after December 15, 2016, and interim periods within those fiscal years.

FASB ASU No. 2015-07 also permits early adoption.

Inquiry—FASB ASC 820-10-35-54B(c) states the following:

> If a reporting entity cannot redeem its investment with the investee at net asset value per share (or its equivalent) at the measurement date but the investment may be redeemable with the investee at a future date (for example, investments subject to a lockup or gate or investments whose redemption period does not coincide with the measurement date), the reporting entity shall take into account the length of time until the investment will become redeemable in determining whether the fair value measurement of the investment shall be categorized within Level 2 or Level 3 of the fair value hierarchy. For example, if the reporting entity does not know when it will have the ability to redeem the investment or it does not have the ability to redeem the investment in the near term at net asset value per share (or its equivalent), the fair value measurement of the investment shall be categorized within Level 3 of the fair value hierarchy.

In most cases, redemptions from alternative investment funds that redeem at NAV are only permitted with advance notice, ranging from 30 to 120 days. In order to classify the investment within level 2 of the fair value hierarchy, must the investor have submitted a previous redemption request effective as of the measurement date or is it sufficient for an investor to have had the ability to redeem on the measurement date, even though it may not have exercised this ability?

Reply—Determining the appropriate level within the fair value hierarchy is a matter of professional judgment. Even though a redemption notice may not have been submitted effective on the measurement date, so long as the reporting entity has the ability to redeem at NAV in the near term (for example, it has the contractual and practical ability to redeem) at the measurement date, then consistent with FASB ASC 820-10-35-54B(a), the investment may be classified within level 2 of the fair value hierarchy.

[Issue Date: December 2009; Revised, September 2013, to reflect conforming changes necessary due to the issuance of FASB ASU No. 2011-04; Revised/superseded May 2016, due to the issuance of FASB ASU No. 2015-07—see note at start of section.]

.25 Impact of "Near Term" on Categorization Within Fair Value Hierarchy

Note: Section 2220.25 is superseded by FASB ASU No. 2015-07, *Fair Value Measurement (Topic 820): Disclosures for Investments in Certain Entities That Calculate Net Asset Value per Share (or Its Equivalent)*, which removed the requirement to categorize within the fair value hierarchy all investments for which fair value is measured using the net asset value per share practical expedient. Consistent with the effective date of FASB ASU No. 2015-07, section 2220.25 is superseded as follows:

- For public business entities—for fiscal years beginning after December 15, 2015, and interim periods within those fiscal years.
- For all other entities—for fiscal years beginning after December 15, 2016, and interim periods within those fiscal years.

FASB ASU No. 2015-07 also permits early adoption.

Inquiry—What is considered "near term" for purposes of determining whether the investment would be categorized as level 2 or level 3? (Refer to the inquiry in section 2220.24 for applicable FASB literature.)

Reply—What is viewed as near term is a matter of professional judgment and depends on the specific facts and circumstances. A redemption period of 90 days or less generally would be considered near term, because any potential discount relative to the time value of money to the next redemption date would be unlikely to be considered a significant unobservable input in accordance with FASB ASC 820. However, other factors (for example, likelihood or actual imposition of gates) may influence the determination of whether the investment will be redeemable in the near term.

[Issue Date: December 2009; Revised/superseded May 2016, due to the issuance of FASB ASU No. 2015-07—see note at start of section.]

.26 Classification of Investments for Disclosure Purposes

Inquiry—The sample disclosure provided in FASB ASC 820-10-55-107 appears to apply to an institutional investor with a diversified portfolio of hedge and real estate funds. Certain entities, however, specialize in one particular investment class or have a significant investment in one such class, such as private equity or venture capital. Should these reporting entities use a different classification than that appearing in the sample disclosure?

Reply—Yes. FASB ASC 820-10-55-107 indicates that "[t]he classes presented ... are provided as examples only and are not intended to be treated as a template. The classes disclosed should be tailored to the nature, characteristics, and risks of the reporting entity's investments."

Accordingly, the disclosure should be tailored to address the concentrations of risk that are specifically attributable to the investments. For example, a private equity fund of funds should not simply classify its investments as "private equity" as this classification is not specific enough to address the nature and risks of the investee funds. In this example, more specific classification, perhaps relating to industry, geography, vintage year, or the strategy of the investees (venture, buyout, mezzanine, and so on), may be more appropriate and more useful to the reader. Such classification is a matter of judgment and should only be made after careful consideration of the specific risks and attributes of the portfolio investments has been made.

[Issue Date: December 2009; Revised, October 2013, to reflect conforming changes necessary due to the issuance of FASB ASU No. 2011-04; Revised, May 2016, to reflect conforming changes necessary due to the issuance of FASB ASU Nos. 2010-06 and 2015-07.]

.27 Determining Fair Value of Investments When the Practical Expedient Is Not Used or Is Not Available

Inquiry—For entities that do not elect to use NAV as a practical expedient to estimate fair value or are unable to adjust the most recently reported NAV to estimate a NAV that is calculated in a manner consistent with the measurement principles of FASB ASC 946 as of the reporting entity's measurement date, what inputs or investment features should be considered in estimating fair value?

Reply—Section 2220.27 distinguishes between redeemable and nonredeemable types of alternative investments, which are defined as follows:

- **Investments with redeemable interests.** Typically consist of hedge funds (based both in the United States and offshore) and some bank common/collective trust funds. These investment funds permit holders periodic opportunities to subscribe for or redeem interests at frequencies that can run from daily to annually. Certain funds may impose lock-up periods after an initial investment, under which an investor agrees that it may not redeem its investment for a specified period of time (in some cases, an early redemption may be permitted upon payment of an early redemption fee).
- **Investments with nonredeemable interests.** Typically consist of private equity, venture capital, and real estate funds. Generally, these investments have an initial subscription period, under which each investor makes a commitment to contribute a specified amount of capital as called for by the investment manager, typically as investments are identified and money is needed to acquire them. Due to the inherent illiquidity of the underlying investments, redemptions are not permitted during the fund's life; however, typically, as investments are sold or experience another liquidity event (for example, an initial public offering), the proceeds of the sale, less any incentives due to the fund sponsor, are often distributed back to the investors in the fund immediately following the sale or liquidity event.

Investment Inputs

A reporting entity might first consider the other market participants to whom it could sell the asset. In accordance with FASB ASC 820-10-35-9, "[a] reporting entity shall measure the fair value of an asset or a liability using the assumptions that market participants would use in pricing the asset or liability, assuming that market participants act in their economic best interest." Based on guidance in FASB ASC 820-10-35-53, in the absence of relevant observable inputs, a reporting entity uses "unobservable inputs [that] shall reflect the assumptions that market participants would use when pricing the asset or liability, including assumptions about risk." FASB ASC 820-10-35-54A states the following:

> A reporting entity shall develop unobservable inputs using the best information available in the circumstances, which might include the reporting entity's own data. In developing unobservable inputs, a reporting entity may begin with its own data, but it shall adjust those data if reasonably available information indicates that other market participants would use different data or there is something particular to the reporting entity that is not available to other market participants (for example, an entity-specific synergy). A reporting entity need not undertake exhaustive efforts to obtain information about market participant assumptions. However, a reporting entity shall take into account all information about market participant assumptions that is reasonably available.

When doing so, the reporting entity is reminded that the FASB ASC glossary defines *market participants* as "knowledgeable, having a reasonable understanding about the asset or liability and the transaction using all available information, including information that might be obtained through due diligence efforts that are usual and customary." Thus, it can be presumed that a market participant would be aware of, and may be willing to accept, limitations on conversion to cash inherent to alternative investments. However, in some cases, those types of limitations may also affect the fair value measurement (see "Investment Features").[6] It also can be presumed that market participants may consider other factors such as the investment manager's track record and potentially limited access to desirable investment opportunities. Finally, it should be acknowledged that market participant assumptions normally result in a range of values. According to FASB ASC 820-10-35-24B, "[a] fair value measurement is the point within that range that is most representative of fair value in the circumstances." See FASB ASC 820-10-35-9 for further guidance. The reporting entity should also consider the guidance in paragraphs 54C–54M of FASB ASC 820-10-35.

Alternative investments may lend themselves to valuation techniques consistent with the income or market approaches. If both of these approaches are used to measure fair value, the results should be evaluated as discussed in FASB ASC 820-10-35-24B. When NAV is not used as a practical expedient, examples of factors that might be used when estimating fair value (depending on the valuation technique(s) and facts and circumstances) are as follows:

- NAV (as one valuation factor)
- Transactions in principal-to-principal or brokered markets (external markets) and overall market conditions
- Features of the alternative investment
- Expected future cash flows appropriately discounted (detailed description is beyond the scope of section 2220.27; however, for many funds with nonredeemable interests, expected future cash flows from the interests might typically coincide with the expected future cash flows from the underlying investments)
- Factors used to determine whether there has been a significant decrease in the volume and level of activity for the asset when compared with normal market activity for the asset (FASB ASC 820-10-35-54C)

The preceding examples are not listed in any order of importance. Rather, the reporting entity might determine the relative weighting and importance of these inputs based on its view of what market participants might consider in estimating fair value.

<u>Investment Features</u>[7]

A valuation technique used to measure the fair value of an asset or a liability should reflect assumptions a market participant might use to price the asset

---

[6] FASB ASC 820-10-35-2C states that "[t]he effect on the measurement arising from a particular characteristic will differ depending on how that characteristic would be taken into account by market participants." [Footnote revised, May 2016, to reflect conforming changes necessary due to the issuance of FASB ASU No. 2011-04.]

[7] The "Investment Features" section contains important information related to features of alternative investments that a reporting entity may consider in determining fair value when the option to utilize the practical expedient is unavailable or not elected. The list of features highlighted in this section is intended to provide some examples to better explain the types of scenarios that could impact fair values. Because individual investments may have additional terms and features, the examples included in the "Investment Features" section should not be viewed as an all-inclusive "checklist." Professional judgment should be applied in evaluating the assumptions appropriate to any individual investment. The actual computation of fair value requires management's professional judgment and is beyond the scope of this Technical Questions and Answers section.

or liability, including assumptions about liquidity and risk, based on the best information available. The following discussion provides a detailed description of features of alternative investments that normally might be expected to be considered by market participants in the estimation of the fair value of an alternative investment. When considering the potential impact of the features of an alternative investment on its fair value, it is important that all relevant features be considered in the aggregate because that is how a market participant might be likely to evaluate them in determining how much it might be willing to pay for an alternative investment.

Other factors that may be considered include observed subscriptions and redemptions in redeemable interests; external market transactions in nonredeemable interests; and other features of the alternative investment. Additionally, a market participant might normally be expected to compare the performance of the alternative investment to publicly available data (for example, benchmarks, indexes, expected returns, and returns of comparable vehicles), and the cash returns of the investment to NAVs reported by the alternative investment during the year. A conclusion may ultimately be reached that the reported NAV is equivalent to fair value, either because no conditions exist to suggest an adjustment is necessary or because factors indicating a discount to the reported NAV may be offset by other factors that might justify a premium. In other cases, however, the investment may be valued at a discount or premium to the reported NAV because factors indicate that the fair value of the investment is less than, or more than, the reported NAV. Regardless of whether or not NAV is determined to be equivalent to fair value, the reporting entity needs to evaluate the relevant individual factors and their potential impact on fair value, and consider the level of documentation in its evaluation.

Among the factors that market participants might be expected to consider are the various terms and features of the alternative investment. Such features generally fall into one of two categories: initial due diligence features or ongoing monitoring features. The magnitude of any adjustment resulting from consideration of ongoing monitoring features is a matter of judgment and should be evaluated based on the facts and circumstances specific to each investee fund.

Initial Due Diligence Features. Generally, *initial due diligence features* are inherent characteristics that may have been considered by the reporting entity as part of its due diligence when making its initial investment in the particular investee fund. The following provides examples of initial due diligence features of an alternative investment. Not every feature may be relevant to every alternative investment, nor does this list necessarily include all assumptions that market participants may apply in any specific situation.

<u>Lock-up periods and redemption fees.</u> (Typically applies only to redeemable interests)

Lock-up period refers to the initial amount of time a reporting entity is contractually required to invest before having the ability to redeem. Typically, when the lock-up period expires, the reporting entity may redeem its interests on any scheduled liquidity date, subject to the other liquidity terms described in the investee fund's governing documents. The length of the lock-up period often depends on the quality and reputation of the fund manager as well as the expected liquidity of the underlying investment portfolio. In some instances, alternative investments may offer reduced fees if an investor agrees to a longer lock-up period. Also, some funds may permit investors to redeem during a lock-up period upon payment of a redemption fee. Such fees are typically imposed on the amount to be redeemed and generally range from 1 percent to 3 percent of the gross redemption amount.

Related to the concept of lock-up periods is the general frequency in which an investor is allowed to redeem or withdraw from a fund. In the absence of a lock-up period, investors with redeemable interests typically may only redeem at prescribed liquidity dates (generally monthly, quarterly, or annually).

<u>Notice periods.</u> (Typically applies only to redeemable interests)

Following the expiration of any applicable lock-up period, a reporting entity may, upon specified prior written notice (generally 45–120 days) to the general partner or manager (redemption notice), elect to redeem all or a portion of its interest as of the last day of a calendar month, quarter, or year (redemption date).

<u>Holdbacks.</u> (Typically applies only to redeemable interests)

When the general partner or investment manager receives a redemption notice, the fund will redeem the interests of an investor as specified in the redemption notice, at the redemption price as of the applicable redemption date. The fund will distribute all or a substantial portion (for example, 90 percent) of the redemption price with respect to the interests being redeemed within a specified number of business days (for example, 30 days) following the applicable redemption date. Any balance (for example, the remaining 10 percent) is distributed within a specific time frame, often following the release of the fund's audited financial statements for the year in which the redemption date falls. Holdback amounts protect the general partner or investment manager from adjustments reducing the NAV of the fund during an audit of the financial statements.

<u>Suspension of redemptions ("gates").</u> (Typically applies only to redeemable interests)

Pursuant to the fund's governing documents, the general partner or investment manager can suspend or restrict the right of any investor to redeem his or her interests (whether in whole or in part). The general partner or investment manager can implement this restriction for certain reasons, including the aggregate amount of redemption requests, certain adverse regulatory or tax consequences, reduced liquidity of portfolio holdings, and other reasons that may render the manager unable to promptly and accurately calculate the fund's NAV. The most common example is the use of a "gate," whereby certain redemption requests are deferred, in whole or in part, because the aggregate amount of redemption requests as of a particular redemption date exceeds a specified level, generally ranging from 15 percent to 25 percent of the fund's net assets. The mere presence of a provision allowing the imposition of a gate might not normally be expected to have an effect on fair value, in the absence of any evidence suggesting that the provision actually may be exercised (see "Ongoing Monitoring Features," which follows).

<u>Lack of redemption option.</u> (Nonredeemable interests and instances where all or a portion of otherwise redeemable interests have been declared nonredeemable)

As discussed earlier, funds investing in private equity, venture capital, or real estate investments generally do not permit withdrawals or redemptions, primarily to match the liquidity provisions of the fund with the liquidity of the investment portfolio. When the fund sells any of its portfolio holdings, it often distributes the proceeds received on the sale to the investors in the fund.

Fund sponsor approval to transfer. (Redeemable and nonredeemable interests)

In virtually all cases, transfers of interests in alternative investments are not permitted under the governing documents of the fund without the written consent of the fund sponsor or general partner, for regulatory or tax reasons or both, and thus, are inherent to the category of investments. Past experiences, as well as the current operating environment, are both considerations in assessing the likelihood of such approval being granted.

In some private equity, venture capital and real estate funds that require investors to make commitments to invest over time and periodically call on the commitments as needed, the fund sponsor or general partner may allow an investor to withdraw or redeem from the fund and, thus, be absolved of future commitments, but the investor may forfeit its existing interest if no other investors (including the fund sponsor or general partner) are willing to assume the withdrawn partner's interest, including future commitments. If forfeiture occurs (which, in practice, is rare), the investor's interest is generally reallocated to the remaining investors in the fund. (The balance of the withdrawing partner's commitment may also be reallocated to the other investors, or the total size of the fund may be reduced).

Use of "side pockets." (Typically applies only to redeemable interests)

Certain funds issuing redeemable interests may be allowed to invest a portion of their assets in illiquid securities. In such cases, a common mechanism used is a "side pocket," whereby, at the time of an investment in an illiquid security, a proportionate share of an investor's capital account, relative to the entire interest of the fund, is assigned to a separate memorandum capital account or designated account. Typically, the investor loses its redemption rights to the designated account, and even a full redemption request is fulfilled only with that capital ascribed to his or her basic capital account (that is, the nondesignated capital account), while the investor continues to hold its proportionate interest in the designated account. Only when the security is sold (or otherwise deemed liquid) by the fund is the amount moved back to each applicable investor's basic capital account (and otherwise withdrawn investors can redeem the designated account balance). This designated account generally does not pay a performance fee[8] (although one may be levied) until the illiquid investment is sold or otherwise deemed liquid. Designated accounts are often referred to as "side pocket accounts" or as "special investment accounts."

---

[8] Consistent with the definition in the AICPA Audit and Accounting Guide *Investment Companies*, a *performance fee* (also referred to as an *incentive fee*) is a fee paid to an investment adviser based upon the fund's performance for the period. It may be an absolute share of the fund's performance or a share of the performance in excess of a specified benchmark.

> Similar to "gates," the mere existence of contractual provisions permitting the use of side pockets typically does not have a material effect on estimating the fair value unless those provisions are actually exercised and access to a portion of the investment is actually limited.

As previously noted, these examples of initial due diligence features are common characteristics of alternative investment funds and, as such, are generally considered and accepted by investors when making investment decisions in these investments. Accordingly, a market participant may or may not require an adjustment to the reported NAV in a transfer of an investment interest in an alternative investment solely due to the existence of these items. However, it is necessary to consider these features in conjunction with other inputs available to the reporting entity. For example, if the reporting entity is valuing redeemable interests and observes that other investors are subscribing for interests at the reported NAV under the same terms as the reporting entity's agreement, that fact may provide evidence that no adjustment to the reported NAV is necessary. However, if other investors are subscribing to the fund at the reported NAV under terms that, in aggregate, are less favorable than those in the reporting entity's agreement (for example, higher fees, greater restrictions on redemption), that fact may provide evidence that the reporting entity's holdings may trade at a premium to the reported NAV. Similarly, if other investors are receiving more favorable terms in aggregate than those in the reporting entity's agreement (for example, lower fees, fewer restrictions on redemption), that fact may provide evidence that the reporting entity's holding may trade at a discount to the reported NAV. An investor may also typically consider whether the fund's terms are more or less restrictive than those prevailing in the current market. For example, terms that are more restrictive may suggest a discount. Alternatively, the quality of the investment manager may command a premium.

In short, if market participants would be expected to place a discount or premium on the reported NAV because of features, risk, or other factors relating to the interest, then the fair value measurement of the interest would need to be adjusted for that risk or opportunity.[9] However, if market participants might accept the same features, risk, and other factors relating to the interest and might transact at the reported NAV without a premium or discount, that fact may suggest that no adjustment is needed for the factors discussed previously to estimate fair value.

Ongoing Monitoring Features. *Ongoing monitoring features* are characteristics related to activity in an investee fund subsequent to a reporting entity's initial investment. Because ongoing monitoring features often include specific events relating to the investee fund, the fund sponsor, the industry or the asset class, they are more likely to result in consideration of a discount or premium to the reported NAV than initial due diligence features. The following provides some examples of ongoing monitoring features for an alternative investment.

As with initial due diligence features, not every feature may be relevant to a particular investment, nor does this list necessarily include all assumptions that market participants may apply in any specific situation. Also, changes in

---

[9] This is consistent with FASB ASC 820-10-35-54, which states, "A measurement that does not include an adjustment for risk would not represent a fair value measurement if market participants would include one when pricing the asset or liability." [Footnote revised, May 2016, to reflect conforming changes necessary due to the issuance of FASB ASU No. 2011-04.]

market conditions may affect the investor's assumptions relating to the significance of any particular feature.

<u>*Imposition of a gate.*</u> (Typically applies only to redeemable interests)

Though an investee fund manager's mere ability to impose a gate on redemption requests is a common initial due diligence feature (as noted previously), the actual imposition of a gate by an investee fund manager may warrant further consideration of whether a discount should be applied to the reported NAV. The act of imposing the gate generally implies that the investee fund manager is experiencing liquidity concerns, either related to specific investments or its portfolio as a whole, which the reporting entity and a market participant normally would be expected to consider in estimating fair value of the interest in the investee fund. Further, the imposition of a gate increases the uncertainty of the ultimate timing of receipt of cash upon redemption, sometimes significantly, and, thus, may impose an additional risk premium on the investment.

<u>*Redemptions from an investee fund.*</u> (Typically applies only to redeemable interests)

Even in the absence of the actual imposition of a gate, when an investee fund experiences material redemption requests this may suggest comparable liquidity issues that could result in a discount from the reported NAV, particularly in situations when the investee fund is leveraged.

<u>*Notification of redemption triggers the assessment of redemption fee.*</u> (Typically applies only to redeemable interests)

Though, as noted previously, an investee fund manager may have the ability to charge redeeming investors a redemption fee, the mere existence of this feature is generally considered to be an initial due diligence feature which, in many instances, may not cause the reported NAV to exceed the fair value of the investment interest. However, if a reporting entity irrevocably agrees to redeem some or all of its interest, the redemption fee normally would be expected to cause the reported NAV to exceed the fair value of the investment interest.

<u>*Significant changes in key terms of the investee fund.*</u> (Redeemable and nonredeemable interests)

The initial due diligence features, as previously noted, represent standard or common characteristics of an alternative investment. They are generally known and accepted by the reporting entity at the time of making an initial investment at the reported NAV. As such, a market participant with full knowledge of these features may also likely transact at the reported NAV, so long as the terms remain within the range prevailing in the market.

If, however, the investee fund makes significant changes to the terms (for example, fees, lock-up periods, notification periods, gates) subsequent to the initial investment, the reporting entity normally would be expected to consider these changes when evaluating whether the reported NAV should be adjusted to arrive at fair value. In some cases, changes may be deemed to have little impact on the investment decisions of a market participant, whereas in other cases, changes to key terms may create a distinct difference between the existing interest and other interests (either in the specific alternative investment or comparable investments), which may result in either a discount or premium to the reported NAV.

Closure of fund to new subscriptions. (Redeemable interests)

Some funds may cease accepting subscriptions from new investors because doing so might cause them to exceed the maximum number of investors they can accept without requiring public filings of financial information under securities laws. In other cases, funds may voluntarily suspend the acceptance of subscriptions from new investors, and even in some cases additional subscriptions from existing investors, because of the adviser's view that opportunities to make further investments under the fund's investment strategy may be limited given the size of the markets involved or that they might not bring acceptable returns, or both. Such an event may suggest that existing interests in the fund could trade at a premium because prospective investors may have no other means of investing in the fund. Further, a large number of investors or the intent not to "dilute" the fund's returns by accepting additional investment funds, or both, may provide evidence that the fund may trade at a premium to the reported NAV.

Ability of fund to identify and make acceptable investments. (Nonredeemable interests)

Venture capital, private equity, and real estate funds typically offer interests on the basis of committed capital, which is only called from investors as investments are identified. Investors agree to commit capital under implicit or explicit understandings that committed capital will be called during an initial investment period, often from one to five years. Depending on the market environment, managers may find that they are unable to identify sufficient investments to utilize committed capital on a timely basis. Such funds often are smaller and less diversified than expected at the time of inception of the fund, which may negatively influence fair value. Further, certain vintages (that is, years when funds were organized) may be identified over time as having represented exceptionally good or poor investment opportunities for the particular investment style, and interests in funds organized in those years may be more likely to incur premiums or discounts, respectively. The fund's potential inability to identify and make acceptable investments will often result in unfunded capital commitments, which may need to be considered when estimating the fair value of an investment interest in the fund.

Allegations of fraud against the investee fund manager. (Redeemable and nonredeemable interests)

If the reporting entity is aware of allegations of fraud, noncompliance with laws and regulations, or other improprieties against the investee fund manager or its affiliates, the reporting entity should consider the potential impact of these allegations on the value of its interest in the investee fund. In many cases, such allegations may result in the unexpected inability to obtain any cash proceeds from the investee fund pending the resolution of the investigation or from a general lack of liquidity resulting from historical misrepresentation of the net assets of the fund. In other cases, the ongoing ability of the investee fund manager to manage the fund may be brought into question.

<u>*Change in financial strength or key personnel of investment manager.*</u> (Redeemable and nonredeemable interests)

In some cases, a key consideration for investment in certain funds is the reputation, and prior investment record, of the investment manager, or specific individuals expected to manage the investee fund's portfolio. In some situations, the desirability of the investment manager or individuals, or both, may influence the nature of the fee, lock-up, and similar terms investors are willing to accept in making an initial investment. If those key personnel no longer provide services to the alternative investment, investors may not be willing to continue to accept those terms. Further, if the advisory organization experiences financial deterioration, it may be less able to retain key personnel or, for certain private equity, venture capital, or real estate funds, to repay previously-received incentive fees to the fund under contractual clawback provisions (if the fund experiences subsequent losses). Those uncertainties may increase the risk of the investment.

[Issue Date: December 2009; Revised, December 2012, to reflect conforming changes necessary due to the issuance of SAS Nos. 122–126; Revised, May 2016, to reflect conforming changes necessary due to the issuance of FASB ASU No. 2011-04.]

Q&A Section 2230

Noncurrent Receivables

[.01] Reserved

.02 Balance Sheet Classification of Deposit on Equipment to Be Purchased

Inquiry—What is the appropriate balance sheet classification of a deposit on machinery which is to be purchased within one year?

Reply—Financial Accounting Standards Board (FASB) *Accounting Standards Codification* (ASC) 210-10-45-4 states, in part:

> The concept of the nature of current assets contemplates the exclusion from that classification of such resources as the following:
>
> *a* Cash and claims to cash that are restricted as to withdrawal or use for other than current operations, are designated for expenditure in the acquisition or construction of noncurrent assets, or are segregated for the liquidation of long-term debts.

Accordingly, the deposit on equipment should be classified as a noncurrent asset even though the equipment will be purchased within one year.

[Revised, June 2009, to reflect conforming changes necessary due to the issuance of FASB ASC.]

Q&A Section 2240

Cash Surrender Value of Life Insurance

.01 Balance Sheet Classification of Life Insurance Policy Loan

Inquiry—A company has secured a short-term loan from an insurance company against the cash surrender value of its life insurance policies.

In Financial Accounting Standards Board (FASB) *Accounting Standards Codification* (ASC) 210-10-45-4(d), cash surrender value of life insurance policies is excluded from the classification of a current asset. This reference does not appear to recommend a different classification if the cash value may have been fully borrowed from the insurance company.

Is it proper to classify a readily liquid asset as noncurrent and simultaneously show the related borrowings as a current liability?

Reply—FASB ASC 210-10-45-4 states, in part:

> This concept of the nature of current assets contemplates the exclusion from that classification of such resources as . . . (*d*) cash surrender value of life insurance policies.

FASB ASC 210-10-45-9(d) states, in part:

> Loans accompanied by pledge of life insurance policies would be classified as current liabilities if, by their terms or by intent, they are to be repaid within 12 months. The pledging of life insurance policies does not affect the classification of the asset any more than does the pledging of receivables, inventories, real estate, or other assets as collateral for a short-term loan. However, when a loan on a life insurance policy is obtained from the insurance entity with the intent that it will not be paid but will be liquidated by deduction from the proceeds of the policy upon maturity or cancellation, the obligation shall be excluded from current liabilities.

FASB ASC 210-20-05-1 states, in part:

> It is a general principle of accounting that the offsetting of assets and liabilities in the balance sheet is improper except if a right of setoff exists.

Therefore, if a company takes out policy loans from the insurance company on life insurance policies which it owns and if there is no intention to repay the loan during the ensuing operating cycle of the business, such loan may be excluded from current liabilities. Furthermore, as the owner of a policy normally has the right to offset the loan against the proceeds received on maturity or cancellation of the policy, it is appropriate to apply the amount of the loan in reduction of the cash surrender value, with disclosure of the amount so offset.

[Revised, June 2009, to reflect conforming changes necessary due to the issuance of FASB ASC.]

.02 Disclosure of Life Insurance on Principal Stockholders

Inquiry—A client corporation, which is a nonpublic entity, maintains life insurance policies on its principal stockholders that will provide for the repurchase of the stock in the event of a stockholder's death. The cash surrender value of these policies appears on the balance sheet. Is further disclosure necessary?

Reply—The rule of informative disclosure requires that the essential facts respecting firm commitments for purchase of a corporation's own stock pursuant to a buy-sell agreement be set forth in a footnote to the financial statements.

The following is an example of a footnote describing such a situation that might appear on the balance sheet in reference to the cash surrender value account:

> The company is the owner and beneficiary of key-man life insurance policies carried on the lives of X, Y, and Z, bearing face value amounts of $500,000, $500,000, and $450,000, respectively. No loans are outstanding against the policies, but there is no restriction in the policy regarding loans.
>
> The life insurance contracts are accompanied by mandatory stock purchase agreements to the amount of the proceeds of the life insurance. In the event of the insured's death, the "fair market value" of the stock will, by previous action, be established by the X Appraisal Company. The insured's estate will be obligated to sell, and the company will be obligated to purchase, the insured's stock up to the appraisal value of the stock or the proceeds of insurance, whichever is the lesser. The purpose is to protect the company against an abrupt change in ownership or management.

[Revised, April 2010.]

.03 Omission of Cash Surrender Value of Life Insurance from Assets

Inquiry—Clearly, cash surrender values of life insurance may be included among the assets in the balance sheet of an enterprise. Is this mandatory, or may management elect to omit this item from the assets on the theory that its inclusion will be misleading since the insurance is carried for the purpose of covering the loss it is anticipated will be sustained as a result of the death of a key official?

Reply—If the enterprise retains all valuable contract rights incident to ownership of the life insurance policy, then it is mandatory from the standpoint of full accountability to reflect the asset status of the cash surrender value of the policy. Not to reflect the cash surrender value would be tantamount to creating a hidden reserve which would be contrary to generally accepted accounting principles.

.04 Corporation's Policy on Life of Debtor Corporation's Officer

Inquiry—A client took out a straight life insurance policy on the life of an officer of another corporation which is indebted to the client. The client corporation hopes to receive the proceeds of the insurance policy tax free and has not deducted the yearly premium payments as expenses. The officer is over 65 years old, and, therefore, there is a great possibility he or she will die prior to the full payment of the outstanding balance of the corporation's debt. The prior CPA reported the accumulated premium payments on the Balance Sheet as "Investment in Life Insurance."

Is it proper to show total premiums paid as an investment under these circumstances?

Reply—Where a corporation takes out a life insurance policy on the life of a debtor corporation's officer (assuming that there is an insurable interest), the manner of accounting for the premiums should not differ from the manner of accounting for premiums paid on the life of the corporation's own officer. The premiums should be broken down between the expense and the cash surrender value elements. Accordingly, the accumulated premiums account should be analyzed to determine the cash surrender value as at the balance sheet date, the expense portion for the period under audit, and the remaining portion which should be treated as a correction of prior period earnings. See Financial Accounting Standards Board (FASB) *Accounting Standards Codification* (ASC) 250, *Accounting Changes and Error Corrections*, for a discussion of correction of an error.

[Revised, June 2009, to reflect conforming changes necessary due to the issuance of FASB ASC.]

[.05] Reserved

.06 Measurement of Cash Value Life Insurance Policy

Inquiry—How should a company measure and record a cash value life insurance policy that it purchases for itself on the company's balance sheet?

Reply—In accordance with FASB ASC 325-30-25-1, "an investment in a life insurance contract shall be reported as an asset."

FASB ASC 325-30-35-1 states

> An asset representing an investment in a life insurance contract shall be measured subsequently at the amount that could be realized under the insurance contract as of the date of the statement of financial position. It is not appropriate for the purchaser of life insurance to recognize income from death benefits on an actuarially expected basis. The death benefit shall not be realized before the actual death of the insured, and recognizing death benefits on a projected basis is not an appropriate measure of the asset.

FASB ASC 325-30-35-3 states

> FASB ASC 325-30-30-1 states that a policyholder shall consider any additional amounts included in the contractual terms of the policy in determining the amount that could be realized under the life insurance contract. When it is probable that contractual terms would limit the amount that could be realized under the life insurance contract, these contractual limitations shall be considered when determining the realizable amounts. Those amounts that are recoverable by the policyholder at the discretion of the insurance entity shall be excluded from the amount that could be realized under the life insurance contract.

FASB ASC 325-30-35-4 states that "amounts that are recoverable by the policyholder in periods beyond one year from the surrender of the policy shall be discounted in accordance with Topic 835."

FASB ASC 325-30-35-5 states

> A policyholder shall determine the amount that could be realized under the life insurance contract assuming the surrender of an individual-life by individual-life policy (or certificate by certificate in

> a group policy). Any amount that ultimately would be realized by the policyholder upon the assumed surrender of the final policy (or final certificate in a group policy) shall be included in the amount that could be realized under the insurance contract. See Example 1 (paragraph 325-30-55-1) for an illustration of this guidance.

FASB ASC 325-30-35-6 states

> A policyholder shall not discount the cash surrender value component of the amount that could be realized under the insurance contract when contractual restrictions on the ability to surrender a policy exist, as long as the holder of the policy continues to participate in the changes in the cash surrender value as it had done before the surrender request. If, however, the contractual restrictions prevent the policyholder from participating in changes to the cash surrender value component, then the amount that could be realized under the insurance contract at a future date shall be discounted in accordance with Topic 835.

FASB ASC 325-30-35-7 states "if a group of individual-life policies or a group policy only allows for the surrender of all of the individual-life policies or certificates as a group, then the policyholder shall determine the amount that could be realized under the insurance contract on a group basis."

[Issue Date: May 2010.]

Q&A Section 2250

Intangible Assets

[.01] Reserved

[.02] Reserved

[.03] Reserved

[.04] Reserved

[.05] Reserved

.06 Accounting Treatment of Agreements Not to Compete

Inquiry—A company enters into an agreement with an outgoing officer whereby the company will make future periodic payments to the officer in return for the officer's agreement not to compete with the company for the period coinciding with the payments.

Would it be appropriate for the company to record a liability for the total future payments to the former officer and a corresponding intangible asset for the covenant?

Reply—The authoritative literature does not provide specific guidance for the treatment of executory contracts, which require future consideration upon the occurrence of certain events.

FASB Concept No. 6, *Elements of Financial Statements—a replacement of FASB Concepts Statement No. 3 (incorporating an amendment of FASB Concepts Statement No. 2)*, paragraph 36 specifies that a characteristic of a liability is that "the transaction or other event obligating the entity has already happened." Because the event that gives rise to the company's obligation is the former officer's forbearance from competition, many accountants believe that the transaction should be recorded prospectively, as the payments are "earned" by the former officer. They would disclose the contractual obligation as a commitment in the company's notes to its financial statements.

FASB Concept No. 6 paragraph 26 provides that a characteristic of an asset is that "it embodies a probable future benefit." Accordingly, the company would only record an intangible asset if the payment to the former officer preceded the period of forbearance.

[.07] Reserved

Q&A Section 2260

Other Assets

[.01] Reserved

[.02] Reserved

.03 Legal Expenses Incurred to Defend Patent Infringement Suit

Inquiry—A company is sued for patent infringement. Should the cost to defend the patent be capitalized or expensed?

Reply—The choice of capitalizing or expensing depends on the outcome of the lawsuit. FASB Concept No. 6, *Elements of Financial Statements—a replacement of FASB Concepts Statement No. 3 (incorporating an amendment of FASB Concepts Statement No. 2)*, paragraph 247 states ". . . the legal and other costs of successfully defending a patent from infringement are 'deferred legal costs' only in the sense that they are part of the cost of retaining and obtaining the future economic benefit of the patent."

If defense of the patent lawsuit is successful, costs may be capitalized to the extent of an evident increase in the value of the patent. Legal costs which relate to an unsuccessful outcome should be expensed.

Q&A Section 3000

LIABILITIES AND DEFERRED CREDITS

TABLE OF CONTENTS

Q&A Section 3100
Current Liabilities

.01 Estimated Liability for Unemployment Claims

Inquiry—Under state law, a corporation has a choice of the method to pay unemployment insurance contributions. The corporation may pay a percentage of gross wages or may reimburse the state employment commission directly for actual unemployment claims. A client chose to reimburse the state for the actual claims which may arise. If no claims against the client are filed, may the client record an expense and a liability for unemployment claims?

Reply—The estimated unemployment insurance costs should be accrued currently based on the client's estimated or past history of unemployment. Unemployment insurance cost should be related to the period worked by the employees. Not recording unemployment costs until claims are actually filed would result in a mismatching of revenues and expenses. Such an approach would be unacceptable under generally accepted accounting principles.

[.02] Reserved

.03 Accounting for Possible Refunds of Leasing Fees

Inquiry—A company franchises distributorships for home and office oxygen inhalator units. The licensees lease the units from the company and pay an initial leasing fee for each unit before receipt of the unit. As stipulated in the franchise agreement, the licensee is entitled to a refund, upon termination of the franchise agreement and return of the units, of a specified amount of the initial leasing fee depending on the period of time that the units are leased out. When units are returned they can usually be redistributed with little or no repair. Is there a liability for the return of a portion of the initial leasing fees?

Reply—The returned units can usually be redistributed with little or no repair. Therefore, accounting for these units would be similar to accounting for returnable containers. Because the licensee pays the initial leasing fee prior to delivery of the units, there is no receivable to be offset by an "allowance account" for the estimated refunds, and so the amounts for estimated refunds should be shown as a liability.

.04 Date for Accrual of Tax Penalties

Inquiry—A company has received certain billings from the federal government for interest and penalties for late filing of federal withholding taxes. Some of these notices were received prior to the balance sheet date, while other notices were received after the balance sheet date, but in either case they apply to periods prior to the balance sheet date. Should liabilities for the interest and penalties be shown on the balance sheet?

Reply—Paragraph .02 of AU-C section 560, *Subsequent Events and Subsequently Discovered Facts* (AICPA, *Professional Standards*), states, in part:

> Financial statements may be affected by certain events that occur after the date of the financial statements … financial reporting frameworks ordinarily identify two types of events:
>
> *a.* Those that provide evidence of conditions that existed at the date of the financial statements
>
> *b.* Those that provide evidence of conditions that arose after the date of the financial statements

The auditor's objective is to determine whether events occurring between the date of the financial statements and the date of auditor's report that require adjustment of, or disclosure in, the financial statements have been identified and are appropriately reflected in the financial statements. Therefore, provision should be made for any billings received for penalties on late filing of federal withholding taxes which were required to be filed prior to the balance sheet date. Similarly, any such interest should be provided for up to the balance sheet date. Interest accrued subsequent thereto would be an expense of the following period.

[Revised, December 2012, to reflect conforming changes necessary due to the issuance of SAS Nos. 122–126.]

[.05] Reserved

[.06] Reserved

[.07] Reserved

[.08] Reserved

.09 Accrual for Employer Co-Insurance Arrangements

Inquiry—A company pays for the medical expenses of its active employees but purchased "stop-gap" or "excess of loss" insurance to cover medical expenses exceeding $10,000, lifetime benefit, per employee. What amount, if any, should the company accrue to cover its liability?

Reply—Although Financial Accounting Standards Board (FASB) *Accounting Standards Codification* (ASC) 450, *Contingencies*, excludes employment-related costs, that accounting guidance may be appropriate for this situation. FASB ASC 450-20-25-2 states that an accrual for a loss contingency is required if the loss is probable and the amount of the loss can be reasonably estimated. Medical expenses incurred by the employee during the reporting period should be accrued. This includes expenses incurred during the reporting period but submitted after the balance sheet date. The accrual should be based on all relevant data (including statistical data), the company's historical experience, and its expectations of the future. Some of this data may be available from insurance administrators or actuaries.

[Revised, June 2009, to reflect conforming changes necessary due to the issuance of FASB ASC.]

.10 Compensated Absences

Inquiry—A company with a June 30 year end has a sick pay policy that states that an employee employed for at least three months is entitled to ten sick days annually. The employee is entitled to these days as of January 1 and any unused sick days as of December 31, are paid to these workers. Should the company accrue a liability as of June 30 for the unused sick days of these workers?

Reply—Yes. Financial Accounting Standards Board (FASB) *Accounting Standards Codification* (ASC) 710, *Compensation—General*, indicates that sick pay that is customarily paid even though the absence from work is not actually the result of an illness, should not be considered sick pay in applying the provisions of paragraphs 6–7 of FASB ASC 710-10-25. In considering necessity for making an accrual, the four criteria in FASB ASC 710-10-25-1 should be considered.

In determining the amount of the accrual, the guidance in FASB ASC 450, *Contingencies*, concerning the probability of future payment should be considered. Specifically, the company should consider its payment history and employee turnover in calculating the accrual.

In this example, if an employee had taken three days through June 30, the remaining accrual would be seven days. If this example were modified, and the days were earned on a pro rata basis throughout the year, the company would record a liability for the expected payment to be made to the employee for only the accumulated right through June 30. With the same three days taken through June 30, the company would have an accrual for the remaining two days in the June 30 financial statements.

[Revised, June 2009, to reflect conforming changes necessary due to the issuance of FASB ASC.]

Q&A Section 3200

Long-Term Debt

[.01] Reserved

[.02] Reserved

[.03] Reserved

[.04] Reserved

[.05] Reserved

.06 Amortization Period for Placement Fee When Mortgage Refinanced

Inquiry—A company paid a $100,000 mortgage placement fee for an eighteen year mortgage. Ten months later, it became apparent that a refinancing of a significantly larger mortgage would be needed. The company negotiated a commitment with a bank for a larger mortgage to be placed one year from the date of this agreement. At the time of the commitment, in accordance with Financial Accounting Standards Board (FASB) *Accounting Standards Codification* (ASC) 350, *Intangibles—Goodwill and Other*, which deals with intangible assets, the company reduced the amortization period of the placement fee to the expected remaining period of the original mortgage.

Two months before the closing date of the original mortgage, at which time almost the entire prepaid mortgage fee had been amortized, the bank was unable to make the loan and exercised an option to extend the closing date of the old mortgage and the placement date of the new mortgage for six more months.

Should the amortization period now be extended to the new settlement date?

Reply—The mortgage placement fee should not be viewed as an intangible asset but as a deferred charge under FASB ASC 835, *Interest*. It is an amortizable cost incurred to secure the mortgage.

The unamortized amount of the fee at the time when the bank exercises the option should be amortized over the remaining six month period. The reasons for the exercise of the option do not change the fact that the period benefited has been extended. The change should be treated as a change in accounting estimate, in accordance with FASB ASC 250, *Accounting Changes and Error Corrections*. If the new mortgage is placed before the end of the six month option period, any balance of the fee should then be written off in accordance with FASB ASC 470-50 and FASB ASC 470-50-45-1, which deal with early extinguishment of debt.

[Revised, June 2009, to reflect conforming changes necessary due to the issuance of FASB ASC.]

[.07] Reserved

[.08] Reserved

.09 Financial Statement Presentation of "Pay Any Day" Loans

Inquiry—Corporation A finances its purchases of equipment through "pay any day" loans. Under this type of financing arrangement, the borrower signs a note and security agreement which sets forth the amount financed, the finance charge, and the amount of monthly payment. This instrument differs from a conditional sales contract or "add-on" loan. The "add-on" loan is a contract calling for a specified number of payments, including interest, and therefore the liability is the total amount to be repaid over the life of the contract; whereas, the "pay any day" loan, or note and security agreement is a simple interest loan and the agreement shows the finance charge in order to disclose the amount of interest that will be paid if each installment payment is made on its exact due date.

What is the appropriate financial statement presentation of "pay any day" loans?

Reply—A "pay any day" loan can be recorded and reported in the financial statements at its face amount plus accrued interest because it is in effect a term loan with interest charged at the current rate. The amount of the loan, if any, expected to be paid within one year would be shown as a current liability.

.10 Determining the Allocation for Lease Payments for a Lease Capitalized at Fair Market Value

Inquiry—According to Financial Accounting Standards Board (FASB) *Accounting Standards Codification* (ASC) 840-30-30-1, a lessee accounting for a capital lease, records an asset and an obligation equal to the present value of the minimum lease payments at the beginning of the lease term, excluding any portion of the payments which represent executory costs (such as insurance and taxes) which will be paid by the lessor. However, if this amount is greater than the fair market value of the leased property, the amount recorded as the asset and obligation should be fair market value. When the asset and obligation are recorded at the fair market value, since the interest rate is not known, how should the amount for the lease payments be recorded?

Reply—FASB ASC 840-30-35-6 states that during the lease term, each minimum lease payment shall be allocated between a reduction of the obligation and interest expense so as to produce a constant periodic rate of interest on the remaining balance of the obligation. This is the "interest" method described in paragraphs 2–3 of FASB ASC 835-30-35.

When the asset to be recorded based on the present value of the minimum lease payments exceeds the fair market value of the asset, it is usually because the incremental borrowing rate used to determine present value is lower than the interest rate implicit in the lease.

[Revised, June 2009, to reflect conforming changes necessary due to the issuance of FASB ASC.]

.11 Effect of Sales Taxes on the Determination of Present Value of Minimum Lease Payments

Inquiry—A company leases a machine for $14,000 a month for 72 months. The monthly invoice received from the lessor includes the stipulated monthly rent plus a charge for state sales taxes. The lease does not meet the 90 percent criterion of a capital lease (i.e., the present value of the minimum lease payments excluding executory costs equals or exceeds 90 percent of the fair value of the leased property) if sales taxes are excluded from minimum lease payments. The criterion is met if both the rent and sales taxes are included as minimum lease payments.

Should the minimum lease payments include sales taxes?

Reply—Practice in this area varies. Financial Accounting Standards Board (FASB) *Accounting Standards Codification* (ASC) 840-10-25 describes, in part, minimum lease payments as the payments that the lessee is obligated to make or can be required to make in connection with the leased property. However, the lessee's obligation to pay (apart from rental payments) executory costs such as insurance, maintenance, and taxes in connection with leased property are excluded. Many accountants interpret this to mean that all taxes, including sales taxes, levied on lease payments are considered executory costs since the lessor is merely acting as a collection agent for the taxing authority.

Other accountants believe that only taxes other than sales taxes (such as property taxes) should be excluded from the minimum lease payments because sales taxes are often capitalized as part of the cost of purchased assets. FASB ASC 840-10-10-1 states that the criteria are derived from the concept that a lease that transfers substantially all of the benefits and risks incident to ownership should be accounted for as the acquisition of an asset and the incurrence of an obligation.

Because the authoritative pronouncements do not specifically address whether sales taxes should be included as part of minimum lease payments, practice varies and should be determined by the company's general policy for accounting for sales taxes on purchased assets.

Regardless of which approach is used, in order to properly apply the 90 percent test referred to in FASB ASC 840-10-25-1(d), the components of the numerator and denominator should be the same. For example, if the sales taxes are included as part of the minimum lease payments (the numerator) then the sales taxes should be included in the fair value of the leased asset (the denominator).

[Revised, June 2009, to reflect conforming changes necessary due to the issuance of FASB ASC.]

.12 Balance Sheet Classification of Revolving Line of Credit

Inquiry—A company has a revolving line of credit with a bank. The company is only required to make monthly interest payments. No principal payments are required. In the event the credit line is terminated, the principal is due 12 months after the date of termination.

Should the principal amount be classified as current or long-term in a classified balance sheet?

Reply—Financial Accounting Standards Board (FASB) *Accounting Standards Codification* (ASC) 210-10-45-9 states that liabilities whose regular and ordinary liquidation is expected to occur within a relatively short period of time, usually 12 months, are intended for inclusion in the current liability classification. If the line of credit has not been terminated at the balance sheet date, the principal amount should be classified as long-term, unless the company intends to repay the outstanding debt within 12 months.

[Revised, June 2009, to reflect conforming changes necessary due to the issuance of FASB ASC.]

.13 Uncertainty Arising From Violation of Debt Agreement

Inquiry—At the end of 20X1, a company was in violation of its long-term debt covenant and was unable to obtain a waiver from the bank. It therefore reclassified its debt to current and appropriate footnote disclosures were made. During 20X2, the violation was cured. What is the proper classification of the debt in the company's 20X2 comparative financial statements?

Reply—Financial Accounting Standards Board (FASB) *Accounting Standards Codification* (ASC) ASC 470-10-45-11 states that:

> Current liabilities shall include long-term obligations that are or will be callable by the creditor either because the debtor's violation of a provision of the debt agreement at the balance sheet date makes the obligation callable or because the violation, if not cured within a specified grace period, will make the obligation callable. Accordingly, such callable obligations shall be classified as current liabilities unless either of the following conditions is met:
>
> *a.* The creditor has waived or subsequently lost (for example, the debtor has cured the violation after the balance sheet date and the obligation is not callable at the time the financial statements are issued) the right to demand repayment for more than one year (or operating cycle, if longer) from the balance sheet date. If the obligation is callable because of violations of certain provisions of the debt agreement, the creditor needs to waive its right with regard only to those violations.
>
> *b.* For long-term obligations containing a grace period within which the debtor may cure the violation, it is probable that the violation will be cured within that period, thus preventing the obligation from becoming callable.

Since the violation was cured in 20X2, the debt should be classified as long-term in the 20X2 financial statements. The debt should not be reclassified to long term in the 20X1 financial statements because it was a current liability based on the facts existing at the 20X1 balance sheet date.

[Revised, June 2009, to reflect conforming changes necessary due to the issuance of FASB ASC.]

[.14] Reserved

.15 Disclosure of Five-Year Maturities on Long-Term Debt

Inquiry—A company entered into a 10-year loan agreement with a lender. The mortgage note contains a variable interest rate based on prime plus one percent. In accordance with Financial Accounting Standards Board (FASB) *Accounting Standards Codification* (ASC) 440, *Commitments*, the company will disclose the maturities on the debt for each of the next five succeeding years. Should the disclosure include principal and interest?

Reply—No. The required disclosure of the amount of scheduled repayments for each of the five succeeding fiscal years relates only to principal repayments and should not include interest. Disclosure is also called for when interest rates vary with the prime rate.

[Revised, June 2009, to reflect conforming changes necessary due to the issuance of FASB ASC.]

.16 Amortization of Premium or Discount in Investment Securities With an Early Call Date

Inquiry—Investment securities may be acquired at par value, at a premium, or at a discount. If the investment securities have an earlier call date, how should the amortization of premium or accretion of discount be recorded?

Reply—Financial Accounting Standards Board (FASB) *Accounting Standards Codification* (ASC) 310-20 applies to the accounting for discounts, premiums, and commitment fees associated with the purchase of loans and other debt securities such as corporate bonds. In accordance with FASB ASC 310-20-35-26, "the calculation of the constant effective yield necessary to apply the interest method shall use the payment terms required by the loan contract, and prepayments of principal shall not be anticipated to shorten the loan term." Accordingly, the period of amortization or accretion is from the purchase date to the maturity date. As provided by FASB ASC 310-20-35-26, in order to amortize the premium or accrete the discount to an early call date, the enterprise must hold a large number of similar loans for which prepayments are probable and the timing and amount of prepayments can be reasonably estimated.

[Revised, June 2009, to reflect conforming changes necessary due to the issuance of FASB ASC.]

.17 Disclosure of Covenant Violation and Subsequent Bank Waiver

Inquiry—At the balance-sheet date, an entity was in violation of certain provisions of the loan covenant associated with its long-term debt. Under the terms of the loan agreement, the obligation is now callable by the creditor. Subsequent to the balance-sheet date, the bank waived its right to demand repayment for more than one year from the balance-sheet date. Therefore, the loan remained classified as long-term, per Financial Accounting Standards Board (FASB) *Accounting Standards Codification* (ASC) 470-10-45-12. Does the covenant violation and subsequent bank waiver need to be disclosed in the financial statements?

Reply—The authoritative literature applicable to nonpublic entities does not address disclosure of debt covenant violations existing at the balance-sheet date that have been waived by the creditor for a stated period of time. Nevertheless, disclosure of the existing violation(s) and the waiver period should be considered for reasons of adequate disclosure. If the covenant violation resulted from nonpayment of principal or interest on the debt, inability to maintain required financial ratios, or other such financial covenants, that information may be vital to users of the financial statements even though the debt is not callable. If the lender has waived the right for greater than one year but retained the future covenant requirements (i.e., covenant requirements will have to be met at interim dates during the next 12 months), the accounting and disclosure provisions of FASB ASC 470, *Debt*, apply.

For SEC registrants, Regulations S-X, Article 4, Section 210-4-08(c), requires disclosure of the amount of the obligation and the period of waiver whenever a creditor has waived its right to call the debt for a stated period of time.

[Revised, June 2009, to reflect conforming changes necessary due to the issuance of FASB ASC.]

Q&A Section 3400

Contingent Liabilities

.01 Contested Liability

Inquiry—A company acquired the entire outstanding stock of another company several years ago. The acquired company was reorganized under IRS Code Section 334(*b*)(2) causing its building and equipment to be written up in value. Inventory was later written down.

An unpaid portion of the original purchase price is claimed by the former owners of the acquired company, but this is contested by the acquiring company on the grounds that the value of the acquired company's stock was misrepresented.

The acquired company's shareholders intend to sue the acquiring company for the unpaid balance, but a suit has not yet been filed. How should the amount due under the original purchase contract and the possible suit be reflected on the acquiring company's financial statements?

Reply—Because the possibility of a suit exists, footnote disclosure describing the entire dispute should be made, including legal counsel's comment that no suit is pending at this time. The amount due under the original purchase contract, plus accrued interest, should still be reported as a liability. No adjustments should be made in the acquiring company's financial records until the dispute is settled or legal counsel advises that a statute of limitations effectively bars filing of the suit in question and the company is not legally liable to pay the debt.

[.02] Reserved

[.03] Reserved

.04 Accounting for Issuance of Cents Off Coupons

Inquiry—A client includes with its consumer product a coupon for cents off on the next purchase of the product. Should the coupon be accounted for as a reduction of the selling price when the second product is sold?

Reply—Financial Accounting Standards Board (FASB) *Accounting Standards Codification* (ASC) 450-20-05-10 would consider the possible future coupon claims as a loss contingency to be evaluated as a future event. More than likely, the redemption of some or all of the coupons would be considered a *probable* event as defined in FASB ASC glossary. The amount to be accrued and charged to earnings at the time the first product is sold should be based on a reasonable estimate of the amount of coupons expected to be presented for redemption. This estimate could be based on experience in previous promotions.

[Revised, June 2009, to reflect conforming changes necessary due to the issuance of FASB ASC.]

[.05] Reserved

[.06] Reserved

Q&A Section 3500

Commitments

.01 Accounting for Contract to Cut Timber

Inquiry—A corporation is engaged in the forest products industry and purchases timber under both "pay as cut" (specifies a rate the buyer will pay per unit of volume cut) and "lump sum" (buyer pays a fixed amount for the right to cut timber on a specific tract of land). The corporation agrees to purchase timber on land which is identified in the contract. The exact amount of timber purchased can vary in total footage as well as species due to the nature of the goods. Is it proper to recognize the transactions as assets and liabilities on the balance sheet?

Reply—It would be improper to recognize a contract to cut timber as an asset and a liability unless the contract, at the time it was entered into, resulted in the purchase of the timber.

A distinction must be made between a contract that is executory in nature and one in which a sale and a purchase of lumber has occurred. Evidence of a purchase would be the transfer of title to the lumber at the time the contract is signed. Such a transfer usually occurs with lump sum contracts and may occur under pay as cut contracts if they include performance guarantees or risk of monetary damages if not performed. Therefore, those contracts would generally be recognized as assets and liabilities.

Receiving title at the time the timber is cut rather than at the time the contract is signed makes the contract executory. It is generally accepted practice to adequately disclose the nature and amounts of commitments relating to executory contracts in the notes to financial statements. Therefore, pay as cut contracts without performance guarantees or risk of monetary damages would generally not be recognized as assets and liabilities until performance occurs.

.02 Liability Under Foreign Bank's Letter of Payment Guarantee

Inquiry—A client, an import-export firm, agreed to purchase goods from a foreign manufacturer. The agreement calls for advance payment with the goods being delivered over the twelve-month period following the date of the agreement. The client arranged to make this advance payment through a letter of credit issued by a U.S. bank. The U.S. bank has received a letter of payment guarantee issued by a bank in the foreign country. If the supplier fails to make shipments under the terms of the agreement, the U.S. bank will look to the foreign bank for any unpaid advances owed to the U.S. bank by the client. The U.S. bank will look to the client for payment of all amounts represented by shipments to the client under the terms of the agreement.

Is the client directly liable for the amount advanced by the U.S. bank through its letter of credit, or does the client become liable only as the goods are received and payment is due the U.S. bank?

Reply—The client is directly liable for the amount advanced to the foreign supplier. It appears from the description of the transactions that the foreign bank is contingently liable if the supplier does not perform under the agreement. The offsetting asset would be classified as an "Advance to Suppliers." Additional footnote disclosure of the financial arrangements would also be required.

[.03] Reserved

.04 Recognition of Losses on Purchase Commitments

Inquiry—Financial Accounting Standards Board (FASB) *Accounting Standards Codification* (ASC) 330-10-35-17 states: "A net loss on firm purchase commitments for goods for inventory, measured in the same way as are inventory losses, shall be recognized in the accounts". FASB ASC 330-10-50-5 further states: "The amounts of net losses on firm purchase commitments accrued under paragraph 330-10-35-17 shall be disclosed separately in the income statement."

Does this statement mean that the measurement of losses cannot be done on an item by item basis but must only be done if there is an overall net loss on purchase commitments?

Reply—Net losses apply to specific purchase commitments and contracts, and not necessarily to components of major categories of inventories, as discussed in FASB ASC 330-10-35-8.

[Revised, June 2009, to reflect conforming changes necessary due to the issuance of FASB ASC.]

.05 Letters of Credit

Inquiry—Should a company report its outstanding letters of credit as a liability in the financial statements?

Reply—Financial Accounting Standards Board (FASB) *Accounting Standards Codification* (ASC) 440-10-50-1 requires disclosure of unused letters of credit. They are commitments and should not be reported as a liability in the financial statements.

[Revised, June 2009, to reflect conforming changes necessary due to the issuance of FASB ASC.]

.06 Covenants Imposed by Loan Agreements

Inquiry—Restrictive covenants under certain loan agreements of Company A require the Company to maintain a special level of working capital, reduce the amount of its debts, and restrict the amount of retained earnings available for dividend payments. Should the restrictive covenants be disclosed?

Reply—FASB ASC 440-10-50-1 requires the disclosure of restrictive covenants.

[Revised, June 2009, to reflect conforming changes necessary due to the issuance of FASB ASC; Revised, December 2012, to reflect conforming changes necessary due to the issuance of SAS Nos. 122–126.]

.07 Disclosure of Unused Lines of Credit

Inquiry—Should nonpublic companies disclose the existence of unused lines of credit that are available as of the balance sheet date?

Reply—Although public companies are required [pursuant to SEC Regulation S-X, section 210.5-02.19(b)] to disclose significant unused lines of credit for short-term financing in the notes, there is no such explicit requirement for nonpublic companies under generally accepted accounting principles. However, under certain circumstances, disclosure by nonpublic companies may be advisable based on the general principle of adequate disclosure.

The notes, as well as the financial statements, should be informative of matters that may affect their use, understanding, and interpretation.

[Amended, June 1995; Revised, October 2009, to reflect conforming changes necessary due to the withdrawal of SAS No. 69; Revised, December 2012, to reflect conforming changes necessary due to the issuance of SAS Nos. 122–126.]

Q&A Section 3600

Deferred Credits

.01 Balance Sheet Presentation of Unearned Revenue

Inquiry—A client, a motor club with an insurance company subsidiary, has annually contended that unearned insurance premiums and membership dues should be presented on the consolidated balance sheet as deferred income immediately preceding the members' equity and should not be included in the amount for total liabilities. The client recognizes the revenues on the insurance premiums and membership dues on a pro rata basis over the period covered by the insurance policy and the memberships, therefore, the auditors have maintained that the unearned portion of the insurance premiums and membership dues represent a liability on the part of the client to render services in the future.

Is it appropriate to show these unearned premiums and dues outside the liability section of the balance sheet?

Reply—FASB Concepts Statement No. 5, *Recognition and Measurement in Financial Statements of Business Enterprises*, paragraph 84, indicates that amounts received for goods or services in advance are not treated as revenue of the period in which they are received but as revenue of the period or periods in which they are earned. These amounts are carried as "unearned revenue"—that is, liabilities to transfer goods or render services in the future—until the earnings process is complete. Therefore, the unearned portions of the insurance premiums and membership dues represent liabilities to provide services in the future. While the description of the liabilities might vary, to present the unearned premiums and membership dues outside of the liability section of the balance sheet would be inappropriate.

[.02] Reserved

[.03] Reserved

Q&A Section 3700

Pension Obligations

.01 Effect of New Mortality Tables on Nongovernmental Employee Benefit Plans (EBPs) and Nongovernmental Entities That Sponsor EBPs

Inquiry—Nongovernmental EBPs and nongovernmental entities that sponsor EBPs (sponsoring entities) incorporate assumptions about participants' mortality in the calculation of the benefit liability for financial reporting purposes. Professional associations of actuaries occasionally publish updated *mortality tables* and mortality improvement projection scales (collectively referred to as mortality tables for purposes of this Technical Question and Answer) to reflect changes in mortality conditions based on recent historical trends and data. Established actuarial companies also may develop mortality tables based on other information and assumptions. For financial reporting purposes, how and when should nongovernmental EBPs and nongovernmental sponsoring entities consider these updated mortality tables if their financial statements have not yet been issued at the time the updated mortality tables are published?

Reply—Nongovernmental EBPs and nongovernmental sponsoring entities should consider the specific requirements of generally accepted accounting principles (GAAP), which require the use of a mortality assumption that reflects the best estimate of the plan's future experience for purposes of estimating the plan's obligation[1] as of the current measurement date (that is, the date at which the obligation is presented in the financial statements). In making this estimate, GAAP requires that all available information through the date the financial statements are available to be issued should be evaluated to determine if the information provides additional evidence about conditions that existed at the balance sheet date.

FASB *Accounting Standards Codification* (ASC) 855-10-55-1 specifies that information that becomes available after the balance sheet date (but before the financial statements are available to be issued) may be indicative of conditions existing at the balance sheet date when that information is a culmination of conditions that existed over a long period of time. Updated mortality tables are based on historical trends and data that go back many years; therefore, the existence of updated mortality conditions is not predicated upon the date that the updated mortality tables are published. Management of a nongovernmental EBP or a nongovernmental sponsoring entity should understand and evaluate the reasonableness of the mortality assumption chosen, even when assisted by an actuary acting as a management's specialist, and document its evaluation and the basis for selecting the mortality tables it decided to use for its current financial reporting period. A management's specialist is defined in paragraph .05 of AU-C section 500, *Audit Evidence* (AICPA, *Professional Standards*), as an individual or organization possessing expertise in a field other than accounting

---

[1] Obligations that use a mortality assumption include, but are not limited to, defined benefit obligations under pension and other postretirement plans, and certain postemployment and deferred compensation arrangements. In accordance with paragraphs 18 and 21 of FASB *Accounting Standards Codification* (ASC) 715-30-35 and FASB ASC 960-20-35-4, changes in actuarial assumptions result in gains and losses that are recognized as they arise, and the comparative obligation amounts that have been previously reported would not be adjusted for issuance of updated mortality tables.

or auditing, whose work in that field is used by the entity to assist the entity in preparing the financial statements.

Many defined benefit pension plans present plan obligations as of the beginning of the plan year, as allowed under FASB ASC 960-205-45-1. Although this presentation is before the balance sheet date, it represents a measurement of an amount that is presented in the financial statements that should reflect management's best estimate of the plan's mortality and other assumptions. The assumptions used to estimate the plan's obligation should be evaluated based on all available information through the date the financial statements are available to be issued, including determining whether updated mortality conditions existed as of the date the obligation is presented in the financial statements (that is, the beginning of the year).

Auditors are required to evaluate the competence, capabilities, and objectivity of a management's specialist; obtain an understanding of the work of that specialist; and evaluate the appropriateness of that specialist's work as audit evidence for the relevant assertion. Considerations may include evaluating the relevance and reasonableness of significant assumptions and methods used by that specialist. Refer to paragraphs .08 and .A35–.A49 of AU-C section 500 and the "Using the Work of a Specialist" section in chapter 2, "Planning and General Auditing Considerations," of the AICPA Audit and Accounting Guide *Employee Benefit Plans*, for further guidance. In addition, the auditor is responsible for evaluating subsequent events under AU-C section 560, *Subsequent Events and Subsequently Discovered Facts* (AICPA, *Professional Standards*). That section requires the auditor to obtain sufficient appropriate audit evidence about whether events occurring between the date of the financial statements and the date of the auditor's report that require adjustment of, or disclosure in, the financial statements are appropriately reflected in those financial statements in accordance with the applicable financial reporting framework.

[Issue Date: February 2015.]

Q&A Section 4000

CAPITAL

TABLE OF CONTENTS

Section

Q&A Section 4110
Issuance of Capital Stock

.01 Expenses Incurred in Public Sale of Capital Stock

Inquiry—A closely held corporation is issuing stock for the first time to the public.

How would costs, such as legal and accounting fees, incurred as a result of this issue, be handled in the accounting records?

Reply—Direct costs of obtaining capital by issuing stock should be deducted from the related proceeds, and the net amount recorded as contributed stockholders' equity. Assuming no legal prohibitions, issue costs should be deducted from capital stock or capital in excess of par or stated value.

Such costs should be limited to the direct cost of issuing the security. Thus, there should be no allocation of officers' salaries, and care should be taken that legal and accounting fees do not include any fees that would have been incurred in the absence of such issuance.

.02 Stock Issued for No Consideration

Inquiry—A corporation issued stock without receiving any consideration and set up goodwill to offset the credit to capital stock. Was this transaction properly recorded?

Reply—This is primarily a legal rather than an accounting question, and it would be advisable to obtain legal advice as to the effect of such issuance. If such stock were legally issued, the appropriate entry would be to show the offset as discount on capital stock issued. Goodwill should only be recognized when acquired, in accordance with Financial Accounting Standards Board (FASB) *Accounting Standards Codification* (ASC) 350, *Intangibles—Goodwill and Other*.

[Revised, June 2009, to reflect conforming changes necessary due to the issuance of FASB ASC.]

.03 Stock Issued for Accounting and Management Services

Inquiry—A newly formed corporation is going public and wishes to issue shares of stock for certain services, such as accounting, legal, underwriting, printing, etc.

How should the value for these services be set up on the books of the corporation?

Reply—It would be appropriate to record the stock issued at the fair value of the stock or services rendered, whichever is the more clearly evident. The recipients should be able to furnish evidence as to such fair value. Since the amounts the Securities and Exchange Commission might consider to be fair value cannot be predicted, a consultation with the staff of the Commission might be advisable before formal submission of the financial statements.

[.04] Reserved

[.05] Reserved

[.06] Reserved

.07 Expenses Incurred in Withdrawn Public Offering

Inquiry—What is the proper accounting for the costs of a public offering that was withdrawn?

Reply—Accounting Research Study No. 15, *Stockholders' Equity*, page 23, discusses accounting for stock issue costs. The Study states that such costs are usually deducted from contributed portions of equity, that is, capital stock or capital in excess of stated or par value, as a reduction in the proceeds from the sale of securities.

Since there were no proceeds from a sale of securities to offset the costs, the costs should be charged to current year's income, but not as an extraordinary item.

[.08] Reserved

.09 Costs Incurred to Acquire Treasury Stock

Inquiry—A company has incurred legal and accounting costs arising from the acquisition of treasury stock. How should the costs be classified in the company's financial statements?

Reply—There is no authoritative literature on this particular subject. Some accountants believe that costs associated with the acquisition of treasury stock should be treated in a manner similar to stock issue costs. Stock issue costs are usually accounted for as a deduction from the gross proceeds of the sale of stock. Costs associated with the acquisition of treasury stock may be added to the cost of the treasury stock.

.10 Costs Incurred in Shelf Registration

Inquiry—A public company incurs legal and other fees in connection with an SEC filing for a stock issue it plans to offer under a shelf registration. How should the company account for these costs?

Reply—The costs should be capitalized as a prepaid expense. When securities are taken off the shelf and sold, a portion of the costs attributable to the securities sold should be charged against paid in capital. Any subsequent costs incurred to keep the filing "alive" should be charged to expense as incurred. If the filing is withdrawn, the related capitalized costs should be charged to expense.

.11 Default on Stock Subscribed

Inquiry—A company entered into a stock subscription agreement to sell its stock. The agreement called for three monthly payments of $10,000 after which the stock would be issued. Although the first payment was received by the company, the subscriber subsequently defaulted on the remaining two payments. According to the agreement, any payments made by the subscriber towards the stock subscription are not refundable. How should the company account for the retention of the first $10,000 payment?

Reply—The payment should be recorded as an addition to shareholders' equity (i.e., a credit to paid-in capital). According to Financial Accounting Standards Board (FASB) *Accounting Standards Codification* (ASC) 505-10-25-2, capital transactions shall be excluded from the determination of net income or the results of operations.

[Revised, June 2009, to reflect conforming changes necessary due to the issuance of FASB ASC.]

Q&A Section 4120
Reacquisition of Capital Stock

[.01] Reserved

[.02] Reserved

.03 Repurchase of Stock in Excess of Retained Earnings and Additional Paid-in Capital

Inquiry—A corporation has contracted to repurchase, over a period, some of its own stock. The corporation does not have sufficient retained earnings and additional paid-in capital from which to charge the excess of amounts paid over par value. How should this repurchase be reflected in the company's financial statements?

Reply—In many states, it would not be legal for a corporation to repurchase shares of its own stock at a cost greater than the amount of retained earnings of the corporation. Competent legal advice as to the effect of the agreement should be obtained. This may be an executory contract, with only amounts currently being paid for considered as repurchases. If this be the case, only amounts disbursed are to be recognized in the accounts, with an offset to treasury stock. There should of course be disclosure in a note to the financial statements of the date, number of shares, and amounts of future payments under the contract. Such future payments would thus include the interest factor, which would be an additional cost of the stock, rather than being interest expense.

However, if legal counsel advises that this is in fact a completed contract and enforceable, the full amount should be shown (excluding interest) as treasury stock, with an offsetting liability. Again, there should be footnote disclosure of the nature of the liability and of the interest rate and maturity dates. Under these circumstances, the interest would be included as a current expense.

[.04] Reserved

.05 Purchase of Treasury Shares for an Amount in Excess of Market Price

Inquiry—A corporation enters into an agreement to purchase a major block of its shares from one of its shareholders at a price in excess of its current market price. These shares represent the controlling interest in the corporation. The purchase price of the treasury stock does not include any other rights or privileges. At what value should the corporation record the treasury stock?

Reply—Financial Accounting Standards Board (FASB) *Accounting Standards Codification* (ASC) 505-30-30-4 states that transactions do arise in which an acquisition of an enterprise's stock may take place at prices different from routine transactions in the open market. A block of shares representing a controlling interest will generally trade at a price in excess of market, and a large block of shares may trade at a price above or below the current market price depending on whether the buyer or seller initiates the transaction. A company's acquisition of its shares in those circumstances is solely a treasury stock transaction and is properly accounted for at the purchase price of the treasury shares.

In this situation, since the purchase price does not include amounts attributable to items other than the shares purchased, the entire purchase price should be accounted for as the cost of treasury shares.

[Revised, June 2009, to reflect conforming changes necessary due to the issuance of FASB ASC.]

Q&A Section 4130

Warrants

[.01] Reserved

[.02] Reserved

.03 Warrants Reacquired

Inquiry—Company A issued, in a prior year, stock warrants with a subordinated note. The value of the warrants as determined at the date of issuance was added to capital in excess of par value and recorded as deferred loan costs to be amortized over the term of the loan. Company A plans to reacquire the warrants for $110,000. Should the $110,000 be:

(*a*) accounted for as additional cost of the loan and amortized over the remaining term of the loan, or

(*b*) accounted for as a capital transaction and deducted from capital in excess of par value, or

(*c*) accounted for in some other manner?

Reply—The purchase price of the warrants should be deducted from either capital in excess of par value or retained earnings.

Q&A Section 4150

Stock Dividends and Stock Splits

[.01] Reserved

.02 Stock Dividend Affecting Market Price of Stock

Inquiry—A company issued a 10 percent stock dividend. May the dividend be treated as a stock split if the dividend resulted in a drop in the market price of the stock?

Reply—Financial Accounting Standards Board (FASB) *Accounting Standards Codification* (ASC) 505-20-25-3 states, in part: "except for a few instances, the issuance of additional shares of less than 20 or 25 percent of the number of previously outstanding shares would call for treatment as a stock dividend as described in paragraph 505-20-30-3." FASB ASC 505-20-30-3 requires a transfer from retained earnings to the category of permanent capitalization in an amount equal to the fair value of the additional shares issued.

In order to treat the 10 percent "stock dividend" as a "split-up effected in the form of a dividend," the company would have to demonstrate that the additional shares issued is "large enough to materially influence the unit market price of the stock" as indicated in FASB ASC 505-20-25-3.

[Revised, June 2009, to reflect conforming changes necessary due to the issuance of FASB ASC.]

[.03] Reserved

Q&A Section 4160

Contributed Capital

.01 Payment of Corporate Debt by Stockholders

Inquiry—Three shareholders own stock in Corporations A and B. They agree to personally pay a debt of Corporation A by giving the creditor stock in Corporation B. How should this transaction be recorded on the books of Corporation A?

Reply—The payments by the three stockholders of Corporation A's debt would represent an additional contribution by the stockholders to Corporation A. This can be recorded as a credit to "additional capital."

[.02] Reserved

Q&A Section 4200

Retained Earnings

.01 Foreign Currency Translation—Retained Earnings

Inquiry—A parent company is translating a foreign subsidiary's financial statements for consolidation purposes. It is the second year of operation for the subsidiary. How should retained earnings be translated?

Reply—For assets and liabilities, Financial Accounting Standards Board (FASB) *Accounting Standards Codification* (ASC) 830-30-45-3 requires the use of the exchange rate at the balance sheet date. For revenues, expenses, gains, and losses, the exchange rate at the dates on which those elements are recognized shall be used. However, an appropriately weighted average exchange rate for the period may be used to translate the income statement.

In year two, net income or loss would be translated at the weighted average exchange rate for the current year and accumulated with the historical opening translated retained earnings. It should be noted there may be a number of other transactions that may affect the subsidiary's retained earnings including the declaration of dividends.

[Revised, June 2009, to reflect conforming changes necessary due to the issuance of FASB ASC.]

Q&A Section 4210

Dividends

.01 Write-Off of Liquidating Dividends

Inquiry—Quite a few years ago, cash dividends were distributed to stockholders in excess of earnings. The company would now like to "clean up" the stockholders' equity section of the balance sheet by removing the account "Prior Years' Liquidation Dividends" which is shown as a reduction of the capital stock account. Can the liquidating dividends account be written off against "retained earnings" or "paid in capital in excess of par value"?

Reply—Essentially, this question is a legal one as to whether cash distribution to stockholders in excess of earnings in prior years may be charged to earnings in subsequent years. When liquidating dividends are declared, the charge is made to accounts such as "capital repayment," "capital returned," or "liquidating dividends" which appear on the balance sheet as offsets to paid-in capital. By this treatment, the amount of capital returned as well as the amount of capital originally paid in can be disclosed. Perhaps the wisest thing to do under the circumstances is to consult legal counsel to determine whether the write-off proposed is legal under the corporate statutes of the state. Perhaps it is legally permissible, under the laws of incorporation, to reduce the par or stated value of the corporation's stock, thereby creating a reduction surplus which may then be used retroactively to absorb the original deficit, on the ground that the excess payments were dividends in partial liquidation.

[.02] Reserved

[.03] Reserved

.04 Accrual of Preferred Dividends

Inquiry—A corporation has cumulative preferred stock. It has not paid any dividends on this stock in the last three years. Should the corporation accrue the preferred dividends in arrears?

Reply—Generally, preferred stock contains a cumulative provision whereby dividends omitted in previous years must be paid prior to the payment of dividends on other outstanding shares. Since dividends do not become a corporate liability until declared, no accrual is needed. Financial Accounting Standards Board (FASB) *Accounting Standards Codification* (ASC) 505-10-50-5 requires entities to disclose within its financial statements (either on the face of the statement of financial position or in the notes thereto) the aggregate and per-share amounts of arrearages in cumulative preferred dividends. Furthermore, FASB ASC 260-10-45-11 states that dividends accumulated for the period on cumulative preferred stock (whether or not earned) should be deducted from income from continuing operations and also from net income when computing earnings per share. If there is a loss from continuing operations or a net loss, the amount of the loss should be increased by those preferred dividends. Preferred dividends that are cumulative only if earned should be deducted only to the extent that they are earned.

If preferred dividends are not cumulative, only the dividends declared should be deducted. In all cases, the effect that has been given to preferred dividends in arriving at income available to common stockholders in computing basic earnings per share should be disclosed for every period for which an income statement is presented.

[Amended, September 1997; Revised, June 2009, to reflect conforming changes necessary due to the issuance of FASB ASC.]

Q&A Section 4230

Capital Transactions

[.01] Reserved

.02 Exchange of No Par Common Shares for Par Value Preferred Shares

Inquiry—The shareholders of Corporation A exchanged their no par common shares for preferred shares with a par value to "freeze" the value of stock ownership for estate tax purposes. How should the difference between the carrying basis of the preferred shares and the carrying basis of the common shares be accounted for?

Reply—The difference should be charged or credited to additional paid-in capital. If there is no additional paid-in capital, any "debit" balance should first be charged to retained earnings and any remaining "debit" balance should be described in the financial statements as a discount on preferred stock. However, in many states the law requires that issued stock must be fully paid and nonassessable and therefore, if the par value of the preferred shares exceeds the market value of the common shares this exchange may have legal implications that should be considered.

.03 Use of Stockholder's Assets to Repay Corporate Loan

Inquiry—The sole owner of a corporation agreed to collateralize the company's bank loan with personal assets. As a result of financial difficulties, the company's bank loan was called and its owner agreed to sell his personal assets collateralizing the company's loan, to repay the bank debt. What is the appropriate accounting of this transaction?

Reply—The monies used to repay the bank loan are in substance a further capital infusion by the individual, which increases his investment in the company. The company would eliminate its liability to the bank and credit paid-in capital.

Q&A Section 5000

REVENUE AND EXPENSE

TABLE OF CONTENTS

Section

Section

Section

Q&A Section 5100
Revenue Recognition

.01 Equipment Sales Net of Trade-Ins

Inquiry—A Client who deals in heavy equipment records all sales at net of trade-ins. Is this an acceptable accounting practice?

Reply—Support for the accounting treatment for trade-ins which this client follows could not be found. Sales should be credited with the nominal or stated contract price, and the difference between *(a)* the trade-in allowance and *(b)* the amount determined by pricing the trade-in at net realizable value minus normal profit margin should be treated as a sales allowance or discount. The traded-in equipment should be set up in inventory at an amount which, when reconditioning costs are added, will allow a margin approximating a normal profit when the sale is made.

.02 Rights to Broadcast Time Received for Services

Inquiry—An advertising agency creates and sells jingles and station identifications to radio and television stations. The agency receives broadcast time credit as part payment. This broadcast time is then resold by the agency to its clients. Should this broadcast time be recognized by the advertising agency:

1. when the agency bills the radio or television station, or
2. when it is subsequently sold to advertisers?

Reply—The broadcast time credit should be recognized as income when the services are billed to the station. It may be necessary to estimate the value of the credits. A corresponding asset account should be charged. This asset would be relieved as the broadcast time is sold by the advertising agency.

[.03] Reserved

.04 Discounts on Prepaid Funeral Arrangement Plans

Inquiry—An incorporated mortuary sells pre-need funeral plans in addition to rendering current mortuary services. These pre-need funeral plans are sold at a discount in order to be attractive to the public. All monies received from the sale of these plans are placed in a trust fund which has been set up at a local bank. The bank is the trustee of the trust and makes investments as it sees fit. The pre-need funeral plan agreements stipulate that all income earned by the trust belong to the mortuary, and withdrawals of such income from the trust may be made by the mortuary periodically. In return for the feature of the agreements calling for the mortuary's entitlement to the trust fund income, purchasers of the pre-need plans are permitted to buy the plans at a substantial discount. The agreements also provide for fully-covered funeral benefits in certain cases, although the plans may not be fully paid at time of death. Another advantage to the purchasers is that the costs of their funerals will not be influenced by increases in the cost of living index.

Certain expenses are met by the mortuary in the selling of its pre-need funeral plans; these are recorded monthly in a separate expense account in its general ledger. Trust fund income earned is also recorded monthly in the mortuary's general ledger, in a separate income account. As pre-need plans are utilized by persons who had purchased them earlier, the special discounts mentioned in the preceding paragraph are recorded in a separate expense account in the mortuary's general ledger. It should be emphasized here that such discounts are not reflected as an expense in the mortuary's operations until such time the plans are actually used, whereas the expenses of the sales of the plans and the income earned by the trust affect operations currently, with no dependency whatsoever on the deaths of the purchasers or holders of the plans.

In order to achieve a better matching of expenses with revenues accruing from the sales of plans, could the trust fund income or the excess of trust fund income over the expenses of selling the plans be deferred until the plans are utilized? Or could the special discounts be charged to income at some date prior to the utilization of the plans?

Reply—It would be more acceptable to currently accrue or recognize selling expenses, fees and commissions, and trust fund income rather than use the "completed contract" or deferral accounting approach. If it is a fact that costs of furnishing services commonly exceed the trust funds expended at time of utilizing a plan, current provision should be made on an estimated basis for the potential or possible losses (more accurately, estimated excess of future servicing costs over monies to be released from trust to defray same) on plans not utilized as yet at the balance sheet date.

The special discounts are more in the nature of sales adjustments rather than costs or expenses.

[.05] Reserved

[.06] Reserved

.07 One-Cent Sales

Inquiry—A client in the fast food business has a "one-cent sale" once a week. For example, the sale might be two cheeseburgers for the price of one (60¢) plus one cent. The company would record the transaction as follows:

Cash (.60 + .01)	$.61	
Advertisement Expense	.59	
Sales (.60 × 2)		$1.20

The company makes this entry so that their "food costs" are not distorted, but should an adjustment be made at the end of the year for financial reporting purposes eliminating this advertising expense against sales?

Reply—The practice of crediting sales and charging advertising expense for the difference between the normal sales price and the "bargain day" sales price of merchandise is not acceptable for financial reporting. Realization of the full sales price cannot properly be imputed under such conditions. To do so would seem to imply that the same quantities would have been sold if the price had not been reduced.

It might however be appropriate to adjust the cost of sales and charge advertising for the cost of the one-cent hamburger. Such cost of sales should include only out-of-pocket expenses.

.08 Life Membership Fees in a Club

Inquiry—A company is engaged in a service club enterprise. What is the proper accounting for life membership fees?

Reply—The life membership fees should be allocated over the time the individual may be expected to require the services of the club.

[.09] Reserved

.10 Members of Country Club Assessed for Debt Retirement

Inquiry—A country club has voted to impose a special yearly assessment on its membership for ten years. The proceeds are to be used to retire a first mortgage on the property of the club.

The assessment is being imposed on all members including voting certificate holders and nonvoting associate members.

Is the proper accounting treatment of this transaction a contribution to capital, or are dues to be reflected in the annual income statement?

Reply—When billing the assessments each year, the receivables from the members can be shown as an asset with a credit to income for the special assessment. Such amounts might then be appropriated to a special membership equity, perhaps entitled "appropriation for retirement of debt." The financial statements should disclose that the directors had voted a special assessment for ten years and the amount of assessment per year. The first or the last year for the assessment, or both, should also be disclosed.

.11 Excise Tax on Club Dues

Inquiry—The members of certain private clubs must pay a federal excise tax in addition to their annual dues. Should the clubs record, as revenues, the dues net of the excise tax, or should revenues include both dues and taxes?

Reply—A club, in collecting excise taxes on dues, is acting as no more than an agent or conduit for the federal government. The amounts paid to the club by members to be turned over as excise taxes should not be construed as dues, and to show them as such on the income statement is erroneous.

[.12] Reserved

[.13] Reserved

.14 Recognition of Fees Earned on Construction Mortgage Placements

Inquiry—A client is in the business of bringing lenders and borrowers together for a fee. When a construction mortgage has been arranged and agreed to, it would appear that the client has earned its fee. However, because of the terms of the fee arrangement, there is some doubt as to when the income should be recognized.

The following is a summary of the types of transactions involved:

1. Negotiable Note

   The company receives a negotiable note in payment of its fees. Generally the note is unsecured and non-interest-bearing and is payable over the same period as the construction draws on the related mortgage are to be made.

2. Nonnegotiable Note

   The terms of the nonnegotiable note are comparable to the negotiable note.

3. Commitment Letter, Not Contingent on Future Events

   The company receives a letter from the borrower indicating that the lender and the borrower have agreed on the terms of the mortgage. In addition, the letter states that the borrower agrees to pay the company a fixed fee by a specified date for services rendered in arranging the loan.

4. Commitment Letter, Contingent on Future Draws

   The company receives commitment letters from the borrower as described in No. 3 in the preceding. However, the commitment letters state that a certain amount of the fee will not be paid unless or until certain construction draws are received from the lender.

When should revenue be recognized as earned by the client?

Reply—Revenue recognition is discussed in Financial Accounting Standards Board (FASB) Concepts Statement No. 5, *Recognition and Measurement in Financial Statements of Business Enterprises*, paragraphs 83 and 84.

Applying the guidelines of Concepts No. 5, paragraphs 83 and 84, to the specific situations, revenue would be recognized as follows:

1. Negotiable Note

   Income would be recognized when the services have been performed and billed which may be prior to receipt of the negotiable note.

2. Nonnegotiable Note

   The terms of the nonnegotiable note are comparable to the negotiable note, and revenue would be recognized in a similar manner.

3. Commitment Letter, Not Contingent on Future Events

   Such a letter would be evidence that the services have been rendered and are now "billable"; therefore, the fee has been earned and income should be recognized.

4. Commitment Letter, Contingent on Future Draws

   From the description, it appears that the agreement between the client, borrower, and lender in this case is such that the parties do not consider all the services rendered until actual borrowings take place even though the client need not physically do anything else. In such a situation, a portion of the fees should be deferred until the stipulated draw provisions have been met.

[.15] Reserved

.16 Rental Revenue Based on Percentage of Sales

Inquiry—A supermarket built an addition to its store to house a liquor store. The rent to the liquor store is to be a percent of its sales. On its income statement, would it be proper for the supermarket to include the liquor store sales as though they were their own sales? The rent would then appear as a gross margin.

Reply—No. In accordance with the FASB *Accounting Standards Codification* (ASC) glossary, this transaction meets the definition of a *lease*, which is "... the right to use property, plant, or equipment (land and/or depreciable assets) usually for a stated period of time."

The revenue received from the liquor store represents rental income to the supermarket and it would be inappropriate for the supermarket to include as its sales the sales of the liquor store. However, it would be appropriate for the supermarket to include the rental income as part of its gross revenues.

[Amended June 1995; Revised, June 2009, to reflect conforming changes necessary due to the issuance of FASB ASC.]

[.17] Reserved

[.18] Reserved

[.19] Reserved

.20 Payment for Termination of License Agreement

Inquiry—A research and development company holds numerous patents. The company derives its income from the sale of products which utilize its patents as well as from the licensing of the patents, for which it receives royalties, and also from the sale of patent rights, for which it receives a single payment for the term of the license.

A licensee desired to terminate its license, since it was no longer using the technology contained in the company's patent, and paid to the company a lump sum termination payment. This payment approximated the amount the company would have earned during the remaining years of the license agreement. How should the termination payment be reflected in the company's financial statements?

Reply—The transaction is similar to sale of a license for the remaining life of a patent and should be accounted for in the same manner. If this is the sole license for a patent, any remaining unamortized cost of such patent should be written off at this time. If the license represents only a portion of the use of the patent, an appropriate portion of the remaining unamortized cost should be written off. The proceeds should be included in this year's current operations, and there should be disclosure that a major source of income from licensing agreements is being terminated.

[.21] Reserved

[.22] Reserved

[.23] Reserved

[.24] Reserved

.25 Finished Parts Held by Manufacturer for Customers

Inquiry—Corporation A, a subcontractor, manufacturers precision parts to customers' specifications. Parts produced by Corporation A are inspected by a customer's quality control representative and then held in a secured area in Corporation A's plant. Corporation A is entitled to full contract payment on parts inspected and held in the secured area. Historically, there has been a short time span between completion date and scheduled shipment date, but recently production efficiency has improved to the extent that contracts are completed significantly in advance of scheduled shipment dates. Based on the recent experience of Corporation A, what is the proper date for revenue recognition?

Reply—FASB Concepts Statement No. 5, *Recognition and Measurement in Financial Statements of Business Enterprises*, paragraph 83, states in part:

> "Revenues are not recognized until earned. An entity's revenue-earning activities involve delivering or producing goods, rendering services, or other activities that constitute its ongoing major or central operations, and revenues are considered to have been earned when the entity has substantially accomplished what it must do to be entitled to the benefits represented by the revenues . . . ."

Revenue should be recognized at the time of inspection and delivery to the secured areas, since the realization criteria have been met. Corporation A should disclose the method followed for income recognition as part of its disclosure of accounting policies.

[.26] Reserved

[.27] Reserved

.28 Revenue From Private Label Sales

Inquiry—Corporation A produces certain products that are sold under Corporation B's label. Corporation B reimburses Corporation A for all direct costs of raw material, ingredients, and packaging plus 10 cents per pound processing fee. Corporation A prepares an invoice for each shipment which itemizes the various direct costs plus 10 cents per pound processing fee. Should Corporation A record the total invoice amount as a sale or should it record the processing fee as revenue and the reimbursed direct costs as a reduction of expenses?

Reply—Corporation A should probably record the total invoice amount as a sale. Accounting for contracts of this type would be treated similar to cost-plus-fixed-fee contracts discussed in FASB ASC 912-605.

[Revised, June 2009, to reflect conforming changes necessary due to the issuance of FASB ASC.]

[.29] Reserved

[.30] Reserved

.31 Accounting for Zero Coupon Bonds

Inquiry—A client purchased a 20-year zero coupon treasury bond for $189, with a maturity value of $1,000, at an 8 1/2 percent yield to maturity.

(1) What authoritative pronouncement would provide guidance for this transaction?

(2) How is the interest income computed for financial reporting purposes?

Reply—(1) FASB ASC 835-30-15-2 states that, "The guidance in this Subtopic applies to receivables and payables that represent contractual rights to receive money or contractual obligations to pay money on fixed or determinable dates, whether or not there is any stated provision for interest . . . Some examples are secured and unsecured notes, debentures, bonds . . ."

(2) FASB ASC 835-30-35-2 states that, "the difference between the present value and the face amount shall be treated as discount or premium and amortized as interest expense or income over the life of the note in such a way as to result in a constant rate of interest when applied to the amount outstanding at the beginning of any given period." This is the "interest" method described in

paragraphs 2–3 of FASB ASC 835-30-35. However, other methods of amortization may be used if the results obtained are not materially different from those which would result from the "interest" method.

The following is an example of the application of the interest method. To calculate the semi-annual amount, multiply the purchase price by 4 1/4 percent (half of 8 1/2 percent) to arrive at the adjusted cost basis for the first six-month period. Then repeat this calculation for the next six-month period using the adjusted cost basis. The total amount of income (accrual) in the first year will be $16.40. Each year the cost basis is increased by the amount of income (accrual) reported in the previous year, as indicated in the following example:

Semi-Annual Period	*Your Purchase Price or Adjusted Cost Basis*	*1/2 Purchase YTM*	*Accrual During Period*	*Adjusted Coast Basis at End of Period*
1	$189.00	4.25%	$8.03	$197.03
2	197.03	4.25%	8.37	205.40
3	205.40	4.25%	8.73	214.13
4	214.13	4.25%	9.10	223.23

The interest income would be reported annually for financial reporting purposes. If the bond is held to maturity, there will be no gain or loss. If sold prior to maturity any gain or loss is determined by the difference between the adjusted cost basis and the selling price.

[Revised, June 2009, to reflect conforming changes necessary due to the issuance of FASB ASC.]

[.32] Reserved

.33 Operating Lease With Rental Payments Rebated Against Purchase Price

Inquiry—A lessor corporation leases construction equipment for periods of six to eighteen months under short-term cancellable leases. The leases provide that during the first six months, 100 percent of the rentals paid may be applied toward the purchase price of the equipment if the lessee decides to purchase the equipment; during the next three months the percentage drops to 80 percent, and after nine months 60 percent may be applied toward the purchase price. The leases do not qualify as capital leases. How should the lessor account for the leases and the respective rebates?

Reply—The authoritative literature does not address this matter. The lessor should record rental income until the lessee decides to purchase the equipment. The lessor should then record the sale of the equipment net of the applicable rebate. The amount recorded as rental income should not be reclassified as sales proceeds.

[.34] Reserved

.35 Involuntary Conversion—Recognition of Gain

Inquiry—A tornado virtually destroys a company's building on June 12, 20X0. The company has insurance and expects to be reimbursed for costs incurred to refurbish the building. The company's fiscal year-end is June 30, 20X0.

On August 15, 20X0, prior to the issuance of the financial statements, the company receives a check in excess of the carrying amount of the building. Should the company recognize the gain on the involuntary conversion in the June 30, 20X0 financial statements?

Reply—No. Since the company was reimbursed for an amount in excess of the carrying amount of the building there was no loss to record on June 30, 20X0. The gain, which was received on August 15, 20X0, was a gain contingency on June 30, 20X0. Per FASB ASC 450-30-25-1, contingencies that might result in gains usually are not reflected in the accounts since to do so might be to recognize revenue prior to its realization.

[Revised, June 2009, to reflect conforming changes necessary due to the issuance of FASB ASC.]

.36 Sales of Investment to Minority Stockholder

Inquiry—A corporation enters into an agreement to sell an investment accounted for on the equity method to a minority stockholder in return for his shares in the corporation. The fair value of the investment exceeds its book value. Would the corporation recognize a gain on this transaction or would the excess be credited to equity?

Reply—FASB ASC 845-10-30-1 states that a transfer of a nonmonetary asset to a stockholder or to another entity in a nonreciprocal transfer should be recorded at the fair value of the asset transferred, and that a gain or loss should be recognized on the disposition of the asset. FASB ASC 845-10-30-2 also indicates that the fair value of an entity's own stock reacquired may be a more clearly evident measure of the fair value of the asset distributed in a nonreciprocal transfer if the transaction involves acquiring stock for the treasury or retirement.

The corporation should recognize as a gain, in the year in which the transaction occurs, the excess of the fair value of the investment transferred over its carrying amount.

[Revised, June 2009, to reflect conforming changes necessary due to the issuance of FASB ASC.]

.37 Sales Price Based on Future Revenue

Inquiry—A company sold one of its direct-mail catalog offices for cash plus a percentage of revenue to be earned over the next five years. The sales agreement limits the percentage of revenue to a stipulated maximum. Management believes the maximum will be earned within the five-year period. When should revenue from this transaction be recorded?

Reply—According to FASB ASC 450-30-25-1, "A contingency that might result in a gain usually should not be reflected in the financial statements because to do so might be to recognize revenue before its realization."

Unless it is assured that adequate revenue will be earned to cause payment of the contingent portion of the sales price, the contingent portion of the sales price should only be accrued as earned. The accuracy and reasonableness of management's projections must be ascertained. If realization is assured, which would be relatively infrequent, revenue should be recorded as of the date of the sale using the present value of the projected cash receipts in accordance with FASB ASC 835, *Interest*.

[Revised, June 2009, to reflect conforming changes necessary due to the issuance of FASB ASC.]

[.38] Reserved

[.39] Reserved

[.40] Reserved

[.41] Reserved

[.42] Reserved

[.43] Reserved

[.44] Reserved

[.45] Reserved

[.46] Reserved

[.47] Reserved

[.48] Reserved

[.49] Reserved

[.50] Reserved

[.51] Reserved

[.52] Reserved

[.53] Reserved

[.54] Reserved

[.55] Reserved

[.56] Reserved

[.57] Reserved

[.58] Reserved

[.59] Reserved

[.60] Reserved

[.61] Reserved

[.62] Reserved

[.63] Reserved

[.64] Reserved

[.65] Reserved

[.66] Reserved

[.67] Reserved

[.68] Reserved

[.69] Reserved

[.70] Reserved

[.71] Reserved

[.72] Reserved

[.73] Reserved

[.74] Reserved

[.75] Reserved

[.76] Reserved

Q&A Section 5210
Depreciation and Depletion

[.01] Reserved

.02 Disclosure of Depreciation Expense

Inquiry—Financial Accounting Standards Board (FASB) *Accounting Standards Codification* (ASC) 360-10-50-1 states that the financial statements should disclose depreciation *expense* for a period. Does *expense* mean the total amount of depreciation accrued (that is, credited to the allowance for depreciation account) for the period or the amount actually expensed after allowing for depreciation included in overhead apportioned to inventories?

Reply—In concerns such as public utilities and trading or commercial enterprises, determination of the total provision for depreciation is usually simple since the amounts of depreciation are generally identified in the expense accounts. In manufacturing concerns, however, there are difficulties in determining the amount of depreciation to be disclosed. Depreciation is usually included in overhead which in turn is distributed over a number of departments and products and finds its way ultimately into cost of sales through inventory accounts. To determine the amount of depreciation which is included as a part of the cost of merchandise sold may require an extensive and usually impracticable, if not impossible, analysis of cost accounts. The auditor usually solves the problem by suggesting that the amount of depreciation charged to manufacturing costs and to expense accounts be taken as representing the amount charged to income. Obviously, this method does not correctly state the depreciation charge which was recovered through sale of goods in which depreciation was an element of cost. From a practical standpoint, in view of the indicated difficulty, if not impossibility, of determining the exact amount of depreciation included in cost of sales, it has become recognized practice to report the amount of depreciation charged in the statement of income as that which has been charged to manufacturing costs and to expense accounts, even when amounts of depreciation included in inventories at the beginning and end of the period vary sufficiently to affect depreciation included in cost of sales. Such practice also is acceptable to the Securities and Exchange Commission.

[Revised, June 2009, to reflect conforming changes necessary due to the issuance of FASB ASC.]

[.03] Reserved

.04 Depreciation of Clothing Rented to Individuals

Inquiry—Company A maintains a stock of tuxedos, shoes and related items which are rented to individuals. Management estimates that this stock will have a useful life of approximately two years. Additional stock will be purchased from time to time as required. At the end of each fiscal year, a complete physical inventory is taken of all items on hand. What is the most appropriate accounting treatment for the stock of rental clothing?

Reply—The clothing represents a fixed asset to be depreciated over its estimated life. The estimated life should be adjusted periodically to reflect experience and should not exceed two years. The depreciation charge should be computed monthly based on inventory at the beginning of the period plus additions during the current year.

Logically it seems that loss and retirement of clothing will relate to that clothing first purchased. Accordingly the first-in first-out basis would appropriately account for such loss and retirement.

.05 Classification of Costs of Constructing a Golf Course

Inquiry—How should the costs of constructing a golf course be broken down into depreciable and nondepreciable classifications?

Reply—For the costs incurred in constructing a golf course, those expenditures made to change the land itself, exclusive of buildings, should be treated as permanent improvements to the land and are not, therefore, depreciable. These costs would include clearing the land, building fairways, changing the contour of the earth by moving and filling, building sand traps, and creating water hazards. If trees are planted, and their lives can be estimated, it would appear to be proper to depreciate these over such lives. In the absence of any reasonable estimate, trees and shrubs should be carried at cost. Any structures such as buildings, shacks or stands should be depreciated along with the costs of any vehicles such as trucks or carts, and any equipment used. A watering system should be depreciated as it is made of material that will not last indefinitely.

[.06] Reserved

[.07] Reserved

.08 Additional First Year Depreciation

Inquiry—A corporation reports depreciation expense on its financial statements at the same amount that it claims on its income tax return. If that amount included the maximum $10,000 deduction for additional first year depreciation (election to expense recovery property) allowed for tax purposes, whereas, normal depreciation was $18,000, would the financial statements be in accordance with generally accepted accounting principles?

Reply—FASB ASC 360-10-35-4 states, in part: ". . . depreciation accounting, a system of accounting which aims to distribute the cost or other basic value of tangible capital assets, less salvage (if any), over the estimated useful life of the unit . . . in a systematic and rational manner . . . ." Accordingly, if any arbitrary additional first year depreciation amount is included in the financial statements and it is material, it would be a departure from generally accepted accounting principles. Refer to paragraph .A5 of AU-C section 705, *Modifications to the Opinion in the Independent Auditor's Report* (AICPA, *Professional Standards*), and paragraph .06 of AU-C section 320, *Materiality in Planning and Performing an Audit* (AICPA, *Professional Standards*), for guidance on materiality.

[Revised, June 2009, to reflect conforming changes necessary due to the issuance of FASB ASC; Revised, December 2012, to reflect conforming changes necessary due to the issuance of SAS Nos. 122–126.]

.09 Amortization of Leasehold Improvement

Inquiry—A zoological society leases property in the city zoo for concession stands. The society plans to construct a new building, which will house several concession stands, on the leased property. When construction is complete the title to the building will be turned over to the city. The lease is not a service concession arrangement within the scope of FASB ASC 853, *Service Concession Arrangements*. How should the building be accounted for by the zoological society?

Reply—The construction of a building on leased property is considered a leasehold improvement. A leasehold improvement is a permanent improvement or betterment that increases the usefulness of the leased property and will revert to the lessor at the end of the lease term. The costs of such improvements are normally amortized either over the life of the improvement or the lease term, whichever is shorter.

[Revised, April 2014, to reflect conforming changes necessary due to revisions to FASB ASC.]

[.10] Reserved

Q&A Section 5220

Interest Expense

.01 Deferral of Payment of Interest

Inquiry—A client experienced problems in meeting its current obligations and reached an agreement with its primary creditor concerning several mortgage loans. Under the agreement, the interest rate on these loans will, for the present, be reduced from 10 percent to 8 percent, but the lender has the option in the future of increasing the interest rate to 11 percent to recover the foregone interest. At the maturity date, any unpaid interest calculated at the original 10 percent rate will be due.

How should the interest expense be recorded on the client's financial statements?

Reply—Interest should be accrued at the rate of 10 percent, the original rate under the mortgage loans. This debit would represent the interest expense charged to income. The credit would be segregated between current liabilities (an amount representing the 8 percent rate) and noncurrent liabilities (an amount representing the *deferred interest*).

[.02] Reserved

.03 Computation of Interest Expense on Long-Term Redeemable Bonds

Inquiry—A bank has issued four year nonnegotiable savings bonds with interest of 7 percent for the first year, 7 1/2 percent for the second year, 8 percent for the third year and 8 1/2 percent for the fourth year. The depositor has the option to request that he or she be paid his interest on a semiannual or annual basis, but few do so, and the normal procedure is that the interest will be compounded and left on deposit for the four years.

If a bond is redeemed prior to maturity, interest is paid to the bondholder at the rate of 5 percent per annum for the period that the bond was held, less 90 days. Few instances of bond redemption prior to maturity are anticipated.

Which of the following methods of accounting for interest expense is appropriate?

(1) Accrue interest at 7 percent for the first year, 7 1/2 percent for the second year (plus the compounding factor), 8 percent for the third year (plus the compounding factor), and 8 1/2 percent for the fourth year (plus the compounding factor), making a debit to the interest expense and a credit to the accrued interest payable on four year bonds.

(2) Determine the total amount of interest that will be due to the holder upon the maturity of the bond and accrue a pro rata share of this amount for each month of the four year period that the bond is in effect.

Reply—A rate of interest should be used which reflects the bank's liabilities and assumes that the bondholders will not redeem their bonds and not withdraw the interest prior to maturity. This is essentially the second approach in the preceding.

[.04] Reserved

.05 Amortization of Prepaid Interest on Discounted Notes

Inquiry—An equipment leasing company will use as of the beginning of the year the interest method to amortize prepaid interest on new discounted notes. But it will continue to use the straight-line method to amortize prepaid interest on notes discounted earlier. Is the adoption of the interest method on a prospective basis a change in accounting principle?

Reply—Financial Accounting Standards Board (FASB) *Accounting Standards Codification* (ASC) 835-30-35 states that the interest method of amortization should be used but that other methods of amortization may be used if the results obtained are not materially different from those which would result from the interest method.

If the results in earlier periods would not have differed materially by using the interest method, the interest method may be adopted for the new notes, disclosed, and not be reported as a change in accounting principle.

If the results in earlier periods would have been materially different by using the interest method, the interest method should be adopted for the old and new notes, and be reported as a correction of an error.

[Revised, June 2009, to reflect conforming changes necessary due to the issuance of FASB ASC.]

.06 Imputed Interest on Shareholder Loans

Inquiry—A section of the Internal Revenue Code requires, under certain circumstances, that a company impute interest on demand loans made to a shareholder of the company. Would this also be required under generally accepted accounting principles? If not, must it be disclosed and would there be an effect on the deferred income tax accounts?

Reply—No. FASB ASC 835-30-15-2 states that the guidance in FASB ASC 835-30 applies to receivables and payables which represent contractual rights to receive money or contractual obligations to pay money on fixed or determinable dates. Imputed interest would not be required on demand loans since they have no fixed or determinable due date.

However, disclosure of this transaction would be required under FASB ASC 850, *Related Party Disclosures*.

There would be no effect on the deferred income tax accounts since this would be considered a permanent difference.

[Revised, June 2009, to reflect conforming changes necessary due to the issuance of FASB ASC.]

.07 Imputed Interest on Note Exchanged for Cash Only

Inquiry—If an enterprise receives cash in exchange for a non-interest bearing long-term note payable with a stated amount equal to the cash received, must interest be imputed on the note in accordance with FASB ASC 835, *Interest*?

Reply—If there are rights or privileges other than cash attendant to the exchange, the value of such rights or privileges should be given accounting recognition pursuant to FASB ASC 835-30-25-6. If the note is issued solely for cash (that is, the cash received is equivalent to the face amount of the note) and no other right or privilege is exchanged, it is presumed to have a present value at issuance measured by the cash proceeds exchanged.

[Amended, June 1995; Revised, June 2009, to reflect conforming changes necessary due to the issuance of FASB ASC.]

Q&A Section 5230

Employee Benefit Plans

[.01] Reserved

[.02] Reserved

[.03] Reserved

[.04] Reserved

[.05] Reserved

.06 Deferred Compensation Payable To Surviving Spouse

Inquiry—Corporation A and its president entered into an employment contract. The contract stipulated that if the president died while employed by Corporation A, Corporation A would pay $500 a month to the president's widow for the rest of her life. Shortly after the contract was signed, the president died. The present value of the estimated future payments by Corporation A to the president's widow is $X. Should Corporation A accrue the $X?

Reply—Under Financial Accounting Standards Board (FASB) *Accounting Standards Codification* (ASC) 710-10-25-11, the estimated amounts to be paid under a compensation contract would normally be accrued over the period of active employment. The president's death accelerates recognition of a liability that is reasonably determinable from actuarial tables. Accordingly, the present value of the estimated future payments not previously recognized should be accrued and recognized as an expense.

[Revised, June 2009, to reflect conforming changes necessary due to the issuance of FASB ASC.]

[.07] Reserved

[.08] Reserved

.09 Deferred Compensation Arrangement Funded by Life Insurance Contracts

Inquiry—A company has a deferred compensation contract with one of its employees. In accordance with FASB ASC 710-10-25-11, the estimated amount of future payments was accrued over the period of active employment. The company purchases a life insurance policy on the employee, naming the company as beneficiary. May the cash surrender value earned on the policy be offset against the liability for the deferred compensation arrangement?

Reply—No. Paragraphs 1–2 of FASB ASC 325-30-35 specify that the cash surrender value on a life insurance contract should be reported on the balance sheet as an asset with any changes in that value reflected as an adjustment of insurance expense for the period. No right of offset or other deviations from the preceding accounting would be appropriate regardless of the funding objective pertaining to the purchase of the insurance contract, as stated in paragraphs 2–3 of FASB ASC 325-30-15.

[Revised, June 2009, to reflect conforming changes necessary due to the issuance of FASB ASC.]

Q&A Section 5240

Cost Allocation

[.01] Reserved

[.02] Reserved

[.03] Reserved

[.04] Reserved

[.05] Reserved

[.06] Reserved

[.07] Reserved

[.08] Reserved

[.09] Reserved

.10 Sale of Research and Development Technology

Inquiry—A company has incurred material research and development costs in the current year. Subsequent to the balance sheet date but prior to issuance of the financial statements, the company commenced negotiations and sold the research and development technology to an unrelated company. May the company capitalize the incurred research and development costs in its annual financial statements in light of the subsequent sale?

Reply—No. Financial Accounting Standards Board *Accounting Standards Codification* 730-10-25 states that research and development costs should be expensed when incurred. There is no justification for capitalizing the costs because the technology will be sold. The company should disclose the subsequent sale of the research and development technology in the footnotes to its financial statements if the amount is material.

[Revised, June 2009, to reflect conforming changes necessary due to the issuance of FASB ASC.]

[.11] Reserved

Q&A Section 5250

Tax Allocation

[.01–.13] Reserved

.14 Application of Financial Accounting Standards Board (FASB) Interpretation No. 48, *Accounting for Uncertainty in Income Taxes* (codified in FASB *Accounting Standards Codification* (ASC) 740-10) to Taxes Other Than Income Taxes

Inquiry—Does FASB Interpretation No. 48, *Accounting for Uncertainty in Income Taxes*, (codified in FASB ASC 740-10) apply to federal or state income taxes only, or does it apply to sales, payroll, and other taxes as well?

Reply—The scope of FASB Interpretation No. 48 or FASB ASC 740-10 applies to income taxes only. Entities should follow FASB ASC 450, *Contingencies*, to account for uncertainties related to payroll, sales, and other taxes.

[Issue Date: May 2010.]

[.15] Reserved

Q&A Section 5260

Estimated Losses

.01 Recognition of Estimated Losses on Uncompleted Contracts

Inquiry—An engineering firm manufactures and sells telemetry components on the basis of bids previously submitted to customers. In some cases, engineering time is required to modify a component to customer specifications. Since the amount of required engineering time is not known at the time a bid is submitted, costs to complete a particular job may exceed the bid price. The firm completes all jobs.

Presently all costs that accumulate on a particular job (direct materials, labor, and applied manufacturing and engineering overhead) are charged to that job and treated as work in process, even though the costs may exceed the selling price. Once the job is completed, it is taken out of work in process inventory and treated as costs of completion in the month that the job is shipped. Therefore, a loss on a job is recognized only when the job is shipped. When cost to complete a job is expected to exceed the bid price, what disclosure should be made on the balance sheet?

Reply—The problem faced by the firm is not primarily one of disclosure but rather that of satisfying the generally accepted accounting principle of "providing for losses which are reasonably certain to occur."

It is assumed that the firm is accounting on the completed-contract basis. With regard to construction companies using this method of accounting, Financial Accounting Standards Board (FASB) *Accounting Standards Codification* (ASC) 605-35-25-89 states, "Although the completed-contract method does not permit the recording of any income prior to completion, provision shall be made for expected losses. See paragraphs 605-35-25-45 through 25-47." The same concept applies to companies accounting under the percentage-of-completion method (paragraphs 5 and 46 of FASB ASC 605-35-25).

A possible journal entry to recognize the loss would be a charge to "Estimated Loss on Uncompleted Contracts" while crediting "Estimated Liability for Loss on Uncompleted Contracts." This estimated liability could then be deducted from any excess of accumulated costs over related billings (or added to any liability arising from billings in excess of accumulated costs) for balance sheet purposes. If the loss is not deductible for tax purposes, part of the income tax paid should be set up as a deferred charge.

[Revised, June 2009, to reflect conforming changes necessary due to the issuance of FASB ASC.]

Q&A Section 5290

Other Expenses

[.01] Reserved

.02 Classification of Expenses Which Are Taxable to Employees

Inquiry—An amendment to the Internal Revenue Code requires, under certain circumstances, that an employer include as income, the fair value for the use of a company automobile, in the employee's wage and tax statement (Form W-2).

Should this be reported in the company's statement of income as compensation to employees?

Reply—No. The fair value is the amount the employee would have paid to use the car if the employee had owned it. The employer should report, as automobile expenses, the amount of actual expenses it incurred as owner of the car.

[.03] Reserved

[.04] Reserved

.05 Accrual of Audit Fee

Inquiry—A CPA has been engaged to audit the financial statements of a client company. The audit is being conducted after year end. Is it proper to accrue the audit fee as an expense of the year under audit?

Reply—According to FASB Concepts Statement No. 6, *Elements of Financial Statements*, paragraph 145, "The goal of accrual accounting is to account in the periods in which they occur for the effects on an entity of transactions and other events and circumstances, to the extent that those financial effects are recognizable and measurable." The audit fee expense was incurred in the period subsequent to year end. Therefore, it is properly recorded as an expense in the subsequent period. However, fees incurred in connection with planning the audit, together with preliminary procedures (for example, confirmation work) would be accruable for the year under audit.

.06 Accounting for a Lease Trial Period

Inquiry—A lease agreement allows a prospective lessee the free use of newly introduced specialized equipment for 30 days prior to entering into a long-term lease agreement for the equipment. The prospective lessee is not committed to enter into a long-term lease agreement at the beginning or during the 30-day trial period and there is no economic penalty to the lessee if the lessee does not enter into that agreement. How should the prospective lessee account for the 30-day trial period?

Reply—The 30-day trial period is part of the lessor's marketing strategy. Therefore, the lessee should not report any lease expense during the 30-day trial period. If the lessee subsequently enters into the lease arrangement, the date of inception should begin on the first day of the lease with no accounting recognition given to the trial period.

Q&A Section 5400

Deleted, May 2016, due to the issuance of FASB ASU No. 2015-01.

Deleted, May 2016, due to the issuance of FASB ASU No. 2015-01.

Q&A Section 5500

Earnings per Share

[.01] Reserved

.02 Earnings Per Share of Wholly-Owned Subsidiaries

Inquiry—The annual report of a holding company with five wholly owned subsidiaries shows the consolidated net income and earnings per share of the companies. If the report also includes the individual income statements of the five subsidiaries, is it necessary to include individual earnings per share figures?

Reply—Financial Accounting Standards Board (FASB) *Accounting Standards Codification* (ASC) 260-10-15-3 does not require presentation of earnings per share in statements of wholly owned subsidiaries.

Therefore, it is not necessary to show earnings per share figures for the subsidiaries.

[Amended, September 1997; Revised, June 2009, to reflect conforming changes necessary due to the issuance of FASB ASC.]

.03 Weighted Average Shares Outstanding for an Interim Period

Inquiry—A company retired some of its common stock during the first quarter of its fiscal year. Should earnings per share for the interim period be based on annualized weighted average shares outstanding or the weighted average shares outstanding during the period?

Reply—The earnings per share computation should be based on the weighted average shares outstanding during the interim period, and not on an annualized weighted average.

[Amended, September 1997; Revised, June 2009, to reflect conforming changes necessary due to the issuance of FASB ASC.]

[.04] Reserved

[.05] Reserved

[.06] Reserved

[.07] Reserved

[.08] Reserved

[.09] Reserved

[.10] Reserved

[.11] Reserved

[.12] Reserved

[.13] Reserved

[.14] Reserved

.15 Stock Dividend Declared But Not Paid at Balance-Sheet Date

Inquiry—A client declared a percent stock dividend to shareholders of record in December 20X4, payable in 20X5. In calculating the weighted average number of shares outstanding for determining the earnings per share for 20X4, how should this stock dividend apply?

Reply—FASB ASC 260-10-55-12 requires the computations of basic and diluted earnings per share to be adjusted retroactively for all periods presented to reflect a change in capital structure resulting from a stock dividend. Therefore, the 5 percent stock dividend should be considered as being outstanding for every month of 20X4, as well as for every month of every preceding period presented.

[Amended, September 1997; Revised, June 2009, to reflect conforming changes necessary due to the issuance of FASB ASC.]

[.16] Reserved

Q&A Section 5600

Leases

[.01] Reserved

[.02] Reserved

[.03] Reserved

.04 Accounting for Subleases

Inquiry—A corporation leased a building and, ultimately, subleased half of the space to a third party with the lease agreement between the two original parties remaining in effect. Management believed that a fairer presentation was made by netting the rental income from the sublease against its own minimum lease payments. Is the corporation properly accounting for its leased property and sublease income?

Reply—No. Financial Accounting Standards Board (FASB) *Accounting Standards Codification* (ASC) 840-30-35-12 states that the original lessee, as sublessor, shall continue to account for the obligation related to the original lease as before. The sublease shall be accounted for in accordance with paragraphs 1, 29–31, and 41–44 of FASB ASC 840-10-25, depending upon which of the criteria the original lease met. If the original lease is an operating lease, the original lessee shall account for both it and the new lease as operating leases.

[Revised, June 2009, to reflect conforming changes necessary due to the issuance of FASB ASC.]

[.05] Reserved

[.06] Reserved

.07 Determining a Lease Term for Accounting Purposes

Inquiry—How should a lessee and lessor determine, for accounting purposes, the lease term of a lease, which is fundamental to determining the appropriate accounting for that lease?

Reply—FASB ASC glossary provides a definition of *lease term* as follows:

The fixed noncancelable lease term plus all of the following, except as noted in the following paragraph:

a. All periods, if any, covered by bargain renewal options

b. All periods, if any, for which failure to renew the lease imposes a penalty on the lessee in such amount that a renewal appears, at lease inception, to be reasonably assured

c. All periods, if any, covered by ordinary renewal options during which any of the following conditions exist:

1. A guarantee by the lessee of the lessor's debt directly or indirectly related to the leased property is expected to be in effect
2. A loan from the lessee to the lessor directly or indirectly related to the leased property is expected to be outstanding

d. All periods, if any, covered by ordinary renewal options preceding the date as of which a bargain purchase option is exercisable *e.* All periods, if any, representing renewals or extensions of the lease at the lessor's option

The lease term shall not be assumed to extend beyond the date a bargain purchase option becomes exercisable.

[Revised, June 2009, to reflect conforming changes necessary due to the issuance of FASB ASC.]

.08 Lease Term for Accounting Purposes Differs From Term Stated in Lease (Part 1)

Inquiry—Can a lease term for accounting purposes begin before an initial fixed noncancelable term stated in a lease agreement?

Reply—Yes. FASB ASC 840 provides that a lease term for accounting purposes includes all periods in which a lessee has access to and control over leased space, even if those periods precede the fixed noncancelable term stated in the lease agreement. For example, a lease agreement is signed on January 1 but the initial fixed noncancelable term begins on April 1. The lease allows the lessee to make improvements to the leased space at any time starting after January 1. In this situation, the lease term for accounting purposes starts on January 1.

[Revised, June 2009, to reflect conforming changes necessary due to the issuance of FASB ASC.]

.09 Lease Term for Accounting Purposes Differs From Term Stated in Lease (Part 2)

Inquiry—Can a lease term for accounting purposes extend beyond an initial fixed noncancelable term stated in a lease agreement?

Reply—Yes. FASB ASC glossary term *lease term* identifies situations in which the lease term for accounting purposes extends beyond the fixed noncancelable term stated in a lease agreement. Section 5600.07 identifies those situations. For example, the lease term for accounting purposes would include renewal periods that at lease inception appear reasonably assured because failure to exercise renewal periods would impose a penalty on the lessee.

[Revised, June 2009, to reflect conforming changes necessary due to the issuance of FASB ASC.]

.10 Rent Expense and Rent Revenue in an Operating Lease—General

Inquiry—In an operating lease, how should a lessee accrue rent expense and a lessor recognize rent revenue?

Reply—FASB ASC 840-20-25-1 says that the lessee should accrue rent expense on a straight line basis over the lease term unless another systematic and rational basis is more representative of the time pattern use of the property.

Paragraphs 1–2 of FASB ASC 840-20-25 say that the lessor should recognize rent revenue on a straight line basis over the lease term unless another systematic and rational basis is more representative of the time pattern use of the property.

Also see section 5600.11, "Rent Expense and Rent Revenue in an Operating Lease—Scheduled Increase in Rental Space."

[Revised, June 2009, to reflect conforming changes necessary due to the issuance of FASB ASC.]

.11 Rent Expense and Rent Revenue in an Operating Lease—Scheduled Increase in Rental Space

Inquiry—Related to sections 5600.08 and 5600.10 assume a lessee has access to and use of one floor of a building as of the beginning of a lease agreement in year 1. In accordance with the agreement and at the start of year 3, the lessee will have access to and the ability to occupy a second floor in addition to the first floor, and will pay an additional rental fee starting at that time. In this situation, how should the lessee accrue rent expense and the lessor recognize rent revenue before the lessee is allowed to occupy the second floor?

Reply—FASB ASC 840 is the applicable guidance. In years 1 and 2, the lessee should accrue rent expense on a straight line basis (unless another systematic and rational basis is more representative of the time pattern use of the property) for the one floor and not include the rental of the second floor in its accrual because the lessee does not have access to and control over the second floor until the start of year 3. Starting in year 3, the lessee should accrue rent expense on a straight line basis for both floors.

The lessor's accounting for revenue is parallel to that of the lessee for expense in this fact pattern.

[Revised, June 2009, to reflect conforming changes necessary due to the issuance of FASB ASC.]

.12 Rent Expense and Rent Revenue in an Operating Lease—Rent Holiday

Inquiry—A lessee has a 120 month lease for $10,000 per month on space owned by a lessor. The lease term for accounting purposes is 120 months. As an incentive to sign the lessee to the lease agreement, the first 6 of those months are rent free. In an operating lease, if a lease term includes a period of free or reduced rent (rent holiday), how does the rent holiday factor into the lessee's recognition of rent expense and the lessor's recognition of rent revenue?

Reply—FASB ASC 840-20-25-2 provides that the lessee should recognize rent expense of $9,500 per month ($10,000 x 114 months/120 month lease term) for 120 months, which is on a straight line basis. Likewise, the lessor should recognize rent revenue of $9,500 per month.

[Revised, June 2009, to reflect conforming changes necessary due to the issuance of FASB ASC.]

.13 Rent Expense and Rent Revenue in an Operating Lease—Scheduled Rent Increases

Inquiry—In an operating lease, how should a lessee accrue rent expense and a lessor recognize rent revenue using the straight line method (see section 5600.10) when the lease agreement contains scheduled rent increases over the lease term?

Reply—FASB ASC 840-20-25-2 provides that the lessee and lessor should add up all rental payments over the lease term and divide that number by the number of periods in the lease term to arrive at the expense/revenue amounts to be accrued/recognized on a straight line basis.

[Revised, June 2009, to reflect conforming changes necessary due to the issuance of FASB ASC.]

.14 Amortization/Depreciation of Leasehold Improvements in an Operating Lease (Part 1)

Inquiry—A lessee enters into an operating lease in which the lease term for accounting purposes is 10 years. Upon signing the lease, the lessee acquires leasehold improvements that have a useful life of 15 years. Over what period should the lessee amortize or depreciate the leasehold improvements?

Reply—For leasehold improvements contemplated at or near the beginning of an initial lease term, the lessee should amortize or depreciate the leasehold improvements over the shorter of the (*a*) useful life of the improvements or (*b*) remaining lease term, which is 10 years in this inquiry. If the leasehold improvements are acquired and placed in service significantly after the inception of a lease, FASB ASC 840-10-35-6 requires that the lessee amortize or depreciate leasehold improvements over the shorter of the useful life of the leasehold assets or a term that includes required lease periods and renewals that are deemed to be reasonably assured at the date the leasehold improvements are acquired. Note that FASB ASC 840-10-35-6 does not apply to preexisting leasehold improvements.

[Revised, June 2009, to reflect conforming changes necessary due to the issuance of FASB ASC.]

.15 Leasehold Improvements and Lease Term in an Operating Lease (Part 2)

Inquiry—A lessee enters into an operating lease in which the initial fixed noncancelable term within the lease agreement is 10 years and the agreement includes three 5-year renewal periods. Upon signing the lease, the lessee plans to acquire leasehold improvements that have a useful life of 15 years. Is the lessee's plan to acquire the leasehold improvements a factor in determining the lease term for accounting purposes?

Reply—Yes, the lessee should consider the impact on the lease term for accounting purposes, if any, of the plan to acquire leasehold improvements. If the leasehold improvements are expected to have a significant value at the end of the initial 10 year term such that the lessee would not be willing to abandon these assets (that is, effectively incur a penalty) resulting in a renewal option being reasonably assured of being exercised, that renewal period would be added to the initial fixed noncancelable term in determining the appropriate lease term for accounting purposes.

.16 Landlord Incentive Allowance in an Operating Lease

Inquiry—A lessee enters into an operating lease in which the landlord offers an incentive allowance towards the cost of the lessee making leasehold improvements. The leasehold improvements are the lessee's assets and cost $1 million, and the incentive allowance totals $500,000. Should the lessee net the $500,000 allowance received from the landlord against the $1 million leasehold improvement asset?

Reply—No. In accordance with FASB ASC 840-20-55-3, the $500,000 allowance should be reported by the lessee as a liability and amortized straight line over the lease term as a reduction of rent expense. Therefore, the lessee's amortization/depreciation calculation is based on the $1 million leasehold improvements.

[Revised, June 2009, to reflect conforming changes necessary due to the issuance of FASB ASC.]

.17 Cash Flows Statement Presentation of Landlord Incentive Allowance in an Operating Lease

Inquiry—Related to section 5600.16, how should a lessee categorize expenditures for leasehold improvements and a related cash incentive allowance received from a landlord in the statement of cash flows?

Reply—In accordance with FASB ASC 230, *Statement of Cash Flows*, a lessee should report expenditures for leasehold improvements in the investing section of a statement of cash flows. Cash allowances received from the landlord should be presented in the lessee's operating activities section of its statement of cash flows. The cash allowances from the lessor are treated for accounting purposes as adjustments of rent. FASB ASC 230 does not identify rent payments on operating leases as investing or financing activities.

[Revised, June 2009, to reflect conforming changes necessary due to the issuance of FASB ASC.]

Q&A Section 5700

Contributions Made

.01 Income Tax Accounting for Contributions to Certain Not-for-Profit Scholarship Funding Entities

Inquiry—A state's corporate income taxpayers are allowed a credit against their state corporate income tax of 100 percent of eligible contributions made during the year to a not-for-profit scholarship funding entity. Unused credits may be carried forward up to 3 years. The taxpayer may not convey, assign, or transfer the credit to another entity unless all of the assets of the taxpayer are conveyed, assigned, or transferred in the same transaction.

Should corporate income taxpayers report contributions that qualify for the tax credit as contributions or as income tax expense in income statements prepared in accordance with generally accepted accounting principles?

Reply—Corporate income taxpayers should report such contributions as contributions in their income statements in accordance with Financial Accounting Standards Board (FASB) *Accounting Standards Codification* (ASC) 720-25.

Such contributions meet the definition of a *contribution* in the FASB ASC glossary. Just as the federal government offering a tax deduction for such a contribution does not change the nonreciprocal nature of the gift, the fact that the state provides a dollar-for-dollar tax credit to the donor for its remittance to the scholarship funding entity does not change the nonreciprocal nature of the gift. Nor does having only the alternative of paying a corresponding, higher tax make the contribution involuntary.

FASB ASC 740, *Income Taxes*, provides that total income tax expense or benefit for the year is the sum of deferred tax expense or benefit and income taxes currently payable or refundable.

Example

Assumptions:

$100 contribution to qualified scholarship funding entity

$5,000 federal taxable income (includes $100 charitable contribution deduction)

Tax rate—5.5 percent

State Tax Computation:

Federal taxable income	$5,000
Contribution	100
State taxable income	5,100
Tax rate	0.055
Pre-credit state income tax	275
Tax credit	(100)
State income taxes payable	$175

Journal Entries:

Journal entries made during the year should achieve the following result:

Dr. Contributions		100
Cr. Cash		100

To record contribution to scholarship fund

Dr. Income tax expense	175	
Cr. State income taxes payable	175	

To record state income tax expense

[Revised, June 2009, to reflect conforming changes necessary due to the issuance of FASB ASC.]

Q&A Section 6000

SPECIALIZED INDUSTRY PROBLEMS

TABLE OF CONTENTS

Section

Section

Q&A Section 6130

Finance Companies

.01 Amortization of Discount on Receivables of Consumer Finance Companies

Inquiry—A client in the consumer finance business loans money for short periods of time. What method should be used to amortize discounts on such loans?

Reply—In determining income from loans receivable which have been issued at a discount, the required method of income recognition for any such discount is the interest method, as described in Financial Accounting Standards Board (FASB) *Accounting Standards Codification* (ASC) 310-20.

[Revised, June 2009, to reflect conforming changes necessary due to the issuance of FASB ASC.]

.02 Method of Recognizing Revenue From Finance Charges

Inquiry—A finance company would like to establish a policy of recognizing 15 percent of the finance charges on discount loans as revenues in the first month of the loan and recognizing the balance of such charges as yield adjustments as the receivables are liquidated. Is this an acceptable method of recognizing revenues from finance charges?

Reply—No. In accordance with FASB ASC 310-20, the interest (actuarial) method should be used to account for interest income. In addition, FASB ASC 310-20-35-2 requires that certain direct loan acquisition costs be deferred and treated as yield adjustments in applying the interest method.

[Revised, June 2009, to reflect conforming changes necessary due to the issuance of FASB ASC.]

.03 Method of Recognizing Revenue From Service Charges

Inquiry—A company finances insurance premiums of individuals through various insurance agents. The company's policy is to receive completed premium finance agreements directly from the insurance agents. The amount financed includes a finance charge and a nonreturnable service charge. The finance charge is recognized in income by the interest method.

How should the service charge be recognized on the records of the company?

Reply—In accordance with FASB ASC 310-20, the service charge should also be recognized in income over the life of the related loan as an adjustment of yield using the interest method.

[Revised, June 2009, to reflect conforming changes necessary due to the issuance of FASB ASC.]

.04 Method of Recognizing Revenue From Commissions on Loan Insurance

Inquiry—A finance company receives commissions for loan insurance. How should the company recognize commission revenues?

Reply—FASB ASC 942-605-25-1 states that the insurance commissions received from independent insurers should be deferred and systematically amortized to income over the life of the related insurance contracts because the insurance and lending activities are integral parts of the same transactions. The method of commission amortization should be consistent with the method of premium income recognition for that type of policy in accordance with FASB ASC 944, *Financial Services—Insurance*.

[Revised, June 2009, to reflect conforming changes necessary due to the issuance of FASB ASC.]

.05 Disclosure of Contractual Maturities of Direct Cash Loans

Inquiry—FASB ASC 944-805-50-4 states

> Disclosures that typically would be required by the preceding paragraph for the various specific elements included in the closed block need not be made separately for the closed block if the nature of the information for the closed block would not differ significantly from that already included for the reporting entity as a whole. For example, it is not necessary to show a separate schedule of contractual maturities of closed block fixed maturity securities if the relative composition of contractual maturities is similar to those of the reporting entity taken as a whole. However, if the relative maturities of the closed block fixed maturities securities differ from those of the reporting entity taken as a whole, separate disclosures shall be made.

At December 31, 20X1, a company has only three loans outstanding of $36,000 each, payable monthly as follows: 12 installments of $3,000 each; 24 installments of $1,500 each; and 36 installments of $1,000 each. How would these contractual maturities properly be shown?

Reply—Appropriate disclosure of the amounts to be received would be: 20X2, $66,000; 20X3, $30,000; and 20X4, $12,000. Refer to FASB ASC 944-805-55 for implementation guidance and illustrations.

[Revised, June 2009, to reflect conforming changes necessary due to the issuance of FASB ASC.]

.06 Balance Sheet Presentation of Subordinated Debt

Inquiry—A consumer finance company, whose financial statements are used only by the company and its banks, would like to include subordinated debt in its balance sheet with the caption "Total Subordinated Notes and Shareholders' Equity." The company believes that presentation would show more clearly the position of the banks with respect to other creditors. Would the presentation be acceptable if the statements were clearly labeled, "For the Use of Banks and Bankers Only"?

Reply—No. Although the total of subordinated long-term debt and stockholders' equity is important to creditors of finance companies, the prominent presentation of this total in balance sheets causes many users of financial statements to interpret this amount as total stockholders' equity, and, for this reason, its use is not acceptable.

The proposed balance sheet presentation would not be in accordance with generally accepted accounting principles even if the financial statements are clearly and conspicuously labeled, "For the Use of Banks and Bankers Only."

[Revised, December 2012, to reflect conforming changes necessary due to the issuance of SAS Nos. 122–126.]

[.07] Reserved

Q&A Section 6140
Not-For-Profit Entities

.01 Inventory Valuation for a Not-for-Profit Scientific Entity

Inquiry—A not-for-profit scientific entity produces products that are sold at a price less than cost. The difference between cost and sale proceeds is covered by contributions. The not-for-profit entity reports inventories in its financial statements at an arbitrary amount and discloses that fact on the face of the financial statements. Is this accounting appropriate?

Reply—No. Financial Accounting Standards Board (FASB) *Accounting Standards Codification* (ASC) 330-10-35-1 states

> A departure from the cost basis of pricing the inventory is required when the utility of the goods is no longer as great as their cost. Where there is evidence that the utility of goods, in their disposal in the ordinary course of business, will be less than cost, whether due to physical deterioration, obsolescence, changes in price levels, or other causes, the difference shall be recognized as a loss of the current period. This is generally accomplished by stating such goods at a lower level commonly designated as *market*.

Accordingly, inventories should be valued at lower of cost or market and not at an arbitrary amount. The fact that the difference between the sales proceeds and the costs is covered by contributions does not change the application of the requirements of FASB ASC 330-10.

[Amended, June 1995; Revised, June 2009, to reflect conforming changes necessary due to the issuance of FASB ASC.]

.02 Income Recognition of Membership Dues by Not-for-Profit Entity

Inquiry—A local not-for-profit entity collects membership dues and does not provide any services to its members in return for the dues. It records the dues as contributions and recognizes them as revenue in the period they are received. The entity provides services, such as seminars, group insurance, and so on, to its members at an extra cost.

Is this the appropriate accounting method?

Reply—Yes. This entity qualifies as a *not-for-profit entity* under the FASB ASC glossary definition. Accordingly, FASB ASC 958-605-25-2 would require that the dues be recognized as contributions revenue when received since the members receive no benefits from the dues. In accordance with FASB ASC 958-605-25-1, if the member did receive benefits from those dues, dues revenue would be recognized over the period of membership.

[Amended, June 1995; Revised, June 2009, to reflect conforming changes necessary due to the issuance of FASB ASC.]

.03 Lapsing of Time Restrictions on Receivables That Are Uncollected at Their Due Date

Inquiry—FASB ASC 958-605-45-5 provides that "receipts of unconditional promises to give with payments due in future periods shall be reported as restricted support unless explicit donor stipulations or circumstances surrounding the receipt of a promise make clear that the donor intended it to be used to support activities of the current period. It is reasonable to assume that by specifying future payment dates donors indicate that their gift is to support activities in each period in which a payment is scheduled. For example, receipts of unconditional promises to give cash in future years generally increase temporarily restricted net assets."

Do time restrictions on contributions receivable lapse when the receivable is due or when it is collected?

Reply—Time restrictions on contributions receivable lapse when the receivable is due. (In some cases, the due date may be explicitly stated. In other cases, circumstances surrounding receipt of the contribution may make clear the implicit due date. In yet other cases, the due date may be unclear. NPEs should consider the facts and circumstances surrounding the promise to give to determine the due date, if any.)

[Revised, June 2009, to reflect conforming changes necessary due to the issuance of FASB ASC.]

.04 Lapsing of Restrictions on Receivables if Purpose Restrictions Pertaining to Long-Lived Assets Are Met Before the Receivables Are Due

Inquiry—FASB ASC 958-605-45-4 provides, in part, that "a restriction on a not-for-profit entity's use of the assets contributed results either from a donor's explicit stipulation or from circumstances surrounding the receipt of the contribution that make clear the donor's implicit restriction on use." These are purpose restrictions. FASB ASC 958-605-45-5 provides that "receipts of unconditional promises to give with payments due in future periods shall be reported as restricted support unless explicit donor stipulations or circumstances surrounding the receipt of a promise make clear that the donor intended it to be used to support activities of the current period. It is reasonable to assume that by specifying future payment dates donors indicate that their gift is to support activities in each period in which a payment is scheduled. For example, receipts of unconditional promises to give cash in future years generally increase temporarily restricted net assets." These are time restrictions. FASB ASC 958-205-45-9 provides, in part, as follows:

> If two or more temporary restrictions are imposed on a contribution, the effect of the expiration of those restrictions shall be recognized in the period in which the last remaining restriction has expired.

FASB ASC 958-205-45-11 further provides, in part

> Temporarily restricted net assets with time restrictions are not available to support expenses until the time restrictions have expired.

FASB ASC 958-205-45-12 further provides

> Time restrictions implied on gifts of long-lived assets pursuant to paragraph 958-605-45-6 expire as the economic benefits of the acquired assets are used up; that is, over their estimated useful lives. In the absence of donor stipulations specifying how long donated assets must be used or a not-for-profit entity's policy of implying time restrictions, restrictions on long-lived assets, if any, or cash to acquire long-lived assets expire when the assets are placed in service.

NPEs may receive promises to give contributions that are restricted by donors for investment in long-lived assets. In some circumstances, the assets may be placed in service, and the purpose restrictions met, prior to the due date of the contribution. For example, an NPE may have a capital campaign, asking for commitments to contribute over the next five years so the entity can build a new facility. A donor may promise to give $100,000 in five years in response to that request.

Are the restrictions met when the assets are placed in service or when the receivable is due?

Reply—NPEs should consider the facts and circumstances surrounding the promise to give and whether those facts and circumstances indicate that the donor intended the contribution to be used to support activities of the current period, with constructing the building or placing it in service considered activities of the current period. If circumstances indicate that the donor intended to support activities of the current period, there is no time restriction and the preceding guidance in paragraphs 9 and 11–12 of FASB ASC 958-205-45 would not be applicable, unless a restriction was placed on the contribution other than constructing the building. If circumstances indicate that the donor's intent is not to support activities of the current period, there are both a time restriction and a purpose restriction. In accordance with FASB ASC 958-205-45-11, the effect of the expiration of restrictions is recognized in the period in which the last remaining restriction has expired.

[Revised, June 2009, to reflect conforming changes necessary due to the issuance of FASB ASC.]

[.05] Reserved

.06 Functional Category of Cost of Sales of Contributed Inventory

Inquiry—How should the cost of sales of contributed inventory be reported? For example, should it be reported as a separate supporting service, as program, or as fund-raising?

Reply—Cost of sales of contributed inventory should be reported as the cost of a separate supporting service, unless the item sold is related to a program activity, in which case, cost of sales is reported as a cost of a program activity. Cost of sales of contributed inventory should not be reported as fund-raising.

.07 Functional Category of Costs of Special Events

Inquiry—FASB ASC 958-720-25-4 provides that "fundraising costs, including the cost of special fundraising events, are incurred to persuade potential donors to make contributions to a not-for-profit entity and shall be expensed as incurred." The FASB ASC glossary defines the term fundraising activities as "activities undertaken to induce potential donors to contribute money, securities, services, materials, facilities, other assets, or time." Chapter 13 of the AICPA Audit and Accounting Guide *Not-for-Profit Entities* provides guidance on accounting for special events and provides that not-for-profit entities may report the gross revenues of special events and other fund-raising activities with the cost of direct benefits to donors (for example, meals and facilities rental) displayed either (1) as a line item deducted from the special event revenues or (2) in the same section of the statement of activities as are other programs or supporting services and allocated, if necessary, among those various functions.

Should all costs of special fund-raising events, such as costs of direct donor benefits that are provided in exchange transactions, be reported as fund-raising?

Reply—The discussion of special fund-raising events in FASB ASC 958-720-25 and 958-720-45 provide that some, but not necessarily all, costs of special fund-raising events should be reported as fund-raising. Certain costs of special fund-raising events, such as costs of direct donor benefits that are provided in exchange transactions, should be reported in categories other than fund-raising.

[Revised, June 2009, to reflect conforming changes necessary due to the issuance of FASB ASC.]

.08 Functional Category of the Costs of Direct Donor Benefits

Inquiry—NPEs may hold special events that provide donor benefits. For example, an entity may hold a special event and provide a meal to donors, which would be a direct donor benefit. Paragraphs 10–15 of FASB ASC 958-720-55 provide guidance on reporting the costs of special events, including the costs of direct donor benefits. Paragraphs 20–22 of FASB ASC 958-720-45 provide that, if cost of sales relates to an item that is program related, cost of sales should be reported as program expense. Otherwise, cost of sales could be reported as a separate supporting service. Also, FASB ASC 958-720-45-19 provides that the cost of premiums provided that are greater than nominal in value should be reported as cost of sales. However, FASB ASC 958 provides no guidance concerning the functional category in which the costs of direct donor benefits should be reported in circumstances in which the benefits are not program related, beyond providing that they should be reported as a supporting service.

In which functional category should the costs of direct donor benefits that are not program related be reported?

Reply—The costs of donor benefits that are not program related and that are provided in exchange transactions should be reported as a separate supporting category, such as cost of sales, and should not be reported as fund-raising.

The costs of donor benefits that are not program related and that are provided in transactions that are other than exchange transactions, such as a fund-raising dinner for which there is no charge to attend, should be reported as fund-raising.

[Revised, June 2009, to reflect conforming changes necessary due to the issuance of FASB ASC.]

.09 Reporting Bad Debt Losses

Inquiry—FASB ASC 958-225-45-7 provides that expenses should be reported as decreases in unrestricted net assets.

FASB ASC 958-225-45-15 provides that "a statement of activities may report gains and losses as net amounts if they result from peripheral or incidental transactions or from other events and circumstances that may be largely beyond the control of the not-for-profit entity and its management."

FASB ASC 958-310-35-7 provides that, if the fair value of contributions arising from unconditional promises to give cash or noncash assets decreases subsequent to initial measurement because of changes in the quantity or nature of assets expected to be received, the decrease should be recognized as expenses or losses (bad debt) in the period(s) in which the expectation changes.[1]

May bad debt *losses* be netted against contribution revenue?

---

[1] The provision that certain decreases in the fair value of contributions arising from unconditional promises to give should be accounted for as losses, rather than as expenses, is an accounting convention. This convention provides that, in circumstances in which the net assets related to receivables are represented as restricted net assets, decreases in net assets should be reported as decreases in restricted net assets, rather than as decreases in unrestricted net assets.

Reply—Bad debt losses are prohibited from being netted against contribution revenue under FASB ASC 958-225-45-15 because losses are permitted to be netted only against gains, and not against revenues.

[Revised, June 2009, to reflect conforming changes necessary due to the issuance of FASB ASC.]

.10 Consolidation of Political Action Committee

Inquiry—Some not-for-profit entities are related to other not-for-profit entities that perform political activities that the reporting entity does not wish to perform, perhaps because performing those activities may threaten the reporting entity's tax exempt status, the reporting entity is precluded from conducting such activities, or for other reasons. For example, a membership entity may establish and sponsor a political action committee (PAC) whose mission is to further the interests of the membership entity. The resources held by the PAC are used for the purposes of the membership entity and the governing board of the PAC is appointed by the board of the membership entity.

Does FASB ASC 958-810 require consolidation of PACs in the circumstances previously described?

Reply—FASB ASC 958-810 requires consolidating PACs in the circumstances described in the preceding. Under FASB ASC 958-810, the threshold issues pertaining to the circumstances previously described are whether there is (1) control through a majority voting interest in the board of the PAC and (2) an economic interest. In the circumstances described in the preceding, both are present. Control through a majority voting interest in the board of the PAC exists because the governing board of the PAC is appointed by the board of the membership entity. An economic interest exists because the PAC holds significant resources that must be used for the purposes of the membership entity.

[Revised, June 2009, to reflect conforming changes necessary due to the issuance of FASB ASC.]

.11 Costs of Soliciting Contributed Services and Time That Do Not Meet the Recognition Criteria in FASB ASC 958

Inquiry—Questions have arisen about the classification of costs of soliciting contributed services and time. The issue focuses on whether those costs should be reported as fundraising in all cases or whether, in circumstances in which the services or time do not meet the recognition criteria in FASB ASC 958-605-25-16, those costs should be reported in the functional category to which the solicited services or time pertain.

According to FASB ASC 958-720-45-9, fundraising activities include the following:

a. Publicizing and conducting fundraising campaigns

b. Maintaining donor mailing lists

c. Conducting special fundraising events

d. Preparing and distributing fundraising manuals, instructions, and other materials

e. Conducting other activities involved with soliciting contributions from individuals, foundations, government agencies, and others.

The FASB ASC glossary defines *contribution* and provides as follows:

> An unconditional transfer of cash or other assets to an entity or a settlement or cancellation of its liabilities in a voluntary nonreciprocal

> transfer by another entity acting other than as an owner. Those characteristics distinguish contributions from exchange transactions, which are reciprocal transfers in which each party receives and sacrifices approximately equal value; from investments by owners and distributions to owners, which are nonreciprocal transfers between an entity and its owners; and from other nonreciprocal transfers, such as impositions of taxes or fines and thefts, which are not voluntary transfers. In a contribution transaction, the value, if any, returned to the resource provider is incidental to potential public benefits. In an exchange transaction, the potential public benefits are secondary to the potential proprietary benefits to the resource provider. The term contribution revenue is used to apply to transactions that are part of the entity's ongoing major or central activities (revenues), or are peripheral or incidental to the entity (gains).

The FASB ASC glossary defines the term *fundraising activities* as follows:

> Activities undertaken to induce potential donors to contribute money, securities, services, materials, facilities, other assets, or time.

FASB ASC 958-605-25-16 discusses recognition criteria for contributed services and provides, in part, as follows:

> Contributions of services shall be recognized if the services received meet any of the following criteria:
>
> *a.* They create or enhance nonfinancial assets
>
> *b.* They require specialized skills, are provided by individuals possessing those skills, and would typically need to be purchased if not provided by donation.

Contributed services that do not meet these criteria are prohibited from being recognized.

As previously mentioned, questions have arisen about the classification of the costs of soliciting contributed services and time that do not meet the recognition criteria in FASB ASC 958-605-25-16.

How should the costs of soliciting contributed services that do not meet the recognition criteria in FASB ASC 958-605-25-16 be reported?

Reply—FASB ASC 958-720-45-10 provides that fundraising activities include soliciting contributions of services from individuals, regardless of whether those services meet the recognition criteria for contributions in paragraphs 2–20 of FASB ASC 958-605-25.[2] For example, costs of soliciting contributed services to be used in program functions should be reported as fundraising, even if the services do not meet the recognition criteria. Similarly, costs of soliciting management and general services should be reported as fundraising, even if the management and general services do not meet the recognition criteria.

Certain contributed services are prohibited from being recognized for practical, rather than conceptual, reasons. Those services are nevertheless contributions, regardless of whether or not they are recognized. Therefore,

[2] NPEs frequently incur other costs in connection with contributed services, such as costs of training and managing volunteers. Costs of training and managing volunteers should not be reported as fund-raising, unless those volunteers are performing fundraising functions.

soliciting those contributions meets the definition of *fundraising* in the FASB ASC glossary.

[Revised, June 2009, to reflect conforming changes necessary due to the issuance of FASB ASC.]

.12 Nondiscretionary Assistance Programs

Inquiry—FASB ASC 958 provides guidance for transactions in which an entity—the *donor*—makes a contribution by transferring assets to a not-for-profit entity—the *recipient entity*, as defined in the FASB ASC glossary—that accepts the assets from the donor and agrees to use those assets on behalf of or transfer those assets, the return on investment of those assets, or both to another entity—the *beneficiary*—that is specified by the donor. It also provides guidance for transactions that take place in a similar manner but are not contributions because the transfers are revocable, repayable, or reciprocal. FASB ASC 958 provides that a recipient entity that (*a*) accepts assets from a donor without variance power and (*b*) agrees to use those assets on behalf of or transfer those assets, the return on investment of those assets, or both to a specified beneficiary that is not financially interrelated is not a donee. The recipient entity should recognize its liability to the specified beneficiary concurrent with its recognition of cash or other financial assets[3] received from the donor. Further, FASB ASC 958 provides that a nondonee recipient entity that receives nonfinancial assets is permitted, but not required, to recognize its liability and those assets provided that the entity reports consistently from period to period and discloses its accounting policy.

FASB ASC 958-605-55-71 discusses transfers that are not contributions and provides as follows:

> Receipts of resources as an agent, trustee, or intermediary of a donor are not contributions received to the agent because the recipient of assets who is an agent or trustee has little or no discretion in determining how the assets transferred will be used. For the same reason, deliveries of resources as an agent, trustee, or intermediary of a donor are not contributions made by the agent. Similarly, contributions of services (time, skills, or expertise) between donors and donees that are facilitated by an intermediary are not contributions received or contributions made by the intermediary.

Some NPEs participate in activities wherein the resource provider (donor) determines the eligibility requirements for the ultimate beneficiaries and the NPE must disburse to any who meet guidelines specified by the resource provider or return the assets. In some of those programs, the NPE receives assets, such as food, food vouchers, public transportation vouchers, and cash and distributes the assets on behalf of the resource provider (donor) in exchange for a fee for performing that service.

---

[3] The Financial Accounting Standards Board (FASB) *Accounting Standards Codification* (ASC) glossary defines financial assets as

> cash, evidence of an ownership interest in an entity, or a contract that conveys to one entity a right to do either of the following:
>
> *a.* Receive cash or another financial instrument from a second entity
>
> *b.* Exchange other financial instruments on potentially favorable terms with the second entity

Should recipient entity NPEs report receipts and disbursements of assets under such programs (other than any fees for performing the service) as revenues and expenses?

Reply—Receipts and disbursements of assets under such programs (other than any fees for performing the service) are agency transactions, and are not contributions to the recipient entity NPE. A recipient entity that receives financial assets, such as cash or vouchers that can be exchanged for cash, should recognize its liability to the beneficiaries concurrent with its recognition of financial assets received from the donor. A recipient entity that receives nonfinancial assets, such as food vouchers or public transportation vouchers that are denominated in either dollar values or in nonfinancial terms, such as pounds of food or bus rides, but that will not be settled in cash, is permitted, but not required, to recognize its liability and those assets provided that the entity reports consistently from period to period and discloses its accounting policy.

[Revised, June 2009, to reflect conforming changes necessary due to the issuance of FASB ASC.]

.13 Note to Sections 6140.14–.18—Implementation of FASB ASC 958—Classification of a Beneficiary's Interest in the Net Assets of a Financially Interrelated Fund-Raising Foundation (in the Beneficiary's Financial Statements)

Some not-for-profit entities have separate fund-raising foundations (commonly referred to as *institutionally related foundations*) that solicit contributions on their behalf. FASB ASC 958 provides guidance on (among other things) the accounting that should be followed by such institutionally related foundations and their related beneficiary entity(ies) with respect to contributions received by the foundation.

Some institutionally related foundations and their beneficiary entities meet the characteristics of financially interrelated entities provided in FASB ASC 958-20-15-2. If entities are financially interrelated, FASB ASC 958 provides that the balance sheet of the beneficiary entity(ies) should reflect that entity's interest in the net assets of the foundation, and that interest should be periodically adjusted to reflect the beneficiary's share of the changes in the net assets of the foundation. This accounting is similar to the equity method of accounting, which is described in FASB ASC 323, *Investments—Equity Method and Joint Ventures*.

FASB ASC 323-10-35-5 requires that the periodic adjustment of the investment be included in the determination of the investor's net income. The purpose of sections 6140.14–.18 (applicable to NPEs other than health care [HC] entities) and sections 6400.36–.42 (applicable to not-for-profit HC entities) is to clarify that in circumstances in which the recipient and the beneficiary are financially interrelated:

- Beneficiary entities should segregate the adjustment into changes in restricted and unrestricted net assets. (NPE TPA [sections 6140.14–.16]; HC TPA [section 6400.36–37 and .39])
- In circumstances in which the beneficiary can influence the financial decisions of the recipient entity to such an extent that the beneficiary can determine the timing and amount of distributions from the recipient to the beneficiary, the existence of the recipient entity should be transparent in determining the net asset classifications in the beneficiary's financial statements. In other words,

the recipient cannot impose time or purpose restrictions beyond those imposed by the donor. (NPE TPA [sections 6140.14 and .16]; HC TPA [sections 6400.36 and .39])

- In circumstances in which the beneficiary cannot influence the financial decisions of the recipient entity to such an extent that the beneficiary can determine the timing and amount of distributions from the recipient to the beneficiary, the existence of the recipient entity creates an implied time restriction on the beneficiary's net assets attributable to the beneficiary's interest in the net assets of the recipient (in addition to any other restrictions that may exist). Accordingly, in recognizing its interest in the net assets of the recipient entity and the changes in that interest, the beneficiary should classify the resulting net assets and changes in those net assets as temporarily restricted (unless donors placed permanent restrictions on their contributions). (NPE TPA [section 6140.15]; HC TPA [section 6400.37])
- In circumstances in which the beneficiary can influence the financial decisions of the recipient entity to such an extent that the beneficiary can determine the timing and amount of distributions from the recipient to the beneficiary and some net assets held by the recipient for the benefit of the beneficiary are subject to purpose restrictions (for example, net assets of the recipient restricted to the beneficiary's purchase of property, plant, and equipment [PPE]), expenditures by the beneficiary that meet those purpose restrictions result in the beneficiary (and recipient) reporting reclassifications from temporarily restricted to unrestricted net assets (assuming that the beneficiary has no other net assets subject to similar purpose restrictions), unless those net assets are subject to time restrictions that have not expired, including time restrictions that are implied on contributed long-lived assets as a result of the beneficiary's accounting policy pursuant to FASB ASC 958-605-45-6. (If those net assets are subject to time restrictions that have not expired and the beneficiary has other net assets with similar purpose restrictions, the restrictions on those other net assets would expire in accordance with FASB ASC 958. These sections do not, however, establish a hierarchy pertaining to which restrictions are released first—restrictions on net assets held by the recipient or purpose restrictions on net assets held by the beneficiary.) (NPE TPA [section 6140.17]; HC TPA [section 6400.40])
- In circumstances in which the beneficiary cannot influence the financial decisions of the recipient entity to such an extent that the beneficiary can determine the timing and amount of distributions from the recipient to the beneficiary and some net assets held by the recipient for the benefit of the beneficiary are subject to purpose restrictions, though not subject to time restrictions other than the implied time restrictions that exist because the beneficiary cannot determine the timing and amount of distributions from the recipient to the beneficiary, expenditures by the beneficiary that are consistent with those purpose restrictions should not result in the beneficiary reporting a reclassification from temporarily restricted to unrestricted net assets, subject to the

exceptions in the following sentence. Expenditures by the beneficiary that are consistent with those purpose restrictions should result in the beneficiary reporting a reclassification from temporarily restricted to unrestricted net assets if (*a*) the recipient has no discretion in deciding whether the purpose restriction is met[4] or (*b*) the recipient distributes or obligates itself to distribute to the beneficiary amounts attributable to net assets restricted for the particular purpose, or otherwise indicates that the recipient intends for those net assets to be used to support the particular purpose as an activity of the current period. In all other circumstances, (*a*) purpose restrictions and (*b*) implied time restrictions on the net assets attributable to the interest in the recipient entity exist and have not yet expired. (However, if the beneficiary has other net assets with similar purpose restrictions, those restrictions would expire in accordance with FASB ASC 958. These TPAs do not establish a hierarchy pertaining to which restrictions are released first—restrictions on net assets held by the recipient or restrictions on net assets held by the beneficiary.) (NPE TPA [section 6140.18]; HC TPA [section 6400.41])

- *For HC NPEs Only.* In circumstances in which the beneficiary can influence the financial decisions of the recipient to such an extent that the beneficiary can determine the timing and amount of distributions from the recipient to the beneficiary, changes in the beneficiary's interest in the net assets of a recipient entity attributable to unrealized gains and losses on investments should be included or excluded from the performance indicator in accordance with FASB ASC 954-10, FASB ASC 954-205-45, FASB ASC 954-320-45, FASB ASC 954-320-55, and FASB ASC 954-605 in the same manner that they would have been had the beneficiary had the transactions itself. Similarly, in applying this guidance, the determination of whether amounts are included or excluded from the performance measure should comprehend that if the beneficiary cannot influence the financial decisions of the recipient entity to such an extent that the beneficiary can determine the timing and amount of distributions from the recipient to the beneficiary, an implied time restriction exists on the beneficiary's net assets attributable to the beneficiary's interest in the net assets of the recipient (in addition to any other restrictions that may exist). Accordingly, in circumstances in which the beneficiary cannot influence the financial decisions of the recipient entity to such an extent that the beneficiary can determine the timing and amount of distributions from the recipient to the beneficiary, the beneficiary should classify the resulting net assets and changes in those

---

[4] In some circumstances, the purpose restrictions may be so broad that the recipient entity has discretion in deciding whether expenditures by the beneficiary that are consistent with those purpose restrictions actually meet those purpose restrictions. For example, the recipient's net assets may have arisen from a contribution that was restricted for the beneficiary's purchase of research equipment, with no particular research equipment specified. Purchasing an XYZ microscope, which is consistent with that purpose restriction, may or may not meet that purpose restriction, depending on the decision of the recipient. In contrast, the net assets may have arisen from a contribution that was restricted for an XYZ microscope. Purchasing an XYZ microscope, which also is consistent with that purpose restriction, would result in the recipient having no discretion in determining whether that purpose restriction is met.

net assets as temporarily restricted (unless donors placed permanent restrictions on their contributions) and therefore exclude those changes from the performance indicator. (HC TPA [section 6400.42])

- *For HC NPEs Only.* In circumstances in which the recipient entity and the beneficiary are both controlled by the same entity, entities should consider the specific facts and circumstances to determine whether the beneficiary can influence the financial decisions of the recipient entity to such an extent that the beneficiary can determine the timing and amount of distributions from the recipient to the beneficiary. (HC TPA [section 6400.38])

Technical Practice Aids for Not-for-Profit Entities Implementation of FASB ASC 958—Classification of a Beneficiary's Interest in the Net Assets of a Financially Interrelated Fund-Raising Foundation (in the Beneficiary's Financial Statements)

HC NPEs			
NPEs that are not HC NPEs			
Can the beneficiary determine the timing and amount of distributions from the recipient to the beneficiary? [Not-for-profit health care entities (HC NPEs) under common control consider HC Technical Practice Aid (TPA) section 6400.38]	**How does the existence of the recipient affect the beneficiary's reporting of its interest?**	**Are any net assets held by the recipient for the benefit of the beneficiary subject to donor-imposed purpose restrictions and has the beneficiary made expenditures that meet those purpose restrictions (in circumstances in which the beneficiary can determine the timing and amount of distributions from the recipient to the beneficiary) or that are consistent with those purpose restrictions (in circumstances in which the beneficiary cannot determine the timing and amount of distributions from the recipient to the beneficiary)?**	**Are any changes in the beneficiary's interest in the net assets of the recipient attributable to unrealized gains and losses on investments?**

(continued)

HC NPEs			
NPEs that are not HC NPEs			
Yes	Existence of recipient is transparent in determining net asset classifications. (NPE TPA [sections 6140.14 and .16]; HC TPA [sections 6400.36 and .39])	Reclass the applicable net assets from temporarily restricted (TR) to unrestricted (UR) unless those net assets are subject to time restrictions that have not expired. (NPE TPA [section 6140.17]; HC TPA [section 6400.40])	Changes in the beneficiary's interest in the net assets of a recipient entity attributable to unrealized gains and losses on investments should be included or excluded from the performance indicator in accordance with FASB ASC 954-10, FASB ASC 954-205-45, FASB ASC 954-320-45, FASB ASC 954-320-55, and FASB ASC 954-605 in the same manner that they would have been had the beneficiary had the transactions itself. (HC TPA [section 6400.42])
No	Existence of the recipient creates an implied time restriction on the beneficiary's net assets attributable to the beneficiary's interest in the net assets of the recipient. (NPE TPA [section 6140.15]; HC TPA [section 6400.37])	Reclass the applicable net assets from TR to UR only if the purpose restriction and the implied time restriction are met. Whether the purpose restriction is met depends in part on (1) whether the recipient has discretion in determining whether the purpose restriction is met and (2) the recipient's decision in exercising that discretion, if any. (NPE TPA [section 6140.18]; HC TPA [section 6400.41])	An implied time restriction exists on the beneficiary's net assets attributable to the beneficiary's interest in the net assets of the recipient. The beneficiary should classify the resulting net assets and changes in those net assets as temporarily restricted (unless donors placed permanent restrictions on their contributions) and therefore exclude those changes from the performance indicator. (HC TPA [section 6400.42])

[Revised, June 2009, to reflect conforming changes necessary due to the issuance of FASB ASC.]

.14 Application of FASB ASC 958—Classification of a Beneficiary's Interest in the Net Assets of a Financially Interrelated Fund-Raising Foundation (The beneficiary can influence the operating and financial decisions of the foundation to such an extent that the beneficiary can determine the timing and amount of distributions from the foundation.)

Inquiry—ABC Research Institute, a not-for-profit entity subject to FASB ASC 958[5] and ABC Foundation are financially interrelated entities as described in FASB ASC 958-20-15-2. ABC Foundation's bylaws state that it is organized for the purpose of stimulating voluntary financial support from donors for the sole benefit of ABC Research Institute. Assume that ABC Research Institute can influence the operating and financial decisions of ABC Foundation to such an extent that ABC Research Institute can determine the timing and amount of distributions from ABC Foundation to ABC Research Institute.

During its most recent fiscal year, ABC Foundation's activities resulted in an increase in net assets (before distributions) of $3,200, comprised of $2,000 in unrestricted contributions, $1,000 in temporarily restricted contributions (purpose restrictions), $500 in unrestricted dividend and interest income, and $300 in expenses. In addition, ABC Foundation distributed $2,500 in cash representing unrestricted net assets to ABC Research Institute. How should this activity be reported in ABC Research Institute's financial statements?

Reply—Because ABC Foundation (the recipient entity) and ABC Research Institute (the beneficiary) are financially interrelated, FASB ASC 958-20-25-2 requires ABC Research Institute to recognize its interest in the net assets of ABC Foundation and periodically adjust that interest for its share of the change in net assets of ABC Foundation. This is similar to the equity method of accounting described in FASB ASC 323.

In recognizing its interest in the net assets of ABC Foundation and the changes in that interest, ABC Research Institute should classify the resulting net assets as if contributions were received by ABC Research Institute directly from the donor, because ABC Research Institute can influence the operating and financial decisions of ABC Foundation to such an extent that ABC Research Institute can determine the timing and amount of distributions from ABC Foundation to ABC Research Institute. In other words, the existence of ABC Foundation should be transparent in determining the net asset classifications in ABC Research Institute's financial statements because ABC Foundation cannot impose time or purpose restrictions beyond those imposed by the donor. (Any instructions given by ABC Foundation are designations, rather than restrictions.)

In the circumstances described in the preceding, ABC Research Institute would initially increase its asset, "Interest in Net Assets of ABC Foundation" for the change in ABC Foundation's net assets ($3,200). ABC Research Institute's Statement of Activity would include "Change in Unrestricted Interest in ABC Foundation" of $2,200, which would be reported as an increase in unrestricted net assets, and "Change in Temporarily Restricted Interest in ABC Foundation" of $1,000 as an increase in temporarily restricted net assets.

---

[5] This section addresses not-for-profit entities subject to FASB ASC 958. Section 6400.36, "Application of FASB ASC 958—Classification of a Beneficiary's Interest in the Net Assets of a Financially Interrelated Fund-Raising Foundation (The beneficiary can influence the operating and financial decisions of the foundation to such an extent that the beneficiary can determine the timing and amount of distributions from the foundation.)," addresses a similar issue for not-for-profit health care entities subject to FASB ASC 954, *Health Care Entities*.

The $2,500 distribution from ABC Foundation to ABC Research Institute would not be reported as an increase in net assets on ABC Research Institute's Statement of Activity. By analogy to equity method accounting, the $2,500 would be reported in a manner similar to a distribution from a subsidiary to its parent (for example, a dividend). ABC Research Institute should report the distribution by increasing cash and decreasing its interest in the net assets of ABC Foundation.

If the distribution represented restricted net assets, ABC Research Institute would not reclassify the net assets from temporarily restricted to unrestricted at the time of the distribution. Instead, ABC Research Institute would reclassify the net assets from temporarily restricted to unrestricted when those restrictions were met.

[Revised, June 2009, to reflect conforming changes necessary due to the issuance of FASB ASC.]

.15 Application of FASB ASC 958—Classification of a Beneficiary's Interest in the Net Assets of a Financially Interrelated Fund-Raising Foundation (The beneficiary cannot influence the operating and financial decisions of the foundation to such an extent that the beneficiary can determine the timing and amount of distributions from the foundation.)

Inquiry—ABC Research Institute, a not-for-profit entity subject to FASB ASC 958[6] and ABC Foundation are financially interrelated entities as described in FASB ASC 958-20-15-2. ABC Foundation's bylaws state that it is organized for the purpose of stimulating voluntary financial support from donors for the sole benefit of ABC Research Institute. Assume that ABC Research Institute cannot, however, influence the operating and financial decisions of ABC Foundation to such an extent that ABC Research Institute can determine the timing and amount of distributions from ABC Foundation to ABC Research Institute.

During its most recent fiscal year, ABC Foundation's activities resulted in an increase in net assets (before distributions) of $3,200, comprised of $2,000 in unrestricted contributions, $1,000 in temporarily restricted contributions (purpose restrictions), $500 in unrestricted dividend and interest income, and $300 in expenses. In addition, ABC Foundation elected to distribute $2,500 in cash representing unrestricted net assets to ABC Research Institute. How should this activity be reported in ABC Research Institute's financial statements?

Reply—Because ABC Foundation (the recipient entity) and ABC Research Institute (the beneficiary) are financially interrelated, FASB ASC 958-20-25-2 requires ABC Research Institute to recognize its interest in the net assets of ABC Foundation and periodically adjust that interest for its share of the change in net assets of ABC Foundation. This is similar to the equity method of accounting described in FASB ASC 323.

ABC Research Institute cannot influence the operating and financial decisions of ABC Foundation to such an extent that ABC Research Institute can

---

[6] This section addresses not-for-profit entities subject to FASB ASC 958. Section 6400.37, "Application of FASB ASC 958—Classification of a Beneficiary's Interest in the Net Assets of a Financially Interrelated Fund-Raising Foundation (The beneficiary cannot influence the operating and financial decisions of the foundation to such an extent that the beneficiary can determine the timing and amount of distributions from the foundation.)," addresses a similar issue for not-for-profit health care entities subject to FASB ASC 954.

determine the timing and amount of distributions from ABC Foundation to ABC Research Institute. Therefore, an implied time restriction exists on ABC Research Institute's interest in the net assets of ABC Foundation (in addition to any other restrictions that may exist). Accordingly, in recognizing its interest in the net assets of ABC Foundation and the changes in that interest, ABC Research Institute should classify the resulting net assets as changes in temporarily restricted net assets (unless donors placed permanent restrictions on their contributions).

In the circumstances described in the preceding, ABC Research Institute would initially increase its asset, "Interest in Net Assets of ABC Foundation" for the change in ABC Foundation's net assets ($3,200). ABC Research Institute's Statement of Activity would include "Change in Temporarily Restricted Interest in ABC Foundation" of $3,200 as an increase in temporarily restricted net assets.

The $2,500 distribution from ABC Foundation to ABC Research Institute would not be reported as an increase in net assets on ABC Research Institute's Statement of Activity. By analogy to equity method accounting, the $2,500 would be treated similar to a distribution from a subsidiary to its parent (for example, a dividend). ABC Research Institute should report the distribution by increasing cash and decreasing its interest in the net assets of ABC Foundation.

ABC Research Institute would reclassify the net assets from temporarily restricted to unrestricted at the time of the distribution, because the time restriction would expire at the time of the distribution. (If those net assets were subject to purpose or time restrictions that remained even after the net assets had been distributed to ABC Research Institute, ABC Research Institute would not reclassify the net assets from temporarily restricted to unrestricted at the time of the distribution. Instead, ABC Research Institute would reclassify the net assets from temporarily restricted to unrestricted when those restrictions were met.)

[Revised, June 2009, to reflect conforming changes necessary due to the issuance of FASB ASC.]

.16 Application of FASB ASC 958—Classification of a Beneficiary's Interest in the Net Assets of a Financially Interrelated Fund-Raising Foundation (More Than One Beneficiary—Some Contributions Are Designated)

Inquiry—DEF Arts Entity is the parent of three brother-sister not-for-profit entities: Ballet, Orchestra, a not-for-profit entity subject to FASB ASC 958[7] and Foundation. Foundation is organized for the purpose of raising contributions for the benefit of both Ballet and Orchestra. The four entities are legally separate not-for-profit entities that are financially interrelated pursuant to the guidance in FASB ASC 958-20-15-2. Assume that Orchestra can influence the financial decisions of Foundation to such an extent that Orchestra can determine the timing and amount of distributions from Foundation to Orchestra.

A donor contributes $5,000 cash to Foundation and stipulates that the contribution is for the benefit of Orchestra. Foundation would record the contribution as temporarily restricted revenue (because Foundation must use the

[7] This section addresses not-for-profit entities subject to FASB ASC 958. Section 6400.39, "Application of FASB ASC 958—Classification of a Beneficiary's Interest in the Net Assets of a Financially Interrelated Fund-Raising Foundation (More Than One Beneficiary—Some Contributions Are Designated)," addresses a similar issue for not-for-profit health care entities subject to FASB ASC 954.

contribution for the benefit of Orchestra). In its separately issued financial statements, Orchestra would recognize its interest in the net assets attributable to that contribution by debiting "Interest in Net Assets of Foundation" for $5,000. Would the offsetting credit be reported as temporarily restricted revenue (because the net assets attributable to the contribution are restricted on Foundation's Balance Sheet) or unrestricted revenue (because there are no donor-imposed time restrictions or purpose restrictions on how Orchestra must use the contribution)?

Reply—Orchestra should report the offsetting credit as unrestricted revenue. Because Orchestra can influence the financial decisions of Foundation to such an extent that Orchestra can determine the timing and amount of distributions from Foundation to Orchestra, no implied time restriction exists on Orchestra's net assets attributable to its interest in the net assets of Foundation. Accordingly, in recognizing its interest in the net assets of Foundation and the changes in that interest, Orchestra should classify the resulting net assets as if contributions were received by Orchestra directly from the donor. In other words, the existence of Foundation should be transparent in determining the net asset classifications in Orchestra's separately issued financial statements because Foundation cannot impose time or purpose restrictions beyond those imposed by the donor. (Any instructions given by Foundation are designations, rather than restrictions.)

Because there are no donor-imposed restrictions on how Orchestra must use the contribution, Orchestra should report the change in its interest in the net assets attributable to the contribution as an increase in unrestricted net assets in its separately issued Statement of Activity. When Foundation actually distributes the funds, Orchestra should increase cash and decrease its interest in net assets of Foundation; the distributions would have no effect on Orchestra's Statement of Activity.

[Revised, June 2009, to reflect conforming changes necessary due to the issuance of FASB ASC.]

.17 Application of FASB ASC 958—Classification of a Beneficiary's Interest in the Net Assets of a Financially Interrelated Fund-Raising Foundation (The beneficiary makes an expenditure that meets a purpose restriction on net assets held for its benefit by the recipient entity—The beneficiary can influence the operating and financial decisions of the recipient to such an extent that the beneficiary can determine the timing and amount of distributions from the recipient.)

Inquiry—ABC Research Institute, a not-for-profit entity subject to FASB ASC 958[8] and ABC Foundation are financially interrelated entities as described in FASB ASC 958-20-15-2. ABC Foundation's bylaws state that it is organized for the purpose of stimulating voluntary financial support from donors for the sole benefit of ABC Research Institute. Assume that ABC Research Institute can influence the operating and financial decisions of ABC Foundation to such an extent that ABC Research Institute can determine the timing and amount of distributions from ABC Foundation to ABC Research Institute.

[8] This section addresses not-for-profit entities subject to FASB ASC 958. Section 6400.40,"Application of FASB ASC 958—Classification of a Beneficiary's Interest in the Net Assets of a Financially Interrelated Fund-Raising Foundation (The beneficiary makes an expenditure that meets a purpose restriction on net assets held for its benefit by the recipient organization—The beneficiary can influence the operating and financial decisions of the recipient to such an extent that the beneficiary can determine the timing and amount of distributions from the recipient.)," addresses a similar issue for not-for-profit health care entities subject to FASB ASC 954.

ABC Foundation's net assets consist of $3,000,000 resulting from cash contributions restricted for the purchase of property, plant, and equipment (PPE) by ABC Research Institute. ABC Research Institute has recorded its interest in those net assets by debiting "Interest in net assets of ABC Foundation" and crediting "Change in interest in ABC Foundation," which is reported as an increase in temporarily restricted net assets. ABC Research Institute's accounting policy is to not imply a time restriction that expires over the useful life of the donated long-lived assets pursuant to FASB ASC 958-605-45-6 and it has no other net assets restricted for the purchase of PPE.[9] ABC Research Institute subsequently purchased and placed into service $3,000,000 of PPE that meets those donor restrictions prior to receiving a distribution from ABC Foundation. Should ABC Research Institute reclassify $3,000,000 from temporarily-restricted net assets to unrestricted net assets as a result of building and placing into service the $3,000,000 of PPE?

Reply—Because ABC Foundation (the recipient entity) and ABC Research Institute (the beneficiary) are financially interrelated, FASB ASC 958-20-25-2 requires ABC Research Institute to recognize its interest in the net assets of ABC Foundation and periodically adjust that interest for its share of the change in net assets of ABC Foundation. This is similar to the equity method of accounting described in FASB ASC 323.

In recognizing its interest in the net assets of ABC Foundation and the changes in that interest, ABC Research Institute should classify the resulting net assets as if contributions were received by ABC Research directly from the donor, because ABC Research Institute can influence the operating and financial decisions of ABC Foundation to such an extent that ABC Research Institute can determine the timing and amount of distributions from ABC Foundation to ABC Research Institute. Accordingly, the net assets representing contributions restricted for the purchase of PPE should be reported as temporarily restricted net assets (purpose restricted) in ABC Research Institute's financial statements. Upon purchasing and placing into service the PPE, ABC Research Institute (and ABC Foundation) should reclassify $3,000,000 from temporarily restricted to unrestricted net assets.[10] In other words, the existence of ABC Foundation should be transparent in determining the net asset classifications in ABC Research Institute's financial statements because ABC Foundation cannot impose time or purpose restrictions beyond those imposed by the donor. (Any instructions given by ABC Foundation are designations, rather than restrictions.)

[Revised, June 2009, to reflect conforming changes necessary due to the issuance of FASB ASC.]

---

[9] The assumption that ABC Research Institute has no other net assets restricted for the purchase of PPE is intended to avoid establishing a hierarchy pertaining to which restrictions are released first—restrictions on net assets held by the recipient or restrictions on net assets held by the beneficiary. That issue is not addressed in this TPA.

[10] In this fact pattern, ABC Research Institute's interest in the net assets of ABC Foundation is subject to only purpose restrictions because the net assets arose from cash contributions with no time restrictions. If instead the net assets arose from promises to give rather than from cash contributions, the net assets might be subject to time restrictions in addition to the purpose restrictions. In determining whether net assets that arose from promises to give are subject to time restrictions, NPEs should consider the guidance in section 6140.04, "Lapsing of Restrictions on Receivables if Purpose Restrictions Pertaining to Long-Lived Assets Are Met Before the Receivables Are Due," which discusses whether restrictions on net assets arising from promises to give that are restricted by donors for investments in long-lived assets are met when the assets are placed in service or when the receivables are due.

.18 Application of FASB ASC 958—Classification of a Beneficiary's Interest in the Net Assets of a Financially Interrelated Fund-Raising Foundation (The beneficiary makes an expenditure that is consistent with a purpose restriction on net assets held for its benefit by the recipient entity—The beneficiary cannot influence the operating and financial decisions of the recipient to such an extent that the beneficiary can determine the timing and amount of distributions from the recipient.)

Inquiry—ABC Research Institute, a not-for-profit entity subject to FASB ASC 958[11] and ABC Foundation are financially interrelated entities as described in FASB ASC 958-20-15-2. ABC Foundation's bylaws state that it is organized for the purpose of stimulating voluntary financial support from donors for the sole benefit of ABC Research Institute. Assume that ABC Research Institute cannot, however, influence the operating and financial decisions of ABC Foundation to such an extent that ABC Research Institute can determine the timing and amount of distributions from ABC Foundation to ABC Research Institute.

ABC Foundation's net assets consist of $3,000,000 resulting from cash contributions restricted for the purchase of property, plant, and equipment (PPE) by ABC Research Institute. ABC Research Institute has recorded its interest in those net assets by debiting "Interest in net assets of ABC Foundation" and crediting "Change in interest in ABC Foundation," which is reported as an increase in temporarily restricted net assets. ABC Research Institute has no other net assets restricted for the purchase of PPE.[12]

ABC Research Institute subsequently built and placed into service the New Modern Wing of the Research Building prior to receiving a distribution from ABC Foundation or any indication that it intends to support building and placing into service the New Modern Wing of the Research Building. Should ABC Research Institute reclassify $3,000,000 from temporarily-restricted net assets to unrestricted net assets as a result of building and placing into service the $3,000,000 of PPE?

Reply—From ABC Research Institute's perspective, its interest in the net assets of ABC Foundation has two restrictions—a purpose restriction (the purchase of the PPE) and an implied time restriction. (ABC Research Institute cannot influence the operating and financial decisions of ABC Foundation to such an extent that ABC Research Institute can determine the timing and amount of distributions from ABC Foundation to ABC Research Institute, including distributions pertaining to expenditures by ABC Research Institute that meet the donor-imposed purpose restrictions. Therefore, an implied time restriction exists on ABC Research Institute's interest in the net assets of ABC Foundation.) FASB ASC 958-205-45-9 provides, in part, as follows:

---

[11] This section addresses not-for-profit entities subject to FASB ASC 958. Section 6400.41, "Application of FASB Statement No. 136—Classification of a Beneficiary's Interest in the Net Assets of a Financially Interrelated Fund-Raising Foundation (The beneficiary makes an expenditure that is consistent with a purpose restriction on net assets held for its benefit by the recipient organization—The beneficiary cannot influence the operating and financial decisions of the recipient to such an extent that the beneficiary can determine the timing and amount of distributions from the recipient.)," addresses a similar issue for not-for-profit health care entities subject to FASB ASC 954.

[12] The assumption that ABC Research Institute has no other net assets restricted for the purchase of PPE is intended to avoid establishing a hierarchy pertaining to which restrictions are released first—restrictions on net assets held by the recipient or restrictions on net assets held by the beneficiary. That issue is not addressed in this section.

> If two or more temporary restrictions are imposed on a contribution, the effect of the expiration of those restrictions shall be recognized in the period in which the last remaining restriction has expired.

FASB ASC 958-205-45-11 further provides, in part, as follows:

> Temporarily restricted net assets with time restrictions are not available to support expenses until the time restrictions have expired.

In considering whether the purpose restriction on ABC Research Institute's interest in the net assets of ABC Foundation is met, ABC Research Institute should determine whether ABC Foundation has discretion in deciding whether an expenditure by ABC Research Institute that is consistent with the purpose restriction satisfies that purpose restriction. For example, if the restricted net assets arose from a contribution that was restricted for "building projects of ABC Research Institute," with no particular building project specified, purchasing and placing into service the New Modern Wing of the Research Building is consistent with the purpose restriction but may or may not meet it, because ABC Foundation has some discretion in deciding which building project releases the purpose restriction. In other words, ABC Foundation may, at its discretion, either release restricted net assets in support of building the New Modern Wing of the Research Building or not, because the purpose restriction imposed by the donor was broad enough to give ABC Foundation discretion in deciding which building projects meet the purpose restriction. If ABC Foundation has such discretion, a purpose restriction and an implied time restriction on ABC Research Institute's interest in the net assets of ABC Foundation exist. Therefore, ABC Research Institute should not reclassify $3,000,000 from temporarily-restricted net assets to unrestricted net assets as a result of building and placing into service the New Modern Wing of the Research Building unless ABC Foundation distributes or obligates itself to distribute to ABC Research Institute amounts attributable to net assets restricted for the purchase of PPE by ABC Research Institute, or ABC Foundation otherwise indicates that it intends for those net assets to be used to support the building and placing into service the New Modern Wing of the Research Building as an activity of the current period (assuming that ABC Research Institute had no other net assets that were restricted for the purchase of PPE).[13,14]

---

[13] In this fact pattern, the expenditure is made prior to meeting the purpose restriction and the implied time restriction that exists because ABC Research Institute cannot determine the timing and amount of distributions from ABC Foundation to ABC Research Institute. FASB ASC 958-205-45-11 provides that in circumstances in which both purpose and time restrictions exist, expenditures meeting the purpose restriction must be made simultaneous with or after the time restriction has expired in order to satisfy both the purpose and time restriction and result in a reclassification of net assets from temporarily restricted to unrestricted. In other words, time restrictions, if any, must be met before expenditures can result in purpose restrictions being met. In this fact pattern, however, the time restriction is an implied time restriction that exists because the beneficiary cannot determine the timing and amount of distributions from the recipient to the beneficiary, rather than an implied time restriction that exists because a promise to give is due in a future period or because of an explicit donor stipulation. Accordingly, in this fact pattern, temporarily restricted net assets with implied time restrictions are available to support expenditures made before the expiration of the time restrictions and the net assets should be reclassified from temporarily restricted to unrestricted in the period in which the last remaining restriction has expired. In other words, in this fact pattern, if the expenditure that meets the purpose restriction is made before meeting the implied time restriction that exists because the beneficiary cannot determine the timing and amount of distributions from the recipient to the beneficiary, all the restrictions should be considered met once the implied time restriction is met.

[14] In this fact pattern, ABC Research Institute's interest in the net assets of ABC Foundation is subject to an implied time restriction that exists because ABC Research Institute cannot determine

(continued)

In contrast to the example in the previous paragraph, if the restricted net assets arose from a contribution that was restricted for "building and placing into service the New Modern Wing of the Research Building," ABC Foundation has no discretion in deciding whether that purpose restriction is met by building and placing into service the New Modern Wing of the Research Building. Therefore, if ABC Research Institute builds and places into service the New Modern Wing of the Research Building, the purpose restriction is met (assuming that ABC Research Institute had no other net assets that were restricted for building and placing into service the New Modern Wing). In addition, the implied time restriction is met because ABC Foundation is required to distribute the funds to ABC in order to meet the donor's stipulations. Therefore, ABC Research Institute (and ABC Foundation) should reclassify $3,000,000 from temporarily-restricted net assets to unrestricted net assets as a result of building and placing into service the New Modern Wing of the Research Building.

In summary, ABC Research Institute should not reclassify $3,000,000 from temporarily-restricted net assets to unrestricted net assets as a result of building and placing into service the New Modern Wing of the Research Building until both the purpose restriction and the implied time restriction are met. If both the purpose restriction and the implied time restriction are met, ABC Research Institute should decrease its interest in the net assets of ABC Foundation and increase cash (or a receivable, if the Foundation has merely obligated itself to make the distribution) by the amount of the distribution, and simultaneously reclassify the same amount from temporarily restricted net assets to unrestricted net assets.

[Revised, June 2009, to reflect conforming changes necessary due to the issuance of FASB ASC.]

.19 Application of FASB ASC 958—Classification of Distributions From a Financially Interrelated Fund-Raising Foundation (Recipient Entity) to a Health Care Beneficiary

Inquiry—How should a fund-raising foundation (recipient), a not-for-profit entity subject to FASB ASC 958 report (in its separately issued financial statements) distributions to a financially interrelated beneficiary that is a health care entity? In other words, should such distributions be reported following (*a*) the guidance on reporting transfers among affiliated health care entities in FASB ASC 954-10, FASB ASC 954-205, FASB ASC 954-605, and FASB ASC 954-810, or (*b*) the guidance in FASB ASC 958.

(footnote continued)

the timing and amount of distributions from ABC Foundation to ABC Research Institute and a purpose restriction. Because the net assets arose from cash contributions with no other donor-imposed time restrictions, no time restrictions other than those imposed by ABC Foundation exist. If instead the net assets arose from promises to give rather than from cash contributions, the net assets might be subject to donor-imposed time restrictions in addition to the time restriction imposed by ABC Foundation and the purpose restriction. In determining whether net assets that arose from promises to give are subject to donor-imposed time restrictions in addition to the time restrictions imposed by ABC Foundation, NPEs should consider the guidance in section 6140.04, which discusses whether restrictions on net assets arising from promises to give that are restricted by donors for investments in long-lived assets are met when the assets are placed in service or when the receivables are due. In circumstances in which the net assets are subject to (*a*) donor-imposed time restrictions in addition to the (*b*) implied time restrictions that exist because ABC Research Institute cannot determine the timing and amount of distributions from ABC Foundation to ABC Research Institute and (*c*) purpose restrictions, the last remaining time restriction should be considered in applying the guidance in FASB ASC 958-205-45-11 that provides that temporarily restricted net assets with time restrictions are not available to support expenses until the time restrictions have expired.

Reply—FASB ASC 958 applies to all not-for-profit entities, except those that are providers of health care services (FASB ASC 958-10-15-3). Therefore, the guidance in FASB ASC 954 generally does not apply to financial statements of recipient entities that are financially interrelated fund-raising foundations. The foundation should follow the accounting and reporting requirements of FASB ASC 958 rather than FASB ASC 954 in the foundation's separately issued financial statements. The foundation should report distributions to beneficiary entities as expenses or distributions to related entities. The guidance in the previous sentence applies regardless of whether the recipient entity and the beneficiary are under common control or whether one controls the other in a parent-subsidiary relationship.

[Revised, June 2009, to reflect conforming changes necessary due to the issuance of FASB ASC.]

.20 NPEs Reporting No Fund-Raising Expenses

Inquiry—Some NPEs with contributions report no fund-raising expense. FASB ASC 958-720-50-1 provides that the financial statements should disclose total fund-raising expense. Do circumstances exist in which an NPE could have contributions but minimal or no fund-raising expense?

Reply—It would be unusual for an NPE to have contributions but have minimal or no fund-raising expense. Examples of circumstances in which an NPE could have contributions but minimal or no fund-raising expense typically include those in which (*a*) because of name recognition or custom, donors contribute to the NPE without the NPE undertaking fund-raising activities,[15] (*b*) fund-raising activities related to those contributions are conducted entirely or almost entirely by volunteers whose contributed services do not meet the recognition criteria for contributed services in FASB ASC 958-605-25-16 or (*c*) other entities that the NPE does not control[16] contribute to the NPE with the NPE undertaking minimal or no fund-raising activity or other participation in relation to those contributions.[17,18] Examples of circumstances in which an NPE with contributions may have no fund-raising expense or minimal fund-raising expense in relation to contributions include:

- A religious entity obtains most or all of its contributions from member tithing.

---

[15] Fund-raising activities include, but are not limited to, compensating another entity for raising funds on behalf of the NPE, such as circumstances in which the fund-raising entity retains an administrative fee for raising funds on behalf of the NPE.

[16] The FASB ASC glossary defines *control* as "the possession, direct or indirect, of the power to direct or cause the direction of the management and policies of an entity through ownership, by contract, or otherwise."

[17] As discussed in FASB ASC 958-720-45-27, "Federated fundraising entities solicit and receive designated and undesignated contributions and make grants and awards to other not-for-profit entities. The fundraising activities of federated fundraising entities, including activities related to fundraising on behalf of others, shall be reported as fundraising expenses."

[18] As discussed in section 6140.22, "In Circumstances in Which the Reporting NPE Undertakes a Transaction in Which Another NPE (Fund-Raising NPE) Raises Contributions on Behalf of the Reporting NPE, and the Reporting NPE Compensates the Fund-Raising NPE for Raising Those Contributions (Compensation Including, But Not Limited to, an Administrative Fee), Should the Reporting NPE Report the Fund-Raising NPE's Compensation Gross as Fund-Raising Expenses, or Net, as a Reduction of Contributions?," reporting NPEs should report fund-raising expenses for compensation to a fund-raising NPE acting as an agent or intermediary in circumstances in which the fund-raising NPE acting as an agent or intermediary retains an administrative fee that will be deducted from all contributions that are to be transferred to the donor's chosen entity. That fact pattern is an example of a circumstance in which other entities that the NPE does not control contribute to the NPE (through an agent or intermediary) with the NPE undertaking minimal or no fund-raising activity or other participation in relation to those contributions, and the NPE would report fund-raising expense.

- Most or all contributions arise from volunteers making phone calls or writing letters on the entity's behalf (and this volunteer activity does not meet the recognition criteria for contributed services in FASB ASC 958-605-25-16).
- An entity has no paid staff, and most or all contributions arise from uncompensated board members soliciting contributions (and this board member activity does not meet the recognition criteria for contributed services in FASB ASC 958-605-25-16).
- The reporting entity is a private foundation or is supported by a private foundation, and the reporting entity expends no or minimal resources in soliciting those contributions.
- The reporting entity obtains most or all of its contributions from one or more entities that it does not control (fund-raising NPE), expends minimal resources, and has minimal participation in soliciting those contributions.[19] For example:
  - — NPE Relief and Development Entity is one of many entities devoted to cause ABC. NPE Relief and Development Entity receives most or all of its contributions from Relief and Development Entities in the USA, Canada, and the United Kingdom that raise support for cause ABC throughout the world.
  - — NPE Religious Entity Denomination International Mission Board receives a substantial portion of its support from the NPE Religious Entity Denomination, which supports various entities and causes, including but not limited to NPE Religious Entity Denomination International Mission Board. NPE Religious Entity Denomination allocates, at its discretion, X percent of its contributions from supporting churches and individuals to NPE Religious Entity Denomination International Mission Board.

The reporting NPE should consider, however, whether it is required to make financial statement disclosures required by FASB ASC 850, *Related Party Disclosures*, and FASB ASC 275, *Risks and Uncertainties*.

[Revised, June 2009, to reflect conforming changes necessary due to the issuance of FASB ASC.]

.21 Should an NPE Report Amounts Charged to the NPE by a Professional Fund-Raiser Gross, as Fund-Raising Expenses, or Net, as a Reduction of Contributions?

Inquiry—In circumstances in which a professional fund-raiser charges an NPE for soliciting contributions on the NPE's behalf, should the NPE report amounts charged to the NPE by the professional fund-raiser gross, as fund-raising expense, or net, as a reduction of contributions?

Reply—In circumstances in which a professional fund-raiser charges an NPE for soliciting contributions on the NPE's behalf, the NPE should report

[19] Footnote 18, in referring to section 6140.22, discusses a circumstance in which other entities that the NPE does not control contribute to the NPE (through an agent or intermediary) with the NPE undertaking minimal or no fund-raising activity or other participation in relation to those contributions, and the NPE would report fund-raising expense.

the amounts charged to the NPE by the professional fund-raiser gross, as fund-raising expense. As discussed in paragraphs 14–15 of FASB ASC 958-225-45, revenues and expenses should be reported gross (except for investment revenues and related expenses, which are permitted to be reported net of related expenses), while gains and losses may be reported net. Accordingly, in circumstances in which an NPE incurs expenses by hiring a professional fund-raiser to solicit contributions on its behalf, the NPE should report those contributions and expenses gross, rather than net. For example, assume NPE A enters into a transaction with Professional Fund-Raiser B, whereby Professional Fund-Raiser B solicits contributions on behalf of NPE A, for a fee of 20 percent of contributions raised. Professional Fund-Raiser B raises $100,000 and remits $80,000 to NPE A after retaining its fee of $20,000. NPE A should report $100,000 contribution revenue and $20,000 fund-raising expense.

[Revised, June 2009, to reflect conforming changes necessary due to the issuance of FASB ASC.]

.22 In Circumstances in Which the Reporting NPE Undertakes a Transaction in Which Another NPE (Fund-Raising NPE) Raises Contributions on Behalf of the Reporting NPE, and the Reporting NPE Compensates the Fund-Raising NPE for Raising Those Contributions (Compensation Including, But Not Limited to, an Administrative Fee), Should the Reporting NPE Report the Fund-Raising NPE's Compensation Gross, as Fund-Raising Expenses, or Net, as a Reduction of Contributions?

Inquiry—In some circumstances, a federated fund-raising entity (or other NPE) (fund-raising NPE) acts as an agent or intermediary rather than a donee. For example, in circumstances in which the fund-raising NPE receives resources from donors who stipulate that those resources should be transferred to a specified NPE, the fund-raising NPE acts as an agent or intermediary rather than a donee.[20] The NPE compensates the fund-raising NPE acting as an agent or intermediary. (Such compensation includes, but is not limited to, the fund-raising NPE retaining an administrative fee that will be deducted from all contributions that are to be transferred to the donor's chosen entity.) Should the reporting NPE report the compensation to the fund-raising NPE acting as an agent or intermediary gross, as fund-raising expenses, or net, as a reduction of contributions?

Reply—The reporting NPE should report fund-raising expenses for the compensation to the fund-raising NPE acting as an agent or intermediary in circumstances in which the reporting NPE compensates the fund-raising NPE acting as an agent or intermediary for raising contributions on behalf of the reporting NPE. (Such compensation includes, but is not limited to, the fund-raising NPE acting as an agent or intermediary retaining an administrative fee that will be deducted from all contributions that are to be transferred to the donor's chosen entity.) Accordingly, the reporting NPE should report the amount retained as compensation by the fund-raising NPE acting as an agent or intermediary gross as fund-raising expenses and report contributions for the gross amount contributed from the donor to the fund-raising NPE acting as an agent or intermediary for the benefit of the reporting NPE.

---

[20] In some circumstances, the fund-raising NPE receives resources from donors without stipulations or with stipulations sufficiently broad such that the fund-raising NPE acts as a donee, rather than as an agent or intermediary.

Paragraphs 84–87 of FASB ASC 958-605-55 discuss, among other matters, circumstances in which a federated fund-raising entity acts as an agent or intermediary, rather than a donee, in raising contributions in which the donor specifies the entity to which the contribution should be transferred. As discussed in FASB ASC 958-605-55-86, in circumstances in which the federated fund-raising entity charges an administrative fee that will be deducted from all contributions that are to be transferred to the donor's chosen entity, the beneficiaries should report the gross amount of the contributions as contribution revenue and the administrative fees withheld by the federated fund-raising entity as expenses. The guidance in paragraphs 84–87 of FASB ASC 958-605-55 would also apply if the fund-raising NPE were other than a federated fund-raising entity. Also, in functionalizing the administrative fees reported as expenses, the reporting NPE beneficiary would classify those expenses as fund-raising.

[Revised, June 2009, to reflect conforming changes necessary due to the issuance of FASB ASC.]

.23 Changing Net Asset Classifications Reported in a Prior Year

Inquiry—In some circumstances, not-for-profit organizations (NFPs) correct net asset classifications previously reported in prior years' financial statements.

The FASB ASC glossary defines an *error in previously issued financial statements* as follows:

> An error in recognition, measurement, presentation, or disclosure in financial statements resulting from mathematical mistakes, mistakes in the application of generally accepted accounting principles (GAAP), or oversight or misuse of facts that existed at the time the financial statements were prepared. A change from an accounting principle that is not generally accepted to one that is generally accepted is a correction of an error.

Are individual net asset classes, rather than net assets in the aggregate (total net assets), relevant in determining whether an NFP's correction of net asset classifications previously reported in prior years' financial statements is an error in previously issued financial statements?

Reply—Individual net asset classes, rather than net assets in the aggregate (total net assets), are relevant in determining whether an NFP's correction of net asset classifications previously reported in prior years' financial statements is an error in previously issued financial statements.

FASB ASC 958-205-45-2, in discussing the financial statement presentation of net asset classes, provides, in part, as follows:

> The usefulness of information provided by financial statements of NFPs can be vastly improved if certain basic information is classified in comparable ways. All NFPs shall … classify and report net assets in three groups—permanently restricted, temporarily restricted, and unrestricted—based on the existence or absence of donor-imposed restrictions and the nature of those restrictions. Information about the nature and amount of restrictions imposed by donors on the use of contributed assets, including their potential effects on specific assets and on liabilities or classes of net assets, is helpful in assessing the financial flexibility of an NFP.

FASB ASC 958-225-45-13, in discussing the circumstances in which net assets should be reclassified, provides as follows:

Reclassifications of net assets—that is, simultaneous increases in one net asset class and decreases in another—shall be made if any of the following events occur:

a. The NFP fulfills the purposes for which the net assets were restricted.

b. Donor-imposed restrictions expire with the passage of time or with the death of a split-interest agreement beneficiary (if the net assets are not otherwise restricted).

c. A donor withdraws, or court action removes, previously imposed restrictions.

d. A donor imposes restrictions on otherwise unrestricted net assets. For example, a donor may make a restricted contribution that is conditioned on the NFP restricting a stated amount of its unrestricted net assets. Such restrictions that are not reversible without donors' consent result in a reclassification of unrestricted net assets to restricted net assets.

Paragraph 74 of FASB Statement No. 117, *Financial Statements of Not-for-Profit Organizations*, which was part of appendix B, "Basis for Conclusions," of FASB Statement No. 117 and not included in FASB ASC, discusses, among other matters, the importance of reporting information beyond totals for the organization as a whole, such as information about which net assets are subject to donor restrictions, and provides as follows:

> In assessing the financial position or performance of a not-for-profit organization, however, the Board believes it is important to avoid focusing attention almost exclusively on net assets, change in net assets, total assets, or other highly simplified and aggregated amounts. For example, in Concepts Statement No. 6, *Elements of Financial Statements*, paragraph 106, the Board says, "Since donor-imposed restrictions affect the types and levels of service a not-for-profit organization can provide, whether an organization has maintained certain classes of net assets may be more significant than whether it has maintained net assets in the aggregate." Similarly, it is important to avoid focusing attention almost exclusively on "the bottom line" or other highly simplified and condensed information about business enterprises. Accordingly, this Statement requires not only summary amounts that focus on a not-for-profit organization as a whole but also information about items and components of those amounts; for example, it generally requires reporting information about the gross amounts of items of revenues and expenses and of cash receipts and cash payments.

[Issue Date: May 2010.]

.24 Contributions of Certain Nonfinancial Assets, Such as Fundraising Material, Informational Material, or Advertising, Including Media Time or Space for Public Service Announcements or Other Purposes

Inquiry—In some circumstances, entities other than an NFP use for the NFP's benefit (or provide at no charge to the NFP) certain nonfinancial assets that encourage the public to contribute to the NFP or help the NFP communicate its message or mission. Examples of such activities include the following:

- An advertising agency, television station, or newspaper provides design services or professional talent services.

- A radio or television station gives an NFP (or uses for the NFP's benefit) commercial air time at no charge.
- An NFP distributes a public service announcement to several radio or television stations and asks the stations to air the announcement. (Some stations air the announcement and report information about the airings to the NFP.)
- A magazine, newspaper, or other print media gives an NFP (or uses for the NFP's benefit) advertising space at no charge.
- An Internet site gives an NFP (or uses for the NFP's benefit) advertising space at no charge.

In circumstances in which fundraising material, informational material, or advertising, including media time or space for public service announcements or other purposes, is used for the NFP's benefit (or provided to the NFP at no charge) and encourages the public to contribute to an NFP or help the NFP communicate its message or mission, should the NFP report a contribution? If so, how should that contribution be measured and reported?

Reply—In circumstances in which fundraising material, informational material, or advertising, including media time or space for public service announcements or other purposes, is used for the NFP's benefit (or provided to the NFP at no charge) and encourages the public to contribute to an NFP or help the NFP communicate its message or mission, NFPs should consider whether they have received a contribution. If they have received a contribution, it should be measured at fair value, pursuant to FASB ASC 958-605-30-2, and the related expense, at the time the expense is recognized, should be reported by function, based on the nature of the contributed item.

As noted in paragraph 5.02 of the AICPA Audit and Accounting Guide *Not-for-Profit Entities*, the FASB ASC glossary defines a *contribution*, in part, as "an unconditional transfer of cash or other assets to an entity or a settlement or cancellation of its liabilities in a voluntary nonreciprocal transfer by another entity acting other than as an owner." As noted in paragraph 5.01 of the Audit and Accounting Guide *Not-for-Profit Entities*, other assets include securities, land, buildings, use of facilities or utilities, material and supplies, intangible assets, and unconditional promises to give in the future.

Paragraph 25 of FASB Concepts Statement No. 6, *Elements of Financial Statements—a replacement of FASB Concepts Statement No. 3 (incorporating an amendment of FASB Concepts Statement No. 2)*, defines *assets* as "probable future economic benefits obtained or controlled by a particular entity as a result of past transactions or events." Paragraph 26 of FASB Concepts Statement No. 6, in discussing the characteristics of assets, provides, in part, as follows:

> An asset has three essential characteristics: (a) it embodies a probable future benefit that involves a capacity, singly or in combination with other assets, to contribute directly or indirectly to future net cash inflows, (b) a particular entity can obtain the benefit and control others' access to it, (c) the transaction or other event giving rise to the entity's right to or control of the benefit has already occurred. ... [A]lthough the ability of an entity to obtain benefit from an asset and to control others' access to it generally rests on a foundation of legal rights, legal enforceability of a claim to the benefit is not a prerequisite for a benefit to qualify as an asset if the entity has the ability to obtain and control the benefit in other ways.

Paragraph 28 of FASB Concepts Statement No. 6 elaborates further on the economic benefits of assets, noting that for NFPs, such benefits may be realized in the form of service potential rather than cash inflows, as follows:

> The common characteristic possessed by all assets (economic resources) is "service potential" or "future economic benefit," the scarce capacity to provide services or benefits to the entities that use them. ... In a not-for-profit organization, that service potential or future economic benefit is used to provide desired or needed goods or services to beneficiaries or other constituents, which may or may not directly result in net cash inflows to the organization.

Paragraph 31 of FASB Concepts Statement No. 6, in discussing the momentary nature of certain assets, provides as follows:

> Services provided by other entities, including personal services, cannot be stored and are received and used simultaneously. They can be assets of an entity only momentarily—as the entity receives and uses them—although their use may create or add value to other assets of the entity. Rights to receive services of other entities for specified or determinable future periods can be assets of particular entities.

Accordingly, in circumstances in which fundraising material, informational material, or advertising, including media time or space for public service announcements or other purposes, is used for the NFP's benefit (or provided to the NFP at no charge) and encourages the public to contribute to an NFP or help the NFP communicate its message or mission, the NFP may have received an unconditional transfer of other assets in a voluntary nonreciprocal transfer from another entity acting other than as an owner.

Paragraphs 5.56–.57 of the Audit and Accounting Guide *Not-for-Profit Entities*, in discussing reporting contributions received, provide as follows:

> FASB ASC 958-605-25-2 states that except as provided (for contributed services and collections), contributions received shall be recognized as revenues or gains in the period received and as assets, decreases of liabilities, or expenses depending on the form of the benefits received. [FN omitted]
>
> Depending on the kind of benefit received, in addition to recognizing contribution revenue, the NFP should also recognize (*a*) an increase in assets (for example, cash, securities, contributions receivable, collections [if capitalized, see chapter 7, "Other Assets," of this guide], and property and equipment); (*b*) a decrease in liabilities (for example, accounts payable or notes payable); or (*c*) an expense (for example, donated legal services).

FASB ASC 958-720-45-2, in discussing reporting expenses, provides as follows:

> To help donors, creditors, and others in assessing an NFP's service efforts, including the costs of its services and how it uses resources, a statement of activities or notes to financial statements shall provide information about expenses reported by their functional classification, such as major classes of program services and supporting activities, for example:
>
> *a.* Program services
>
> *b.* Supporting activities
>
> *c.* Management and general activities

d. Fundraising activities

e. Membership development activities

Accordingly, expenses related to such fundraising material, informational material, or advertising, including media time or space for public service announcements or other purposes, used for the NFP's benefit (or provided to the NFP at no charge) that encourages the public to contribute to an NFP or help the NFP communicate its message or mission should be reported by function at the time the expense is recognized, based on the nature of the contributed item.

[Issue Date: May 2010.]

.25 Multiyear Unconditional Promises to Give—Measurement Objective and the Effect of Changes in Interest Rates

Inquiry—FASB ASC 958-605-25-8 provides that promises to give should be recognized when received.

What is the measurement objective for multiyear unconditional promises to give, and what is the effect of changes in interest rates on that objective?

Reply—The measurement objective for multiyear unconditional promises to give (both the revenue and contribution receivable) is fair value at initial recognition, consistent with FASB ASC 958-605-30-2. The measurement objective for contributions receivable at subsequent measurement depends on whether the NFP has elected the fair value option, pursuant to FASB ASC 825-10. If the NFP has elected the fair value option, pursuant to FASB ASC 825-10, the measurement objective for contributions receivable at subsequent measurement is fair value. If the NFP has not elected the fair value option, pursuant to FASB ASC 825-10, the measurement objective for contributions receivable at subsequent measurement is as described in FASB ASC 958-310-35-4.

The model in FASB ASC 825-10-50-3 is not a fair value model.[21]

As discussed in paragraph 5.20 of the Audit and Accounting Guide *Not-for-Profit Entities*, "[p]resent value techniques are one valuation technique for measuring the fair value of the contribution ... or receivable; other valuation techniques also are available, as described in FASB ASC 820, *Fair Value Measurements and Disclosures*."

Paragraph 5.112 of the Audit and Accounting Guide *Not-for-Profit Entities*, in discussing the discount rate to be used if present value techniques are used to measure fair value, provides, in part, as follows:

> FASB ASC 958-605-30-5 discusses the determination of the discount rate if present value techniques are used to measure fair value. The present value of unconditional promises to give should be measured using a discount rate that is consistent with the general principles for present value measurement discussed in paragraphs 5–9 of FASB

[21] FASB ASC 825-10-50 requires various disclosures, including disclosures of fair value and carrying amounts for all financial instruments (which include contributions receivable) for which it is practicable to estimate that value and the method(s) and significant assumptions used to estimate the fair value of financial instruments. FASB ASC 825-10-55-3 states that disclosures required by the "General" subsection of FASB ASC 825-10-50 are optional if an entity meets all of the following 3 criteria: (*a*) the entity is a nonpublic entity; (*b*) the entity's total assets are less than $100 million on the date of the financial statements; and (*c*) the entity has no instrument that, in whole or in part, is accounted for as a derivative instrument.

ASC 820-10-55-5. In conformity with FASB ASC 835-30-25-11, the discount rate should be determined at the time the unconditional promise to give is initially recognized and should not be revised subsequently unless the NFP has elected to measure the promise to give at fair value in conformity with the "Fair Value Option" subsections of FASB ASC 825-10.

Accordingly, in circumstances in which the NFP

- has not elected the fair value option, pursuant to FASB ASC 825-10, and market interest rates change in periods subsequent to initial recognition, the discount rate used in a present value technique should not be revised to reflect such changes in market rates.
- has elected the fair value option, pursuant to FASB ASC 825-10, and market interest rates change in periods subsequent to initial recognition, the discount rate used in a present value technique should be revised to reflect such changes in market rates.

[Issue Date: May 2010.]

.26 Not-for-Profit Entity With For-Profit Subsidiary and Adoption of FASB ASU No. 2014-02 on Goodwill

Inquiry—A not-for-profit entity has a for-profit subsidiary that it consolidates under GAAP. This for-profit subsidiary is considered a private company and would elect to amortize goodwill as permitted by FASB Accounting Standards Update (ASU) No. 2014-02, *Intangibles—Goodwill and Other (Topic 350): Accounting for Goodwill (a consensus of the Private Company Council)*. Is this accounting alternative permitted in the consolidated financial statements since the accounting alternative in ASU No. 2014-02 is not permitted to be used by not-for-profit entities?

Reply—No. A *private company* is defined in the FASB ASC glossary as "an entity other than a public business entity, a not-for-profit entity, or an employee benefit plan within the scope of Topics 960 through 965 on plan accounting." When FASB utilizes the broad term *entity* in this context, it implies the reporting entity (for example, consolidated entity), rather than the legal entity. In this case, because the reporting entity is the consolidated not-for-profit entity, which is not permitted to adopt the accounting alternative in ASU No. 2014-02, the for-profit subsidiary that is part of that consolidated reporting entity is not permitted to use the amortization accounting alternative in the consolidated financial statements. The for-profit subsidiary could adopt the accounting alternative in ASU No. 2014-02 in its standalone financial statements.

[Issue Date: January 2015.]

Q&A Section 6300

Insurance Companies

.01 Recognition of Commission Income by Insurance Agency

Inquiry—Insurance agents and brokers receive commissions on the insurance policies that they place for their clients with insurance companies. Commissions consist of a percentage of the premiums that the clients pay for the policies. On policies that are cancelled before the end of their term, usually one year, the insurance company charges back the portion of the commissions related to the unearned premiums to the originating agent or broker. In addition, some brokers may receive contingent commissions from underwriters based on the profitability of policies placed with an underwriter. How should an insurance agent or broker account for revenue from such commissions?

Reply—Commissions should be recognized on the date on which (*a*) the client is afforded protection under the policy (effective date), (*b*) the premium due under the policy can be reasonably estimated, and (*c*) the premium is billable to the client. A provision should be made for expected adjustments relating to policy cancellations when they can be reasonably estimated in accordance with Financial Accounting Standards Board (FASB) *Accounting Standards Codification* (ASC) 450, *Contingencies*. Contingent commissions should generally be recognized when the insurance agent or broker is notified by the underwriter of the amount to be received.

[Amended; Revised, June 2009, to reflect conforming changes necessary due to the issuance of FASB ASC.]

.02 Method of Recognizing Revenue From Commissions on Credit Life Insurance

Inquiry—Under arrangements with a lending institution, an insurance agency provides credit life insurance to mortgagors. The borrower pays the premium for the entire term of the insurance (as much as eight years) when the loan is made, and the insurance agency remits to the insurance company this entire sum less a commission.

Should this commission income be recognized when it is received, or should it be recognized over the term of the policy?

Reply—Generally, credit life insurance appears to have more of the characteristics of casualty insurance than it does of life insurance. In particular, from the agent's viewpoint, payment for the policy usually occurs in a lump sum from which agent commissions are deducted. Generally, the efforts of the agency in connection with any individual policy terminate when collection is made or, at least, when the proceeds from the collections are remitted to the insurance company. It would therefore seem that the recognition of income should occur when proceeds of the policy are received.

However, as there is a potential liability for returned premiums, it would appear that a reasonable allowance should be provided at this time for estimated commissions on the portion of the policies that may be cancelled in future years. Most finance companies should have adequate statistics upon which to base such estimates. If the finance company is new, there may be statistics available from similar enterprises.

.03 Recognition of Income on Unclaimed Refunds Due Policyholders on Policy Cancellations

Inquiry—An insurance agency has a material amount of accounts payable legally due to policyholders who have cancelled their insurance prior to the end of the policy term. The company does not notify these policyholders that these amounts are due them. When, if ever, should these credits be taken into income?

Reply—These accounts payable should continue to be reported as liabilities until such time as the individuals involved legally lose their claim to these amounts. Legal counsel should be consulted for an opinion as to whether these amounts would have to be paid over to the state under an escheat law.

Consideration should also be given to the appropriateness of notifying these policyholders that this money is due them.

.04 Reserve for Future Claims of Title Insurance Company

Inquiry—A title insurance company must place part of its premiums in a reserve for future claims. When should this reserve be recognized as income?

Reply—The jurisdiction under which a title insurance company operates usually requires that a stipulated percentage of premiums collected must be deferred in an unearned premium account. Generally, the unearned premium is taken into income over a ten-year period since most claims against title policies tend to occur during this ten-year period. However, actual claims are not charged to the unearned premium account. Actual claims are charged against income (title claims account) with the credit to "Reserve for Claims." The reserve for claims represents reported claims that have surfaced. The unearned premium account is intended to cover unsurfaced claims.

[.05] Reserved

[.06] Reserved

[.07] Reserved

.08 Definition of an Insurance Benefit Feature

Inquiry—FASB ASC 944-605-25-8 states "If the amounts assessed against the contract holder each period for the insurance benefit feature of an insurance contract are assessed in a manner that is expected to result in profits in earlier years and losses in subsequent years from the insurance benefit function, a liability for unearned revenue shall be recognized in addition to the account balance." What constitutes the *insurance benefit function* in performing the test described previously?

Reply—The test should be applied separately to the base mortality or morbidity feature and, in addition, separately to each other individual mortality or morbidity feature. Other individual mortality or morbidity features that would need to be tested separately are those features that create incremental mortality or morbidity risk to the base contract (for example, no lapse guarantees or long term care riders in a universal life insurance contract). Indicators that a mortality or morbidity feature should be evaluated separately may include

- explicit incremental charges,
- offered separately in the market place,
- described in the contract as a separate benefit, or
- the contract holder has a choice to accept or reject the additional benefit without rejecting the base contract.

Other insurance benefit features that provide for fixed and guaranteed benefits and premiums, and offered as a rider or an addition to a universal life contract, in practice typically would have been and should continue to be, separately accounted for under FASB ASC 944. Those features that have not been accrued for under FASB ASC 944 should be evaluated under the guidance of FASB ASC 944-20-10-2, paragraphs 20–25 of FASB ASC 944-40-30, and paragraphs 1–2 of FASB ASC 944-605-30.

[Revised, June 2009, to reflect conforming changes necessary due to the issuance of FASB ASC.]

.09 Definition of an Assessment

Inquiry—In performing the test in FASB ASC 944-605-25-8 (that is, have amounts assessed against the contract holder in a manner that is expected to result in profits in earlier years and losses in subsequent years from the insurance benefit function), what assessments should be used in the comparison of the amount and timing of expected assessments and the related benefits for determining whether amounts are assessed in a manner that is expected to result in profits in earlier years and losses in subsequent years from the insurance benefit function?

Reply—If an insurance benefit function has an explicit fee, there is a presumption that the terms and conditions of a contract entered into between two parties dealing at arms length are representative of their agreement. Therefore, there is a rebuttable presumption that the explicit fee should be used for the test in FASB ASC 944-605-25-8. However, there may be circumstances where the presumption may be overcome if evidence indicates that the substance of the agreement is not captured in the explicit terms of the contract. It is unlikely the presumption can be rebutted in the situation in which the assessment is explicitly incremental upon election of a separate insurance benefit feature and for which the policyholder has the choice to not pay if the election is not made.

In circumstances in which an insurance benefit function has no corresponding explicit fee or if the explicit fee does not capture the substance of the agreement, another method of determining assessments should be used for the test in FASB ASC 944-605-25-8. For example, in some universal life policies, the product's base mortality function may have been designed and priced on an integrated basis with the other functions, such as, administration and asset management. In such products, while the explicit cost of insurance charge is not expected to be sufficient to cover the death benefit risk in all periods, the product may be designed such that other assessments, including administrative fees, asset management fees, and investment margins, are expected to result in profits in subsequent years sufficient to offset the losses from the explicit cost of insurance charges designed shortfalls. In this example, it may be appropriate to include such additional implicit assessments in the test in FASB ASC 944-605-25-8 for the base mortality function. The analysis of implicit assessments would need to appropriately consider the pricing and cost of all components of the product. Indicators that implicit assessments are appropriately allocated to product components are

- allocation is not inconsistent with documentation, if any, of pricing at contract inception,
- assessments are allocated considering the recovery of all costs of each product component,

- allocation does not contradict external information on the market value of an individual product component on a stand-alone basis, and
- allocation method is applied consistently.

There is a presumption that the minimum guaranteed death benefit of a variable annuity and the no-lapse guarantee mortality feature of a universal life or a variable universal life contract will result in profits in earlier years and losses in subsequent years. This pattern of profits followed by losses results from the design and capital markets risks of these benefit features.

[Revised, June 2009, to reflect conforming changes necessary due to the issuance of FASB ASC.]

.10 Level of Aggregation of Additional Liabilities Determined Under FASB ASC 944

Inquiry—At what level of aggregation should additional liabilities, determined in accordance with FASB ASC 944-40-30-20, be calculated?

Reply—It is presumed that the level of aggregation generally should be consistent with the level at which the entity's DAC amortization ratios and associated DAC balances are calculated. This is the level at which products with common features have been aggregated. It is not appropriate to combine DAC-level groups for aggregation purposes in FASB ASC 944-40-30-20. Aggregation at a more detailed level than the level at which the entity's DAC amortization ratios and associated DAC balances are calculated may be warranted based on an individual entity's facts and circumstances including, but not limited to, the risk characteristics of the corresponding insurance benefit features, such as, variable annuities with a ratchet minimum guaranteed death benefit (MGDB) and variable annuities with a return of premium MGDB, or universal life products with and without secondary guarantees.

[Revised, June 2009, to reflect conforming changes necessary due to the issuance of FASB ASC.]

.11 Losses Followed by Losses

Inquiry—Should the guidance in FASB ASC 944-605-25-8 be applied if amounts assessed against the contract holder for an insurance benefit feature are expected to result in losses in earlier and subsequent years?

Reply—Yes, the concept underlying FASB ASC 944-605-25-8 is that the insurance entity may be required to establish a liability if it provides an insurance benefit in future periods for which it charges amounts in such periods that are less than the expected value of the insurance benefits to be provided. Consequently, the insurance enterprise should recognize a liability. This concept is applicable in situations in which charges attributable to an insurance benefit feature are less than the expected cost of the insurance benefit in all periods.

[Revised, June 2009, to reflect conforming changes necessary due to the issuance of FASB ASC.]

.12 Reinsurance

Inquiry—How should a ceding entity account for reinsurance contracts that meet the risk transfer criteria of FASB ASC 944 and that reinsure the insurance benefit features accounted for under FASB ASC 944-20-10-2, paragraphs 20–25 of FASB ASC 944-40-30, and paragraphs 1–2 of FASB ASC 944-605-30?

Reply—The accounting for reinsurance should be separate from the accounting for the direct contracts of the ceding entity in accordance with paragraphs 3–4 of FASB ASC 944-20-40, FASB ASC 944-310-25-2, FASB ASC 944-310-45-7, FASB ASC 944-340-25-1, FASB ASC 944-605-45-1, and FASB ASC 944-605-50-1. Reinsurance recoverables arising from the reinsurance contract should be reported as assets. As stated in FASB ASC 944-40-25-34, the recoverable should be calculated using methods and assumptions consistent with those used to establish the direct contract holder's liability. Therefore, a benefit ratio using the same assumptions and scenarios used to establish the direct contract liability, as required in FASB ASC 944-40-30-20 should be used to establish a reinsurance recoverable with excess benefit payments ceded under the terms of the reinsurance contract as the numerator and direct assessments as the denominator. As required by FASB ASC 944-605-35-14, the cost of reinsurance shall be amortized over the remaining life of the underlying reinsured contracts if the reinsurance contract is long-duration, or over the contract period of the reinsurance if the reinsurance contract is short-duration. The cost of reinsurance may be recognized based on total direct assessments or another reasonable manner such as estimated gross profits.

[Revised, June 2009, to reflect conforming changes necessary due to the issuance of FASB ASC.]

.13 Accounting for Contracts That Provide Annuitization Benefits

Inquiry—Are the provisions of paragraphs 26–27 and 40–41of FASB ASC 944-40-25, paragraphs 26–29 of FASB ASC 944-40-30, paragraphs 10 and 12–16 of FASB ASC 944-40-35, and FASB ASC 944-40-45-2, dealing with accounting for contracts that provide annuitization benefits, limited only to universal life-type, limited-payment, and investment contracts?

Reply—No. The provisions of FASB ASC 944 relating to accounting for contracts that provide annuitization benefits applies to all insurance and investment contracts that have annuitization benefits. Therefore, any product that includes an annuitization benefit should be evaluated. This includes, but is not limited to, products where the base contracts are accounted for under FASB ASC 944 and where the annuitization benefit has not already been included in establishing the liability. To the extent annuitization benefits features have not already been included in benefit or premium deficiency liabilities, the provisions of paragraphs 26–27 and 40–41 of FASB ASC 944-40-25, paragraphs 26–29 of FASB ASC 944-40-30, paragraphs 10 and 12–16 of FASB ASC 944-40-35, and FASB ASC 944-40-45-2 should be applied.

[Revised, June 2009, to reflect conforming changes necessary due to the issuance of FASB ASC.]

.14 Note to Sections 6300.15–.24—Accounting by Noninsurance Enterprises for Property and Casualty Insurance Arrangements That Limit Insurance Risk

Insurance enables a company (the insured) to transfer insurance risk to an insurer for a specified premium. Insurance may be purchased for a number of economic reasons generally with the underlying goal of transferring insurance risk, including property damage, injury to others, and business interruption.

The following series of questions and answers (sections 6300.15–.24) focus on certain aspects of finite insurance products that are utilized by noninsurance enterprises. Due to the diverse nature of contracts in the marketplace, the guidance in these questions and answers is designed to assist practitioners in identifying the relevant literature to consider in addressing their specific facts and circumstances. The sections contain many excerpts of applicable guidance, but readers should be familiar with all the guidance contained in that literature not only the specific paragraphs listed.

GAAP guidance for an insurance enterprise's purchase of reinsurance is more extensive than guidance on accounting by noninsurance enterprises for insurance contracts. The accounting guidance for reinsurance addresses transactions between an insurer (the contract holder) and a reinsurer (the issuer of the contract). Sections 6300.15–.24 address property and casualty insurance contracts between a policyholder and an insurance enterprise, which is similar to the relationship between an insurer and a reinsurer.

.15 Finite Insurance

Inquiry—What are "finite" insurance transactions?

Reply—Finite insurance contracts are contracts that transfer a clearly defined and restricted amount of insurance risk from the policyholder to the insurance company, and the policyholder retains a substantial portion of the related risks under most scenarios. Nevertheless, under certain finite contracts there may be a reasonable possibility that the insurance company will incur a loss on the contract.

.16 Insurance Risk Limiting Features

Inquiry—What types of insurance risk limiting features do finite insurance contracts normally contain?

Reply—Contractual features that serve to limit insurance risk transfer are found in both traditional and finite insurance contracts; however, the degree to which these features limit risk is relatively higher in finite insurance. All contractual provisions that limit risk transfer need to be considered when reviewing insurance contracts. Common features that may limit the transfer of insurance risk include:

- *Sliding scale fees and profit sharing formulae*. These features adjust cash flows between the policyholder and insurance company based on loss experience (for example, increasing payments from the insured enterprise as losses increase and decreasing payments as losses decrease, subject to maximum and minimum limits).
- *Experience refunds*. These arrangements allow the policyholder to share in the favorable experience of the underlying contracts by reference to an "experience account" that typically tracks premiums paid, less fees, less losses incurred, plus interest. Experience provisions also can require the policyholder to share in unfavorable experience by requiring additional payments to the insurer in the event that the experience account is negative.
- *Caps*. Caps are used to limit the insurer's aggregate exposure by imposing a dollar limit, or a limit expressed as a percentage of premiums paid, on the amount of claims to be paid by the insurer. For example, the insurer will not be responsible for losses beyond 150 percent of the premiums paid. While commercial insurance policies usually have limits on the amount of coverage provided, there may be significant risk mitigation for the insurer if the premium paid is a substantial percentage of the maximum coverage provided.
- *Loss Corridors*. This feature, which may exist in various forms, serves to eliminate or limit the risk of loss for a specified percentage or dollar

amount of claims within the contract coverage. For example, in a contract providing coverage for a policyholder's first $3,000,000 of losses, the insurer will pay the first million and last million of losses but will exclude the corridor from $1,000,000 to $2,000,000.

- *Dual-triggers*. This feature requires the occurrence of both an insurable event and changes in a separate pre-identified variable to trigger payment of a benefit/claim. An example is a policy entered into by a trucking company that insures costs associated with rerouting trucks over a certain time period if snowfall exceeds a specified level during that time period.
- *Retrospectively-Rated Premiums*. Such premiums are determined after the inception of the policy based on the loss experience under the policy.
- *Reinstatement Premiums*. To the extent the coverage provided by a contract is absorbed by losses incurred, the contract provides for the policyholder to reinstate coverage for the balance of the contract period for a stated additional premium. To the extent reinstatement is required rather than optional, the additional premium may mitigate risk to the insurer.
- *Termination Provisions*. These provisions can be structured to reduce the risk of the insurer, for example, by allowing for termination by the insurer at a discounted amount under certain circumstances.
- *Payment Schedules*. Features that delay timely reimbursement of losses by the insurer prevent the transfer of insurance risk.

There may be other features and provisions, in addition to the list of common insurance risk transfer limiting features in the preceding, that exist in a contract. Determining the appropriate accounting requires a full understanding of all of the features and provisions of the contract.

.17 Transfer of Insurance Risk

Inquiry—Why is transfer of insurance risk important under GAAP?

Reply—If a contract does not provide for the indemnification of the insured by the insurer, it is accounted for as a deposit (financing) rather than as insurance as noted in FASB ASC 720-20-25-1.

[Revised, June 2009, to reflect conforming changes necessary due to the issuance of FASB ASC.]

.18 Accounting Guidance for Transfer of Insurance Risk

Inquiry—What GAAP accounting literature provides guidance related to transfer of insurance risk?

Reply—The assessment of transfer of insurance risk requires significant judgment and a complete understanding of the insurance contract and other related contracts between the parties. The greater the number, or degree, or both, of insurance risk limiting features that exist in a contract, the more difficult it becomes to assess whether or not the insurance risk transferred is sufficient to permit the contract to be accounted for as insurance rather than as a deposit.

FASB ASC 720-20-25-1 provides the following guidance on insurance contracts that do not provide for indemnification of the insured by the insurer against loss or liability:

> To the extent that an insurance contract or reinsurance contract does not, despite its form, provide for indemnification of the insured or the ceding entity by the insurer or reinsurer against loss or liability, the premium paid less the amount of the premium to be retained by the insurer or reinsurer shall be accounted for as a deposit by the insured or the ceding entity. Those contracts may be structured in various ways, but if, regardless of form, their substance is that all or part of the premium paid by the insured or the ceding entity is a deposit, it shall be accounted for as such.

FASB ASC 944 establishes the conditions required for a contract between an insurer and a reinsurer to be accounted for as reinsurance and prescribes accounting and reporting standards for those contracts. FASB ASC 944-20-15-41 notes, in part, the following:

> Unless the condition in paragraph 944-20-15-53 is met, indemnification of the ceding entity against loss or liability relating to insurance risk in reinsurance of short-duration contracts exists under paragraph 944-20-15-37(a) only if both of the following conditions are met:
>
> *a.* Significant insurance risk. The reinsurer assumes significant insurance risk under the reinsured portions of the underlying insurance contracts. Implicit in this condition is the requirement that both the amount and timing of the reinsurer's payments depend on and directly vary with the amount and timing of claims settled under the reinsured contracts.
>
> *b.* Significant loss. It is reasonably possible that the reinsurer may realize a significant loss from the transaction.

FASB ASC 944 looks to the present value of all cash flows between the parties, however characterized, under reasonably possible outcomes in determining whether it is reasonably possible that the reinsurer may realize a significant loss from the contract.

FASB ASC 720-20-25-2 suggests that noninsurance entities look to the risk transfer guidance in FASB ASC 944, and states, in part, the following:

> Entities may find the conditions in Section 944-20-15 useful in assessing whether an insurance contract transfers risk.

FASB ASC 944-20-25-1 states that a multiple-year retrospectively rated insurance contract must indemnify the insured as required by FASB ASC 944-20-15-36 to be accounted for as insurance. FASB ASC 944-20 also indicates that there may be certain situations in which the guarantee accounting in accordance with FASB ASC 460, *Guarantees*, is applicable.

FASB ASC 815, *Derivatives and Hedging*, addresses scenarios where there are dual-triggers and includes a number of relevant examples.

[Revised, June 2009, to reflect conforming changes necessary due to the issuance of FASB ASC.]

.19 Differences Between Retroactive and Prospective Insurance

Inquiry—What are the differences between retroactive and prospective insurance?

Reply—FASB ASC 944-605-05-7 states that for property and casualty insurance: The distinction between prospective and retroactive reinsurance contracts is based on whether the contract reinsures future or past insured events covered by the underlying contracts.

[Revised, June 2009, to reflect conforming changes necessary due to the issuance of FASB ASC.]

.20 Accounting for Prospective Insurance

Inquiry—How does a noninsurance enterprise account for prospective insurance contracts that qualify for insurance accounting?

Reply—A noninsurance enterprise amortizes the premiums over the contract period in proportion to the amount of insurance protection provided. If an insured loss occurs, and if it is probable that the policy will provide reimbursement for the loss and the amount of the loss can be reasonably estimated, the noninsurance enterprise records a receivable from the insurance enterprise and a recovery of the incurred loss in the income statement. If it is not probable[1] that the policy will provide reimbursement, then the receivable and recovery are not recorded.

[Revised, June 2009, to reflect conforming changes necessary due to the issuance of FASB ASC.]

.21 Accounting for Retroactive Insurance

Inquiry—How does a noninsurance enterprise account for retroactive insurance contracts that qualify for insurance accounting?

Reply—Paragraphs 3–4 of FASB ASC 720-20-25 state the following:

> Notwithstanding that Topic 944 applies only to insurance entities, purchased retroactive insurance contracts that indemnify the insured shall be accounted for in a manner similar to the manner in which retroactive reinsurance contracts are accounted for under Subtopic 944-605. The guidance in that Subtopic shall be applied, as appropriate, based on the facts and circumstances of the particular transaction. That is, amounts paid for retroactive insurance shall be expensed immediately. Simultaneously, a receivable shall be established for the expected recoveries related to the underlying insured event.
>
> If the receivable established exceeds the amounts paid for the insurance, the resulting gain is deferred. Immediate gain recognition and liability derecognition are not appropriate because the liability has not been extinguished (the entity is not entirely relieved of its obligation). Additionally, the liability incurred as a result of a past insurable event and amounts receivable under the insurance contract do not meet the criteria for offsetting under paragraph 210-20-45-1.

FASB ASC 720-20-35-2 further states the following:

> If the amounts and timing of the insurance recoveries can be reasonably estimated, the deferred gain shall be amortized using the interest method over the estimated period over which the entity expects to recover substantially all amounts due under the terms of the insurance contract. If the amounts and timing of the insurance recoveries cannot be reasonably estimated, then the proportion of actual recoveries to total estimated recoveries shall be used to determine the amount of the amortization.

[1] According to the Financial Accounting Standards Board (FASB) *Accounting Standards Codification (ASC)* glossary, *probable* means that the future event or events are likely to occur.

Paragraphs 22–23 of FASB ASC 944-605-25 state the following:

> Amounts paid for retroactive reinsurance of short-duration contracts that meets the conditions for reinsurance accounting shall be reported as reinsurance receivables to the extent those amounts do not exceed the recorded liabilities relating to the underlying reinsured contracts. If the recorded liabilities exceed the amounts paid, reinsurance receivables shall be increased to reflect the difference and the resulting gain deferred.
>
> If the amounts paid for retroactive reinsurance for short-duration contracts exceed the recorded liabilities relating to the underlying reinsured short-duration contracts, the ceding entity shall increase the related liabilities or reduce the reinsurance receivable or both at the time the reinsurance contract is entered into, so that the excess is charged to earnings.

FASB ASC 944-605-35-9 further states the following:

> Any gain deferred under paragraph 944-605-25-22 shall be amortized over the estimated remaining settlement period. If the amounts and timing of the reinsurance recoveries can be reasonably estimated, the deferred gain shall be amortized using the effective interest rate inherent in the amount paid to the reinsurer and the estimated timing and amounts of recoveries from the reinsurer (the interest method). Otherwise, the proportion of actual recoveries (the recovery method) shall determine the amount of amortization.

[Revised, June 2009, to reflect conforming changes necessary due to the issuance of FASB ASC.]

.22 Accounting for Multiple-Year Retrospectively Rated Insurance

Inquiry—How does a noninsurance enterprise account for a multiple-year retrospectively rated insurance contract?

Reply—As noted in FASB ASC 720-20-05-10, multiple-year retrospectively rated contracts

> include a "retrospective rating" provision that provides for at least one of the following based on contract experience:
>
> *a.* Changes in the amount or timing of future contractual cash flows, including premium adjustments, settlement adjustments, or refunds to the noninsurance entity
>
> *b.* Changes in the contract's future coverage

FASB ASC 720-20-05-9 also states, in part:

> A critical feature of these contracts is that part or all of the retrospective rating provision is obligatory such that the retrospective rating provision creates for each party to the contract future rights and obligations as a result of past events.

FASB ASC 944-20-25-2 also discusses the accounting for retrospective adjustments and states:

> For a multiple-year retrospectively rated insurance contract accounted for as insurance, the insurer shall both:

a. Recognize an asset to the extent that the insured has an obligation to pay cash (or other consideration) to the insurer that would not have been required absent experience under the contract

b. Recognize a liability to the extent that any cash (or other consideration) would be payable by the insurer to the insured based on experience to date under the contract.

Paragraphs 3–4 of FASB ASC 944-20-35 further state:

> The amount recognized under paragraph 944-20-25-4 in the current period shall be computed, using a with-and-without method, as the difference between the ceding entity's total contract costs before and after the experience under the contract as of the reporting date, including costs such as premium adjustments, settlement adjustments, and impairments of coverage.
>
> The amount of premium expense related to impairments of coverage shall be measured in relation to the original contract terms. Future experience under the contract (that is, future losses and future premiums that would be paid regardless of past experience) shall not be considered in measuring the amount to be recognized.

FASB ASC 944-20-25-4 also further states:

> For contracts that meet all of the conditions described in paragraph 944-20-15-55:
>
> *a.* The ceding entity shall recognize a liability and the assuming entity shall recognize an asset to the extent that the ceding entity has an obligation to pay cash (or other consideration) to the reinsurer that would not have been required absent experience under the contract (for example, payments that would not have been required if losses had not been experienced).
>
> *b.* The ceding entity shall recognize an asset and the assuming entity shall recognize a liability to the extent that any cash (or other consideration) would be payable from the assuming entity to the ceding entity based on experience to date under the contract.

[Revised, June 2009, to reflect conforming changes necessary due to the issuance of FASB ASC.]

.23 Deposit Accounting

Inquiry—What is deposit accounting?

Reply—Deposit accounting essentially treats the contract as a financing transaction similar to a loan taking into account the time value of money. FASB ASC 340 provides guidance on how to account for insurance and reinsurance contracts that do not transfer insurance risk.

[Revised, June 2009, to reflect conforming changes necessary due to the issuance of FASB ASC.]

.24 Identifying Accounting Model for Insurance Transactions

The accompanying chart depicts the basic decision process in identifying the appropriate accounting model for insurance transactions.

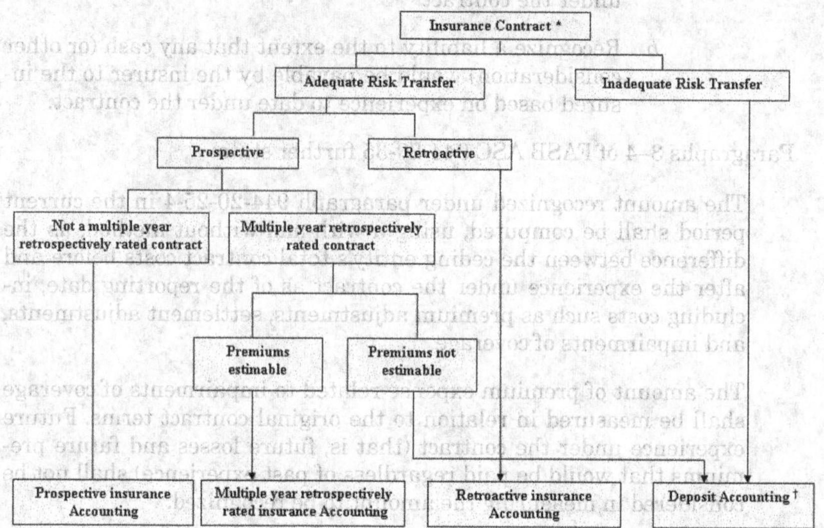

* The insurance model discussed in this series of technical practice aids is based on property and casualty and other short-duration contracts, as defined in Financial Accounting Standards Board (FASB) *Accounting Standards Codification* (ASC) 944, *Financial Services—Insurance*.

† FASB ASC 944-20 should also be considered in determining the accounting for multiple-year retrospectively rated contracts that do not transfer risk.

[Revised, June 2009, to reflect conforming changes necessary due to the issuance of FASB ASC.]

.25 Integrated/Nonintegrated Contract Features in Applying FASB ASC 944-30

Inquiry—If there are contract features that do not meet the definition of nonintegrated contract features contained in the FASB ASC glossary, how should the contract features be evaluated under FASB ASC 944-30?

Reply—The flowchart in FASB ASC 944-30-55-11, titled "Summary of Internal Replacement Transactions Accounting Model," asks the question, "Does the contract modification involve the addition of or changes to a nonintegrated contract feature?" If the answer is *Yes*, the nonintegrated contract feature is evaluated separately from the base contract. All other modifications need to be evaluated to determine if the contract modification results in a substantially changed replacement contract in accordance with the criteria in FASB ASC 944-30-35-37.

When applying the guidance in FASB ASC 944-30 to determine whether a feature is integrated or nonintegrated, one indicator of a nonintegrated contract feature is that it is distinguishable as a separate component from the base contract.

[Revised, June 2009, to reflect conforming changes necessary due to the issuance of FASB ASC.]

.26 Evaluation of Significance of Modification in Applying FASB ASC 944-30

Inquiry—When analyzing a contract feature under FASB ASC 944-30-35-37(a), how should the significance of the change in the degree of mortality risk, morbidity risk, or other insurance risk be determined?

Reply—In assessing the significance of a change in the degree of mortality, morbidity, or other insurance risk, the insurance enterprise should consider the specific facts and circumstances of the modification as well as which approach or approaches it considers most appropriate to analyze the substance of the change. It is the substance of the contract between the insurance enterprise and the contract holder that is to be evaluated, and not just the economics to the insurance enterprise that is critical to determining whether an internal replacement results in a substantially changed contract.

FASB ASC 944-30 does not require any one specific approach for analyzing the significance of a change in insurance risk; rather, it provides examples of several approaches that may be used in assessing changes in the degree of insurance risk. Factors to consider in determining whether there are significant changes in insurance risks may include changes in actuarially estimated costs for that benefit feature (for example, changes in the death benefit provided) or, alternatively, changes in the FASB ASC 944 benefit ratio related to that benefit feature (for example, giving consideration to the change in the relationship between the actuarially estimated future costs of the benefit feature and estimated total future fees to be charged for the contract). Another example of assessing the significance of a change for a universal life contract is by comparing the change in the relationship between the expected cost of the benefit and the charges for the benefit. Another potential comparison would be the change in the net amount at risk before and after the modification. Reunderwriting an entire contract generally would indicate a significant change in the kind or degree of insurance risk.

Different approaches utilized to assess the significance of a change in the degree of mortality, morbidity, or other insurance risk could result in different conclusions. Therefore, it may be necessary to consider multiple approaches to evaluate the significance of a change. For example, a change from a 20-pay life insurance contract to a 10-pay life insurance contract, where the two premiums are determined to be actuarially equivalent amounts, is an internal replacement that may or may not result in the replacement contract being determined to be substantially changed from the replaced contract. Using actuarially estimated cost before and after the modification would not result in a significant change (for example, the death benefit remains the same, only the premium payment period is changing). Comparing the relationship of the present value of estimated cost and the present value of the actuarially equivalent premiums also would not result in a significant change. However, if one used the net amount at risk as the basis for comparison, the change could be considered significant, given that the net amount at risk would differ for contracts with different premium collection periods.

While all these approaches, and perhaps others, would be appropriate in analyzing the significance of the change in this specific example, not all of these approaches would be appropriate in all circumstances. Any approach utilized should consider the substance of the change between the insurance enterprise and the contract holder. For instance, a minimum guaranteed death benefit (MGDB) is essentially a combination of mortality and investment risk and, therefore, it generally would not be appropriate to analyze the change in a MGDB based on a comparison of net expected cost (expected costs net of expected charges for the MGDB benefit) or the change in the relationship between the expected cost and charges for the MGDB benefit due to the interaction of the mortality and investment risk.

The approach or approaches determined to be appropriate to evaluate the substance of a change should be applied consistently in analyzing similar types of modifications for similar contracts.

[Revised, June 2009, to reflect conforming changes necessary due to the issuance of FASB ASC.]

.27 Changes in Investment Management Fees and Other Administrative Charges in Applying FASB ASC 944-30

Inquiry—How should changes in investment management fees and other administrative charges be evaluated under the guidance in FASB ASC 944-30?

Reply—Changes in accordance with terms and within ranges specified in the contract, without any other change in benefits or coverages, are not modifications to the contract.

Changes in investment management fees and charges that are not in accordance with terms specified in the contract should be evaluated under the guidance in FASB ASC 944-30-35-37(b) based on the substance of the fees and consider whether the change in fees is significant in the context of the overall investment return rights. Changes in the structure of investment management fees and charges (for example, between flat fee, sliding scale, or percentage of assets), whether made by the insurance entity or investment advisor, may or may not result in a significant change to the nature of investment return rights.

[Revised, June 2009, to reflect conforming changes necessary due to the issuance of FASB ASC.]

.28 Definition of Reunderwriting for Purposes of Applying FASB ASC 944-30

Inquiry—Is the performance of limited examination procedures in conjunction with the election of a benefit, feature, right, or coverage by the contract holder considered underwriting or reunderwriting as contemplated by FASB ASC 944-30-35-26(b)?

Reply—It depends. The performance of examination procedures with respect to specific risks or components of a contract would not represent underwriting or reunderwriting as long as the procedures are limited in nature and do not involve judgment or discretion with respect to acceptance or price. For example, examination procedures undertaken to confirm data used to calculate benefit amounts, such as the income verification procedures undertaken as part of a benefit step-up in a disability policy, or to gather information to verify representations made by the contract holder with respect to the election being made, such as limited procedures to validate an insured's claim of currently being a nonsmoker, would not be considered underwriting or reunderwriting.

The lack of underwriting is not, by itself, determinative that an election is not a modification or that a change is not substantial. The election should be evaluated against the other conditions of FASB ASC 944-30.

[Revised, June 2009, to reflect conforming changes necessary due to the issuance of FASB ASC.]

.29 Contract Reinstatements in Applying FASB ASC 944-30

Inquiry—How should insurance enterprises apply the guidance in FASB ASC 944-30 to contract reinstatements?

Reply—If an insurance enterprise determines it has no further obligation to pay claims due to the lapse of a contract, the related contract would be considered extinguished. If the insurance contract is later reinstated, it would be accounted for as a newly issued contract in the period in which the reinstatement occurs. Unamortized deferred acquisition costs, unearned revenue liabilities, and deferred sales inducement assets related to the terminated contract should not be reestablished in connection with the newly issued contract.

[Revised, June 2009, to reflect conforming changes necessary due to the issuance of FASB ASC.]

.30 Commissions Paid on an Increase in Insurance Coverage or Incremental Deposits in Applying FASB ASC 944-30

Inquiry—Should additional commissions incurred on either an increase in insurance coverage or incremental deposits not provided for in the replaced contract, related to a contract modification determined to result in a substantially unchanged replacement contract under FASB ASC 944-30, be accounted for as maintenance costs?

Reply—No. If commissions are paid on either an increase in insurance coverage or incremental deposit, not previously provided for in the contract, related to a contract modification determined to result in a substantially unchanged replacement contract, the commissions should be accounted for as acquisition costs in accordance with the provisions of FASB ASC 944, as appropriate.

For example, an increase in face amount of a universal life-type contract results in a replacement contract that is determined to be substantially unchanged. The modification is an integrated feature because the universal life-type contract has only a single account value and the death benefit is the excess of face amount over account value. In this situation, the commission incurred on what is essentially the sale of new insurance coverage should not be considered maintenance expense, but rather should be accounted for as acquisition costs in accordance with the provisions of FASB ASC 944. The substance of the modification in this example is the sale of additional insurance.

[Revised, June 2009, to reflect conforming changes necessary due to the issuance of FASB ASC.]

.31 Participating Dividends and the Interaction of Guidance in FASB ASC 944

Inquiry—How are paid up additions funded by dividends on participating policies evaluated under FASB ASC 944-30, and what is the impact on estimated gross margins?

Reply—Paid up additions funded by dividends on participating policies that meet the conditions of FASB ASC 944-30-35-26 would not be considered internal replacements subject to the guidance in FASB ASC 944-30. Paid up additions that do not meet the conditions of FASB ASC 944-30-35-26 would be considered nonintegrated contract features under FASB ASC 944-30.

For paid up additions that do not meet the conditions of FASB ASC 944-30-35-26, FASB ASC 944 addresses the accounting and the impact of various dividend options, including paid up additions, on estimated gross margins. Under FASB ASC 944-30-35-15, the estimated gross margins should include an insurance company's best estimate of the dividend options that policyholders will elect, which would include the option to use dividends to fund paid up additions. FASB ASC 944-30 does not amend or affect that guidance in FASB ASC 944.

[Revised, June 2009, to reflect conforming changes necessary due to the issuance of FASB ASC.]

.32 Premium Changes to Long Duration Contracts in Applying FASB ASC 944-30

Inquiry—Are changes in premiums to long-duration insurance contracts for which the insurer has the right to make changes in premium rates considered modifications as contemplated in FASB ASC 944-30?

Reply—It depends.

FASB ASC 944-20-55-5 states:

> . . . individual and group insurance contracts that are . . . guaranteed renewable (renewable at the option of the insured), or collectively renewable (individual contracts within a group are not cancelable), ordinarily are long-duration contracts.

The AICPA Audit and Accounting Guide *Life and Health Insurance Entities* defines a guaranteed renewable contract as:

> An insurance contract whereby the insured has the right to continue in force by the timely payment of premiums for a period that coincides approximately with the average working lifetime (for federal income tax purposes at least until age sixty), with the right reserved by the insurer to make changes in premium rates by classes.

The right to adjust premium rates for group long-duration insurance contracts generally would not meet the characteristics of a modification under FASB ASC 944-30 as long as all of the following conditions are met:

- The right to adjust premium rates is provided for under the terms of the insurance contract,
- The change to premium rates for a contract holder is the same change in premium rates that is applicable to the entire class of contract holders,
- Changes to premium rates do not involve consideration by the insurer of specific experience of the contract holder, and
- No other changes in benefits or coverages occur.

Further, the determination of rates based on a formula specified within the contract that does not involve insurer discretion would not be considered a modification as contemplated under FASB ASC 944-30.

Changes to a contract that involve the adjustment of rates or benefits based on a judgmental review of actual experience of the contract holder or the renegotiation of rates or benefits with that contract holder, even if no reunderwriting has occurred, generally would be considered a modification that is subject to the guidance in FASB ASC 944-30.

[Revised, June 2009, to reflect conforming changes necessary due to the issuance of FASB ASC.]

.33 Evaluation of Changes Under FASB ASC 944-30-35-37(a)

Inquiry—How should changes in the period of coverage or insured risk under FASB ASC 944-30-35-37(a) be evaluated?

Reply—A change in the period of coverage should be evaluated based on a comparison of the remaining period of coverage of the replaced contract to the remaining period of coverage of the replacement contract when assessing the significance of that change. Similarly, when determining whether there are significant changes in insurance risk under FASB ASC 944-30-35-37(a) the evaluation should be based on a comparison of the remaining insurance coverage of the replaced contract to the remaining insurance coverage of the replacement contract.

[Revised, June 2009, to reflect conforming changes necessary due to the issuance of FASB ASC.]

.34 Nature of Investment Return Rights in FASB ASC 944-30-35-37(b)

Inquiry—What constitutes the *nature of the investment return rights* in FASB ASC 944-30-35-37(b)?

Reply—The phrase *nature of the investment return rights* encompasses the manner in which the contract's investment return is determined. For pass-through contracts, the addition of a floor or the capping of the returns, such that actual returns (net of fees and charges) are not passed through to the policyholder, fundamentally changes the nature of the investment return rights.

If the contract is referenced to a pool of assets or otherwise indexed (for example, S&P 500 or LIBOR), the underlying referenced pool of assets or index is an inherent component of the nature of investment return rights, and changes in these provisions would result in a change to the nature of investment return rights between the insurance enterprise and the contract holder under FASB ASC 944-30-35-37(b). This differs from a contract holder reallocation of funds among multiple investment alternatives provided for in the contract in which the investment performance of the investments passes through to the contract holder.

Contract holder liquidity rights related to investment guarantees (for example, variable annuity guaranteed minimum accumulation benefits, guaranteed minimum income benefits, and guaranteed minimum withdrawal benefits) are inherent components of the nature of investment return rights, and the addition of a different investment guarantee with substantively different timing of cash flow accessibility to the contract holder would result in a change to the nature of investment return rights between the insurance enterprise and the contract holder under FASB ASC 944-30-35-37(b).

Changes to a component (or components) of an investment return formula (for example, the strike price of the guarantee for a variable annuity with a guaranteed minimum accumulation benefit or other modification to an existing investment guarantee) should be evaluated in a manner similar to changes in minimum guarantees for contracts subject to periodic discretionary declaration.

[Revised, June 2009, to reflect conforming changes necessary due to the issuance of FASB ASC.]

[.35] Reserved

.36 Prospective Unlocking

Inquiry—Certain insurance contracts classified as long-duration insurance contracts under FASB ASC 944, may include provisions that allow for premium rate increases by class of customer, subject to regulatory approval. Policies with these provisions may include long-term care, Medicare supplements, and certain other guaranteed renewable contracts.

Is an insurance company permitted to "unlock" its original FASB ASC 944 assumptions after contract inception for collected, approved, or expected premium rate increases for the contracts previously described in situations other than in premium deficiency?

Reply—No, FASB ASC 944 policyholder benefit liability assumptions cannot be unlocked for collected, approved, or expected premium rate increases for the contracts described in situations other than in the premium deficiency situations described in paragraphs 7–9 of FASB ASC 944-60-25.

FASB ASC 944 requires that best estimate assumptions (with a provision for adverse deviation) be determined at contract inception and used to calculate the long duration policy benefit liability. Paragraphs 5–6 of FASB ASC 944-40-35 state the following:

> Original assumptions shall continue to be used in subsequent accounting periods to determine changes in the liability for future policy benefits (often referred to as the lock-in concept) unless a premium deficiency exists subject to paragraphs 944-60-25-7 through 25-9.
>
> Changes in the liability for future policy benefits that result from its periodic estimation for financial reporting purposes shall be recognized in income in the period in which the changes occur.

FASB ASC 944-60-25-7 describes the premium deficiency situations that can exist. As FASB ASC 944-60-30-1 describes, the first situation occurs when the present value of future payments for benefits and related expenses less the present value of future gross premiums (both determined using revised assumptions based on actual and expected experience) exceed the existing liability for future policy benefits reduced by unamortized acquisition costs. As FASB ASC 944-60-25-9 describes, a premium deficiency can also exist when the liability on a particular line of business is not deficient in the aggregate, but circumstances are such that profits would be recognized in early years and losses in later years.

[Issue Date: December 2008; Revised, June 2009, to reflect conforming changes necessary due to the issuance of FASB ASC.]

.37 Application of Accounting Standards Update No. 2010-26, *Financial Services—Insurance (Topic 944): Accounting for Costs Associated with Acquiring or Renewing Insurance Contracts (a consensus of the FASB Emerging Issues Task Force)*

Inquiry—How should Accounting Standards Update (ASU) No. 2010-26, *Financial Services—Insurance (Topic 944): Accounting for Costs Associated with Acquiring or Renewing Insurance Contracts (a consensus of the FASB Emerging Issues Task Force)*, be applied?

Reply—The application of ASU No. 2010-26 will be based on an election of the entity and could be applied in either of the following ways:

a. Prospectively

b. Retrospectively, as described in FASB ASC 250-10

If an entity decides to retrospectively apply, paragraph BC16 of ASU No. 2010-26 discusses that the task force did not believe that an entity is necessarily expected to reperform its detailed capitalization, amortization, and premium deficiency calculations for every prior year that is restated. Specifically, paragraph BC16 states that the

> Task Force members stated that an entity may need to make reasonable estimates of the effect on prior years on the basis of its specific circumstances in order to adopt the amendments retrospectively. In electing retrospective application, the Task Force did not believe that

an entity is necessarily expected to reperform its detailed capitalization, amortization, and premium deficiency calculations for every prior year if it has ways to reasonably estimate those amounts in accordance with Subtopic 250-10, *Accounting Changes and Error Corrections—Overall*.

[Issue Date: July 2011.]

.38 Retrospective Application of ASU No. 2010-26

Inquiry—If different levels of historical information are available for various products, how should this information be included when retrospectively applying ASU No. 2010-26? Can ASU No. 2010-26 be applied retrospectively to different points in time for various products?

Reply—If the entity has determined that it is impracticable to determine the cumulative effect of applying a change in accounting principle to all prior periods (as discussed in paragraphs 5–7 of FASB ASC 250-10-45) for all contracts subject to ASU No. 2010-26 and is applying the new accounting principle as if the change was made prospectively as of the earliest date practicable (in accordance with FASB ASC 250-10), the effect of applying a change in accounting principle for deferral of acquisition costs should be applied at a single point in time to contracts that were entered into from the point of retrospective application and forward.

Determining the earliest practicable date of retrospective application of ASU No. 2010-26 is a matter of judgment. Accordingly, the entity will need to make a determination, based on individual facts and circumstances, about what single point in time to use as a starting point for retrospective application for all products. The guidance on reporting a change in accounting principle made in an interim period in FASB ASC 250-10-45-14 should also be considered.

The entity will adopt the deferral guidance in ASU No. 2010-26 for contracts entered into from the date of retrospective application and forward. Therefore, the acquisition costs that were previously deferred relating to periods prior to the date of retrospective application will be based upon the previous applicable guidance under FASB ASC 944-30 for deferral of acquisition costs. It is recommended that the entity disclose the types of costs deferred under ASU No. 2010-26 and whether differences exist in the costs deferred under the previous guidance of FASB ASC 944-30 and ASU No. 2010-26.

For example, an insurance entity only sells product A and product B, and they are both material to the entity for all prior periods. For product A, the entity has sufficient information going back three years; however, for product B, the entity has sufficient information going back seven years. In this example, the entity would be limited to three years of retrospective application (that is, the earliest date practicable) of ASU No. 2010-26, and all years prior to the three years that would be retrospectively adjusted would continue to follow the previous accounting policy used to defer acquisition costs.

The guidance in ASU No. 2010-26 does not change the required amortization methods for acquisition costs that are deferrable; therefore, all deferrable cost will be amortized in the same manner, notwithstanding that the types of cost deferred for certain periods may be different. However, ASU No. 2010-26 requires that advertising costs that meet the capitalization criteria for direct-response advertising in FASB ASC 340-20 should be included in deferred acquisition costs and amortized in the same manner as all other deferred acquisition costs.

[Issue Date: July 2011.]

.39 Cumulative Effect of Change in Accounting Principle—ASU No. 2010-26

Inquiry—If an entity is retrospectively applying the guidance in ASU No. 2010-26, what effects of a change in accounting principle should be included in the cumulative effect?

Reply—As stated in FASB ASC 250-10-45-8:

> Retrospective application shall include only the direct effects of a change in accounting principle, including any related income tax effects. Indirect effects that would have been recognized if the newly adopted accounting principle had been followed in prior periods shall not be included in the retrospective application. If indirect effects are actually incurred and recognized, they shall be reported in the period in which the accounting change is made.

In addition to the impact on deferrals and amortization of acquisition costs, including any impact to income taxes, the following are some items to consider when evaluating the direct effects of retrospective application of ASU No. 2010-26:

- *Premium deficiency (loss recognition).* If a premium deficiency was recognized in prior financial statements, an entity should determine whether the amount of the premium deficiency loss that was recognized would change if deferred acquisition costs had been measured based on the guidance in ASU No. 2010-26. In those situations when the application of this accounting change results in additional acquisition costs being deferred in prior periods, entities should evaluate whether a premium deficiency is needed based on the revised DAC amount.
- *Shadow accounts.* Adjustments made to DAC as a result of ASU No. 2010-26 may also require adjustments to shadow DAC[2] or shadow premium deficiency amounts.
- *Limited payment contracts.* For limited pay contracts, the calculation of deferred profit liability includes capitalizable acquisition costs.[3] Therefore, changes in the amount of DAC due to the adoption of ASU No. 2010-26 will result in changes to the deferred profit liability.
- *Equity method investee that is an insurance entity.* The amount recognized relating to an equity method investment in an insurance entity may be affected by an investee's retrospective adoption of ASU No. 2010-26.

---

[2] As discussed in FASB ASC 320-10-S99-2:

> [A]sset amounts that are amortized using the gross-profits method, such as deferred acquisition costs accounted for under FASB ASC 944-30-35-4 and certain intangible assets arising from insurance contracts acquired in business combinations, should be adjusted to reflect the effects that would have been recognized had the unrealized holding gains and losses actually been realized.
>
> Also, loss recognition assessments due to the impact of unrealized gains or losses may need to be adjusted to reflect the revised deferred cost. These adjustments, due to the unrealized investment gains and losses, are commonly referred to in practice as *shadow deferred acquisition cost* or *shadow premium deficiency adjustments*.

[3] As discussed in paragraph 9 of FASB ASC 944-30-25, capitalizable acquisition costs should be included in the calculation of net premiums and for purposes of determining the deferred profit for limited payment contracts.

- *Noncontrolling interest of an insurance subsidiary.* The noncontrolling interest balance should be adjusted to reflect the adoption of ASU No. 2010-26 to the extent that the noncontrolling interest relates to an entity with DAC.
- *Divested operations.* Adjustments made to DAC of a divested entity may affect a gain or loss previously recorded on the sale of an insurance entity, as well as the amounts reported in the financial statements prior to sale (for example, assets and liabilities held for sale, income (loss) from discontinued operations).
- *Reinsurance.* Adjustments made to DAC due to the adoption of ASU No. 2010-26 may also require adjustments to amounts related to reinsurance transactions involving long duration reinsurance contracts.[4]
- *Foreign exchange.* Entities that conduct business in multiple currencies should consider the impact of ASU No. 2010-26 on foreign exchange translation adjustments, as well as foreign exchange transactions (for example, the remeasurement of DAC from nonfunctional currency to functional currency).[5]

[Issue Date: October 2012.]

.40 Deferrable Commissions and Bonuses Under ASU No. 2010-26

Inquiry—Under the guidance of ASU No. 2010-26, are all commissions and bonuses deferrable?

Reply—Commissions and bonuses are not deferrable solely due to an insurance entity having a sales transaction. To be deferrable as an incremental direct acquisition cost, the costs must result directly from, and be essential to, the sales transaction(s) and would not have been incurred by the insurance entity had the sales transaction(s) not occurred.

Entities will need to use judgment to determine whether acquisition costs related to commissions and bonuses for employees or nonemployees meet the criterion to be deferrable under ASU No. 2010-26 of resulting directly from, and being essential to, the sale transaction.

FASB ASC 944-30-55-1F and 944-30-55-1G provide examples of some of the types of activities for which related costs are deferrable and those that are not. Chapter 10, "Commissions, General Expenses, and Deferred Acquisition Costs," of the AICPA Audit and Accounting Guide *Life and Health Insurance Entities* contains discussion of the guidance in ASU No. 2010-26.

[Issue Date: October 2012.]

---

[4] FASB ASC 944-30-35-64 provides that "proceeds from reinsurance transactions that represent recovery of acquisition costs shall reduce applicable unamortized acquisition costs in such a manner that net acquisition costs are capitalized and charged to expense in proportion to net revenue recognized." The remainder is deferred and amortized as part of the estimated cost of reinsurance under FASB ASC 944-605-30-4. Changes to deferrable amounts will, therefore, affect the estimated cost of reinsurance.

[5] FASB ASC 830-10-45-18 describes nonmonetary items as being "[o]ther intangible assets, deferred charges and credits, except policy acquisition costs for life insurance companies," thus, requiring that in remeasurements to functional currency, capitalized acquisition costs of life insurance companies should be accounted for as if they were monetary. FASB ASC 255-10-55-1 notes that deferred property and casualty insurance policy acquisition costs related to unearned premiums should be accounted for as nonmonetary items.

Q&A Section 6400

Health Care Entities

[.01] Reserved

[.02] Reserved

[.03] Reserved

.04 Hospital as Collecting Agent for Physicians [Amended]

Inquiry—Under an agreement with several physicians, a hospital acts as collecting agent for the physicians' fees, and the physicians, in return, provide professional services at the hospital. These physicians are not employees; payroll taxes are not paid for them, and the hospital cannot exercise any of the prerogatives of an employer. To enable it to collect the physicians' Medicare fees, the hospital holds valid assignments. Should the amounts collected as physicians' fees be included in the income and expenses of the provider hospital?

Reply—No. As discussed in Financial Accounting Standards Board (FASB) *Accounting Standards Codification* (ASC) 954-305-45-4, health care entities may receive and hold assets owned by others under agency relationships; for example, they may perform billing and collection services for physicians. In accepting responsibility for those assets, an entity incurs a liability to the principal under the agency relationship to return the assets in the future. In the preceding example, the hospital is functioning as a conduit with respect to the physicians' fees. As a result, the fees should be reported as a liability to the physicians and not recognized in the statement of revenues and expenses. Agency funds are reported as unrestricted assets.

[Amended, September 1997; Revised, June 2009, to reflect conforming changes necessary due to the issuance of FASB ASC.]

[.05] Reserved

[.06] Reserved

[.07] Reserved

[.08] Reserved

[.09] Reserved

[.10] Reserved

[.11] Reserved

.12 General Obligation Bonds Issued for Current Use by City Owned Hospital [Amended]

Inquiry—A hospital is a city municipal enterprise. The city council issued general obligation bonds to provide funds for the hospital's operations, without restriction. The hospital's assets will not be used to pay principal or interest on the bonds. Should the general obligation bond liability be reported in the hospital's financial statements?

Reply—No. FASB ASC 954-470-25-1 states that if a health care entity has no obligation to make payments of principal and interest on the debt, the entity should not reflect the liability on its balance sheet. The proceeds from the bond issue are contributions from the city. Therefore, the hospital should not report the bonds as a liability in its financial statements.

[Amended, September 1997; Revised, June 2009, to reflect conforming changes necessary due to the issuance of FASB ASC.]

[.13] Reserved

[.14] Reserved

[.15] Reserved

[.16] Reserved

.17 Elimination of Profit on Intercompany Sales

Inquiry—FASB ASC 810-10-45-1 addresses the elimination of intercompany profit or loss on assets remaining within a combined or consolidated group. FASB ASC 980-810-45-1 indicates the following with regard to intercompany profit:

> Profit on sales to regulated affiliates shall not be eliminated in general-purpose financial statements if both of the following criteria are met:
>
> *a.* The sales price is reasonable.
>
> *b.* It is probable that, through the rate-making process, future revenue approximately equal to the sales price will result from the regulated affiliate's use of the products.

Because health care providers are, in certain cases, reimbursed for operating costs, it is possible that, assuming they meet certain related party tests under third-party regulations, an entity could receive reimbursement on intercompany sales that include a profit. Thus, one could argue that under that circumstance, it would not be appropriate to eliminate profit on intercompany sales using the criteria set forth in FASB ASC 980, *Regulated Operations*.

Reply—In some instances health care entities may encounter situations where they fall under FASB ASC 980-10-15-2. Generally, however, as explained in FASB ASC 980-10-15-7, the normal Medicare and Medicaid arrangements are excluded from the scope of FASB ASC 980 on the basis that the "regulator" is also a party to the contract. Accordingly, gains or losses on sale of assets within the group should be eliminated in combined or consolidated financial statements. However, these gains or losses would be recognized and disclosed as appropriate in the separate financial statements of the members of the group.

[Revised, June 2009, to reflect conforming changes necessary due to the issuance of FASB ASC.]

[.18] Reserved

.19 Offsetting of Limited Use Assets

Inquiry—Can limited-use assets of one entity be offset against the related liability of another entity in combined or consolidated financial statements?

Reply—Unless a *right of setoff* exists as defined in the FASB ASC glossary, assets, in general, should not be offset against related liabilities in any financial statement presentation.

[Amended; Revised, June 2009, to reflect conforming changes necessary due to the issuance of FASB ASC.]

.20 Format of Combined or Consolidated Financial Statements

Inquiry—When presenting combined or consolidated financial statements of various health care entities, is there a prescribed or recommended presentation format?

Reply—No. The sample financial statements contained in FASB ASC 954, *Health Care Entities*, do not prescribe the format of statements. In addition, no single format for combined or consolidated financial statements has been considered appropriate in all circumstances.

[Revised, June 2009, to reflect conforming changes necessary due to the issuance of FASB ASC.]

[.21] Reserved

[.22] Reserved

[.23] Reserved

[.24] Reserved

.25 Accounting for Transfer of Assets From Not-for-Profit to For-Profit Entities

Inquiry—How should subsequent transfers of assets, evidenced as additional investment, from not-for-profit entities to for-profit entities be accounted for by the transferee and transferor?

Reply—Additional investments in for-profit entities (subsequent to the original transfer of assets) should be reflected by the transferee as an increase in capital stock or paid-in capital, or both. The transferor would record a corresponding increase in its investment account in the for-profit entity, if a financial interest was received (for example, additional capital stock).

.26 Transfer of Assets From Subsidiary For-Profit Entity to Not-for-Profit Stockholder Parent

Inquiry—How should transfers of assets from a "subsidiary" for-profit entity (F) to a not-for-profit entity (N) that is a minority stockholder of F be recorded?

Reply—This transaction would generally be recorded as a dividend, which would be reported as a reduction in F's retained earnings. Any dividend in excess of retained earnings is a "liquidating" dividend; as such, it would be reported as a reduction in F's paid-in capital account. If N accounts for its investment in F using the equity method, then the not-for-profit entity would report all dividends received as a reduction of its investment account, in accordance with FASB ASC 323, *Investments—Equity Method and Joint Ventures*. If N's investment in F is accounted for using the cost method, because the conditions for applying the equity method are not met, the dividends would be reported as income.

[Revised, June 2009, to reflect conforming changes necessary due to the issuance of FASB ASC.]

[.27] Reserved

[.28] Reserved

.29 Timing of Recording Transfers Between Related Entities

Inquiry—When should a transfer of assets between related entities be recorded—only when the transfer is actually made, or at some earlier point?

Reply—In most situations, transfers should be recorded at the time they are formally obligated to occur (formal board resolutions, legal notes, passage of title to real estate, and so on). This would be the case when each of the entities have independent governance, and the timing of the transfer is controlled by the governing board of the transferor. Yet, in situations where there is clear, common control of the related entities, it would be appropriate to record transfers at the time when both (*a*) the transfer amount is known and (*b*) the receiving entity is given control over the timing of the transfer.

.30 Accounting for Transactions Involving Medicaid Voluntary Contribution or Taxation Programs [Amended]

Inquiry—The Medicaid program is set up on a state-by-state basis to provide medical assistance to the indigent. Although state-administered, the program is actually a joint federal and state program for which the federal government picks up a portion of the cost. Under this arrangement, the federal government "matches" a percentage of the total amount paid by the state to health care providers. This matching is referred to as federal financial participation.

States have attempted to increase the amount of federal matching funds for which they are eligible by increasing the amount of medical assistance they provide. In order to pay for the increased medical assistance, some states have imposed a tax on health care entities, sought donations or other voluntary payments from them, or both. As a result, the states have been able to generate additional federal matching funds without expending additional state funds. How should a health care entity account for these taxes or donations made to the state?

Reply—Congress has passed legislation prohibiting the use of health care entity taxes or donations except in limited situations.

The accounting for these types of programs is dependent on the individual facts and circumstances. For example, if there is a guarantee that specific monies given to the state by the health care entity will be 'returned' to the entity from the state, those amounts should be recorded as receivables. In addition, if the health care entity has met all requirements to be legally entitled to additional funds from the state, the revenue/gain should be recognized.

However, if the monies go into a pool with other contributions which are then disbursed based on factors over which the health care entity has little or no control, the payments should be recognized as an expense. Any subsequent reimbursements would be recognized as revenue/gain when the provider is entitled to them and payment is assured.

Care should be taken to avoid delayed recognition of expenses or to improperly recognize contingent gains. Because of complexities involved, it may be necessary to consult with legal counsel.

[Revised, June 2009, to reflect conforming changes necessary due to the issuance of FASB ASC.]

[.31] Reserved

[.32] Reserved

.33 Accounting for a Joint Operating Agreement

Inquiry—Two not-for-profit health care systems enter into a Joint Operating Agreement whereby both (the Venturers) agree to jointly operate and control certain of their hospitals while sharing in the operating results and residual interest upon dissolution based upon an agreed-upon ratio. Neither of the Venturers receives cash or other monetary assets as part of entering into the Agreement. How should the Venturers account for the Agreement?

Reply—Joint Operating Agreements are similar to joint ventures and typically are characterized by factors such as:

- Common purpose (for example, to share risks and rewards; to develop a new market, health service or program; to pool resources)
- Joint funding: all parties contribute resources toward its accomplishment
- Defined relationship: typically governed by an agreement
- Joint control: control is not derived from holding a majority of the voting interest

Even though the Agreement does not provide for a separate legal entity (such as a corporation or partnership), the same principles apply. For example, because there is joint control (that is, neither party controls the venture), consolidation would not be appropriate. Instead, such agreements should be accounted for similar to a corporate joint venture using the equity method of accounting (see FASB ASC 323). Because the transaction did not reflect the culmination of the earnings process, the Venturers' basis in the investment would be recorded at net book value.

[Revised, June 2009, to reflect conforming changes necessary due to the issuance of FASB ASC.]

.34 Accounting for Computer Systems Costs Incurred in Connection With the Health Insurance Portability and Accountability Act of 1996 (HIPAA)

Inquiry—The Health Insurance Portability and Accountability Act of 1996 (HIPAA) was enacted by the federal government with the intent to assure health insurance portability, improve the efficiency and effectiveness of the health care system, reduce health care fraud and abuse, help ensure security and privacy of health information, and enforce standards for transacting health information. HIPAA addresses issues of security and confidentiality in the transfer of electronic patient information and facilitates the reduction of administrative costs by standardizing health care electronic transactions.

How should health care entities account for computer systems costs incurred in connection with HIPAA?

Reply—Costs associated with upgrading and improving computer systems to comply with HIPAA should follow the guidance set forth in FASB ASC 350-40. The accounting for specific compliance costs depends on whether the costs relate to "upgrades and enhancements" or maintenance. The following summarizes the financial reporting requirements for each type of cost:

- *Upgrades* are defined in the FASB ASC glossary as, "an improvement to an existing product that is intended to extend the life or improve significantly the marketability of the original product through added functionality, enhanced performance, or both. The terms upgrade and enhancement are used interchangeably to describe improvements to software products; however, in different segments of the software industry, those terms may connote different levels of packaging or improvements. This definition does not include platform-transfer rights."

For example, if the changes increase the security of the data from tampering or alteration or reduce the ability of unauthorized persons to gain access to the data, those changes would be tasks that the software previously could not perform and the associated qualifying costs of application development stage activities should be capitalized. Conversely, if the changes merely reconfigure existing data to conform to the HIPAA standard or regulatory requirements, such changes would not result in the capability to perform of additional tasks and the associated costs therewith should be expensed as incurred. Because many of the costs associated with HIPAA relate to compliance with the Act and do not result in "additional functionality," those costs should be expensed as incurred.

- *Maintenance costs* should be expensed as incurred. Training costs and data conversion costs, except for costs to develop or obtain software that allows for access or conversion of old data by new systems, should also be expensed as incurred.

[Revised, June 2009, to reflect conforming changes necessary due to the issuance of FASB ASC.]

.35 Note to Sections 6400.36–.42—Implementation of FASB ASC 958—Classification of a Beneficiary's Interest in the Net Assets of a Financially Interrelated Fund-Raising Foundation (in the Beneficiary's Financial Statements)

Some not-for-profit entities have separate fund-raising foundations (commonly referred to as "institutionally related foundations") that solicit contributions on their behalf. FASB ASC 958, *Not-for-Profit Entities*, provides guidance on (among other things) the accounting that should be followed by such institutionally related foundations and their related beneficiary entity(ies) with respect to contributions received by the foundation.

Some institutionally related foundations and their beneficiary entities meet the characteristics of financially interrelated entities provided in FASB ASC 958-20-15-2. If entities are financially interrelated, FASB ASC 958 provides that the balance sheet of the beneficiary entity(ies) should reflect that entity's interest in the net assets of the foundation, and that interest should be periodically adjusted to reflect the beneficiary's share of the changes in the net assets of the foundation. This accounting is similar to the equity method of accounting, which is described in FASB ASC 323.

FASB ASC 323-10-35-5 requires that the periodic adjustment of the investment be included in the determination of the investor's net income. The purpose of sections 6140.14–.18 (applicable to not-for-profit entities [NPEs] other than health care [HC] entities) and sections 6400.36–.42 (applicable to not-for-profit health care entities) is to clarify that in circumstances in which the recipient and the beneficiary are financially interrelated:

- Beneficiary entities should segregate the adjustment into changes in restricted and unrestricted net assets. (NPE sections 6140.14–.16; HC sections 6400.36–.37 and .39)
- In circumstances in which the beneficiary can influence the financial decisions of the recipient entity to such an extent that the beneficiary can determine the timing and amount of distributions from the recipient to the beneficiary, the existence of the recipient entity should be

transparent in determining the net asset classifications in the beneficiary's financial statements. In other words, the recipient cannot impose time or purpose restrictions beyond those imposed by the donor. (NPE section 6140.14 and .16; HC sections 6400.36 and .39)

- In circumstances in which the beneficiary cannot influence the financial decisions of the recipient entity to such an extent that the beneficiary can determine the timing and amount of distributions from the recipient to the beneficiary, the existence of the recipient entity creates an implied time restriction on the beneficiary's net assets attributable to the beneficiary's interest in the net assets of the recipient (in addition to any other restrictions that may exist). Accordingly, in recognizing its interest in the net assets of the recipient entity and the changes in that interest, the beneficiary should classify the resulting net assets and changes in those net assets as temporarily restricted (unless donors placed permanent restrictions on their contributions). (NPE section 6140.15; HC section 6400.37)
- In circumstances in which the beneficiary can influence the financial decisions of the recipient entity to such an extent that the beneficiary can determine the timing and amount of distributions from the recipient to the beneficiary and some net assets held by the recipient for the benefit of the beneficiary are subject to purpose restrictions [for example, net assets of the recipient restricted to the beneficiary's purchase of property, plant, and equipment (PPE)], expenditures by the beneficiary that meet those purpose restrictions result in the beneficiary (and recipient) reporting reclassifications from temporarily restricted to unrestricted net assets (assuming that the beneficiary has no other net assets subject to similar purpose restrictions), unless those net assets are subject to time restrictions that have not expired, including time restrictions that are implied on contributed long-lived assets as a result of the beneficiary's accounting policy pursuant to FASB ASC 958-605-45-6. (If those net assets are subject to time restrictions that have not expired and the beneficiary has other net assets with similar purpose restrictions, the restrictions on those other net assets would expire in accordance with FASB ASC 958. These sections do not, however, establish a hierarchy pertaining to which restrictions are released first—restrictions on net assets held by the recipient or purpose restrictions on net assets held by the beneficiary.) (NPE section 6140.17; HC section 6400.40)
- In circumstances in which the beneficiary cannot influence the financial decisions of the recipient entity to such an extent that the beneficiary can determine the timing and amount of distributions from the recipient to the beneficiary and some net assets held by the recipient for the benefit of the beneficiary are subject to purpose restrictions, though not subject to time restrictions other than the implied time restrictions that exist because the beneficiary cannot determine the timing and amount of distributions from the recipient to the beneficiary, expenditures by the beneficiary that are consistent with those purpose restrictions should not result in the beneficiary reporting a reclassification from temporarily restricted to unrestricted net assets, subject to the exceptions in the following sentence. Expenditures by the beneficiary that are consistent with those purpose restrictions should result in the beneficiary reporting a reclassification from temporarily restricted to unrestricted net assets if (*a*) the recipient has no discretion

in deciding whether the purpose restriction is met[1] or (*b*) the recipient distributes or obligates itself to distribute to the beneficiary amounts attributable to net assets restricted for the particular purpose, or otherwise indicates that the recipient intends for those net assets to be used to support the particular purpose as an activity of the current period. In all other circumstances, (*a*) purpose restrictions and (*b*) implied time restrictions on the net assets attributable to the interest in the recipient entity exist and have not yet expired. (However, if the beneficiary has other net assets with similar purpose restrictions, those restrictions would expire in accordance with FASB ASC 958. These sections do not establish a hierarchy pertaining to which restrictions are released first—restrictions on net assets held by the recipient or restrictions on net assets held by the beneficiary.) (NPE section 6140.18; HC section 6400.41)

- *For HC NPEs Only.* In circumstances in which the beneficiary can influence the financial decisions of the recipient to such an extent that the beneficiary can determine the timing and amount of distributions from the recipient to the beneficiary, changes in the beneficiary's interest in the net assets of a recipient entity attributable to unrealized gains and losses on investments should be included or excluded from the performance indicator in accordance with FASB ASC 954-10, FASB ASC 954-205-45, FASB ASC 954-320-45, FASB ASC 954-320-55, and FASB ASC 954-605, in the same manner that they would have been had the beneficiary had the transactions itself. Similarly, in applying this guidance, the determination of whether amounts are included or excluded from the performance measure should comprehend that if the beneficiary cannot influence the financial decisions of the recipient entity to such an extent that the beneficiary can determine the timing and amount of distributions from the recipient to the beneficiary, an implied time restriction exists on the beneficiary's net assets attributable to the beneficiary's interest in the net assets of the recipient (in addition to any other restrictions that may exist). Accordingly, in circumstances in which the beneficiary cannot influence the financial decisions of the recipient entity to such an extent that the beneficiary can determine the timing and amount of distributions from the recipient to the beneficiary, the beneficiary should classify the resulting net assets and changes in those net assets as temporarily restricted (unless donors placed permanent restrictions on their contributions) and therefore exclude those changes from the performance indicator. (HC section 6400.42)
- *For HC NPEs Only.* In circumstances in which the recipient entity and the beneficiary are both controlled by the same entity, entities should consider the specific facts and circumstances to determine whether the

[1] In some circumstances, the purpose restrictions may be so broad that the recipient entity has discretion in deciding whether expenditures by the beneficiary that are consistent with those purpose restrictions actually meet those purpose restrictions. For example, the recipient's net assets may have arisen from a contribution that was restricted for the beneficiary's purchase of research equipment, with no particular research equipment specified. Purchasing an XYZ microscope, which is consistent with that purpose restriction, may or may not meet that purpose restriction, depending on the decision of the recipient. In contrast, the net assets may have arisen from a contribution that was restricted for an XYZ microscope. Purchasing an XYZ microscope, which also is consistent with that purpose restriction, would result in the recipient having no discretion in determining whether that purpose restriction is met.

beneficiary can influence the financial decisions of the recipient entity to such an extent that the beneficiary can determine the timing and amount of distributions from the recipient to the beneficiary. (HC section 6400.38)

Technical Practice Aids for Not-for-Profit Entities Implementation of FASB ASC 958—Classification of a Beneficiary's Interest in the Net Assets of a Financially Interrelated Fund-Raising Foundation (in the Beneficiary's Financial Statements)

HC NPEs			
NPEs that are not HC NPEs			
Can the beneficiary determine the timing and amount of distributions from the recipient to the beneficiary? (Not-for-profit health care entities [HC NPEs] under common control consider section 6400.38)	**How does the existence of the recipient affect the beneficiary's reporting of its interest?**	**Are any net assets held by the recipient for the benefit of the beneficiary subject to donor-imposed purpose restrictions and has the beneficiary made expenditures that meet those purpose restrictions (in circumstances in which the beneficiary can determine the timing and amount of distributions from the recipient to the beneficiary) or that are consistent with those purpose restrictions (in circumstances in which the beneficiary cannot determine the timing and amount of distributions from the recipient to the beneficiary)?**	**Are any changes in the beneficiary's interest in the net assets of the recipient attributable to unrealized gains and losses on investments?**

(continued)

HC NPEs			
NPEs that are not HC NPEs			
Yes	Existence of recipient is transparent in determining net asset classifications. (NPE sections 6140.14 and .16; HC sections 6400.36 and .39)	Reclass the applicable net assets from temporarily restricted (TR) to unrestricted (UR) unless those net assets are subject to time restrictions that have not expired. (NPE section 6140.17; HC section 6400.40)	Changes in the beneficiary's interest in the net assets of a recipient entity attributable to unrealized gains and losses on investments should be included or excluded from the performance indicator in accordance with FASB ASC 954-10, FASB ASC 954-205-45, FASB ASC 954-320-45, FASB ASC 954-320-55, and FASB ASC 954-605, in the same manner that they would have been had the beneficiary had the transactions itself. (HC section 6400.42)
No	Existence of the recipient creates an implied time restriction on the beneficiary's net assets attributable to the beneficiary's interest in the net assets of the recipient. (NPE section 6140.15; HC section 6400.37)	Reclass the applicable net assets from TR to UR only if the purpose restriction and the implied time restriction are met. Whether the purpose restriction is met depends in part on (1) whether the recipient has discretion in determining whether the purpose restriction is met and (2) the recipient's decision in exercising that discretion, if any. (NPE section 6140.18; HC section 6400.41)	An implied time restriction exists on the beneficiary's net assets attributable to the beneficiary's interest in the net assets of the recipient. The beneficiary should classify the resulting net assets and changes in those net assets as temporarily restricted (unless donors placed permanent restrictions on their contributions) and therefore exclude those changes from the performance indicator. (HC section 6400.42)

[Revised, June 2009, to reflect conforming changes necessary due to the issuance of FASB ASC.]

.36 Application of FASB ASC 958—Classification of a Beneficiary's Interest in the Net Assets of a Financially Interrelated Fund-Raising Foundation (The beneficiary can influence the operating and financial decisions of the foundation to such an extent that the beneficiary can determine the timing and amount of distributions from the foundation.)

Inquiry—ABC Hospital, a not-for-profit health care entity subject to FASB ASC 954,[2] and ABC Foundation are financially interrelated entities as described in FASB ASC 958-20-15-2. ABC Foundation's bylaws state that it is organized for the purpose of stimulating voluntary financial support from donors for the sole benefit of ABC Hospital. Assume that ABC Hospital can influence the operating and financial decisions of ABC Foundation to such an extent that ABC Hospital can determine the timing and amount of distributions from ABC Foundation to ABC Hospital.

During its most recent fiscal year, ABC Foundation's activities resulted in an increase in net assets (before distributions) of $3,200, comprised of $2,000 in unrestricted contributions, $1,000 in temporarily restricted contributions (purpose restrictions), $500 in unrestricted dividend and interest income, and $300 in expenses. In addition, ABC Foundation distributed $2,500 in cash representing unrestricted net assets to ABC Hospital. How should this activity be reported in ABC Hospital's financial statements?

Reply—Because ABC Foundation (the recipient entity) and ABC Hospital (the beneficiary) are financially interrelated, FASB ASC 958-20-25-2 requires ABC Hospital to recognize its interest in the net assets of ABC Foundation and periodically adjust that interest for its share of the change in net assets of ABC Foundation. This is similar to the equity method of accounting described in FASB ASC 323.

In recognizing its interest in the net assets of ABC Foundation and the changes in that interest, ABC Hospital should classify the resulting net assets as if contributions were received by ABC Hospital directly from the donor, because ABC Hospital can influence the operating and financial decisions of ABC Foundation to such an extent that ABC Hospital can determine the timing and amount of distributions from ABC Foundation to ABC Hospital. In other words, the existence of ABC Foundation should be transparent in determining the net asset classifications in ABC Hospital's financial statements because ABC Foundation cannot impose time or purpose restrictions beyond those imposed by the donor. (Any instructions given by ABC Foundation are designations, rather than restrictions.)

In the circumstances described previously, ABC Hospital would initially increase its asset, "Interest in Net Assets of ABC Foundation" for the change in ABC Foundation's net assets ($3,200). ABC Hospital's Statement of Operations would include "Change in Unrestricted Interest in ABC Foundation" of $2,200 (which would be included in the performance indicator in accordance with FASB ASC 954-10, FASB ASC 954-205, FASB ASC 954-310, 954-405, and FASB ASC 954-605) and "Change in Temporarily Restricted Interest in ABC

[2] This section addresses not-for-profit health care entities subject to Financial Accounting Standards Board (FASB) *Accounting Standards Codification* (ASC) 954, *Health Care Entities.* Section 6140.14, "Application of FASB ASC 958—Classification of a Beneficiary's Interest in the Net Assets of a Financially Interrelated Fund-Raising Foundation (The beneficiary can influence the operating and financial decisions of the foundation to such an extent that the beneficiary can determine the timing and amount of distributions from the foundation.)," addresses a similar issue for not-for-profit entities subject to FASB ASC 958, *Not-for-Profit Entities.*

Foundation" of $1,000 which would be reported in the Statement of Changes in Net Assets.

The $2,500 distribution from ABC Foundation to ABC Hospital would not be reported as an increase in net assets on ABC Hospital's Statement of Operations or its Statement of Changes in Net Assets. By analogy to equity method accounting, the $2,500 would be reported in a manner similar to a distribution from a subsidiary to its parent (for example, a dividend). ABC Hospital should report the distribution by increasing cash and decreasing its interest in the net assets of ABC Foundation.

If the distribution represented restricted net assets, ABC Hospital would not reclassify the net assets from temporarily restricted to unrestricted at the time of the distribution. Instead, ABC Hospital would reclassify the net assets from temporarily restricted to unrestricted when those restrictions were met.

[Revised, June 2009, to reflect conforming changes necessary due to the issuance of FASB ASC.]

.37 Application of FASB ASC 958—Classification of a Beneficiary's Interest in the Net Assets of a Financially Interrelated Fund-Raising Foundation (The beneficiary cannot influence the operating and financial decisions of the foundation to such an extent that the beneficiary can determine the timing and amount of distributions from the foundation.)

Inquiry—ABC Hospital, a not-for-profit health care entity subject to FASB ASC 954,[3] and ABC Foundation are financially interrelated entities described in FASB ASC 958-20-15-2. ABC Foundation's bylaws state that it is organized for the purpose of stimulating voluntary financial support from donors for the sole benefit of ABC Hospital. Assume that ABC Hospital cannot, however, influence the operating and financial decisions of ABC Foundation to such an extent that ABC Hospital can determine the timing and amount of distributions from ABC Foundation to ABC Hospital.

During its most recent fiscal year, ABC Foundation's activities resulted in an increase in net assets (before distributions) of $3,200, comprised of $2,000 in unrestricted contributions, $1,000 in temporarily restricted contributions (purpose restrictions), $500 in unrestricted dividend and interest income, and $300 in expenses. In addition, ABC Foundation elected to distribute $2,500 in cash representing unrestricted net assets to ABC Hospital. How should this activity be reported in ABC Hospital's financial statements?

Reply—Because ABC Foundation (the recipient entity) and ABC Hospital (the beneficiary) are financially interrelated, FASB ASC 958-20-25-2 requires ABC Hospital to recognize its interest in the net assets of ABC Foundation and periodically adjust that interest for its share of the change in net assets of ABC Foundation. This is similar to the equity method of accounting described in FASB ASC 323.

ABC Hospital cannot influence the operating and financial decisions of ABC Foundation to such an extent that ABC Hospital can determine the timing and

[3] This section addresses not-for-profit health care entities subject to FASB ASC 954. Section 6140.15, "Application of FASB ASC 958—Classification of a Beneficiary's Interest in the Net Assets of a Financially Interrelated Fund-Raising Foundation (The beneficiary cannot influence the operating and financial decisions of the foundation to such an extent that the beneficiary can determine the timing and amount of distributions from the foundation.)," addresses a similar issue for not-for-profit entities subject to FASB ASC 958.

amount of distributions from ABC Foundation. Therefore, an implied time restriction exists on ABC Hospital's interest in the net assets of ABC Foundation (in addition to any other restrictions that may exist). Accordingly, in recognizing its interest in the net assets of ABC Foundation and the changes in that interest, ABC Hospital should classify the resulting net assets as changes in temporarily restricted net assets (unless donors placed permanent restrictions on their contributions).

In the circumstances previously described, ABC Hospital would initially increase its asset, "Interest in Net Assets of ABC Foundation" for the change in ABC Foundation's net assets ($3,200). ABC Hospital's Statement of Changes in Net Assets would include "Change in Temporarily Restricted Interest in ABC Foundation" of $3,200 as an increase in temporarily restricted net assets.

The $2,500 distribution from ABC Foundation to ABC Hospital would not be reported as an increase in net assets on ABC Hospital's Statement of Operations or its Statement of Changes in Net Assets. By analogy to equity method accounting, the $2,500 would be treated similar to a distribution from a subsidiary to its parent (for example, a dividend). ABC Hospital should report the distribution by increasing cash and decreasing its interest in the net assets of ABC Foundation.

ABC Hospital would reclassify the net assets from temporarily restricted to unrestricted at the time of the distribution, because the time restriction would expire at the time of the distribution. The reclassification would be reported as "net assets released from restrictions" and included in the performance indicator in the statement of operations. (If those net assets were subject to purpose or time restrictions that remained even after the net assets had been distributed to ABC Hospital, ABC Hospital would not reclassify the net assets from temporarily restricted to unrestricted at the time of the distribution. Instead, ABC Hospital would reclassify the net assets from temporarily restricted to unrestricted when those restrictions were met and the reclassification would be included in or excluded from the performance indicator in accordance with FASB ASC 954-10, FASB ASC 954-205, FASB ASC 954-310, FASB ASC 954-405, and FASB ASC 954-605.)

[Revised, June 2009, to reflect conforming changes necessary due to the issuance of FASB ASC.]

.38 Application of FASB ASC 958—Classification of a Beneficiary's Interest in the Net Assets of a Financially Interrelated Fund-Raising Foundation—Does Common Control Lead to the Conclusion That the Beneficiary Can Determine the Timing and Amount of Distributions from the Recipient?

Inquiry—ABC Holding Company (a not-for-profit entity) has two not-for-profit subsidiaries (ABC Hospital and ABC Foundation) that it controls and consolidates in accordance with the guidance in FASB ASC 954-10, FASB ASC 954-205, FASB ASC 954-605, and FASB ASC 954-810. ABC Hospital and ABC Foundation are brother-sister entities that are financially interrelated entities as described in FASB ASC 958-20-15-2. ABC Hospital issues separate financial statements in connection with a loan agreement. ABC Foundation's bylaws state that it is organized for the purpose of stimulating voluntary financial support from donors for the sole benefit of ABC Hospital.

Because ABC Hospital and ABC Foundation are under common control, does that lead to the conclusion that ABC Hospital can influence the financial decisions of ABC Foundation (either directly or indirectly) to such an extent that ABC Hospital can determine the timing and amount of distributions from ABC Foundation to ABC Hospital?

Reply —In some circumstances ABC Hospital, though a subsidiary of ABC Holding Company, may be able to influence the financial decisions of ABC Foundation (either directly or indirectly) to such an extent that ABC Hospital can determine the timing and amount of distributions from ABC Foundation to ABC Hospital. For example, if ABC Hospital formed ABC Holding Company as a nominally-capitalized shell with no real operating powers, a rebuttable presumption exists that ABC Hospital can influence the financial decisions of ABC Foundation (either directly or indirectly) to such an extent that ABC Hospital can determine the timing and amount of distributions from ABC Foundation to ABC Hospital. On the other hand if, for example, ABC Hospital formed ABC Holding Company to be an operating entity with substance, other factors would need to be considered in determining whether ABC Hospital can influence the financial decisions of ABC Foundation (either directly or indirectly) to such an extent that ABC Hospital can determine the timing and amount of distributions from ABC Foundation to ABC Hospital. Therefore, it is necessary to consider the facts and circumstances surrounding the relationships between ABC Holding Company and ABC Hospital, and ABC Hospital and ABC Foundation, to determine whether ABC Hospital exerts enough influence over ABC Foundation to determine the timing and amount of distributions from ABC Foundation to ABC Hospital. Indicators to consider may include, but are not limited to, the following:

- What is the extent of overlap among the boards of ABC Hospital, ABC Holding Company, and ABC Foundation (for example, do a majority of the individuals who govern ABC Hospital also govern ABC Foundation; do a majority of the individuals who govern ABC Hospital also govern ABC Holding Company; are the boards of ABC Hospital, ABC Foundation and ABC Holding Company substantially independent of one another)? The greater the overlap among the boards of ABC Hospital and either ABC Holding Company or ABC Foundation, the more likely that ABC Hospital can influence the financial decisions of ABC Foundation (either directly or indirectly) to such an extent that ABC Hospital can determine the timing and amount of distributions from ABC Foundation to ABC Hospital.

- What is the extent of overlap among management teams of ABC Hospital, ABC Holding Company, and ABC Foundation (for example, do the individuals who manage ABC Hospital also manage ABC Foundation; do the individuals who manage ABC Hospital also manage ABC Holding Company; does ABC Holding Company have a separate management team that exercises significant authority over both ABC Hospital and ABC Foundation)? The greater the overlap between ABC Hospital's management and management of either ABC Holding Company or ABC Foundation, the more likely that ABC Hospital can influence the financial decisions of ABC Foundation (either directly or indirectly) to such an extent that ABC Hospital can determine the timing and amount of distributions from ABC Foundation to ABC Hospital.

- What are the origins of the parent/holding company structure? For example, were ABC Holding Company and ABC Foundation created by

ABC Hospital through a corporate restructuring, which may indicate that ABC Hospital, as the original entity, can influence the financial decisions of ABC Foundation (either directly or indirectly) to such an extent that ABC Hospital can determine the timing and amount of distributions from ABC Foundation to ABC Hospital. Alternatively, were ABC Hospital and ABC Foundation independent entities that merged and created ABC Holding Company to govern the combined entity, which may indicate that ABC Hospital cannot influence the financial decisions of ABC Foundation (either directly or indirectly) to such an extent that ABC Hospital can determine the timing and amount of distributions from ABC Foundation to ABC Hospital.

- What is the number of entities under common control? The greater the number of entities under ABC Holding Company's control, the less likely it is that any one subsidiary, such as ABC Hospital, can influence the financial decisions of another brother-sister subsidiary, such as ABC Foundation, (either directly or indirectly) to such an extent that ABC Hospital can determine the timing and amount of distributions from ABC Foundation to ABC Hospital

Other relevant facts and circumstances should also be considered.

[Revised, June 2009, to reflect conforming changes necessary due to the issuance of FASB ASC.]

.39 Application of FASB ASC 958—Classification of a Beneficiary's Interest in the Net Assets of a Financially Interrelated Fund-Raising Foundation (More Than One Beneficiary—Some Contributions Are Designated)

Inquiry—DEF Health Entity is the parent company of three brother-sister not-for-profit entities: Health A, a not-for-profit health care entity subject to FASB ASC 954,[4] Health B, and Foundation. Foundation is organized for the purpose of raising contributions for the benefit of both Health A and Health B. The four entities are legally separate not-for-profit entities that are financially interrelated pursuant to the guidance in FASB ASC 958-20-15-2. Assume that Health A can influence the financial decisions of Foundation to such an extent that Health A can determine the timing and amount of distributions from Foundation to Health A.

A donor contributes $5,000 cash to Foundation and stipulates that the contribution is for the benefit of Health A. Foundation would record the contribution as temporarily restricted revenue because Foundation must use the contribution for the benefit of Health A. In its separately issued financial statements, Health A would recognize its interest in the net assets attributable to that contribution by debiting "Interest in Net Assets of Foundation" for $5,000. Would the offsetting credit be reported as temporarily restricted revenue (because the net assets attributable to the contribution are restricted on Foundation's Balance Sheet) or unrestricted revenue (because there are no donor-imposed time

[4] This section addresses not-for-profit health care entities subject to FASB ASC 954. Section 6140.16, "Application of FASB ASC 958—Classification of a Beneficiary's Interest in the Net Assets of a Financially Interrelated Fund-Raising Foundation (More Than One Beneficiary—Some Contributions Are Designated)," addresses a similar issue for not-for-profit entities subject to FASB ASC 958.

restrictions or purpose restrictions on how Health A must use the contribution)?

Reply —Health A should report the offsetting credit as unrestricted revenue. Because Health A can influence the financial decisions of Foundation to such an extent that Health A can determine the timing and amount of distributions from Foundation to Health A, no implied time restriction exists on Health A's net assets attributable to its interest in the net assets of Foundation. Accordingly, in recognizing its interest in the net assets of Foundation and the changes in that interest, Health A should classify the resulting net assets as if contributions were received by Health A directly from the donor. In other words, the existence of Foundation should be transparent in determining the net asset classifications in Health A's separately issued financial statements because Foundation cannot impose time or purpose restrictions beyond those imposed by the donor. (Any instructions given by Foundation are designations, rather than restrictions.)

Because no donor-imposed restrictions exist on how Health A must use the contribution, Health A should report the change in its interest in the net assets attributable to the contribution as an increase in unrestricted net assets that is included in its performance indicator (in accordance with FASB ASC 954-10, FASB ASC 954-205, FASB ASC 954-310, FASB ASC 954-405, and FASB ASC 954-605) in its separately issued Statement of Operations. When Foundation actually distributes the funds, Health A should increase cash and decrease its interest in net assets of Foundation; the distributions would have no effect on Health A's Statement of Operations or its Statement of Changes in Net Assets.

[Revised, June 2009, to reflect conforming changes necessary due to the issuance of FASB ASC.]

.40 Application of FASB ASC 958—Classification of a Beneficiary's Interest in the Net Assets of a Financially Interrelated Fund-Raising Foundation (The beneficiary makes an expenditure that meets a purpose restriction on net assets held for its benefit by the recipient entity—The beneficiary can influence the operating and financial decisions of the recipient to such an extent that the beneficiary can determine the timing and amount of distributions from the recipient.)

Inquiry —ABC Hospital, a not-for-profit health care entity subject to FASB ASC 954,[5] and ABC Foundation are financially interrelated entities as described in FASB ASC 958-20-15-2. ABC Foundation's bylaws state that it is organized for the purpose of stimulating voluntary financial support from donors for the sole benefit of ABC Hospital. Assume that ABC Hospital can influence the operating and financial decisions of ABC Foundation to such an extent that ABC Hospital can determine the timing and amount of distributions from ABC Foundation to ABC Hospital.

ABC Foundation's net assets consist of $3,000,000 resulting from cash contributions restricted for the purchase of PPE by ABC Hospital. ABC Hospital

[5] This section addresses not-for-profit health care entities subject to FASB ASC 954. Section 6140.17, "Application of FASB ASC 958—Classification of a Beneficiary's Interest in the Net Assets of a Financially Interrelated Fund-Raising Foundation (The beneficiary makes an expenditure that meets a purpose restriction on net assets held for its benefit by the recipient entity—The beneficiary can influence the operating and financial decisions of the recipient to such an extent that the beneficiary can determine the timing and amount of distributions from the recipient.)," addresses a similar issue for not-for-profit entities subject to FASB ASC 958.

has recorded its interest in those net assets by debiting "Interest in net assets of ABC Foundation" and crediting "Change in interest in ABC Foundation," which is reported as an increase in temporarily restricted net assets. ABC Hospital's accounting policy is to not imply a time restriction that expires over the useful life of the donated long-lived assets pursuant to FASB ASC 958-605-45-6 and it has no other net assets restricted for the purchase of PPE.[6] ABC Hospital subsequently purchased and placed into service $3,000,000 of PPE that meets those donor restrictions prior to receiving a distribution from ABC Foundation. Should ABC Hospital reclassify $3,000,000 from temporarily-restricted net assets as a result of building and placing into service the $3,000,000 of PPE?

Reply —Because ABC Foundation (the recipient entity) and ABC Hospital (the beneficiary) are financially interrelated, FASB ASC 958-20-25-2 requires ABC Hospital to recognize its interest in the net assets of ABC Foundation and periodically adjust that interest for its share of the change in net assets of ABC Foundation. This is similar to the equity method of accounting described in FASB ASC 323.

In recognizing its interest in the net assets of ABC Foundation and the changes in that interest, ABC Hospital should classify the resulting net assets as if contributions were received by ABC Hospital directly from the donor, because ABC Hospital can influence the operating and financial decisions of ABC Foundation to such an extent that ABC Hospital can determine the timing and amount of distributions from ABC Foundation to ABC Hospital. Accordingly, the net assets representing contributions restricted for the purchase of PPE should be reported as temporarily restricted net assets (purpose restricted) in ABC Hospital's financial statements. Upon purchasing and placing into service the PPE, ABC Hospital (and ABC Foundation) should reclassify $3,000,000 from temporarily restricted to unrestricted net assets,[7] reported separately from the performance indicator in the statement of operations in accordance with the guidance in FASB ASC 954-10, FASB ASC 954-205, FASB ASC 954-310, FASB ASC 954-405, and FASB ASC 954-605. In other words, the existence of ABC Foundation should be transparent in determining the net asset classifications in ABC Hospital's financial statements because ABC Foundation cannot impose time or purpose restrictions beyond those imposed by the donor. (Any instructions given by ABC Foundation are designations, rather than restrictions.)

[Revised, June 2009, to reflect conforming changes necessary due to the issuance of FASB ASC.]

---

[6] The assumption that ABC Hospital has no other net assets restricted for the purchase of PPE is intended to avoid establishing a hierarchy pertaining to which restrictions are released first—restrictions on net assets held by the recipient or restrictions on net assets held by the beneficiary. That issue is not addressed in this section.

[7] In this fact pattern, ABC Research Institute's interest in the net assets of ABC Foundation is subject to only purpose restrictions because the net assets arose from cash contributions with no time restrictions. If instead the net assets arose from promises to give rather than from cash contributions, the net assets might be subject to time restrictions in addition to the purpose restrictions. In determining whether net assets that arose from promises to give are subject to time restrictions, NPEs should consider the guidance in section 6140.04, *Lapsing of Restrictions on Receivables if Purpose Restrictions Pertaining to Long-Lived Assets are Met Before the Receivables are Due*, which discusses whether restrictions on net assets arising from promises to give that are restricted by donors for investments in long-lived assets are met when the assets are placed in service or when the receivables are due.

.41 Application of FASB ASC 958—Classification of a Beneficiary's Interest in the Net Assets of a Financially Interrelated Fund-Raising Foundation (The beneficiary makes an expenditure that is consistent with a purpose restriction on net assets held for its benefit by the recipient entity—The beneficiary cannot influence the operating and financial decisions of the recipient to such an extent that the beneficiary can determine the timing and amount of distributions from the recipient.)

Inquiry—ABC Hospital, a not-for-profit health care entity subject to FASB ASC 954,[8] and ABC Foundation are financially interrelated entities as described in FASB ASC 958-20-15-2. ABC Foundation's bylaws state that it is organized for the purpose of stimulating voluntary financial support from donors for the sole benefit of ABC Hospital. Assume that ABC Hospital cannot, however, influence the operating and financial decisions of ABC Foundation to such an extent that ABC Hospital can determine the timing and amount of distributions from ABC Foundation to ABC Hospital.

ABC Foundation's net assets consist of $3,000,000 resulting from cash contributions restricted for the purchase of PPE ABC Hospital. ABC Hospital has recorded its interest in those net assets by debiting "Interest in net assets of ABC Foundation" and crediting "Change in interest in ABC Foundation," which is reported as an increase in temporarily restricted net assets. ABC Hospital has no other net assets restricted for the purchase of PPE.[9]

ABC Hospital subsequently built and placed into service the New Modern Hospital Wing (at a cost of $3,000,000) prior to receiving a distribution from ABC Foundation or any indication from ABC Foundation that it intends to support building and placing into service the New Modern Hospital Wing. Should ABC Hospital reclassify $3,000,000 from temporarily-restricted net assets to unrestricted net assets as a result of building and placing into service the New Modern Hospital Wing?

Reply—From ABC Hospital's perspective, its interest in the net assets of ABC Foundation has two restrictions—a purpose restriction (the purchase of the PPE) and an implied time restriction. (ABC Hospital cannot influence the operating and financial decisions of ABC Foundation to such an extent that ABC Hospital can determine the timing and amount of distributions from ABC Foundation to ABC Hospital, including distributions pertaining to expenditures by ABC Hospital that meet the donor-imposed purpose restrictions. Therefore, an implied time restriction exists on ABC Hospital's interest in the net assets of ABC Foundation.) FASB ASC 958-205-45-9 provides, in part, as follows:

> If two or more temporary restrictions are imposed on a contribution, the effect of the expiration of those restrictions is recognized in the period in which the last remaining restriction has expired.

[8] This section addresses not-for-profit health care entities subject to FASB ASC 954. Section 6140.18, "Application of FASB ASC 958—Classification of a Beneficiary's Interest in the Net Assets of a Financially Interrelated Fund-Raising Foundation (The beneficiary makes an expenditure that is consistent with a purpose restriction on net assets held for its benefit by the recipient entity—The beneficiary cannot influence the operating and financial decisions of the recipient to such an extent that the beneficiary can determine the timing and amount of distributions from the recipient.)," addresses a similar issue for not-for-profit entities subject to FASB ASC 958.

[9] The assumption that ABC Hospital has no other net assets restricted for the purchase of PPE is intended to avoid establishing a hierarchy pertaining to which restrictions are released first—restrictions on net assets held by the recipient or restrictions on net assets held by the beneficiary. That issue is not addressed in this section.

FASB ASC 958-205-45-11 further provides, in part:

> Temporarily restricted net assets with time restrictions are not available to support expenses until the time restrictions have expired.

In considering whether the purpose restriction on ABC Hospital's interest in the net assets of ABC Foundation is met, ABC Hospital should determine whether ABC Foundation has discretion in deciding whether an expenditure by ABC Hospital that is consistent with the purpose restriction satisfies that purpose restriction. For example, if the restricted net assets arose from a contribution that was restricted for "building projects of ABC Hospital," with no particular building project specified, purchasing and placing into service the New Modern Hospital Wing is consistent with the purpose restriction but may or may not meet it, because ABC Foundation has some discretion in deciding which building project releases the purpose restriction. In other words, ABC Foundation may, at its discretion, either release restricted net assets in support of building the New Modern Hospital Wing or not, because the purpose restriction imposed by the donor was broad enough to give ABC Foundation discretion in deciding which building projects meet the purpose restriction. If ABC Foundation has such discretion, a purpose restriction and an implied time restriction on ABC Hospital's interest in the net assets of ABC Foundation exist. Therefore, ABC Hospital should not reclassify $3,000,000 from temporarily-restricted net assets to unrestricted net assets as a result of building and placing into service the New Modern Hospital Wing unless ABC Foundation distributes or obligates itself to distribute to ABC Hospital amounts attributable to net assets restricted for the purchase of PPE by ABC Hospital, or ABC Foundation otherwise indicates that it intends for those net assets to be used to support the building and placing into service the New Modern Hospital Wing as an activity of the current period (assuming that ABC Hospital had no other net assets that were restricted for the purchase of PPE).[10,11]

---

[10] In this fact pattern, the expenditure is made prior to meeting the purpose restriction and the implied time restriction that exists because ABC Hospital cannot determine the timing and amount of distributions from ABC Foundation to ABC Hospital. FASB ASC 958-205-45-11 provides that in circumstances in which both purpose and time restrictions exist, expenditures meeting the purpose restriction must be made simultaneous with or after the time restriction has expired in order to satisfy both the purpose and time restriction and result in a reclassification of net assets from temporarily restricted to unrestricted. In other words, time restrictions, if any, must be met before expenditures can result in purpose restrictions being met. In this fact pattern, however, the time restriction is an implied time restriction that exists because the beneficiary cannot determine the timing and amount of distributions from the recipient to the beneficiary, rather than an implied time restriction that exists because a promise to give is due in a future period or because of an explicit donor stipulation. Accordingly, in this fact pattern, temporarily restricted net assets with implied time restrictions are available to support expenditures made before the expiration of the time restrictions and the net assets should be reclassified from temporarily restricted to unrestricted in the period in which the last remaining restriction has expired. In other words, in this fact pattern, if the expenditure that meets the purpose restriction is made before meeting the implied time restriction that exists because the beneficiary cannot determine the timing and amount of distributions from the recipient to the beneficiary, all the restrictions should be considered met once the implied time restriction is met.

[11] In this fact pattern, ABC Hospital's interest in the net assets of ABC Foundation is subject to an implied time restriction that exists because ABC Hospital cannot determine the timing and amount of distributions from ABC Foundation to ABC Hospital and a purpose restriction. Because the net assets arose from cash contributions with no other donor-imposed time restrictions, no time restrictions other than those imposed by ABC Foundation exist. If instead the net assets arose from promises to give rather than from cash contributions, the net assets might be subject to donor-imposed time restrictions in addition to the time restriction imposed by ABC Foundation and the purpose restriction. In determining whether net assets that arose from promises to give are subject to donor-imposed time restrictions in addition to the time restrictions imposed by ABC Foundation, NPEs should consider the

(continued)

In contrast to the example in the previous paragraph, if the restricted net assets arose from a contribution that was restricted for "building and placing into service the New Modern Hospital Wing," ABC Foundation has no discretion in deciding whether that purpose restriction is met by building and placing into service the New Modern Hospital Wing. Therefore, if ABC Hospital builds and places into service the New Modern Hospital Wing, the purpose restriction is met (assuming that ABC Hospital had no other net assets that were restricted for building and placing into service the New Modern Hospital Wing). In addition, the implied time restriction is met because ABC Foundation is required to distribute the funds to ABC Hospital in order to meet the donor's stipulation. Therefore, ABC Hospital (and ABC Foundation) should reclassify $3,000,000 from temporarily-restricted net assets as a result of building and placing into service the New Modern Hospital Wing.

In summary, ABC Hospital should not reclassify $3,000,000 from temporarily-restricted net assets to unrestricted net assets as a result of building and placing into service the New Modern Hospital Wing until both the purpose restriction and the implied time restriction are met. If both the purpose restriction and the implied time restriction are met, ABC Hospital should decrease its interest in the net assets of ABC Foundation and increase cash (or a receivable, if the Foundation has merely obligated itself to make the distribution) by the amount of the distribution, and simultaneously reclassify the same amount from temporarily restricted net assets to unrestricted net assets. The reclassification should be reported separately from the performance indicator in the statement of operations in accordance with the guidance in FASB ASC 954-10, FASB ASC 954-205, FASB ASC 954-310, FASB ASC 954-405, and FASB ASC 954-605.

[Revised, June 2009, to reflect conforming changes necessary due to the issuance of FASB ASC.]

.42 Application of FASB ASC 958—Classification of a Beneficiary's Interest in the Net Assets of a Financially Interrelated Fund-Raising Foundation (Recipient Entity)—Accounting for Unrealized Gains and Losses on Investments Held by the Foundation

Inquiry —FASB ASC 958 provides that if entities are financially interrelated, the balance sheet of the beneficiary entity should reflect that entity's beneficial interest in the net assets of the recipient entity, and that that interest should be adjusted periodically to reflect the changes in the net assets of the recipient entity. This accounting is similar to the equity method of accounting. FASB ASC 954-10, FASB ASC 954-205-45, FASB ASC 954-320-45, FASB ASC 954-320-55, and FASB ASC 954-605 provide guidance pertaining to the classification of investment returns in the financial statements of health care entities.

(footnote continued)

guidance in section 6140.04, *Lapsing of Restrictions on Receivables if Purpose Restrictions Pertaining to Long-Lived Assets are Met Before the Receivables are Due*, which discusses whether restrictions on net assets arising from promises to give that are restricted by donors for investments in long-lived assets are met when the assets are placed in service or when the receivables are due. In circumstances in which the net assets are subject to (*a*) donor-imposed time restrictions in addition to the (*b*) implied time restrictions that exist because ABC Hospital cannot determine the timing and amount of distributions from ABC Foundation to ABC Hospital and (*c*) purpose restrictions, the last remaining time restriction should be considered in applying the guidance in FASB ASC 958-205-45-11 that provides that temporarily restricted net assets with time restrictions are not available to support expenses until the time restrictions have expired.

ABC Hospital and ABC Foundation are financially interrelated entities. How should changes in ABC Hospital's interest in the net assets of ABC Foundation attributable to unrealized gains and losses on Foundation's investments be classified in ABC Hospital's financial statements?

Reply—In circumstances in which ABC Hospital can influence the financial decisions of ABC Foundation to such an extent that ABC Hospital can determine the timing and amount of distributions from Foundation to ABC Hospital, changes in ABC Hospital's interest in the net assets of ABC Foundation attributable to unrealized gains and losses on investments should be classified in the same manner that they would have been had ABC Hospital held the investments and had the transactions itself. In accordance with the guidance in FASB ASC 954-10, FASB ASC 954-205-45, FASB ASC 954-320-45, FASB ASC 954-320-55, and FASB ASC 954-605, ABC Hospital should include in the performance indicator the portion of the change attributable to unrealized gains and losses on trading securities that are not restricted by donors or by law, and should exclude from the performance indicator the portion of the change attributable to all other unrealized gains and losses.

In circumstances in which ABC Hospital cannot influence the financial decisions of Foundation to such an extent that ABC Hospital can determine the timing and amount of distributions ABC Hospital receives from Foundation, an implied time restriction exists on ABC Hospital's net assets attributable to its interest in the net assets of Foundation (in addition to any other restrictions that many exist). Accordingly, ABC Hospital should classify all changes in that interest, including the portion of the change attributable to unrealized gains and losses on investments, as changes in temporarily restricted net assets (unless donors placed permanent restrictions on investment gains and losses pertaining to their contributions) and therefore should exclude those changes from the performance indicator.

[Revised, June 2009, to reflect conforming changes necessary due to the issuance of FASB ASC.]

.43 Application of FASB ASC 958—Classification of Distributions From a Financially Interrelated Fund-Raising Foundation (Recipient Entity) to a Health Care Beneficiary

Inquiry—How should a fund-raising foundation (recipient), a not-for-profit entity subject to FASB ASC 958, report (in its separately issued financial statements) distributions to a financially interrelated beneficiary that is a health care entity? In other words, should such distributions be reported following (*a*) the guidance on reporting transfers among affiliated health care entities in FASB ASC 954-10, FASB ASC 954-205, FASB ASC 954-605, and FASB ASC 954-810 or (*b*) the guidance in FASB ASC 958.

Reply—FASB ASC 958 applies to all not-for-profit entities, except those that are providers of health care services (FASB ASC 958-10-15-3). Therefore, the guidance in FASB ASC 954 generally does not apply to financial statements of recipient entities that are financially interrelated fund-raising foundations. The foundation should follow the accounting and reporting requirements of FASB ASC 958 rather than FASB ASC 954 in the foundation's separately issued financial statements. The foundation should report distributions to beneficiary entities as expenses or distributions to related entities. The guidance in the previous sentence applies regardless of whether the recipient entity and the beneficiary are under common control or whether one controls the other in a parent-subsidiary relationship.

[Revised, June 2009, to reflect conforming changes necessary due to the issuance of FASB ASC.]

[.44] Reserved

.45 Applicability of FASB ASC 460—Accounting and Disclosure Requirements for Guarantees, Including Indirect Guarantees of Indebtedness of Others

Inquiry—In order to attract a physician into a community to meet community needs, a hospital may loan the physician an amount to be forgiven over a set period as long as the physician remains in practice in the community. The hospital (generally a not-for-profit) is precluded from requiring the physician to refer patients to or treat patients at that facility, although the hospital hopes to be the primary referral location. Is this arrangement subject to FASB ASC 460, *Guarantees*?

Reply—No. The contract does not constitute a guarantee contract under FASB ASC 460-10-15-4.

[Revised, June 2009, to reflect conforming changes necessary due to the issuance of FASB ASC.]

.46 Applicability of FASB ASC 460—Guarantor's Accounting and Disclosure Requirements for Guarantees, Including Indirect Guarantees of Indebtedness of Others—Mortgage Guarantees

Inquiry—In order to recruit a physician, a hospital may guarantee the physician's home mortgage. The physician may be recruited either as an employee of the hospital or as an independent contractor. Is this arrangement considered a guarantee under FASB ASC 460?

Reply—If the physician becomes an employee of the hospital, the arrangement is not covered by FASB ASC 460; see the discussion of "other employment-related costs" in FASB ASC 460-10-55-17. If the physician is not an employee, then the arrangement is considered a guarantee under FASB ASC 460. The contract requires the guarantor (hospital) to make a payment (in cash) to the guaranteed party (mortgage lender) based on changes in an underlying (occurrence or nonoccurrence of a specified event such as a scheduled payment under mortgage contract not made by physician) that is related to an asset (mortgage loan) of the guaranteed party (mortgage lender).

As an example, a physician obtains a mortgage guarantee from a hospital. The presence of the hospital's guarantee, obtained through a local bank, reduces the interest rate on the physician's mortgage loan by one-half point. No loan default is expected to occur (and as a result, no cash is expected to be paid out). At inception, the hospital would record an obligation to stand ready to perform in an amount equal to the fair value of the guarantee. FASB ASC 460 does not prescribe where the offsetting debit should go (for example, expense, asset, or adjustment to a gain or loss on sale), instead stating that it depends on the circumstances in which the guarantee was issued (FASB ASC 460-10-55-23).

FASB ASC 460 does not describe in detail how the guarantor's liability for its obligations under the guarantee would be measured subsequent to initial recognition, but notes (paragraph 12) that the liability typically would be reduced by a credit to earnings as the guarantor is released from risk under the guarantee. In the situation described previously, the hospital would be released from risk as the physician's outstanding mortgage obligation is reduced.

[Revised, June 2009, to reflect conforming changes necessary due to the issuance of FASB ASC.]

.47 Application of Accounting Standards Update No. 2011-07, *Presentation and Disclosure of Patient Service Revenue, Provision for Bad Debts, and the Allowance for Doubtful Accounts for Certain Health Care Entities*, in Consolidated Financial Statements

Inquiry—Health System consists of a parent holding company and two operating subsidiaries. Subsidiary A is an acute care hospital that has a policy of providing services to patients regardless of their ability to pay. Subsidiary A records patient service revenue at the time services are rendered and, thus, typically recognizes significant amounts of patient service revenue associated with uninsured self-pay patients prior to assessing its collectability. Subsidiary B is an ambulatory surgery center that does not have a policy of providing services to patients regardless of their ability to pay; thus, its provision for bad debts is a reflection of its credit risk. Health System issues consolidated financial statements. In addition, each subsidiary issues standalone financial statements.

FASB Accounting Standards Update (ASU) No. 2011-07, *Health Care Entities (Topic 954): Presentation and Disclosure of Patient Service Revenue, Provision for Bad Debts, and the Allowance for Doubtful Accounts for Certain Health Care Entities (a consensus of the FASB Emerging Issues Task Force)*, amended FASB ASC 954-605-45 to require that a health care entity present all bad debts associated with patient service revenue as a deduction from revenue if a significant amount of patient service revenue is recognized at the time services are rendered and the entity does not assess the patient's ability to pay. Thus, in the separate subsidiary statements, Subsidiary A's statement of operations presents bad debts associated with patient service revenue as a deduction from patient service revenue, while Subsidiary B's statement of operations displays bad debts related to patient service revenue as an operating expense.

In determining how to present bad debts in Health System's consolidated statement of operations, should the assessment of significance be made at the consolidated reporting entity level (regardless of the presentation in the separate subsidiary financial statements), or should the determinations made at the separate subsidiary reporting level be retained in consolidation?

Reply—Because ASU No. 2011-07 does not address this issue, the determination of whether the presentation of bad debts at the consolidated reporting entity level should be based on an entity-wide assessment of significance or on significance determined at the level of each individual subsidiary is an accounting policy election. If Health System decides to retain the presentations determined based on assessments made at the individual subsidiary reporting level (based on FASB ASC 810-10-25-15, which states that the application of guidance in an industry-specific topic of FASB ASC to a subsidiary within the scope of that topic shall be retained in consolidation), the consolidated statement of operations would reflect bad debts related to Subsidiary A's patient service revenue as a deduction from patient service revenue and the bad debts related to Subsidiary B's patient service revenue as an operating expense.

Alternatively, Health System may elect to assess "significance" at the consolidated reporting entity level regardless of the presentations used in the separate subsidiary financial statements. In that case, if consolidated patient service revenues are deemed to include a significant amount of revenue recognized under a policy in which services are provided to patients regardless of their ability to pay, then the entire provision for bad debts related to consolidated patient service (that is, the combined bad debts of Subsidiaries A and B) would be presented as a deduction from the consolidated net patient service revenues. If such revenues are not deemed to be significant at the consolidated reporting entity level, the entire provision for bad debts related to consolidated patient service revenues should be presented as an operating expense.

Application of the disclosure requirements would be consistent with the policy that is elected. Whichever policy is elected should be disclosed in the notes to the financial statements in accordance with FASB ASC 230-10-50-1 and consistently applied.

It is recommended that Securities and Exchange Commission (SEC) registrants consider consultations with the SEC staff if they are considering accounting for transactions similar to those described in this inquiry.

[Issue Date: February 2012. Revised, March 2012.]

.48 Accounting for Costs Incurred During Implementation of ICD-10

Inquiry—The U.S. health care system is scheduled to transition from the International Classification of Diseases, 9th Edition (ICD-9) code sets used to report medical diagnoses and inpatient procedures to the International Classification of Diseases, 10th Edition (ICD-10). ICD-10 expands the number of available codes from 24,000 to greater than 155,000. With its expanded capacity and complexity, ICD-10 enables the documentation of many different types of diseases and conditions and the capture of diagnostic information with a higher level of specificity. The transition from ICD-9 to ICD-10 is expected to produce several distinct benefits for health care entities, including the following:

- Improved precision in documentation of clinical care, which is expected to result in greater accuracy in the processing of claims and reimbursements
- Higher quality and more specific data that can be tracked and used to improve disease management programs and clinical outcomes

Implementing ICD-10 by October 1, 2013, is mandatory.[12] Health care entities that do not comply are expected to be unable to submit claims to third-party payors for payment. Costs expected to be incurred in connection with the conversion include those to (*a*) modify existing computer systems to accept the ICD-10 fields or to replace systems that cannot be made ICD-10 compliant, (*b*) enhance electronic medical records, (*c*) train clinical coders to use ICD-10, and (*d*) train clinicians to improve their documentation practices so that medical documentation contains the details necessary to support the higher level of specificity that ICD-10 enables.

How should a health care entity account for costs incurred in connection with the implementation of ICD-10?

Reply—ICD-10 conversion is expected to require changes to both business processes and information systems. When a project involves both process engineering and software development or modification, the guidance in FASB ASC

[12] In April 2012, the U.S. Department of Health and Human Services officially proposed delaying the International Classification of Diseases, 10th Edition implementation deadline to October 1, 2014. More information on the proposed rule is available on fact sheets at www.cms.gov/apps/media/fact_sheets.asp. The proposed rule may be viewed at www.ofr.gov/inspection.aspx.

720-45 should be considered. FASB ASC 720-45 requires that project costs be segregated among process reengineering activities, activities that develop or modify software, and costs associated with acquisition of fixed assets. The costs associated with process reengineering (for example, assessing the current state of business processes, process redesign or reengineering, or work force restructuring) are expensed as incurred. The costs associated with developing or modifying internal-use software are capitalized or expensed based on FASB's internal-use software guidance (discussed further in the text that follows). Costs associated with acquisition of fixed assets are accounted for in accordance with an entity's policy for capitalizing long-lived productive assets. If an outside consultant is engaged to conduct the project, the total consulting contract price should be allocated among these activities based on the relative fair values of each component (which are not necessarily the separate prices stated within the contract for each element). FASB ASC 720-45-55-1 provides a helpful table that summarizes the accounting for typical components of a business process reengineering and information technology transformation project and the guidance that applies to each component.

Significant expenses also are likely to be incurred in connection with training coders and clinicians to comply with the ICD-10 requirements. According to paragraphs 4 and 6 of FASB ASC 350-40-25, all training costs should be expensed as incurred, even those that are incurred during the application development stage.

The guidance set forth in FASB ASC 350-40 should be followed when accounting for the portion of project costs associated with either acquisition of new ICD-10 compliant systems or modification of existing software to become ICD-10 compliant. Health care entities should determine the extent to which those modifications result in "additional functionality"—that is, whether the modifications enable the software to perform tasks that it was previously incapable of performing.

The specific facts and circumstances of each entity should be considered in evaluating whether any of the modifications result in additional functionality, and professional judgment should be applied in assessing whether modifications to an entity's system result in additional functionality beyond the original software's capabilities and qualify as an upgrade or enhancement. Factors to consider in the assessment might include, but are not limited to, the following:

- The extent and types of changes being made to the software design. A significant amount of changes may be indicative of additional functionality.
- The amount of additional software coding required and the new software processes developed. Less software coding or few additional software processes may point toward maintenance rather than additional functionality.
- The extent to which billing system data will be used for new purposes, including its ability to use the additional coding capabilities beyond submitting claims to Medicare (for example, to track data in order to improve disease management programs and clinical outcomes or to enhance the quality of patient care or pay-for-performance contracts), may be indicative of additional functionality.
- Whether the changes are part of normal maintenance provided by the vendor at no additional cost. If the entity was billed

separately for an upgrade, or if the maintenance fee with the vendor significantly increased in the period of the change, that may be indicative of additional functionality.

- The entity's historical experience with clinical coding system upgrades (for example, the number of years since the last upgrade, the amount of changes made, whether that upgrade qualified for capitalization). An entity should consider the criteria applied to previous upgrades, including its experience to determine whether they resulted in additional functionality, and compare those criteria to the facts and circumstances associated with the proposed or planned upgrade.
- Increase in the number and complexity of the interfaces between the central billing system and downstream departmental systems. The greater the complexity of the system, the more likely that significant changes will be required, resulting in additional functionality.

Modifications of software that do not result in additional functionality are expensed as maintenance costs. Modifications that result in additional functionality are considered upgrades or enhancements of the existing system and are expensed or capitalized in accordance with the criteria set forth in paragraphs 1–6 of FASB ASC 350-40-25.

[Issue Date: July 2012.]

.49 Presentation of Claims Liability and Insurance Recoveries—Contingencies Similar to Malpractice

Inquiry—ASU No. 2010-24, *Health Care Entities (Topic 954): Presentation of Insurance Claims and Related Insurance Recoveries (a consensus of the FASB Emerging Issues Task Force)*, addressed the presentation of a health care entity's insurance claims and related insurance recoveries. The ASU specifically addressed malpractice claims but also referenced similar contingent liabilities. What is meant by *similar contingent liabilities*?

Reply—Similar contingent liabilities within the scope of ASU No. 2010-24 include liabilities of a similar nature, such as workers compensation and director and officers claims.

[Issue Date: October 2012.]

.50 Accrual of Legal Costs Associated With Contingencies Other Than Malpractice

Inquiry—FASB ASC 954-450 requires health care entities to estimate and accrue the legal costs that are expected to be incurred in connection with litigating a malpractice claim in the period the malpractice incident arises. In accounting for legal costs associated with contingency claims other than malpractice, some health care entities have followed guidance in FASB ASC 450-20-S99-2 that permits making a policy election to either expense claims-related legal fees in the period(s) in which the costs are actually incurred or to estimate and accrue them in the period in which the associated claim arises. Although that guidance specifically applies to entities required to apply the SEC's rules and regulations, other entities have also looked to that guidance as a basis for establishing an accounting policy election.

Health System GHI has contingent liabilities associated with workers compensation claims. Based on the guidance in FASB ASC 450-20-S99-2, Health System GHI established an accounting policy of expensing legal costs incurred in connection with its workers compensation claims in the periods in which the legal costs are actually incurred. Does the adoption of ASU No. 2010-24 require Health System GHI to change its method of accounting for legal costs incurred in connection with its workers compensation claims to be consistent with the method used for legal costs associated with its malpractice claims?

Reply—The adoption of ASU No. 2010-24 should not cause an entity to change its accounting for legal costs associated with contingencies other than medical malpractice liabilities. Because Health System GHI's established accounting policy is to expense such costs in the period(s) in which they are actually incurred, it would continue to apply that policy subsequent to its adoption of ASU No. 2010-24. Similarly, an entity that utilized FASB ASC 450-20-S99-2 as a basis for establishing a policy of estimating and accruing expected legal costs in the period in which the incident that gives rise to the claim occurs would continue to apply its policy election subsequent to adoption of the ASU. The appropriateness of any changes by an entity in its policy for accounting for legal costs incurred in connection with contingent liabilities other than malpractice would be evaluated in accordance with FASB ASC 250-10.

[Issue Date: October 2012.]

.51 Presentation of Insurance Recoveries When Insurer Pays Claims Directly

Inquiry—Prior to the issuance of ASU No. 2010-24, most health care entities that carried professional liability insurance only reported liabilities related to malpractice claims that were not covered by insurance (in effect, netting anticipated insurance recoveries against the related liability). ASU No. 2010-24 amended FASB ASC 954-450-25-2 to provide that a health care entity should not net insurance recoveries against related insurance claim liabilities and that the claim liability should be determined without consideration of insurance recoveries. The amendments are consistent with the guidance on netting receivables and payables in FASB ASC 210-20 that are more broadly applicable for other industries.

ABC Hospital's medical malpractice insurance policy provides that the insurer will handle all aspects of claims handling and settlement for ABC Hospital's covered malpractice claims, including making payments to plaintiffs directly on behalf of ABC Hospital. Thus, ABC Hospital neither pays its own malpractice claims nor receives insurance recoveries. How do the amendments to FASB ASC 954-450-25-2 made by ASU No. 2010-24 apply to ABC Hospital's malpractice liabilities?

Reply—Unless ABC Hospital has a valid right of setoff (which is not common), as described in FASB ASC 210-20-45, ABC Hospital should report the gross amount of its claims liabilities (including legal costs) as its obligations, regardless of whether covered by insurance, and should record a receivable as if it were entitled to receive insurance recoveries to offset those obligations, as discussed in FASB ASC 954-450-25-2. It is expected that in most cases, this results in reporting a receivable that mirrors the amount of estimated losses accrued that are covered by insurance.

This situation is discussed in paragraph BC4 of ASU No. 2010-24. Despite the fact that an insurance entity is paying for the defense of the claim and ultimately paying for some or all of the award or settlement, ABC Hospital is the primary obligor for payment of the claim (because if the insurer was unable to pay, ABC Hospital would still be liable). Thus, the guidance in the amendments made by ASU No. 2010-24 applies to ABC Hospital's malpractice liabilities.

[Issue Date: October 2012.]

.52 Insurance Recoveries From Certain Retrospectively Rated Insurance Policies

Inquiry—GHI Health System's (GHI's) program of medical malpractice risk management includes a retrospectively rated insurance policy (that is, a policy with a premium that is adjustable based on actual claims experience during the policy term). The total annual premium consists of a minimum premium (representing the insurance company's expenses and profits) and an additional amount for estimated claims that is adjusted based on GHI's actual malpractice loss experience. The policy is also subject to a maximum premium amount. How would GHI apply the guidance in ASU No. 2010-24 to claims that are covered by an insurance policy with a retrospectively related premium that reflects GHI's own experience?

Reply—ASU No. 2010-24 requires GHI to report the gross amount of liability for its estimated malpractice claims without regard to any insurance coverage that may exist and to record a receivable to the extent it is indemnified against risk of financial loss through an insurance policy. The existence of an insurance policy, in itself, is no assurance that GHI has been indemnified against risk of financial loss. To the extent that an insurance contract does not, despite its form, provide for indemnification of the insured against loss, the insured entity must account for it as a deposit (financing) arrangement rather than insurance, as discussed in FASB ASC 720-20 and 340-30.

Therefore, at policy inception, GHI should determine the extent to which its retrospectively rated policy actually provides indemnification against risk of financial loss associated with malpractice claims. Because the premium is based on GHI's own loss experience, the economic substance of the arrangement may more closely resemble a claims funding mechanism than a contract that indemnifies GHI against risk of financial loss. The facts and circumstances of the terms of the insurance arrangement must be carefully evaluated in making this assessment. For example, a premium that adjusts dollar for dollar to ultimate loss experience during the coverage period and for which the loss experience has only a remote chance of exceeding the maximum premium is likely indicative of a self-insurance funding program and would be accounted for as a financing arrangement based on the guidance in FASB ASC 340-30. In that situation, there would typically be no insurance recoveries to record because claims are being paid from GHI's own resources on deposit with the insurer. This is consistent with FASB ASC 954-720-25-1 that states that "[i]nsurance recoveries from a retrospectively rated insurance policy whose ultimate premium is based primarily on the health care entity's loss experience shall not be recognized until the estimated losses exceed the stipulated maximum premium." However, if it is reasonably possible that GHI's ultimate loss experience will exceed the maximum premium, the policy is more likely to have indemnified GHI against a certain level of loss. In that situation, insurance recoveries associated with that indemnification, if any, would be determined and presented separately as a receivable.

[Issue Date: October 2012.]

Q&A Section 6500

Extractive Industries

[.01–.03] Reserved

Q&A Section 6500

Extractive Industries

[.01-.03] Reserved

Q&A Section 6600

Real Estate

.01 Method of Recognizing Revenue From Commissions by Real Estate Brokerage Firm

Inquiry—A client is a real estate broker and also manages real estate. The client is the exclusive broker for all its affiliates and acts as broker for outside parties as well. All of the affiliates invest in raw land for appreciation and occasionally improve and subdivide parcels. None of the properties are extensive enough to be considered "retail land sales companies." Sales are probably half for second home sites and half for larger parcels bought for investment. Sales are usually for cash with an occasional mortgage taken by the seller. The client usually receives a gross brokerage commission of 10 percent to 15 percent, which is shared with its salesmen and cobrokers, retaining an average of 5 percent. Commissions are received at closing and cobrokers are paid shortly after the closing. Salesmen draw against firm purchase and sale agreements and are credited with the commission on closing. If a buyer fails to complete a purchase, his deposit is usually retained by the client in lieu of the brokerage commission, which legal counsel indicates is permitted under law.

The client records brokerage commission income when a firm purchase and sale agreement is accepted. This is an agreement which specifies price and all terms of sale, has no unusual or difficult conditions, and is secured by a deposit of 10 percent or more of the purchase price. This method was adopted by the client to more closely match revenues and expenses. Indirect selling expenses, including advertising, are treated as period costs. The costs of cobrokerage and salesmen's commissions are also accrued at that time. The client's contention is that the earnings process has been substantially completed, and the wait until closing (usually 30–90 days but occasionally longer) is a legal formality rather than an integral part of the broker's work. Very few sales are not closed, and the price and terms of sale rarely change. From an audit point of view, many of the open sales at year-end have closed by completion of the audit field work. The client's financial statements do disclose the method of accounting employed for brokerage commissions.

Is this present method of accounting for brokerage commissions considered acceptable?

Reply—Revenue recognition is discussed in Financial Accounting Standards Board (FASB) Concepts Statement No. 5, *Recognition and Measurement of Business Enterprises*, paragraphs 83–84. Paragraph 83 states in part:

> "Revenues are not recognized until earned. An entity's revenue-earning activities involve delivering or producing goods, rendering services, or other activities that constitute its ongoing major or central operations, and revenues are considered to have been earned when the entity has substantially accomplished what it must do to be entitled to the benefits represented by the revenues."

Therefore, the client's method of accounting for commission income at the time when a firm purchase and sale agreement is entered into would be acceptable. However, because of state laws governing real estate operations, recognition of commission income might have to be postponed, depending on the particular legal requirements of a given state, until such time as the broker is legally entitled to receive that commission.

[.02] Reserved

.03 Accounting for Sale of Property With Option to Repurchase

Inquiry—A corporation sold a parcel of land to a bank. The corporation has an option to repurchase the land for a period of three years. The corporation received the full purchase price at the time of sale.

What is the proper accounting treatment for this transaction?

Reply—The conclusion in FASB *Accounting Standards Codification* (ASC) 360-20-40-38 is that a transaction whereby a seller has an obligation or an option to repurchase the property must be accounted for as a financing, leasing, or profit sharing arrangement. A right of first refusal based on a bona fide offer by a third party is ordinarily not an obligation or an option to repurchase.

[Revised, June 2009, to reflect conforming changes necessary due to the issuance of FASB ASC.]

.04 Method of Recognizing Profit on Sale of Undeveloped Land With a Release Provision

Inquiry—One hundred acres of undeveloped land was sold for $10,000 per acre for a total consideration of $1,000,000. The buyer made a cash down payment of $250,000, and the balance of $750,000 is payable in three annual installments of $250,000. The agreement has a release provision that title to the acreage will be released to the buyer on a basis of 115 percent of the sales price. Therefore, of the $250,000 down payment, $217,000 would be applicable to the release of 21.7 acres, and the balance of $33,000 would be applicable to the remaining acreage. At this point, there would be a balance due on the sales agreement of $750,000 against which $33,000 would apply. The buyer would have this privilege every year, and the only security would be the land underlying the agreement.

What is the proper accounting treatment?

Reply—FASB ASC 360-20-40-23 states the following:

> If the amounts applied to unreleased portions do not meet the initial and-continuing-investment criteria as applied to the sales value of those unreleased portions, profit shall be recognized on each released portion when it meets the criteria in paragraph 360-20-40-5 as if each release were a separate sale.

FASB ASC 360-20-40-5 states, in part:

> Profit on real estate sales transactions shall not be recognized by the full accrual method until all of the following criteria are met:
>
> *a.* A sale is consummated.
>
> *b.* The buyer's initial and continuing investments are adequate to demonstrate a commitment to pay for the property.
>
> *c.* The seller's receivable is not subject to future subordination.
>
> *d.* The seller has transferred to the buyer the usual risks and rewards of ownership in a transaction that is in substance a sale and does not have a substantial continuing involvement with the property.

Presumably, the tests referred to would have to be met continuously; that is, at the time of closing and at each release date.

The relationship of the $33,000 to the $750,000 is not sufficient "to constitute an adequate initial and continuing investment" related to the unreleased property. Therefore, "profit shall be recognized on each released portion when it meets the criteria in paragraph 360-20-40-5 as if each release were a separate sale" as stated in FASB ASC 360-20-40-23.

[Amended; Revised, June 2009, to reflect conforming changes necessary due to the issuance of FASB ASC.]

[.05] Reserved

[.06] Reserved

[.07] Reserved

[.08] Reserved

Q&A Section 6700

Construction Contractors

.01 Distinction Between Long-Term and Short-Term Construction Contracts

Inquiry—A construction company considers all contracts that are less than one year in duration as short-term contracts and accounts for them on a completed contract method. Long-term contracts are accounted for on the completed-contract method or the percentage of completion method depending on other factors.

Does the distinction made by the company conform with generally accepted accounting principles?

Reply—Financial Accounting Standards Board (FASB) *Accounting Standards Codification* (ASC) 605-35-25-92 states that the completed-contract method may be used as the basic accounting method only if the financial position and results of operations reported on that basis would not vary from those resulting from the use of the percentage-of-completion method, "for example, in circumstances in which an entity has primarily short-term contracts." FASB ASC 605-35-25-95 also states that an entity using the completed-contract method as its basic accounting method should depart from that policy for a single contract or a group of contracts not having the features described in paragraphs 92–93 of FASB ASC 605-35-25. Thus, it appears that the distinction made by the company conforms to generally accepted accounting principles.

[Amended; Revised, June 2009, to reflect conforming changes necessary due to the issuance of FASB ASC.]

[.02] Reserved

[.03] Reserved

[.04] Reserved

[.05] Reserved

[.06] Reserved

[.07] Reserved

[.08] Reserved

[.09] Reserved

.10 Payments for Landfill Rights

Inquiry—A construction contractor pays for rights allowing the contractor to extract a specified volume of landfill from a third party's property for a period of three years. How should the payment for landfill rights be classified in the contractor's balance sheet?

Reply—Until the landfill is extracted, the contractor should classify the payment for landfill rights as a deferred charge. The portion of the landfill payment related to the volume of landfill extracted should be reclassified as project costs. A deferred charge remaining at the termination of the agreement should be written off as an expense.

Q&A Section 6910
Investment Companies

[.01] Reserved

[.02] Reserved

[.03] Reserved

[.04] Reserved

[.05] Reserved

[.06] Reserved

[.07] Reserved

[.08] Reserved

[.09] Reserved

[.10] Reserved

[.11] Reserved

[.12] Reserved

[.13] Reserved

[.14] Reserved

[.15] Reserved

.16 Presentation of Boxed Investment Positions in the Condensed Schedule of Investments of Nonregistered Investment Partnerships

Inquiry—Should long and short positions in the same security (*boxed positions*) be disclosed on a gross or net basis in the schedule of investments?

Reply—Although there may be a perfect economic hedge in boxed positions, the determination of which components of the boxed position would be required to be presented in the schedule of investments should be evaluated on a gross basis for the purposes of the 5 percent of net assets test as described in FASB *Accounting Standards Codification* (ASC) 946-210-50-6. To the extent that one (or both) of the components is (are) required to be disclosed, such component(s) should be disclosed on the schedule of investments because there may be market risk if one position is removed before the other or experiences settlement costs or losses upon disposition. In the event that only one of the positions is required to be disclosed, a nonregistered investment partnership is not precluded from disclosing both positions.

[Revised, June 2009, to reflect conforming changes necessary due to the issuance of FASB ASC.]

.17 Disclosure of Long and Short Positions

Inquiry—If a nonregistered investment partnership has a long position that exceeds 5 percent of net assets and a short position in the same issuer that is less than 5 percent of net assets, is the investment partnership required to disclose both the long and short position in the condensed schedule of investments?

Reply—No. The guidance in FASB ASC 946-210-50-6 indicates that, in applying the 5 percent test to determine the investments to be disclosed in the condensed schedule of investments, total long and total short positions in any one issuer should be considered separately. Because the value of the long position exceeds 5 percent of net assets, disclosure of the long position is required; however, disclosure of the short position is not required because the short position does not exceed 5 percent of net assets. Although not required, a nonregistered investment partnership is not precluded from disclosing both positions

[Revised, June 2009, to reflect conforming changes necessary due to the issuance of FASB ASC.]

.18 Disclosure of an Investment in an Issuer When One or More Securities or One or More Derivative Contracts Are Held—Nonregistered Investment Partnerships

Inquiry—A nonregistered investment partnership may hold one or more securities of the same issuer and one or more derivative contracts for which the underlying is a security of the same issuer. How should such securities and derivative contracts be presented in the condensed schedule of investments when applying FASB ASC 946-210-50-6?

Reply—When applying the guidance in FASB ASC 946-210-50-6, the disclosure on the condensed schedule of investments relating to securities should be consistent with the classification of the securities on the statement of assets and liabilities. It is important to note, however, that derivative contracts may be netted for statement of assets and liabilities presentation when the right of offset exists under FASB ASC 210-20 and FASB ASC 815-10, although the disclosures in the condensed schedule of investments should reflect all open contracts by their economic exposure (that is, long exposure derivative versus short exposure derivative). The netting concepts allowed by FASB ASC 210-20 and FASB ASC 815-10 are not considered for purposes of presentation in the condensed schedule of investments. Those securities (market value) and derivative contracts (appreciation or fair value) that are classified as period-end assets on a gross basis (for derivative contracts, regardless of whether they represent long or short exposures) should be aggregated. To the extent that the sum constitutes more than 5 percent of net assets, the positions should be disclosed in accordance with FASB ASC 946-210-50-6. The investment company should similarly sum all of the positions classified as liabilities on a gross basis and determine whether they exceed 5 percent of net assets. Separate computations should be performed for assets and liabilities. The following are illustrative examples of how to apply the disclosure guidelines. Positions representing gross liabilities are presented in parentheses.

Example 1:

- U.S. Treasury Bond (long)—4 percent of net assets
- U.S. Treasury Bond (short)—(1 percent) of net assets
- U.S. Treasury Bond futures contract—Appreciation equals 2 percent of net assets

In the preceding example, the investment company should present separately the long bond and the futures contract in the condensed schedule of investments because, in aggregate, the gross asset position for this issuer exceeds 5 percent of net assets. The short bond position, which represents the only liability position associated with the issuer, is not required to be disclosed separately because the gross liability position is not more than 5 percent of net assets. This assessment for derivatives is made regardless of whether the exposure to the underlying is long or short. Assessments are based solely on the value of the derivative contract (that is, either a long or short position with depreciation or a negative fair value would be considered a liability and aggregated with other liabilities for the purpose of this test). The preparer may consider whether disclosure of all positions, including those 5 percent or less, would be appropriate or meaningful to the reader in the circumstances.

Example 2:

- Various bonds of X company (long)—4 percent of net assets
- Stock of X company (short)—(3 percent) of net assets
- Long exposure equity swap (X company is the underlying)—Fair value equals 2 percent of net assets
- Short exposure equity swap (X company is the underlying)—Fair value equals (1 percent) of net assets

The guidance in paragraphs 6(e)–6(f) of FASB ASC 946-210-50 relates to 5 percent disclosures for any derivative position. That guidance states, "In applying the 5-percent test, total long and total short positions in any one issuer shall be considered separately." This guidance contemplates situations such as the preceding example 2 in which an investment company holds both a long and short exposure to the same derivative without closing out either derivative position. In such cases, the long and short exposure to the same derivative should be considered separately and should not be netted for the purpose of the 5 percent issuer exposure calculation. This is consistent with the approach for boxed security positions.

In the preceding example 2, the investment company should present separately the various long bond positions and the long exposure equity swap contract in the condensed schedule of investments because, in aggregate, the gross asset position for this issuer exceeds 5 percent of net assets. Because none of the long bond positions is individually more than 5 percent of net assets, FASB ASC 946-210-50-6(c)(2) permits the reporting of all the long bond positions of that issuer in the aggregate (that is, naming the issuer but showing a range of maturities, interest rates, and other applicable bond disclosures as opposed to individually listing out the details of each of the long bond positions), although the preparer may consider whether disclosure of individual positions provides more meaningful information to the reader of the financial statements. The short stock position and the short exposure equity swap contract are not required to be disclosed separately because the gross liability position is, in aggregate, not more than 5 percent of net assets. Again, the investment company is not precluded from disclosing separately the short stock position and the short exposure equity swap position if the disclosure of such positions is deemed to provide more meaningful information to the reader. The preparer should consider both the long exposure and short exposure in the equity swaps separately and should not net them for the purpose of the 5 percent exposure calculation if both equity swap contracts have not been closed out.

Example 3:

- Bond of X company (long)—3 percent of net assets
- Stock of X company (short)—(1 percent) of net assets

- Swap (X company is the underlying)—Fair value equals (2 percent) of net assets

In the preceding example 3, the investment company would not be required to present separately any of the positions in the condensed schedule of investments because the gross asset position of the issuer (represented by the bond) is not more than 5 percent of net assets, and the gross liability position (represented by the combined total values of the short stock position and the swap) is also not more than 5 percent of net assets.

Example 4:

- Bond of X company (long)—4 percent of net assets
- Stock of X company (short)—(2 percent) of net assets
- Swap (X company is the underlying)—Fair value equals 2 percent of net assets
- Swap (X company is the underlying)—Fair value equals (4 percent) of net assets

In the preceding example 4, the investment company should present separately each of the positions in the condensed schedule of investments because the gross asset position of the issuer (represented by the combined total values of the bond and the appreciated swap) and the gross liability position of the issuer (represented by the combined total values of the short stock position and the depreciated swap) are both greater than 5 percent of net assets.

[Revised, June 2009, to reflect conforming changes necessary due to the issuance of FASB ASC; Revised, October 2010, by the Planning Subcommittee of FinREC.]

.19 Information Required to Be Disclosed in Financial Statements When Comparative Financial Statements of Nonregistered Investment Partnerships Are Presented

Inquiry—When comparative financial statements of a nonregistered investment partnership are presented, should the schedule of investment be presented as of the end of each period presented, or only as of the most recent date of the statement of assets and liabilities? Additionally, when comparative financial statements of a nonregistered investment partnership are provided, should the financial highlights be presented for each period provided, or only for the most recent period?

Reply—FASB ASC 946 does not require comparative financial statements for nonregistered investment partnerships. However, if an entity elects to prepare comparative financial statements, the general guidance for the presentation of comparative financial statements as found in paragraphs 2 and 4 of FASB ASC 205-10-45 indicate the following:

> In any one year it is ordinarily desirable that the statement of financial position, the income statement, and the statement of changes in equity be presented for one or more preceding years, as well as for the current year.
>
> Notes to financial statements, explanations, and accountants' reports containing qualifications that appeared on the statements for the preceding years shall be repeated, or at least referred to, in the comparative statements to the extent that they continue to be of significance.

Because the schedule of investments would continue to be considered of significance relative to the statement of assets and liabilities for the prior year, the schedule of investments for the prior year should be included as a part of the comparative statements. Additionally, FASB ASC 946-205-45-1 states that "at a minimum, a condensed schedule of investments (as discussed in paragraphs 946-210-50-4 through 50-10) should be provided for each statement of assets and liabilities." Therefore, comparative schedules of investments are required to be presented when comparative statements of assets and liabilities are reported.

Consistent with the requirements of FASB ASC 205-10-45, comparative financial highlights should be presented when comparative statements of operations are provided because they would also be considered a significant disclosure for the prior periods of operation included in the financial statements.

[Revised, June 2009, to reflect conforming changes necessary due to the issuance of FASB ASC.]

.20 Presentation of Purchases and Sales/Maturities of Investments in the Statement of Cash Flows

Inquiry—Should the value of securities purchased by a nonregistered investment partnership during the period presented be reported in the statement of cash flows separately from the proceeds received on the sale/maturity of securities by the nonregistered investment partnership or may the nonregistered investment partnership report only the net difference?

Reply—In general, a nonregistered investment partnership should present purchases and sales/maturities of long-term investments (securities purchased with no stated maturity or with a stated maturity of greater than one year at the date of acquisition) on a gross basis in the statement of cash flows pursuant to FASB ASC 230, *Statement of Cash Flows*, although the nonregistered investment partnership may consider the provisions in FASB ASC 230-10-45-9 in determining whether or not certain purchases and sales/maturities qualify for net reporting. Purchases and sales/maturities of short-term investments (securities purchased with a stated remaining maturity of one year or less at the date of acquisition), however, may be presented on a net basis, as described in FASB ASC 230-10-45-18. Additionally, proceeds and costs reported for transactions in short positions are reflected separately from proceeds and costs associated with long positions.

[Revised, June 2009, to reflect conforming changes necessary due to the issuance of FASB ASC.]

.21 Recognition of Premium/Discount on Short Positions in Fixed-Income Securities

Inquiry—An investment company enters into short positions on various fixed-income securities, where the short sale price is at a premium or discount to the par value of the bond. The Audit and Accounting Guide *Investment Companies* discusses, in chapter 2, the requirement that an investment company amortize premiums/discounts on its investments, referring to long positions, but is silent as to whether similar accounting is required for short positions. The investment company currently recognizes all payments of coupon interest as interest expense on its short positions. Is the investment company also required under generally accepted accounting principles to amortize the premium and discount on the short position?

Reply—Yes. As when recognizing interest income on long positions, when recognizing interest expense on short positions, the investment company should recognize all economic elements of interest, including premium and discount.

[Revised, June 2009, to reflect conforming changes necessary due to the issuance of FASB ASC.]

.22 Presentation of Reverse Repurchase Agreements

Inquiry—An investment company enters into a *reverse repurchase agreement*, which is defined in chapter 3 of the Audit and Accounting Guide *Investment Companies* as "the sale of a security at a specified price with an agreement to purchase the same or substantially the same security from the same counterparty at a fixed or determinable price at a future date." The investment company receives cash and initially records the amount payable as a liability. Should reverse repurchase agreements be presented in the financial statements of investment companies at the amount payable or at fair value?

Reply—Investment companies present their debt obligations at amounts payable. Because reverse repurchase agreements represent a fixed, determinable obligation of the investment company, such agreements should also be presented at amounts payable. A reverse repurchase agreement denominated in a currency that differs from the reporting currency should be translated at the current exchange rate.

.23 Accounting Treatment of Offering Costs Incurred by Investment Partnerships

Inquiry—According to FASB ASC 946-20-25-6 and FASB ASC 946-20-35-5, all open-end registered investment companies and those closed-end registered investment companies with a continuous offering period should defer offering costs and amortize them to expense over 12 months on a straight-line basis. However, FASB ASC 946-20-25 does not indicate whether an investment partnership should apply the same treatment. Should an investment partnership that continually offers its interests also defer and amortize such costs over 12 months?

Reply—Yes, an investment partnership that continually offers its interests should defer offering costs incurred prior to the commencement of operations and then amortize them to expense over the period that it continually offers its interests, up to a maximum of 12 months. The straight-line method of amortization should generally be used. If the offering period terminates earlier than expected, the remaining deferred balance should be charged to expense.

[Revised, June 2009, to reflect conforming changes necessary due to the issuance of FASB ASC.]

.24 Meaning of "Continually Offer Interests"

Inquiry—How should an investment partnership determine if it continually offers its interests?

Reply—An investment partnership is deemed to continually offer its interests if an eligible, new investor may enter into an agreement to purchase an interest in the partnership on any business day or on a series of specified business days over a continuous period of time. A new investor is one that does not already own any interest in the investment partnership at the time of purchase.

Some investment partnerships may offer their interests at a single point in time and require new investors to commit to providing capital contributions over a period of time. As interests are not available for purchase over a continuous period, such investment partnerships would not be deemed to have a continuous offering period.

.25 Considerations in Evaluating Whether Certain Liabilities Constitute "Debt" for Purposes of Assessing Whether an Investment Company Must Present a Statement of Cash Flows

Inquiry—FASB ASC 230-10-15-4 exempts investment companies (both registered and unregistered) from the requirement to provide a statement of cash flows, if all of the following conditions are met:

a. During the period, substantially all of the entity's investments were carried at fair value and classified as level 1 or level 2 measurements in accordance with FASB ASC 820.[1]

b. *The enterprise had little or no debt, based on the average debt outstanding*[2] *during the period, in relation to average total assets. (emphasis added)*

c. The enterprise provides a statement of changes in net assets.[3]

Because FASB ASC 230-10-15-4(c)(3) specifically states that covered options written would generally not be considered debt for purposes of determining whether an investment company meets these conditions, does that imply that *uncovered options* and *short sales of securities and reverse repos* must, by inference, be treated as debt? If not, under what circumstances may they be excluded from *debt* in determining whether the investment company must present a statement of cash flows?

Reply—Although presented in the liabilities section of the statement of assets and liabilities, options sold/written (whether covered or uncovered), short sales of securities, and other liabilities recorded as a result of investment practices are not necessarily debt; rather, their classification depends on the nature of the activity. Certain transactions (for example, securities lending, mortgage dollar rolls, or short sale transactions) may have a practice of being entered into solely for operating purposes (similarly to unsettled purchases of securities) or as an investing strategy (similarly to covered options written), and the investment company either retains the proceeds in cash accounts or uses them to invest in securities that are cash equivalents under FASB ASC 230. In such cases, the proceeds from the transaction would not be considered debt for purposes of assessing whether the conditions in FASB ASC 230 are met.

[Issue Date: May 2008; Revised, June 2009, to reflect conforming changes necessary due to the issuance of FASB ASC; Revised, October 2013, to reflect conforming changes necessary due to the issuance of FASB ASU No. 2012-04.]

---

[1] [Footnote deleted, October 2013, to reflect conforming changes necessary due to the issuance of FASB ASU No. 2012-04.

[2] FASB *Accounting Standards Codification* (ASC) 230-10-15-4(c)(3) states, "For the purpose of determining average debt outstanding, obligations resulting from redemptions of shares by the entity from unsettled purchases of securities or similar assets, or from covered options written generally may be excluded. However, any extension of credit by the seller that is not in accordance with standard industry practices for redeeming shares or for settling purchases of investments shall be included in average debt outstanding."

[3] FASB ASC 946-205-45-5 states, "For investment partnerships, the statement of changes in net assets may be combined with the statement of changes in partners' capital if the information in paragraph 946-205-45-3 is presented."

.26 Additional Guidance on Determinants of Net Versus Gross Presentation of Security Purchases and Sales/Maturities in the Statement of Cash Flows of a Nonregistered Investment Company

Inquiry—Under what circumstances, if any, may purchases and sales/maturities of securities presented in the operating section of the statement of cash flows of a nonregistered investment company be shown on a *net*, rather than a *gross*, basis?

Reply—Chapter 7 of the AICPA Audit and Accounting Guide *Investment Companies* states:

> Cash flows from operating activities should include the fund's investing activities. Cash flows from operating activities include (***bold ital*** added for emphasis)—
>
> *a.* Interest and dividends received.
>
> *b.* Operating expenses paid.
>
> *c.* ***Purchases of long-term investments*** (at cost).
>
> *d.* ***Sales of long-term investments*** (proceeds).
>
> *e.* ***Net sales or purchases of short-term investments***.
>
> *f.* Cash flows for other types of investing activities related to changes in margin accounts and collateral status, such as written options, financial futures contracts, securities lending, and so forth.

Section 6910.20 provides the following guidance:

> In general, a nonregistered investment partnership should present purchases and sales/maturities of long-term investments (securities purchased with no stated maturity or with a stated maturity of greater than one year at the date of acquisition) on a gross basis in the statement of cash flows pursuant to FASB ASC 230, *Statement of Cash Flows*, although the nonregistered investment partnership may consider the provisions in FASB ASC 230-10-45-9 in determining whether or not certain purchases and sales/maturities qualify for net reporting. Purchases and sales/maturities of short-term investments (securities purchased with a stated remaining maturity of one year or less at the date of acquisition), however, may be presented on a net basis, as described in FASB ASC 230-10-45-18. Additionally, proceeds and costs reported for transactions in short positions are reflected separately from proceeds and costs associated with long positions.

One of the requirements of FASB ASC 230-10-45-9 is that the original maturity of assets and liabilities qualifying for net reporting is 3 months or less. However, FASB ASC 230-10-45-18 permits "banks, brokers and dealers in securities, and other entities [that] carry securities and other assets in a trading account" to classify cash receipts and cash payments from such activities as operating cash flows, while cash flows from transactions in "available for sale" securities are reported gross as investing activities.[4] In other industries, operating cash flows relating to trading account securities typically are reported on a net basis.

---

[4] Refer to paragraphs 11 and 18–20 of FASB ASC 230-10-45 and FASB ASC 310-10-45-11 for additional guidance.

If a nonregistered investment company presents a statement of cash flows, the investment company's trading style, investment objectives stated in its offering memorandum, and portfolio turnover should be the primary determinants of net versus gross reporting. Where the investment company's overall activities comport with *trading*, as discussed in FASB ASC 230 and FASB ASC 320, *Investments—Debt and Equity Securities*,[5] netting is permissible; otherwise, gross reporting of purchases and sales/maturities is required.

Regardless of whether net or gross reporting is appropriate based on the stated criteria, an entity should separately report its activity related to long positions from activity related to short positions; that is, changes/activity in account balances reported as assets should not be netted against changes/activity in account balances reported as liabilities.

[Issue Date: May 2008; Revised, June 2009, to reflect conforming changes necessary due to the issuance of FASB ASC.]

.27 Treatment of Deferred Fees

Inquiry—The governing documents of an offshore fund provide that the investment adviser may elect to defer payment of its management fee, incentive fee, or both. Based on the documents, the deferred fees that are payable to the investment adviser do not take the form of a legal capital account and are settled exclusively in cash. Under this arrangement, the fund retains the fee amount and is obligated to pay the investment adviser the deferred fees at a later date adjusted for the fund's rate of return (whether positive or negative). How should the deferred fees and the appreciation or depreciation on the deferred fees be presented on the statement of assets and liabilities, on the statement of operations, and on the financial highlights? What additional disclosures, if any, should be included in the financial statements or the notes to the financial statements?

Reply—In accordance with guidance from paragraph 35 of FASB Statement of Financial Accounting Concepts No. 6, *Elements of Financial Statements*, the fund should record the cumulative deferred fees as a liability. The indexing of this liability to the fund's rate of return represents a hybrid instrument that has a host debt instrument with an embedded derivative, which has attributes of a total return contract. Although FASB ASC 815-15-25-1 and FASB ASC 815-15-55-190 require the embedded total return contract to be bifurcated from the host debt instrument, the Securities and Exchange Commission staff has previously indicated[6] that the bifurcation requirements of FASB ASC 815 do not extend beyond measurement to financial statement presentation, if the embedded

---

[5] FASB ASC glossary defines *trading securities* as follows:

> Securities that are bought and held principally for the purpose of selling them in the near term and therefore held for only a short period of time. Trading generally reflects active and frequent buying and selling, and trading securities are generally used with the objective of generating profits on short-term differences in price.

Although investment companies do not apply FASB ASC 320 and, therefore, do not normally categorize securities as trading, available for sale, or held to maturity, the concepts of whether the securities are held for trading purposes and whether the related cash flows would be classified as operating cash flows under paragraphs 11 and 18–20 of FASB ASC 230-10-45 and FASB ASC 310-10-45-11 are relevant in determining whether cash flows from purchases and sales of securities should be presented gross or net by investment companies.

[6] Twenty-Eighth Annual National Conference on Current SEC Developments December 4–6, 2000. Remarks by E. Michael Pierce.

derivative and host debt instrument, together, represent the principal and interest obligations of a debt instrument. While the fund should fair value the embedded return component of the deferral arrangement according to the guidance from FASB ASC 815-10-25-1, FASB ASC 815-10-30-1, and FASB ASC 815-10-35-1, generally, the fair value of such return component would be the same as the appreciated or depreciated return of the fund because (1) the fund fair values all of its investments, whether assets or liabilities, which generally represent substantially all of its net assets, and (2) if the deferred fee liability was transferred, the transfer would likely be transacted at the current net asset value.[7] The deferred fees and the embedded total return contracts associated with deferred fees that are at an appreciated or depreciated position as of the reporting date may be presented as one amount titled "Deferred incentive fees payable" on the statement of assets and liabilities.

FASB ASC 946-225-45-1 states, in part, "The objective of the statement of operations is to present the increase or decrease in net assets resulting from all of the company's investment activities, by reporting investment income from dividends, interest, and other income less expenses, the amounts of realized gains or losses from investment and foreign currency transactions, and changes in unrealized appreciation or depreciation of investments and foreign-currency-denominated assets and liabilities for the period." Because the fund directly earns or incurs the income, expenses, net realized gains or losses, and unrealized appreciation or depreciation on the deferred fee retained in the fund, such amounts should be presented within their respective line items in the investment company's statement of operations. The net change in unrealized appreciation or depreciation on the total return contracts associated with the deferred fees should be reported in earnings; that is, reflected as an expense (appreciation of deferred fees) or negative expense (depreciation of deferred fees) of the fund rather than as an allocation of earnings or losses and, following the guidance from FASB ASC 850, *Related Party Disclosures*, should be presented separately from the current period management or incentive fee.

FASB ASC 946-205-50-7 states, in part, "the caption descriptions in the per-share data shall be the same captions used in the statement of operations . . . to allow the reader to determine which components of operations are included in or excluded from various per-share data." FASB ASC 946-205-50-14 adds "generally, the determination of expenses for computing those ratios shall follow the presentation of expenses in the fund's statement of operations." The per share information, net investment income ratio, and net expense ratio included in the financial highlights should reflect the amounts presented on the statement of operations including the adjustment associated with the deferred fee amount. In order to reflect the effect of the adjustment on the fund's expense ratio, the fund may also present an expense ratio that excludes the amount of deferred fee expense or negative expense reported in the statement of operations. Consistent with guidance from FASB ASC 946, *Financial Services—Investment Companies*, the fund should disclose the nature of the deferred fee arrangement, including the priority of claim in the event of liquidation, the current period and cumulative amounts deferred, the cumulative earnings or losses on the deferral, the terms of payment, the date that the deferral payments commence (or the next payment date), and the manner in which the deferral will be invested.

---

[7] All concepts of FASB ASC 820, *Fair Value Measurement*, should be considered.

The following is an illustration of a deferred incentive fee presentation in the financial statements and the related disclosures:

Statement of Assets and Liabilities

Assets	
Cash and cash equivalents	$206,000
Investments, at fair value	166,585,000
Total assets	$166,791,000
Liabilities	
Management fee payable	$400,000
Redemptions payable	1,000,000
Accrued expenses	100,000
Deferred incentive fees payable	4,800,000
Total liabilities	6,300,000
Net assets	$160,491,000

Statement of Operations

Investment income	
Interest income	$5,576,000
Dividend income	1,766,000
Total investment income	$7,342,000
Expenses	
Incentive fee	$2,680,000
Management fee	1,831,000
Change in net appreciation on deferred incentive fees	650,000
Administration fee	60,000
Professional fees and other	75,000
Total expenses	5,296,000
Net investment income	$2,046,000

(continued)

Realized and unrealized gains (losses) from investment activities	
Net realized gain on securities	$2,773,000
Net realized gain on swap and forward contracts	509,000
Net change in unrealized appreciation on securities	1,515,000
Net change in unrealized appreciation on swap and forward contracts	852,000
Net realized and unrealized gain from investment activities	$5,649,000
Net increase in net assets resulting from operations	$7,695,000

Notes to Financial Statements

Note X—Investment Management and Incentive Fees

Pursuant to an investment advisory agreement, the Fund pays to the Adviser a quarterly management fee of $\frac{1}{4}$ of 1 percent (1 percent per annum) of the net assets of the Fund on the last day of each quarter. The Adviser also is entitled to an annual incentive fee equal to 20 percent of the net profits attributable to each series of common shares, subject to a loss carry forward. If there is a net loss for the year, the incentive fee will not apply to future years until such net loss has been recovered, adjusted for redemptions.

The Adviser may elect to defer receipt of all or a portion of the management or incentive fees earned for a particular fiscal year, and such amounts will be indexed to the Fund's return. In the event of liquidation of the Fund, any deferred amount, as adjusted for the appreciation or depreciation resulting from indexing, the deferred fee to the Fund's return has a priority claim over the interests of the equity holders of the Fund.

For the [year/period] ended December 31, 20XX, payment of 50 percent of the incentive fee incurred by the Fund was deferred for X years. Cumulative deferred incentive fees as of December 31, 20XX totaled $3,850,000, and cumulative net appreciation on such amounts totaled $950,000. The net change in appreciation or depreciation of deferred incentive fees is recorded on a separate line item under "Expenses" within the statement of operations. Distributions of 20XX and prior year deferred incentive fees are scheduled for the period from [DATE RANGE]. During the year ended December 31, 20XX, the distribution of previously deferred incentive fees amounted to $500,000.

The following is an example disclosure of a roll forward of deferred incentive fees payable, which is a best practice disclosure.

The deferred incentive fees payable balance as of December 31, 20XX is comprised of the following:

Deferred incentive fees payable at January 1, 20XX	$3,310,000
Appreciation on deferred incentive fees for the year ended December 31, 20XX	650,000
Incentive fees deferred for the year ended December 31, 20XX	1,340,000
Deferred incentive fees paid for the year ended December 31, 20XX	(500,000)
Deferred incentive fees payable at December 31, 20XX	$4,800,000

Note X—Financial Highlights

The following represents the per share information, ratios to average net assets, and other supplemental information for the year ended December 31, 20XX:

	Class A Initial series	*Class B Initial series*
Per share operating performance:		
Beginning net asset value	$1,130.35	$1,123.80
Income from investment operations:		
Net investment income	11.01	6.76
Net realized and unrealized gain from investment activities	141.50	145.64
Total income from operations	152.51	152.40
Ending net asset value	$1,282.86	$1,276.20
Ratios to average net assets:		
Expenses other than incentive fee	1.43%	1.46%
Incentive fee	1.46	1.49
Total expenses	2.89	2.95
Change in net appreciation on deferred incentive fees	(0.40)	(0.43)
Total expense excluding change in net appreciation on deferred incentive fees	2.49%	2.52%
Net investment income	1.12%	1.09%
Total return prior to incentive fee	17.07%	16.93%
Incentive fee	(3.58)	(3.37)
Total return after incentive fee	13.49%	13.56%

The per share operating performance and total return are calculated for the initial series of each share class. The ratios to average net assets are calculated for each class taken as a whole. An individual investor's per share operating performance, total return, and ratios to average net assets may vary from these per share amounts and ratios based on participation in new issues and different management fee and incentive fee arrangements and the timing and amount of capital transactions.

[Issue Date: May 2008; Revised, June 2009, to reflect conforming changes necessary due to the issuance of FASB ASC.]

.28 Reporting Financial Highlights, Net Asset Value (NAV) Per Share, Shares Outstanding, and Share Transactions When Investors in Unitized Nonregistered Funds Are Issued Individual Classes or Series of Shares

Inquiry—Some unitized nonregistered funds issue a separate series of shares to each individual investor in the fund, which remains outstanding so long as the investor maintains its investment in the fund and is not closed until the investor fully redeems. These series may be issued within multiple classes of shares with each series within a class bearing the same economic characteristics. The shares are legally issued and outstanding until redemption (that is, they are not notional interests), but will not be converted or otherwise consolidated into an identifiable "permanent" series of shares in a "series roll-up."[8] Essentially, these unitized funds apply partnership accounting.

How should financial highlights (per share data, ratios, and total return) be presented in this situation, and how should each series of shares outstanding at period-end and share transactions during the period be disclosed in the financial statements?

Reply—

Presentation of Financial Highlights

The issuance of a separate series of shares to each individual investor is done for operational purposes because this enables a fund to allocate profit and loss to each investor in the same manner as a limited partnership allocates profit and loss to an individual partner's capital account. The definition of *nonregistered investment partnership—financial highlights* in the FASB ASC glossary—states, in part, that for unitized funds, "permanent series of a class of share shall be the basis for which that share's financial highlights are determined and presented." When a separate series of shares is issued to each individual investor and remains outstanding until the investor fully redeems, reporting the financial highlights for each outstanding series of shares could result in financial highlights presented for up to 500 investors and would be the substantive equivalent of presenting the financial highlights in a limited partnership for each limited partner.

The financial highlights should be presented at the aggregate level for the entire permanent series of shares from which the individual series of shares has been issued. Because the fund operates like a partnership, the financial

[8] A series roll up typically occurs at the end of the year when a temporary series of shares has increased above its high watermark (for example, the highest level in value a series has achieved, adjusted for subscriptions and redemptions) at which time the outstanding shares of a temporary series of shares are converted (or rolled up) into the permanent series of shares.

highlights should include only those financial highlights applicable to a partnership, which are the ratios to average net assets and total return, but not per share data.

When a separate series of shares is issued to each individual investor and remains outstanding until the investor fully redeems, the permanent series of shares will be the fund as a whole, excluding managing investor interests, if the shares otherwise have substantially similar terms. There are situations when a fund will issue multiple classes of shares, which contain multiple series of shares, due to differing fee arrangements or restrictions affecting an investor's ability to participate in the profits and losses generated by "new issue" securities. When a fund issues multiple classes of shares, and in each class of shares, a series of shares is issued to each individual investor and remains outstanding until the investor fully redeems, financial highlights should be presented at the aggregate level for each permanent class of shares from which the individual series of shares have been issued. For example, if a fund has outstanding, at year-end, Class A shares, Series 1–40, which have a 1 percent management fee; Class B shares Series 1–300, which have a 2 percent management fee; and Class C shares, which are only held by the managing investor, the fund would present financial highlights information for Class A, taken as a whole and Class B, taken as a whole. There is no requirement to present financial highlights for Class C because FASB ASC 946-205-50-4 requires financial highlights to be presented only for nonmanaging investors.

It would be acceptable for a fund to present supplemental financial highlights data for a single series of shares, which the fund determines to be "representative." Such financial highlights may be labeled as representing supplemental information and may only be presented in addition to those financial highlights that are required. Factors to consider when determining the representative series of shares include the following:

1. The series of shares was outstanding for the entire fiscal period (or, if all units of a series of shares outstanding at the beginning of the fiscal period were redeemed during the period, the series of shares at period-end outstanding for the longest period of time).
2. The fees and other offering terms of the series of shares most closely conform to those which may be described in the fund's offering documents.
3. The series of shares represent the largest ownership interest in the fund.

The basis of presentation of the financial highlights and the criteria used to determine the most representative series of shares should be disclosed in a note to those highlights and should be consistently applied.

If appropriate, a fund may present other supplemental information if determined to be informative and not misleading.

Presentation of Shares Outstanding and Share Transactions

FASB ASC 946-210-45-4 indicates that net asset value per share and shares outstanding should be reported for each class. Because a fund which issues a separate series of shares to each investor operates like a partnership, presenting the net asset value per share and the shares outstanding for each series of shares would be the substantive equivalent of presenting each partner's capital balance in the financial statements of a partnership, which is not required by FASB ASC 946 for nonunitized partnership interests. Chapter 7 of the guide discusses the requirement for the unitized funds to disclose units of capital, including the title and par value of each class of shares, and the number of shares authorized, outstanding, and dollar amount of such shares. FASB ASC 946-505-50-2 requires disclosure of the number and value of shares sold, the number and value of shares issued in reinvestment of distributions, the number and cost of shares reacquired, and the net change in shares. For funds which issue a separate series of shares to each investor, such funds should satisfy the disclosure requirements in FASB ASC 946-210-45-4 and 946-505-50-2 by presenting such disclosures on an aggregate share basis. For funds which issue multiple classes of shares which contain multiple series of shares, such disclosure requirements should be presented at the aggregate level for each permanent class of shares from which the individual series of shares have been issued.

EXAMPLE

A fund issues Class A and Class B nonvoting shares to investors and, within each class, a separate series of shares is issued to each individual investor. Class A shares have a 1 percent management fee and a 20 percent incentive fee, while Class B shares are issued to related party investors and, therefore, are not charged a management fee or an incentive fee. Class C voting shares are management shares and do not participate in the profits or losses of the fund. As of December 31, 20X7, there are 15,100 total shares outstanding totaling $1,517,600. The following shows such amounts outstanding as of December 31, 20X7 by class and series:

Class A Series 1–5,000 shares outstanding, NAV $500,000

Class A Series 2–7,500 shares outstanding, NAV $765,000

Class B Series 1–2,500 shares outstanding, NAV $252,500

Class C–100 shares outstanding, NAV $100

In the prior year, as of December 31, 20X6, there were 10,100 total shares outstanding totaling $970,100. The following shows such amounts outstanding as of December 31, 20X6 by class and series:

Class A Series 1–6,000 shares outstanding, NAV $588,000

Class B Series 1–3,000 shares outstanding, NAV $288,000

Class B Series 2–1,000 shares outstanding, NAV $94,000

Class C–100 shares outstanding, NAV $100

Example Statement of Assets and Liabilities

Statement of Assets and Liabilities
December 31, 20X7

Assets	
Cash and cash equivalents	$100,100
Investments, at fair value	1,550,000
Total assets	$1,650,100

Liabilities	
Redemptions payable	94,000
Management fees payable	4,000
Incentive fee payable	3,000
Accrued expenses	31,500
Total liabilities	132,500
Net assets (based on 12,500 Class A shares, 2,500 Class B shares, and 100 Class C shares outstanding)	$1,517,600

Example Footnote Disclosures

Capital Share Transactions

As of December 31, 20X7, 5,000,000 shares of capital stock were authorized. Class A and Class B shares have $0.01 par value, and Class C shares have $1.00 par value. Transactions in capital stock were as follows:

	Shares		*Amount*	
Class A	*20X7*	*20X6*	*20X7*	*20X6*
Shares sold	7,500	6,000	$750,000	$600,000
Shares redeemed	(1,000)	—	$(99,500)	—
Net increase	6,500	6,000	$650,500	$600,000

	Shares		*Amount*	
Class B	*20X7*	*20X6*	*20X7*	*20X6*
Shares sold	—	4,000	—	$400,000
Shares redeemed	(1,500)	—	($148,750)	—
Net increase	(1,500)	4,000	($148,750)	$400,000

	Shares		*Amount*	
Class C	*20X7*	*20X6*	*20X7*	*20X6*
Shares sold	—	100	—	$100
Shares redeemed	—	—	—	—
Net increase	—	100	—	$100

Financial Highlights

The ratios to average net assets and total return are presented below for each class taken as a whole, excluding managing shareholder interests, for the year ended December 31, 20X7. The ratios and total return are not annualized.

The computation of similar financial information for other participating shareholders may vary based on the timing of their respective capital transactions.

Annual ratios to average net assets and total return for the year ended December 31, 20X7 are as follows:

	Class A	*Class B*
Ratios to average net assets:		
Expenses other than incentive fee	2.26%	1.26%
Incentive fee	0.31%	0.00%
Total expenses	2.57%	1.26%
Net investment income	0.93%	1.93%
Total return prior to incentive fee	3.48%	5.02 %
Incentive fee	(0.40)%	(0.00)%
Total return after incentive fee	3.08%	5.02%

[Issue Date: May 2008; Revised, June 2009, to reflect conforming changes necessary due to the issuance of FASB ASC.]

.29 Allocation of Unrealized Gain (Loss), Recognition of Carried Interest, and Clawback Obligations

Inquiry—The governing documents of some nonregistered investment partnerships (as defined in chapter 7 of the AICPA Audit and Accounting Guide *Investment Companies*), may contain provisions which do not allow allocations of unrealized gains or losses, or do not require the recognition of carried interest (also referred to as *carry*, *incentive*, or *performance fees and allocations*), and clawback obligations (also referred to as *lookback*, *negative carried interest*, or *general partner*[9] *giveback*) until a specified date or time (for example, at the time of the partnership's liquidation or termination), or until the occurrence of a specific event (such as the actual disposition of an investment). Often, in these cases, the partnership's investments are either not marketable or are of such limited liquidity that interim valuations are highly subjective, and the intent of the provision is to delay the general partner's receipt of incentive allocations in cash until the gains can be measured objectively. In preparing financial statements of an investment partnership in accordance with U.S. generally accepted accounting principles, in which capital is reported by investor class, how should cumulative unrealized gains (losses), carried interest, and clawback be reflected in the equity balances of each class of shareholder or partner at the balance sheet date? In particular, should cumulative period-end unrealized gains and losses, nonetheless, be allocated as if realized in accordance

[9] Various terms may be used by different legal structures as the equivalents of *general partner* and *limited partner* (for example, *managing member* and *member* for limited liability companies). For convenience, the terms *partnership*, *general partner*, and *limited partner* are used throughout, but are intended to refer to any equivalent structure.

with the partnership's governing documents prior to the date, time, or event specified in the partnership agreement?

Reply—If a nonregistered investment partnership reports capital by investor class, cumulative unrealized gains (losses), carried interest, and clawback provisions would be reflected in the equity balances of each class of shareholder or partner at the balance sheet date, as if the investment company had realized all assets and settled all liabilities at the fair values reported in the financial statements, and allocated all gains and losses and distributed the net assets to each class of shareholder or partner at the reporting date consistent with the provisions of the partnership's governing documents. Further discussion of the presentation of each item follows.

Certain partnerships record an expense for fees (including incentive fees) due a general partner, whereas others allocate net income from limited partner capital accounts to the general partner capital account. These amounts could either be considered a disproportionate income allocation or a compensation arrangement, and the accounting should conform to the structure of the partnership agreement, with the financial statement disclosures set forth in FASB ASC 946.

A basic premise for the preparation and presentation of the financial statements of an investment company is to reflect each class of shareholders' or partners' interest in the net assets of the reporting entity as of the reporting date. Another objective is to present total return for nonmanaging investor classes after incentive allocations and fees, as expressed in FASB ASC 946.

Other accounting literature related to the presentation of data similar to total return is consistent with FASB ASC 946. FASB ASC 260, *Earnings per Share*, refers to allocating earnings or undistributed earnings for a period to participating securities "as if all of the earnings for the period had been distributed."

Although this guidance does not relate specifically to the presentation of capital accounts, measuring period-end capital balances for those classes under the same methodology appears consistent with this guidance. Accordingly, if an entity reports capital by investor class, cumulative unrealized gains (losses), carried interest, and clawback provisions would be reflected in the equity balances of each class of shareholder or partner at the balance sheet date, as if the investment company had realized all assets and settled all liabilities at the fair values reported in the financial statements, and allocated all gains and losses and distributed the net assets to each class of shareholder or partner at the reporting date consistent with the provisions of the partnership's governing documents. Further discussion of the presentation of each item follows.

Cumulative Unrealized Gains (Losses)

Cumulative unrealized gains (losses) would be included in the ending balances of each class of shareholders' or partners' interest in the reporting entity at the reporting date, and the changes in such amounts would be reported in the changes in net asset value and partners' capital for the reporting period.

Carried Interest

The carried interest generally is due to the investment manager, an affiliated entity, or both, and is either in the form of a fee (usually for offshore funds) or as an allocation from the limited partners' capital accounts, pro rata, to the general partner's capital account (usually for domestic funds). Although many variations exist, the investment manager is often entitled to receive its carry on a "deal-by-deal" basis. On this basis, as individual investments are sold, the investment proceeds are allocated based on a specific methodology defined in the governing documents to determine the amount of carry, if any, to which the investment manager is entitled.

In presenting each class of shareholders' or partners' interest in the net assets as of the reporting date, the financial statements would consider the carry formula as if the investment company had realized all assets and settled all liabilities at their reported fair value, and allocated all gains and losses and distributed the net assets to each class of shareholder or partner at the reporting date.

Clawback

Although all classes of shareholder or partner may be subject to clawback provisions in the governing documents, a clawback most frequently involves an obligation on the part of the investment manager to return previously received incentive allocations to the investment fund due to subsequent losses. Such clawback amounts, when paid, are typically distributed to other investors.

Consistent with the previously discussed principle to reflect each class of shareholders' or partners' interest in the net assets of the reporting entity as of the reporting date, the impact of a clawback would be calculated as of each reporting date under the methodology specified in the fund's governing documents.

Consistent with FASB ASC 310-10-45-14, such an obligation would not be recognized as an asset (receivable) in the entity's financial statements unless substantial evidence exists of ability and intent to pay within a reasonably short period of time. Rather, in most instances, the obligation would be reflected as a deduction from the general partner's capital account.

The specific circumstances, including whether the clawback represents a legal obligation to return or contribute funds to the reporting entity, require consideration before determining whether a clawback, resulting in a negative general partner capital balance (that is, contra-equity), is recognized in the financial statements. A careful reading of the governing documents ordinarily is required. Additionally, it may not be appropriate to reflect a negative general partner capital balance (and a corresponding increase to limited partner capital balances) if the general partner does not have the financial resources to make good on its obligation. It may be helpful to consult with the entity's legal counsel for clarification before recording a negative general partner capital balance.

Even if not recognized within the capital accounts, at a minimum, it would be appropriate to disclose the existence of a clawback in the footnotes to the financial statements because in almost all cases, the existence of the clawback would modify the manner in which future distributions are made.

[Issue Date: January 2009; Revised, June 2009, to reflect conforming changes necessary due to the issuance of FASB ASC.]

.30 Disclosure Requirements of Investments for Nonregistered Investment Partnerships When Their Interest in an Investee Fund Constitutes Less Than 5 Percent of the Nonregistered Investment Partnership's Net Assets

Inquiry—Nonregistered investment partnerships (as defined in the AICPA Audit and Accounting Guide *Investment Companies* [the guide]) are subject to the disclosure requirements of FASB ASC 946-210-50-6 related to investments in the partnership's portfolio. These disclosures require reporting investment partnerships to individually disclose an investment by name, type, and so on if the reporting investment partnership's investment constitutes more than 5 percent of its net assets. In accordance with paragraphs 8–9 of FASB ASC 946-210-50, nonregistered investment partnerships that own interests in another investment partnership[10] (investee fund) are required to disclose the investment partnership's proportional share of any underlying investment owned (either directly or through an investee fund) in any issuer that exceeds 5 percent of the reporting investment partnership's net assets at the reporting date. If the nonregistered investment partnership owns an interest in an investee fund that constitutes less than 5 percent of the nonregistered investment partnership's net assets, should the reporting investment partnership apply the guidance in paragraphs 8–9 of FASB ASC 946-210-50?

Reply—Yes. Even though the amount of the investment in the investee fund does not exceed 5 percent of the reporting investment partnership's net assets, the reporting investment partnership's proportional share of the investee fund's investments in an individual issuer may nonetheless exceed 5 percent of the reporting investment partnership's net assets because an investee fund may have issued debt (recourse or nonrecourse) to purchase investments or may have significant short positions or other liabilities. Paragraphs 8–9 of FASB ASC 946-210-50 do not establish any minimum investment size below which a reporting investment company need not determine its proportional share of an investment owned by an individual investee. Rather, paragraph 9 states that if such proportional share "of *any* investment owned by any individual investee exceeds 5 percent of the reporting investment company's net assets at the reporting date, each such investment shall be named and categorized" (*emphasis added*). The intent of the disclosure of positions exceeding 5 percent of net assets, as documented in paragraph .18 of Statement of Position 95-2, *Financial Reporting by Nonpublic Investment Partnerships*, in which this guidance originally appears, and paragraph 7.17 of the guide, is to "enable users to make their decisions focusing on the risk and opportunities associated with the type of investment, a geographical area, and industry by investee." In situations when the information about the investee fund's portfolio is not available, that fact shall be disclosed, which is consistent with the guidance in FASB ASC 946-210-50-10.

[Issue Date: July 2009.]

.31 The Nonregistered Investment Partnership's Method for Calculating Its Proportional Share of Any Investments Owned by an Investee Fund in Applying the "5 Percent Test" Described in Q&A Section 6910.30

Inquiry—What method should a nonregistered reporting investment partnership (as defined in the AICPA Audit and Accounting Guide *Investment Companies*) use to calculate its proportional share of any investments owned by an investee fund in applying the "5 percent test" described in Q&A section 6910.30, "Disclosure Requirements of Investments for Nonregistered Investment Partnerships When Their Interest in an Investee Fund Constitutes Less Than 5 Percent of the Nonregistered Investment Partnership's Net Assets," and where should the disclosure be located within the financial statements?

---

[10] Such investment partnerships include, but are not limited to, investment partnerships, funds of funds, special purpose vehicles, disregarded entities, and limited liability companies.

Reply—The reporting investment partnership should calculate its proportional share of any investments owned by the investee fund as its percentage ownership of the investee fund. Additionally, consistent with the provisions related to direct investments, indirect long and short positions of the same issuer held by the investee fund should not be netted. The disclosure of investments in issuers exceeding 5 percent of reporting investment partnership net assets should be made either on the face of the (condensed) schedule of investments or within the financial statement footnotes.

[Issue Date: July 2009.]

.32 Additional Financial Statement Disclosures for Nonregistered Investment Partnerships When the Partnership Has Provided Guarantees Related to the Investee Fund's Debt

Inquiry—What additional disclosures should a nonregistered reporting investment partnership (as defined in the AICPA Audit and Accounting Guide *Investment Companies*) consider within the financial statements when the reporting investment partnership has provided guarantees related to the investee fund's debt (also see Q&A section 6910.30)?

Reply—In addition to considering the recognition provisions described in FASB ASC 460-10-50, the reporting investment partnership should further disclose any guarantees it has provided on investee fund debt even though the risk of loss may be remote. These disclosure requirements are described in FASB ASC 460-10-50 and FASB ASC 946-20-50 and include the following:

- Loss contingencies, such as guarantees of indebtedness of others, including indirect guarantees of indebtedness of others and the nature and amount of the guarantee
- Guarantor's obligation, including the nature of the guarantee, the approximate term of the guarantee, the primary reasons for providing the guarantees, and the events or circumstances that would require the guarantor to perform under the guarantee

[Issue Date: July 2009; Revised, April 2014, to reflect conforming changes necessary due to revisions to FASB ASC.]

.33 Certain Financial Reporting, Disclosure, Regulatory, and Tax Considerations When Preparing Financial Statements of Investment Companies Involved in a Business Combination

Inquiry—FASB ASC 805-10-50 requires the following, among other things, when a transaction or other event meets the definition of a *business combination*:

- The identification of the acquiree
- Recognizing and measuring identifiable assets acquired and liabilities assumed, at the acquisition date, generally at their fair values
- Disclosure, by the acquirer, of information that enables users of its financial statements to evaluate the nature and financial effect of a business combination that occurs during the current reporting period

What are some of the financial reporting, disclosure, regulatory, and tax guidance that should be considered in preparing financial statements of investment companies involved in a business combination?

Reply—When investment companies engage in a business combination, shares of one company typically are exchanged for substantially all the shares or assets of another company (or companies). Most mergers of registered investment companies are structured as tax-free reorganizations. Following a business combination, portfolios of investment companies are often realigned, subject to tax limitations, to fit the objectives, strategies, and goals of the surviving company. Typically, shares of the acquiring fund are issued at an exchange ratio determined on the acquisition date, essentially equivalent to the acquiring fund's net asset value (NAV) per share divided by the NAV per share of the fund being acquired, both as calculated on the acquisition date. Adjusting the carrying amounts of assets and liabilities is usually unnecessary because virtually all assets of the combining investment companies (investments) are stated at fair value, in accordance with FASB ASC 820, *Fair Value Measurement*, and liabilities are generally short-term so that their carrying values approximate their fair values.[11] However, conforming adjustments may be necessary when funds have different valuation policies (for example, valuing securities at the bid price versus the mean of the bid and asked price) in order to ensure that the exchange ratio is equitable to shareholders of both funds.

Only one of the combining companies can be the legal survivor. In certain instances, it may not be clear which of the two funds constitutes the acquirer for financial reporting purposes. Although the legal survivor would normally be considered the acquirer, continuity and dominance in one or more of the following areas might lead to a determination that the fund legally dissolved should be considered the acquirer for financial reporting purposes:

- Portfolio management
- Portfolio composition
- Investment objectives, policies, and restrictions
- Expense structures and expense ratios
- Asset size

A registration statement on Form N-14 is often filed in connection with a merger of management investment companies registered under the Investment Company Act of 1940 (the Act), or of business development companies as defined by the Act. Form N-14 is a proxy statement in that it solicits a vote from the (legally) acquired fund's shareholders to approve the transaction, and a prospectus, in that it registers the (legally) acquiring fund's shares that will be issued in the transaction. Form N-14 frequently requires the inclusion of pro forma financial statements reflecting the effect of the merger.

Tax implications must be considered and monitored carefully in the planning, execution, and postmerger stages of a business combination. The tax rules that must be considered include those related to the determination that the transaction is tax-free to the funds involved and their shareholders,[12] the qualification tests affecting regulated investment companies (RICs),[13] and the accounting for tax attributes of specific accounts such as earnings and profits,[14]

---

[11] If the carrying value of the acquired investment company's liabilities differs materially from fair value on the acquisition date, refer to FASB ASC 805-30-30-8 for guidance on recognition of the liabilities by the surviving entity.

[12] See IRC Section 368(a) and IRS Notice 88-19.

[13] See IRC Section 851.

[14] See section 1.852-12(b) of Title 26, Internal Revenue, of U.S. *Code of Federal Regulations*.

capital loss carryforwards, and methods of tax accounting.[15] Management may consider obtaining a private letter ruling from the IRS or an opinion of counsel on the tax-free treatment. Upon completion of the acquisition, the portfolio securities obtained from the acquiree generally should be monitored because substantial turnover of the acquiree's portfolio securities may jeopardize the tax-free status of the reorganization. There are important differences in the tax rules affecting business combinations of RICs and non-RIC investment companies.

Merger-related expenses (mainly legal, audit, proxy solicitation, and mailing costs) are addressed in the plan of reorganization and are often paid by the fund incurring the expense, although the adviser may waive or reimburse certain merger-related expenses. Numerous factors and circumstances should be considered in determining which entity bears merger-related expenses.

In accordance with FASB ASC 805-10-25-23, acquisition related costs are accounted for as expenses in the periods in which the costs are incurred and the services are received, except that costs to issue equity securities are recognized in accordance with other applicable U.S. generally accepted accounting principles.

If the combination is a taxable reorganization, the fair value of the assets acquired on the date of the combination becomes the assets' new cost basis. For financial reporting purposes, assets acquired in a tax-free reorganization may be accounted for in the same manner as a taxable reorganization. However, investment companies carry substantially all their assets at fair value as an ongoing reporting practice and cost basis is principally used and presented solely for purposes of determining realized and unrealized gain and loss. Accordingly, an investment company, which is an acquirer in a business combination structured as a tax-free exchange of shares, may make an accounting policy election to carry forward the historical cost basis of the acquiree's investment securities for purposes of measuring realized and unrealized gain or loss for statement of operations presentation in order to more closely align the subsequent reporting of realized gains by the combined entity with tax-basis gains distributable to shareholders. The basis for such policy election should be disclosed in the notes to the financial statements, if material.

Instructions to Forms N-1A and N-2 state that, for registered investment companies, costs of purchases and proceeds from sales of portfolio securities that occurred in the effort to realign a combined fund's portfolio after a merger should be excluded in the portfolio turnover calculation. The amount of excluded purchases and sales should be disclosed in a note.[16]

FASB ASC 805-10-50-1 states that disclosures are required when business combinations occur during the reporting period or after the reporting date but before the financial statements are issued.

In accordance with FASB ASC 805-10-50, 805-20-50, and 805-30-50, disclosures for all business combinations should include a summary of the essential elements of the combination; that is, the name and description of the acquiree, the acquisition date, the percentage of voting equity interests acquired, the primary reasons for the combination and the manner in which control was obtained, the nature of the principal assets acquired, the number and fair value

---

[15] See IRC Section 381.

[16] See Form N-1A, Item 13, Instruction 4(d)(iii) and Form N-2, Item 4, Instruction 17c.

of shares issued by the acquiring company, and the exchange ratio. In addition, public business enterprises are required to disclose supplemental pro forma information consisting of the revenue and earnings of the combined entity for the current reporting period as though the acquisition date for all business combinations had been as of the beginning of the acquirer's annual reporting period.

Public business enterprises are also required to report, if practicable, the amounts of revenue and earnings of the acquiree since the acquisition date included in the combined entity's income statement for the reporting period. In many cases, investments acquired are absorbed into and managed as an integrated portfolio by an investment company upon completion of an acquisition; therefore, providing this information will not be practicable. That fact, along with an explanation of the circumstances, should be disclosed.

Because of the importance of investment company taxation to amounts distributable to shareholders, certain additional disclosures are recommended for combinations of investment companies, including the tax status and attributes of the merger. Additionally, if the merger is a tax-free exchange, separate disclosure of the amount of unrealized appreciation or depreciation and the amount of undistributed investment company income of the acquiree at the date of acquisition, if significant, may provide meaningful information about amounts transferred from the acquiree, which may be distributable by the combined fund in future periods.

See the following exhibits under "Illustrative Financial Statement Presentation for Tax-Free Business Combinations of Investment Companies" for an example of the calculation of an exchange ratio in an investment company merger, as well as merger-related financial statement disclosures.

Illustrative Financial Statement Presentation for Tax-Free Business Combinations of Investment Companies

The following financial statements and disclosures illustrate a tax-free business combination of an investment company. The illustrative notes are unique to a business combination. The exhibits assume that Fund B merges into Fund A as of the close of business on December 31, 20X4, and that both Fund A and Fund B have a January 31 fiscal year-end. Exhibit 1 presents the financial position of each fund immediately before the acquisition and of the combined fund immediately after the acquisition. Exhibit 2 presents the results of operations and changes in net assets of each fund for the 11-month fiscal period immediately before the acquisition, and the results of operations and summary changes in net assets information for the combined fund for the 1-month period subsequent to the acquisition. Exhibit 3 presents the statement of operations, statement of changes in net assets, and appropriate notes of the combined entity immediately after the acquisition. (The January 31, 20X5, statement of net assets of the combined entity is not presented as it will be identical in form to the December 31, 20X4, statement.)

Exhibit 1

Financial Position of Each Fund Immediately Before Acquisition

Statement of Net Assets
December 31, 20X4

	Fund A	*Fund B*
Investments in securities, at fair value	$20,000,000	$10,000,000
(Cost: Fund A—$18,000,000 Fund B—$ 9,000,000)		
Other assets	1,000,000	500,000
	21,000,000	10,500,000
Liabilities	1,000,000	500,000
Net assets	$20,000,000	$10,000,000
Shares outstanding	2,000,000	1,000,000
Net asset value per share	$ 10.00	$ 10.00

Calculation of Exchange Ratio:

Net assets of Fund B	$10,000,000
Divided by Fund A net asset value per share	$10.00
Fund A shares issuable	**1,000,000**
Fund B shares outstanding	1,000,000
Exchange ratio (Fund A shares issuable/Fund B shares outstanding)	**1-for-1**

Financial Position of Combined Entity Immediately After Acquisition

Statement of Net Assets
December 31, 20X4

Investments in securities, at fair value (Cost—$27,000,000)	$30,000,000
Other assets	1,500,000
	31,500,000
Liabilities	1,500,000
Net assets	$30,000,000
Shares outstanding	3,000,000
Net asset value per share	$10.00

Note: The individual components of net assets (paid-in capital, undistributed income and capital gains, and unrealized appreciation and depreciation) are not presented in this example but are similarly combined.

Exhibit 2

Statement of Operations
Eleven Months Ended December 31, 20X4

	Fund A	*Fund B*
Dividend and interest income	$3,200,000	$1,600,000
Management fee	100,000	50,000
Transfer agent fee	50,000	25,000
Other expenses	50,000	25,000
	200,000	100,000
Investment income—net	3,000,000	1,500,000
Realized and unrealized gain on investments		
Net realized gain on investments	1,000,000	500,000
Change in unrealized appreciation	1,000,000	500,000
Net realized and unrealized gain on investments	2,000,000	1,000,000
Net increase in net assets resulting from operations	$5,000,000	$2,500,000

Statement of Changes in Net Assets
Eleven Months Ended December 31, 20X4

	Fund A	*Fund B*
Increase (decrease) in net assets		
Operations		
Investment income—net	$3,000,000	$1,500,000
Net realized gain on investments	1,000,000	500,000
Change in unrealized appreciation	1,000,000	500,000
	5,000,000	2,500,000
Dividends to shareholders from		
Investment income—net	(3,000,000)	(1,500,000)
Net realized gain on investments	(1,000,000)	(500,000)
Capital shares transactions	2,000,000	250,000
Total increase	3,000,000	750,000
Net assets		
Beginning of year	17,000,000	9,250,000
End of year	$20,000,000	$10,000,000

Statement of Operations of Combined Entity
Month Ended January 31, 20X5

Dividend and interest income	$ 400,000
Management fee	15,000
Transfer agent fee	5,000
Other expenses	5,000
	25,000
Investment income–net	$ 375,000
Realized and unrealized gain on investments	
Net realized gains on investments	100,000
Change in unrealized appreciation	100,000
Net gain on investments	200,000
Net increase in net assets resulting from operations	$ 575,000

Other Changes in Net Assets Information
Month Ended January 31, 20X5

a) No dividends were paid during the month.

b) Capital shares transactions were as follows:

	Shares	*Amount*
Shares sold	20,000	$200,000
Shares redeemed	(10,000)	($100,000)
	10,000	$100,000

Exhibit 3

Statements of Operations and Changes in Net Assets of the Combined Entity Immediately After Acquisition

Fund A
Statement of Operations
Year Ended January 31, 20X5

Dividend and interest income ($3,200,000 + $400,000)		$3,600,000
Management fee ($100,000 + $15,000)	$ 115,000	
Transfer agent fee ($50,000 + $5,000)	55,000	
Other expenses ($50,000 + $5,000)	55,000	
		225,000
Investment income—net		3,375,000
Realized and unrealized gain on investments		
Net realized gain on investments ($1,000,000 + $100,000)	1,100,000	
Change in unrealized appreciation ($1,000,000 + $100,000)	1,100,000	
Net gain on investments		2,200,000
Net increase in net assets resulting from operations		$5,575,000

Fund A
Statement of Changes in Net Assets
Year Ended January 31, 20X5

	20X5	*20X4*
Increase (decrease) in net assets		
Operations		
Investment income—net	$3,375,000	$2,400,000
Net realized gain on investments	1,100,000	700,000
Change in unrealized appreciation	1,100,000	300,000
	5,575,000	3,400,000
Dividends to shareholders from		
Investment income—net	(3,000,000)	(2,400,000)
Net realized gain on investments	(1,000,000)	(700,000)
Capital share transactions (Notes 6 and 7)	12,100,000	1,100,000
Total increase	13,675,000	1,400,000
Net assets		
Beginning of year	17,000,000	15,600,000
End of year	$30,675,000	$17,000,000

Notes to Financial Statements of the Combined Entity Immediately After Acquisition

Note 6—Acquisition of Fund B

On December 31, 20X4, Fund A acquired all of the net assets of Fund B, an open-end investment company, pursuant to a plan of reorganization approved by Fund B shareholders on December 26, 20X4. The purpose of the transaction was to combine 2 funds managed by Investment Advisor C with comparable investment objectives and strategies. The acquisition was accomplished by a tax-free exchange of 1 million shares of Fund A, valued at $10 million, for 1 million shares of Fund B outstanding on December 31, 20X4. The investment portfolio of Fund B, with a fair value of $10 million and identified cost of $9 million at December 31, 20X4, was the principal asset acquired by Fund A. For financial reporting purposes, assets received and shares issued by Fund A were recorded at fair value; however, the cost basis of the investments received from Fund B was carried forward to align ongoing reporting of Fund A's realized and unrealized gains and losses with amounts distributable to shareholders for tax purposes.[17] Immediately prior to the merger, the net assets of Fund A were $20 million.

Note: The following paragraph is required for public business enterprises, as defined in the FASB ASC glossary, only. For purposes of this disclosure and consistent with FASB ASC 805-10-50-2(h), assume that, had the acquisition occurred February 1, 20X4, the beginning of Fund A's fiscal year, $10,000 of the transfer agent fee and $15,000 of other expenses—a total of $25,000—would have been eliminated.

Assuming the acquisition had been completed on February 1, 20X4, the beginning of the annual reporting period of Fund A, Fund A's pro forma results of operations for the year ended January 31, 20X5,[18] are as follows:

Net investment income	$4,900,000[19]
Net gain (loss) on investments	$3,200,000[20]
Net increase (decrease) in net assets resulting from operations	$8,100,000

Because the combined investment portfolios have been managed as a single integrated portfolio since the acquisition was completed, it is not practicable

[17] If material amounts of undistributed net investment income or undistributed realized gains are transferred to the acquirer (which the acquirer will be required to distribute), those amounts should also be disclosed. Material acquired loss carryovers should also be disclosed or cross-referenced to related income tax disclosures.

[18] FASB ASC 805-10-50-2 states that, if comparative financial statements are presented, supplemental pro forma information should be presented as if the business combination had occurred as of the beginning of the comparable prior annual reporting period. Investment companies should base application of this provision on whether they are required to present comparative statements of operations in their financial statements. Typically, business development companies registered with the Securities and Exchange Commission are required to present comparative statements of operations, but other registered open-end and closed-end investment companies are not required to do so.

[19] $3,375,000 as reported, plus $1,500,000 Fund B premerger, plus $25,000 of pro-forma eliminated expenses.

[20] $2,200,000 as reported plus $1,000,000 Fund B premerger.

to separate the amounts of revenue and earnings of Fund B that have been included in Fund A's statement of operations since December 31, 20X4.

Note 7—Capital Share Transactions

As of January 31, 20X5, 100 million shares of $1 par value capital stock were authorized. Transactions in capital stock were as follows:

	Shares		*Amount*	
	20X5	*20X4*	*20X5*	*20X4*
Shares sold	520,000	300,000	$5,000,000	$3,000,000
Shares issued in connection with acquisition of Fund B	1,000,000		10,000,000	
Shares issued in reinvestment of dividends	300,000	250,000	3,000,000	2,400,000
	1,820,000	550,000	18,000,000	5,400,000
Shares redeemed	610,000	450,000	5,900,000	4,300,000
Net increase	1,210,000	100,000	$12,100,000	$1,100,000

[Issue Date: December 2009.]

.34 Application of the Notion of Value Maximization for Measuring Fair Value of Debt and Controlling Equity Positions

Inquiry—Private equity funds or business development companies (collectively, a fund) may hold a controlling interest in an investee company and hold both equity and debt instruments issued by the investee. From a business strategy perspective, in this circumstance, the fund's management generally views their investment in the debt and equity instruments as an aggregate position rather than as separate financial instruments. The fund's management rarely, if ever, exits an investment by selling an individual financial instrument (that is, debt separate from equity or vice versa); rather, the instruments are generally exited in their entirety as a group (and the debt is typically redeemed at the amount owed, which we will assume to be par). When a fund has a controlling[21] interest in an investee and holds both debt and equity positions in that investee for which there are not observed trades,[22] is it appropriate to apply the notion of value maximization discussed in paragraph BC49 of Accounting Standards Update (ASU) No. 2011-04, *Fair Value Measurement (Topic 820): Amendments to Achieve Common Fair Value Measurement and Disclosure Requirements in U.S. GAAP and IFRSs*, and, as a result, value the debt and equity positions together using an enterprise value approach?[23]

[21] This question and answer does not address facts and circumstances in which an entity does not have a controlling financial interest in an investee company.

[22] Observed trades would be an indicator that market participants may transact separately for the debt and equity; thus, further consideration of the facts and circumstances would be necessary to conclude whether the fair value maximization guidance is relevant. FASB ASC 820-10-35-41 indicates that "a quoted price in an active market provides the most reliable evidence of fair value and shall be used without adjustment to measure fair value whenever available."

[23] Such an approach might result in a fair value of the debt and equity positions that differs from the result from selling the debt and equity positions in separate transactions. See footnote 24 of this question and answer that references Agenda Paper 2E that includes an example that illustrates how fair value might differ.

Reply—This inquiry relates to the unit of account for investments within the scope of FASB ASC 946 and was discussed at a joint meeting between FASB and the International Accounting Standards Board during their deliberations of the fair value project.[24] Specifically, the boards considered whether to provide unit of account guidance for investments within the scope of FASB ASC 946. The boards concluded that unit of account guidance was outside the scope of the fair value project. However, the boards agreed to include language in paragraph BC49 of ASU No. 2011-04 that indicated that an entity assumes that

> market participants seek to maximize the fair value of a financial or nonfinancial asset or to minimize the fair value of a financial or nonfinancial liability by acting in their economic best interest in a transaction to sell the asset or to transfer the liability in the principal (or most advantageous) market for the asset or liability. Such a transaction might involve grouping assets and liabilities in a way in which market participants would enter into a transaction, if the unit of account specified in other Topics does not prohibit that grouping.

This language provides fair value measurement guidance in situations when the unit of account is not specified. Because FASB ASC 946 does not specify the unit of account for measuring fair value, it might be appropriate to consider how fair value would be maximized, which may be in a transaction that involves both the debt and controlling equity position if this is how market participants would transact.[25] Consistent with the guidance in paragraph BC49 of ASU No. 2011-04, this transaction (and, thus, fair value) might be measured using an enterprise value approach measured in accordance with the guidance in FASB ASC 820 (that is, an exit price from the perspective of market participants under current conditions at the measurement date).

Because the enterprise value approach results in a fair value for the entire capital position (that is, both debt and equity), an allocation to the individual units of account would be necessary. FASB ASC 820 does not prescribe an allocation approach, but FASB ASC 820-10-35-18F discusses that a "reporting entity shall perform such allocations on a reasonable and consistent basis using a methodology appropriate in the circumstances." Facts and circumstances, such as relevant characteristics of the debt and equity instruments, must be considered when making this allocation. Generally, the allocation method should be consistent with the overall valuation premise used to measure fair value.

[Issue Date: February 2013.]

.35 Assessing Control When Measuring Fair Value

Inquiry—Is it appropriate to aggregate positions across multiple reporting entities (multiple funds) to assess control[26] for purposes of whether a control premium might be appropriate in a fair value measurement, or does control have to reside in a single fund for the enterprise value approach to be acceptable? Also, is it appropriate to consider "club deals" in which a group of unrelated investors jointly make an investment when assessing control?

---

[24] Refer to the International Accounting Standards Board (IASB)/FASB Agenda Paper 2E prepared for the October 2010 IASB/FASB joint meeting. (See www.ifrs.org/Current-Projects/IASB-Projects/Fair-Value-Measurement/Summaries/Pages/IASB-October-2010.aspx.)

[25] This assessment would include a consideration of the entity's prior history in selling similar investments. Consideration of specific terms of the instruments that are considered characteristics, as discussed in FASB ASC 820, is also necessary (for example, change in control provisions).

[26] This question and answer does not address consolidation matters. Control in this question and answer refers to the ability to cause a controlling financial interest in the investee to be sold.

Reply—Control of an investee company may be achieved by virtue of a single fund holding a controlling financial interest, through multiple funds in the same fund complex[27] under common control being allocated financial interests in the investee company, or through "club deals" in which a group of unrelated investment managers jointly make controlling investments in a private company on behalf of funds they manage. For example, a single adviser may decide to make a controlling financial investment in an investee and then allocate that investment across multiple legal and reporting entities. Individually, no one entity may control the investee (this question and answer assumes this is the case); however, the entities in aggregate may have a controlling financial interest in the investee.

It is not consistent with the fair value measurement framework in FASB ASC 820 for a reporting entity to aggregate positions across multiple reporting entities (multiple related funds or unrelated club deals) to assess control[28] for purposes of whether a control premium might be appropriate in a fair value measurement. However, when determining the fair value of the position the reporting entity holds, that determination should consider whether other premiums and discounts (relative to the price of a noncontrolling interest) are appropriate. For example, observed transaction data for similar investments may indicate that market participants pay a premium multiple relative to the multiples observed for the guideline companies because some market participants place additional value on being part of the controlling group that has the right to determine the company's strategy.

A reporting entity should consider all available evidence about how a market participant would exit the investments (and the prices it would receive) in determining the principal (or most advantageous) market and whether premiums to noncontrolling interests are appropriate.

[Issue Date: February 2013.]

.36 Determining Whether Loan Origination Is a Substantive Activity When Assessing Whether an Entity Is an Investment Company

Inquiry—If an entity originates loans to third parties for the purposes of maximizing its returns from capital appreciation, investment income, or both, how does the entity determine whether the loan origination activity represents a substantive activity that precludes the entity from qualifying as an investment company under FASB ASC 946-10-15-6?

Reply—In performing its assessment, the entity should consider its design, business purpose (see FASB ASC 946-10-55-4 through 946-10-55-7), and the reason for performing the activities (see FASB ASC 946-10-55-10), including how the entity is marketed and presented to current and potential investors. If an entity believes it is an investment company under FASB ASC 946, the entity's design, business purpose, and how it holds itself out to investors should be consistent with those of an investment company.

Determining whether loan origination activity represents a substantive activity may require significant judgment. Loan origination would generally be considered inconsistent with the business purpose of capital appreciation,

---

[27] Fund complex refers to a group of funds managed by the same investment adviser.

[28] This is not consistent because it does not consider that, for example, kick-out rights may prevent a reporting entity from having unilateral control (even though the fund is part of a complex with the same adviser). Said another way, control is not a characteristic of the individual fund's investment in these assumed facts and circumstances.

investment income, or both (investing income). Significance of the income generated from the entity's origination and syndication of loans as compared to the income generated through capital appreciation, investment income, or both, is an important factor for entities to consider. Paragraph 4 of FASB ASC 946-10-55 indicates that an investment company should have no substantive activities other than its investing activities and should not have significant assets or liabilities other than those relating to investing activities. The evaluation of loan origination activities generally would include a quantitative and qualitative assessment of the significance of those activities relative to the entity's investing activities. Often, the entity's business strategy with respect to originating loans (for example, if the entity originates and holds the loans versus originating and selling the loans), would correspond to the quantitative significance of loan origination income relative to investing income.

As an example, assume an entity (potential investment company) originates a $100 loan with a 10-year maturity, an expected life of five years, a coupon rate of 6 percent, an origination fee of 1.50 percent, and the entity expects to hold the loan until repayment by the borrower. In this example, the entity receives a $1.50 origination fee ($100 × 1.50%), expects to receive $30 dollars in interest payments ($100 × 6% × 5 years) over the expected holding period of the loan, and expects no capital gain or loss. Because the loan origination fee represents 4.76 percent ($1.50 / $31.50) of the total estimated income over the expected holding period of the loan, this quantitative analysis may indicate that loan origination fees are not a significant source of income. If the entity has investing income from other investments, including loans that are not originated by the entity, it would reduce the percentage of loan origination income to total estimated income (investing income plus other income, such as loan origination fees) over the expected life of the originated loans because the denominator would include the investing income from these other investments. Although an entity may have a significant amount of loan origination income to total income in a particular year (for example, in the early stages of the life of the entity as it expands its portfolio of investments), it would generally be appropriate to consider loan origination income relative to total income over the anticipated holding period of the originated loans. Management should have a reasonable basis for estimating loan origination income relative to total estimated income. For example, management should not estimate long or extended holding periods for loans (a decrease in loan origination activity) that is inconsistent with historical experience, except when warranted by changes in the entity's operations.

Contrast the preceding example with the origination of the same loan; however, assume the loan is expected to be sold in one year at a price of par (no gain or loss). In this example, the loan origination fee of $1.50 would represent 20 percent of the $7.50 total estimated income over the expected holding period of the loan ($1.50 origination fee plus $6 of coupon interest) and indicates that loan origination fees are significant. Although the quantitative analysis should be performed based on all income generated by the entity, as opposed to an individual loan, the preceding simplistic examples are intended to demonstrate the importance of the quantitative analysis in determining whether loan origination is a substantive business activity.

The fee income generated as part of loan origination activities relative to total income represents an important factor for entities to consider. An entity would generally also perform a qualitative analysis in determining whether the loan origination represents a substantive activity of the entity. The following factors are not all-inclusive, and judgment should be applied in determining the importance of each factor in specific circumstances:

- *Investing activity*. The nature and extent of the entity's sale of originated loans relative to purchases and sales of non-originated loans and other investments may be an indicator of whether the loan origination activities are substantive.
- *Regulatory considerations*. The regulations to which an entity is subject may provide an indicator of the entity's purpose and design.
- *Entity ownership and management*. The ownership of the entity and who manages the entity (for example, investment adviser) may be an indicator of whether the loan origination activities are substantive.
- *Customization of the loans*. Whether the loans are uniquely customized and specific to each borrower may be an indicator of whether the loans are originated for an investment purpose rather than to earn origination fees.
- *Loan retention*. When an entity holds loans as part of its investment portfolio to match its investment horizon, rather than selling loans (through securitizations or otherwise) shortly after origination, it may be an indicator that loan origination services are not a separate substantial business activity for the entity.
- *Embedded features*. Embedded features, particularly those that would indicate the loan is more akin to equity than debt (for example, conversion feature, dividend participation rights, and so on), may be an indicator that the entity's intent is for investment purposes, rather than to earn a loan origination fee.

FASB ASC 946-10-25-1 indicates that an entity shall reassess whether it is an investment company only if there is a subsequent change in the purpose and design of the entity. A change in the level of loan origination activity or holding period for self-originated loans that would affect the preceding quantitative analysis, as well as changes to the qualitative factors listed previously, may indicate that the purpose and design of the entity have changed.

Appendix A—Factors to Consider in Determining Whether Loan Origination Represents a Substantive Activity of the Entity

Factor	*Example*	
	More indicative of an investment company	***Less indicative of an investment company***
Fees	Fee income generated from the entity's loan origination activities is insignificant relative to total income.	Fee income generated from the entity's loan origination activities is significant to total income.
Investing activity	The entity's purchases and sales of non-originated securities are significant in relation to its origination of loans.	The entity may originate loans and sell them primarily for the purpose of generating origination fees. Loans originated by the entity are its primary investments.
Regulatory considerations	The party that manages the entity is registered with the SEC or a state as an investment adviser.	The entity is required to operate like a bank by a banking authority, for example, licensing and capital requirements.
Entity ownership and management	The entity is managed by an investment adviser, and substantially all investors are unrelated third parties.	The entity is a bank, an entity owned by a bank, or a captive finance company.
Customization of the loans	Loans are originated with unique features specific to each individual loan.	Loans are originated using standard terms and agreements (generally in higher volumes).
Loan retention	Loans are created and held as part of the investment portfolio to match the investment horizon of the entity.	Loans are sold shortly after origination through securitizations or otherwise.
Embedded features	Originated loans include embedded features that are more akin to equity.	Originated loans do not include equity-like features.

[Issue Date: October 2016.]

.37 Considering the Length of Time It Will Take an Investment Company[29] to Liquidate Its Assets and Satisfy Its Liabilities When Determining If Liquidation Is Imminent

Inquiry—FASB ASC 205-30-25-1 states that an entity shall prepare financial statements in accordance with the requirements of the liquidation basis of accounting when liquidation is imminent, unless the liquidation follows a plan for liquidation that was specified in the entity's governing documents at the entity's inception. FASB ASC 205-30-25-2 defines when liquidation is imminent based on the occurrence of events and does not include a time element. Should an investment company consider the length of time it will take to liquidate its assets and satisfy its liabilities when determining if liquidation is imminent?

Reply—No. FASB ASC 205-30-25-2 defines *imminent* as when either of the following occurs:

a. A plan for liquidation has been approved by the person or persons with the authority to make such a plan effective, and the likelihood is remote that any of the following will occur:
   1. Execution of the plan will be blocked by other parties (for example, those with shareholder rights)
   2. The entity will return from liquidation.
b. A plan for liquidation is imposed by other forces (for example, involuntary bankruptcy), and the likelihood is remote that the entity will return from liquidation.

The definition of *imminent* is intended to coincide with the timing of the decision to liquidate, or the imposition of a plan for liquidation by other forces and, therefore, a change in the needs of the users of financial statements. The length of time it will take to liquidate an investment company's assets and satisfy its liabilities is not a criterion for consideration in determining if liquidation is imminent. However, an investment company may consider whether the length of time it will take to liquidate its assets and satisfy its liabilities affects the assessment of whether the likelihood is remote that the investment company will return from liquidation or that execution of the plan will be blocked by other parties.

[Issue Date: October 2016.]

.38 Determining If Liquidation Is Imminent When the Only Investor in an Investment Company[30] Redeems Its Interest, and the Investment Company Anticipates Selling All of Its Investments and Settling All of Its Assets and Liabilities

Inquiry—When the only investor in an investment company redeems its interest, and, as a result, the investment company anticipates selling all of its investments and settling all of its assets and liabilities, should liquidation be considered imminent? Must it be anticipated that the legal entity will be dissolved in order for liquidation to be imminent?

Reply—It depends on the intent of the sponsor or investment adviser. Factors to consider include whether the sponsor or investment adviser of the investment company anticipates continuing to operate the investment company

---

[29] FASB ASC 205-30 does not apply to investment companies regulated under the Investment Company Act of 1940.

[30] See footnote 29.

using the same or a similar investment strategy, and whether the lack of investors is expected to be temporary. It may also depend on the terms of the governing documents as they relate to this situation.

For example, if the sole investor in an investment company redeems its interest and if management does not intend to continue (or may not continue, according to the fund's governing documents) to solicit new investors and does not expect the investment company to continue its previous operations (that is, continue with an investment strategy consistent with its governing documents), the liquidation basis of accounting may be appropriate because this may be considered a plan for liquidation imposed by other forces, and the likelihood may be remote the entity will return from liquidation. However, if management intends to continue to solicit investors under its existing investment strategy, the temporary lack of investors does not necessarily indicate that a forced liquidation is being imposed on the investment company and that liquidation is imminent. There may be situations in which the investment adviser retains the legal entity and uses it to offer investors an investment company with a new name and different investment strategy. In these cases, the activities of the original investment company have ceased, and utilizing the legal entity for a new purpose could indicate that the original entity has effectively liquidated.

[Issue Date: October 2016.]

.39 Presentation of Stub Period Information by an Investment Company[31]

Inquiry—Should an investment company (subject to presentation of liquidation-basis financial statements) present information for the stub period, which is the period from the most recent balance sheet date to the date liquidation becomes imminent?

Reply—Paragraph BC18 of the basis for conclusions in FASB ASU No. 2013-07, *Presentation of Financial Statements (Topic 205): Liquidation Basis of Accounting*, indicates that the guidance in FASB ASC 205-30 requires the liquidation basis of accounting to be applied prospectively from the date that liquidation becomes imminent. However, FASB ASC 205-30 does not provide guidance about whether an entity should present information for the stub period. Paragraph BC18 further indicates that in deciding whether to present information about the stub period, an entity should consider the requirements of its regulator and the needs of any other anticipated users of the entity's financial statements. The governing documents for many nonpublic investment companies require audited financial statements to be provided to investors. Furthermore, the investment adviser may use the financial statements to satisfy regulatory requirements, such as Rule 206(4)-2 under the Investment Advisers Act of 1940 (Custody Rule), regulations of the Commodity Futures Trading Commission, requirements of the Cayman Islands Monetary Authority, OCC or state regulations for bank collective funds, and so on. Therefore, if the date of adoption of liquidation basis differs from year-end, an investment company would most likely present stub period financial statements up to the adoption date of the liquidation basis because such information is either required by legal or regulatory requirements or is considered relevant to users of the financial statements.

[Issue Date: October 2016.]

---

[31] See footnote 29.

.40 Applying the Financial Statement Reporting Requirements in FASB ASC 946-205-45-1 When an Investment Company[32] Presents a Stub Period

Inquiry—How should an investment company apply the financial statement presentation requirements in FASB ASC 946-205-45-1 when the investment company presents a stub period (the period of time from the most recent balance sheet date to the date liquidation becomes imminent) together with the liquidation basis financial statements?

Reply—When an investment company presents stub period going concern basis financial statements together with its liquidation basis financial statements, the stub period financial statements under the going concern basis of accounting would generally be consistent with FASB ASC 946-205-45-1, including (1) a statement of operations, (2) a statement of changes in partners' capital (or members' capital or net assets, as applicable), (3) a statement of cash flows (when required), and (4) financial highlights, as well as required disclosures. When an investment company presents a stub period, the investment company may include a cumulative-effect adjustment in the statement of changes in net assets in liquidation. This adjustment would bridge the investment company's ending equity balance under the going concern basis of accounting, with its opening equity balance under the liquidation basis of accounting. An investment company may, instead, disclose the cumulative-effect adjustment in the notes to the liquidation basis financial statements. If a stub period is not presented, the cumulative-effect adjustment generally would be disclosed in the notes to the financial statements.

The cumulative-effect adjustment includes the adjustment necessary to record assets and liabilities at their liquidation basis carrying amounts, including the accrual of income and expenses through liquidation. The initial statement of changes in net assets in liquidation presents only changes in net assets that occurred during the period since liquidation became imminent. The entity should consider appropriate disclosures about the cumulative-effect adjustment.

Regardless of whether a stub period is presented, the investment company should provide in its liquidation basis financial statement disclosures required by paragraphs 1–2 of FASB ASC 205-30-50, including, among others

1. the methods and significant assumptions used to measure assets and liabilities,
2. any subsequent changes to those methods and assumptions,
3. the type and amount of costs and income accrued in the statement of net assets in liquidation, and
4. the period over which those costs are expected to be paid or income earned.

FASB ASC 205-30-50-1 indicates an entity would make disclosures required by other GAAP topics that are relevant to understanding the entity's statement of net assets in liquidation and statement of changes in net assets in liquidation. For example, because a schedule of investments is part of the statement of net assets of an investment company, a reporting entity generally would include a schedule of investments with the statement of net assets in liquidation to the extent the investment company holds investments at the reporting date.

[32] See footnote 29.

An investment company would not be required by FASB ASC 205-30 to present a statement of assets and liabilities (or similar statement) and a (condensed) schedule of investments as of the last day under the going concern basis (the day prior to the date liquidation became imminent). However, the investment company may determine that those statements are meaningful to the users of the financial statements under certain circumstances or may be required to present those statements (for example, by regulation or contract).

The following example assumes that liquidation was deemed to be "imminent" on July 1, and the investment company is reporting as of December 31.[33]

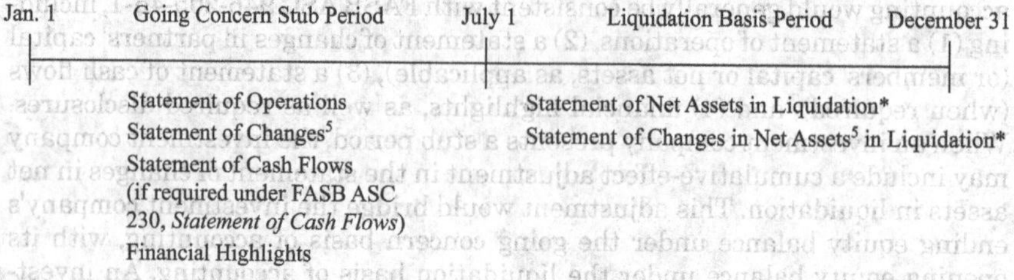

* FASB ASC 205-30-45-1 indicates that an entity applying the liquidation basis of accounting shall, at a minimum, prepare a statement of net assets in liquidation and a statement of changes in net assets in liquidation. The statement of net assets in liquidation generally would include a schedule of investments.

[Issue Date: October 2016.]

.41 Separation of Final-Period Financial Statements Between Going Concern and Liquidation Periods for Certain Investment Companies[34] That Liquidate Over a Short Period of Time

Inquiry—Some investment companies liquidate over a short period of time because their investments are easily traded. Financial statements for the investment company's last fiscal period may be required to be issued under various regulatory or contractual requirements.[35] In this circumstance, would an investment company be required to apply liquidation basis of accounting and separate the financial information for the liquidation period from the going concern period?

Reply—FASB ASC 205-30-45-2 states that the liquidation basis of accounting shall be applied prospectively from the day that liquidation becomes imminent. Regardless of the amount of time it takes to liquidate, separation of final-period financial information between going concern and liquidation periods is required unless it is determined that the effects of adopting the liquidation basis of accounting are immaterial to the financial statements taken as a whole (under the premise that GAAP requirements need not be applied to immaterial items). Any materiality determination should be made based on the specific facts and circumstances of the entity and its liquidation. Because the final-period financial statements will indicate that the investment company is

---

[33] In Net Assets or Members' (or Partners') Capital.

[34] See footnote 29.

[35] Examples of such requirements may include Rule 206(4)-2 under the Investment Advisers Act of 1940 (Custody Rule), regulations of the Commodity Futures Trading Commission, requirements of the Cayman Islands Monetary Authority, OCC or state regulations for bank collective funds, and so on.

in liquidation or has liquidated, if management has concluded that the effects of adopting the liquidation basis of accounting were not material, the notes to the financial statements generally should include an affirmative statement to that effect.

[Issue Date: October 2016.]

.42 Presenting Financial Highlights Under the Liquidation Basis of Accounting for an Investment Company[36]

Inquiry—Should an investment company present total return or internal rate of return (IRR) after adopting the liquidation basis of accounting? Should an investment company present net investment income or expense ratios after adopting the liquidation basis of accounting?

Reply—Once an entity adopts the liquidation basis of accounting, the entity is required to present, at a minimum, a statement of net assets in liquidation and a statement of changes in net assets in liquidation. In addition, FASB ASC 205-30-50-1 states that an entity shall make all disclosures required by other topics that are relevant to understanding the entity's statement of net assets in liquidation and statement of changes in net assets in liquidation. The disclosures shall convey information about the amount of cash or other consideration that an entity expects to collect and the amount that the entity is obligated or expects to be obligated (in the case of the accruals described in paragraphs 6–7 of FASB ASC 205-30-25) to pay during the course of liquidation. Upon adoption of the liquidation basis of accounting, an entity accrues estimated costs and income and recognizes assets that it might not have previously. Subsequent to the adoption of the liquidation basis of accounting, an entity shall remeasure its assets and liabilities (if required under the relevant topic for those liabilities) and the accruals of disposal or other costs at period end.

In determining whether financial highlights should be presented for periods subsequent to the initial application of the liquidation basis of accounting, the reporting entity should consider whether and how the accrual of costs and income and recognition of other assets that were recorded as of the adoption of the liquidation basis (for example, the cumulative-effect adjustment) would affect the financial highlights information and whether the result would be meaningful to a user of the entity's financial statements.

The board noted in paragraph BC13 of ASU No. 2013-07 that "...financial statements that are prepared using the liquidation basis of accounting provide users of those financial statements with specialized information because the **emphasis shifts from reporting about the entity's economic performance and position to reporting about the amount of cash or other consideration that an investor might reasonably expect to receive after liquidation**..." [emphasis added]. Accordingly, given the shift in focus (and measurement basis of assets and some liabilities), an entity should consider whether financial highlights continue to be relevant and useful to understanding the entity's statement of net assets in liquidation or statement of changes in net assets in liquidation. Financial highlights information may no longer be relevant and useful in understanding the liquidation basis statements. Additionally, if the financial highlights are deemed necessary, consideration should

[36] See footnote 29.

be given to whether different descriptions or disclosures should be used, rather than those that are used for going concern financial statements of investment companies.

Factors to consider when determining whether total return is relevant to understanding the entity's statement of net assets in liquidation or statement of changes in net assets in liquidation may include the following:

- How does the use of liquidation basis of accounting by the investment company affect comparability of the total return, and is the resulting performance information relevant and informative?
- Will the total return be meaningful on a comparative basis given that certain income and costs are accelerated, and other assets may be recorded as of the adoption of the liquidation basis of accounting?
- Would total return for the liquidation period be relevant and meaningful for the users of financial statements in understanding the changes in net assets in liquidation?
- What additional disclosures would be necessary when presenting total return under the liquidation basis of accounting for a user of the financial statements to understand the differences between the going concern basis total return and the liquidation basis amounts?

  IRR is less likely to be the performance measure used by a fund applying the liquidation basis of accounting because many private equity, venture capital, and real estate funds have a plan of liquidation in their governing documents at inception. However, when IRR is the performance measure used by a fund in liquidation because IRR is a cash-based metric, it would generally be more relevant than total return to users of investment company liquidation basis financial statements. IRR is based on the timing of cash inflows and outflows from investments, and the liquidation value of the asset is based on the amount of cash or other consideration that an investor might reasonably expect to receive.

Factors to consider when determining whether net investment income or expense ratios are relevant to understanding the entity's statement of net assets in liquidation or statement of changes in net assets in liquidation may include the following:

- Under the liquidation basis of accounting, income and costs and other assets would be accrued as of the adoption of the liquidation basis. Consider whether and how any cumulative-effect adjustment would be included in ratio information and whether users of the financial statements would find such information meaningful given the change in recognition of income and expense.
- Would the changes in estimated income and costs recorded in the statement of changes in net assets in liquidation after adoption of liquidation basis be relevant and useful in the form of income and expense ratios? Often, users of the financial statements will use such information to compare investment companies or determine whether the investment company is operating consistent

with its investment objective. However, such use of financial highlights information may no longer be relevant as a result of the liquidation.

- Are additional disclosures necessary when presenting the net investment income and expense ratios in liquidation basis financial statements for those metrics to be meaningful?

[Issue Date: October 2016.]

.43 Accrued Income When Using the Liquidation Basis of Accounting[37]

Inquiry—FASB ASC 205-30-25-7 states that an entity should accrue costs and income that it expects to incur or earn through the end of its liquidation if and when it has a reasonable basis for estimation. Would an investment company accrue income related to estimated earnings on the investments held by the investment company?

Reply—Income for investment companies is generally derived from investments that are measured at fair value under the going concern basis of accounting. Fair value may be determined based on the discounted value of cash payments expected to be received. Under the liquidation basis of accounting, FASB ASC 205-30-30-3 requires that the income be accrued on an undiscounted basis.

FASB ASC 205-30-30-1 requires an entity to measure assets to reflect the estimated amount of cash or other consideration that it expects to collect in settling or disposing of those assets (liquidation value) in carrying out its plan for liquidation. In some cases, fair value may approximate the amount that an entity expects to collect. However, an entity shall not presume this to be true for all assets.

Due to the inherent uncertainty in determining the cash to be received upon selling an investment, an entity's best estimate of the liquidation value of an investment may be equal to (or derived from) its current fair value. An entity is not precluded from using fair value to measure its assets in liquidation as long as it represents the best estimate of liquidation value. However, if, for example, a less liquid investment is expected to be disposed of in a short time at a discount to its fair value, that estimated liquidation value should be recorded upon adopting the liquidation basis. Regardless of the valuation method used, management should be careful to accrue the costs to dispose of its investments, such as commissions, as required by FASB ASC 205-30-25-6.

FASB ASC 205-30-25-7 requires an entity to accrue income that it expects to earn through the end of liquidation, if and when it has a reasonable basis for estimation. Evaluating whether an entity has a reasonable basis for estimating investment income is specific to an entity's particular circumstances and the nature of the investment. Factors that could be considered when making this evaluation include investment-specific characteristics (for example, credit quality, leverage rate, operating expectations, dividend history and expectations), general market conditions (for example, market interest rates, investor sentiment), and the estimated disposal date for the investment. Although it is generally more likely that an entity may have a reasonable basis to estimate income from a fixed income security rather than from an equity security, an

[37] See footnote 29.

investment company should consider whether it has a reasonable basis to estimate income from all types of investments.

For example, an entity may determine that fair value is the best estimate of liquidation value. In addition, an entity may conclude it has a reasonable basis to estimate interest income on a fixed income security based on the contractual nature of the income stream, its analysis of the credit quality of the issuer, general market conditions, and its expected disposal date. Although the fair value of the fixed income security generally includes the discounted future interest payments, FASB ASC 205-30-30-3 requires that the income be accrued on an undiscounted basis. If the entity expects to liquidate the investment in a short period of time, it may determine that the accrual of income on an undiscounted basis is not material. In considering whether and for what period to accrue income upon adoption of the liquidation basis of accounting, an entity may not be able to reasonably estimate the precise date of disposal for each of its investments. However, the entity may be able to reasonably estimate the minimum time it plans to hold these investments until it begins to dispose of them. These estimates should be reevaluated at each reporting date. If upon entering liquidation, an entity expects to dispose of an investment at a future date and uses fair value as its best estimate of liquidation value because, for example, it does not have a reasonable basis to determine the proceeds from investment disposal, management should carefully consider the net effect of 1) the income accrual already reflected in the fair value measurement and 2) the effect of discounting all other future cash flows from the expected disposal date to the date the entity entered liquidation, because such amounts should be removed from the fair value.

If the entity determines that fair value is its best estimate of liquidation value, that fair value and liquidation value would represent only the amount the entity expects to collect on the future disposal date, and the entity may still need to accrue the income from the date that liquidation became imminent until that future disposal date.

It may be possible for an entity to perform an analysis of the overall portfolio based on the premiums or discounts on securities, expected time to disposition, and estimated changes in yield to determine whether the difference between liquidation value and fair value could be material and whether to perform a more detailed calculation. Liquidity, credit quality, and other factors may also need to be considered.

Paragraphs 1–2 of FASB ASC 205-30-50 require certain disclosures to be made. In particular, the investment company would be required to disclose the type and amount of income accrued in the statement of net assets in liquidation and the period over which that income is expected to be collected or earned.

Example

Assume that an investment company with a December 31 year-end has one fixed income investment. The investment company determines that liquidation is imminent on January 1, 2015, and the entity, after consideration of factors specific to its security and general market conditions, will likely dispose of its investment on December 31, 2015. The fixed income instrument matures in 15 years on December 31, 2029, has a par value of $100, and a coupon of 10 percent per annum paid annually on December 31. The current market rate of interest (yield) for the fixed income investment is 9 percent. On January 1, 2015, when liquidation is determined to be imminent, the fair value of the fixed income investment is determined to be $108.06. The fair value was determined by discounting the future cash flows at the market rate of interest as follows:

	Cash Flows	
Present value of cash flows discounted at 9% on January 1, 2015	*December 31, 2015 to 2028*	*December 31, 2029*
$108.06	$10/year	$110

On January 1, 2015, the investment company estimates the expected sales proceeds on the date it expects to dispose of the fixed income investment (December 31, 2015) as the discounted value of the cash flows of the security expected to be received subsequent to December 31, 2015. The investment company concludes that 9 percent (the current market rate) is the best estimate of the market rate for this investment as of December 31, 2015. Based on this determination, the estimated sales proceeds (or liquidation value) are $107.79, calculated as follows on January 1, 2015, for expected disposition on December 31, 2015:

	Estimated Cash Flows as of January 1, 2015	
Present value of future cash flows discounted at 9% as of December 31, 2015	*December 31, 2016 to 2028*	*December 31, 2029*
$107.79	$10/year	$110

In this example, the fair value (as of January 1, 2015) and the liquidation value (estimated sales proceeds at December 31, 2015) are different due to the cash flows incorporated into each calculation, the difference between the coupon rate and the current market rate, and fact that the cash flows are being discounted over different periods. As the expected disposition date is December 31, 2015, the cash flow occurring on this date is not incorporated into the liquidation value.

After arriving at liquidation value, the investment company also concludes, for this security, that it has a reasonable basis to estimate the interest income through liquidation and accrues, as of January 1, 2015, the undiscounted interest coupon payment of $10, expected to be received during the period from January 1, 2015, to expected disposition on December 31, 2015. As a result, on January 1, 2015, the investment company would measure its total position (investment and accrued interest income) at the amount of cash it expects to receive during the period through liquidation on December 31, 2015 of $117.79. (The $10 coupon payment is recorded as accrued income, and the $107.79 of expected sales proceeds from disposition of the fixed income investment would be recorded as the liquidation value of the security). Other approaches for estimating the liquidation value of the security (or a portfolio of similar securities) at the expected disposition date may be acceptable, but an entity should ensure that its liquidation basis financial statements reflect (*a*) the entity's best estimate of the cash expected to be collected at the disposition of the security, and (*b*) the expected future income from the date liquidation became imminent through the expected disposition date, when the entity has a reasonable basis to estimate that amount.

[Issue Date: October 2016.]

Q&A Section 6930

Employee Benefit Plans

.01 When Does a Plan Have to File a Form 11-K?

Inquiry—When is a plan subject to the requirements of the Securities Act of 1933, thus requiring a Form 11-K filing under the Securities Exchange Act of 1934?

Reply—Section 3(a)(2) of the Securities Act of 1933 provides exemptions from registration requirements for defined benefit plans and defined contribution plans not involving the purchase of employer securities with employee contributions. All other plans are subject to the requirements, provided they are both voluntary and contributory. For further guidance, see the "Securities and Exchange Commission Reporting Requirements" section in chapter 12 of the AICPA Audit and Accounting Guide *Employee Benefit Plans*. Advice of ERISA counsel should be obtained to determine if the registration requirements apply to the plan.

[Revised, June 2009, to reflect conforming changes necessary due to the issuance of recent authoritative literature.]

.02 Defined Benefit Plan Measurement of a Life Insurance Policy

Inquiry—How should a defined benefit plan measure a cash value life insurance policy?

Reply—Financial Accounting Standards Board (FASB) *Accounting Standards Codification* (ASC) 715-30-35-60 indicates that for defined benefit plans, insurance contracts with insurance entities (other than those that are, in substance, annuities) should be accounted for as investments and measured at fair value.

FASB ASC 715-30-35-60 also states that for some contracts, the best available evidence of fair value may be contract value; if a contract has a determinable cash surrender value or conversion value, that is presumed to be its fair value.

[Issue Date: May 2010.]

Q&A Section 6931

Financial Statement Reporting and Disclosure—Employee Benefit Plans

> **NOTE**
>
> Question and Answer 3700.01, "Effect of New Mortality Tables on Nongovernmental Employee Benefit Plans (EBPs) and Nongovernmental Entities That Sponsor EBPs," relates to both employer and plan pension obligations and addresses how and when nongovernmental employee benefit plans and nongovernmental sponsoring entities consider updated mortality tables if their financial statements have not yet been issued at the time the updated tables are published.

[.01] Reserved

.02 Benefits Payable to Terminated Participants of a Defined Contribution Plan

Inquiry—Should benefits payable to terminated participants of a DC plan [such as profit sharing or 401(k)] be classified as a liability in the plan financial statements?

Reply—No. Classifying benefits payable to participants as a liability is inappropriate because, by definition, net assets available for benefits (the difference between plan assets and liabilities) represent benefits owed to all participants—both active and terminated. Therefore, only amounts owed to nonparticipants (that is, third parties) should be classified as liabilities.

However, benefits payable to terminated participants should be disclosed in accordance with FASB ASC 962-205-50-1, which states the following, in part:

> The financial statements shall also disclose, if applicable,
>
> *i.* Amounts allocated to accounts of persons who have elected to withdraw from the plan but have not yet been paid. These amounts shall not be reported as a liability on the statement of net assets available for benefits in financial statements prepared in accordance with generally accepted accounting principles (GAAP). A footnote to reconcile the audited financial statements to Form 5500 may be necessary to comply with the Employee Retirement Income Security Act.

[Amended, June 1995; Revised, June 2009, to reflect conforming changes necessary due to the issuance of FASB ASC; Revised, December 2012, to reflect conforming changes necessary due to the issuance of SAS Nos. 122–126; Revised, June 2009, to reflect conforming changes necessary due to the issuance of FASB ASC; Revised, April 2014, to reflect conforming changes necessary due to revisions to FASB ASC.]

[.03] Reserved

.04 Depreciation of a Real Estate Investment Owned by a Defined Benefit Pension Plan

Inquiry—A DB plan has invested in real estate which owns and receives rents from various stores in a shopping center. The financial statements include an expense for depreciation based on original cost. FASB ASC 960-325-35-1 requires that plan investments in real estate be presented at their fair value at the reporting date. Consequently, by providing for depreciation expense, the unrealized appreciation on this asset is increased.

Should depreciation expense be reflected for this plan investment?

Reply—No. Depreciation expense is normally an adjustment of the valuation of fixed assets reported at cost, in accordance with FASB ASC 960-360-35-1, which requires plan assets used in plan operations to be presented at cost less accumulated depreciation or amortization. Accordingly, since plan investments in real estate are to be reported at fair value, there is no requirement to provide for depreciation expense.

[Revised, June 2009, to reflect conforming changes necessary due to the issuance of FASB ASC.]

.05 Accounting and Disclosure Requirements for Single-Employer Employee Benefit Plans Related to the Medicare Prescription Drug, Improvement and Modernization Act of 2003

Inquiry—On December 8, 2003, the president signed into law the Medicare Prescription Drug, Improvement and Modernization Act of 2003 (the act) for employers that sponsor postretirement health care plans that provide prescription drug benefits. The act introduces a prescription drug benefit under Medicare (Medicare Part D) as well as a federal subsidy to sponsors of retiree health care benefit plans that provide a benefit that is at least actuarially equivalent to Medicare Part D.1. FASB ASC 715-60 and FASB ASC 740-10 address the issue of whether an employer that provides postretirement prescription drug coverage should recognize the effects of the act on its accumulated postretirement benefit obligation (APBO) and net postretirement benefit costs and, if so, when and how to account for those effects. FASB ASC 715-60 and FASB ASC 740-10 say that the APBO and net periodic postretirement benefit costs should reflect the effects of the act. FASB ASC 715-60 and FASB ASC 740-10 do not address accounting for the subsidy by health and welfare benefit plans.

For a single-employer health and welfare benefit plan, should the effects of the plan sponsor's (employer's) Medicare prescription drug subsidy (Medicare subsidy) be taken into consideration when calculating the health and welfare plan's postretirement benefit obligation?

Reply—No, the effects of the employer's Medicare subsidy should not be reflected in the plan's obligations. The primary objective of the financial statements of a health and welfare benefit plan is to provide financial information that is useful in assessing the plan's present and future ability to pay its benefit obligations when due. The Medicare subsidy amount is paid to the plan sponsor and does not flow into the plan. The plan sponsor is not required to use the subsidy amount to fund the postretirement benefits and may use the subsidy for any valid business purpose. As a result, the Medicare subsidy does not reduce the amount of benefits that need to be covered by plan assets and future employer contributions. Therefore, the APBO, without reduction for the Medicare subsidy, is a more meaningful measure of the benefits. Further, the information necessary to calculate the gross measure should be readily available for sponsors who are subject to income taxes, because those plan sponsors should maintain gross and net measures of the APBO in order to properly account for income taxes under FASB ASC 740.

Disclosures

The plan should disclose the following:

a. The existence of the act

b. The fact that the APBO and the changes in the benefit obligation do not reflect any amount associated with the Medicare subsidy because the plan is not directly entitled to the Medicare subsidy

c. Until the plan sponsor (employer) is able to determine whether benefits provided by its plan are actuarially equivalent to Medicare Part D.1, that the employer is not able to determine whether the benefits provided by its plan are actuarially equivalent to Medicare Part D.1. If the plan sponsor (employer) has included the effects of the Medicare subsidy in measuring its APBO and changes in benefit obligation, the plan should disclose the fact that the amount of the APBO differs from that disclosed by the plan sponsor (employer) because the plan sponsor's amounts are net of the Medicare subsidy.

[Revised, June 2009, to reflect conforming changes necessary due to the issuance of FASB ASC.]

.06 Accounting and Disclosure Requirements for Multiemployer Employee Benefit Plans Related to the Medicare Prescription Drug, Improvement and Modernization Act of 2003

Inquiry—On December 8, 2003, the president signed into law the Medicare Prescription Drug, Improvement and Modernization Act of 2003 (the act) for employers that sponsor postretirement health care plans that provide prescription drug benefits. The act introduces a prescription drug benefit under Medicare (Medicare Part D) as well as a federal subsidy to sponsors of retiree health care benefit plans that provide a benefit that is at least actuarially equivalent to Medicare Part D.1. FASB ASC 715-60 and FASB ASC 740-10 address the issue of whether an employer that provides postretirement prescription drug coverage should recognize the effects of the act on its APBO and net postretirement benefit costs and, if so, when and how to account for those effects. FASB ASC 715-60 and FASB ASC 740-10 say that the APBO and net periodic postretirement benefit costs should reflect the effects of the act. FASB ASC 715-60 and 740-10 do not address accounting for the subsidy by multiemployer health and welfare benefit plans or by the sponsors or participating employers of those plans.

For multiemployer health and welfare benefit plans, should the effects of the Medicare prescription drug subsidy (Medicare subsidy) be taken into consideration when calculating the health and welfare plan's postretirement benefit obligation?

Reply—Yes, the multiemployer plan's benefit obligations should be reduced by the effects of the Medicare subsidy because the multiemployer plan trust receives the subsidy amount directly and not the individual employers. Because the primary objective of the financial statements of a health and welfare benefit plan is to provide financial information that is useful in assessing the plan's present and future ability to pay its benefit obligations when due, and because the Medicare subsidy amount flows into the multiemployer plan trust, the APBO net of the Medicare subsidy is a more meaningful measure of those benefits.

Disclosures

Until the multiemployer plan is able to determine whether benefits provided by its plan are at least actuarially equivalent to Medicare Part D.1, the plan should disclose the following in the notes to its financial statements:

a. The existence of the act

b. The fact that measures of the APBO and changes in the benefit obligation do not reflect any amount associated with the subsidy because the plan is unable to conclude whether the benefits provided by the plan are actuarially equivalent to Medicare Part D under the act.

If the multiemployer plan has included the effects of the Medicare subsidy in measuring its APBO and changes in the benefit obligation, the plan should disclose the following:

a. The existence of the act

b. The reduction in the APBO for the subsidy related to benefits attributed to past service

c. The effect of the subsidy on the changes in the benefit obligation for the current period

d. An explanation of any significant change in the benefit obligation or plan assets not otherwise apparent in the other disclosures

e. The gross benefit payments (paid and expected, respectively) including prescription drug benefits, and separately the gross amount of the subsidy receipts (received and expected, respectively)

[Revised, June 2009, to reflect conforming changes necessary due to the issuance of FASB ASC.]

.07 Financial Statement Presentation of Underwriting Deficits

Inquiry—The administrator of an employee health and welfare benefit plan has questioned an item on the plan's statement of net assets available for benefits. The item appears in the liabilities section as follows:

Reserve for underwriting deficit—(Note 3) $10,000

Note 3 reads as follows:

Reserve for underwriting deficit represents a liability with the XYZ Life Insurance Company for claims paid in excess of premiums during the current policy year. This liability will be applied to reduce any refunds which may accrue in the future. Such a refund was received during the current year.

The related debit to the credit setting up the liability was to "Underwriting Deficit," and is included in health claims deductions in the "Statement of Changes in Net Assets Available for Benefits."

The administrator takes the position that this item should be excluded entirely from the financial statements because:

1. The policy provides that any underwriting deficit in one policy year is not immediately recoverable by the insurance company but only recoverable against underwriting "gains" of succeeding years, if any.
2. Upon cancellation of the policy by the underwriter, the fund is relieved of any liability for any unrecovered underwriting deficit existing on date of cancellation.

3. Although there were usually underwriting "gains" in past years, there is no assurance that future underwriting "gains" will occur to permit recovery of the deficit.

Should the underwriting loss be reflected in the financial statements in the year in which it occurs?

Reply—Yes, if certain criteria are met. FASB ASC 965-30-25-5 states experience ratings determined by the insurance company or by estimates, may result in a premium deficit. Premium deficits should be included in the benefit obligations if (*a*) it is probable that the deficit will be applied against the amounts of future premiums or future experience-rating refunds and (*b*) the amount can be reasonably estimated. If no obligation is included for a premium deficit because either or both of the conditions are not met, or if an exposure to loss exists in excess of the amount accrued, disclosure of the premium deficit should be made if it is reasonably possible that a loss or an additional loss has been incurred. They should not be shown as liabilities on the plan's statement of net assets available for benefits.

Considerations in determining whether it is probable that a premium deficit will be applied against future premiums or refunds include (*a*) the extent to which the insurance contract requires payment of such deficits and (*b*) the plan's intention, if any, to transfer coverage to another insurance company.

[Amended, June 1995; Amended, June 2001; Revised, June 2009, to reflect conforming changes necessary due to the issuance of FASB ASC; Revised, April 2014, to reflect conforming changes necessary due to revisions to FASB ASC.]

[.08] Reserved

[.09] Reserved

[.10] Reserved

.11 Fair Value Measurement Disclosures for Master Trusts

Inquiry—Employee benefit plans often hold investments under master trust arrangements. According to the Department of Labor's Form 5500 instructions, a *master trust* is a trust for which a regulated financial institution serves as trustee or custodian and in which assets of more than one plan, sponsored by a single employer or by a group of employers under common control, are held.

In a typical master trust arrangement, the plan does not hold units or shares of the master trust but has an undivided interest in the assets of the master trust. However, for participant directed DC plans, the plan typically has a divided interest in the individual assets of the master trust based upon participant direction. The "Master Trusts" sections in chapters 5, 6, and 8 of the AICPA Audit and Accounting Guide *Employee Benefit Plans* (guide) discusses the requirement for investments in master trusts to be shown as a single line item on the statement of net assets available for benefits; however, the plan does not "purchase" and "dispose" of its interest in the master trust but is allocated an interest once the plan sponsor chooses to transfer the plan's assets into the master trust. The guide also discusses the requirement for master trust investments to be shown by general type in the footnotes.

For employee benefit plan financial statements, are the disclosure requirements of FASB ASC 820-10-50 required for the plan's total interest in the master trust or the individual investments under the master trust arrangement?

Reply—The disclosures required by FASB ASC 820-10-50 are required for individual investments under a master trust arrangement and are not required for the plan's total interest in the master trust.

According to FASB ASC 820-10-50, for assets that are measured at fair value on a recurring basis in periods subsequent to initial recognition, the reporting entity shall disclose information that enables users of its financial statements to assess the valuation techniques and inputs used to develop those measurements, and for recurring fair value measurements using significant unobservable inputs (level 3), the effect of the measurements on earnings (or changes in net assets) for the period.

Because of the nature of the plan's ownership interest in the master trust—that is, the plan does not hold units or shares of a master trust—the disclosures in FASB ASC 820 should be presented for the underlying master trust investments.

Consideration should be given to combining, or reconciling, or both, the master trust FASB ASC 820 disclosures as described previously with the current master trust disclosures as described in chapters 5, 6, and 8 of the guide.

[Issue Date: March 2009; Revised, June 2009, to reflect conforming changes necessary due to the issuance of FASB ASC; Revised, April 2010.]

[.12] Reserved

[.13] Reserved

[.14] Reserved

[.15] Reserved

[.16] Reserved

[.17] Reserved

NOTE

Sections 6931.18–.30 have been issued as a set in September 2014 to provide nonauthoritative guidance about the effects of FASB Accounting Standards Update No. 2013-07, *Presentation of Financial Statements—Liquidation Basis of Accounting*, on the accounting for primarily single-employer defined benefit pension and defined contribution retirement plans. Readers are encouraged to read these sections as a collective set of guidance.

.18 Definition of "Imminent" Under Liquidation Basis of Accounting for Single-Employer Defined Benefit and Defined Contribution Retirement Employee Benefit Plans

Inquiry—"Pending Content" in paragraph 2 of FASB ASC 205-30-25, *Presentation of Financial Statements—Liquidation Basis of Accounting*, states that liquidation is imminent when either of the following occurs:

a. A plan for liquidation has been approved by the person or persons with the authority to make such a plan effective, and the likelihood is remote that any of the following will occur:

1. Execution of the plan will be blocked by other parties.
2. The entity will return from liquidation.

b. A plan for liquidation is imposed by other forces (for example, involuntary bankruptcy), and the likelihood is remote that the entity will return from liquidation.

For a single-employer DB plan or DC plan, could liquidation be considered imminent upon approval by the governing body with authority over the plan (for example, board approval or executed plan amendment)?

(Although the information contained in the following reply is specific to single-employer DB and DC plans, the information may be relevant when considering the termination of a single-employer health and welfare benefit plan, or a multiemployer plan.)

Reply—Determining whether liquidation is imminent is a matter of judgment, based on facts and circumstances. In accordance with "Pending Content" in paragraph 2 of FASB ASC 205-30-25, liquidation is imminent when a plan for liquidation has been approved by the persons with authority to make such a plan effective, and the likelihood is remote that execution of the plan will be blocked by other parties. For a single-employer DB or DC plan, this would mean that the likelihood would need to be remote that other parties, such as the Pension Benefit Guarantee Corporation (PBGC) or the IRS, would block the liquidation. Such evaluation often depends on whether the termination is a standard termination, or a distressed or involuntary termination. Further, approval for the termination of a DB plan is different and often more complex than that of a DC plan. For all types of plans, consultation with legal counsel, plan actuaries (if applicable), and service organizations (for example, trustees or record keepers) may be necessary in order to make a judgment about whether the likelihood is remote that other parties would block the termination of a plan. This evaluation may change over time, depending upon the stage of the termination process.

The following paragraphs discuss the different types of terminations and the related processes, which may be helpful when determining whether liquidation is imminent.

Defined Benefit Pension Plans

Standard Termination

Terminating a DB plan is a detailed process covered by the Employee Retirement Income Security Act of 1974 (ERISA) that involves the PBGC and IRS. A DB plan may terminate only if certain rules and procedures are followed. These rules and procedures for terminating a single-employer DB plan in a standard or distressed termination are set forth in Title 29, *Labor*, U.S. Code of Federal Regulations (CFR) part 4041 of ERISA. Failure to comply with the standard termination requirements or failure to meet the deadlines may cause the proposed termination to be nullified. If the termination is nullified, the plan administrator may not make a final distribution of assets and the plan is an ongoing plan for all purposes. If the plan administrator still intends to terminate the plan, the process will need to be started again with a new proposed termination date. See the PBGC Pension Plan Termination Fact Sheet[1] and the PBGC Standard Termination Filing Instructions[2] for further information.

[1] www.pbgc.gov/res/factsheets/page/termination.html

[2] www.pbgc.gov/documents/500-instructions.pdf

The following is not a detailed description of the entire termination process but rather an overview of the standard termination process of a DB plan.[3] This overview is based upon the regulations in effect as of September 2014 and is subject to change. Actual code sections and the PBGC Standard Termination Filing Instructions should be consulted.

- Select a proposed termination date. This is typically done by a resolution of the plan's governing body or an amendment to the DB plan.
- Provide a "Notice of Intent to Terminate" to affected parties (other than the PBGC) at least 60 days and not more than 90 days before the proposed termination date.
- Provide a "Notice of Plan Benefits" to participants, beneficiaries of deceased participants, and alternative payees no later than the time the plan administrator files the "Standard Termination Notice" (PBGC Form 500) with the PBGC. (*Note*: If the plan administrator wants to qualify for the distribution deadline linked to receipt of the IRS determination letter, the determination letter request must be submitted to the IRS no later than the time the plan administrator files the Form 500 with the PBGC.)
- File a "Standard Termination Notice" (PBGC Form 500) with the PBGC on or before the 180th day after the proposed termination date. The PBGC has 60 days after receiving a complete Form 500 to review the termination for compliance with laws and regulations.
- The plan administrator may not distribute plan assets in connection with the termination until the PBGC review period ends. Under a standard termination, complete distribution must occur within the later of (*a*) 180 days after expiration of the PBGC's 60-day review period or (*b*) 120 days after receipt of a favorable IRS determination letter provided that the plan administrator submitted a valid request for an IRS determination letter by the time the Form 500 was filed with the PBGC.
- File a "Post Distribution Certification" (PBGC Form 501) with the PBGC no later than 30 days after all plan benefits are distributed.
- Apply for a determination letter from the IRS (Form 5310, "Application for Determination for Terminating Plan") as to whether the plan termination affects the qualified status of the plan. (*Note*: This filing is optional. If filed, it must be filed with the IRS within one year of the proposed termination date.)

Distressed or Involuntary Termination

A distressed termination occurs when a DB plan has insufficient assets to pay all benefits owed and the employer proves to the PBGC that it is unable to financially support the DB plan. In these situations, the PBGC takes over the DB plan as trustee and "uses its own assets and any remaining assets in the DB plan to make sure current and future retirees of the DB plan receive their pension benefits, within the legal limits."[4]

---

[3] See the PBGC Standard Termination Filing Instructions at www.pbgc.gov/documents/500-instructions.pdf.

[4] See the PBGC website at www.pbgc.gov/prac/terminations/distress-terminations.html.

An involuntary termination occurs when initiated by the PBGC if any of the following occurs:

- The DB plan has not met minimum funding requirements.
- The plan cannot pay benefits when due.
- A lump sum payment has been made to a participant who is a substantial owner of the sponsoring company.
- The loss to the PBGC is expected to increase unreasonably if the DB plan is not terminated.

The PBGC must terminate a DB plan if assets are not available to pay currently due benefits.

Defined Contribution Plans

Generally, the termination process for a DC plan, including a money purchase pension plan, includes the following:

- Select a proposed termination date. This is typically done by a resolution by the plan's governing body or an amendment to the DC plan.
- Amend the DC plan to terminate and cease benefit accruals.
- Notify affected parties concerning the termination.
- Apply for a determination letter from the IRS (Form 5310) about whether the DC plan termination affects the qualified status of the plan. The application for a determination letter is optional for a DC plan. If filed, it must be filed with the IRS within one year of the proposed termination date. The employer or trustee is not required to hold the assets until a favorable determination letter is issued, but usually will do so as a safety feature to ensure that distributions will receive the favorable tax treatment to which qualified plan distributions are entitled.
- Distribute the DC plan's assets as soon as it is administratively feasible. (*Note*: If actions are taken to terminate a DC plan but the assets are not distributed as soon as administratively feasible, the DC plan is not considered terminated for purposes of Internal Revenue Code 401(a), *Qualified Pension, Profit-Sharing, and Stock Bonus Plans*. The DC plan's qualified status must be maintained until the DC plan is terminated in fact. In accordance with "IRS Retirement Plans FAQs regarding Plan Terminations," whether distributions are made as soon as it is administratively feasible is determined under all the facts and circumstances of a given case, but generally the IRS views this to mean within one year after DC plan termination.[5]

[Issue Date: September 2014.]

.19 Applicability of Using Liquidation Basis of Accounting for Partial Plan Terminations or Plan Mergers for Single-Employer DB Plans

Inquiry—Is a single-employer DB plan required to apply the liquidation basis of accounting in accordance with FASB ASC 205-30-25 in either of the following situations?

[5] This document is available at www.irs.gov/Retirement-Plans/Retirement-Plans-FAQs-regarding-Plan-Terminations.

a. The DB plan is partially terminated (for example, an employer closes a particular plant or division that results in the termination of employment of a substantial portion of DB plan participants, or an employer stops or reduces future benefit accruals under a DB plan).

b. A DB plan ceases to exist by merging into a successor plan.

(Although the information contained in the following reply is specific to single-employer DB plans, the information may be relevant when considering the termination of a DC plan, a health and welfare plan, or a multiemployer plan.)

Reply—In accordance with "Pending Content" in FASB ASC glossary, *liquidation* is defined as the process by which an entity converts its assets to cash or other assets and settles its obligations with creditors in anticipation of the entity ceasing all activities. Upon cessation of the entity's activities, any remaining cash or other assets are distributed to the entity's investors or other claimants (albeit sometimes indirectly). Liquidation may be compulsory or voluntary. Dissolution of an entity as a result of that entity being acquired by another entity or merged into another entity in its entirety and with the expectation of continuing its business does not qualify as liquidation.

Partial Plan Termination

In a partial plan termination, judgment is required to assess whether the plan is ceasing all plan activities. Generally, this is not the case; therefore, a partial plan termination generally is not an event that would trigger the application of the liquidation basis of accounting.

Transfer of Plan Assets and Obligations (Plan Merger)

A plan merger generally occurs in connection with or as a result of the acquisition of an entity by another entity, or when an entity merges two plans for which it is the sponsor. Such plan mergers generally would not use the liquidation basis of accounting in FASB ASC 205-30 because the plan obligations are not being settled with the participant; rather, the DB plan's assets and obligations are being transferred to another plan. Accordingly, a plan merger would not be accounted for using the liquidation basis of accounting.

[Issue Date: September 2014.]

.20 Use of Beginning-of-Year Benefit Information Date Versus End-of-Year Benefit Information Date When Using the Liquidation Basis of Accounting for Single-Employer DB Plans

Inquiry—Paragraph 4 of FASB ASC 960-205-45 permits the actuarial present value of accumulated plan benefits to be presented as of the beginning or end of the plan year; however, an end-of-year benefit information date is considered preferable. When a single-employer DB plan uses a beginning-of-year benefit information date and is required to prepare its financial statements using the liquidation basis of accounting in accordance with FASB ASC 205-30, is the DB plan required to change to an end-of-year benefit information date?

Reply—Using a beginning-of-year benefit information date is not the most meaningful or useful to a reader of the financial statements for a terminating plan. The use of an end-of-year benefit information date is considered preferable and plans are encouraged to develop procedures to enable them to use that date. Paragraph 4 of FASB ASC 960-205-45 was not amended by FASB ASU No. 2013-07 because an entity should measure liabilities in accordance with the measurement provisions of other FASB ASC topics that otherwise would apply to those liabilities[6] (in this case, FASB ASC 960-205-45). Accordingly, DB plans continue to be permitted to present the actuarial present value of accumulated plan benefits as of the beginning of year or end of year.

In accordance with paragraph 1(h) of FASB ASC 960-205-50, plans are required to disclose unusual or infrequent events or transactions occurring after the latest benefit information date but before the financial statements are issued or are available to be issued that might significantly affect the usefulness of the financial statements in an assessment of the plan's present and future ability to pay benefits. If reasonably determinable, the effects of such events or transactions should be disclosed. If such effects are not quantified, the reasons why they are not reasonably determinable should be disclosed. Therefore, DB plans that continue to use a beginning-of-year benefit information date are still required to disclose the effects of the plan termination if it is reasonably determinable.

[Issue Date: September 2014.]

.21 Presentation of the Actuarial Present Value of Accumulated Plan Benefits of Single-Employer DB Plans When Using the Liquidation Basis of Accounting

Inquiry—Paragraph 2 of FASB ASC 960-20-45 permits the information regarding a defined benefit pension plan's actuarial present value of accumulated plan benefits and changes therein to be presented on the face of one or more financial statements or in the notes thereto.

When a single-employer DB plan prepares its financial statements using the liquidation basis of accounting in accordance with FASB ASC 205-30, may the DB plan continue to choose to report obligations either in a separate financial statement, combined with the statement of net assets available for benefits and the year-to-year changes therein, or in the notes to the financial statements?

(Although the information contained in the following reply is specific to single-employer DB plans, the information may be relevant when considering the termination of a single-employer defined benefit health and welfare plan as it relates to its benefit obligations, or a multiemployer plan.)

Reply—Yes. The conclusions reached in FASB ASU No. 2013-07 explain that the objective of the project was to provide guidance about when and how an entity should apply the liquidation basis of accounting. It does not change the provisions in FASB ASC 960-20-45 that allow the present value of accumulated plan benefits to be presented on the face of one or more financial statements or in the notes thereto.

When liquidation basis financial statements are presented, practice may vary regarding the presentation of a DB plan's benefit obligations. Typically, the DB plan's financial statements continue to be presented as prescribed in FASB ASC 960, *Plan Accounting*. That is, the benefit obligation information, estimated using the liquidation basis of accounting, would be presented in a separate statement, combined with the statement of net assets available for benefits and the year-to-year changes therein, or in the notes to the financial

[6] See "Pending Content" in paragraph 2 of FASB ASC 205-30-30.

statements. Exhibits 1–4 illustrate a DB plan using the liquidation basis of accounting following the FASB ASC 960 format:

Exhibit 1—C&H Company Pension Plan, Statements of Net Assets Available for Benefits as of December 31, 20X2 (in Liquidation) and 20X1 (Ongoing)

Exhibit 2—C&H Company Pension Plan, Statement of Changes in Net Assets Available for Benefits in Liquidation

Exhibit 3—C&H Company Pension Plan, Statements of Accumulated Plan Benefits as of December 31, 20X2 (in Liquidation) and 20X1 (Ongoing)

Exhibit 4—C&H Company Pension Plan, Statement of Changes in Accumulated Plan Benefits in Liquidation

Also acceptable would be to present the plan's benefit obligation, estimated using the liquidation basis of accounting, as liabilities on the face of the statement of net assets (or liabilities) in liquidation even though the benefit obligations previously reported for the ongoing plan were presented in the notes to the financial statements or in a separate statement. When using the liquidation basis of accounting, the plan's assets and liabilities are shown in a "statement of net assets (or liabilities) in liquidation." Under this approach, the statement of net assets in liquidation would include the plan's benefit obligations, as actuarially determined using end-of-year benefit information, with appropriate disclosures of termination and liquidation assumptions. The prior year benefit obligation(s) would be presented either in a separate statement or in the notes to the financial statements, along with information regarding the effects, if significant, of certain factors affecting the year-to-year change in the benefit obligation(s) adjusted to reflect the liability now presented in the statement of net assets in liquidation (see subsequent exhibit D). Exhibits A–D illustrate a DB plan's financial statements using the liquidation basis of accounting when not following the FASB ASC 960 format:

Exhibit A—C&H Company Pension Plan, Statements of Net Assets in Liquidation as of December 31, 20X2, and Statement of Net Assets Available for Benefits as of December 31, 20X1 (Ongoing)

Exhibit B—C&H Company Pension Plan, Statement of Changes in Net Assets in Liquidation

Exhibit C—C&H Company Pension Plan, Statements of Accumulated Plan Benefits as of December 31, 20X1 (Ongoing)

Exhibit D—C&H Company Pension Plan, Statement of Changes in Accumulated Plan Benefits in Liquidation

The following are illustrative DB plan financial statements presented using the liquidation basis of accounting under both scenarios discussed previously.

I. Illustrations of a Single-Employer DB Plan Using the Liquidation Basis of Accounting (Assuming an End-of-Year Benefit Information Date) Following the FASB ASC 960 Financial Statement Format

[The notes to the financial statements are not illustrated.]

Circumstances include the following:

- C&H Company Pension Plan is a single-employer, cash balance, defined benefit pension plan providing retirement, disability, and death benefits.
- The plan was terminated in 20X2 as a standard termination and the plan has changed its basis of accounting from the ongoing plan basis, used in presenting the 20X1 financial statements, to the liquidation basis used in presenting the 20X2 financial statements, in accordance with FASB ASC 205-30. As of December 31, 20X2, all assets of the plan have not yet been fully liquidated.
- The plan presents separate statements of net assets available for benefits as of December 31, 20X2 (in liquidation) and 20X1 (ongoing), statement of changes in net assets available for benefits for the year ended December 31, 20X2 (in liquidation), statements of accumulated plan benefits as of December 31, 20X2 (in liquidation) and 20X1 (ongoing), and statement of changes in accumulated plan benefits (in liquidation).

  Note: If the comparative benefit obligations are presented in the notes to the financial statements (as permitted by paragraph 2 of FASB ASC 960-20-45 [see section 6931.26, "Comparative Financial Statements When Using the Liquidation Basis of Accounting of a Single-Employer DB Plan"]), then exhibits 3–4 would not be necessary and the related information would be presented in the notes to the financial statements.
- The financial statements use an end-of-year benefit information date.
- The financial statements follow the format as prescribed under FASB ASC 960 and 205-30.
- The plan's assets are sufficient to cover the obligation and, therefore, the employer is not required to contribute additional funding into the plan (no employer receivable).
- The statement of net assets available for benefits as of December 31, 20X2 (in liquidation), includes accrued interest expected to be earned through the end of its liquidation on the money market fund. (*Note*: The liquidation valuation of the money market fund does not include interest income expected to be earned through the end of its liquidation. See section 6931.25, "Accrued Income When Using the Liquidation Basis of Accounting for a Single-Employer DB Plan.")
- The statement of net assets available for benefits as of December 31, 20X2 (in liquidation), includes accrued expenses expected to be incurred through the end of its liquidation. (See section 6931.24, "Accrued Costs When Using the Liquidation Basis of Accounting for a Single-Employer DB Plan.")

- For purposes of this illustration, the statement of changes in net assets available for benefits for the year ended December 31, 20X2 (in liquidation), reflects an adjustment to the liquidation basis in the aggregate as a separate line item; however, other presentations may be acceptable.
- The changes in actuarial assumptions included in the statement of changes in accumulated plan benefits in liquidation reflect the changes due to the change to liquidation basis of accounting.

Exhibit 1

C&H Company Pension Plan
Statements of Net Assets Available for Benefits as of December 31, 20X2 (in Liquidation) and 20X1 (Ongoing)

	December 31,	
	20X2 (in Liquidation)	*20X1 (Ongoing)*
Assets		
Investments		
Money Market Fund	$14,334,000	$1,860,000
C&H Company common stock	0	880,000
Guaranteed investment contract with insurance company	0	890,000
Corporate bonds	0	3,670,000
U.S. government securities	0	270,000
Hedge fund	0	460,000
Real estate fund	0	240,000
Total investments	14,334,000	8,270,000
Receivables		
Employer's contribution	0	35,000
Due from broker for securities sold	0	175,000
Accrued interest and dividends	0	76,000
Accrued interest expected to be earned in liquidation	443,000	0
Total receivables	443,000	286,000
Cash—noninterest bearing	200,000	90,000
Total assets	14,977,000	8,646,000
Liabilities		
Due to broker for securities purchased	0	460,000
Accrued expenses	42,000	40,000
Accrued expenses expected to be incurred in liquidation	23,000	0
Total liabilities	65,000	500,000
Net assets available for benefits	$14,912,000	$8,146,000

See accompanying notes to the financial statements.

Exhibit 2

C&H Company Pension Plan
Statement of Changes in Net Assets Available for Benefits in Liquidation

	Year Ended December 31, 20X2
Investment income:	
Net appreciation in fair value of investments	$3,735,000
Interest	325,000
Dividends	5,000
	4,065,000
Less investment expenses	39,000
Total investment income	4,026,000
Employer contributions	3,359,000
Total additions	7,385,000
Benefits paid directly to participants	740,000
Purchases of annuity contracts	257,000
Total benefits paid	997,000
Administrative expenses	42,000
Total deductions	1,039,000
Net increase	6,346,000
Adjustment to liquidation basis	420,000
Net assets available for benefits:	
Beginning of year (ongoing)	8,146,000
End of year (in liquidation)	$14,912,000

See accompanying notes to the financial statements.

Exhibit 3

C&H Company Pension Plan
Statements of Accumulated Plan Benefits as of December 31, 20X2 (in Liquidation) and 20X1 (Ongoing)

	December 31,	
	20X2 (in Liquidation)	*20X1 (Ongoing)*
Actuarial present value of accumulated plan benefits		
Vested benefits:		
Participants currently receiving payments	$3,040,000	$2,950,000
Other participants	10,840,000	6,530,000
	13,880,000	9,480,000
Nonvested benefits	0	2,400,000
Total actuarial present value of accumulated plan benefits	$13,880,000	$11,880,000

See accompanying notes to the financial statements.

Exhibit 4

C&H Company Pension Plan
Statement of Changes in Accumulated Plan Benefits in Liquidation

	Year Ended December 31, 20X2
Actuarial present value of accumulated plan benefits at beginning of year (ongoing)	$11,880,000
Increase (decrease) during the year attributable to:	
Change in actuarial assumptions[7]	1,359,500
Benefits accumulated	895,000
Increase for interest[8]	742,500
Benefits paid	(997,000)
Net increase	2,000,000
Actuarial present value of accumulated plan benefits at end of year (in liquidation)	$13,880,000

See accompanying notes to the financial statements.

[7] The changes in actuarial assumptions reflect the changes due to the change to liquidation basis of accounting.

[8] The actuarial report will often refer to this amount as the "increase for interest due to the decrease in the discount period."

II. Illustrations of a Defined Benefit Pension Plan Using the Liquidation Basis of Accounting (Assuming an End-of-Year Benefit Information Date)—Other Acceptable Method

[The notes to the financial statements are not illustrated.]

Note: When using the liquidation basis of accounting, the plan's assets and liabilities are shown in a statement of net assets (or liabilities). Under this method, the statement of net assets in liquidation is presented in place of a statement using an ongoing basis and includes all liabilities, including benefit obligations, as actuarially determined using end-of-year benefit information.

Circumstances include the following:

- C&H Company Pension Plan is a single-employer, cash balance, defined benefit pension plan providing retirement, disability, and death benefits.
- The plan was terminated in 20X2 as a standard termination and the plan has changed its basis of accounting from the ongoing plan basis, used in presenting the 20X1 financial statements, to the liquidation basis used in presenting the 20X2 financial statements, in accordance with FASB ASC 205-30. As of December 31, 20X2, all assets of the plan have not yet been fully liquidated.
- The adjustment to liquidation for estimated payments to participants upon liquidation (the plan benefit obligation in liquidation) is presented in the statements of net assets in liquidation and changes in net assets in liquidation.
- In the prior year (20X1), the plan presented separate statements of accumulated plan benefits and changes in accumulated plan benefits. Accordingly, when presenting comparative financial statements, the 20X1 accumulated plan benefits continue to be presented in such statements.

  Note: If the comparative benefit obligations are presented in the notes to the financial statements (as permitted by paragraph 2 of FASB ASC 960-20-45 [see section 6931.26]), then exhibits C–D would not be necessary and the related information would be presented in the notes to the financial statements.
- The financial statements use an end-of-year benefit information date.
- The statement of net assets in liquidation as of December 31, 20X2, includes accrued interest expected to be earned through the end of its liquidation on the money market fund. (*Note*: The liquidation valuation of the money market fund does not include interest income expected to be earned through the end of its liquidation. See section 6931.25.)
- The statement of net assets in liquidation as of December 31, 20X2, includes accrued expenses expected to be incurred through the end of its liquidation. (See section 6931.24.)
- For purposes of this illustration, the statement of changes in net assets in liquidation for the year ended December 31, 20X2,

reflects an adjustment to the liquidation basis (other presentations may be acceptable).

- The changes in actuarial assumptions included in the statement of changes in accumulated plan benefits in liquidation reflect the changes due to the change to liquidation basis of accounting.

Exhibit A

C&H Company Pension Plan
Statement of Net Assets in Liquidation as of December 31, 20X2, and Statement of Net Assets Available for Benefits as of December 31, 20X1 (Ongoing)

	December 31,	
	20X2 (in Liquidation)	*20X1 (Ongoing)*
Assets		
Investments		
Money Market Fund	$14,334,000	$1,860,000
C&H Company common stock	0	880,000
Guaranteed investment contract with insurance company	0	890,000
Corporate bonds	0	3,670,000
U.S. government securities	0	270,000
Hedge fund	0	460,000
Real estate fund	0	240,000
Total investments	14,334,000	8,270,000
Receivables		
Employer's contribution	0	35,000
Due from broker for securities sold	0	175,000
Accrued interest and dividends	0	76,000
Accrued interest expected to be earned in liquidation	443,000	0
Total receivables	443,000	286,000
Cash—noninterest bearing	200,000	90,000
Total assets	14,977,000	8,646,000
Liabilities		
Estimated payments to participants upon liquidation	13,880,000	0
Due to broker for securities purchased	0	460,000
Accrued expenses	42,000	40,000
Accrued expenses expected to be incurred in liquidation	23,000	0
Total liabilities	13,945,000	500,000
Net assets available for benefits (ongoing)		$8,146,000
Net assets in liquidation	$1,032,000	

See accompanying notes to the financial statements.

Exhibit B

C&H Company Pension Plan
Statement of Changes in Net Assets in Liquidation

	Year Ended December 31, 20X2
Investment income:	
Net appreciation in fair value of investments	$3,735,000
Interest	325,000
Dividends	5,000
	4,065,000
Less investment expenses	39,000
Total investment income	4,026,000
Employer contributions	3,359,000
Total additions	7,385,000
Benefits paid directly to participants	740,000
Purchases of annuity contracts	257,000
Total benefits paid	997,000
Administrative expenses	42,000
Total deductions	1,039,000
Net increase	6,346,000
Adjustment to liquidation basis	
Estimated payments to participants upon liquidation[9]	(13,880,000)
Accrued interest and expenses	420,000
Beginning of year (net assets available for benefits [ongoing])	8,146,000
End of year (net assets in liquidation)	$1,032,000

See accompanying notes to the financial statements.

[9] See exhibit D.

Exhibit C

C&H Company Pension Plan
Statement of Accumulated Plan Benefits as of December 31, 20X1 (Ongoing)

Actuarial present value of accumulated plan benefits	
Vested benefits:	
Participants currently receiving payments	$2,950,000
Other participants	6,530,000
	9,480,000
Nonvested benefits	2,400,000
Total actuarial present value of accumulated plan benefits	$11,880,000

See accompanying notes to the financial statements.

Exhibit D

C&H Company Pension Plan
Statement of Changes in Accumulated Plan Benefits in Liquidation

	Year Ended December 31, 20X2
Actuarial present value of accumulated plan benefits at beginning of year (ongoing)	$11,880,000
Increase (decrease) during the year attributable to:	
Change in actuarial assumptions[10]	1,359,500
Benefits accumulated	895,000
Increase for interest[11]	742,500
Benefits paid	(997,000)
Net increase	2,000,000
Actuarial present value of accumulated plan benefits at end of year (in liquidation)	$13,880,000
Adjustment to liquidation basis–estimated payments to participants upon liquidation	(13,880,000)
	0

See accompanying notes to the financial statements.

[Issue Date: September 2014.]

---

[10] See footnote 7.

[11] See footnote 8.

.22 Contribution Receivable From the Plan Sponsor in a Standard Termination of a Single-Employer DB Plan

Inquiry—When using the liquidation basis of accounting in accordance with FASB ASC 205-30 for a standard termination, should a single-employer DB plan record a contribution receivable from the plan sponsor for the amount that the plan sponsor is expected to contribute to the plan as part of its obligation to settle the plan?

(Although the information contained in the following reply is specific to single-employer DB plans, the information may be relevant when considering the termination of a single-employer DC plan, a health and welfare plan, or a multiemployer plan.)

Reply—"Pending Content" in paragraph 4 of FASB ASC 205-30-25 states that when using the liquidation basis of accounting, an entity should recognize other items that it previously had not recognized but that it expects to either sell in liquidation or use to settle liabilities. Further, "Pending Content" in paragraph 7 of FASB ASC 205-30-25 requires an entity to accrue income that it expects to earn through the end of its liquidation if and when it has a reasonable basis for estimation. The DB plan would record a receivable from the plan sponsor if such amounts are expected to be used to settle benefits and the DB plan has a reasonable basis to estimate the amount. As part of a standard termination, the plan sponsor would need to obtain from the actuary an estimated settlement liability and required contributions (as of the termination date) in order to have a reasonable basis to determine that it has adequate resources to fund the obligation to settle the DB plan. The actuary determines the amount of any minimum required contributions up to the DB plan's termination date. A receivable would typically be recorded for any such minimum required contribution (see the recommendation of the AICPA Financial Reporting Executive committee in the "Contributions and Contributions Receivable" section of the "Defined Benefit Pension Plans" chapter of the AICPA Audit and Accounting Guide *Employee Benefit Plans*). An additional contribution may be necessary to fully fund the obligation. Such additional contribution should be recorded as a receivable if and when the DB plan has a reasonable basis for estimation, in accordance with "Pending Content" in paragraph 7 of FASB ASC 205-30-25. The additional contribution estimated by the actuary may be as of a date other than the DB plan's measurement date and, therefore, may need to be updated to reflect changes in assumptions and the investment performance of the DB plan's assets as of the plan's measurement date.

[Issue Date: September 2014.]

.23 Overfunded Single-Employer DB Plan When Using the Liquidation Basis of Accounting

Inquiry—Should an overfunded single-employer DB plan that is using the liquidation basis of accounting, in accordance with FASB ASC 205-30, and expects to have excess assets, accrue the excess assets as a payable to the plan sponsor?

(Although the information contained in the following reply is specific to single-employer DB plans, the information may be relevant when considering the termination of a single-employer DC plan, a health and welfare plan, or a multiemployer plan.)

Reply—The DB plan's provisions may direct excess assets at termination to be distributed in a number of ways (for example, allocated to participants in the form of an increased benefit, used to pay the DB plan's expenses, transferred to another plan, or reverted to the plan sponsor). The decision to accrue the excess assets as a payable to the plan sponsor is affected by the DB plan's provisions for termination and whether there is a reasonable basis for estimation. "Pending Content" in paragraph 7 of FASB ASC 205-30-25 states that an entity should accrue costs that it expects to incur through the end of its liquidation if and when it has a reasonable basis for estimation. Until the DB plan is fully liquidated, it may not be possible to estimate whether there will be excess assets. Further, reversion of excess assets to the plan sponsor would have tax implications for the plan sponsor and, therefore, is not common. Plan management may want to disclose the DB plan's provisions for the treatment of excess plan assets in the notes to the financial statements.

[Issue Date: September 2014.]

.24 Accrued *Costs* When Using the Liquidation Basis of Accounting for a Single-Employer DB Plan

Inquiry—"Pending Content" in paragraph 7 of FASB ASC 205-30-25 states that an entity should accrue costs and income that it expects to incur or earn through the end of its liquidation if and when it has a reasonable basis for estimation. Would a single-employer DB plan accrue estimated future expenses such as trustee fees, audit fees, actuarial fees, and PBGC premiums?

(Although the information contained in the following reply is specific to single-employer DB plans, the information may be relevant when considering the termination of a single-employer DC plan, a health and welfare plan, or a multiemployer plan.)

Reply—When a DB plan uses the liquidation basis of accounting, management needs to consider the period over which the liquidation will occur as well as the nature of expenses that will be incurred and reported by the DB plan during the liquidation period. These future expense amounts should be accrued in the financial statements provided there is a reasonable basis for their estimation. For DB plans, care should be taken that future expenses are not double counted in the course of estimating the amounts to be accrued though the end of liquidation and the amounts included in the benefit obligation. "Pending Content" in paragraphs 1–2 of FASB ASC 205-30-50 requires certain disclosures to be made. In particular, the DB plan would be required to disclose the type and amount of costs accrued in the statement of net assets in liquidation and the period over which those costs are expected to be paid.

[Issue Date: September 2014.]

.25 Accrued *Income* When Using the Liquidation Basis of Accounting for a Single-Employer DB Plan

Inquiry—"Pending Content" in paragraph 7 of FASB ASC 205-30-25 states that an entity should accrue costs and income that it expects to incur or earn through the end of its liquidation if and when it has a reasonable basis for estimation. Would a DB plan accrue income related to estimated earnings on the investments held by the DB plan?

(Although the information contained in the following reply is specific to single-employer DB plans, the information may be relevant when considering the termination of a single-employer DC plan, a health and welfare plan, or a multiemployer plan.)

Reply—Income for a DB plan is primarily related to its investments, which are generally measured at fair value under the ongoing basis of accounting. "Pending Content" in paragraph 7 of FASB ASC 205-30-25 requires an entity to accrue income that it expects to earn through the end of liquidation if and when it has a reasonable basis for estimation. Because the DB plan invests in various investment securities and the mix of the plan's investment portfolio is likely to change as the liquidation progresses, there may not be a reasonable basis for which to estimate changes in fair value of the investment portfolio and, therefore, accrual of such appreciation or depreciation of the investments generally would not be necessary.

In some circumstances, liquidation value may not differ from fair value (for example, because it assumes the related dispositions would be conducted in an orderly manner) and, therefore, an entity would not be precluded from measuring those assets at fair value. Management should be careful not to double count income that is already reflected in the fair value of the investments. For example, the fair value of a common stock generally would already include dividends expected to be declared in the future. Similarly, the fair value of a bond generally would already include interest expected to be earned from the measurement date through the maturity date. Consistent with the ongoing basis of accounting, dividends and interest earned through the measurement date but not yet received would be accrued if these amounts are not reflected in the fair value of the investments.

If the fair value or the liquidation value does not include future expected earnings, the entity should accrue income that it expects to earn through the end of liquidation if and when it has a reasonable basis for estimation. For example, the interest earned on a money market account or interest-bearing cash generally would not be included in the fair value, so those amounts would be estimated and reported on the financial statements if and when the DB plan has a reasonable basis for estimation. "Pending Content" in paragraphs 1–2 of FASB ASC 205-30-50 requires certain disclosures to be made. In particular, the DB plan would be required to disclose the type and amount of income accrued in the statement of net assets in liquidation and the period over which that income is expected to be earned.

[Issue Date: September 2014.]

.26 Comparative Financial Statements When Using the Liquidation Basis of Accounting of a Single-Employer DB Plan

Inquiry—"Pending Content" in paragraph 2 of FASB ASC 205-30-45 states that the liquidation basis of accounting should be applied prospectively from the day that liquidation becomes imminent. ERISA requires comparative statements of net assets available for benefits and a full year statement of changes in net assets available for benefits. Is a single-employer DB plan able to present the current year financial statements in liquidation comparatively on the same financial statements with the prior period statements prepared on the ongoing plan basis?

(Although the information contained in the following reply is specific to single-employer DB plans, the information may be relevant when considering the termination of a single-employer DC plan, a health and welfare plan, or a multiemployer plan.)

Reply—Yes, the DB plan may present comparative financial statements, as required by ERISA, clearly labeled as to the basis on which they have been prepared. See the illustrative financial statements included in section 6931.21, "Presentation of the Actuarial Present Value of Accumulated Plan Benefits of Single-Employer DB Plans When Using the Liquidation Basis of Accounting," for an illustration of possible column headings. "Pending Content" in paragraph

1 of FASB ASC 205-30-50 states that the entity should make all disclosures required by other FASB ASC topics that are relevant to understanding the entity's statements of net assets in liquidation and changes in net assets in liquidation. This would include the disclosure required by FASB ASC 205 relating to changes affecting comparability. Paragraph 1 of FASB ASC 205-10-50 states that if, because of reclassifications or for other reasons, changes have occurred in the manner of or basis for presenting corresponding items for two or more periods, information should be furnished that will explain the change. This procedure is in conformity with the well-recognized principle that any change in practice that affects comparability of financial statements should be disclosed.

[Issue Date: September 2014.]

.27 Presentation of a Stub Period in a Single-Employer DB Plan When Using the Liquidation Basis of Accounting

Inquiry—In accordance with "Pending Content" in paragraph 2 of FASB ASC 205-30-45 , the initial statement of changes in net assets in liquidation should present only changes in net assets that occurred during the period since liquidation became imminent. The FASB ASC does not provide guidance about whether an entity should present information for the period of time that preceded the determination that liquidation is imminent (referred to as a *stub period*). Is a single-employer DB plan required to present a stub period for the period of time that preceded the determination that liquidation is imminent?

(Although the information contained in the following reply is specific to single-employer DB plans, the information may be relevant when considering the termination of a single-employer DC plan, a health and welfare plan, or a multiemployer plan.)

Reply—No. Paragraph BC18 of FASB ASU No. 2013-07 states that the objective of the project was to provide guidance about when and how the entity should apply the liquidation basis of accounting. In deciding whether to present information about a stub period, an entity should consider the requirements of its regulator and the needs of any other anticipated users of the entity's financial statements.

Further, "Pending Content" in paragraph 1 of FASB ASC 960-40-25 states that if liquidation of a plan is deemed to be imminent before the end of the plan year, the plan's *year-end* financial statements should be prepared using the liquidation basis of accounting (*emphasis added*). Accordingly, because ERISA requires a full year presentation of comparative statements of net assets available for benefits and a full year statement of changes in net assets available for benefits, a DB plan would typically present a full year statement of changes in net assets available for benefits in liquidation for the current year (regardless of the date that the DB plan entered into liquidation during the year) and a statement of net assets available for benefits in liquidation as of the end of the current year and a statement of net assets available for benefits using the ongoing basis as of the prior year end.

For DB plans that present the benefit obligation information in primary financial statements, the statements prepared using the liquidation basis of accounting may be presented comparatively (as applicable) with the prior period statements on an ongoing plan basis labeled accordingly.

(*Note*: A plan year may be less than 12 months depending upon the date of complete distribution of plan assets.)

[Issue Date: September 2014.]

.28 Presentation of Fully Benefit-Responsive Investment Contracts in Single-Employer DC Plans When Using the Liquidation Basis of Accounting

Inquiry—Should single-employer DC plans that hold fully benefit-responsive investment contracts present both fair value and contract value on the face of the financial statements, as required by paragraphs 2–3 and 6 of FASB ASC 962-205-45, when the plan is using the liquidation basis of accounting in accordance with FASB ASC 205-30?

(Although the information contained in the following reply is specific to single-employer DC plans, the information may be relevant when considering the termination of a single-employer health and welfare plan or a multiemployer plan that holds fully benefit-responsive investment contracts.)

Reply—When a DC plan is using the liquidation basis of accounting, as required by FASB ASC 205-30, the plan accounts for its assets using the liquidation basis of accounting. Therefore, the plan would no longer show the fair value of such investments and an adjustment to contract value. Rather, the liquidation basis valuation is what the plan expects to collect for that contract (for example, a surrender value). For comparative financial statements, if the prior year is presented on an ongoing basis, the plan would continue to present fair value adjusted to contract value in the prior year. See section 6931.29, "FASB ASC 820 Fair Value Disclosures When a Single-Employer Defined Benefit Pension Plan is Using the Liquidation Basis of Accounting," for guidance on whether the disclosures required by FASB ASC 820, *Fair Value Measurement*, apply. (*Note*: A DC plan that is using the liquidation basis of accounting may need to re-evaluate whether an investment contract that was considered fully benefit-responsive on an ongoing basis continues to meet the criteria to be considered fully benefit-responsive when using the liquidation basis of accounting.)

[Issue Date: September 2014.]

.29 FASB ASC 820 Fair Value Disclosure When an Employee Benefit Plan is Using the Liquidation Basis of Accounting

Inquiry—If an employee benefit plan is using the liquidation basis of accounting in accordance with FASB ASC 205-30, do the fair value disclosures required by FASB ASC 820 still apply?

Reply—In accordance with "Pending Content" in paragraph 1 of FASB ASC 205-30-50, disclosures required by other FASB ASC topics relevant to understanding an employee benefit plan's liquidation basis financial statements continue to be required. For example, in some circumstances, liquidation value may not differ from fair value (for example, because it assumes the related dispositions would be conducted in an orderly manner) and, therefore, an entity would not be precluded from measuring those assets at fair value. In such cases, the FASB ASC 820 disclosures would be required.

[Issue Date: September 2014.]

.30 Single-Employer DB Plan Disclosures When Using the Liquidation Basis of Accounting

Inquiry—When a single-employer DB plan presents its financial statements using the liquidation basis of accounting in accordance with FASB ASC 205-30, what effect would this have on the disclosures the DB plan is required to make by other FASB ASC topics?

(Although the information contained in the following reply is specific to single-employer DB plans, the information may be relevant when considering the termination of a single-employer DC plan, a health and welfare plan, or a multiemployer plan.)

Reply—In addition to the required disclosures in "Pending Content" in paragraphs 1–2 of FASB ASC 205-30-50, plan management should consider the required disclosures of other FASB ASC topics and ERISA to determine which disclosures are relevant. Often, it would be appropriate to revise current required disclosures to reflect plan provision changes, accounting policy changes, and laws and regulations affected by the plan termination. For example, disclosures such as the DB plan's tax status, PBGC information, disclosure of vesting provisions, eligibility, and distribution provisions will likely be affected.

[Issue Date: September 2014.]

Q&A Section 6932

ERISA Reporting and Disclosures

.01 Employee Benefit Security Administration Guidance on Insurance Company Demutualizations

Inquiry—Insurance contract policyholders receive demutualization proceeds in connection with a proposed plan of demutualization of an insurance company. What alternatives are available with respect to receipt by policyholders of demutualization proceeds?

Reply—On February 15, 2001, Employee Benefit Security Administration (EBSA) issued a letter regarding alternatives available under the trust requirement of Title I of ERISA with respect to receipt by policyholders of demutualization proceeds belonging to an ERISA-covered plan in connection with the proposed plan of demutualization of an insurance company (the company). In its letter, the DOL noted that the application of ERISA's trust requirements would depend on whether demutualization proceeds received by a policyholder constitute plan assets. The DOL stated that, in the case of an unfunded or insured welfare plan in which participants pay a portion of the premiums, the portion of the demutualization proceeds attributable to participant contributions must be treated as plan assets. In the case of a pension plan, or where any type of plan or trust is the policyholder or where the policy is paid for out of trust assets, the DOL stated that all of the proceeds received by the policyholder in connection with the demutualization would constitute plan assets. Auditors should take care to identify those plans with contracts with insurance companies that have demutualized and ensure that the proceeds are properly recorded as plan assets. Plan sponsors may not be familiar with EBSA's letter regarding alternatives available with respect to receipt by policyholders of demutualization proceeds. In addition, it has been noted that demutualization proceeds are often deposited into a separate account or trust and may be overlooked in financial reporting for the plan.

[Revised, May 2017.]

.02 When Should Participant Contributions Be Considered Late Remittances?

Inquiry—For purposes of reporting on line 4(a) of Form 5500, from what date should remittances be deemed late; the date the remittances can reasonably be made, or 15 days after the end of the month in which the funds were withheld?

Reply—Participant contributions are required to be remitted as soon as they can reasonably be segregated from an employer's general assets. DOL Regulation 2510.3-102 states that an employer is required to segregate employee contributions from its general assets as soon as practicable, but in no event more than (*a*) 90 days after the contributions are paid by employees or withheld from their wages for a welfare benefit plan or (*b*) the 15th business day following the end of the month in which amounts are contributed by employees or withheld from their wages for a pension benefit plan. The definition of what constitutes as soon as practicable will vary from plan sponsor to plan sponsor. DOL Field Assistance Bulletin 2003-2 states that the process for segregating participant contributions must be taken into account when determining when participant contributions can be reasonably segregated from the employer's general assets. Plan sponsors, under their fiduciary responsibility, also should consider how costly to the plan a more expeditious process would be. Those costs should be balanced against any additional income and security the plan and plan participants would realize from a faster system.

In considering whether remittances are delinquent, an understanding of the plan sponsor's process to segregate and remit contributions should be obtained. If the plan has several entities and payroll processes that comprise the remittance process, their timeframe to remit may be longer than a plan sponsor with only one location and one payroll system. Similarly, facts and circumstances that occur in the year (for example, a change in payroll processing or new service provider) may change the timeframe in which remittances are made. If a process has been established and the plan sponsor deviates from such a process, an understanding of the reasons why the remittance of the contributions for the period or periods did not comply with the established process should be obtained. Based on that understanding, a determination as to whether the plan sponsor remitted contributions as soon as it could reasonably segregate them from general assets should be made. The plan sponsor also may want to consult ERISA counsel in making that determination. In any case, any contributions remitted after the 15th business day after the end of the month in which the funds were withheld should be reported on Form 5500, Schedule H, Line 4a.

.03 How Should Delinquent Loan Remittances Be Reported on the Form 5500?

Inquiry—How should delinquent loan remittances be reported on the Form 5500?

Reply—In Advisory Opinion 2002-02A, the DOL stated that participant loan repayments paid to or withheld by an employer for purposes of transmittal to an employee benefit plan are sufficiently similar to participant contributions to justify, in the absence of regulations providing otherwise, the application of principles similar to those underlying the participant contribution regulation for purposes of determining when such repayments become assets of the plan. Delinquent forwarding of participant loan repayments is eligible for correction under the Voluntary Filer Correction Program and PTE 2002-51 on terms similar to those that apply to delinquent participant contributions. Accordingly, the DOL will not reject a Form 5500 report based solely on the fact that delinquent forwarding of participant loan repayments is included on Line 4a of the Schedule H or Schedule I. Filers that choose to include such participant loan repayments on Line 4a must apply the same supplemental schedule and independent public accountant disclosure requirements to the loan repayments as apply to delinquent transmittals of participant contributions. If the plan does not report delinquent loan remittances on Line 4a, those payments should be reported on Schedule G.

.04 How Should Participant Loans Be Reported on Defined Contribution Plan Master Trust Form 5500 Filings?

Inquiry—How should participant loans be reported on defined contribution plan master trust Form 5500 filings?

Reply—The face of Schedule H Form 5500 instructs master trust investment accounts not to complete line 1c(8) participant loans. In practice, many master trusts for defined contribution plans include participant loans as part of their master trust agreement. However, even though these loans may be included as part of the master trust agreement, the Form 5500 instructs the preparer not to include them as part of the master trust assets. Thus, the plan's financial statements would require a supplemental schedule, Schedule of Assets (Held at End of Year), to report participant loans as a nonmaster trust investment. The plan's Form 5500 filing would require the participant loans to be broken out separately from the investment in the master trust on the Schedule H.

.05 How Should Investments in Brokerage Accounts Be Reported in the Financial Statements and Form 5500?

Inquiry—Investments in individually directed brokerage accounts can be aggregated in a single line item on the Form 5500. Can they be listed as a single line item on the supplemental schedule of assets, or do the individual underlying investments have to be listed?

Reply—As described in the Form 5500 instructions, individually directed brokerage accounts may be aggregated in a single line item on the statement of net assets available for benefits and on the supplemental schedule of assets, provided the investments are not loans, partnership or joint-venture interests, real property, employer securities, or investments that could result in a loss in excess of the account balance of the participant or beneficiary who directed the transaction. In addition, the total investment income or loss for individually directed brokerage accounts may be aggregated in a single line item in the Form 5500; however, the financial statements must separate interest and dividends from net appreciation (depreciation) in fair value on the statement of changes in net assets available for benefits.

[Revised, May 2017.]

.06 Do All Types of Reconciling Items Between the Financial Statements and the Form 5500 Require a Reconciling Footnote in the Financial Statements?

Inquiry—Does ERISA require a footnote to the audited financial statements reconciling amounts reported in the Statement of Changes in Net Assets Available for Benefits to those reported in the Form 5500 for differences in the way income and expense amounts are classified in the two reports?

Reply—Generally, a reconciliation would be required for differences occurring because certain income and expense items are netted against each other and disclosed as one amount in one statement and reported separately in the other (for example, the amount reported as contributions in the financial statements may differ from that reported in the 5500 because excess contributions are recorded net on the financial statements but gross on the Form 5500). However, frequently the classification of line items comprising certain income and expense items (for example, investments and investment interest, dividends, gains and losses, and self-directed brokerage accounts) reported in the Form 5500 differ from the classifications shown in the financial statements. In such situations, a reconciling footnote may not be necessary.

For further guidance, see the "Reports Issued Prior to Form 5500 Filing" section in chapter 12 of the AICPA Audit and Accounting Guide *Employee Benefit Plans*.

[Revised, June 2009, to reflect conforming changes necessary due to the issuance of recent authoritative literature.]

.07 What is the Requirement to Report Certain Transactions Under Individual Account Plans on the Schedule of Reportable Transactions?

Inquiry—Under Form 5500 (Schedule H, Part IV, line 4j), there is a special rule whereby transactions under an individual account plan that a participant directs should not be taken into account for purposes of preparing the Schedule of Reportable Transactions. What about situations where an individual account plan is participant-directed but has certain transactions that appear to be nonparticipant-directed (for example, pass-through account for contributions)?

Reply—If the plan is an individual account plan and the overall structure of the plan is participant-directed, pass-through account transactions would not be required to be included on the Schedule of Reportable Transactions. Another example would be a participant-directed individual account plan that liquidates its investment options as a result of a plan termination, merger, or change in service provider. Often such changes result in the plan sponsor directing the plan trustee to liquidate the current balance in the participant-directed investment options into a short-term fund before the transfer to new investment options. Such transactions would be not be required to be included on the Schedule of Reportable Transactions.

.08 Is Noninterest-Bearing Cash an Asset on the Supplemental Schedule of Assets (Held at End of Year)?

Inquiry—Should noninterest-bearing cash be included as an asset on the supplemental Schedule of Assets (Held at End of Year)?

Reply—Generally, only assets held for investment are included on the supplemental Schedule of Assets (Held at End of Year); thus noninterest-bearing cash would not be included. Interest-bearing cash accounts would be included on the supplemental schedule.

.09 Is Netting of Investments on the Schedule of Assets (Held at End of Year) Permitted?

Inquiry—Can immaterial investments be netted together as "other" on the supplemental Schedule of Assets (Held at End of Year)?

Reply—No, each investment must be separately listed on the supplemental schedule.

.10 Is the Schedule of 5 Percent Reportable Transactions Required for Defined Benefit Plans?

Inquiry—Is the schedule of 5 percent reportable transactions required for defined benefit plans?

Reply—As defined benefit plans generally are not participant-directed, the reportable transactions schedule would be required.

Q&A Section 6933

Auditing Employee Benefit Plans

.01 Initial Audit of a Plan

Inquiry—In an initial audit of a plan that has been in existence for several years, to what extent does the auditor need to audit information from previous years?

Reply—In an initial audit of a plan which has been in existence in previous years, ERISA requires that the audited financial reports contain a comparative Statement of Net Assets Available for Benefits and, as such, there should be some consideration of the accumulation of data from prior years, and the effect on current year balances. The auditor can choose to compile, review, or audit the opening Statement of Net Assets Available for Benefits. It is important to note, however, that if the opening Statement of Net Assets Available for Benefits is not audited, the auditor must satisfy himself or herself as to the reasonableness of the amounts reported in that statement because material errors in that information may materially impact the Statement of Changes in Net Assets Available for Benefits under audit.

The auditor should apply appropriate audit tests and procedures to the opening balances in the Statement of Net Assets Available for Benefits to determine that those balances are not materially misstated. The auditor should make inquiries of the plan's management and outside service organizations, as applicable, regarding the plan's operations during those earlier years. The auditor also may wish to obtain relevant information (for example, trust statements, recordkeeping reports, reconciliations, minutes of meetings, and service auditors' reports issued under Statement on Standards for Attestation Engagements [SSAE] No. 16, *Reporting on Controls at a Service Organization* [AICPA, *Professional Standards*, AT sec. 801], or Statement on Auditing Standards No. 70, *Service Organizations*, as amended (now superseded),[1] for earlier years, as applicable, to determine whether there appears to be any errors during those years that could have a material effect on current year balances. Further, the auditor should gain an understanding of the accounting practices that were followed in prior years to determine that they have been consistently applied in the current year. Based on the results of the auditor's inquiries, review of relevant information, and evidence gathered during the current year audit, the auditor would determine the necessity of performing additional substantive procedures (including detailed testing or substantive analytics) on earlier years' balances.

See the "Initial Audits of Plans" sections in chapters 2 and 11 of the AICPA Audit and Accounting Guide *Employee Benefit Plans*.

[Revised, June 2009, to reflect conforming changes necessary due to the issuance of recent authoritative literature; Revised, August 2011, to reflect

---

[1] Prior to the issuance of Statement on Standards for Attestation Engagements (SSAE) No. 16, *Reporting on Controls at a Service Organization* (AICPA, *Professional Standards*, AT sec. 801), the requirements and guidance for service auditors reporting on controls at a service organization were contained in Statement on Auditing Standards No. 70, *Service Organizations*, as amended (now superseded). SSAE No. 16 is effective for service auditor's reports for periods ending on or after June 15, 2011, with earlier implementation permitted. [Footnote added, August 2011, to reflect conforming changes necessary due to the issuance of SSAE No. 16. Footnote revised, December 2012, to reflect conforming changes necessary due to the issuance of SAS Nos. 122–126.]

conforming changes necessary due to the issuance of SSAE No. 16; Revised, December 2012, to reflect conforming changes necessary due to the issuance of SAS Nos. 122–126.]

.02 Investment Allocations Testing in an Electronic Environment

Inquiry—How should the auditor test for proper investment allocation in situations where changes may be made by participants electronically, via phone or internet, on a daily basis?

Reply—Where participants make contributions or investment elections by telephone or electronic means (such as the Internet), the auditor should consider confirming the contribution percentage, source, and investment election directly with the participant, or compare that information to detail of the transaction (for example, a copy of the transaction confirmation) if maintained by the plan sponsor or service organization. Alternatively, if a service organization has a type 2 SSAE No. 16 report that provides evidence that controls over the investment allocation process were operating effectively, the auditor may place some reliance on those controls to assess the risks of material misstatement at less than maximum and thereby reduce (not eliminate) substantive testing.

See the "General Auditing Procedures" section in chapter 7 of the AICPA Audit and Accounting Guide *Employee Benefit Plans*.

[Revised, June 2009, to reflect conforming changes necessary due to the issuance of recent authoritative literature; Revised, August 2011, to reflect conforming changes necessary due to the issuance of SSAE No. 16.]

.03 Auditor's Responsibility for Detecting Nonexempt Transactions

Inquiry—What is the auditor's responsibility for detecting nonexempt transactions resulting from participant contributions that are not remitted to the plan within the guidelines established by DOL regulations?

Reply—An audit performed in accordance with generally accepted auditing standards (GAAS) cannot be expected to provide assurance that all party-in-interest transactions will be discovered. Nevertheless, during the audit the auditor should be aware of the possible existence of party-in-interest transactions. During the planning phase of the audit, the auditor should inquire about the existence of any party-in-interest or nonexempt transactions. If any issues relating to late remittances are brought to the auditor's attention, the auditor may consider obtaining a schedule of employee contributions detailing payroll withholding date and date of deposit to the plan. A sample of deposits can then be traced to the supporting payroll register and wire transfer advice or check. Further, the auditor should have the client include in the management representation letter a representation that there are no party-in-interest transactions that have not been disclosed in the supplemental schedules.

.04 Nonexempt Transactions

Inquiry—If a nonexempt transaction related to the preceding is noted, is materiality of the transaction taken into consideration in determining the need for the supplemental schedule of nonexempt transactions?

Reply—There is no materiality threshold for the inclusion on the supplemental schedule. All known events must be reported.

.05 Testing of Plan Qualification Tests Prepared by TPA

Inquiry—What responsibility does the auditor have in testing plan qualification tests (for example, ACP and ADP) prepared by a client's third-party administrator?

Reply—An audit in accordance with generally accepted auditing standards (GAAS) is not designed to ensure compliance with all legislative and regulatory provisions. However, plans must be designed and comply with certain operating tests to maintain their qualified status. If specific information comes to the auditor's attention that provides evidence concerning the existence of possible violations affecting the financial statements, the auditor should apply auditing procedures specifically directed to ascertaining whether a violation has occurred. The auditor is also expected to inquire of, and obtain representation from, management concerning compliance with laws and regulations and the prevention of violations that may cause disqualification.

.06 Audit Procedures for Plan Mergers

Inquiry—What audit procedures should be performed for material plan mergers into a plan? What audit procedures are required when the prior plan was audited? What if the prior plan was never audited?

Reply—If the prior plan was audited, the auditor should obtain the audited financial statements to ensure that the balance transferred from the prior plan reconciles to the balance that is reflected on the new plan's financial statements. Also, the auditor will generally perform procedures to ensure that participant accounts were properly set up under the new plan. If the prior plan was not audited, the auditor will generally perform audit procedures to determine that the equity that is transferred from the prior plan is reasonable based upon an analysis of historical activity. (Other audit procedures relating to plan mergers can be found in the "Plan Mergers" section in chapter 12 of AICPA Audit and Accounting Guide *Employee Benefit Plans*.

[Revised, June 2009, to reflect conforming changes necessary due to the issuance of recent authoritative literature.]

.07 Audit Requirements for Remaining Portion of a Split Plan

Inquiry—For the year ended December 31, 20X1, an audit was performed for AB Plan with more than 100 participants that covered two related companies (Company A and Company B). In July 20X2, Company A was sold, and the plan assets related to those participants were transferred to a new unrelated plan (Plan C). What are the audit requirements for the remaining portion of the AB Plan which, as of July 20X2, covers only employees at Company B and had fewer than 100 participants?

Reply—Audit for the AB Plan is required for the year ended December 31, 20X2, because the plan had over 100 participants at the beginning of the plan year. For the year ended December 31, 20X3, an audit of plan AB may not be required if the number of participants at January 1, 20X3, is under 100 and the plan meets the criteria for the Small Pension Plan Audit Waiver.

.08 Audit Requirements for Frozen and Terminated Plans

Inquiry—Are frozen and terminated plans that are still paying out benefits required to have an audit?

Reply—An audit is required if the plan has more than 100 participants at the beginning of the plan year. Chapter 5 of the AICPA Audit and Accounting Guide *Employee Benefit Plans*, provides guidance with regard to the definition of "participants." When a plan has been terminated or frozen, complete and prominent disclosure of the relevant circumstances is essential in all subsequent financial statements issued by the plan. If the number of participants falls below 100, auditors should consider whether the plan meets the criteria for the Small Pension Plan Audit Waiver.

For further guidance, see the "Terminating Plans" section in chapter 2 and the "Small Pension Plan Audit Waiver (SPPAW) Summary" flowchart in chapter 5 of the guide.

[Revised, June 2009, to reflect conforming changes necessary due to the issuance of recent authoritative literature.]

.09 Audit Procedures When Plan Operates in a Decentralized Environment

Inquiry—When a plan operates in a decentralized environment, what additional audit procedures should be considered?

Reply—The auditor should consider the controls at each decentralized location as well as the overall mitigating controls that may be performed on a centralized basis. Taking into consideration the materiality of the activity at each decentralized location, the auditor may choose to expand participant level and substantive testing to incorporate these decentralized locations.

.10 Is the Master Trust Required to Be Audited?

Inquiry—Is the master trust required to be audited?

Reply—While the DOL does not require the master trust to be audited, the plan administrator normally engages an auditor to report only on the financial statements of the individual plans. If the master trust is not audited, the plan auditor should perform those procedures necessary to obtain sufficient audit evidence to support the financial statement assertions as to the plan's investments or qualify or disclaim his or her report.

Q&A Section 6934
Limited-Scope Audits—Employee Benefit Plans

.01 Certifications by "Agent of"

Inquiry—Can the plan sponsor accept a certification from the plan's recordkeeper if the recordkeeper certifies the investment information to be complete and accurate on behalf of the plan's trustee/custodian as "agent for"?

Reply—According to the Department of Labor, such a certification generally would be acceptable if there is in fact a legal arrangement between the trustee and the recordkeeper to be able to provide the certification on the trustee's behalf. Care should be taken by the plan administrator to obtain such legal documentation. Additionally the plan auditor might consider adding wording to the standard limited-scope report to include reference to such an arrangement. Sample language might include the following: "... any auditing procedures with respect to the information described in Note X, which was certified by ABC, Inc., the recordkeeper of the Plan as agent for XYZ Bank, the trustee of the Plan, ... We have been informed by the plan administrator that the trustee holds the Plan's investment assets and executes investment transactions. The plan administrator has obtained a certification from the agent on behalf of the trustee, as of and for the year ended December 31, 20XX, that the information provided to the plan administrator by the agent for the trustee is complete and accurate." The third paragraph of the report should also be modified.

.02 Limited-Scope Audit on a Portion of the Plan's Investments

Inquiry—Is it permissible to perform a limited-scope audit on a portion of the plan's investments but not all (some investments did not meet the DOL 29 CFR 2520.103-8 criteria for a limited-scope audit)? If yes, what form does the auditors' report take?

Reply—Yes, it is permissible to perform a limited-scope audit on only a portion of a plan's investments and audit the remaining investments. The auditors' report is the same as that used for a limited-scope audit. However, the note that is referenced in the auditor report should clearly identify the investments that were not audited.

.03 Limited-Scope Audit—Plan Certifications for Master Trusts

Inquiry—If a limited-scope audit is to be performed for a plan funded under a master trust arrangement or other similar vehicle, should separate individual plan certifications from the trustee or the custodian be obtained for the allocation of the assets and the related income activity to the specific plan?

Reply—Yes, if a limited-scope audit is to be performed for a plan funded under a master trust arrangement or other similar vehicle, separate individual plan certifications from the trustee or the custodian should be obtained for the allocation of the assets and the related income activity to the specific plan.

[DOL regulation 2520.103-8]

.04 In a Limited-Scope Audit Is it Necessary to Test the Allocation of Investment Earnings at the Participant Account Level?

Inquiry—For a DOL limited-scope audit, is it necessary to test the allocation of investment earnings at the participant account level?

Reply—The testing of allocation of investment earnings at the participant level is part of the participant data testing and is recommended for a limited-scope audit.

Q&A Section 6935

SSAE No. 16 Reports—Employee Benefit Plans

.01 Audit Procedures When SSAE[1] No. 16 Reports Are Not Available

Inquiry—What procedures need to be performed in an audit of a plan if the service organization does not provide the plan with a type 1 or type 2 service auditor's report,[2] as described in Statement on Standards for Attestation Engagements (SSAE) No. 16, *Reporting on Controls at a Service Organization* (AICPA, *Professional Standards*, AT sec. 801)?

Reply—Service organizations are not required to furnish SSAE No. 16 reports. However, this does not relieve the auditor of his or her responsibility to obtain a sufficient understanding of the plan and its environment, including components of the plan's internal control that are maintained by the service organization. This understanding enables the plan auditor to assess the risks of material misstatement of financial statement assertions affected by transactions executed by the service organization, and to design the nature, timing, and extent of further audit procedures. When an SSAE No. 16 report is not available, other sources, such as user manuals, system overviews, technical manuals, the contract between the user organization and the service organization, and reports on the service organization's controls issued by internal auditors or regulatory authorities, may provide sufficient information about the nature of the services provided by the service organization that are part of the plan's information system and the service organization's controls over those services. If both the services provided and the service organization's controls over those services are highly standardized, information obtained through the plan auditor's prior experience with the service organization may be helpful in assessing risk. The plan auditor may wish to consider the specific control objectives and selected controls outlined in exhibit B-1 of appendix B of the AICPA Accounting and Audit Guide *Employee Benefit Plans*, in obtaining his or her understanding. If the plan auditor concludes that the available information is not adequate to obtain a sufficient understanding of the service organization's controls to assess the risks of material misstatement of financial statement assertions affected by the service organization's services, consideration should be given to contacting the service organization through the user organization to obtain adequate internal control information, or request that a service auditor be engaged to perform procedures at the service organization.

The level of substantive testing that should be performed depends on the amount of reliance the auditor can place on controls at the service

---

[1] Statement on Standards for Attestation Engagements (SSAE) No. 16, *Reporting on Controls at a Service Organization* (AICPA, *Professional Standards*, AT sec. 801), establishes the requirements and application guidance for a service auditor reporting on controls at a service organization that are relevant to user entities' internal control over financial reporting, and also describes the contents of such reports. AU-C section 402, *Audit Considerations Relating to an Entity Using a Service Organization* (AICPA, *Professional Standards*), contains the requirements and guidance for auditors of the financial statements of entities that use a service organization. [Footnote revised, August 2011, to reflect conforming changes necessary due to the issuance of SSAE No. 16. Footnote revised, December 2012, to reflect conforming changes necessary due to the issuance of SAS Nos. 122–126.]

[2] In SSAE No. 16, a *type 1 report* is a report on management's description of a service organization's system and the suitability of the design of controls, and a *type 2 report* is a report on management's description of a service organization's system and the suitability of the design and operating effectiveness of controls. [Footnote added, August 2011, to reflect conforming changes necessary due to the issuance of SSAE No. 16.]

organization. Thus, if a type 2 SSAE No. 16 report is not available, the auditor would need to increase substantive testing or consider testing controls at the service organization.

Auditing procedures applied to data maintained by the service organization may include tests of participant data, payroll data, or benefits data to determine that they agree with the information obtained and maintained by the employer. If the data is not available at the employer, consideration should be given to confirming the information directly with participants or to reviewing hard copy information obtained from the service organization, if available.

Individual participant accounts in 401(k) plans or other defined contribution pension plans should be tested for proper allocation of plan assets, contributions, income, and expenses. As such, the auditor should consider confirming contribution percentages and investment elections directly with the participants in situations where transactions are performed electronically or by phone. In addition, record keepers may maintain back up documentation of participant transactions, which may be requested as audit evidence to test participant data.

Procedures that should be considered in the audit of benefit payments, particularly those initiated by telephone or electronic methods, include confirming disbursements directly with participants, or comparing the disbursement to a transaction report if one is maintained, and testing the documentation underlying the benefit payment transactions.

For further guidance, see chapters 7 and 9–10 of the AICPA Audit and Accounting Guide *Employee Benefit Plans*.

[Revised, June 2009, to reflect conforming changes necessary due to the issuance of recent authoritative literature; Revised, June and August 2011, to reflect conforming changes necessary due to the issuance of SSAE No. 16.]

.02 Allocations Testing of Investment Earnings When a Type 2 SSAE No. 16 Report Is Available

Inquiry—In plan audits in which the auditor uses a type 2 SSAE No. 16 report, how extensively should the allocation of investment earnings at the participant level be tested? What are commonly used methods for testing this information?

Reply—In plan audits in which the plan auditor uses a type 2 SSAE No. 16 report, the extent of testing of the allocation of investment earnings at the participant level will be determined based on the plan auditor's assessment of the risk that earnings have not been allocated in accordance with the plan instrument. The type 2 SSAE No. 16 report can provide information about the service auditor's tests of the operating effectiveness of the service organization's controls over the investment allocation process and the results of those tests to help the auditor assess this risk. However, the auditor should not use the type 2 SSAE No. 16 report to completely eliminate substantive testing.

One commonly used method of testing this information is comparing the yield in the participants' accounts (selecting a sample of funds) for a certain period of time to the yield that the plan reported as a whole (as compared to published sources) for those funds for the same period of time.

[Revised, June and August 2011, to reflect conforming changes necessary due to the issuance of SSAE No. 16.]

Q&A Section 6936

Auditing Defined Contribution Plans

.01 Auditor's Responsibility for Testing a Plan's Compliance With Qualification Issues

Inquiry—What is the auditor's responsibility for testing a plan's compliance with top heavy rules, the Average Deferral Percentage Test, and other qualification issues?

Reply—An audit in accordance with generally accepted auditing standards (GAAS) is not designed to ensure compliance with all legislative and regulatory provisions. However, a plan must be designed to comply with all provisions, and must meet certain operating tests in order to maintain its qualified status. If specific information comes to the auditor's attention that provides evidence concerning the existence of possible violations of provisions that may affect the financial statements, he or she should apply auditing procedures specifically directed to ascertaining whether a violation has occurred. The auditor also is expected to inquire of, and obtain representation from, management concerning compliance with laws and regulations, and the controls in place to prevent violations of those laws and regulations that may cause the plan to lose its qualified status.

For further guidance, see chapter 11 and the "Plan Tax Status" section of chapter 12 of AICPA Audit and Accounting Guide *Employee Benefit Plans*.

[Revised, June 2009, to reflect conforming changes necessary due to the issuance of recent authoritative literature.]

.02 Merger Date for Defined Contribution Plans

Inquiry—If a defined contribution plan has an effective merger date, per the merger agreement, of December 31, 20X1, but a significant portion of the plan's assets have not been transferred as of December 31, 20X1, should the audit be done as of the December date, or when the majority of the assets were transferred? Would the answer be any different for a defined benefit plan? Would a liability representing the assets due to the acquiring plan be reflected on the statement of net assets if the audit date is December 31, 20X1?

Reply—For defined contribution plans, if there is a significant difference between the effective merger date per the merger agreement and the actual date assets were transferred, consideration should be given to performing an audit through the date of the actual transfer. However, all facts and circumstances should be considered, including management's intent, before determining the proper merger date.

For defined benefit plans, the merger typically is recorded on the effective merger date per the merger agreement because legal title to the assets, liabilities, and benefit obligations has transferred. In certain circumstances, it may be appropriate to record a liability representing the assets due the acquiring plan at year-end (for example, if the physical transfer from one plan to another has been requested and is pending).

Q&A Section 6937

Auditing Defined Benefit Plans

.01 General Conditions Requiring an Audit of Pension Plan Financial Statements

Inquiry—What are the general conditions requiring an audit of pension plan financial statements?

Reply—An audit generally is required if the plan is covered under Title I of ERISA and there are over 100 participants as of the beginning of the plan year. Exhibit 5-2 in chapter 5 of the AICPA Audit and Accounting Guide *Employee Benefit Plans* provides guidance on determining who is considered a participant. In addition, DOL regulations permit plans that have between 80 and 120 participants at the beginning of the plan year to complete the Form 5500 in the same category (large plan or small plan) as was filed in the previous year.

Q&A Section 6938

Auditing Health and Welfare Plans

.01 When Does a Health and Welfare Plan Require an Audit?

Inquiry—When does a health and welfare plan require an audit?

Reply—A health and welfare plan is required to have an audit when the plan has more than 100 participants at the beginning of the plan year (this can be expanded to 120 if the 80–120-participant rule applies) and the plan is funded. According to DOL Regulation 2520.104-44, the existence of a separate fund or account for the plan by the employer or a third-party administrator can cause the requirement that funds be paid directly from the general assets of the sponsor not to be met. For example, if a separate account is maintained that would be deemed to be a trust under state law, the related plan would be deemed to be funded under ERISA. It is not always easy to determine when a plan is considered funded. The auditor may wish to consult with legal counsel, plan actuaries, or the DOL to determine if a plan meets the definition of funded.

.02 Audit Requirements for Health and Welfare Plans

Inquiry—Assume a partially insured H&W plan where the employer pays claims to a certain level and then reinsurance assumes the liability. There are over 100 participants, and the employer and employees each pay a portion of the premiums. The employee's share is paid on a pretax basis through a Section 125 plan. There is no trust established, but at year end there may be a minimal payable to the third party administrator for regular monthly charges and a small reinsurance receivable, depending on timing. Does this plan require an audit?

Reply—No, the plan does not require an audit. According to the fact pattern described, no separate trust exists to hold the assets of this plan, and therefore it is not a funded plan for ERISA purposes. ERISA exempts unfunded plans from the requirement to perform an annual audit. Participant contributions made through a Section 125 cafeteria plan are not required to be held in trust per DOL Technical Release 92-1, and as long as no trust is being utilized, no audit requirement exists.

For further guidance, see the "Welfare Benefit Plans" and "PWBA Technical Release 92-1" sections in appendix A of the AICPA Audit and Accounting Guide *Employee Benefit Plans*.

[Revised, June 2009, to reflect conforming changes necessary due to the issuance of recent authoritative literature.]

.03 HIPAA Restrictions

Inquiry—In recent audits of health and welfare plans, our firm has been denied access to personnel files because of Health Insurance Portability and Accountability Act of 1996 (HIPAA) rules. In such cases, it has prohibited us from performing certain procedures necessary to render our opinion on the financial statements, such as testing of birth date, hire date, elections, and other such information. How can we overcome this obstacle?

Reply—The items mentioned (birth date, hire date, elections) are not "protected health information" (PHI) under the HIPAA rules.

PHI is individually identifiable health information that is created or received from a health care provider, health plan, employer, or health care clearinghouse; that either identifies or can be used to identify an individual; and relates to the individual's past, present, or future physical or mental health, to the provision of health care to an individual, or to the payment for the provision of health care to the individual. In other words, there are two components to PHI: (*a*) the identification of an individual, and (*b*) health information. Identification of an individual without the corresponding health information is not PHI, nor is health information without identifying the corresponding individual to whom it relates.

The first step is to understand what information is needed for the audit and whether it constitutes PHI. If access to PHI is necessary for the audit, HIPAA regulations allow for that access.

HIPAA privacy regulations indicate that a plan sponsor may not use or disclose protected health information except as permitted or required by the regulations. The regulations permit use of the "minimum necessary" information for use in health care operations, including conducting audits. If the auditor has signed a business associate agreement with the plan sponsor, then that auditor is considered a business associate under the regulations, and access to such minimum necessary information required for the audit should not be restricted by HIPAA.

Discussion with the plan sponsor may be necessary to demonstrate that the requested information is the minimum necessary for the audit and, if such information is not obtained, would result in a disclaimer of opinion.

For more information, call the Department of Labor Office of Health Plan Standards and Compliance Assistance at (202) 693-8335, or call EBSA's toll free inquiry line at 1-866-444-EBSA (3272). Health and Human Service (HHS) also has a toll-free number dealing with HIPAA privacy related issues. That number is 1-866-627-7748. You also may wish to visit the HHS Web site, www.hhs.gov/ocr/hipaa.

.04 Is a Health and Welfare Plan Required to Be Audited if Participants Are Contributing to the Plan?

Inquiry—If participants are contributing to a health and welfare plan, is an audit required?

Reply—According to DOL Technical Release Nos. 88-1 and 92-1, participant contributions to a welfare plan that has an Internal Revenue Code (IRC) Section 125 cafeteria plan feature do not have to be held in trust. If contributions are not through a Section 125 plan and they are not used for the payment of insurance or health maintenance organization (HMO) premiums, generally, they will be required to be held in trust. If the plan is funded voluntarily or as required by DOL regulation, then the plan would require an audit.

.05 Audit Requirement When Only Medical Is Funded Through a VEBA Trust

Inquiry—If a plan offers several benefits under the plan document, and only the medical component is funded through the voluntary employees' beneficiary association (VEBA) trust, what is the audit requirement?

Reply—The reporting entity and thus the audit requirement is of the entire plan; not the trust. All benefits covered by the plan should be included in the audited financial statements.

.06 Audit of Plan When VEBA Trust Is a Pass-Through

Inquiry—If a VEBA trust is used as a pass-through for claims payment during the year, but there are no monies in the VEBA trust at year end, is an audit of the plan required?

Reply—If a plan is deemed to be funded for a part of a plan year, the entire plan year is subject to the audit requirement. All plan activity for the entire year would have to be included in the audited financial statements.

.07 When Multiple Plans Use a VEBA Trust, Can the Audit Be Performed At the Trust Level?

Inquiry—If multiple plans use a VEBA trust, can an audit be performed at the VEBA trust level?

Reply—The audit requirement is of the plan, not the trust. Each plan would require a separate audit if it individually met the audit requirement (see previous question). The auditor may be engaged to audit the VEBA trust in order to assist with the plan level allocation reporting, but this would not fulfill the plan level audit requirement.

.08 Audit Requirement for Health and Welfare Plan Funded Through a 401(h) Account

Inquiry—Does the funding of a health and welfare benefit plan through a 401(h) account, when the plan was otherwise unfunded, cause the plan to require an audit?

Reply—If the plan was otherwise unfunded, the 401(h) account association will not cause the health and welfare benefit plan to be considered funded for audit determination purposes.

Q&A Section 6939

Auditor's Reports—Employee Benefit Plans

[.01] Reserved

.02 Audit Opinion to Be Issued When Discrimination Testing Has Not Been Completed

Inquiry—We have completed the audit of a plan except for reviewing the 401(k) and 401(m) discrimination testing, which has not yet been done and, quite possibly may not ever be done. If such testing is not performed, what type of audit opinion should be issued?

Reply—Independent auditors should inquire if the plan has complied with the annual limitation tests to determine if the plan has met the requirements in order to maintain its tax exempt status. Since the nondiscrimination requirements under 401(k) and 401(m) are required to be met annually, the independent auditor should understand the results of similar tests performed in the past and the reasons why the associated testing has not been performed in the current year. The auditor should be aware that any corrections, corrective distributions, or qualified nonelective contributions (QNECs) that would result from the failure of these compliance tests must be made before the end of the following plan year to preserve the plan's qualified status. If correction is to be made through refunds then a correction made within two and a half months after the plan's year end will avoid potential excise tax and preserve the plan's qualified tax status. In contrast, a refund after two and a half months triggers an excise tax payable by the plan sponsor. In the event that testing has not been completed for the year under audit, the auditor should consider the results of testing performed in the past and any corrections that were made and whether significant changes in the plan's demographics have occurred. The client should determine whether or not it is expected that a correction will be necessary, and should make an estimate for accrual purposes of the amount required for correction. Consideration should be given to modifying the tax note in the financial statements to indicate that the plan sponsor will take the necessary steps, if any, to bring the plan's operations into compliance with the Code. Similar wording also should be included in the management representation letter. If the results of the testing, when completed, are expected to be material based on similar issues in the past or discussions with the client and a correction amount cannot be reasonably estimated, the auditor should consider withholding his or her report until the testing is completed and the appropriate accruals recorded. If, however, the financial statements are issued and the client doesn't remedy or complete the tests by the next audit, the auditor should consider the effect on the financial statements as well as other implications as described in AU-C section 250, *Consideration of Laws and Regulations in an Audit of Financial Statements* (AICPA, *Professional Standards*), since the plan's tax qualified status may be in jeopardy.

For further guidance, see the "Plan Tax Status" section in chapter 12 of AICPA Audit and Accounting Guide *Employee Benefit Plans*.

[Revised, June 2009, to reflect conforming changes necessary due to the issuance of recent authoritative literature; Revised, December 2012, to reflect conforming changes necessary due to the issuance of SAS Nos. 122–126.]

Q&A Section 6940
Franchisors

.01 Method of Accounting for Sale of Territorial Franchise Right

Inquiry—A client sells territorial franchise rights to region managers for $30,000 with ten percent taken in cash and the remainder as a note. The region manager in turn sells franchises in his territory. The note is payable at the rate of $1,000 per franchise sold in the territory but is due in three years regardless of the number of franchises sold.

The collectibility of the notes depends on the performance of the region managers. The company has been able to resell territories of managers who have been unsuccessful, and the down payments have been refunded in these instances.

What is the proper method of accounting for these franchise fees and the related costs of selling the territories?

Reply—In discussing initial franchise fees for area franchises, Financial Accounting Standards Board (FASB) *Accounting Standards Codification* (ASC) 952-605-25-5 states, in part: ". . . revenue ordinarily shall be recognized when all material services or conditions relating to the sale(s) have been substantially performed or satisfied by the franchisor." FASB ASC 952-605-25-2 describes substantial performance as follows:

> Substantial performance for the franchisor means that all of the following conditions have been met:
>
> *a.* The franchisor has no remaining obligation or intent—by agreement, trade practice, or law—to refund any cash received or forgive any unpaid notes or receivables.
>
> *b.* Substantially all of the initial services of the franchisor required by the franchise agreement have been performed.
>
> *c.* No other material conditions or obligations related to the determination of substantial performance exist.

Therefore, the sale of the regions is not a completed transaction which would allow the recognition of income when the sale is made (for example, when the down payment and notes are received) since the company's practice of refunding down payments to region managers and, in effect, excusing nonpayment of their notes would violate item (*a*).

Since payment of the notes is on the basis of specific performance (for example, at the rate of $1,000 per franchise sold in the region), as a practical matter, a reasonable basis for recognizing deferred revenue would be over the estimated number of franchises to be opened in a region.

With regard to the costs of selling the territories, paragraphs 1–3 of FASB ASC 952-340-25 state the following:

> Direct (incremental) costs relating to franchise sales for which revenue has not been recognized shall be deferred until the related revenue is recognized.
>
> Deferred costs shall not exceed anticipated revenue less estimated additional related costs.

> Costs yet to be incurred shall be accrued and charged against income no later than the period in which the related revenue is recognized . . .

Therefore, deferral and amortization of costs "incurred to produce the region sales" could be accounted for in a manner similar to the deferral and recognition of revenue discussed in the preceding paragraph. The operating expenses of the company should be charged off as a period cost.

[Revised, June 2009, to reflect conforming changes necessary due to the issuance of FASB ASC.]

.02 Revenue Recognition for Franchisors

Inquiry—A franchise agreement is entered into whereby the franchisor agrees to provide to a franchisee the technical information necessary to manufacture a product. In addition, the franchisor agrees to provide consultation needed to produce the product for the next five years. The agreement states that 80 percent of the franchise fee is to be paid in the first year of the agreement, and five percent is to be paid in each of the next four years. How should the franchisor recognize the revenue from this agreement?

Reply—This issue is addressed in FASB ASC 952. FASB ASC 952-605-25-4 states that "if it is probable that the continuing fee will not cover the cost of the continuing services to be provided by the franchisor and a reasonable profit on those continuing services, then a portion of the initial franchise fee shall be deferred and amortized over the life of the franchise. The portion deferred shall be an amount sufficient to cover the estimated cost in excess of continuing franchise fees and provide a reasonable profit on the continuing services." The FASB ASC glossary defines *continuing franchise fees* as "consideration for the continuing rights granted by the franchise agreement and for general or specific services during its life."

In the preceding situation, it is unlikely the five percent of revenues the franchisor will receive in years two through five is sufficient to cover the costs, and a reasonable profit, on the raw materials and services provided. Therefore, the franchisor should defer a portion of the first year's franchise fee and amortize it over the next four years at a rate that will cover costs and provide a reasonable profit.

[Revised, June 2009, to reflect conforming changes necessary due to the issuance of FASB ASC.]

Q&A Section 6950

State and Local Governments

[.01] Reserved

[.02] Reserved

[.03] Reserved

[.04] Reserved

[.05] Reserved

[.06] Reserved

[.07] Reserved

[.08] Reserved

[.09] Reserved

[.10] Reserved

[.11] Reserved

[.12] Reserved

[.13] Reserved

[.14] Reserved

[.15] Reserved

[.16] Reserved

[.17] Reserved

.18 Accounting for the Issuance of Zero-Coupon Bonds and Other Deep Discount Debt by a Governmental Entity

Inquiry—A governmental entity issues zero-coupon bonds due in 10 years. Even though bond interest and principal is not due until the end of the bond's term, a sinking fund was established. When should interest expense be recognized and principal payments be deducted from the debt?

Reply—The treatment by governmental entities of the bond discount related to deep-discount debt has not been specifically addressed in authoritative literature. As discussed in *Governmental Accounting, Auditing and Financial Reporting*, by the Government Finance Officers Association, the accrual of principal and interest payments for zero-coupon bonds and other deep-discount debt is not recommended because the requirement that payments be due "early in the next year" is not met. The face amount of the debt less the discount presented as a direct deduction should be presented in the general long-term debt account group. The net value of the bonds should be accreted (the discount reduced) over the life of the bonds in the long-term debt account group. This presentation shows what amount would be payable if the debt were required to be paid today. The interest method provides an acceptable means of amortizing the discount. However, the straight line amortization method may also be used if its application would not produce amounts that differ materially from those that would be achieved if the interest method were applied.

[.19] Reserved

[.20] Reserved

.21 Auditor's Reports on Local Governments

Inquiry—A state law referring to the audit of local governments requires every auditor's report to state that the audit was conducted in accordance with generally accepted auditing standards and with the auditing standards prescribed by the state auditor. The law also requires the auditor's report to conform with the standard report form and to contain a reference to a report of comments and recommendations.

May a CPA include such wording in the opinion if he or she has followed the standards prescribed by the state auditor and he or she has included a report of comments and recommendations?

Reply—A CPA may state in the report that the audit has been conducted in accordance with generally accepted auditing standards and with the standards prescribed by the state treasurer if the audit was in fact conducted in accordance with these standards.

Also a CPA may include in the auditor's report a reference to a report of comments and recommendations if such a report has in fact been issued. [Amended June 1995; Revised, December 2012, to reflect conforming changes necessary due to the issuance of SAS Nos. 122–126.]

.22 State Accounting Guide Differs From GAAP

Inquiry—Are reports on financial statements conforming to the State accounting guide requirements considered auditor's reports on special purposes financial statements in accordance with AU-C section 800, *Special Considerations—Audits of Financial Statements Prepared in Accordance With Special Purpose Frameworks* (AICPA, *Professional Standards*)?

Reply—Yes. Reports on financial statements conforming to the State accounting guide requirements are considered auditor's reports on special purposes financial statements. Paragraph .07 of AU-C section 800 states that a basis of accounting that an entity uses to comply with the requirements or financial reporting provisions of a regulatory agency to whose jurisdiction the entity is subject is a special purpose framework. Paragraph .A35 of AU-C section 800 contains illustrations of auditor's reports on special purpose financial statements. In addition, chapter 14 of Audit and Accounting Guide *State and Local Governments* discusses auditor reporting when law or regulation requires a government to prepare and file with a regulatory agency financial statements that do not constitute a complete presentation of all the financial statements required by GASB Statement No. 34, *Basic Financial Statements—and Management's Discussion and Analysis—for State and Local Governments*, but that otherwise are prepared in accordance with GAAP.

[Amended, June 1995; Amended, December 2004; Revised, December 2012, to reflect conforming changes necessary due to the issuance of SAS Nos. 122–126.]

Q&A Section 6960

Colleges and Universities

[.01] Reserved

[.02] Reserved

[.03] Reserved

[.04] Reserved

[.05] Reserved

[.06] Reserved

[.07] Reserved

[.08] Reserved

[.09] Reserved

[.10] Reserved

[.11] Reserved

.12 Allocation of Overhead

Inquiry—A private college has many individual restricted programs funded from federal, state and private contributions. One of the programs was charged a $97,000 overhead expense amount, with the credit going to revenue in another program. Is it appropriate under generally accepted accounting principles to record revenue based on the overhead allocation?

Reply—No, it is inappropriate. The allocation of overhead is an interprogram transaction that should not be reported as revenue of the program providing the services but rather as a reduction of expense of such program. For additional information related to this topic, see chapter 16 of Audit and Accounting Guide *Not-for-Profit Entities*.

[Amended, June 1995.]

Q&A Section 6970

Entertainment Industry

.01 Changes in Film Impairment Estimates During Quarters Within a Fiscal Year (Part I)

Inquiry—Company A produced a film that is subject to the requirements of Financial Accounting Standards Board (FASB) *Accounting Standards Codification* (ASC) 926, *Entertainment—Films*. In accordance with paragraphs 12–17 of FASB ASC 926-20-35, Company A determined at the end of the first quarter of 20X1 that the film was impaired. Company A wrote down the film's cost basis by $2 million, which represents the amount that the film's net book value exceeded the film's fair value. Company A determined the film's fair value by using a discounted cash flow model. At the end of the second quarter of 20X1, Company A determines based on updated information that the film's estimated net cash flows will be greater than anticipated at the end of the first quarter. Is the change in the estimated net cash flows a circumstance under FASB ASC 926 that requires Company A to restore all or a portion of the film's cost basis that was written off in the first quarter of 20X1?

Reply—Yes. FASB ASC 926-20-35-3 requires that changes in estimates during the fiscal year be applied retroactively from the beginning of the fiscal year.

In this situation, Company A would use the new information regarding the film's estimated net cash flows gathered in the second quarter as if it were available in the first quarter to determine what the amount of the impairment loss would have been in the first quarter. Company A would record this adjustment to the impairment loss in the second quarter. Company A also would adjust the film's cost amortization for the first and second quarters to reflect the revised impairment loss. Company A should not restate the first quarter. In accordance with FASB ASC 926-20-35-13, the amount of the impairment write down restored cannot result in the adjusted net book value exceeding the film's fair value at the end of the second quarter. For example, if the revised first quarter calculation indicates that the impairment loss was only $1 million at the end of the first quarter, the actual adjustment at the end of the second quarter would be different than the $1 million because of the effect on the film's cost amortization using the individual-film-forecast-computation method, and possibly the film's fair value at the end of the second quarter. In addition, restorations of impairment write downs on a film should not exceed previous impairment write downs taken on that film.

FASB ASC 270-10-45-14 requires that Company A disclose the effect of the change in estimate in the period that the change occurred. For public registrants, the Management Discussion and Analysis should address material restorations of prior impairment write downs.

Note that had the change in estimated net cash flows occurred in the subsequent fiscal year, FASB ASC 926-20-35-13 would prohibit Company A from adjusting the impairment write down taken in 20X1.

[Revised, June 2009, to reflect conforming changes necessary due to the issuance of FASB ASC.]

.02 Changes in Film Impairment Estimates During Quarters Within a Fiscal Year (Part II)

Inquiry—Assume the same facts in section 6970.01 with the following exception. The film's actual net cash inflow for the second quarter was as expected by Company A at the end of the first quarter. Company A, as expected, spent most of its advertising budget to promote the film during the second quarter. The film's estimated net cash inflow for subsequent periods also did not change. As a result of the advertising expenditures, using a discounted cash flow model at the end of the second quarter, the film's fair value increased from the amount determined at the end of the first quarter. Is that a circumstance under FASB ASC 926, for which Company A should restore all or a portion of the film's cost basis that was previously written off in the first quarter of 20X1?

Reply—No. In this situation the film's estimated net cash flows did not change from those used to estimate the film's fair value at the end of the first quarter. Accordingly, the guidance in FASB ASC 926-20-35-3 is not applicable.

[Revised, June 2009, to reflect conforming changes necessary due to the issuance of FASB ASC.]

Q&A Section 6980

Brokers and Dealers

.01 Auditor's Report on Internal Control for Broker-Dealer [Amended]

Inquiry—Some state regulatory agencies are requesting that their name be included in the restrictive paragraph of the auditor's report on internal accounting control for broker-dealers. Because most broker-dealers must comply with Securities and Exchange Commission (SEC) regulations, the report on internal accounting control from their auditors includes a report on the additional requirements of Rule 17a-5(g) as well as a report on their study and evaluation as part of an audit. The restriction paragraph of the report illustrated in the AICPA Audit and Accounting Guide *Brokers and Dealers in Securities* appendix C therefore includes the SEC as a designated recipient of the report and reads as follows:

> This report is intended solely for the information and use of the Board of Directors, management, the SEC, *[designated self-regulatory organization]*, and other regulatory agencies that rely on Rule 17a-5(g) under the Securities Exchange Act of 1934 in their regulation of registered brokers and dealers, and should not be used for any other purpose.

One state agency suggested revising the paragraph to reflect other agencies as recipients as follows:

> This report is intended solely for the information and use of the Board of Directors, management, the SEC, *[designated self-regulatory organization]*, and other regulatory agencies and should not be used for any other purpose.

Is this proposed revised wording appropriate in view of the fact that not all regulatory agencies use the SEC's Rule 17a-5(g) criteria or other established criteria for the evaluation of the adequacy of internal accounting control procedures for their purposes?

Reply—No. The previous suggested wording is not appropriate because the report would then be distributable to all other non-SEC regulatory agencies, and as stated, most agencies, including those of the 50 states, do not establish criteria in reasonable detail and in terms susceptible to objective application for the auditor's study, evaluation and report on the control procedures for the agencies' purposes.

[Amended, September 1997.]

[.02] Reserved

Q&A Section 6985

U.S. Department of Housing and Urban Development (HUD) Programs

[.01] Reserved

Q&A Section 6990

Common Interest Realty Associations

.01 Personal Property of Timeshares

Inquiry—Should a common interest realty association (CIRA) that is a timeshare development report as assets personal property that it owns and uses as internal unit furnishings for timeshare units?

Reply—Yes. Financial Accounting Standards Board *Accounting Standards Codification* 972-360-25-5 states, "Common interest realty associations shall recognize common personal property, such as furnishings, recreational equipment, maintenance equipment, and work vehicles, that is used by the common interest realty association in operating, preserving, maintaining, repairing, and replacing common property and providing other services, as assets." Personal property that is owned by a CIRA and used as internal unit furnishings for timeshare units is common personal property that is used by the CIRA in providing other services.

[Revised, June 2009, to reflect conforming changes necessary due to the issuance of FASB ASC.]

Q&A Section 6995

Credit Unions

.01 Financial Reporting Issues Related to Actions Taken by the National Credit Union Administration on January 28, 2009 in Connection With the Corporate Credit Union System and the National Credit Union Share Insurance Fund

Inquiry—On January 28, 2009, the National Credit Union Administration (NCUA) announced certain actions it was taking to stabilize the corporate credit union system. The NCUA indicated that the expense of the actions would be passed on proportionately to all federally-insured credit unions through the partial (currently estimated by NCUA to be 51 percent) write-off of such credit unions' existing deposits with the National Credit Union Share Insurance Fund (NCUSIF), as well as the assessment of an insurance premium sufficient to return the NCUSIF's equity to insured shares ratio to 1.30 percent.

Federally insured credit unions (including corporate credit unions) are required to maintain a refundable deposit with the NCUSIF in an amount equal to one percent of the credit union's total insured shares. The amount on deposit in the insurance fund is periodically adjusted for changes in the balance of a credit union's insured shares. In addition, a credit union is required to pay an additional annual insurance premium equal to one-twelfth of one percent of its insured shares.

Credit unions also have their own financial system, the Corporate Credit Union Network, consisting of the U.S. Central Federal Credit Union (USC) and its member corporate credit unions. These state or regional corporate credit unions make available a wide range of investments and correspondent financial services for credit unions, and the USC serves as a financial intermediary for corporate credit unions. The USC and many of the corporate credit unions made investments in asset-backed securities that became impaired during 2008.

In a letter to federally-insured credit unions (NCUA Letter No. 09-CU-02) issued on January 28, 2009, the NCUA stated that the corporate credit union system is now facing unprecedented strains on its liquidity and capital due to credit market disruptions and the current economic climate, and that given the importance of the USC as a liquidity and payment systems provider to both corporate credit unions and, by extension, natural person credit unions, NCUA is taking decisive action to stabilize the USC's financial position and provide stability for the liquidity needs of the corporate system. In the letter, the NCUA announced two significant actions it was taking to address the current status of the corporate credit union system, as follows:

- The NCUA is injecting $1 billion in cash from the NCUSIF into the USC in the form of capital. The NCUA has stated that while a capital infusion has cost implications for all credit unions, it is a lower cost alternative than liquidation and sale of the distressed securities held by the USC in today's market. The staff notes that in the *unaudited* January 2009 financial statements of the NCUSIF, this investment in the USC was immediately written off.
- The NCUA is offering a voluntary temporary NCUSIF guarantee of member shares in corporate credit unions through December 31, 2010. The guarantee will cover all shares, but does not include

paid-in capital and membership capital accounts. The NCUA believes the guarantee helps provide stability to meet the liquidity needs of the corporate system, which will allow for the orderly pay down of stressed securities and, in turn, reduces the overall resolution cost. The NCUA's initial estimate of the liability attributable to this guarantee is $3.7 billion, based on current corporate credit union balance sheets (that is, the holdings of impaired asset-backed securities) and the modeling of various market scenarios. The NCUA has indicated that this estimate could change significantly depending on a host of factors including, but not limited to, credit loss estimates.

In consideration of AU-C section 560, *Subsequent Events and Subsequently Discovered Facts* (AICPA, *Professional Standards*), do the actions of the NCUA with regard to the valuation of a federally-insured credit union's NCUSIF deposit at December 31, 2008, constitute a subsequent event that provides evidence of conditions that existed at the date of the financial statements (commonly referred to as a "type 1" subsequent event), or of conditions that arose after the date of the financial statements (commonly referred to as a "type 2" subsequent event)? Secondly, when and how should the obligation for the insurance premium be recognized for financial reporting purposes?

Reply—

Issue 1: NCUSIF Deposit. The AICPA staff believes that there is diversity in opinion on this issue and based on the facts known at the time this question and answer was issued, the staff does not express a preference for either of the views discussed in the following paragraphs.

Existing authoritative guidance for the accounting for the NCUSIF deposit is in Financial Accounting Standards Board (FASB) *Accounting Standards Codification* (ASC) 942-325-25-3, which states the following:

> For credit unions and corporate credit unions, amounts deposited with the National Credit Union Share Insurance Fund shall be accounted for and reported as assets as long as such amounts are fully refundable.

FASB ASC 942-325-35-4 further states the following:

> The refundability of National Credit Union Share Insurance Fund deposits shall be reviewed for impairment. When the refundability of a deposit is evaluated, the financial condition of both the credit union and of the National Credit Union Share Insurance Fund shall be considered. Deposits may be returned to solvent credit unions for a number of reasons, including termination of insurance coverage, conversion to insurance coverage from another source, or transfer of operations of the insurance fund from the National Credit Union Administration Board. However, insolvent or bankrupt credit unions shall not be entitled to a return of their deposits. To the extent that National Credit Union Share Insurance Fund deposits are not refundable, they shall be charged to expense in the period in which the deposits are made or the assets become impaired.

- Alternative A—Type 1 Subsequent Event

AU-C section 560 addresses the auditor's responsibilities relating to subsequent events occurring between the date of the financial statements and the date of the auditor's report that require adjustment of, or disclosure in, the financial statements. AU-C section 560 describes one type of subsequent event as an event that provides evidence of conditions that existed at the date of the financial statements. Proponents of type 1 subsequent event accounting maintain that the actions taken by the NCUA on January 28, 2009 constitute additional evidence regarding strained liquidity and capital deterioration conditions that existed at December 31, 2008, and that the NCUA announcement on January 28, 2009 of the partial write-off of the NCUSIF deposit is a confirmation of those conditions at December 31, 2008.

Proponents of this view also believe that Emerging Issues Task Force (EITF) Issue No. 87-22, "Prepayments to the Secondary Reserve of the FSLIC," addresses a situation that may be considered relevant. Similar to the NCUSIF, the Federal Savings and Loan Insurance Corporation (FSLIC) required insured institutions to make annual prepayments of their regular future insurance premiums. In May 1987, the Federal Home Loan Bank Board eliminated the secondary reserve of the FSLIC as of December 31, 1986. The Task Force reached a consensus that the impairment of the secondary reserve of the FSLIC was a type 1 subsequent event.

- Alternative B—Type 2 Subsequent Event

AU-C section 560 describes a second type of subsequent event as an event that provides evidence of conditions that arose after the date of the financial statements.

Proponents of type 2 subsequent event accounting refer to the NCUA's disclosures that it had no obligation to undertake the actions approved on January 28, 2009, and that the NCUSIF deposits were refundable under the circumstances noted in FASB ASC 942-325-25 and FASB ASC 942-325-35 until January 28, 2009. As such, proponents of this view believe that the NCUSIF deposits did not become impaired until January 28, 2009.

Proponents of this view also believe that EITF Topic No. D-47, "Accounting for the Refund of Bank Insurance Fund and Savings Association Insurance Fund Premiums," in which the Financial Accounting Standards Board (FASB) staff expressed their belief that insured institutions should not accrue a liability for a potential special assessment of deposit insurance premium until the period in which any proposed legislation is enacted, can be used by analogy to support their view regarding the NCUSIF deposit.

Issue 2: Premium Assessment.

- View A—Record in 2009. Proponents of this view support recognition of the obligation to pay the insurance premium when assessed, at January 28, 2009, and refer to FASB ASC 942-325-35-4(c), which states that to the extent that the NCUA Board assesses premiums to cover prior operating losses of the insurance fund or to increase the fund balance to "normal operating levels," credit unions should expense those premiums when assessed.

Further reference is made to the aforementioned EITF Topic No. D-47, in which the FASB staff expressed their belief that insured institutions should not accrue a liability for a potential special assessment of deposit insurance premium until the period in which any proposed legislation is enacted.

- View B—Record in 2008. If NCUSIF deposit impairment is recognized in 2008, proponents of view B believe that both the NCUSIF deposit impairment and the additional premium assessment relate to the same event and conditions that caused the deposit impairment that existed at December 31, 2008, and that both should be recorded as of December 31, 2008.

[Issue Date: March 2009; Revised, June 2009, to reflect conforming changes necessary due to the issuance of FASB ASC; Revised, December 2012, to reflect conforming changes necessary due to the issuance of SAS Nos. 122–126.]

.02 Evaluation of Capital Investments in Corporate Credit Unions for Other-Than-Temporary Impairment

Inquiry—In a letter to its shareholders on February 2, 2009, the U.S. Central Federal Credit Union (USC) explained its financial position to other corporate credit unions that have direct capital investments in the USC in the form of membership capital shares (MCS) and paid-in capital (PIC). The letter also explained that on December 31, 2008, $450 million of members' MCS were converted to a new form of capital, paid-in capital II (PIC II). On January 28, 2009, the USC announced that it would record other-than-temporary impairment (OTTI) charges of approximately $1.2 billion for 2008 in relation to its portfolio of asset-backed securities as a result of severe deterioration in economic and market data during the fourth quarter of 2008, and that this charge resulted in an accumulated deficit (negative retained earnings) for the USC of approximately $493 million. The staff notes that audited financial statements of the USC as of and for the year ended December 31, 2008 were not available at the time of issuance of this question and answer. On January 28, 2009, the National Credit Union Administration (NCUA) announced that it was injecting $1.0 billion from the National Credit Union Share Insurance Fund (NCUSIF) in the form of new PIC to the USC, which is senior to all other forms of USC capital. The staff notes that in the *unaudited* January 2009 financial statements of the NCUSIF, this investment in the USC was immediately written off.

According to the NCUA Rules and Regulations, *membership capital* means funds contributed by members that are

- adjustable balance with a minimum withdrawal notice of three years or are term certificates with a minimum term of three years.
- available to cover losses that exceed retained earnings and PIC.
- not insured by the NCUSIF or other share or deposit insurers.
- cannot be pledged against borrowings.

Paid-in capital means accounts or other interests of a corporate credit union that are

- perpetual, noncumulative dividend accounts.
- available to cover losses that exceed retained earnings.
- not insured by the NCUSIF or other share or deposit insurers.
- cannot be pledged against borrowings.

How should a corporate credit union evaluate its MCS and PIC in the USC for OTTI at December 31, 2008? Similarly, how should a natural person credit union evaluate its MCS and PIC investments in other corporate credit unions for OTTI at December 31, 2008?

Reply—The staff believes the following authoritative literature is helpful in making that evaluation.

FASB ASC 320, *Investments—Debt and Equity Securities*, addresses equity securities that have readily determinable fair values. As there is no active market for MCS or PIC investments, FASB ASC 320 would not apply. FASB ASC 323, *Investments—Equity Method and Joint Ventures*, generally requires that investments in common stock that result in the investor having the ability to exert significant influence over the issuer be accounted for using the equity method. Otherwise, the cost method would apply. FASB ASC 323 also indicates that a series of operating losses of an investee or other factors may indicate that a decrease in value of the investment has occurred, which is other than temporary and should accordingly be recognized, and reference is then made to FASB ASC 320. MCS and PIC do not represent common stock investments; however, the concepts of FASB ASC 323 can be considered. According to the aforementioned USC letter to corporate credit unions, the ownership of MCS or PIC, or both, by any particular corporate credit union would not provide it the opportunity to exert significant influence over the USC, particularly given "one member, one vote." As such, it appears appropriate to consider investments in MCS and PIC cost method equity investments and that evaluation for impairment by corporate credit unions is required.

Although FASB ASC 320 does not specifically apply to MCS and PIC, FASB ASC 320 addresses issues of impairment and includes within its scope cost method equity investments. FASB ASC 958-325-35-8 states that the guidance in this Subtopic is applicable for investments in equity securities that are not subject to the scope of FASB ASC 320 and not accounted for under the equity method pursuant to FASB ASC 958-810-05-5. FASB ASC 320-10-35-25 provides guidance on how to determine impairment on such cost-basis investments without readily determinable fair values.

Step 1 of the impairment framework detailed in paragraphs 20–29 of FASB ASC 320-10-35 requires an investor to determine whether or not the fair value of the investment is less than its cost basis. FASB ASC 320-10-35-25 regarding cost-method investments (that have no readily determinable fair value) states the following:

> Because the fair value of cost-method investments is not readily determinable, the evaluation of whether an investment is impaired shall be determined as follows:
>
> a. If an entity has estimated the fair value of a cost-method investment (for example, for disclosure under Section 825-10-50, that estimate shall be used to determine if the investment is impaired for the reporting periods in which the entity estimates fair value. If the fair value of the investment is less than its cost, proceed to Step 2.
>
> b. For reporting periods in which an entity has not estimated the fair value of a cost-method investment, the entity shall evaluate whether an event or change in circumstances has occurred in that period that may have a significant adverse

> effect on the fair value of the investment (an impairment indicator).

FASB ASC 320-10-35-27 further states the following:

> Impairment indicators include, but are not limited to:
>
> a. A significant deterioration in the earnings performance, credit rating, asset quality, or business prospects of the investee
>
> b. A significant adverse change in the regulatory, economic, or technological environment of the investee
>
> c. A significant adverse change in the general market condition of either the geographic area or the industry in which the investee operates
>
> d. A bona fide offer to purchase (whether solicited or unsolicited), an offer by the investee to sell, or a completed auction process for the same or similar security for an amount less than the cost of the investment
>
> e. Factors that raise significant concerns about the investee's ability to continue as a going concern, such as negative cash flows from operations, working capital deficiencies, or noncompliance with statutory capital requirements or debt covenants.

FASB ASC glossary defines *fair value* as "the price that would be received to sell an asset or paid to transfer a liability in an orderly transaction between market participants at the measurement date." The staff understands that, in practice, fair value disclosures under FASB ASC 825-10-50 for MCS and PIC have generally reflected redemption values (at par), and have recognized that such investments were interest-earning at assumed market rates of interest. This is similar to historical fair value disclosures for investments in Federal Home Loan Bank stock.

FASB ASC 320-10-35-30 states the following:

> When the fair value of an investment is less than its cost at the balance sheet date of the reporting period for which impairment is assessed, the impairment is either temporary or other than temporary. An entity shall apply the following guidance and other guidance that is pertinent to the determination of whether an impairment is other than temporary, such as the guidance in Section 325-40-35, as applicable. *Other than temporary* does not mean permanent.

The staff notes that entities holding MSC or PIC should first determine whether fair values are believed to be less than the cost bases of the respective holdings at the balance sheet date. If so, such impairment is assessed as either temporary or other than temporary. In this regard, SEC Staff Accounting Bulletin Topic 5M indicates the following:

> The value of investments in marketable securities classified as either available-for-sale or held-to-maturity may decline for various reasons. The market price may be affected by general market conditions which reflect prospects for the economy as a whole or by specific information pertaining to an industry or an individual company. Such declines require further investigation by management. Acting upon the premise that a write-down may be required, management should consider all available evidence to evaluate the realizable value of its investment.

There are numerous factors to be considered in such an evaluation and their relative significance will vary from case to case. The staff believes that the following are only a few examples of the factors which, individually or in combination, indicate that a decline is other than temporary and that a write-down of the carrying value is required:

a. The length of the time and the extent to which the market value has been less than cost;

b. The financial condition and near-term prospects of the issuer, including any specific events which may influence the operations of the issuer such as changes in technology that may impair the earnings potential of the investment or the discontinuance of a segment of the business that may affect the future earnings potential; or

c. The intent and ability of the holder to retain its investment in the issuer for a period of time sufficient to allow for any anticipated recovery in market value.

Unless evidence exists to support a realizable value equal to or greater than the carrying value of the investment, a write-down to fair value accounted for as a realized loss should be recorded. In accordance with the guidance of paragraph 16 of Statement 115, such loss should be recognized in the determination of net income of the period in which it occurs and the written down value of the investment in the company becomes the new cost basis of the investment.

Accordingly, investors should consider an evaluation of the financial position of the USC and its ability to redeem the MSC or PIC within anticipated time frames. The staff believes the audited financial statements of the USC as of and for the year ended December 31, 2008 would be useful evidence to appropriately evaluate MSC or PIC for other-than-temporary impairment. The evaluation for impairment should consider the specific facts and circumstances, including consideration of the regulatory capital requirements of the USC. However, the staff does not believe that regulatory capital requirements should be the primary consideration for assessing whether impairment is other than temporary. As noted earlier in this question and answer, the NCUSIF has immediately written off the investment in the USC. The staff believes this action by the NCUSIF should be considered in the assessment of whether impairment is deemed to be other than temporary.

The staff also notes that a natural person credit union that invests in a corporate credit union whose direct investment may be impaired, should evaluate that investment for other-than-temporary impairment using the same guidance noted earlier. The staff notes that the evaluation for impairment in any of these cases should be determined in view of the specific facts and circumstances.

[Issue Date: March 2009; Revised, June 2009, to reflect conforming changes necessary due to the issuance of FASB ASC.]

Q&A Section 7000

SPECIALIZED ORGANIZATIONAL PROBLEMS

TABLE OF CONTENTS

Section

Q&A Section 7000

SPECIALIZED ORGANIZATIONAL PROBLEMS

TABLE OF CONTENTS

Q&A Section 7200
Partnerships

.01 Balance Sheet Presentation of Drawings in Excess of Capital Contributions

Inquiry—Two partners each contributed capital of $100 to form a partnership for the construction of a shopping center. The partnership has obtained several loans to fund the construction, but no payments on these loans are due for two years. The partners each withdrew excess funds of $50,000 from the partnership out of the proceeds of the loans.

How would the balance sheet show the $200 of capital and $100,000 of withdrawals?

Reply—Whether the $50,000 payments to the partners are permissible depends on the terms of the construction loan commitment. If the partnership agreement is silent concerning these payments, and they are, in fact, not loans to the partners, the $50,000 withdrawn by each partner represents drawings in anticipation of profits. As drawing accounts, they would normally be closed to the partners' capital accounts. In the situation presented, it would result in a "negative" capital account for each partner in the amount of $49,900 in the partners' equity section of the balance sheet. Full disclosure of the circumstances causing the negative balance should also be included.

.02 Provision for Income Taxes on Partnership Income

Inquiry—A partnership agreement provides that in computing net profits, there will be a provision for income taxes, and the amount of the provision for income taxes will be considered an expense of the partnership. In the preparation of the income statement, would the net profit figure after income taxes be considered as having been determined according to generally accepted accounting principles?

Reply—Between themselves, partners may agree to compute net profits in any fashion they wish; but for financial presentation purposes, a provision for income taxes should not be set up. The absence of this item in the financial statement can be explained in the form of a footnote to the income statement. If the income statement shows a net profit figure after income taxes, the statement is not prepared in accordance with generally accepted accounting principles.

[.03] Reserved

[.04] Reserved

[.05] Reserved

[.06] Reserved

[.07] Reserved

.08 Income Allocation of Limited Partnership

Inquiry—A real estate limited partnership allocates the depreciation deduction entirely to the limited partners in accordance with the provisions of the partnership agreement. This is done in order to induce investment in the venture by the limited partners. Would such an allocation in the financial statements conform with generally accepted accounting principles (GAAP)?

Reply—Yes. Allocation of partnership income is determined by the partnership agreement. Therefore, in computing the income allocable to the limited and general partners, the depreciation deduction may be allocated entirely to the limited partners, in financial statements prepared in accordance with GAAP.

[Revised, December 2012, to reflect conforming changes necessary due to the issuance of SAS Nos. 122–126.]

Q&A Section 7400

Related Parties

[.01] Reserved

[.02] Reserved

[.03] Reserved

[.04] Reserved

[.05] Reserved

.06 Exchange of Interest Bearing Note for Non-Interest Bearing Note

Inquiry—Corporation A has an interest bearing note receivable from an officer/shareholder. Corporation A plans to exchange the present note for a non-interest bearing note. Should the non-interest bearing note be discounted in accordance with Financial Accounting Standards Board (FASB) *Accounting Standards Codification* (ASC) 835, *Interest*?

Reply—Yes. The non-interest bearing note should be discounted in accordance with FASB ASC 835, and there should be recognition of compensation or a dividend distribution, depending on what the unstated right or privilege represents.

[Revised, June 2009, to reflect conforming changes necessary due to the issuance of FASB ASC.]

Q&A Section 7500

Estates and Trusts

[.01] Reserved

Q&A Section 7600

Business Combinations—General

[.01–.09] Reserved

Q&A Section 7610
Purchase Method

[.01–.24] Reserved

Q&A Section 7620

Applicability of Pooling of Interests Method

[.01–.18] Reserved

Q&A Section 7630

Application of Pooling of Interests Method

[.01–.02] Reserved

Q&A Section 8000

AUDIT FIELD WORK

TABLE OF CONTENTS

Section

Section

Section

Q&A Section 8100
Generally Accepted Auditing Standards

.01 Determining the Effective Date of a New Statement on Auditing Standards for Audits of a Single Financial Statement

Inquiry—The Auditing Standards Board issues a Statement on Auditing Standards (SAS) and the effective date is as follows: "This standard is effective for audits of financial statements for periods beginning on or after December 15, 2006." If an auditor is engaged to perform an audit of only the balance sheet as of December 31, 2006, would the new standard be effective?

Reply—In determining whether the standard is effective to an audit of a single statement, the auditor needs to determine whether the standard would be effective if the auditor was engaged to audit the entity's complete set of financial statements. If the standard would be effective when auditing a complete set of financial statements, the standard is effective when auditing a single statement. If the standard would not be effective when auditing a complete set of financial statements, the standard is not effective when auditing a single statement. To illustrate, refer to the following examples:

Example 1—Entity's year began January 1, 2006, and ends December 31, 2006; would the standard apply to an audit of only the balance sheet as of December 31, 2006?

No, because the standard is not effective until periods beginning on or after December 15, 2006. Because the standard would not be effective if engaged to audit the complete set of financial statements, the standard is not effective if engaged to audit only the balance sheet.

Example 2—Entity's year begins November 1, 2006, and ends October 31, 2007; would the standard apply to an audit of only the balance sheet as of June 30, 2007 (or as of any date during their year)?

No, for same reason as stated in Example 1.

Example 3—Entity's year begins December 25, 2006, and ends December 21, 2007 (52–53 weeks); would the standard be effective if the auditor is engaged to audit only the balance sheet as of December 31, 2006?

Yes, because the fiscal period began after December 15, 2006, the standard would be effective if engaged to audit a complete set of financial statements for this period. Therefore, the standard is effective for an audit of the balance sheet only.

Example 4—Entity's year begins January 1, 2007, and ends December 31, 2007; would the standard be effective if the auditor is engaged to audit only the balance sheet as of January 31, 2007?

Yes, for the same reason as stated in Example 3.

.02 Determining the Effective Date of a New Statement of Auditing Standards for Audits of Interim Periods

Inquiry—The Auditing Standards Board issues a SAS and the effective date is as follows: "This standard is effective for audits of financial statements for periods beginning on or after December 15, 2006." If an auditor is engaged to perform an "interim audit" of an entity's financial statements, would the standard apply?

Reply—The auditor would refer to the entity's normal fiscal year to determine whether the standard is effective. To illustrate, refer to the following examples:

> *Example 1*—Entity's year begins January 1, 2007. The standard would be effective for an audit of financial statements for the three-month period ending March 31, 2007, because the interim period began after December 15, 2006.
>
> *Example 2*—Entity's year begins October 1, 2006. The standard would not be effective for an audit of financial statements for the six-month period ending March 31, 2007, because the interim period began prior to December 15, 2006.

.03 Using Current Auditing Standards for Audits of Prior Periods

Inquiry—An auditor is engaged to perform an audit of financial statements that are as of or for a period that ended prior to the effective date of the clarified auditing standards. May an auditor use the clarified auditing standards that are currently effective at the time the audit is performed even though the standards were not effective for that prior period?

Reply—Yes. Because the clarified auditing standards are now effective and comprise auditing standards generally accepted in the United States of America (GAAS), the auditor may perform and report on an entity's prior period financial statements using the clarified auditing standards. The auditor's documentation should indicate whether the auditor followed GAAS currently in effect or whether the auditor followed GAAS that existed for the period under audit.

[Issue Date: December 2013.]

Q&A Section 8200
Internal Control

.01 [Reserved]

.02 Determining Accuracy of Cash Collections for Coin-Operated Machines

Inquiry—How can the accuracy of the cash collections be determined for a chain of laundromats with several thousand machines? The coin-operated machines do not employ the use of meters, counters, locked boxes, or any other devices that would provide a basis for control.

Reply—One method to determine if the machines' receipts are being surrendered intact is to occasionally fill selected coin-operated machines with marked coins. The subsequent collections can then be reviewed to make sure the same coins have been turned in. It may also be possible to correlate revenues with consumption of water and electricity by these machines. Furthermore, it may be possible to determine the expected revenues from an installation and the extent to which the machines are being used by observation of the activities of selected installations.

.03 [Reserved]

.04 [Reserved]

.05 Testing the Operating Effectiveness of Internal Control

Inquiry—Where the auditor anticipates the entity may not have effective internal control, does AU-C section 315, *Understanding the Entity and Its Environment and Assessing the Risks of Material Misstatement* (AICPA, *Professional Standards*), require the auditor to obtain an understanding of internal control even if the auditor intends to design a substantive audit approach and not rely on controls?

Reply—Yes. Paragraph .13 of AU-C section 315 states

> The auditor should obtain an understanding of internal control relevant to the audit. Although most controls relevant to the audit are likely to relate to financial reporting, not all controls that relate to financial reporting are relevant to the audit. It is a matter of the auditor's professional judgment whether a control, individually or in combination with others, is relevant to the audit.[1]

Paragraph .14 of AU-C section 315 further states

> When obtaining an understanding of controls that are relevant to the audit, the auditor should evaluate the design of those controls and determine whether they have been implemented by performing procedures in addition to inquiry of the entity's personnel.

The nature and extent of the auditor's understanding of relevant controls is described in paragraph .A68 of AU-C section 315, which states

> Evaluating the design of a control involves considering whether the control, individually or in combination with other controls, is

[1] [Footnote deleted, December 2012, to reflect conforming changes necessary due to the issuance of SAS Nos. 122–126.]

> capable of effectively preventing, or detecting and correcting, material misstatements. Implementation of a control means that the control exists and that the entity is using it. Assessing the implementation of a control that is not effectively designed is of little use, and so the design of a control is considered first. An improperly designed control may represent a significant deficiency or material weakness in the entity's internal control.

When the auditor believes, based on the understanding of controls, that controls are capable of effectively preventing or detecting and correcting material misstatements at the assertion level, the auditor may initially assess control risk at a low level during the risk assessment phase of the audit. This initial assessment of control risk is subject to the satisfactory results of the tests of the operating effectiveness of those controls to support that control risk assessment. Whether an auditor initially assesses control risk at a low level, and the degree thereof, is a matter of professional judgment.

In contrast, when the auditor believes, based on the understanding of controls, that controls are not capable of preventing or detecting and correcting material misstatements, the auditor would assess control risk as high, and the auditor would plan and perform substantive procedures to appropriately respond to the identified risks. In this situation, the auditor may identify missing or ineffective controls. The auditor is required to evaluate identified control deficiencies and determine whether these deficiencies, individually or in combination, are significant deficiencies or material weaknesses. Control deficiencies identified during the audit that upon evaluation are considered significant deficiencies or material weaknesses under this section should be communicated in writing to management and those charged with governance.[2] Also, in this circumstance, the auditor needs to be satisfied that performing substantive procedures alone would enable the auditor to design and perform an appropriate audit strategy and provide sufficient appropriate audit evidence to support his or her audit opinion.

[Issue Date: February 2008; Revised, January 2010, to reflect conforming changes necessary due to the issuance of SAS No. 115; Revised, December 2012, to reflect conforming changes necessary due to the issuance of SAS Nos. 122–126.]

.06 The Meaning of *Expectation That the Controls Are Operating Effectively*

Inquiry—Paragraph .08 of AU-C section 330, *Performing Audit Procedures in Response to Assessed Risks and Evaluating the Audit Evidence Obtained* (AICPA, *Professional Standards*), requires the auditor to design and perform tests of controls to obtain sufficient appropriate audit evidence about the operating effectiveness of relevant controls if the auditor's assessment of risks of material misstatement at the relevant assertion level includes an expectation that the controls are operating effectively or if substantive procedures alone cannot provide sufficient appropriate audit evidence at the relevant assertion level. What does *expectation that the controls are operating effectively* mean?

Reply—The phrase *expectation that the controls are operating effectively* means that the auditor's understanding of the five components of internal control has enabled him or her to initially assess control risk at a low level, and the

---

[2] See AU-C section 265, *Communicating Internal Control Related Matters Identified in an Audit* (AICPA, *Professional Standards*). [Footnote revised, December 2012, to reflect conforming changes necessary due to the issuance of SAS Nos. 122–126.]

auditor's strategy contemplates a combined approach of designing and performing tests of controls and substantive procedures. As stated above, the auditor's initial assessment of control risk is preliminary and subject to the satisfactory results of the tests of the operating effectiveness of those controls.

[Revised, December 2012, to reflect conforming changes necessary due to the issuance of SAS Nos. 122–126.]

.07 Considering a Substantive Audit Strategy

Inquiry—Paragraph .A4 of AU-C section 330 states, in part

> The auditor may determine that performing only substantive procedures is appropriate for particular assertions, and therefore, the auditor excludes the effect of controls from the relevant risk assessment. This may be because the auditor's risk assessment procedures have not identified any effective controls relevant to the assertion or because testing controls would be inefficient, and therefore, the auditor does not intend to rely on the operating effectiveness of controls in determining the nature, timing, and extent of substantive procedures.

Does this mean that an all substantive audit approach may be followed even if the auditor's understanding of internal control causes him or her to believe that controls are designed effectively?

Reply—Yes. After the auditor identifies and assesses the risks of material misstatement, the auditor's decision about whether to test the operating effectiveness of controls may be considered within a cost-benefit framework. If the auditor believes that the benefit of testing control operating effectiveness—both in terms of audit efficiency and effectiveness—is less than the cost of testing controls, the auditor may be inclined to adopt an audit strategy (or modify a preliminary strategy) that excludes testing controls. If testing the operating effectiveness of controls would not be effective or efficient, it will then be necessary to perform substantive procedures that respond to the assessed risks for specific assertions.

However, even in smaller entities, there may be well-designed controls that are operating effectively. For example, there may be controls over revenues that, if tested, could reduce the extent of substantive procedures.

The extent of substantive testing cannot be reduced based on the premise of effective controls, unless the effective operation of such controls has been tested.

[Revised, December 2012, to reflect conforming changes necessary due to the issuance of SAS Nos. 122–126.]

.08 Obtaining an Understanding of the Control Environment

Inquiry—In smaller entities, the control environment might be less formal than larger entities. Is the auditor required to obtain an understanding of these less formal controls, and when do these controls need to be tested?

Reply—AU-C section 315 addresses the auditor's responsibility to identify and assess the risks of material misstatement in the financial statements through understanding the entity and its environment, including the entity's internal control as described in *Internal Control—Integrated Framework*, published by the Committee of Sponsoring Organizations of the Treadway Commission. This includes obtaining a sufficient understanding of the design of controls such as those that are part of the control environment to evaluate the design of controls relevant to an audit of financial statements and to determine whether they have been implemented.

Even in audits of smaller entities, auditors may rely on the control environment to determine the nature, timing, and extent of further auditor procedures. If an auditor chooses to rely on these controls, then the auditor is presumptively required[3] to test those controls.[4]

It is preferable to evaluate the control environment early on in the audit process. This is because the results of the auditor's evaluation of these controls could affect the nature, timing, and extent of other planned audit procedures. For example, weaknesses in the control environment may undermine the effectiveness of other control components and, therefore, be negative factors in the auditor's assessment of the risks of material misstatement, in particular in relation to the risks of fraud.

[Revised, December 2012, to reflect conforming changes necessary due to the issuance of SAS Nos. 122–126.]

.09 Assessing Inherent Risk

Inquiry—Paragraph .14 of AU-C section 200, *Overall Objectives of the Independent Auditor and the Conduct of an Audit in Accordance With Generally Accepted Auditing Standards* (AICPA, *Professional Standards*), defines *inherent risk* as "the susceptibility of an assertion about a class of transaction, account balance, or disclosure to a misstatement that could be material, either individually or when aggregated with other misstatements, before consideration of any related controls." In situations in which the auditor's methodology makes separate assessments of inherent risk and control risk, does this mean that an auditor can ignore the assessment of control risk in his or her assessment of the combined risks of material misstatement if inherent risk is assessed as low?

Reply—No. Paragraph .26 of AU-C section 315 states, in part

> To provide a basis for designing and performing further audit procedures, the auditor should identify and assess the risks of material misstatement at[5]
>
> *b.* the relevant assertion level for classes of transactions, account balances, and disclosures.

Because an auditor is required to assess the combined risk of material misstatement, an auditor can not ignore control risk regardless of his or her assessment of inherent risk. While auditing standards do not require separate assessments to be performed, they do require an assessment of risk of material misstatement that includes control risk.

While not required by generally accepted auditing standards, some audit methodologies may express the assessment of inherent risk in quantitative

---

[3] See paragraph .08 of AU-C section 330, *Performing Audit Procedures in Response to Assessed Risks and Evaluating the Audit Evidence Obtained* (AICPA, *Professional Standards*). [Footnote revised, December 2012, to reflect conforming changes necessary due to the issuance of SAS Nos. 122–126.]

[4] Chapter 4 of the AICPA Audit Guide *Assessing and Responding to Audit Risk in a Financial Statement Audit* provides further guidance about obtaining an understanding of the entity and its environment, including its internal control, and about evaluating and testing entity level controls, including the control environment.

[5] [Footnote deleted, December 2012, to reflect conforming changes necessary due to the issuance of SAS Nos. 122–126.]

terms (for example, percentages) or nonquantitative terms (for example, high, medium, or low). Because the definition of *inherent risk* excludes the effect of any related controls, the auditor's assessment of inherent risk should exclude the effect of any related controls. Therefore, if an auditor assesses inherent risk as low, an auditor has to be careful whether his or her judgment was influenced by the effect of certain controls.

For example, assume an auditor is auditing a balance sheet account that the auditor expects to have only one adjustment per month posted to it. The auditor believes that the monthly adjustment is relatively easy to calculate. Assume further that the auditor's methodology calls for the auditor, as part of performing risk assessment procedures, to assess inherent risk at the assertion level as high, medium, or low. The auditor assesses the susceptibility of inherent risk as low because the auditor believes that the amount is relatively easy to calculate, but also partially because the auditor has not identified a misstatement in this account in prior year audits and believes that the bookkeeper is capable of recording the correct monthly amount.

In this example, the auditor's professional judgment as to the assessment of inherent risk was influenced by the auditor's belief that the bookkeeper is competent and has never made an error in prior years in posting the monthly adjustment. As a result, the auditor's assessment of inherent risk did not assume that there are no controls because there are some controls in place that the bookkeeper applies in making his or her monthly adjustment.

Therefore, an auditor has to be careful when assessing inherent risk as "low" because the auditor may be assuming that certain basic controls are in place and operating effectively. In such cases, the auditor may actually be making a combined assessment of the risks of material misstatement rather than assessing only inherent risk.

As discussed in section 8200.05, *Testing the Operating Effectiveness of Internal Control*, an initial assessment of effective controls (even a basic control) is subject to the satisfactory results of the tests of the operating effectiveness of those controls.

[Issue Date: March 2008; Revised, December 2012, to reflect conforming changes necessary due to the issuance of SAS Nos. 122–126.]

.10 Assessing Control Risk

Inquiry—Is defaulting to a high control risk level still permitted under AU-C section 315?

Reply—No. AU-C section 315 addresses the auditor's responsibility to identify and assess the risks of material misstatement in the financial statements through understanding the entity and its environment, including the entity's internal control. As the auditor obtains that understanding, the auditor may identify material weaknesses in the design of controls and, as a result, end up assessing control risk as high for some financial statement accounts and relevant assertions. Also, as discussed in section 8200.07, "Considering a Substantive Audit Strategy," after identifying and assessing the risk of material misstatement at the assertion level, the auditor may adopt a substantive audit strategy. In this circumstance, the auditor may assess control risk as high. Finally, the auditor might initially assess control risk at low level only to find out later, after testing the operating effectiveness of controls, that controls were not effective and would then reassess control risk as high.[6]

[Issue Date: March 2008; Revised, December 2012, to reflect conforming changes necessary due to the issuance of SAS Nos. 122–126.]

.11 Ineffective Controls

Inquiry—If, based on his or her knowledge of the entity, an auditor believes, in advance of performing risk assessment procedures, that controls over financial reporting are nonexistent or ineffective, could the evaluation and documentation of such controls (including the walk-through) be skipped?

Reply—No. AU-C section 315 requires the auditor to obtain an understanding of internal control relevant to the audit, and to evaluate the design of those controls and determine whether they have been implemented. In addition, AU-C section 315 requires auditors to identify and assess the risks of material misstatement at the relevant assertion level as the basis for designing and performing further audit procedures.

[Issue Date: March 2008; Revised, December 2012, to reflect conforming changes necessary due to the issuance of SAS Nos. 122–126.]

.12 Use of Walkthroughs

Inquiry—AU-C section 315 requires the auditor to obtain an understanding of internal control relevant to the audit. An auditor might perform walk-throughs to confirm his or her understanding of internal control. If the auditor decides to use walk-throughs to confirm his or her understanding of internal control, how often do walk-throughs need to occur?

Reply—In accordance with AU-C section 315, the auditor is required to obtain an understanding of internal control relevant to the audit to evaluate the design of controls and to determine whether they have been implemented. To do that, performing a walk-through would be a good practice. Accordingly, auditors might perform a walk-through of significant accounting cycles every year. In some situations, AU-C section 315 allows the auditor to rely on audit evidence obtained in prior periods. In those situations, the auditor is required to perform audit procedures to establish the continued relevance of the audit evidence obtained in prior periods (for example, by performing a walk-through). So, an auditor might perform walk-throughs every year in order to update his or her understanding.

[Issue Date: March 2008; Revised, December 2012, to reflect conforming changes necessary due to the issuance of SAS Nos. 122–126.]

.13 Documenting Internal Control

Inquiry—Does a control have to be documented for it to be tested?

Reply—No. However, it is recommended that an entity document its controls so that the auditor can efficiently obtain an understanding of controls, assess the risks of material misstatement, and test them for operating effectiveness and reliance thereon (if the auditor chooses to test controls). If the entity does not document a control, and it is an important control, AU-C section 315 paragraph .33 requires the auditor to document the control as part of the auditor's risk assessment procedures to identify and assess the risks of material misstatement. The auditor is required to perform risk assessment

---

[6] [Footnote deleted, December 2012, to reflect conforming changes necessary due to the issuance of SAS Nos. 122–126.]

procedures to identify and assess the risks of material misstatements. In addition, it may not be practical to test the operating effectiveness of controls (if the auditor chooses to do so) throughout the audit period without some level of documentation of the control by the client.

[Issue Date: March 2008; Revised, December 2012, to reflect conforming changes necessary due to the issuance of SAS Nos. 122–126.]

.14 Suggesting Improvements in Internal Control

Inquiry—When performing a walk-through of controls, may an auditor suggest improvements in internal control to the client?

Reply—Yes. A byproduct of obtaining an understanding of internal control is making suggestions for improvement to the client. That brings value to the audit process.

[Issue Date: March 2008]

.15 Identifying Significant Deficiencies

Inquiry—If the auditor decides not to test controls, does that mean there is a control deficiency that is required to be evaluated under AU-C section 265, *Communicating Internal Control Related Matters Identified in an Audit* (AICPA, *Professional Standards*)?

Reply—No, not necessarily. It depends on the reasons the auditor decides not to test the control. The auditor's decisions about the nature, timing, and extent of further audit procedures are based on the assessment of the risks of material misstatement. Communications under AU-C section 265 are based on control deficiencies that the auditor has identified. If the auditor decides not to test a control because it is nonexistent or is not properly designed, then that would represent a control deficiency that would need to be assessed as to severity to determine whether it is a significant deficiency or material weakness. If the design of the control is appropriate, but the auditor decides not to test it for another reason (for example, because the control is redundant), then the auditor has not identified a control deficiency.

[Issue Date: March 2008; Revised, January 2010, to reflect conforming changes necessary due to the issuance of SAS No. 115; Revised, December 2012, to reflect conforming changes necessary due to the issuance of SAS Nos. 122–126.]

.16 Examining Journal Entries

Inquiry—Paragraph .21 of AU-C section 330 states, in part

> The auditor's substantive procedures should include audit procedures related to the financial statement closing process, such as
>
> - agreeing or reconciling the financial statements with the underlying accounting records and
> - examining material journal entries and other adjustments made during the course of preparing the financial statements.

Does the phrase *adjustments made during the course of preparing the financial statements* refer to journal entries and other adjustments prepared by the client during the process of drafting the financial statements, or does it refer to journal entries recorded during the year?

Reply—The requirement to examine material journal entries and other adjustments made during the course of preparing the financial statements in paragraph .21 of AU-C section 330 refers to those journal entries and adjustments prepared by the entity during the process of preparing its financial statements (for example, consolidating entries or elimination entries between divisions). It does not refer to the journal entries recorded by the entity in the general ledger during the year. However, paragraph .32*a* of AU-C section 240, *Consideration of Fraud in a Financial Statement Audit* (AICPA, *Professional Standards*), requires auditors to design and perform audit procedures to test the appropriateness of journal entries recorded by the entity in the general ledger during the year.

[Issue Date: March 2008; Revised, December 2012, to reflect conforming changes necessary due to the issuance of SAS Nos. 122–126.]

.17 Obtaining an Understanding of Business Processes Relevant to Financial Reporting and Communication

Inquiry—Are auditors required to obtain an understanding of business processes relevant to financial reporting and communication in every audit engagement?

Reply—Yes. AU-C section 315 states that the auditor should obtain an understanding of the information system, including the related business processes and communication relevant to financial reporting.[7]

Business processes and communication, which are part of an entity's information system, are different than the control activities relevant to the audit. Business processes are the activities designed to

- develop, purchase, produce, sell, and distribute an entity's products and services;
- ensure compliance with laws and regulations; and
- record information, including accounting and financial reporting information.

Business processes result in the transactions that are recorded, processed, and reported by the information system. Obtaining an understanding of the entity's business processes, which includes how transactions are originated, assists the auditor in obtaining an understanding of the entity's information system relevant to financial reporting in a manner that is appropriate to the entity's circumstances.[8]

It is important for auditors to understand that business processes are different than control activities. Control activities, generally speaking, are those steps put in place by the entity to ensure that the financial transactions are correctly recorded and reported. The auditor is required to obtain an understanding of only those control activities that are considered to be relevant to the audit. Accordingly, there are differing requirements in every audit for obtaining an understanding of business processes versus control activities.

[Issue Date: April 2017]

---

[7] Paragraph .19 of AU-C section 315, *Understanding the Entity and Its Environment and Assessing the Risks of Material Misstatement* (AICPA, *Professional Standards*).

[8] Paragraph .A95 of AU-C section 315.

.18 Obtaining an Understanding of Internal Control Relevant to the Audit

Inquiry—AU-C section 315 states that the auditor should obtain an understanding of internal control relevant to the audit.[9] Does this understanding of internal control relevant to the audit encompass more than control activities?

Reply—Yes. In obtaining an understanding of the entity and its environment, including its internal control in accordance with the requirements of AU-C section 315, the auditor is required to obtain an understanding of each component of internal control. Each component of internal control is therefore relevant to all audits and is required to be understood. These components include all of the following:

a. Control environment

b. The entity's risk assessment process

c. The information system, including the related business processes relevant to financial reporting and communication

d. Control activities relevant to the audit

e. Monitoring of controls

The auditor is required to document, among other things, his or her understanding of each of the components of internal control on every audit engagement. The auditor's responsibilities related to understanding control activities relevant to the audit are also discussed in AU-C section 315.[10]

[Issue Date: April 2017]

.19 Obtaining an Understanding of the Controls Relevant to the Audit

Inquiry—Does an understanding of controls relevant to the audit require the auditor to evaluate the design of controls relevant to the audit and determine whether they have been implemented every year?

Reply—Yes. When obtaining an understanding of controls that are relevant to the audit, AU-C section 315 requires the auditor, when obtaining an understanding of controls that are relevant to the audit, to evaluate the design of those controls and determine whether they have been implemented by performing procedures in addition to inquiry of the entity's personnel.[11] This understanding applies to each component of internal control. When obtaining an understanding of controls that are relevant to the audit, the auditor is required to perform procedures in addition to inquiry of the entity's personnel. These additional procedures may consist of one or more of the following: observations, inspections, or tracing transactions through the information system relevant to financial reporting. Determining which of the corroborating procedures (other than inquiry) should be performed to evaluate responses received to inquiries related to relevant controls is a matter for the auditor's professional judgment.

The auditor's previous experience with the entity and audit procedures performed in previous audits provide the auditor with an understanding of controls that also may be relevant to the current audit. When the auditor intends to use information obtained from the auditor's previous experience with the entity

---

9 Paragraph .13 of AU-C section 315.

10 See paragraphs .21–.22 of AU-C section 315.

11 Paragraph .14 of AU-C section 315.

and the results from audit procedures performed in previous audits, the auditor should determine whether changes affecting the control environment have occurred since the previous audit that may affect that information's relevance to the current audit.[12] The auditor's previous experience in combination with the procedures performed to determine whether such changes have occurred assist the auditor with the requirement to evaluate the design and determine the implementation of relevant controls in each audit. The auditor's procedures to update the auditor's understanding of controls may not need to be as extensive as those the auditor performed to obtain his or her initial understanding of controls. Although an auditor would still be required to perform inquiries combined with other risk assessment procedures, such as observation and inspection, those procedures would be less extensive if the auditor's procedures are limited to confirming that the processes and controls have not changed as opposed to obtaining the understanding of controls.

Nevertheless, the procedures need to be sufficient for the auditor to be able to appropriately assess the risks of material misstatement and design further audit procedures responsive to assessed risks.

[Issue Date: April 2017]

.20 Control Activities That Are Always Relevant to the Audit

Inquiry—The auditor is required to obtain an understanding of control activities relevant to the audit, including the process of reconciling detailed records to the general ledger for material account balances.[13] What control activities are always considered to be relevant in every audit?

Reply—As discussed in paragraph .21 of AU-C section 315, control activities relevant to the audit are those control activities the auditor judges it necessary to understand in order to make a preliminary assessment of control risk which together with the assessment of inherent risk comprise the risks of material misstatement at the assertion level and design further audit procedures responsive to assessed risks. However, there are situations in which the auditor would be required to consider control activities relevant to the audit and, accordingly, obtain an understanding of those control activities. The following are controls activities that, if present, are always relevant to the audit:

- Control activities that address significant risks[14]
- Control activities, relevant to fraud risks[15]
- Control activities that address risks for which substantive procedures alone do not provide sufficient appropriate audit evidence[16] (note that in such circumstance, the operating effectiveness of the control is required to be tested)[17]
- Control activities that address risks for which the auditor intends to rely on the operating effectiveness of controls in determining the nature, timing, and extent of substantive procedures[18]

---

[12] Paragraph .10 of AU-C section 315.

[13] Paragraph .21 of AU-C section 315.

[14] Paragraph .30 of AU-C section 315.

[15] Paragraph .27 of AU-C section 240, *Consideration of Fraud in a Financial Statement Audit* (*AICPA, Professional Standards*).

[16] Paragraph .31 of AU-C section 315.

[17] Paragraph .08 of AU-C section 330.

[18] Paragraph .A101 of AU-C section 315 and paragraph .08a of AU-C section 330.

- Control activities over journal entries, including nonstandard journal entries used to record nonrecurring, unusual transactions, or adjustments[19]

For control activities determined to be relevant to the audit whether required by the standards or based on auditor judgment, the auditor should understand how the entity has responded to risks arising from IT that may impact the design or implementation of the entity's control activities.[20] In addition, if applicable to the audit, control activities meeting any of the criteria stated above over the entity's use of a service organization are relevant to the audit.[21]

[Issue Date: April 2017]

.21 Control Activities That May Be Relevant to the Audit

Inquiry—What are the control activities that may vary from audit engagement to audit engagement and may be relevant to the audit (based on the auditor's judgment)?

Reply—In addition to the controls activities that are always relevant to the audit, other control activities may exist that might be considered relevant to the audit by the auditor based on his or her professional judgment.[22] An audit does not require an understanding of all control activities related to each significant class of transactions, account, balance, and disclosure in the financial statements, or to every assertion relevant to them.[23] The control activities relevant to the audit will vary according to the nature, size, and complexity of the entity and its operations and the circumstances of the engagement. For example, the concepts underlying control activities in smaller entities are likely to be similar to those in larger entities, but the formality with which they operate may vary. The following factors may assist the auditor in identifying whether other control activities are relevant to the audit:

- Materiality and inherent risk (for example, the auditor's emphasis may be on identifying and obtaining an understanding of control activities that address the areas in which the auditor considers that risks of material misstatement are likely to be higher)[24]
- The understanding of other internal control components (for example, the presence or absence of control activities obtained from the understanding of other components of internal control assists the auditor in determining whether it is necessary to devote additional attention to obtaining an understanding of control activities)[25]
- The implementation of any new systems and the effectiveness of general IT controls (for example, deficiencies in general IT controls may have an effect on the effective design and operation of application controls)[26]

---

[19] Paragraph .19*f* of AU-C section 315.

[20] Paragraph .22 of AU-C section 315.

[21] Paragraph .10 of AU-C section 402, *Audit Considerations Relating to an Entity Using a Service Organization* (AICPA, *Professional Standards*).

[22] Paragraph .A100 of AU-C section 315.

[23] See footnote 13

[24] Paragraphs .A101–.A102 of AU-C section 315.

[25] Paragraph .A103 of AU-C section 315.

[26] Paragraph .A108 of AU-C section 315.

- Lack of segregation of duties (for example, in a smaller entity, fewer employees may limit the extent to which segregation of duties is possible; relevant control activities may be more limited to, for example, understanding controls performed by management)
- Legal and regulatory requirements (for example, governmental entities often have additional responsibilities with respect to internal control)[27]

The following are controls activities that may be considered relevant to the audit (based on the factors listed previously):

- Control activities over the completeness and accuracy of information produced by the entity if the auditor intends to make use of the information in designing and performing further audit procedures[28]
- Control activities relating to operations or compliance objectives if such controls relate to data the auditor evaluates or uses in applying audit procedures[29]
- Control activities over safeguarding of assets to the extent such controls are relevant to the reliability of financial reporting[30]
- Control activities that are dependent on other controls (that is, indirect controls)[31]

[Issue Date: April 2017]

---

[27] Paragraph .A74 of AU-C section 315.

[28] Paragraph .A70 of AU-C section 315.

[29] Paragraph .A71 of AU-C section 315.

[30] Paragraph .A72 of AU-C section 315.

[31] Paragraph .10*b* of AU-C section 315.

Q&A Section 8220

Sampling

.01 Application of AU-C Section 530

Inquiry—When would the auditor apply the audit sampling principles in AU-C section 530, *Audit Sampling* (AICPA, *Professional Standards*)?

Reply—Audit sampling is only one of many tools used by auditors to obtain sufficient, appropriate evidence to support an opinion regarding financial statements. AU-C section 530 outlines design, selection, and evaluation considerations to be applied by the auditor when using audit sampling. As a general rule, audit sampling can be used—

- in performing tests of controls that provide an audit trail of documentary evidence,
- in performing substantive procedures to test details of transactions and balances, and
- in dual purpose tests that test a control that provides documentary evidence of performance and whether the recorded monetary amount of transactions or balances is correct.

Sampling applies when the auditor needs to decide whether the rate of deviation from a prescribed procedure is no greater than a tolerable rate, for example in testing a matching process or an approval process. However, risk assessment procedures performed to obtain an understanding of internal control do not involve sampling. Sampling concepts also do not apply for some tests of controls. Tests of automated application controls are generally tested only once or a few times when effective (IT) general controls are present, and thus do not rely on the concepts of risk and tolerable deviation as applied in other sampling procedures. Sampling generally is not applicable to analyses of controls for determining the appropriate segregation of duties or other analyses that do not examine documentary evidence of performance. In addition, sampling may not apply to tests of certain documented controls or to analyses of the effectiveness of security and access controls. Sampling also may not apply to some tests directed toward obtaining audit evidence about the operation of the control environment or the accounting system, for example, inquiry or observation of explanation of variances from budgets when the auditor does not desire to estimate the rate of deviation from the prescribed control, or when examining the actions of those charged with governance for assessing their effectiveness.

Thus, AU-C section 530 applies when sampling techniques are used to test either the operating effectiveness of the controls or to test details of transactions or balances.

Paragraph .05 of AU-C section 530 defines *audit sampling* as

> The selection and evaluation of less than 100 percent of the population of audit relevance such that the auditor expects the items selected (the sample) to be representative of the population and, thus, likely to provide a reasonable basis for conclusions about the population. In this context, *representative* means that evaluation of the sample will result in conclusions that, subject to the limitations of sampling risk,

are similar to those that would be drawn if the same procedures were applied to the entire population

A key to understanding that definition is the intent of the auditor in applying the audit procedure. As noted in paragraph .A3 of AU-C section 530, the auditor may examine fewer than 100 percent of the items comprising an account balance or class of transactions for reasons other than evaluating a characteristic of the balance or class. For example, the auditor is not performing audit sampling in the following situations:

- An auditor traces several sales transactions through a client's accounting system to gain an understanding of the manner in which transactions are processed. AU-C section 530 would not apply because the auditor's intent was to gain an understanding of the processing of these transactions by the accounting system, not to evaluate a characteristic of all sales transactions processed by the accounting system.
- The auditor might examine several large sales invoices that comprise a significant portion of the account balance and leave the remaining portion of the balance untested or test the remaining items by other means, such as the application of analytical procedures. Again, AU-C section 530 does not apply because the auditor does not intend to evaluate all items in the account balance based on the examination of the large items.

Another consideration in determining whether AU-C section 530 is applicable to circumstances in which an auditor examines fewer than 100 percent of the items comprising an account balance or class of transactions is the purpose of the test being applied. If the auditor intends to project the test results to the entire account balance or class of transactions for the purpose of evaluating a characteristic of the balance or class, AU-C section 530 applies. For example, if the auditor intends to examine selected sales invoices to draw a conclusion as to whether sales are overstated, AU-C section 530 applies—the auditor intends to draw a conclusion about all sales. On the other hand, if the auditor selects several large sales invoices for certain audit tests and then applies analytical procedures to the remaining invoices, the auditor is not sampling according to AU-C section 530—the auditor's examination of the large items is not intended to lead the auditor to a conclusion about the other items. In that case, any conclusion about whether sales are overstated would be based on the combined results of the test of large sales invoices, inquiry and observations, analytical procedures, and other auditing procedures performed related to overstatement of sales.

In determining whether AU-C section 530 applies to a given audit procedure, the auditor would also consider the population in which the auditor is interested. The auditor might choose to divide a single reporting line on the financial statements into several populations. For example, accounts receivable might be divided into wholesale receivables, retail receivables and employee receivables. Each of these populations can be tested using a different audit strategy. The sampling concepts in AU-C section 530 apply only to populations for which audit sampling is used. Use of audit sampling on one population does not mandate its use on remaining populations.

[Revised, May 2007; Revised, December 2012, to reflect conforming changes necessary due to the issuance of SAS Nos. 122–126.]

[.02] Reserved

.03 Adequate Size for Nonstatistical Samples

Inquiry—Is there a rule-of-thumb for determining an adequate size for nonstatistical samples for substantive audit tests?

Reply—There is no rule-of-thumb that is appropriate for all applications. AU-C section 530 imposes no requirement to use quantitative aids, such as sample size tables, to determine sample size. Nor does AU-C section 530 impose a rule regarding minimum sample size. Just as before the issuance of AU-C section 530, professional judgment is the key. Auditors often use benchmarks or starting points such as sample sizes used in prior years or in similar circumstances in other audit engagements in determining what sample size is appropriate for a given sampling application. Paragraph .A13 of AU-C section 530 lists factors that influence the auditor's professional judgment in determining sample size. Those factors include

- for tests of controls,
  - — the tolerable rate of deviation of the population to be tested.
  - — the expected rate of deviation of the population to be tested.
  - — the desired level of assurance (complement of risk of overreliance) that the tolerable rate of deviation is not exceeded by the actual rate of deviation in the population; the auditor may decide the desired level of assurance based on the extent to which the auditor's risk assessment takes into account relevant controls.
  - — the number of sampling units in the population if the population is very small.
- for substantive tests of details,
  - — the auditor's desired level of assurance (complement of risk of incorrect acceptance) that tolerable misstatement is not exceeded by actual misstatement in the population; the auditor may decide the desired level of assurance based on
    - the auditor's assessment of the risk of material misstatement.
    - the assurance obtained from other substantive procedures directed at the same assertion.
  - — tolerable misstatement.
  - — expected misstatement for the population.
  - — stratification of the population when performed.
  - — for some sampling methods, the number of sampling units in each stratum.

An auditor who applies statistical sampling uses tables or formulas to compute sample size based on these judgments. An auditor who applies nonstatistical sampling uses professional judgment to relate these factors in determining the appropriate sample size.

If the auditor considered factors such as these in determining sample size in prior years or in other engagements, there may be no reason to believe that sample sizes based on these benchmarks or starting points are inadequate. Individual firms or auditors often prefer to set their own rules regarding a benchmark or starting point for determining sample size. AU-C section 530 does not prohibit such policies. It merely alerts the auditor to factors the auditor should consider in judging the adequacy of sample size.

[Revised, May 2007; Revised, December 2012, to reflect conforming changes necessary due to the issuance of SAS Nos. 122–126.]

.04 Documentation Requirements of AU-C Section 530

Inquiry—Does AU-C section 530 impose any new documentation requirements?

Reply—No, AU-C section 530 contains no new specific documentation requirements. AU-C section 230, *Audit Documentation* (AICPA, *Professional Standards*), applies to audit sampling applications just as it applies to other auditing applications. For example, AU-C section 300, *Planning an Audit* (AICPA, *Professional Standards*), requires the auditor to include in the audit documentation the audit plan, and AU-C section 230 requires the auditor to prepare audit documentation that is sufficient to enable an experienced auditor, having no previous connection with the audit, to understand (*a*) the nature, timing, and extent of the audit procedures performed to comply with generally accepted auditing standards and applicable legal and regulatory requirements; (*b*) the results of the audit procedures performed, and the audit evidence obtained; and (*c*) significant findings or issues arising during the audit, the conclusions reached thereon, and significant professional judgments made in reaching those conclusions. Thus, with regard to audit sampling applications, the auditor's audit program might document such items as the objectives of the sampling application and the audit procedures related to those objectives. The auditor's record of the work performed might include

- the definition of the population and the sampling unit, including how the auditor considered completeness of the population.
- the definition of misstatement.
- the method of sample selection.
- a list of misstatements identified in the sample.
- an evaluation of the result of the sampling application.
- conclusions reached by the auditor.

[Revised, May 2007; Revised, December 2012, to reflect conforming changes necessary due to the issuance of SAS Nos. 122–126.]

.05 Methods to Select Representative Sample

Inquiry—What are some selection methods that can be used to select a representative sample?

Reply—There is no requirement in AU-C section 530, as amended, that random sampling selection methods be used. Representative sampling methods used by auditors include

- haphazard sampling.
- systematic sampling.
- random-number sampling.

Haphazard sampling consists of selecting sampling units without any conscious bias, that is, without any special reason for including or omitting items from the sample. Haphazard sampling does not imply that units can be selected in a careless manner. Rather, a haphazard sample is selected in a manner that can be expected to be representative of the population. For example, where the physical representation of the population is a file cabinet drawer of vouchers, a haphazard sample of all vouchers processed for the year 19XX might include any of the vouchers that the auditor pulls from the drawer, regardless of each voucher's size, shape, location, or other physical features. The auditor using haphazard selection would want to be careful to avoid distorting the sample by selecting, for example, only unusual or physically small items or by omitting items such as the first or last items in the physical representation of the population.

Systematic sampling consists of determining a uniform interval, and one item is selected throughout the population at each of the uniform intervals from the starting point.

Random-number sampling entails matching random numbers generated by a computer or selected from a random-number table with, for example, document numbers.

Another method sometimes used in practice is block sampling. Block sampling consists of selecting groups of sequential transactions (for example, all vouchers processed on several selected dates). Using block samples may be inefficient because in order for a block sample to be adequate to lead to an audit conclusion, a relatively larger number of blocks would be selected. If an auditor decides to use block sampling, the auditor may want to exercise special care to control sampling risk in designing the auditor's sample.

[Revised, May 2007; Revised, December 2012, to reflect conforming changes necessary due to the issuance of SAS Nos. 122–126.]

Q&A Section 8310

Audit Evidence: Securities

[.01] Reserved

.02 Confirmation of Securities Held in Street Name

Inquiry—A CPA firm has been engaged to perform the initial audit of a pension plan and trust. Most of the trust assets are investments held in street name by a brokerage house. Some negotiable bearer bonds, held in a bank, are in denominations not traceable to the trust account since the bond may represent investments by more than one customer. In addition to its monthly account statements the broker will certify details and ownership of investments at the statement date and will permit examination of certain of its internal records. The bank will also certify details and ownership of investments held for the trust.

Would the fact that the securities are held in "street name" and in some cases in denominations which cannot be traced to the trust's account preclude obtaining sufficient appropriate audit evidence on which to base an opinion on the financial statements of the pension plan and trust?

Reply—AU-C section 500, *Audit Evidence* (AICPA, *Professional Standards*), discusses audit evidence. Physical inspection and count of the securities in this case appear to be impracticable; therefore, audit evidence concerning the securities would presumably consist primarily of confirmations received from the brokerage houses and other financial institutions which have possession of the securities. Whether or not confirmations would represent sufficient appropriate audit evidence is really a matter for the auditor's professional judgment.

[Revised, May 2007; Revised, December 2012, to reflect conforming changes necessary due to the issuance of SAS Nos. 122–126.]

Q&A Section 8320
Audit Evidence: Inventories

.01 Reliance on Observation of Inventories at an Interim Date

Inquiry—Although its fiscal year ends on March 31, a client has always counted its physical inventory on December 31. The March 31 ending inventory has always been calculated by the gross profit method which has proven over the past to be quite accurate. No perpetual inventory records are kept.

Can the auditor rely on an observation of inventory that takes place three months prior to the balance sheet date?

Reply—AU-C section 501, *Audit Evidence—Specific Considerations for Selected Items* (AICPA, *Professional Standards*), addresses evidence regarding inventory. Paragraph .11 of AU-C section 501 requires the auditor to attend physical inventory counting, unless impracticable, to observe the performance of management's count procedures, and to perform audit procedures over the entity's final inventory records to determine whether they accurately reflect actual inventory count results. Paragraph .13 indicates that if attendance at physical inventory counting is impracticable, the auditor should make or observe some physical counts on an alternate date and perform audit procedures on intervening transactions.

Paragraph .A31 of AU-C section 501 further states, in part

> For practical reasons, the physical inventory counting may be conducted at a date, or dates, other than the date of the financial statements. This may be done irrespective of whether management determines inventory quantities by an annual physical inventory counting or maintains a perpetual inventory system.

Normally, observing an inventory-taking on December 31 when a client has a March 31 year-end and perpetual records are used as the basis of the March 31 inventories, would present no unusual problems since tests of intervening transactions referred to in paragraph .13 of AU-C section 315, *Understanding the Entity and Its Environment and Assessing the Risks of Material Misstatement* (AICPA, *Professional Standards*), usually can be readily applied. However, if the client keeps no perpetual records of inventory, the tests of the intervening transactions would, in effect, cause the auditor to create the perpetual records as a basis for the March 31 inventory.

[Revised, December 2012, to reflect conforming changes necessary due to the issuance of SAS Nos. 122–126.]

.02 Observation of Physical Inventory on an Initial Audit

Inquiry—A company maintains large inventories of tractor parts in five different locations. The quantities of each part may be quite small, averaging six or seven pieces; but there are approximately 5000 different parts on hand, some as much as twenty years old. The company has been taking complete physical inventories at the end of each year. In the past, the parts inventories have been valued at the current catalogue prices.

A CPA has been engaged to perform the company's initial audit. What procedures may be followed in establishing the value of the parts inventory?

Reply—It would appear necessary under paragraph .11 of AU-C section 501; paragraph .A13 of AU-C section 510, *Opening Balances—Initial Audit*

Engagements, Including Reaudit Engagements (AICPA, *Professional Standards*); and paragraph .07*b* of AU-C section 705, *Modifications to the Opinion in the Independent Auditor's Report* (AICPA, *Professional Standards*), that the auditor observe the client's count of the parts inventory. Presumably tests would be made in each of the five locations.

Inventory pricing should be based on historical cost, rather than current selling price. While it may not be practicable to determine cost individually for the large number of parts on hand, it might be appropriate to determine the ratio of cost to catalogue price to obtain an approximation of the cost of current inventory. Also, some allowance, based on experience, should be made for obsolescence. Presumably a part will have little current value if there is a probability it will not be sold within five years. Costs of warehousing items for such a period may often approach the discounted value of the sales price.

Based upon observations and upon discussions with the client's employees, the auditor may be able to obtain some impressions as to the reliability of the earlier inventories. This would be supported by a comparison of this year's inventory with the prior year's, and by knowledge of sales and production in the current year.

[Revised, December 2012, to reflect conforming changes necessary due to the issuance of SAS Nos. 122–126.]

.03 Cost of Inventories Acquired From Principal Stockholder

Inquiry—A corporation purchased merchandise from a stockholder who owns 99 percent of the corporation's stock and executed a chattel mortgage in favor of the stockholder. The merchandise was acquired by the stockholder prior to the formation of the corporation.

How can the CPA be sure the purchase price of this merchandise is reasonable?

Reply—The "seller's" cost can be ascertained through the examination of his cost records, invoices, etc., and comparing his total cost with the selling price to the corporation. Also, the taking of inventory can be observed and verified against physical quantities and classifications of inventory, against transfer documents and against the transferor's cost records and invoices. If the latter records are not available, the auditor can price the inventory at the current replacement cost which can be obtained by reference to recent invoices, communication with suppliers, or references to recent merchandise catalogs.

A basic consideration in this case is the fact that, upon incorporation, there is a continuance of beneficial interest in the inventory transferred and in the proceeds from its eventual disposition by virtue of the chattel mortgage and the 99 percent stock ownership. Accordingly, the transferor's cost should be carried over and continued on the books of the newly organized corporation.

.04 Reliance on Estimates of Coal Inventories by Experts

Inquiry—An electric utility maintains a large stockpile of coal. The auditors rely on the calculations of an engineering firm in their test of this inventory. The amount of coal by weight is estimated by multiplying the volume of the coal pile, calculated in cubic feet, by the estimated average density of the coal, measured in pounds per cubic foot. The calculated amount is then compared with the utility's perpetual inventory records, and, if the variance is not considered material, the perpetual inventory is accepted as the accurate amount.

Because of the uncertainties involved in this method, particularly in the estimation of the average density of the coal, the engineers are reluctant to render an opinion on the amount of coal on hand. Other methods of calculating the amount of coal such as the "two coal-pile" theory are uneconomical.

In all cases, this inventory is a material item in the accounts of the utility. What alternative auditing procedures might be used in these circumstances?

Reply—While a slight change in density of the coal might result in a change in computed quantity of coal on hand, the effect would most likely not be material in relation to the balance sheet or statement of operations of the utility company. Perhaps, using the criteria of statistical sampling, the engineers would be willing to state that there is a X% probability that the quantity of coal is a certain amount plus or minus X% (or some other measure of variability).

.05 Dates of Observation of Inventories Which Are Kept on Perpetual Records

Inquiry—A retail dealer in tires and tubes has twenty-two stores. Each month the dealer takes inventory at two stores. The dealer's auditor has observed the inventory taking at ten locations. To avoid the need for extra help at year end, January 31, the auditor proposes to visit the remaining locations shortly after December 31 and:

- Count the tires on hand at that time.
- Reconcile the count back to the daily report at December 31.

Do the above described procedures constitute an adequate observation of inventories?

Reply—Paragraphs .11–.15 of AU-C section 501 require the auditor to obtain sufficient appropriate audit evidence regarding the existence and condition of inventory. Paragraph .A31 of AU-C section 501 states, in part

> For practical reasons, the physical inventory counting may be conducted at a date, or dates, other than the date of the financial statements. This may be done irrespective of whether management determines inventory quantities by an annual physical inventory counting or maintains a perpetual inventory system.

Presumably the dealer has the necessary perpetual records which allow the taking of inventory at two stores each month during the year. Therefore, the proposed procedures would be acceptable and meet the requirement for inventory observation.

[Revised, December 2012, to reflect conforming changes necessary due to the issuance of SAS Nos. 122–126.]

.06 Observation of Consignment Inventories

Inquiry—Corporation A sells supplies and equipment for manufacturing jewelry. Silver on consignment from a supplier is kept in a vault adjacent to where Corporation A keeps its silver inventory. The supplier employs an independent warehouse firm to protect the consigned silver. The bonded employee of the warehouse firm has sole access to the consignment silver and performs the duties of warehouse manager for Corporation A. The warehouse firm pays the salary of the bonded employee but is reimbursed by Corporation A. Since the possibility for substitutions between Corporation A's silver inventories and the consignment silver exists, the auditors of Corporation A, in conducting a physical observation of Corporation A's silver inventories, also want to conduct a physical observation of the consignment silver. Is it necessary for the auditors of Corporation A to observe the consignment silver?

Reply—AU-C section 501 addresses specific considerations by the auditor in obtaining sufficient appropriate audit evidence regarding certain aspects of inventory, including inventory owned by a third party. Paragraph .A38 of AU-C section 501 provides that the auditor may consider it appropriate to perform other audit procedures instead of, or in addition to, confirmation with the third party. Among the steps recommended for the auditor to follow, depending on the circumstances, is to attend, or arrange for another auditor to attend, the third party's physical counting of inventory, if practicable.

Because of the relationship which Corporation A has with the warehouse and the bonded employee, and the possibility for substitutions of inventory between Corporation A and the supplier, the auditors would observe the consignment inventory and Corporation A's inventory at the same time.

[Revised, December 2012, to reflect conforming changes necessary due to the issuance of SAS Nos. 122–126.]

Q&A Section 8330
Audit Evidence: Fixed Assets

.01 Verification of Real Estate Ownership

Inquiry—What procedures may be followed in the verification of real property accounts? Is it sufficient to examine the documents involved in the purchase of the property, to examine the real estate tax bills, and to communicate with the holders of any mortgages or trusts secured by the property? Should the client be required to assume the expense of a title search by an attorney?

Reply—It is generally conceded that examination of public records which contain the history of transactions relating to realty, as well as the current status of that property, is normally the function of an attorney or title company rather than that of an auditor. Accordingly if it is feasible for the client to obtain a letter from an attorney or title company which defines the interest the company holds in the land based upon a title search, this appears to be the best evidence available as to title and encumbrances.

If this procedure is too costly, then the following other audit procedures may supply sufficient indicia of title as to enable the auditor to assume that the client does, in fact, own the land subject to named liens.

1. Compare legal description of land found in deed with that found in the title insurance policy, abstract of deed, tax receipts, etc.
2. Verify current payment of carrying expenses of land in question, such as insurance premiums, tax payments, payments to mortgagee, etc.
3. Examine any rent receipts which may show evidence of continuing ownership.
4. Visit the land in question, if this is practicable.
5. Request an attorney's letter describing any conveyances or encumbrances of real property that may have been effected during the period covered in the audit, as well as his opinion regarding present status of title.
6. Obtain statement from client as to condition of title and encumbrance.
7. Check municipal or county records for evidence of ownership.

Use of a property map in connection with undertaking these procedures would also be helpful.

.02 Examination of Assets of a Rental Company

Inquiry—A lessor is in the business of leasing autos, large trucks, tractors, and trailers. Is it necessary for the auditors to make physical observations of the rolling stock which is scattered across the country? What other audit procedures might be employed in the verification of this equipment? Must the titles to all equipment be examined?

Reply—It is not necessary, unless some extraordinary situation or circumstances were brought to light, to examine titles to all the equipment. Random test verifications of title certificates or proper registration of vehicles should be made. The fact that the client is receiving rent for the vehicles and is currently making payments on its time-purchase contracts would also be verified in regular course. Any tax and insurance payments which the client is required to make in connection with the vehicles can be checked. Also, test confirmations of possession of vehicles with the lessee should be made. Audit responsibility would not necessarily extend to physical observation of the equipment at its numerous shifting locations.

Q&A Section 8340

Audit Evidence: Confirmation Procedures

[.01] Reserved

[.02] Reserved

.03 Confirmation of Balances Due on Loans

Inquiry—A bank arranges mortgage loans whereby the borrower instructs the bank to make payments to the contractor or developer. Payment booklets, which specify the periodic amounts due, are sent twice yearly to the borrower. In addition, each borrower receives an annual statement which shows his total yearly payments as well as the various yearly charges. Many of the debtors are unable to verify the correctness of the accrued charges and are unable to check the outstanding balances of their loans because of the complex interest rates. How can these loan balances be confirmed when the debtor cannot determine the total amount of the debt?

Reply—While the debtor may not be able to calculate the balance of the loan due, there are details of the loan which he or she should know and which can be confirmed. A request that the debtor confirm the original amount of the loan and the payments he or she has made would properly serve the purpose of a confirmation. Confirmation of the interest rate might also be requested as this affects the balance of the loan and should be known by the debtor.

[.04] Reserved

[.05] Reserved

[.06] Reserved

[.07] Reserved

[.08] Reserved

.09 Insurance Claims

Inquiry—Should an auditor communicate with an insurance company, or the insurance company's attorneys, when trying to obtain sufficient appropriate audit evidence about insured claims outstanding against management?

Reply—The auditor should obtain appropriate audit evidence about claims outstanding (*a*) from management and (*b*) by communicating with the entity's external legal counsel in accordance with AU-C section 501, *Audit Evidence—Specific Considerations for Selected Items* (AICPA, *Professional Standards*). The auditor may encounter situations where neither management nor the entity's external legal counsel is able to provide sufficient information regarding outstanding claims handled by insurance companies. In those situations, the auditor may consider communicating directly with the insurance company or its attorneys appropriate.

[Revised, December 2012, to reflect conforming changes necessary due to the issuance of SAS Nos. 122–126.]

.10 Letter of Inquiry to Management's External Legal Counsel

Inquiry—When an auditor requested management to send a letter of inquiry to management's external legal counsel, management objected because its external legal counsel would charge for answering the letter of inquiry. Management also believed that an inquiry about legal matters was not necessary because it had not used the services of its external legal counsel in the current year for any matters concerning litigation, claims or assessments. Rather, management paid fees to its external legal counsel in connection with other matters such as corporate registrations. Do generally accepted auditing standards require that a letter of inquiry be sent to management's external legal counsel?

Reply—No. Paragraph .16 of AU-C section 501 states that

> The auditor should design and perform audit procedures to identify litigation, claims, and assessments involving the entity that may give rise to a risk of material misstatement, including (Ref: par. .A39–.A45)
>
> *a.* inquiring of management and, when applicable, others within the entity, including in-house legal counsel;
>
> *b.* obtaining from management a description and evaluation of litigation, claims, and assessments that existed at the date of the financial statements being reported on and during the period from the date of the financial statements to the date the information is furnished, including an identification of those matters referred to legal counsel;
>
> *c.* reviewing minutes of meetings of those charged with governance; documents obtained from management concerning litigation, claims, and assessments; and correspondence between the entity and its external legal counsel; and
>
> *d.* reviewing legal expense accounts and invoices from external legal counsel.

Paragraph .18 of AU-C section 501 further states, in part

> Unless the audit procedures required by paragraph .16 indicate that no actual or potential litigation, claims, or assessments that may give rise to a risk of material misstatement exist, the auditor should, in addition to the procedures required by other AU-C sections, seek direct communication with the entity's external legal counsel.

If information contrary to management's assertion is discovered, in addition to requesting management to send an inquiry letter to management's external legal counsel in accordance with paragraph .18 of AU-C section 501, the auditor should consider the effects of the erroneous assertion on the ability to rely on other written representations from management.

In situations where no letter of inquiry is sent to management's external legal counsel, the auditor may consider including in the written representation letter from management a specific representation that no attorney had been consulted regarding litigation, claims, and assessments.

[Revised, December 2012, to reflect conforming changes necessary due to the issuance of SAS Nos. 122–126.]

.11 Receivables in Special Purpose Financial Statements

Inquiry—If accounts receivable and escrow balances are included in special purpose financial statements, should the accounts receivable and escrow balances be confirmed?

Reply—The generally accepted auditing standards, including confirmation, that apply to financial statements prepared in accordance with generally accepted accounting principles apply to financial statements prepared in accordance with a special purpose framework.

[Revised, December 2012, to reflect conforming changes necessary due to the issuance of SAS Nos. 122–126.]

[.12] Reserved

[.13] Reserved

[.14] Reserved

[.15] Reserved

.16 Retention of Returned Confirmations When a Schedule of Confirmation Results is Prepared

Inquiry—AU-C section 505, *External Confirmations* (AICPA, *Professional Standards*), addresses the auditor's use of external confirmation procedures to obtain audit evidence, in accordance with the requirements of AU-C section 330, *Performing Audit Procedures in Response to Assessed Risks and Evaluating the Audit Evidence Obtained* (AICPA, *Professional Standards*), and AU-C section 500, *Audit Evidence* (AICPA, *Professional Standards*). Similarly, AU-C section 230, *Audit Documentation* (AICPA, *Professional Standards*), addresses the form, content, and extent of audit documentation. When written confirmations are received, should they be retained as part of audit documentation or is a schedule of confirmation results sufficient?

Reply—Paragraph .A4 of AU-C section 230 sets forth factors that the auditor may consider in determining the form, content, and extent of the documentation. As indicated in paragraph .03 of AU-C section 505, confirmations are typically used for accounts with higher risks of material misstatement, they often serve as significant evidence to the assertions being tested, and seasoned judgment is often needed in evaluating confirmations that identify the nature and extent of exceptions. These reasons, among others, support retaining returned confirmations even though a schedule of confirmation results is prepared.

[Revised, June 2009; Revised, December 2012, to reflect conforming changes necessary due to the issuance of SAS Nos. 122–126.]

Q&A Section 8345

Audit Evidence: Destruction of Documents

.01 Audit Considerations When Client Evidence and Corroborating Evidence in Support of the Financial Statements Have Been Destroyed by Fire, Flood, or Natural Disaster

Inquiry—Prior to the completion of audit procedures, some or all of the accounting books and records of the entity subject to audit are destroyed by a fire, flood, or natural disaster. The evidence that might be destroyed includes general and subsidiary ledgers, accounting manuals, worksheets and spreadsheets supporting cost allocations, computations, checks, minutes of meetings, and a variety of other different types of audit evidence. What are the auditor reporting considerations when client evidence has been destroyed?

Reply—Paragraph .06 of AU-C section 200, *Overall Objectives of the Independent Auditor and the Conduct of an Audit in Accordance With Generally Accepted Auditing Standards* (AICPA, *Professional Standards*), states, in part, that "as the basis for the auditor's opinion, GAAS require the auditor to obtain reasonable assurance about whether the financial statements as a whole are free from material misstatement, whether due to fraud or error. Reasonable assurance ... is obtained when the auditor has obtained sufficient appropriate audit evidence to reduce audit risk (that is, the risk that the auditor expresses an inappropriate opinion when the financial statements are materially misstated) to an acceptably low level."

If substantially all of an entity's evidence and corroborating evidence in support of their financial statements has been destroyed and the auditor has been unable to complete audit procedures with respect to financial statement amounts and assertions,[1] the auditor should disclaim an opinion on the financial statements as the auditor is unable to form an opinion as to the fairness of presentation of the financial statements in accordance with the applicable financial reporting framework. If the auditor disclaims an opinion due to an inability to obtain sufficient appropriate audit evidence, the auditor should include in the basis of modification paragraph all the reasons for that inability.

When the auditor disclaims an opinion due to an inability to obtain sufficient appropriate audit evidence, the auditor should amend the introductory paragraph of the auditor's report to state that the auditor was engaged to audit the financial statements. The auditor should also amend the description of the auditor's responsibility and the description of the scope of the audit to state only the following: "Our responsibility is to express an opinion on the financial statements based on conducting the audit in accordance with auditing standards generally accepted in the United States of America. Because of the matter(s) described in the basis for disclaimer of opinion paragraph, however, we were not able to obtain sufficient appropriate audit evidence to provide a basis for an audit opinion." Paragraph .A32 of AU-C section 705, *Modifications to the Opinion in the Independent Auditor's Report* (AICPA, *Professional Standards*), contains an illustration of an auditor's report containing a disclaimer

[1] The auditor should design and perform substantive procedures for all relevant assertions related to each material class of transactions, account balance, and disclosure.

of opinion due to the auditor's inability to obtain sufficient appropriate audit evidence about multiple elements of the financial statements.[2]

In the case where the evidence and corroborating evidence is available for some, but not all, of the financial statement accounts and assertions, the auditor would explain which evidence has been destroyed (such as evidence supporting the cost of inventory, the valuation of amounts in accounts receivable, and so on).

If so engaged by an entity, the auditor may express an opinion on one or more specified elements, accounts, or items of a financial statement (such as a schedule of accounts receivable or fixed assets). If the auditor is so engaged, the guidance in AU-C section 805, *Special Considerations—Audits of Single Financial Statements and Specific Elements, Accounts, or Items of a Financial Statement* (AICPA, *Professional Standards*), should be followed. The auditor should not express an opinion on specified elements, accounts, or items included in a financial statement on which he or she has disclaimed an opinion, if such reporting would be tantamount to expressing a piecemeal opinion on the financial statements. However, an auditor would be able to express an opinion on one or more specified elements, accounts, or items of a financial statement provided that matters to be reported on and the related scope of the audit were not intended to and did not encompass so many elements, accounts, or items as to constitute a major portion of the financial statements. For example, it may be appropriate for an auditor to express an opinion on an entity's schedule of accounts receivable or fixed assets even if the auditor has disclaimed an opinion on the financial statements taken as a whole. However, the report on the specified element, account, or item should be presented separately from the financial statements of the entity.

[Revised, December 2012, to reflect conforming changes necessary due to the issuance of SAS Nos. 122–126.]

.02 Considerations When Audit Documentation Has Been Destroyed by Fire, Flood, or Natural Disaster

Inquiry—Prior to issuance of an auditor's report on financial statements, and either prior to or after the completion of fieldwork, the audit documentation is destroyed by a fire, flood, or natural disaster. To what extent is the auditor required to recreate the audit documentation in order to express an opinion on the financial statements?

Reply—Audit documentation is the principal record of auditing procedures applied, evidence obtained, and conclusions reached by the auditor in the engagement. In addition, certain Statements on Auditing Standards contain specific documentation requirements. Paragraph .02 of AU-C section 230, *Audit Documentation* (AICPA, *Professional Standards*), states that audit documentation provides (*a*) evidence of the auditor's basis for a conclusion about the achievement of the overall objectives of the auditor;[3] and (*b*) evidence that the audit was planned and performed in accordance with generally accepted auditing standards (GAAS) and applicable legal and regulatory requirements. Oral

---

[2] [Footnote deleted, December 2012, to reflect conforming changes necessary due to the issuance of SAS Nos. 122–126.]

[3] Paragraph .12 of AU-C section 200, *Overall Objectives of the Independent Auditor and the Conduct of an Audit in Accordance With Generally Accepted Auditing Standards* (AICPA, *Professional Standards*). [Footnote revised, December 2012, to reflect conforming changes necessary due to the issuance of SAS Nos. 122–126.]

explanations cannot serve as the principal support for the work performed or the conclusions reached.

Because audit documentation is an essential element of an audit performed in accordance with generally accepted auditing standards, the auditor cannot state that he or she has performed an audit in accordance with generally accepted auditing standards without the required audit documentation. In cases where the audit documentation has been destroyed by fire, flood, or a natural disaster prior to the issuance of the auditor's report, it will be necessary for the auditor to either recreate the audit documentation in support of the audit procedures performed or re-perform the audit procedures and create new audit documentation.

In making the determination as to whether to recreate the destroyed audit documentation or to re-perform the audit procedures, the auditor may keep in mind the ultimate objective of the auditing procedures. That is, to obtain sufficient appropriate audit evidence to afford a reasonable basis for expressing an opinion on the financial statements. For example, the auditor may be able to recreate the documentation that supports certain assertions about accounts receivable by using information contained in the audit documentation with respect to sales revenue (assuming that the sales documentation was not destroyed). In addition, the auditor may be able to recreate the audit program and prepare memorandums sufficient to explain the procedures performed and the results obtained. When considering the sufficiency of such documentation, the auditor is required by paragraph .08 of AU-C section 230 to prepare audit documentation that is sufficient to enable an experienced auditor, having no previous connection with the audit, to understand (*a*) the nature, timing, and extent of the audit procedures performed to comply with GAAS and applicable legal and regulatory requirements; (*b*) the results of the audit procedures performed, and the audit evidence obtained; and (*c*) significant findings or issues arising during the audit, the conclusions reached thereon, and significant professional judgments made in reaching those conclusions. Except for perhaps the smallest of audits, it will prove difficult for the auditor to amass sufficient audit documentation by referring to documentation for a related account or by recreating the audit documentation. Consequently, the auditor will usually have to re-perform the audit procedures and create new audit documentation.

[Revised, December 2012, to reflect conforming changes necessary due to the issuance of SAS Nos. 122–126.]

Q&A Section 8350

Audit Evidence: Audit Documentation

.01 Current Year Audit Documentation Contained in the Permanent File

Inquiry—Paragraph .06 of AU-C section 230, *Audit Documentation* (AICPA, *Professional Standards*), defines *audit documentation* as the record of audit procedures performed, relevant audit evidence obtained, and conclusions the auditor reached. AU-C section 230 is applicable to all audit documentation supporting the current year's auditor's report. Do the provisions of AU-C section 230 with respect to documentation completion and retention apply to current year audit documentation maintained in the permanent file?

Reply—Yes. AU-C section 230 applies to current year audit documentation maintained in any type of file if such documentation serves as support for the current year's audit report.

[Revised, December 2012, to reflect conforming changes necessary due to the issuance of SAS Nos. 122–126.]

Q&A Section 8700
Subsequent Events

> ***Note:*** Additional Questions and Answers on subsequent events can be found in section 9070, *Subsequent Events*.

[.01] Reserved

.02 Auditor Responsibilities for Subsequent Events

Inquiry—FASB ASC 855-10-50-1 states, "An entity shall disclose the date through which subsequent events have been evaluated, as well as whether that date is the date the financial statements were issued or the date the financial statements were available to be issued." How does the entity's responsibility to disclose the date through which subsequent events have been evaluated affect the auditor's responsibilities for subsequent events?

Reply—FASB ASC 855 does not change the auditor's responsibilities under AU-C section 560, *Subsequent Events and Subsequently Discovered Facts* (AICPA, *Professional Standards*), which requires the auditor to perform subsequent event procedures from the date of the financial statements to the date of the audit report or as near as practicable thereto.[1] Because AU-C section 700, *Forming an Opinion and Reporting on Financial Statements* (AICPA, *Professional Standards*), requires the auditor's report to be dated no earlier than the date on which the auditor has obtained sufficient appropriate audit evidence on which to base the auditor's opinion on the financial statements,[2] the auditor's report date can never be earlier than management's subsequent event note date. Because the auditor is concerned with events occurring through the date of the auditor's report that may require adjustment to, or disclosure in, the financial statements, the specific management representations relating to information concerning subsequent events should be made as of the date of the auditor's report.[3] In most cases, this will result in the date that management discloses as the date through which they have evaluated subsequent events being the same date as the auditor's report. In order to coordinate that these dates (note date, representation letter date, and auditor report date) are the same, the auditor may want to discuss these dating requirements with management in advance of beginning the audit and may also want to include, in the auditor's written understanding with the client regarding the terms of the engagement (engagement letter), that management will not date the subsequent event note earlier than the date of their management representation letter (also the date of the auditor's report).

---

[1] See paragraph .10 of AU-C section 560, *Subsequent Events and Subsequently Discovered Facts* (AICPA, *Professional Standards*). [Footnote revised, December 2012, to reflect conforming changes necessary due to the issuance of SAS Nos. 122–126.]

[2] See paragraph .41 of AU-C section 700, *Forming an Opinion and Reporting on Financial Statements* (AICPA, *Professional Standards*). [Footnote revised, December 2012, to reflect conforming changes necessary due to the issuance of SAS Nos. 122–126.]

[3] See paragraph .20 of AU-C section 580, *Written Representations* (AICPA, *Professional Standards*). [Footnote revised, December 2012, to reflect conforming changes necessary due to the issuance of SAS Nos. 122–126.]

[Issue Date: September 2009; Revised, December 2012, to reflect conforming changes necessary due to the issuance of SAS Nos. 122–126.]

.03 Auditor's Responsibilities for Subsequent Events Relative to a Conduit Debt Obligor[4]

Inquiry—Entity A is a nonprofit conduit debt obligor with conduit debt securities that are traded in a public market. The entity has a June 30 year-end. Management of the nonprofit has scheduled its annual meeting for early August. During its annual meeting, audited financial statements will be distributed to the board of trustees, as well as to all other persons in attendance. At the same time, entity A will post a notice to its website that alerts the general public regarding the method(s) available for obtaining a copy of its audited financial statements. Entity A plans to file its audited financial statements with the Electronic Municipal Market Access system in late September, after other filing information has been prepared.

FASB ASC 855-10-25-1A states, in part

> [a]n entity that meets either of the following criteria shall evaluate subsequent events through the date the financial statements are issued:
>
> *a.* It is an SEC filer.
>
> *b.* It is a conduit bond obligor for conduit debt securities that are traded in a public market (a domestic or foreign stock exchange or an over-the-counter market, including local or regional markets).

The FASB ASC glossary defines *financial statements are issued* as follows: "Financial statements are considered issued when they are widely distributed to shareholders and other financial statement users for general use and reliance in a form and format that complies with GAAP."

Management has asserted that the financial statements will be widely distributed as of the date of the annual meeting (and, therefore, would be considered issued) because the financial statements (in a form and format that complies with generally accepted accounting principles [GAAP]) are distributed to the board of trustees at the meeting, as well as made available to anyone else as of that date (either through their attendance at the annual meeting or through their being able to obtain a copy through the method(s) described on entity A's website).

How does FASB ASC 855-10 affect the auditor's responsibility and the date of the auditor's report?

Reply—Because entity A is a conduit debt obligor with conduit debt securities that trade in a public market, management is required to evaluate subsequent events through the date the financial statements are first widely distributed (that is, issued).

The auditor, exercising professional judgment, needs to evaluate management's assertion about the financial statement issuance date and decide whether the manner in which entity A has made its financial statements available does or does not constitute issuance for purposes of complying with GAAP

[4] This inquiry and response assumes an entity's financial statements have been prepared in accordance with generally accepted accounting principles promulgated by the Financial Accounting Standards Board. The accounting and disclosures for subsequent events may be different for other accounting standard setters.

and completing the auditor's subsequent event procedures. The auditor is required, in accordance with AU-C section 560, to perform subsequent event procedures at or near the date of the auditor's report. As discussed more fully in section 8700.02, "Auditor Responsibilities for Subsequent Events," in most cases, this will be the same date that management discloses as the date through which they have evaluated subsequent events. In accordance with paragraph .12 of AU-C section 560, the auditor is not required to perform any audit procedures regarding the financial statements after the date of the auditor's report. If, however, a subsequently discovered fact becomes known to the auditor after the report release date, the auditor is required to perform the requirements in paragraph .15 of AU-C section 560.

[Issue Date: June 2010; Revised, December 2012, to reflect conforming changes necessary due to the issuance of SAS Nos. 122–126.]

Q&A Section 8800

Audits of Group Financial Statements and Work of Others

.01 Applicability of AU-C Section 600

Inquiry—Do the requirements of AU-C section 600, *Special Considerations—Audits of Group Financial Statements (Including the Work of Component Auditors)* (AICPA, *Professional Standards*), apply only when the auditor makes reference to the audit of another auditor in his or her report on the group financial statements?

Reply—No. AU-C section 600 applies to all audits of group financial statements. Certain requirements (detailed in paragraphs .50–.64 of AU-C section 600) are applicable to all components, except those for which the auditor of the group financial statements is making reference to the work of a component auditor. (See paragraph .08 of AU-C section 600.)

[Issue Date: November 2012.]

.02 Making Reference to Any or All Component Auditors

Inquiry—If the group engagement partner decides to make reference to one component auditor in the audit report on the group financial statements, is he or she required to make reference to all component auditors in that report?

Reply—No. The decision to make reference to the audit of a component auditor is made individually for each component auditor. The auditor of the group financial statements may make reference to any, all, or none of the component auditors. (See paragraphs .24 and .A52 of AU-C section 600.)

[Issue Date: November 2012.]

.03 Deciding to Act as Auditor of Group Financial Statements

Inquiry—What factors determine whether an auditor decides to act as the auditor of a group's financial statements?

Reply—The group engagement partner decides to act as the auditor of the group financial statements and report as such on the group financial statements upon evaluating whether the group engagement team will be able to obtain sufficient appropriate audit evidence through the group engagement team's work or use of the work of component auditors. Relevant factors in making this determination include, among other things, the (*a*) individual financial significance of the components for which the auditor of the group financial statements will be assuming responsibility, (*b*) extent to which significant risks of material misstatements of the group financial statements are included in the components for which the auditor of the group financial statements will be assuming responsibility, and (*c*) extent of the group engagement team's knowledge of the overall financial statements. (See paragraphs .15 and .A18 of AU-C section 600.)

In audits of state and local governments, additional factors to consider include (*a*) engagement by the primary government as the auditor of the financial reporting entity and (*b*) responsibility for auditing the primary government's general fund (or other primary operating fund). (See paragraph .A21 of AU-C section 600.)

[Issue Date: November 2012.]

.04 Factors to Consider Regarding Component Auditors

Inquiry—What factors might the group engagement partner consider when deciding to use the work of a component auditor and whether to make reference to the component auditor in the auditor's report on the group financial statements?

Reply—In all group audits, the group engagement team is required to obtain an understanding of the component auditor, and the group engagement partner uses this and his or her understanding of the component when deciding to use the work of a component auditor and whether to make reference to the component auditor in the auditor's report on the group financial statements. Factors affecting this decision include (*a*) differences in the financial reporting framework applied in preparing the component and group financial statements, (*b*) whether the audit of the component financial statements will be completed in time to meet the group reporting schedule, (*c*) differences in the auditing and other standards applied by the component auditor and those applied in the audit of the group financial statements, and (*d*) whether it is impracticable for the group engagement team to be involved in the work of the component auditor. (See paragraphs .22 and .A40 of AU-C section 600.)

[Issue Date: November 2012.]

[.05] Reserved

[Deleted, March 2013, due to the issuance of SAS No. 127, *Omnibus Statement on Auditing Standards—2013*. See section 8800.27, "Circumstances in Which Making Reference Is Inappropriate."]

.06 Governmental Financial Statements That Include a GAAP-Basis Component

Inquiry—When a governmental university includes a nongovernmental foundation as a component unit in its financial statements, as required by the Governmental Accounting Standards Board (GASB) financial reporting framework (that is, a not-for-profit foundation that appropriately uses accounting principles generally accepted in the United States of America [GAAP] as promulgated by the Financial Accounting Standards Board [FASB]), may the auditor's report on the university's group financial statements make reference to the auditor of the foundation's financial statements when the group engagement team identifies the foundation as a component?

Reply—Yes. In this situation, because the university (the primary government) is required by the GASB financial reporting framework to include the foundation as a component unit in the financial reporting entity (the group financial statements) and because GASB provides guidance on how to present component unit information that does not conform to GASB reporting standards, the financial statements of the foundation (a component) are deemed to be in accordance with the GASB financial reporting framework.

It is important to note that reference to a component auditor in these circumstances is appropriate only when the provisions established by GASB that require inclusion of the component unit in the financial statements of the primary government have been followed (see section 8800.27).

[Issue Date: November 2012; Revised: March 2013.]

[.07] Reserved

[Deleted, March 2013, due to the issuance of SAS No. 127. See section 8800.27.]

.08 Component Audit Performed in Accordance With *Government Auditing Standards*

Inquiry—When a component auditor conducts an audit of a component's financial statements using *Government Auditing Standards* (GAS), and the group engagement team conducts the audit of the group financial statements using generally accepted auditing standards (GAAS), may the auditor's report on the group financial statements make reference to the component auditor?

Reply—Yes. Financial audits performed under the 2011 revision of GAS incorporate AICPA Statements on Auditing Standards by reference, as well as establish additional requirements. Further, the audit reports issued to meet GAS requirements often refer separately to GAAS, as well. Therefore, the audit of the component would be deemed to have been performed in accordance with GAAS, and the audit report on the group financial statements may make reference to the component auditor. Such reference is appropriate only when the component auditor follows the requirements established by GAAS when conducting the financial audit of the component under GAS. (See paragraphs .25 and .A54 of AU-C section 600.)

[Issue Date: November 2012.]

.09 Component Audit Performed by Other Engagement Teams of the Same Firm

Inquiry—Do the requirements of AU-C section 600 apply when a CPA firm uses auditors in different offices of the firm to perform various audit procedures related to the audit of a single entity's financial statements?

Reply—If the group engagement team identifies components in the financial statements of a single entity, it is a group audit, and AU-C section 600 applies. As defined in AU-C section 600, a *component auditor* may be part of the group engagement partner's firm, a network firm of the group engagement partner's firm, or another firm. (See paragraph .11 of AU-C section 600.)

[Issue Date: November 2012.]

.10 Terms of the Group Audit Engagement

Inquiry—What matters are required to be included in the terms of the group audit engagement?

Reply—The auditor of the group financial statements is required to agree upon the terms of the group audit engagement. In addition to the matters identified in AU-C section 210, *Terms of Engagement* (AICPA, *Professional Standards*), other matters may be included in the terms of a group audit, including whether reference will be made to the audit of a component auditor in the auditor's report on the group financial statements. The terms of the engagement may also include arrangements to facilitate (*a*) unrestricted communication between the group engagement team and component auditors to the extent permitted by law or regulation and (*b*) communication to the group engagement team of important communications between (i) component auditors, those charged with governance of the component, and component management and (ii) regulatory authorities and components related to financial reporting matters. (See paragraphs .17 and .A28 of AU-C section 600.)

[Issue Date: November 2012.]

.11 Equity Method Investment Component

Inquiry—If a company has an investment accounted for using the equity method, is the equity method investment considered a component for applying AU-C section 600?

Reply—Yes. An investment accounted for under the equity method constitutes a component for purposes of AU-C section 600. As such, the requirements of AU-C section 600 apply; however, paragraphs .50–.64 of AU-C section 600 only apply when the group engagement partner assumes responsibility for the work of a component auditor. (See paragraphs .11 and .A2 of AU-C section 600.)

[Issue Date: November 2012.]

.12 Criteria for Identifying Components

Inquiry—What criteria might the group engagement team use to identify components?

Reply—A *component* is defined as "[a]n entity or business activity for which group or component management prepares financial information that is required by the applicable financial reporting framework to be included in the group financial statements." The structure of a group and the nature of the financial information and the manner in which it is reported affect how the group engagement team identifies components. Components can be separate entities or may be identified on the basis of the group financial reporting system that may be (*a*) a parent, one or more subsidiaries, and so on; (*b*) a head office and one or more divisions or branches; or (*c*) both. (See paragraphs .11 and .A1 of AU-C section 600.)

In audits of state and local governments, a component may be a separate legal entity reported as a component unit or part of the governmental entity, such as a business activity, department, or program. (See paragraph .A5 of AU-C section 600.)

[Issue Date: November 2012.]

.13 Criteria for Identifying Significant Components

Inquiry—What criteria might the group engagement team use to identify significant components?

Reply—A *significant component* is a component of individual financial significance to the group or likely to include significant risks of material misstatement of the group financial statements due to its specific nature or circumstances. As the individual financial significance of a component increases relative to the group financial statements, the risks of material misstatement of the group financial statements (posed by the financial information pertaining to that component) typically increase. The group engagement team may apply a percentage to one or more chosen benchmarks to identify components that are of individual financial significance. Appropriate benchmarks might include group assets, liabilities, cash flows, revenues, expenditures, net income, or a combination of these. Components engaging in complex transactions, such as foreign currency transactions, derivatives, alternative investments, complex financing arrangements, and so on, may expose the group to a significant risk of material misstatement even though they are not otherwise of individual financial significance to the group. The group engagement team may consider such components as significant components due to these risks. (See paragraphs .11, .A6, and .A77 of AU-C section 600.)

In audits of governmental entities, appropriate quantitative benchmarks for identifying significant components might include net costs or total budget.

Qualitative considerations may involve matters of heightened public sensitivity (for example, national security issues, donor-funded projects, or reporting of tax revenue).

[Issue Date: November 2012.]

.14 No Significant Components Are Identified

Inquiry—Do the requirements of AU-C section 600 apply when the group engagement team does not identify any significant components?

Reply—Yes. AU-C section 600 is applicable to audits of group financial statements, and group financial statements include financial information for more than one component, regardless of whether any component is identified as a significant component. When a group consists only of components not considered significant components, the group engagement partner can reasonably expect to obtain sufficient appropriate audit evidence (on which to base the group audit opinion) if the group engagement team will be able to (*a*) perform work on the financial information of some of these components and (*b*) use the work performed by component auditors on the financial information of other components to the extent necessary to obtain sufficient appropriate audit evidence. In addition, when no component is identified as significant, it is more likely that appropriate responses to assessed risks of material misstatement for some or all accounts or classes of transactions may be implemented at the group level without the involvement of component auditors. (See paragraphs .A19, .A65, and .A83 of AU-C section 600.)

[Issue Date: November 2012.]

.15 Restricted Access to Component Auditor Documentation

Inquiry—When a component auditor restricts the group engagement team's access to relevant documentation, will the auditor of the group financial statements be able to report on the group financial statements?

Reply—Yes. As long as the group engagement team is able to obtain sufficient appropriate audit evidence, the group engagement partner is able to report on the group financial statements. However, this is less likely as the significance of the component increases. (See paragraphs .16 and .A23 of AU-C section 600.)

[Issue Date: November 2012.]

.16 Responsibilities With Respect to Fraud in a Group Audit

Inquiry—Does AU-C section 600 change the auditor's responsibilities with respect to fraud in the audit of a group's financial statements?

Reply—No. The group engagement team is required to gain an understanding of the group and its environment and to identify and assess the risks of material misstatement of the group financial statements due to error or fraud. In addition, the group engagement team is required to design and implement appropriate responses to the assessed risks. (See paragraphs .20 and .A35 of AU-C section 600.)

[Issue Date: November 2012.]

.17 Inclusion of Component Auditor in Engagement Team Discussions

Inquiry—Is the engagement team required to include the component auditor in its discussions of the entity's susceptibility to material misstatements of the financial statements due to error or fraud?

Reply—No. Key members of the group engagement team are required to discuss the susceptibility of an entity to material misstatements of the financial statements due to error or fraud, specifically emphasizing the risks due to fraud. The group engagement partner may choose to include the component auditor in certain discussions, including those to discuss the susceptibility of the entity to material misstatements of the financial statements. (See paragraphs .20 and .A36 of AU-C section 600.)

[Issue Date: November 2012.]

.18 Determining Component Materiality

Inquiry—If the group engagement partner decides to make reference to a component auditor in the auditor's report on the group financial statements, does the group engagement team establish materiality for the component auditor to use in the separate audit of the component's financial statements?

Reply—No. Reference in the group auditor's report to the fact that part of the audit was conducted by a component auditor is intended to communicate that the group auditor is not assuming responsibility for the work of the component auditor. In that case, the component auditor is responsible for establishing materiality as part of performing the audit of the component's financial statements.

However, if the group engagement partner assumes responsibility for the work of a component auditor, the group engagement team is required to evaluate the appropriateness of materiality at the component level. In addition, the group engagement team is required to communicate the relevant component materiality to that component auditor. The component auditor uses component materiality to evaluate whether uncorrected detected misstatements are material, individually or in the aggregate. (See paragraphs .31, .52–.53, .55, and .A73–.A74 of AU-C section 600.)

[Issue Date: November 2012.]

.19 Understanding of Component Auditor Whose Work Will Not Be Used

Inquiry—Is the group engagement team required to obtain an understanding of a component auditor for a component that is not a significant component if the group engagement team does not plan to use the work of the component auditor and plans only to perform analytical procedures at a group level?

Reply—No. It is not necessary to obtain an understanding of the auditors of those components for which the group auditor will not be using the work of the component auditor to provide audit evidence for the group audit. (See paragraphs .22, .29, and .A41 of AU-C section 600.)

[Issue Date: November 2012.]

.20 Involvement in the Work of a Component Auditor

Inquiry—When the group engagement partner decides to assume responsibility for the work of a component auditor, is the group engagement team required to be involved in the work of the component auditor?

Reply—Yes. The group engagement team is required to determine the type of work to be performed by the group engagement team (or a component auditor on behalf of the group engagement team) on the financial information of a component. The group engagement team is also required to determine the nature, timing, and extent of its involvement in the work of the component auditor. (See paragraph .51 of AU-C section 600.)

[Issue Date: November 2012.]

.21 Factors Affecting Involvement in the Work of a Component Auditor

Inquiry—What factors might affect the group engagement team's involvement in the work of a component auditor?

Reply—Factors that may affect the group engagement team's involvement in the work of a component auditor include (*a*) the significance of the component, (*b*) identified significant risks of material misstatement of the group financial statements, and (*c*) the group engagement team's understanding of the component auditor. (See paragraph .A84 of AU-C section 600.)

[Issue Date: November 2012.]

.22 Form of Communications With Component Auditors

Inquiry—When the group engagement partner decides to assume responsibility for the work of a component auditor, are all communications between the group engagement team and component auditor required to be in writing?

Reply—No. Communication between the group engagement team and a component auditor need not necessarily be in writing. For example, the group engagement team may visit the component auditor to discuss identified significant risks or review relevant parts of the component auditor's audit documentation. In all audits of group financial statements, however, communications between the group engagement team and component auditors about the group engagement team's requirements should be written. (See paragraphs .49, .59–.60, and .A87 of AU-C section 600.)

[Issue Date: November 2012.]

.23 Use of Component Materiality When the Component Is Not Reported On Separately

Inquiry—Is it necessary to use a component materiality lower than group materiality when the component will not be reported on separately, and the audit of the entire group is being performed by the group engagement team as one audit?

Reply—If the component is a significant component on which the group engagement team will be performing audit procedures, the group engagement team is required to determine component materiality. (See paragraph .31 of AU-C section 600.) To reduce the risk that uncorrected and undetected misstatements in each component's financial statements, when aggregated, exceeds the materiality for the group's financial statements as a whole, component materiality should be less than the materiality for the group financial statements as a whole. In circumstances when appropriate responses to assessed risks of material misstatement for some or all accounts or classes of transactions may be implemented at the group level, for example when accounts receivable for the parent and subsidiaries use the same system and the consolidated accounts receivable are audited as one aggregated amount, there is no risk of aggregation error and, therefore, no need to allocate materiality to components.

[Issue Date: November 2012; Revised, February 2013.]

.24 Applicability of AU-C Section 600 When Only One Engagement Team Is Involved

Inquiry—Company X consolidates the operations of Entity A. The same group engagement team that audits Company X also audits Entity A. Because only one engagement team is involved, does AU-C section 600 apply? If so, what does AU-C section 600 require that is not already covered by other auditing standards?

Reply—AU-C section 600 applies to all audits of *group financial statements*, which are financial statements that contain more than one component. In the circumstances when the same engagement team audits all components of the group, the considerations addressed in AU-C section 600 that relate to component auditors are not relevant. However, considerations addressed in AU-C section 600, such as understanding the components; identifying components that are significant due to individual financial significance and the significant risk of material misstatement; determining component materiality; understanding the consolidation process; and addressing the risks, including aggregation risk, of material misstatement in the group financial statements; are relevant in all group audits.

[Issue Date: February 2013.]

.25 Applicability of AU-C Section 600 When Making Reference to the Audit of an Equity Method Investee

Inquiry—When the group engagement partner decides to make reference to the audit of the component auditor of an equity investee in the auditor's report on the group financial statements, is the group auditor still required to determine component materiality for those components for which reference to component auditors will be made?

Reply—Once the group engagement partner has decided to make reference to the audit of the component auditor, paragraph .26 of AU-C section 600 requires the group engagement team to obtain sufficient appropriate audit evidence with regard to the equity investee by

- performing the procedures required by AU-C section 600, except those required by paragraphs .50–.64.
- reading the equity investee's financial statements and component auditor's report thereon to identify significant findings and issues and, when considered necessary, communicating with the component auditor in this regard.

Therefore, when the group engagement partner has decided to make reference to the audit of a component auditor, the group engagement team is not required to determine component materiality for that component.

[Issue Date: February 2013.]

.26 Procedures Required When Making Reference to the Audit of an Equity Method Investee

Inquiry—The auditor of Company A has decided to make reference to the audit of the component auditor of an equity investee in the report on Company A's financial statements. In addition to obtaining and reading the equity investee's financial statements and component auditor's report thereon, what additional procedures may be necessary in order to determine that the equity investment has been properly recorded?

Reply—In determining that the equity investment has been properly recorded, the group engagement team may conclude that additional audit evidence is needed because of, for example, significant differences in fiscal year-ends, changes in ownership, or changes in conditions affecting the use of the equity method of accounting. Examples of procedures that the group engagement team may perform include, but are not limited to, reviewing information in the group's (investor's) files that relates to the equity investee, such as investee minutes, budgets, and cash flows information, and making inquiries of investor management about the equity investee's financial results.

[Issue Date: February 2013.]

.27 Circumstances in Which Making Reference Is Inappropriate

Inquiry—Are there any circumstances in which it would be inappropriate to make reference to the audit of a component auditor of an equity investee in the auditor's report on the group financial statements?

Reply—AU-C section 600 precludes the auditor of the group financial statements from making reference to the audit of the component auditor in the following circumstances:

- When the group engagement team has serious concerns about the component auditor's professional competency or independence. (In this circumstance, the group auditor is precluded from using the work of the component auditor at all.)
- The component auditor's report on the equity investee's financial statements is restricted regarding use.
- The audit of the component was not performed in accordance with the relevant requirements of GAAS or, if applicable, the standards promulgated by the Public Company Accounting Oversight Board (PCAOB).
- The financial statements of the component (that is, the equity investee) and group are prepared in accordance with different financial reporting frameworks, unless certain conditions are met.

Determining if the Audit of the Component Was Performed in Accordance With the Relevant Requirements of GAAS

When the component auditor has performed an audit of the component financial statements in accordance with auditing standards other than GAAS or the standards promulgated by the PCAOB, the group auditor is precluded from making reference, unless the group engagement partner has determined that the component auditor has performed an audit of the financial statements of the component in accordance with the relevant requirements of GAAS. Relevant requirements of GAAS in this context are those that pertain to planning and performing the audit of the component financial statements and do not include those related to the form of the auditor's report. Audits performed in accordance with International Standards on Auditing (ISAs) promulgated by the International Auditing and Assurance Standards Board (IAASB) are more likely to meet the relevant requirements of GAAS than audits performed in accordance with auditing standards promulgated by bodies other than the IAASB. The group engagement team may provide the component auditor with AU-C appendix B, *Substantive Differences Between the International Standards on Auditing and Generally Accepted Auditing Standards* (AICPA, *Professional Standards*), that identifies substantive requirements of GAAS that are not requirements in ISAs.

The component auditor may perform additional procedures in order to meet the relevant requirements of GAAS. When the component auditor's report on the component's financial statements does not state that the audit of the component's financial statements was performed in accordance with GAAS or the standards promulgated by the PCAOB, and the group engagement partner has determined that the component auditor performed additional audit procedures in order to meet the relevant requirements of GAAS, the auditor's report on the group financial statements should clearly indicate

a. the set of auditing standards used by the component auditor and

b. that additional audit procedures were performed by the component auditor to meet the relevant requirements of GAAS.

Making Reference When Different Financial Reporting Frameworks Have Been Used

Conditions that, if met, permit the group auditor to make reference when the component financial statements are prepared in accordance with a different financial reporting framework than that used for the group financial statements are the following:

- The applicable financial reporting framework provides for the inclusion of component financial statements that are prepared in accordance with a different financial reporting framework, and as such, the component financial statements are deemed to be in accordance with the applicable financial reporting framework. For example, the financial reporting frameworks established by GASB and the Federal Accounting Standards Advisory Board have such provisions.
- The measurement, recognition, presentation, and disclosure criteria that are applicable to all material items in the component's financial statements under the financial reporting framework used by the component are similar to the criteria applicable to all material items in the group's financial statements under the financial reporting framework used by the group, and the group engagement team has obtained sufficient appropriate audit evidence for purposes of evaluating the appropriateness of the adjustments to convert the component's financial statements to the financial reporting framework used by the group without the need to assume responsibility for, and, thus, be involved in, the work of the component auditor.

When reference is made to a component auditor's report on financial statements prepared using a different financial reporting framework, the auditor's report on the group financial statements should disclose that the auditor of the group financial statements applied audit procedures on the conversion adjustments.

[Issue Date: February 2013.]

.28 Lack of Response From a Component Auditor

Inquiry—Paragraph .40 of AU-C section 600 requires the group engagement team to communicate to the component auditor and ask for his or her cooperation. Paragraph .41 of AU-C section 600 requires the group engagement team to ask the component auditor for certain information. If the component auditor does not respond to the group engagement team, is the auditor of the group financial statements precluded from making reference to the audit of a component auditor?

Reply—Lack of response from a component auditor to the communication and request for information from the group engagement team does not, in and of itself, preclude the group engagement partner from deciding to make reference to the audit of a component auditor. However, the group engagement team is required to obtain an understanding of the component auditor, in accordance with paragraph .22 of AU-C section 600, including

a. whether a component auditor understands and will comply with the ethical requirements that are relevant to the group audit and, in particular, is independent.

b. a component auditor's professional competence.

c. whether the group engagement team will be able to obtain from a component auditor information affecting the consolidation process.

d. whether a component auditor operates in a regulatory environment that actively oversees auditors.

Obtaining this understanding may be more difficult when the component auditor does not respond to the communication from the group engagement team. When a component auditor does not meet the independence requirements that are relevant to the group audit, or the group engagement team has serious concerns about the other matters previously listed, the group engagement team should obtain sufficient appropriate audit evidence relating to the financial information of the component without making reference to the audit of that component auditor in the auditor's report on the group financial statements or otherwise using the work of that component auditor.

[Issue Date: February 2013.]

.29 Equity Investee's Financial Statements Reviewed, and Investment Is a Significant Component

Inquiry—Company X has an equity investment in Entity A that the group engagement team has identified as a significant component. If the management of Entity A has their financial statements reviewed but refuses to allow an audit or any other work to be performed on Entity A's financial statements, does a scope limitation exist?

Reply—Yes. If Entity A is a significant component, and no auditing procedures can be performed on Entity A's financial statements, a scope limitation exists, and the effect of the group engagement team's inability to obtain sufficient appropriate audit evidence is considered in terms of AU-C section 705, *Modifications to the Opinion in the Independent Auditor's Report* (AICPA, *Professional Standards*).

[Issue Date: February 2013.]

.30 Making Reference to Review Report

Inquiry—Is it ever appropriate to make reference to another CPA's review report in an auditor's report on group financial statements?

Reply—No, it is never appropriate to make reference to the review report on the component's financial statements in the auditor's report on group financial statements. AU-C section 600 only provides for making reference to the audit of a component auditor.

[Issue Date: February 2013.]

.31 Review of Component That Is Not Significant Performed by Another Practitioner

Inquiry—Company X has an equity investment in Entity A that is not considered a significant component. A review of the financial statements of Entity A has been performed by another practitioner. Can the group engagement team use the work of the practitioner as part of the audit evidence for the audit of the group financial statements?

Reply—Paragraphs .54–.55 of AU-C section 600 discuss certain procedures to be performed on a component when the component is not a significant component. In certain circumstances, a review of a component's financial statements may be sufficient audit evidence. Therefore, a group auditor may use the work of another practitioner if the review meets the needs of the group auditor. Although the group auditor may use the review as part of the auditor's evidence for the audit of the group financial statements, the group auditor is not permitted to make reference to the practitioner's review report.

[Issue Date: February 2013.]

.32 Issuance of Component Auditor's Report

Inquiry—Company X has an investment in Entity A accounted for under the equity method of accounting. Company X is audited by one firm, and a CPA from a different firm performs audit procedures at Entity A sufficient to provide the auditor of Company X with appropriate audit evidence relative to the equity investee's financial information. Is it necessary for the auditor of Company X to obtain an auditor's report on Entity A's financial statements from the component auditor?

Reply—Although an audit report is typically obtained when an independent CPA performs work for a group auditor of a different firm, there is no requirement that such report be obtained if the group auditor assumes responsibility for the component auditor's work. When the auditor of Company X will assume responsibility for, and, thus, be involved in, the work of a component auditor, a component auditor's communication with the group engagement team may take the form of a memorandum or report of work performed. Alternatively, the auditor of Company X may decide to review the component auditor's working papers documenting the audit procedures performed. However, in order for the auditor of Company X to make reference to the audit of the component auditor, it is necessary for the component auditor to issue an auditor's report on Entity A.

[Issue Date: February 2013.]

.33 Structure of Component Auditor Engagement

Inquiry—Company X has an investment in Entity A accounted for under the equity method of accounting. Entity A is not willing to pay for an audit of its financial statements. Would an agreed-upon procedures engagement performed by an independent CPA for Entity A be sufficient to provide the auditor of Company X with appropriate audit evidence relative to the investment in the equity investee?

Reply—The auditor of Company X is responsible for determining the nature and extent of the procedures necessary to provide the auditor of Company X with sufficient appropriate audit evidence relative to the investment in the equity investee. The nature and extent of the necessary procedures are based on the significance of the component to the group. A component auditor may perform specified audit procedures relating to the likely significant risks of material misstatement of the group financial statements on behalf of the auditor of Company X. However, the structure of the engagement for the component auditor to perform the necessary procedures is not addressed by the standard.

[Issue Date: February 2013.]

.34 Subsequent Events Procedures Relating to a Component

Inquiry—Company X has an investment in Entity A that is accounted for by the equity method of accounting. Company X and Entity A are audited by different auditors. The audit of Entity A was completed before the audit of Company X began, and the auditor of Company X's financial statements has decided to make reference to the report of the auditor of Entity A. In such circumstances, who is responsible for performing auditing procedures relating to subsequent events at Entity A that may require adjustment to, or disclosure in, the group financial statements?

Reply—The auditor of the group financial statements is responsible for obtaining sufficient appropriate audit evidence that the group financial statements are free from material misstatement, regardless of whether reference is made to the audit of a component auditor. Paragraph .39 of AU-C section 600 states that for components that are audited, the group engagement team or component auditors should perform procedures designed to identify events at those components that occur between the dates of the financial information of the components and the date of the auditor's report on the group financial statements and that may require adjustment to, or disclosure in, the group financial statements.

When the audit of the component is completed before the date of the auditor's report on the group financial statements, the group engagement team may communicate with the component auditor and ask the component auditor to perform procedures to identify subsequent events that would require adjustment to, or disclosure in, the group financial statements. Alternatively, the group engagement team may work with group management to obtain the necessary information and perform procedures themselves. Examples of procedures the group engagement team may perform include, but are not limited to, reviewing information in group management's files that relates to the component, such as component minutes, budgets, and cash flows information, and making inquiries of group management about the component's financial results.

If the group engagement team is unable to obtain sufficient appropriate audit evidence about subsequent events to make a determination about whether the group financial statements are materially misstated, then a scope limitation exists, and the effect of the group engagement team's inability to obtain sufficient appropriate audit evidence is considered in terms of AU-C section 705.

[Issue Date: February 2013.]

.35 Component and Group Have Different Year-Ends

Inquiry—Company X has a component comprising an investment in Entity A accounted for by the equity method of accounting. Entity A is audited by a component auditor. Entity A has a different year-end than Company X. The auditor of the group financial statements has decided to make reference to the audit of the component auditor. What procedures, if any, would be appropriate for the group engagement team perform as a result of the difference in year-ends?

Reply—FASB *Accounting Standards Codification* (ASC) 323-10-35-6 states that "[i]f financial statements of an investee are not sufficiently timely for an investor to apply the equity method currently, the investor ordinarily shall record its share of the earnings or losses of an investee from the most recent available financial statements. A lag in reporting shall be consistent from period to period." When a time lag in reporting between the date of the financial statements of the group and that of the component exists, appropriate procedures performed by the group engagement team include consideration of whether the time lag is consistent with the prior period in comparative statements and, as discussed in section 8800.15, "Restricted Access to Component Auditor Documentation," whether a significant transaction occurred during the time lag that would require adjustment to, or disclosure in, the group financial statements. The group engagement team may also perform auditing procedures on the information from the period audited by the component auditor to Company X's year-end (stub period). If the group engagement team is unable to obtain sufficient appropriate audit evidence about the stub period information, a scope limitation exists, and the effect of the group engagement team's inability to obtain sufficient appropriate audit evidence is considered in terms of AU-C section 705. If a change in stub period occurs that has a material effect on the group's financial statements, the auditor should consider the consistency of the financial statements for the periods presented, in accordance with AU-C section 708, *Consistency of Financial Statements* (AICPA, *Professional Standards*), because of the change in reporting period.

[Issue Date: February 2013.]

.36 Investments Held in a Financial Institution Presented at Cost or Fair Value

Inquiry—Paragraph .11 of AU-C section 600 defines a component as "[a]n entity or business activity for which group or component management prepares financial information that is required by the applicable financial reporting framework to be included in the group financial statements." Is an investment in a certificate of deposit or other types of cash investments held by a financial institution (for example, an overnight repurchase agreement) deemed a component for purposes of AU-C section 600?

Reply—No. A certificate of deposit or other cash investments held by a financial institution or bank do not constitute components.

[Issue Date: February 2013.]

.37 Employee Benefit Plan Using Investee Results to Calculate Fair Value

Inquiry—Do the investments in an employee benefit plan that rely on the investee results to calculate fair value constitute components under AU-C section 600?

Reply—No. Generally, the investments held by an employee benefit plan are required to be accounted for at fair value, with limited exceptions, and do not constitute a *component*, as defined under AU-C section 600; therefore, AU-C section 600 would not apply.

[Issue Date: February 2013.]

.38 Using Net Asset Value to Calculate Fair Value

Inquiry—Paragraphs 59–62 of FASB ASC 820-10-35 permit a reporting entity to estimate the fair value of an investment using net asset value (NAV) per share of the investment (or its equivalent) if NAV is calculated in a manner consistent with the measurement principles of FASB ASC 946, *Financial Services—Investment Companies*, as of the reporting entity's measurement date. If an entity uses the NAV of an investment as a practical expedient to estimate the fair value of that investment, is that investment considered a component under AU-C section 600?

Reply—No. Paragraph .A2 of AU-C section 600 states that an investment accounted for under the equity method constitutes a component for purposes of AU-C section 600. AU-C section 600 does not specifically identify what other, if any, types of investments may be considered components under the definition in that section.

When an entity elects to use NAV as a practical expedient, paragraph .04 of AU-C section 501, *Audit Evidence—Specific Considerations for Selected Items* (AICPA, *Professional Standards*), generally applies because it addresses situations when investments in securities are valued based on an investee's financial results, excluding investments accounted for using the equity method of accounting.

Paragraph .04 of AU-C section 501 states that when investments in securities are valued based on an investee's financial results, excluding investments accounted for using the equity method of accounting, the auditor should obtain sufficient appropriate audit evidence in support of the investee's financial results, as follows:

a. Obtain and read available financial statements of the investee and the accompanying audit report, if any, including determining whether the report of the other auditor is satisfactory for this purpose.

b. If the investee's financial statements are not audited or if the audit report on such financial statements is not satisfactory to the auditor, apply or request that the investor entity arrange with the investee to have another auditor apply appropriate auditing procedures to such financial statements, considering the materiality of the investment in relation to the financial statements of the investor entity.

c. If the carrying amount of the investment reflects factors that are not recognized in the investee's financial statements or fair values of assets that are materially different from the investee's carrying amounts, obtain sufficient appropriate audit evidence in support of such amounts.

d. If the difference between the financial statement period of the entity and investee has or could have a material effect on the entity's financial statements, determine whether the entity's management has properly considered the lack of comparability, and determine the effect, if any, on the auditor's report.

[Issue Date: February 2013.]

.39 Disaggregation of Account Balances or Classes of Transactions

Inquiry—Company X consolidates the operations of Entity A. The same group engagement team audits Company X and the operations of Entity A; no other auditors or engagement teams are involved. Are there any requirements in AU-C section 600 to disaggregate account balances or classes of transactions for purposes of auditing the consolidated financial statements of Company X? For example, is the auditor required to disaggregate accounts receivable for purposes of confirmation procedures, or can the consolidated group of accounts be treated as one population?

Reply—AU-C section 600 does not require the auditor to disaggregate account balances or classes of transactions. The group auditor should design an audit plan that is responsive to the risks of material misstatements to the consolidated financial statements. The less similar the risks of material misstatement at the group and component level, the less appropriate it may be to perform audit procedures for some or all accounts or classes of transactions at the group level. Additionally, the more complex the group (for example, decentralized systems, fewer groupwide controls, differing jurisdictions, or diverse product lines), the less likely that testing in the aggregate will sufficiently and appropriately address the risks of material misstatement.

[Issue Date: February 2013.]

.40 Variable Interest Entities (VIEs) as a Component

Inquiry—Company X consolidates the financial information of Entity A, a variable interest entity of which Company X is the primary beneficiary. Is Entity A considered a component for purposes of AU-C section 600?

Reply—Yes. Paragraph .11 of AU-C 600 defines a component as "[a]n entity or business activity for which group or component management prepares financial information that is required by the applicable financial reporting framework to be included in the group financial statements." Because Entity A's financial information is required to be consolidated into Company X's financial statements, Entity A constitutes a component for purposes of AU-C section 600. As such, the requirements of AU-C section 600 apply.

[Issue Date: March 2013.]

.41 Component Using a Different Basis of Accounting Than the Group

Inquiry—A component whose financial information is required to be consolidated into group financial statements maintains its financial information on the tax basis of accounting. The group financial statements are prepared using GAAP. What is the group auditor's responsibility regarding the consolidation of the component's financial information into the group financial statements?

Reply—When a component's financial information is prepared on the tax basis of accounting, and the group financial statements are prepared using GAAP, the auditor is required by paragraph .36 of AU-C section 600 to evaluate whether the financial information of the component has been appropriately adjusted. Appropriate adjustments are adjustments that convert the tax basis of information to GAAP basis. An example of this is converting depreciation under the method used for tax purposes by the component to depreciation calculated using the method used for the group financial statements.

[Issue Date: March 2013.]

.42 Component Audit Report of Balance Sheet Only

Inquiry—Company X prepares consolidated financial statements that include the operations of entity A. The auditor for entity A has audited the balance sheet only and has disclaimed an opinion on the other financial statements. May the group auditor of Company X, who was engaged to issue an opinion on the consolidated financial statements of the group, make reference in the report on the group financial statements to the audit of the balance sheet of entity A?

Reply—No. A component auditor's report on a balance sheet only does not provide sufficient appropriate audit evidence on revenues, expenses, and cash flows of the component to enable the group engagement partner to make reference. Accordingly, the group engagement team would have to perform procedures on the financial information of entity A in order to obtain sufficient appropriate audit evidence.

[Issue Date: June 2013.]

.43 Using Another Accounting Firm to Perform Inventory Observations

Inquiry—An accounting firm outsources its year-end inventory observation procedures for an audit to another accounting firm due to location of the inventory. Is the other accounting firm considered a component auditor in accordance with AU-C section 600?

Reply—The other auditor performing inventory observation is not considered a component auditor. However, paragraph .02 of AU-C section 600 states that "an auditor may find this section, adapted as necessary in the circumstances, useful when that auditor involves other auditors in the audit of financial statements that are not group financial statements. For example, an auditor may involve another auditor to observe the inventory count or inspect fixed assets at a remote location." Paragraph .16 of AU-C section 220, *Quality Control for an Engagement Conducted in Accordance With Generally Accepted Auditing Standards* (AICPA, *Professional Standards*), requires the engagement partner to be satisfied that those performing the audit possess the appropriate competence and capabilities. In accordance with paragraph .17 of AU-C section 220, the engagement partner is responsible for the direction, supervision, and performance of the audit engagement. The requirements and application material in AU-C section 600 relating to understanding a component auditor, setting materiality, determining the type of work to be performed, and involvement in the work performed by component auditors provide relevant guidance for meeting the requirements in AU-C section 220 with regard to the other auditor.

[Issue Date: June 2013.]

Q&A Section 8900
Predecessor Auditors

[.01] Reserved

.02 Communications Between Predecessor Auditors and Auditors

Inquiry—A client has decided to restate, for comparative purposes, the statement of changes in financial position reported on by the predecessor auditor to a statement of cash flows. The predecessor auditor's audit report will not be presented.

a. Should the auditor notify the predecessor auditor as part of the auditor's procedures to prepare or evaluate restatements permitted or mandated by new accounting standards?

b. How will the restatement affect the auditor's report?

Reply—Paragraph .12 of AU-C section 510, *Opening Balances—Initial Audit Engagements, Including Reaudit Engagements* (AICPA, *Professional Standards*), states

> If the auditor becomes aware of information that leads the auditor to believe that financial statements reported on by the predecessor auditor may require revision, the auditor should request management to inform the predecessor auditor of the situation and arrange for the three parties to discuss this information and attempt to resolve the matter.

In cases where revisions result from an accounting change required or permitted by a new Financial Accounting Standards Board or AICPA pronouncement, the auditor is not required to consult with the predecessor auditor. However, the auditor may find that communication with the predecessor auditor is desirable in order to obtain any additional information or audit documentation that may be needed to prepare or evaluate the restatement. To maintain audit efficiency, such communications may be made as part of the auditor's routine request for review of selected audit documentation.

Paragraph .55 of AU-C section 700A, *Forming an Opinion and Reporting on Financial Statements* (AICPA, *Professional Standards*), requires that if the prior period financial statements are restated, and the predecessor auditor agrees to issue a new auditor's report on the restated financial statements of the prior period, the auditor should express an opinion only on the current period.

[Revised, December 2012, to reflect conforming changes necessary due to the issuance of SAS Nos. 122–126.]

.03 Communications With a Predecessor Auditor Who Has Ceased Operations[1]

Inquiry—AU-C section 210, *Terms of Engagement* (AICPA, *Professional Standards*), requires an auditor to attempt certain communications with the

[1] AR section 400, *Communication Between Predecessor and Successor Accountants* (AICPA, *Professional Standards*), provides guidance to a successor accountant who decides to communicate with a predecessor accountant regarding acceptance of an engagement to compile or review the financial statements of a nonpublic company. In situations in which the predecessor accountant has ceased operations and the successor accountant decides to engage in such communications, the guidance in this paragraph may be useful.

predecessor auditor prior to acceptance of an engagement. How should the auditor fulfill this responsibility when the predecessor auditor has ceased operations?

Reply—Even when the predecessor auditor has ceased operations, AU-C section 210 obligates an auditor to attempt certain communications with the predecessor auditor prior to acceptance of an engagement. The auditor should attempt the required communications, about matters that the auditor believes will assist the auditor in determining whether to accept the engagement, with the individual who had final responsibility for the audit (for example, the engagement partner). Paragraph .12 of AU-C section 210 requires the auditor to evaluate the predecessor auditor's response, or consider the implications if the predecessor auditor provides no response or a limited response, in determining whether to accept the engagement.

[Revised, December 2012, to reflect conforming changes necessary due to the issuance of SAS Nos. 122–126.]

.04 Unavailability of the Audit Documentation of a Predecessor Auditor Who Has Ceased Operations

Inquiry—An auditor's initial audit may be facilitated by reviewing the predecessor auditor's audit documentation. What is the effect on the auditor's initial audit when the audit documentation of a predecessor auditor who has ceased operations is not available for review?

Reply—Paragraph .08 of AU-C section 510 requires the auditor to obtain sufficient appropriate audit evidence about whether the opening balances contain misstatements that materially affect the current period's financial statements, and states that the auditor should perform one or both of the following to obtain evidence regarding opening balances:

a. Review the predecessor auditor's audit documentation

b. Perform specific audit procedures

Paragraph .15 of AU-C section 510 requires that if the auditor is unable to obtain sufficient appropriate audit evidence regarding the opening balances, the auditor should express a qualified opinion or disclaim an opinion on the financial statements, as appropriate, in accordance with AU-C section 705, *Modifications to the Opinion in the Independent Auditor's Report* (AICPA, *Professional Standards*).

[Revised, December 2012, to reflect conforming changes necessary due to the issuance of SAS Nos. 122–126.]

.05 Significant Audit Procedures Performed by a Predecessor Auditor Who Has Ceased Operations

Inquiry—If a predecessor auditor has performed significant audit procedures, such as the observation of inventory or the confirmation of accounts receivable, and subsequently has ceased operations, to what extent may this work be used by the auditor?

Reply—Because a report on the financial statements has not been issued by the predecessor auditor and the auditor cannot complete the procedures required by AU-C section 600, *Special Considerations—Audits of Group Financial Statements (Including the Work of Component Auditors)* (AICPA, *Professional Standards*), the auditor can neither assume responsibility for the work of the predecessor auditor nor issue a report that reflects divided responsibility for the audit, as described in AU-C section 600. The auditor should perform audit procedures sufficient to reduce audit risk to an acceptably low level and thereby enable the auditor to draw reasonable conclusions on which to base the auditor's opinion on the financial statements under audit. However, review of the predecessor auditor's audit documentation may have an effect on the nature, timing and extent of those procedures.

[Revised, December 2012, to reflect conforming changes necessary due to the issuance of SAS Nos. 122–126.]

.06 Auditor Becomes Aware of Information During the Audit That Leads the Auditor to Believe That Financial Statements Reported On by a Predecessor Auditor Who Has Ceased Operations May Require Revision

Inquiry—Paragraph .12 of AU-C section 510 states that if the auditor becomes aware of information during the audit that leads the auditor to believe that financial statements reported on by the predecessor auditor may require revision, the auditor should request management to inform the predecessor auditor of the situation and arrange for the three parties to discuss the situation and attempt to resolve the matter. What actions may an auditor take when the auditor becomes aware of information during the audit that leads the auditor to believe that financial statements reported on by a predecessor auditor require revision when the predecessor auditor has ceased operations?

Reply—When the auditor becomes aware of information that leads the auditor to believe that the financial statements reported on by a predecessor auditor who has ceased operations may require revision, in accordance with paragraph .12 of AU-C section 510, the auditor should discuss the information with management and attempt to resolve the matter. In attempting to resolve the matter, the auditor may request that management inform the individual who had final responsibility for the audit of the financial statements reported on by the predecessor auditor (for example, the engagement partner) of the situation and arrange for that individual to discuss the information with the auditor and management. If it is determined that the financial statements require revision, the auditor may request that management disclose the information to the party responsible for winding up the affairs of the predecessor auditor. If the auditor is not satisfied with the resolution of the matter, in accordance with paragraph .13 of AU-C section 510, the auditor should evaluate (*a*) the implications on the current engagement and (*b*) whether to withdraw from the engagement or, when withdrawal is not possible under applicable law or regulation, disclaim an opinion on the financial statements. The auditor may decide to consult with legal counsel in determining an appropriate course of action.

[Revised, December 2012, to reflect conforming changes necessary due to the issuance of SAS Nos. 122–126.]

[.07] Reserved

[.08] Reserved

[.09] Reserved

.10 Successor Accountant Becomes Aware of Information During the Performance of a Compilation or Review That Leads the Successor Accountant to Believe That Financial Statements Reported On by a Predecessor Accountant Who Has Ceased Operations May Require Revision

Inquiry—Paragraph .10 of AR section 400, *Communications Between Predecessor and Successor Accountants* (AICPA, *Professional Standards*), provides guidance to a successor accountant who, during an engagement to compile or review current-period financial statements, becomes aware of information that leads him or her to believe that financial statements reported on by a predecessor accountant may require revision. Paragraph .10 of AR section 400 states that the successor accountant should request that his or her client communicate this information to the predecessor accountant. How may the successor accountant fulfill this responsibility when the predecessor accountant has ceased operations?

Reply—When the successor accountant becomes aware of information that leads him or her to believe that financial statements reported on by a predecessor accountant may require revision, the successor accountant should discuss the information with management. In attempting to resolve the matter, the successor accountant may request that management inform the individual who had final responsibility for the prior-period engagement (for example, the engagement partner) of the situation and arrange for that individual to discuss the information with management. If it is determined that the financial statements require revision, the successor accountant may request that management disclose the information to the party responsible for winding up the affairs of the predecessor accountant. If the successor accountant is not satisfied with the resolution of the matter, in accordance with paragraph .11 of AR section 400, the successor accountant should evaluate (*a*) possible implications for the current engagement and (*b*) whether to resign from the engagement. The successor accountant may decide to consult with legal counsel in determining an appropriate course of action.

[Revised, December 2012, to reflect conforming changes necessary due to the issuance of SAS Nos. 122–126.]

.11 Management Representations Regarding Prior Periods Presented That Were Audited by Predecessor Auditor

Inquiry—Paragraph .20 of AU-C section 580, *Written Representations* (AICPA, *Professional Standards*), requires that written representations be obtained for all financial statements and period(s) referred to in the auditor's report. Paragraph .52 of AU-C section 700A states that "as required by section 580, *Written Representations*, the auditor should request written representations for all periods referred to in the auditor's opinion."

The prior period financial statements were audited by a predecessor auditor, and the predecessor auditor's report on the prior period's financial statements is not reissued. The auditor's report will express an opinion on the current period's financial statements and will include an other-matter paragraph in accordance with paragraph .54 of AU-C section 700A. Is the auditor required to obtain a representation letter covering the prior period financial statements?

Reply—No. Written representations confirm audit evidence used by the auditor in arriving at the conclusions on which the auditor's opinion is based. Because the auditor is not opining on the prior year when making reference to the prior period that was audited by a predecessor auditor, the auditor is not required to obtain a representation letter covering the prior period financial statements.

However, the auditor may request current-year written representations with respect to audit work that the auditor performs relative to opening balances and may include written representations for such items as consistency in accounting policies, prior year internal control deficiencies, and matters relating to report modifications. Additional representations may be necessary in the current year's letter if the successor auditor discovers material misstatements in the prior year's financial statements; restatement is necessary; and the auditor audits the restatement adjustments.

[Issue Date: September 2014.]

Q&A Section 9000

AUDITORS' REPORTS

TABLE OF CONTENTS

Section

Section

Section

Q&A Section 9030
Accounting Changes

[.01] Reserved

[.02] Reserved

.03 Change in Service Lives of Fixed Assets

Inquiry—A reevaluation of the lives of depreciable property resulted in an increase in the remaining lives of certain properties. The company would like to include the cumulative, net of tax, effect of this change in income. Is this in accordance with generally accepted accounting principles?

Reply—Financial Accounting Standards Board (FASB) *Accounting Standards Codification* (ASC) 250, *Accounting Changes and Error Corrections*, is quite specific regarding the treatment of changes in estimated service lives of depreciable assets. Such a change is considered a change in an accounting estimate and should be recorded prospectively, that is, in the period of the change and future periods as appropriate. Therefore, the proposed accounting would not be in accordance with generally accepted accounting principles. If the change in service lives of depreciable property were accounted for as suggested, the independent auditors would have to issue a qualified or adverse opinion depending upon materiality of the item.

[Revised, June 2009, to reflect conforming changes necessary due to the issuance of FASB ASC.]

[.04] Reserved

[.05] Reserved

[.06] Reserved

[.07] Reserved

[.08] Reserved

[.09] Reserved

.10 Change From Generally Accepted Accounting Principles (GAAP) to a Special Purpose Framework or From a Special Purpose Framework to GAAP

Inquiry—A company that has previously issued financial statements prepared in accordance with GAAP has decided to change to the income tax basis (or vice versa). How should the change in accounting basis be accounted for and reported in the financial statements and how does the change impact the auditor's or accountant's report?

Reply—Accounting issues:

Authoritative literature does not address accounting for a change in accounting basis. FASB ASC 250 provides guidance for reporting accounting changes within the same basis. However, the situation described above is considered to be a change in accounting basis rather than an accounting change.

When only current year financial statements are presented, it is common practice to present the effect of the change in the accounting basis by showing beginning retained earnings as previously reported with an adjustment to convert to the new basis. Although not as common in practice, precedent also exists for either showing opening retained earnings on the new basis or showing the effects of the change as a cumulative-effect adjustment in the income statement.

However, if comparative financial statements are presented, the prior year(s) should be restated and presented under the basis to which the company has changed. Restatement is necessary to ensure comparability with all periods presented.

In both cases, the change in accounting basis should be disclosed in the notes to the financial statements.

—Reporting issues:

Auditing literature states that a change in accounting basis does not represent a lack of consistency and, consequently, that report modification is not required. However, the literature allows for the inclusion of an emphasis-of-matter paragraph in the auditor's report to emphasize a matter regarding the financial statements.

A summary of the relevant authoritative references follows:

Paragraph .A1 of AU-C section 708, *Consistency of Financial Statements* (AICPA, *Professional Standards*), indicates that the consistency reference in the auditor's report refers to consistent application of principles within a basis of presentation. The standards do not address the consistent use of a basis of presentation; therefore, a change in accounting basis does not require the auditor to modify the report for a lack of consistency.

Paragraph .06 of AU-C section 706, *Emphasis-of-Matter Paragraphs and Other-Matter Paragraphs in the Independent Auditor's Report* (AICPA, *Professional Standards*), indicates that an auditor should include an emphasis-of-matter paragraph in the auditor's report if the auditor considers it necessary to draw users' attention to a matter appropriately presented or disclosed in the financial statements that, in the auditor's professional judgment, is of such importance that it is fundamental to users' understanding of the financial statements.

A sample emphasis-of-matter paragraph for an audit report on comparative financial statements in the year of change to a special purpose framework follows:

(emphasis-of-matter paragraph)

> As discussed in Note A to the financial statements, in 20X4 the Company adopted a policy of preparing its financial statements on the accrual method of accounting used for federal income tax purposes, which is a comprehensive basis of accounting other than generally accepted accounting principles. Accordingly, the accompanying financial statements are not intended to present financial position and results of operations in accordance with accounting principles generally accepted in the United States of America. The financial statements for 20X3 have been restated to reflect the income tax basis of accounting accrual method adopted in 20X4.

Accountants performing review or compilation engagements may also consider adding an explanatory paragraph for these basis changes.

[Amended, February 1995; Revised, June 2009, to reflect conforming changes necessary due to the issuance of FASB ASC; Revised, December 2012, to reflect conforming changes necessary due to the issuance of SAS Nos. 122–126.]

[.11] Reserved

[.12] Reserved

Q&A Section 9060
Uncertainties

[.01] Reserved

[.02] Reserved

[.03] Reserved

[.04] Reserved

[.05] Reserved

.06 Possible Effect of Divorce Proceedings on Credit Rating

Inquiry—A client and his wife who are co-owners and co-managers of a business are involved in divorce proceedings. The auditor believes a divorce will adversely affect the business's credit rating. Is it necessary to include a reference in the financial statements to the divorce proceedings and their potentially adverse effects?

Reply—The auditor should not include references in his report to currently litigated divorce proceedings. The independent auditor should refrain from mentioning the client's involvements of a personal nature which might effectively disparage (or even stimulate the slander of) his business reputation or credit standing. It is possible that a divorce settlement could adversely affect the credit standing of the client, but in the absence of a final determination of the litigation or a determinative event which directly affects the financial condition of the entity under audit, the rule of informative disclosure does not compel the independent accountant to contribute in advance to a possible adverse effect on the client's credit standing.

[.07] Reserved

.08 Going Concern Problem—Financial Statements Prepared on the Income Tax Basis of Accounting

Inquiry—A client prepares its financial statements on the income tax basis of accounting. The client is experiencing financial difficulties and its ability to continue as a going concern is questionable. Since the financial statements are prepared on a special purpose framework, is the CPA's audit report required to include an emphasis-of-matter paragraph that refers to this uncertainty?

Reply—Yes. AU-C section 570A, *The Auditor's Consideration of an Entity's Ability to Continue as a Going Concern* (AICPA, *Professional Standards*), applies to all audits of financial statements, regardless of whether the financial statements are prepared in accordance with a general purpose or a special purpose framework. Therefore, when the auditor concludes that there is substantial doubt about the entity's ability to continue as a going concern for a reasonable period, regardless of whether the financial statements are prepared in accordance with a general purpose or a special purpose framework, the auditor should include an emphasis-of-matter paragraph (following the opinion paragraph) to reflect that conclusion.

[Revised, December 2012, to reflect conforming changes necessary due to the issuance of SAS Nos. 122–126.]

.09 Audit Report for Development Stage Enterprise

Inquiry—Is an emphasis-of-matter paragraph in the auditor's report for a going concern uncertainty always required for a development stage enterprise because there is doubt as to recovery of costs from future operations?

Reply—No. A going concern uncertainty does not automatically arise because an enterprise is in the development stage. In accordance with AU-C section 570A, the auditor should consider whether the results of the procedures performed during the course of the audit identify conditions or events that, when considered in the aggregate, indicate there could be substantial doubt about the entity's ability to continue as a going concern for a reasonable period of time. If such conditions or events are identified, the auditor should obtain information about management's plans that are intended to mitigate the adverse effects of such conditions or events, and assess whether it is likely that such plans can be effectively implemented.

If the auditor concludes that substantial doubt about the entity's ability to continue as a going concern for one year after the balance sheet date remains after considering conditions or events and management's plans, the going concern issue should be adequately disclosed in the financial statements, and the auditor's report should include an emphasis-of-matter paragraph to reflect this conclusion.

[Revised, December 2012, to reflect conforming changes necessary due to the issuance of SAS Nos. 122–126.]

Q&A Section 9070

Subsequent Events

> ***Note:*** Additional Questions and Answers on subsequent events can be found in section 8700, *Subsequent Events*.

.01 Failure to Remit Withholding Taxes in Subsequent Period

Inquiry—In the course of an examination of the financial statements, the auditor has discovered that in the period subsequent to the balance sheet date the company has not remitted to the appropriate agencies the taxes currently withheld from employees' wages. Assuming the amount is material, is it necessary that this matter be disclosed in the auditor's report?

Reply—Paragraph .02 of AU-C section 560, *Subsequent Events and Subsequently Discovered Facts* (AICPA, *Professional Standards*), states, in part

> Financial statements may be affected by certain events that occur after the date of the financial statements...financial reporting frameworks ordinarily identify two types of events:
>
> *a.* Those that provide evidence of conditions that existed at the date of the financial statements
>
> *b.* Those that provide evidence of conditions that arose after the date of the financial statements

The auditor's objective is to determine whether events occurring between the date of the financial statements and the date of auditor's report that require adjustment of, or disclosure in, the financial statements have been identified and are appropriately reflected in the financial statements. Even if it is determined that the financial statements are not directly affected, it is possible that the situation indicated future serious difficulties that might require disclosures.

If the delinquent obligations are not evidence of serious financial difficulties, there usually would be no reason why obligations incurred subsequent to the balance sheet date need be reported in financial statements as of such date. In such a case, it should be expected that the delinquent payments will soon be remitted.

[Revised, December 2012, to reflect conforming changes necessary due to the issuance of SAS Nos. 122–126.]

.02 Disclosure of Note Receivable Covering Previous Account of Bankrupt Company

Inquiry—Company A reports on a fiscal year ending January 31. Company A's accounts receivable include a material amount due from a bankrupt company. To avoid legal action, several individuals formed a new company. The new company and the individuals signed a note which would pay the accounts receivable of the bankrupt company over a three year period. The note was signed on March 1, subsequent to the balance sheet date. Should the note receivable, assumed to be collectible, be presented in the balance sheet at January 31?

Reply—AU-C section 560 and Financial Accounting Standards Board (FASB) *Accounting Standards Codification* (ASC) 855, *Subsequent Events*, deal with subsequent events. Paragraph 1 of FASB ASC 855-10-55 states, in part

> Subsequent events affecting the realization of assets, such as receivables and inventories or the settlement of estimated liabilities, should be recognized in the financial statements when those events represent the culmination of conditions that existed over a relatively long period of time.

Accordingly, the accounts receivable should be reported as a note receivable at January 31, with adequate disclosure of the financial arrangements made after the balance sheet date.

[Revised, December 2012, to reflect conforming changes necessary due to the issuance of SAS Nos. 122–126.]

.03 Discovery of Potential Liability in Subsequent Period

Inquiry—In the period subsequent to the balance sheet date, the auditors discovered that an employee of the client had used a company purchase order to obtain merchandise for his personal business. This transaction resulted in a material potential liability of the client. Negotiations with the creditor ensued and the client's attorney was successful in securing a complete release from any obligation on the part of the client.

Is it necessary to disclose this matter on the client's financial statements?

Reply—According to paragraph .02 of AU section 560, the resolution of this matter appears to constitute a subsequent event which is evidence of a condition that existed at the balance sheet date, but since no transaction in fact occurred which involved the client, it is not necessary to disclose the matter in the financial statements. However, a condition which did affect the client and which did exist at the balance sheet date is the future legal costs of settling the matter. Provisions for these costs (if they are material) should be made on the financial statements, and the reasons for incurring these costs should be disclosed.

[Revised, December 2012, to reflect conforming changes necessary due to the issuance of SAS Nos. 122–126.]

[.04] Reserved

.05 Consideration of Impact of Losses From Natural Disasters Occurring After Completion of Audit Field Work and Signing of the Auditor's Report But Before Issuance of the Auditor's Report and Related Financial Statements

Inquiry—An auditor completes the field work with respect to an audit of financial statements, performs all of the post-field work procedures required by the firm's quality control standards and signs the audit report but does not immediately issue the auditor's report and the related financial statements to the client. During the period that the report was signed but not issued, the client suffers a significant loss due to a natural disaster. What are the auditor's responsibilities with respect to consideration of a material subsequent event that occurs after completion of field work and after the signing of the auditor's report but before issuance of the auditor's report and the audited financial statements?

Reply—AU-C section 560 defines *subsequent events* as events occurring between the date of the financial statements and the date of the auditor's report. Paragraph .12 of AU-C section 560 states that the auditor is not required to perform any audit procedures regarding the financial statements after the date of the auditor's report. However, if a subsequently discovered fact becomes known to the auditor after the report release date, the auditor is required to perform certain procedures. Paragraph .02 of AU-C section 560 indicates that there are two types of events: (*a*) those that provide evidence of conditions that existed at the date of the financial statements, and (*b*) those that provide evidence of conditions that arose after the date of the financial statements.

A loss from a natural disaster occurring after year end would be considered the second type subsequent event. These events should not result in an adjustment to the financial statements. Some of these events, however, may be of such a nature that disclosure of them is required to keep the financial statements from being misleading. In addition, the auditor should always remember that the financial statements belong to the client and the client may wish to disclose the event in the notes to the financial statements even if not required to do so.

Management and the auditor should consider whether a subsequent event that provides evidence of conditions that arose after the date of the financial statements would be of such a nature that disclosure of the event is necessary in order to keep the financial statements from being misleading. Management and the auditor should also consider whether the event affects the entity's ability to continue as a going concern.

For example, if the auditee owns a major distribution center in an area that is declared a disaster area by a local, state, or federal government due to natural disaster (e.g. hurricane, earthquake, tornado), management and the auditor should assess the damage done to that asset and the impact on the entity's current and future operations and determine whether disclosure of the impact of the disaster is required to keep the financial statements from being misleading. Occasionally such an event may be so significant that disclosure can best be made by supplementing the historical financial statements with pro forma financial data giving effect to the event as if it had occurred on the date of the balance sheet. It may be desirable to present pro forma statements, usually a balance sheet only, in columnar form on the face of the historical statements.

The auditor may conclude that the event has such a material impact on the entity that it would be appropriate to include an emphasis of matter paragraph in the auditor's report directing the reader's attention to the event and its effects. As paragraph .06 of AU-C section 706, *Emphasis-of-Matter and Other-Matter Paragraphs in the Independent Auditor's Report* (AICPA, *Professional Standards*), notes, emphasis-of-matter paragraphs are included in the auditor's report if the auditor considers it necessary to draw users' attention to a matter appropriately presented or disclosed in the financial statements that, in the auditor's professional judgment, is of such importance that it is fundamental to users' understanding of the financial statements.

If the auditor concludes that the effects of the disaster are such that substantial doubt exists as to the entity's ability to continue as a going concern for a reasonable period of time, the auditor should include an emphasis-of-matter paragraph (following the opinion paragraph) to reflect that conclusion. Paragraph .A6 of AU-C section 570A, *The Auditor's Consideration of an Entity's*

Ability to Continue as a Going Concern (AICPA, *Professional Standards*), provides an example of such an emphasis-of-matter paragraph.

[Revised, December 2012, to reflect conforming changes necessary due to the issuance of SAS Nos. 122–126.]

.06 Decline in Market Value of Assets Subsequent to the Balance Sheet Date

Inquiry—In light of overall market decline, should the decline in market value of an asset subsequent to the balance sheet date result in the adjustment of the financial statements?

Reply—FASB ASC 855-10-25-1 states that "[a]n entity shall recognize in the financial statements the effects of all subsequent events that provide additional evidence about conditions that existed at the date of the balance sheet, including the estimates inherent in the process of preparing financial statements."

FASB ASC 855-10-25-3 states that "[a]n entity shall not recognize subsequent events that provide evidence about conditions that did not exist at the date of the balance sheet but arose after the balance sheet date but before financial statements are issued or are available to be issued."

FASB ASC 855-10-55-2 provides a list of examples of nonrecognized subsequent events, including changes in the fair value of assets or liabilities (financial or nonfinancial) after the balance sheet date but before financial statements are issued or are available to be issued.

[Issue Date: May 2010.]

Q&A Section 9080

Audited Financial Statements

[.01] Reserved

.02 Going Concern Assumption for Venture With Limited Life

Inquiry—A corporation has recently been organized with the sole purpose of constructing a shopping center which will take several years to complete, after which the company will be liquidated. The company uses the completed contract method to recognize income and will have only one operating cycle.

Should there be an emphasis-of-matter paragraph in the auditor's report now or near the final years of operations on the assumption that after a certain fixed period it will no longer be a "going concern"?

Reply—AU-C section 570A, *The Auditor's Consideration of an Entity's Ability to Continue as a Going Concern* (AICPA, *Professional Standards*), requires that an emphasis-of-matter paragraph (following the opinion paragraph) be included in the audit report when the auditor concludes that substantial doubt about the entity's ability to continue as a going concern for a reasonable period of time remains. A *reasonable period of time* is defined as "a period of time not to exceed one year beyond the date of the financial statements being audited." Therefore, when the auditor has substantial doubt that the corporation will continue as a going concern for one year from the date of the financial statements under audit, an emphasis-of-matter paragraph (following the opinion paragraph) reflecting that conclusion should be included in the audit report.

However, if the corporation has presented its financial statements on the assumption of liquidation, AU-C section 570A does not apply and therefore an emphasis-of-matter paragraph reflecting the auditor's conclusion that substantial doubt exists about the corporation's ability to continue as a going concern is not necessary.

[Revised, December 2012, to reflect conforming changes necessary due to the issuance of SAS Nos. 122–126.]

.03 Opinion on Balance Sheet Only

Inquiry—Occasionally, a client will request from a CPA only an audited balance sheet with footnotes even though the CPA has examined and reported on all the financial statements. The usual purpose of this statement is for presentation by the client to a supplier for securing credit.

How may the CPA comply with the client's request while remaining in compliance with the reporting requirements in AU-C section 700, *Forming an Opinion and Reporting on Financial Statements* (AICPA, *Professional Standards*)?

Reply—AU-C sections 200–700 apply in an audit of financial statements and are to be adapted as necessary in the circumstances when applied to audits of other historical financial information. AU-C section 805, *Special Considerations—Audits of Single Financial Statements and Specific Elements, Accounts, or Items of a Financial Statement* (AICPA, *Professional Standards*), addresses special consideration in the application of those AU-C sections to an audit of a single financial statement. Examples of an auditor's report on a single financial statement can be found in illustrations 1–2 of the exhibit to AU-C section 805.

[Revised, June 2009, to reflect conforming changes necessary due to the issuance of FASB ASC; Revised, December 2012, to reflect conforming changes necessary due to the issuance of SAS Nos. 122–126.]

.04 Opinion on Balance Sheet With Disclaimer on Income Statement

Inquiry—A CPA firm has been engaged to perform the initial audit of a company. Since the firm did not observe the inventory taking at the beginning of the period and it is not practicable for it to satisfy itself by other means as to the beginning inventory, the firm plans to issue an opinion only on the balance sheet and disclaim an opinion on the income statement. Would this be in accordance with paragraphs .11 and .15 of AU-C section 705, *Modifications to the Opinion in the Independent Auditor's Report* (AICPA, *Professional Standards*)?

Reply—Paragraph .11 of AU-C section 705 addresses scope limitations imposed by management after the engagement has been accepted, and does not apply when the scope limitation arises from circumstances relating to the timing of the auditor's work, such as the inability to observe beginning inventory in an initial audit.

Paragraph .15 of AU-C section 705 states, in part, that "when the auditor considers it necessary to …disclaim an opinion on the financial statements as a whole, the auditor's report should not also include an unmodified opinion with respect to the same financial reporting framework on a single financial statements…" Paragraph .A17 of AU-C section 705 addresses initial audits and states "[i]n an initial audit, it is acceptable for the auditor to express an unmodified opinion regarding financial position and disclaim an opinion regarding the results of operations and cash flows, when relevant. In this case, the auditor has not disclaimed an opinion on the financial statements as a whole." An example of such an auditor's report can be found in illustration 8 of the exhibit to AU-C section 705.

[Revised, December 2012, to reflect conforming changes necessary due to the issuance of SAS Nos. 122–126.]

[.05] Reserved

.06 Reference in Financial Statements to Auditor's Report

Inquiry—Audited financial statements often contain a note such as:

> The accompanying notes are an integral part of this financial statement.

or a note sometimes reads

> The accompanying notes and auditor's report are an integral part of this financial statement.

The only difference between the two notes is the inclusion of the phrase, "and auditor's report." Is a reference to the auditor's report necessary?

Reply—Paragraph .04 of AU-C section 200, *Overall Objectives of the Independent Auditor and the Conduct of an Audit in Accordance With Generally Accepted Auditing Standards* (AICPA, *Professional Standards*), states, in part, "…an audit in accordance with GAAS is conducted on the premise that management and, when appropriate, those charged with governance, have acknowledged certain responsibilities that are fundamental to the conduct of an audit."

These responsibilities are defined as including the responsibility for the preparation and fair presentation of the financial statements. Therefore, the auditor's report cannot be an integral part of the financial statements, and it is inappropriate to include it by reference.

[Revised, December 2012, to reflect conforming changes necessary due to the issuance of SAS Nos. 122–126.]

[.07] Reserved

[.08] Reserved

.09 Arrangement of References to Financial Statements in Auditor's Report

Inquiry—The examples of auditor's opinions in the Statements on Auditing Standards all seem to refer to the statement of financial position first, followed by the statement of results of operations, and finally the statement of cash flows. Is it necessary that the financial statements be presented in this order and the statements be referred to in the auditor's report in this order?

Reply—The order in which the financial statements are referred to in the independent auditor's report need not follow the order in which the statements are physically arranged. The illustrative standard report such as shown in the exhibit of AU-C section 700 can be used regardless of the order in which the financial statements are presented.

[Revised, December 2012, to reflect conforming changes necessary due to the issuance of SAS Nos. 122–126.]

[.10] Reserved

[.11] Reserved

[.12] Reserved

.13 Classification of Certain Callable Obligations

Inquiry—In some situations in which there is a violation of a debt agreement that makes a long-term obligation callable, management continues to classify the obligation as long-term because it asserts that it is probable that the violation will be cured during the grace period, while the auditor does not agree with that assertion. In such a situation, does an uncertainty exist that might cause the auditor to add an other-matter paragraph (after the opinion paragraph) to his report?

Reply—No. Financial Accounting Standards Board (FASB) *Accounting Standards Codification* (ASC) 470-10-45-12 requires that long-term obligations be classified as current liabilities if they are, or will be, callable because of the debtor's violation of a provision of the debt agreement unless certain conditions are met. These conditions occur when (1) the creditor waives or loses the right to demand payment for more than one year from the balance sheet date or (2) it is probable that the violation will be cured within the grace period specified in the loan agreement.

The circumstances described above do not constitute an uncertainty as described in AU-C section 705 because they do not involve matters in which the outcome and related audit evidence are prospective (paragraph .A13 of AU-C section 705). If the auditor, on the basis of available evidence, disagrees with management's assertion, a qualified or adverse opinion because of a departure from generally accepted accounting principles should be considered.

[Revised, June 2009, to reflect conforming changes necessary due to the issuance of FASB ASC; Revised, December 2012, to reflect conforming changes necessary due to the issuance of SAS Nos. 122–126.]

[.14] Reserved

.15 Condensed Financial Statements of a Nonpublic Entity

Inquiry—A client prepares condensed financial statements that name the auditor and state that they have been derived from audited financial statements. The condensed statements incorporate the audited financial statements by reference and indicate such statements and auditor's report thereon may be obtained. Is the auditor required to report on the condensed financial statements?

Reply—Paragraph .28 of AU-C section 810, *Engagements to Report on Summary Financial Statements* (AICPA, *Professional Standards*), states that if the auditor becomes aware that the entity plans to make a statement in a document that refers to the auditor and the fact that summary financial statements are derived from the financial statements audited by the auditor, the auditor should be satisfied that

a. the reference to the auditor is made in the context of the auditor's report on the audited financial statements; and

b. the statement does not give the impression that the auditor has reported on the summary financial statements.

If these conditions are met, the auditor need not do anything further. If these conditions are not met, the auditor should request management to change the statement or delete the reference to the auditor's report. Alternatively, the entity may engage the auditor to report on the summary financial statements.

[Revised, December 2012, to reflect conforming changes necessary due to the issuance of SAS Nos. 122–126.]

Q&A Section 9100
Signing and Dating Reports

.01 Use of Successor Firm Name in Signing Registration Statement

Inquiry—A CPA firm has been requested to provide an opinion on the consolidated financial statements of a client covering a five-year period. During this five-year period, the CPA firm has undergone several changes in its organization and its name:

1. Opinions for the first two years were issued by John Doe & Co.
2. In the third year, the accounting practice merged with another firm and the opinions for years three and four were signed by Doe, Roe & Co. Primary responsibility for the client was retained by the partners of John Doe & Co.
3. This partnership was later dissolved and the opinion in year five was signed by John Doe & Co., who, under the dissolution agreement, retained the working papers for this client.

Since it is impracticable to obtain the consent of each partner of the dissolved partnership, may the opinion on the five-year statements be issued by John Doe & Co.?

Reply—This situation is discussed in paragraph .A46 of AU-C section 700A, *Forming an Opinion and Reporting on Financial Statements* (AICPA, *Professional Standards*). Since the partners of John Doe & Co., as it presently exists, retained primary responsibility for the publicly held company in question during the merger period, and since the firm is a successor in interest to the engagement and has retained all working papers for this client, it appears that, after consideration of these circumstances, the statements of consolidated income for the five-year period may be released solely in the name of John Doe & Co.

[Revised, December 2012, to reflect conforming changes necessary due to the issuance of SAS Nos. 122–126.]

.02 Reporting on Companies With Different Fiscal Years

Inquiry—A CPA has a client whose fiscal year ends on June 30. A parent company of this client now wishes to go public and must file consolidated financial statements with the SEC. The parent company, however, observes a fiscal year ending on December 31.

The CPA has been asked by the parent to provide financial statements with an auditor's opinion for the year ending December 31, 20X3. To do this, the auditor needs to assemble figures for the period January 1, 20X3, to June 30, 20X3, from the financial statements for the year ended June 30, 20X3, and figures for the period July 1, 20X3, to December 31, 20X3, from the financial statements for the year ended June 30, 20X4.

The CPA has been having difficulty in segregating the financial information into these six-month periods because of the condition of the accounting records. Furthermore, the inventories were not observed nor were the receivables confirmed at the December 31 dates.

Under these conditions, should the CPA express his opinion for the year ended June 30, 20X3, and disclaim an opinion for the six months ended December 31, 20X3?

Reply—In order for an auditor to express an opinion on financial statements for prior periods, it is generally not necessary to observe all audit procedures required for the most recent financial statements. Paragraphs .A9–.A11 of AU-C section 705, *Modifications to the Opinion in the Independent Auditor's Report* (AICPA, *Professional Standards*), indicate that an inability to perform a specific procedure, such as observation of inventories, does not constitute a limitation on the scope of an audit if the auditor is able to obtain sufficient appropriate audit evidence by performing alternative procedures.

Generally, if the client's records are reasonably well kept and the auditor has satisfied himself as to year-end financial statements, review of ratios of sales to cost of sales and determination that accruals have been properly recognized at the interim date will enable an auditor to satisfy himself that the financial statements at an intervening interim date are fairly presented. On the other hand, if no perpetual inventory records are kept and if the client has not prepared inventories as of the interim date, it may not be practicable to reconstruct such inventory, and a disclaimer of opinion should be expressed on the reconstructed statements. In such circumstances, it would appear necessary that the auditor indicate in a basis for disclaimer paragraph that, due to the fact that he was not engaged to make an audit of financial statements as of such date until June 30, 20X4, he was not in a position to observe the amount of inventory at such date and is unable to satisfy himself thereto by the application of other auditing procedures. If this be the case, the SEC would probably be willing to accept combined income statements based on statements of the subsidiary company as of a date six months different than the parent and to accept unconsolidated balance sheets, with the balance sheet of the subsidiary being presented as of its appropriate year-end. The absence of correspondence with debtors and creditors would probably not cause similar problems.

[Revised, December 2012, to reflect conforming changes necessary due to the issuance of SAS Nos. 122–126.]

[.03] Reserved

[.04] Reserved

.05 Signing of Independent Auditor's Report

Inquiry—Should the independent auditor's report be manually signed?

Reply—Paragraph .39 of AU-C section 700 states that the auditor's report should include the manual or printed signature of the auditor's firm.

Although AU-C section 700 does not require a manual signature, Department of Labor and Securities and Exchange Commission regulations require manual signatures in certain circumstances.

[Revised, December 2012, to reflect conforming changes necessary due to the issuance of SAS Nos. 122–126.]

.06 The Effect of Obtaining the Management Representation Letter on Dating the Auditor's Report

Inquiry—AU-C section 580, *Written Representations* (AICPA, *Professional Standards*), establishes a requirement that the auditor request written representations from management as part of an audit of financial statements performed in accordance with generally accepted auditing standards. Additionally, paragraph .41 of AU-C section 700 states that the auditor's report should be dated no earlier than the date on which the auditor has obtained sufficient appropriate audit evidence on which to base the auditor's opinion. Among other things, sufficient appropriate audit evidence includes evidence that the audit documentation has been reviewed, and that the entity's financial statements, including the related notes, have been prepared and that management has asserted that it has taken responsibility for them. Is the auditor required to have the signed management representation in hand as of the date of the auditor's report?

Reply—Paragraph .A27 of AU-C section 580 addresses this issue and states that occasionally, circumstances may prevent management from signing the representation letter and returning it to the auditor on the date of the auditor's report. In those circumstances, the auditor may accept management's oral confirmation, on or before the date of the auditor's report, that management has reviewed the final representation letter and will sign the representation letter without exception as of the date of the auditor's report thereby providing sufficient appropriate audit evidence for the auditor to date the report. However, possession of the signed management representation letter prior to releasing the auditor's report is necessary because paragraph .21 of AU-C section 580 requires that the representations be in the form of a written letter from management. Furthermore, when there are delays in releasing the report, a fact may become known to the auditor that, had it been known to the auditor at the date of the auditor's report, might affect the auditor's report and result in the need for updated representations. AU-C section 560, *Subsequent Events and Subsequently Discovered Facts* (AICPA, *Professional Standards*), addresses the auditor's responsibilities in such circumstances.

[Revised, December 2012, to reflect conforming changes necessary due to the issuance of SAS Nos. 122–126.]

.07 Naming the City and State Where the Auditor Practices

Inquiry—Paragraph .40 of AU-C section 700 states that the auditor's report should "name the city and state where the auditor practices." May the auditor comply with this requirement by issuing his or her report on the firm's letterhead that contains the city and state where the auditor practices?

Reply—Yes. The city and state where the auditor practices is not required to be placed under the auditor's signature and may be named in the firm's letterhead on which the report is issued.

[Issue Date: February 2013.]

.08 Audit Firm With Multiple Offices on Their Company Letterhead and Effect on Report

Inquiry—According to paragraph .40 of AU-C section 700, the auditor's report should name the city and state where the auditor practices. If an auditor's letterhead denotes multiple office locations, has this requirement been met by issuing the report on the firm's letterhead?

Reply—No. If the firm's letterhead includes multiple office locations, it will not be clear which location is the issuing office, and, therefore, the auditor would need to indicate the city and state where the auditor practices in the auditor's report.

[Issue Date: June 2013.]

Q&A Section 9110

Special Reports

.01 Determination of Sales Price Based on Auditor's Report

Inquiry—A CPA has been designated by a contract of sales to prepare a statement of "net current assets" and a statement of net income of the selling firm. Both are elements in the determination of the sales price.

A disagreement has arisen between the seller and the buyer as to the pricing of the inventory which represents the major portion of the "net current assets." The seller relies on a formula represented as "heretofore agreed . . . ." The buyer demands a formula "based upon good accounting practice."

The CPA believes he may have to submit two inventory values to comply with the contract provisions—one to describe the "net current assets" which will use the formula set forth in the contract, and a second using the normal pricing methods of prior years. There is a major variation between the two. The formula in the contract was not represented as being based on good accounting methods but was developed by management after the date of their latest audit.

Can the CPA express an unmodified opinion on each of the two statements if different price bases are used provided full disclosure is made?

Reply—This is a special report situation and these are special circumstances in which the auditor may have a certain reporting latitude he might not otherwise have. Since seller and buyer were both parties to the contract, the CPA was designated by the contract to prepare specified statements, and the contract apparently describes a special formula to be used in pricing inventories, the CPA would ordinarily perform strictly according to the terms of the engagement and report on one set of statements as being fairly presented or correctly presented in accordance with the specified contractual formula.

However, since the CPA is aware of the basic disagreement between seller and buyer, he might be much more helpful towards ultimately resolving the issue if he were to prepare statements on both bases.

The auditor may properly report on the two statements prepared in accordance with different inventory pricing bases, full disclosure, of course, being assumed. A more significant question, under the circumstances, is whether he has (or can obtain) consent from both parties modifying the terms of the engagement to allow preparation of the statements on a dual basis.

[Revised, December 2012, to reflect conforming changes necessary due to the issuance of SAS Nos. 122–126.]

[.02] Reserved

.03 Audit of Sales for Percentage-of-Sales Lease Agreements

Inquiry—Tenants' lease agreements with a large shopping center provide for a minimum annual rental plus a percentage rent for sales in excess of a certain dollar amount. In accordance with the leases, the shopping center has engaged the services of a CPA to verify that sales exceeding the specified minimum base are being reported. If the CPA is satisfied that the internal control of a tenant is good, may he or she rely on copies of sales tax returns filed with the state as sufficient evidence for his examination? Is any further verification necessary if a tenant submits a written confirmation of its annual sales from its CPA?

Reply—The degree of reliance which the auditor can place on the work of a tenant's CPA will depend upon many considerations such as those described in AU-C section 600, *Special Considerations—Audits of Group Financial Statements (Including the Work of Component Auditors)* (AICPA, *Professional Standards*). Comparison of the sales figure reported to the client with the figure reported on the tenant's sales tax return would not in itself be sufficient verification, and additional procedures will be necessary.

An audit program suitable for determining the annual sales of the tenants will have to be highly flexible. Flexibility is required so as to enable the field auditors involved to adjust the audit procedures employed from store to store, as dictated by changes in types of merchandise sold, selling policies employed, sufficiency of records maintained, adequacy of internal control, etc. Accordingly, the depth of the examination will vary to some extent with almost every tenant audited.

Procedures might include examining weekly cash reports submitted by store managers and comparing these reports with general ledger entries, bank statements, and state and federal tax returns, and test checking consecutively numbered sales invoices.

Perhaps the most important documents to play a role in such an examination of the tenants' sales will be the lease agreements which provide the very basis for such examination and which may well contain restrictions on the number and type of records and reports that each tenant will be required to make available.

[Revised, December 2012, to reflect conforming changes necessary due to the issuance of SAS Nos. 122–126.]

[.04] Reserved

[.05] Reserved

[.06] Reserved

.07 Statement of Cash Receipts and Disbursements

Inquiry—What is the appropriate language for audit, review, and compilation reports on a statement of cash receipts and disbursements?

Reply—Report language will vary depending on the level of service performed. A statement of cash receipts and disbursements is a financial statement prepared in accordance with a special purpose framework (see paragraph .07 of AU-C section 800, *Special Considerations—Audits of Financial Statements Prepared in Accordance With Special Purpose Frameworks* [AICPA, *Professional Standards*]), also referred to as an other comprehensive basis of accounting (see paragraph .04 of AR section 60, *Framework for Performing and Reporting on Compilation and Review Engagements* [AICPA, *Professional Standards*]). It is a pure cash-basis financial statement that summarizes cash activity of the entity, including the individual sources and uses of cash, and may be the only financial statement prepared for the period.

Audit reports on this financial statement should contain an emphasis-of-matter paragraph that states the cash receipts and disbursements basis of accounting is being used and that it represents a basis of accounting other than accounting principles generally accepted in the United States of America (see paragraph .19 of AU-C section 800). This extra paragraph is not required for full-disclosure compilation and review reports.

Illustrations of audit, review, and compilation reports on statements of cash receipts and disbursements follow:

A) *Audit*

We have audited the accompanying financial statements of ABC Partnership, which comprise the statement of assets and liabilities arising from cash transactions as of December 31, 20X1, and the related statement of revenue collected and expenses paid for the year then ended, and the related notes to the financial statements.

Management's Responsibility for the Financial Statements

Management is responsible for the preparation and fair presentation of these financial statements in accordance with the cash basis of accounting described in Note X; this includes determining that the cash basis of accounting is an acceptable basis for the preparation of the financial statements in the circumstances. Management is also responsible for the design, implementation, and maintenance of internal control relevant to the preparation and fair presentation of financial statements that are free from material misstatement, whether due to fraud or error.

Auditor's Responsibility

Our responsibility is to express an opinion on these financial statements based on our audit. We conducted our audit in accordance with auditing standards generally accepted in the United States of America. Those standards require that we plan and perform the audit to obtain reasonable assurance about whether the financial statements are free from material misstatement.

An audit involves performing procedures to obtain audit evidence about the amounts and disclosures in the financial statements. The procedures selected depend on the auditor's judgment, including the assessment of the risks of material misstatement of the financial statements, whether due to fraud or error. In making those risk assessments, the auditor considers internal control relevant to the partnership's preparation and fair presentation of the financial statements in order to design audit procedures that are appropriate in the circumstances, but not for the purpose of expressing an opinion on the effectiveness of the partnership's internal control. Accordingly, we express no such opinion. An audit also includes evaluating the appropriateness of accounting policies used and the reasonableness of significant accounting estimates made by management, as well as evaluating the overall presentation of the financial statements.

We believe that the audit evidence we have obtained is sufficient and appropriate to provide a basis for our audit opinion.

Opinion

In our opinion, the financial statements referred to above present fairly, in all material respects, the assets and liabilities arising from cash transactions of ABC Partnership as of December 31, 20X1, and its revenue collected and expenses paid during the year then ended in accordance with the cash basis of accounting described in Note X.

Basis of Accounting

We draw attention to Note X of the financial statements, which describes the basis of accounting. The financial statements are prepared on the cash basis of accounting, which is a basis of accounting other than accounting principles generally accepted in the United States of America. Our opinion is not modified with respect to this matter.

B) *Review*

I (We) have reviewed the accompanying statements of cash receipts and disbursements of XYZ Company for the years ended December 31, 20X2, and 20X1. A review included primarily applying analytical procedures to management (owners') financial data and making inquiries of company management (owners). A review is substantially less in scope than an audit, the objective of which is the expression of an opinion regarding the financial statements as a whole. Accordingly, I (we) do not express such an opinion. Management (owners) is (are) responsible for the preparation and fair presentation of the financial statements in accordance with cash receipts and disbursements basis of accounting described in Note X and for designing, implementing, and maintaining internal control relevant to the preparation and fair presentation of the financial statements.

My (our) responsibility is to conduct the review in accordance with Statements on Standards for Accounting and Review Services issued by the American Institute of Certified Public Accountants. Those standards require me (us) to perform procedures to obtain limited assurance that there are no material modifications that should be made to the financial statements. I (We) believe that the results of my (our) procedures provide a reasonable basis for our report.

Based on my (our) review, I am (we are) not aware of any material modifications that should be made to the accompanying financial statements in order for them to be in conformity with the cash receipts and disbursements basis of accounting described in Note X.

C) *Compilation With Full Disclosure*

I (We) have compiled the accompanying statements of cash receipts and disbursements of XYZ Company for the years ended December 31, 20X2, and 20X1. I (we) have not audited or reviewed the accompanying financial statements and, accordingly, do not express an opinion or provide any assurance about whether the financial statements are in accordance with the cash receipts and disbursements basis of accounting described in Note X.

Management (owners) is (are) responsible for the preparation and fair presentation of the financial statements in accordance with the cash receipts and disbursements basis of accounting described in Note X and for designing, implementing, and maintaining internal control relevant to the preparation and fair presentation of the financial statements.

My (our) responsibility is to conduct the compilation in accordance with Statements on Standards for Accounting and Review Services issued by the American Institute of Certified Public Accountants. The objective of a compilation is to assist management in presenting financial information in the form of financial statements without undertaking to obtain or provide any assurance that there are no material modifications that should be made to the financial statements.

D) *Compilation With Substantially All Disclosures Omitted Including Disclosure of the Basis of Accounting Used*

I (We) have compiled the accompanying statements of cash receipts and disbursements of XYZ Company for the years ended December 31, 20X2, and 20X1. I (we) have not audited or reviewed the accompanying financial statements and, accordingly, do not express an opinion or provide any assurance about whether the financial statements are in accordance with the cash receipts and disbursements basis of accounting.

Management (owners) is (are) responsible for the preparation and fair presentation of the financial statements in accordance with the cash receipts and disbursements basis of accounting and for designing, implementing, and maintaining internal control relevant to the preparation and fair presentation of the financial statements.

My (our) responsibility is to conduct the compilation in accordance with Statements on Standards for Accounting and Review Services issued by the American Institute of Certified Public Accountants. The objective of a compilation is to assist management in presenting financial information in the form of financial statements without undertaking to obtain or provide any assurance that there are no material modifications that should be made to the financial statements.

Management has elected to omit substantially all of the informative disclosures ordinarily included in financial statements prepared on the cash receipts and disbursements basis of accounting. If the omitted disclosures were included in the financial statements, they might influence the user's conclusion about the Company's cash receipts and disbursements. Accordingly, these financial statements are not designed for those who are not informed about such matters.

[Amended, February 1995; Revised, June 2009, to reflect conforming changes necessary due to the issuance of recent authoritative literature; Revised, December 2010, to reflect conforming changes necessary due to the issuance of SSARS No. 19; Revised, December 2012, to reflect conforming changes necessary due to the issuance of SAS Nos. 122–126.]

.08 Statutory Basis Financial Statements Differ From GAAP

Inquiry—Financial statements filed with a state regulatory agency are prepared on a statutory basis which differs from generally accepted accounting principles (GAAP). How should the accountant report on the financial statements if he or she knows they will be distributed to third parties other than the regulatory agency?

Reply—Paragraph .21 of AU-C section 800 addresses this situation and indicates that the auditor should express a qualified or adverse opinion regarding the application of GAAP and, in a separate paragraph, express an opinion about whether the financial statements are presented in accordance with the prescribed basis of accounting mandated by the state regulatory agency. In accordance with paragraph .16 of AU-C section 705, *Modifications to the Opinion in the Independent Auditor's Report* (AICPA, *Professional Standards*), the auditor's report would include a basis for modification paragraph that provides an explanation in full of the differences between GAAP and the state mandated policies, or alternatively, a brief description of the differences with a reference to a footnote identifying these differences in detail.

The exhibit of AU-C section 800 includes an illustration of an auditor's report on a complete set of financial statements prepared in accordance with a regulatory basis of accounting when the financial statements together with the auditor's report are intended for general use.

[Revised, December 2012, to reflect conforming changes necessary due to the issuance of SAS Nos. 122–126.]

[.09] Reserved

[.10] Reserved

[.11] Reserved

[.12] Reserved

.13 Report Distribution Restriction Related to Financial Statements Prepared on a Basis of Accounting Prescribed in an Agreement

Inquiry—An auditor was asked to report on special purpose financial statements of a corporation prepared in accordance with contractual basis of accounting. Certain assets, such as receivables, inventories, and other properties, have been valued on a basis specified in the agreement (fair market value). Is the auditor required to issue a report containing a paragraph that restricts the distribution of the report?

Reply—Yes. Paragraph .20 of AU-C section 800 indicates that in such circumstances, the auditor's report on special purpose financial statements should include an other-matter paragraph, under an appropriate heading, that restricts the use of the auditor's report when the special purpose financial statements are prepared in accordance with

a. a contractual basis of accounting,

b. a regulatory basis of accounting, or

c. an other basis of accounting when required pursuant to paragraph .06*a*–*b* of AU-C section 905, *Alert That Restricts the Use of the Auditor's Written Communication* (AICPA, *Professional Standards*).

[Revised, December 2012, to reflect conforming changes necessary due to the issuance of SAS Nos. 122–126.]

.14 Liquidation Basis Financial Statements

Inquiry—The stockholders of a corporation adopted a plan of complete liquidation. The liquidation will occur over a period of three years. What constitutes the basic financial statements following the adoption of the plan, and on what basis should those statements be presented?

Reply—Interpretation No. 1, "Reporting on Financial Statements Prepared on a Liquidation Basis of Accounting," of AU-C section 700, *Forming an Opinion and Reporting on Financial Statements* (AICPA, *Professional Standards*, AU-C sec. 9700 par. .01–.05), states that a liquidation basis of accounting may be considered GAAP for entities in liquidation or for which liquidation appears imminent.

The financial statements of entities adopting a plan of liquidation may be presented with financial statements of a prior period that were prepared on a going concern assumption. The basic financial statements following the adoption of a plan of liquidation consist of a statement of net assets in liquidation, and the related statement of changes in net assets in liquidation.

[Revised, December 2012, to reflect conforming changes necessary due to the issuance of SAS Nos. 122–126.]

.15 Reporting on Medicaid/Medicare Cost Reports

Inquiry—Third-party payors may require health care entities to prepare and submit "cost reports" as a condition of participation in a payor's program. The most common examples are Medicare and Medicaid. Sometimes, a specific payor (such as a state Medicaid program) will require health care entities to obtain an audit of their financial statements and further, will require some form of independent auditor association with or "certification" of cost reports submitted by the health care entity. No standards exist that define or specify what is meant by "certification" of a cost report. A financial statement audit conducted in accordance with generally accepted auditing standards (GAAS) does not include rendering an opinion or any form of assurance on the entity's compliance with laws and regulations, nor does it provide any assurance on an entity's cost report. Consequently, auditors have expressed concern that providing such certification might erroneously imply that they are providing assurance on the entity's cost report or on its compliance with cost report rules or regulations. When an auditor has been engaged to perform an audit of a health care entity's basic financial statements, what form of report should the auditor issue to comply with the certification requirement?

Reply—The auditor could enter into a separate engagement to examine the cost report under AT section 601, *Compliance Attestation* (AICPA, *Professional Standards*). However, typically states do not require such extensive services and therefore, health care entities may be reluctant to engage the auditor to perform such an examination. If a health care entity includes their cost report as supplementary information to their audited basic financial statements, an auditor may report on the cost report as supplementary information in accordance with AU-C section 720, *Other Information in Documents Containing Audited Financial Statements* (AICPA, *Professional Standards*).[1] AU-C section 725, *Supplementary Information in Relation to the Financial Statements as a Whole* (AICPA, *Professional Standards*), addresses those situations where the auditor is engaged to report on whether certain cost report amounts or statistics are fairly stated, in all material respects, in relation to those basic financial statements as a whole. The following is an illustration of an other matter paragraph that the auditor may include in the auditor's report on the audited financial statements or a separate report that the auditor can issue on certain data within a cost report:

> Our audit was made for the purpose of forming an opinion on the financial statements as a whole. The financial and statistical data on pages x–x, designated with the tickmark "#"[2] that are excerpted from ABC Health System's [*identify title of cost report, such as "Annual Report of Hospitals and Hospital Health Care Complexes"*][3] for the year ended December 31, 200X, identified by Declaration Control Number xxxxxxx and prepared as of [*insert date that cost report was*

[1] [Footnote deleted, December 2010, to reflect conforming changes necessary due to the issuance of SAS Nos. 118–120.]

[2] It should be clear from the description in the auditor's report and/or the specific page numbers referenced as to which data is, and which data is not, covered by the "in relation to" opinion.

[3] This wording presumes that the supplementary information is comprised of specific pages or schedules excerpted from the cost report. If the entire cost report is included as supplementary information, this sentence might be reworded to read "Certain supplementary financial and statistical data designated with the tickmark "#" in ABC Health System's [*identify title of cost report, such as "Annual Report of Hospitals and Hospital Health Care Complexes"*] for the year ended December 31, 200X..."

submitted][4] are presented for purposes of additional analysis and are not a required part of the financial statements. The financial and statistical data, designated with the tickmark "#," is the responsibility of management and was derived from and relates directly to the underlying accounting and other records used to prepare the financial statements. The information has been subjected to the auditing procedures applied in the audit of the financial statements and certain additional procedures, including comparing and reconciling such information directly to the underlying accounting and other records used to prepare the financial statements or to the financial statements themselves, and other additional procedures in accordance with auditing standards generally accepted in the United States of America. In our opinion, the information is stated fairly in all material respects in relation to ABC Health System's financial statements taken as a whole.

The financial and statistical data, designated with the tickmark "#," has been subjected to the auditing procedures applied in the audit of the basic financial statements and, in our opinion, is stated fairly in all material respects in relation to ABC Health System's basic financial statements taken as a whole. Those auditing procedures applied in the audit of the financial statements were not intended to determine compliance with, and therefore would not detect compliance with or deviations from, the applicable instructions furnished by the [*identify related regulators, such as "XYZ State Department of Health"*] relating to the preparation of the cost report or the reporting requirements contained in the [*identify related regulations, such as "XYZ State Medicaid Accounting and Reporting Manual*].[5] None of the other information included in the accompanying schedules excerpted from [*identify source*] has been subjected to the auditing procedures applied in our audit of the basic financial statements referred to above and, accordingly, we express no opinion or any other form of assurance thereon.[6]

This report is intended solely for the information and use of Management and the Board of Directors of ABC Health System and the [*identify requesting organization, such as "XYZ State Department of Health"*] and is not intended to be and should not be used by anyone other than these specified parties.[7]

[4] A provider's as-filed cost report may subsequently be revised; therefore, the auditor's report should clearly identify the specific version of the cost report to which the "in relation to" report applies, such as by identifying specific control numbers and/or date of preparation/filing. Doing so will eliminate any future misunderstanding as to the version of the cost report/cost report excerpts covered by the "in relation to" opinion.

[5] An auditor engaged to perform a financial statement audit in accordance with auditing standards generally accepted in the United States of America would not be in a position to express an opinion, or provide any form of assurance, regarding compliance with cost report preparation instructions or rules and regulations covering reimbursement as promulgated by the government program. [Footnote revised, December 2010, to reflect conforming changes necessary due to the issuance of SAS Nos. 118–120.]

[6] A disclaimer should be included as to any other data included in the supplementary information.

[7] Restrictive use language should be included in the report. Paragraph .06 of AU-C section 905, *Alert as to the Intended Use of the Auditor's Written Communication* (AICPA, *Professional Standards*), states that the auditor should include an alert that restricts the use of an auditor's written communication when the subject matter of the auditor's written communication is based on (*a*) measurement or disclosure criteria that are determined by the auditor to be suitable only for a limited number of users

(continued)

Because this is a restricted-use report, the auditor should consider the guidance in paragraphs .A5–.A6 of AU-C section 905 before deciding whether to combine this report with the auditor's report on the basic financial statements.

[Revised, June 2009, to reflect conforming changes necessary due to the issuance of recent authoritative literature; Revised, December 2010, to reflect conforming changes necessary due to the issuance of SAS Nos. 118–120; Revised, December 2012, to reflect conforming changes necessary due to the issuance of SAS Nos. 122–126.]

.16 Example Reports on Federal Deposit Insurance Corporation Loss Sharing Purchase and Assumption Transactions

Inquiry—The Federal Deposit Insurance Corporation's (FDIC's) Resolutions Handbook (Handbook) states that a loss sharing *transaction* is a purchase and assumption (P&A) transaction that the FDIC commonly uses as a resolution tool for handling failed institutions with more than $500 million in assets. A *P&A* is a resolution transaction in which a healthy institution purchases some or all of the assets of a failed bank or thrift and assumes some or all of the liabilities, including all insured deposits. The Handbook also states that a loss sharing P&A uses the basic P&A structure, except for the provision regarding transferred assets. Instead of selling some or all of the assets to the acquirer at a discounted price, the FDIC agrees to share in future loss experienced by the acquirer on a fixed pool of assets.

How may an independent auditor respond to the requirement in the Handbook for P&A agreements that "[w]ithin 90 days after each calendar year end, the acquiring bank must furnish the FDIC a report signed by its independent public accountants containing specified statements[8] relative to the accuracy of any computations made regarding shared loss assets"?

Reply—When the FDIC requirement applies to an engagement covering an FDIC loss sharing P&A transaction, the auditor may respond to the requirement by issuing a report in accordance with the requirements of AU-C section 806, *Reporting on Compliance With Aspects of Contractual Agreements or Regulatory Requirements in Connection With Audited Financial Statements* (AICPA, *Professional Standards*). The following are illustrations of auditor reports for three possible outcomes for which the independent auditor might report:

Example A—Independent Auditor's Report on Compliance With Contractual Provisions

Independent Auditor's Report

[*To the Board of Directors of* ABC Bank]

We have audited, in accordance with auditing standards generally accepted in the United States of America, the financial statements of

---

(footnote continued)

who can be presumed to have an adequate understanding of the criteria, (*b*) measurement or disclosure criteria that are available only to the specified parties, or (*c*) matters identified by the auditor during the course of the audit engagement when the identification of such matters is not the primary objective of the audit engagement (commonly referred to as a by-product report). [Footnote revised, December 2012, to reflect conforming changes necessary due to the issuance of SAS Nos. 122–126.]

[8] The term *specified statements* is not defined in the Federal Deposit Insurance Corporation's (FDIC's) Resolutions Handbook. The practitioner is advised to read the terms of the loss share agreement and confirm that the audit requirement in that agreement provides for the receipt of a report expressing negative assurance.

ABC Bank (the "Bank") as of [*insert date—e.g.* December 31, 20XY], and the related statements of income, changes in stockholder's equity, and cash flows for the year then ended, and the related notes to the financial statements, and have issued our report thereon dated [*insert date*].

In connection with our audit, nothing came to our attention that caused us to believe that the Bank failed to comply with the computational provisions of Exhibit 4.15A Single Family Shared-Loss Agreement, Article II section 2.1(b), [[and] Exhibit 4.15B, Commercial Shared-Loss Agreement, Article II section 2.1(a)][9] of the Purchase and Assumption agreement between the Bank and the Federal Deposit Insurance Corporation dated [*insert date*], insofar as they relate to accounting matters. However, our audit was not directed primarily toward obtaining knowledge of such noncompliance. Accordingly, had we performed additional procedures, other matters may have come to our attention regarding the Bank's noncompliance with the above-referenced provisions, insofar as they relate to accounting matters.

This report is intended solely for the information and use of the Bank and the Federal Deposit Insurance Corporation and is not intended to be and should not be used by anyone other than these specified parties.

[*Signature*]
[*Auditor's city and state*]
[*Date of the auditor's report*]

Example B—Independent Auditor's Report on Compliance With Contractual Provisions: Assuming Amended Computations Are Attached

Independent Auditor's Report

[*To the Board of Directors of* ABC Bank]

We have audited, in accordance with auditing standards generally accepted in the United States of America, the financial statements of *ABC Bank* (the "Bank"), which comprise the balance sheet as of [*insert date—e.g. December 31, 20XY*], and the related statements of income, changes in stockholders' equity, and cash flows for the year then ended, and the related notes to the financial statements, and have issued our report thereon dated [*insert date*].

In connection with our audit, after giving effect to the attached corrected computations, nothing came to our attention that caused us to believe that the Bank failed to comply with the computational provisions of Exhibit 4.15A Single Family Shared-Loss Agreement, Article II section 2.1(b), [[and] Exhibit 4.15B, Commercial Shared-Loss Agreement, Article II section 2.1(a)][10] of the Purchase and Assumption agreement between the Bank and the Federal Deposit Insurance Corporation dated [*insert date*], insofar as they relate to accounting

[9] Applicable depending on the nature of the agreement between the acquiring bank and the FDIC.

[10] Applicable depending on the nature of the agreement between the acquiring bank and the FDIC.

matters. However, our audit was not directed primarily toward obtaining knowledge of such noncompliance. Accordingly, had we performed additional procedures, other matters may have come to our attention regarding the Bank's noncompliance with the above-referenced provisions, insofar as they relate to accounting matters.

This report is intended solely for the information and use of the Bank and the Federal Deposit Insurance Corporation and is not intended to be and should not be used by anyone other than these specified parties.

[*Signature*]
[*Auditor's city and state*]
[*Date of the auditor's report*]

Example C—Independent Auditor's Report on Compliance With Contractual Provisions: Noncompliance

Independent Auditor's Report

[*To the Board of Directors of* ABC Bank]

We have audited, in accordance with auditing standards generally accepted in the United States of America, the financial statements of *ABC Bank* (the "Bank"), which comprise the balance sheet as of [*insert date—e.g. December 31, 20XY*], and the related statements of income, changes in stockholders' equity, and cash flows for the year then ended, and the related notes to the financial statements, and have issued our report thereon dated [*insert date*].

In connection with our audit, we noted that the Bank did not comply with [*state computational provision not met*] Our audit was not directed primarily toward obtaining knowledge as to whether the Bank failed to comply with the computational provisions of Exhibit 4.15A Single Family Shared-Loss Agreement, Article II section 2.1(b), [[and] Exhibit 4.15B, Commercial Shared-Loss Agreement, Article II section 2.1(a)][11] of the Purchase and Assumption agreement between the Bank and the Federal Deposit Insurance Corporation dated [*insert date*], insofar as they relate to accounting matters. Accordingly, had we performed additional procedures, other matters may have come to our attention regarding the Bank's noncompliance with the above-referenced provisions, insofar as they relate to accounting matters.

This report is intended solely for the information and use of the Bank and the Federal Deposit Insurance Corporation and is not intended to be and should not be used by anyone other than these specified parties.

[*Signature*]
[*Auditor's city and state*]
[*Date of the auditor's report*]

[Issue Date: February 2010; Revised, December 2012, to reflect conforming changes necessary due to the issuance of SAS Nos. 122–126.]

[11] Applicable depending on the nature of the agreement between the acquiring bank and the FDIC.

.17 Application of Financial Accounting Standards Board (FASB) *Accounting Standards Codification* 740-10 (previously, FASB Interpretation No. 48, *Accounting for Uncertainty in Income Taxes*) to Other Comprehensive Basis of Accounting Financial Statements—Recognition and Measurement Provisions

Inquiry—Does an auditor need to consider the recognition and measurement provisions of Financial Accounting Standards Board (FASB) *Accounting Standards Codification* (ASC) 740-10 (previously, FASB Interpretation No. 48, *Accounting for Uncertainty in Income Taxes*) when auditing financial statements prepared in accordance with a special purpose framework?

Reply—Ordinarily, the recognition and measurement provisions of FASB ASC 740-10 (previously, FASB Interpretation No. 48) would not apply to special purpose financial statements because a liability for an uncertain tax position would not be reported on an entity's income tax return, nor would it be based on cash receipts or disbursements. However, FASB ASC 740-10 may apply in order for an entity's financial statements to comply with the financial reporting provisions of a governmental regulatory agency to whose jurisdiction the entity is subject. If the recognition and measurement provisions do apply and the financial statements contain items that are the same as, or similar to, those in financial statements prepared in accordance with GAAP, then the auditor should consider whether the financial statements (including the accompanying notes) include all informative disclosures that are appropriate for the basis of accounting used.

[Issue Date: June 2010; Revised, December 2012, to reflect conforming changes necessary due to the issuance of SAS Nos. 122–126.]

.18 Small Business Lending Fund Auditor Certification Guidance

Inquiry—Enacted into law on September 27, 2010, as part of the Small Business Jobs Act of 2010, the Small Business Lending Fund (SBLF) encourages lending to small businesses by providing capital to community banks with under $10 billion in assets. The United States Department of the Treasury will make SBLF funding available by purchasing senior preferred stock or equivalents in institutions that apply, and are approved, to participate in the SBLF. Generally speaking, the dividend rate paid by institutions on SBLF funding decreases as the institution's *qualified small business lending*, as defined by the Treasury Department, increases.

Under the terms of the SBLF, a participating community bank is required to calculate and report the amount of its qualified small business lending in a supplemental report. In addition to requiring the institution's management to certify to the Treasury Department that the information provided in each supplemental report is accurate, the institution is also required to receive and submit within 90 days of the end of each fiscal year following the investment date a certification from its external auditors that the processes and controls used to generate the supplemental reports are satisfactory.

How may an independent auditor respond to this requirement?

Reply—An independent auditor may satisfy this requirement by issuing a report in accordance with the requirements of AU-C section 806. This assurance, relative to the supplemental reports, may be provided in a separate report or in one or more paragraphs of the auditor's report accompanying the audited financial statements. Such assurance should not be provided unless the auditor has audited the financial statements and subjected the supplemental reports to audit procedures applied in the audit of the financial statements. Professional judgment needs to be applied by the auditor in determining the nature, timing, and extent of those audit procedures. In addition, when the auditor has expressed an adverse opinion or disclaimed an opinion on the financial statements, the auditor should issue a report on compliance only when instances of noncompliance are identified. When the auditor has identified one or more items of noncompliance, the report on compliance should describe such noncompliance.

The following is an illustration of a report that an auditor may use when, as a result of the auditor's audit procedures, nothing has come to the auditor's attention to indicate that the bank failed to comply with the terms of the SBLF:

> Independent Auditor's Report
>
> [*To the Board of Directors of* Institution Name]
> [*Address*]
> [*City, State*]
>
> We have audited, in accordance with auditing standards generally accepted in the United States of America, the financial statements of [*Institution Name*] (the "Bank"), which comprise the balance sheet as of [Date], and the related statements of income, changes in stockholders' equity, and cash flows for the year then ended, and the related notes to the financial statements, and have issued our report thereon dated [*Date*].
>
> In connection with our audit, nothing came to our attention that caused us to believe that the Bank failed to comply with the Small Business Lending Fund Securities Purchase Agreement (the Agreement) between the Bank and the United States Department of the Treasury (Treasury) dated [*Date*], insofar as the Agreement relates to accounting matters provided on the Bank's Supplemental Reports filed with Treasury during the year ended [*Date*] under sections 1.3(j) and 3.1(d) of the Agreement, including that nothing came to our attention that caused us to believe that the Bank's Supplemental Reports did not set forth a complete and accurate statement of loans held by the Bank in each of the categories described therein for the time period(s) specified therein. However, our audit was not directed primarily toward obtaining knowledge of such noncompliance. Accordingly, had we performed additional procedures, other matters may have come to our attention regarding the Bank's compliance with the above-referenced provisions, insofar as they relate to accounting matter
>
> This report is intended solely for the information and use of the Bank and Treasury and is not intended to be and should not be used by anyone other than these specified parties.
>
> [*Signature*]
> [*Date*]

[Issue Date: October 2011; Revised, December 2012, to reflect conforming changes necessary due to the issuance of SAS Nos. 122–126.]

.19 Lender Comfort Letters

Inquiry—No-documentation or low-documentation loans remain popular options within the lending community, especially in lending to the self-employed. The information a prospective borrower is asked to furnish in connection with such loans is limited; however, lenders or brokers still attempt to assess a borrower's creditworthiness and verify the accuracy of information provided to them by the borrower.

Examples of requested information include

- confirmation of a client's self-employed status.
- verification of income from self-employment.
- profitability of a client's business.
- the impact on a client's business if money is withdrawn to fund the down payment on a real estate purchase.

How may an accountant respond to a request from a client, lender, or loan broker to confirm client information in connection with a pending loan application?

Reply—When presented with such requests, the accountant should consider the guidance in Interpretation No. 2, "Responding to Requests for Reports on Matters Relating to Solvency," of AT section 101, *Attest Engagements* (AICPA, *Professional Standards*, AT sec. 9101 par. .23–.33). Paragraph .27 of Interpretation No. 2 states that a practitioner is precluded from giving any form of assurance on matters relating to solvency or any financial presentation of matters relating to solvency. Paragraph .25 of Interpretation No. 2 defines matters relating to solvency as whether an entity (*a*) is not insolvent at the time the debt is incurred or would not be rendered insolvent thereby, (*b*) does not have unreasonably small capital, or (*c*) has the ability to pay its debts as they mature.

In response to a request to confirm client information in connection with a pending loan application, an accountant may provide a client with various professional services that may be useful with a financing. Those services include

- an audit, a review, or a compilation of personal financial statements.
- an examination, a review, or a compilation of pro forma personal financial information.
- an examination or a compilation of prospective personal financial statements.
- an agreed-upon procedures report, as long as the agreed-upon procedures do not provide any assurance on matters related to solvency.

Additionally, a broker or lender may be satisfied with a copy of the client's income tax return and a letter from the accountant, including an acknowledgment that the income tax return was prepared by the accountant. Obtaining client consent before providing any confidential information to a third party is required under professional ethics standards, the Gramm-Leach-Bliley Act, the Internal Revenue Code, and federal and state privacy statutes and regulations. The following is a sample letter that may be used in this situation:

Date

ABC Company
Address
City, State Zip

Dear Mr. _______:

I am writing to you at the request of Mr. & Mrs. __________.

The purpose of this letter is to confirm to you that I prepared the 20XX federal income tax return of Mr. & Mrs. _______ and delivered this return to them for filing with the IRS. At their request, I have attached a copy of the tax return and related schedules provided to them for filing.

This return was prepared from information furnished to me by Mr. & Mrs. _______. This information was neither audited nor verified by me, and I make no representation nor do I provide any assurance regarding the accuracy of this information or the sufficiency of this tax return for your credit decision-making purposes.

I prepared Mr. & Mrs. _______ tax return in accordance with the applicable IRS rules and regulations solely for filing with the IRS. As a result, the tax return does not represent any assessment on my part regarding creditworthiness and does not include any statement of their financial position or income and expense for the year 20XX, in accordance with accounting principles generally accepted in the United States of America, and should not be construed to do so.

As you know, a credit decision should be based on a lender's exercise of due diligence in obtaining and considering multiple factors and information. Any use by you of Mr. & Mrs. _______ 20XX federal income tax return and this letter is solely a matter of your responsibility and judgment. This letter is not intended to establish a client relationship with you nor is it intended to establish any obligation on my part to provide any future information to you with regard to Mr. & Mrs. _______.

Sincerely,

_______(Firm Name)

cc: Mr. & Mrs. _______ (Client)

[Issue Date: July 2012.]

[.20] Reserved

.21 Reporting on Current-Value Financial Statements That Supplement Historical-Cost Financial Statements in Presentations of Real Estate Entities

Inquiry—A real estate entity presents current-value financial statements[12] to supplement historical-cost financial statements. May an auditor accept an engagement to report on current-value financial statements that supplement historical-cost financial statements and, if so, how should the auditor report?

Reply—An auditor may accept an engagement to report on current-value financial statements that supplement historical-cost financial statements of a real estate entity only if the auditor believes the following two conditions exist:

- The measurement and disclosure criteria used to prepare the current-value financial statements are reasonable.
- Competent persons using the measurement and disclosure criteria would ordinarily obtain materially similar measurements or disclosures.

[12] Generally accepted accounting principles require the use of current-value accounting for financial statements of certain types of entities (for example, investment companies, employee benefit plans, personal financial statements, and mutual and common trust funds). This interpretation does not apply to reports on current-value financial statements of such entities.

If these conditions are satisfied, an auditor may report on such current-value financial statements in a manner similar to that discussed in paragraph .22 of AU-C section 800. However, because the current-value financial statements only supplement the historical-cost financial statements and are not presented as a stand-alone presentation, it is not necessary to restrict the use of the auditor's report on the presentation as required by that paragraph.

The following is an example of a report an auditor might issue when reporting on current-value financial statements that supplement historical-cost financial statements of a real estate entity.

Independent Auditor's Report

[*Appropriate Addressee*]

Report on the Financial Statements[13]

We have audited the accompanying historical-cost financial statements of X Company, which comprise the historical-cost balance sheets as of December 31, 20X3, and 20X2, and the related historical-cost statements of income, shareholders' equity, and cash flows for the years then ended, and the related notes to the historical-cost financial statements. We also have audited the supplemental current-value financial statements of X Company, which comprise the current-value balance sheets as of December 31, 20X3, and 20X2, and the related supplemental current-value statements of income and shareholders' equity for the years then ended, and the related notes to the current-value financial statements.

Management's Responsibility for the Financial Statements

Management is responsible for the preparation and fair presentation of the historical-cost financial statements in accordance with accounting principles generally accepted in the United States of America; this includes the design, implementation, and maintenance of internal control relevant to the preparation and fair presentation of historical-cost financial statements that are free from material misstatement, whether due to fraud or error.

Management is responsible for the preparation and fair presentation of the supplemental current-value financial statements in accordance with the basis of accounting described in Note 1; this includes determining that the basis of accounting described in Note 1 is an acceptable basis for the preparation of the supplemental current-value financial statements in the circumstances. Management is also responsible for the design, implementation, and maintenance of internal control relevant to the preparation and fair presentation of supplemental current-value financial statements that are free from material misstatement, whether due to fraud or error.

Auditor's Responsibility

Our responsibility is to express an opinion on these financial statements based on our audits. We conducted our audits in accordance with auditing standards generally accepted in the United States of America. Those standards require that we plan and perform the audit to

[13] The subtitle "Report on the Financial Statements" is unnecessary in circumstances when the second subtitle, "Report on Other Legal and Regulatory Requirements," is not applicable.

obtain reasonable assurance about whether the financial statements are free from material misstatement.

An audit involves performing procedures to obtain audit evidence about the amounts and disclosures in the financial statements. The procedures selected depend on the auditor's judgment, including the assessment of the risks of material misstatement of the financial statements, whether due to fraud or error. In making those risk assessments, the auditor considers internal control relevant to the entity's preparation and fair presentation of the financial statements in order to design audit procedures that are appropriate in the circumstances, but not for the purpose of expressing an opinion on the effectiveness of the entity's internal control.[14] Accordingly, we express no such opinion. An audit also includes evaluating the appropriateness of accounting policies used and the reasonableness of significant accounting estimates made by management, as well as evaluating the overall presentation of the financial statements.

We believe that the audit evidence we have obtained is sufficient and appropriate to provide a basis for our audit opinions.

Opinion on the Historical-Cost Financial Statements

In our opinion, the historical-cost financial statements referred to above present fairly, in all material respects, the financial position of X Company as of December 31, 20X3, and 20X2, and the results of its operations and its cash flows for the years then ended in accordance with accounting principles generally accepted in the United States of America.

Opinion on the Supplemental Current-Value Financial Statements

In our opinion, the supplemental current-value financial statements referred to above present fairly, in all material respects, the financial position of X Company as of December 31, 20X3, and 20X2, and the results of its operations for the years then ended in accordance with the basis of accounting described in Note 1.

Basis of Accounting for the Supplemental Current-Value Financial Statements

As described in Note 1, the supplemental current-value financial statements have been prepared by management to present relevant financial information that is not provided by the historical-cost financial statements and are not intended to be a presentation in conformity with accounting principles generally accepted in the United States of America. In addition, the supplemental current-value financial statements do not purport to present the net realizable, liquidation, or market value of X Company as a whole. Furthermore, amounts ultimately realized by X Company from the disposal of properties may vary significantly from the current values presented. Our opinion on the

[14] In circumstances when the auditor also has responsibility to express an opinion on the effectiveness of internal control in conjunction with the audit of the financial statements, this sentence would be worded as follows: "In making those risk assessments, the auditor considers internal control relevant to the entity's preparation and fair presentation of the financial statements in order to design audit procedures that are appropriate in the circumstances." In addition, the next sentence, "Accordingly, we express no such opinion," would not be included.

supplemental current-value financial statements is not modified with respect to this matter.

Report on Other Legal and Regulatory Requirements

[*Form and content of this section of the auditor's report will vary depending on the nature of the auditor's other reporting responsibilities.*]

[*Signature*]

[*Date*]

In accordance with paragraph .17 of AU-C section 800, the auditor should also consider the adequacy of disclosures relating to the current-value financial statements. Adequate disclosures describe the accounting policies applied and such matters as the basis of presentation, nature of the reporting entity's properties, status of construction-in-process, valuation bases used for each classification of assets and liabilities, and sources of valuation, in a sufficiently clear and comprehensive manner that enables a knowledgeable reader to understand the current-value financial statements.

[Issue Date: March 2013.]

.22 Use of Restricted Alert Language When Financial Statements Are Audited in Accordance With GAAS and *Government Auditing Standards*

Inquiry—Paragraph .11 of AU-C section 905,[15] states that the restricted alert language required by paragraph .07 of AU-C section 905 should not be used when

a. the engagement is performed in accordance with *Government Auditing Standards*, and

b. the auditor's written communication (commonly referred to as a by-product report) pursuant to that engagement is issued in accordance with

   i. AU-C section 265, *Communicating Internal Control Related Matters Identified in an Audit* (AICPA, *Professional Standards*);

   ii. AU-C section 806; or

   iii. AU-C section 935.

Assume an entity's financial statements are audited in accordance with both GAAS and *Government Auditing Standards*. If the auditor issues a compliance report in accordance with AU-C section 806 but that report is not required to be issued in accordance with *Government Auditing Standards* and the report does not refer to *Government Auditing Standards*, is the auditor prohibited from using the restricted alert language required by paragraph .07 of AU-C section 905?

Reply—No, use of the restricted alert language is not prohibited. An auditor may include a restricted alert paragraph using the language required by paragraph .07 in AU-C section 905 as long as the compliance report is not required to be issued in accordance with *Government Auditing Standards* and the report does not refer to *Government Auditing Standards*.

For example, a not-for-profit organization is required to have a financial statement audit conducted in accordance with GAAS and *Government Auditing*

[15] All referenced AU-C sections can be found in AICPA *Professional Standards*.

Standards because the organization receives federal funds. In addition to the reports required by *Government Auditing Standards*, the auditor of the not-for-profit organization is requested to provide a compliance report in accordance with AU-C section 806 to the organization's financial institution about whether the auditor identified any instances of noncompliance with the covenants of a loan agreement. Because this compliance report is not required to be issued in accordance with *Government Auditing Standards* and the report would be issued only in accordance with GAAS and would not refer to *Government Auditing Standards*, the auditor may use the restricted alert language required by paragraph .07 of AU-C section 905.

[Issue Date: March 2013.]

.23 Modification of Compliance Report When Financial Statements Are Audited in Accordance With GAAS

Inquiry—The exhibit, "Illustrations of Reports on Compliance With Aspects of Contractual Agreements or Regulatory Requirements in Connection With Audited Financial Statements," in AU-C section 806 provides illustrative reports on compliance based on a financial statement audit conducted in accordance with auditing standards generally accepted in the United States of America. Based on the facts in section 9110.22, "Use of Restricted Alert Language When Financial Statements Are Audited in Accordance With GAAS and Government Auditing Standards," does the auditor need to modify this language to indicate that the financial statement audit was also conducted in accordance with *Government Auditing Standards*?

Reply—No. In the example in section 9110.22, the auditor's compliance report about whether the auditor identified any instances of noncompliance with the covenants of a loan agreement would be issued only in accordance with GAAS and would not be issued in accordance with *Government Auditing Standards*. Therefore, the illustrative language would not need to be modified and could refer only to the audit being conducted in accordance with auditing standards generally accepted in the United States of America.

[Issue Date: March 2013.]

Q&A Section 9120

Reliance on Others

[.01] Reserved

.02 Responsibility for Audit of Dividend Fund Managed by Agent

Inquiry—A mutual fund employs a management company to act as its dividend disbursing agent and transfer agent. Dividend checks to the individual shareholders of the mutual fund are drawn from a "dividend disbursing agency fund." This account, however, does not appear as an asset or liability on the books of either the mutual fund or the management company.

Is it the responsibility of the mutual fund's auditors or the management company's auditors to audit the dividend disbursing agency fund?

Reply—Since it is one of the primary responsibilities of the management company for the mutual fund, to draw and pay individual dividend checks to the fund's shareholders, it would be appropriate for, if not incumbent upon, the management company's auditors, in connection with their audit, to see that this function is being properly discharged, even though the account from which these checks are disbursed does not appear as an asset or liability on the books of either the fund or the management company.

[.03] Reserved

.04 Reliance on State Grain Inspectors for Inventory Measurements

Inquiry—A grain company operates several storage elevators. The company maintains perpetual inventory records for all facilities—both at the elevators and the home office. State grain inspectors measure the stored grain and in effect perform the same audit functions as the CPA firm. Past experience has been that the differences between the measurements of the state inspectors, the CPA firm, and the perpetual inventory records are immaterial. The state inspectors are qualified with years of experience. Can the CPA firm accept the findings of the state inspectors as adequate inventory observation in accordance with generally accepted auditing standards?

Reply—Paragraph .A29 of AU-C section 501, *Audit Evidence—Specific Considerations for Selected Items* (AICPA, *Professional Standards*), can be applied to this situation. The CPA firm could use the measurements and calculations of the state grain inspectors but not as a complete substitute for its own independent inventory observation.

[Revised, December 2012, to reflect conforming changes necessary due to the issuance of SAS Nos. 122–126.]

[.05] Reserved

.06 Use of Other Auditors' Work When They Are Not Independent

Inquiry—AU-C section 600, *Special Considerations—Audits of Group Financial Statements (Including the Work of Component Auditors)* (AICPA, *Professional Standards*), provides guidance when component auditors are involved in an audit of group financial statements. How does the lack of independence of the component auditors affect the use of their work and reports by the group engagement team?

Reply—In these circumstances, the work and reports of the component auditors cannot be used in accordance with AU-C section 600. The responsibility for the audit report on the financial statements rests solely with the group engagement partner.

Therefore, judgments about assessments of inherent and control risk, the materiality of misstatements, the sufficiency of tests performed, the evaluation of significant accounting estimates, and other matters affecting the auditor's report should always be those of the group engagement team.

The group engagement team, however, may use professional judgment in evaluating the work of the component auditors who are lacking in independence in the way an auditor would consider the work performed by internal auditors.

[Revised, December 2012, to reflect conforming changes necessary due to the issuance of SAS Nos. 122–126.]

.07 Reference to Other Auditors in Accompanying Information Report

Inquiry—An audit report is based in part on the report of component auditors. If the group engagement partner makes reference to component auditors' audit in the audit report, is the report on accompanying information, which includes data audited by component auditors, required to include a reference to component auditors' audit?

Reply—Yes. If a portion of the financial statements was audited by component auditors and the group engagement partner's report refers to the component auditors, the group engagement partner's report on the accompanying information, which includes data audited by component auditors, also should refer to component auditors' audit.

[Revised, December 2012, to reflect conforming changes necessary due to the issuance of SAS Nos. 122–126.]

[.08] Reserved

Q&A Section 9130
Limited Scope Engagements

[.01] Reserved

.02 Auditor's Report if Inventories Not Observed

Inquiry—An auditor has been asked to perform an audit for an entity on a limited scope basis. The entity is required by regulation to have an audit performed, and a disclaimer of opinion is acceptable to the regulator. The engagement does not include any independent verification of the inventory. The auditor will not be present at any physical inventory taking and the pricing and clerical accuracy of the inventory will not be tested. The inventory is material in relation to the other accounts on the client's financial statements.

May the auditor accept the engagement on a limited scope basis? What type of opinion can the auditor give under these circumstances?

Reply—A disclaimer of opinion is appropriate when the scope limitation precludes inventory observation and any other audit tests of the inventories. Paragraph .07 of AU-C section 210, *Terms of Engagement* (AICPA, *Professional Standards*), specifies that if management or those charged with governance impose a limitation on the scope of the auditor's work in the terms of the proposed audit engagement, such that the auditor believes the limitation will result in disclaiming an opinion on the financial statements as a whole, the auditor is not permitted to accept such a limited engagement as an audit engagement. However, if the entity is required by regulation to have an audit, and a disclaimer of opinion is acceptable to the regulator, the auditor is permitted, but not required, to accept the engagement.

[Revised, December 2012, to reflect conforming changes necessary due to the issuance of SAS Nos. 122–126.]

[.03] Reserved

[.04] Reserved

[.05] Reserved

[.06] Reserved

.07 Inadequate Internal Control and Financial Records

Inquiry—How should the auditor report that he or she has been unable, because of inadequate internal control and financial records, to obtain sufficient appropriate audit evidence that all transactions were recorded?

Reply—AU-C section 705, *Modifications to the Opinion in the Independent Auditor's Report* (AICPA, *Professional Standards*), addresses the auditor's inability to obtain sufficient appropriate audit evidence (also referred to as a limitation on the scope of an audit). In accordance with paragraphs .08 and .10 of AU-C section 705, the inability of the auditor to obtain sufficient appropriate audit evidence results in one of the following modifications to the opinion in the auditor's report:

a. A qualified opinion when the auditor concludes that the possible effects on the financial statements of undetected misstatements, if any, could be material but not pervasive.

b. A disclaimer of opinion when the auditor concludes that auditor concludes that the possible effects on the financial statements of undetected misstatements, if any, could be both material and pervasive.

A disclaimer of opinion in this situation would be appropriate under AU-C section 705 if the effects of the inadequacy of internal control and the accounting records are sufficiently pervasive. Otherwise, a qualified opinion may be appropriate.

Paragraph .20 of AU-C section 705 requires that when a modification to the auditor's opinion results from an inability to obtain sufficient appropriate audit evidence, the auditor should include in the basis of modification paragraph the reasons for that inability.

[Revised, May 2007; Revised, December 2012, to reflect conforming changes necessary due to the issuance of SAS Nos. 122–126.]

[.08] Reserved

[.09] Reserved

.10 Effect of Generally Accepted Accounting Principles (GAAP) Departures on Limited Scope Engagements

Inquiry—The auditor of a company is unable to observe physical inventory at year end due to a restriction imposed by the client. Because the inventory is material, the auditor plans to issue a disclaimer of opinion on the financial statements in accordance with paragraph .10 of AU-C section 705.

The auditor also discovers significant mathematical errors in the client's last-in, first-out provision in the prior year. The auditor advises the client to report the error as a prior period adjustment in accordance with Financial Accounting Standards Board *Accounting Standards Codification* 250, *Accounting Changes and Error Corrections*. If the client refuses to do so, the auditor is now faced with a GAAP departure and a disclaimer of opinion—both related to the company's inventory.

How would the GAAP departure affect the auditor's disclaimer of opinion?

Reply—Assuming the auditor decided not to withdraw from the engagement, the requirement in paragraph .22 of AU-C section 705 should be followed. That paragraph requires the auditor, even if the auditor has expressed an adverse opinion or disclaimed an opinion on the financial statements, to "... describe in the basis of modification paragraph any other matters of which the auditor is aware and that would have required a modification to the opinion and the effects thereof."

[Revised, June 2009, to reflect conforming changes necessary due to the issuance of FASB ASC; Revised, December 2012, to reflect conforming changes necessary due to the issuance of SAS Nos. 122–126.]

Q&A Section 9150

Preparation, Compilation and Review Engagements

[.01] Reserved

[.02] Reserved

[.03] Reserved

.04 Financial Statements Marked As "Unaudited"

Inquiry—Is it required that each page of financial statements subjected to a preparation, compilation or review engagement be marked "unaudited"?

Reply—No. There is no requirement in AR-C section 70, *Preparation of Financial Statements* (AICPA, *Professional Standards*), AR-C section 80, *Compilation Engagements* (AICPA, *Professional Standards*), or AR-C section 90, *Review of Financial Statements* (AICPA, *Professional Standards*), that each page of financial statements be marked as "unaudited." However, nothing precludes the preparer from labeling such financial statements as "unaudited."

[Amended, February 1995; Revised, June 2009, to reflect conforming changes necessary due to the issuance of recent authoritative literature; Revised, December 2010, to reflect conforming changes necessary due to the issuance of SSARS No. 19; Revised, March 2016, to reflect conforming changes necessary due to the issuance of SSARS No. 21.]

[.05] Reserved

[.06] Reserved

[.07] Reserved

.08 Supplementary Information

Inquiry—Does the accountant have a reporting obligation when supplementary information, such as supporting schedules of balance sheet or income statement accounts, are presented separately from the financial statements and the accountant's compilation or review report thereon?

Reply—No, the accountant does not have a reporting requirement unless supplementary information *accompanies* the basic financial statements and the accountant's compilation or review report thereon. Pursuant to paragraph .32 of AR-C section 80 and paragraph .80 of AR-C section 90, when supplementary information *accompanies* the basic financial statements and the accountant's report thereon, the accountant is required to clearly indicate the degree of responsibility, if any, the accountant is taking with respect to such information.

[Revised, June 2009, to reflect conforming changes necessary due to the issuance of recent authoritative literature; Revised, December 2010, to reflect conforming changes necessary due to the issuance of SSARS No. 19; Revised, March 2016, to reflect conforming changes necessary due to the issuance of SSARS No. 21.]

[.09] Reserved

[.10] Reserved

[.11] Reserved

[.12] Reserved

[.13] Reserved

[.14] Reserved

[.15] Reserved

[.16] Reserved

[.17] Reserved

.18 Bank Engaged an Accountant to Perform a Compilation Engagement on a Financial Statement of Another Entity

Inquiry—A bank has engaged an accountant to perform a compilation engagement on a balance sheet for another entity. The bank has possession of the books and records of the entity. Can the accountant issue a compilation report under such circumstances?

Reply—Yes. There is nothing in the Statements on Standards for Accounting and Review Services (SSARSs) that precludes the CPA firm from issuing a compilation report under such circumstances assuming that the accountant is able to adhere to the requirements of AR-C section 80.

[Revised, June 2009, to reflect conforming changes necessary due to the issuance of recent authoritative literature; Revised, December 2010, to reflect conforming changes necessary due to the issuance of SSARS No. 19; Revised, March 2016, to reflect conforming changes necessary due to the issuance of SSARS No. 21.]

[.19] Reserved

.20 Reissuance of a Review Report When the Accountant's Independence Is Impaired After the Date of the Accountant's Review Report

Inquiry—An accountant's independence is impaired after the date of the accountant's review report. May the accountant reissue his or her review report on the prior year financial statements?

Reply—Yes. Paragraph .07 of AR-C section 90 states that the accountant must be independent of the entity when performing a review of financial statements in accordance with SSARSs. Paragraph .39*i* of AR-C section 90 requires that the accountant's review report be dated no earlier than the date on which the accountant completed procedures sufficient to obtain limited assurance as a basis for reporting whether the accountant is aware of any material modifications that should be made to the financial statements for them to be in accordance with the applicable financial reporting framework. Therefore, the accountant is no longer performing a review after the date of the financial statements. If the accountant reissues his or her review report on prior year financial statements, there is no requirement to disclose the subsequent independence impairment in the accountant's review report.

[Revised, December 2010, to reflect conforming changes necessary due to the issuance of SSARS No. 19; Revised, March 2016, to reflect conforming changes necessary due to the issuance of SSARS No. 21.]

[.21] Reserved

[.22] Reserved

[.23] Reserved

.24 Issuing a Compilation Report on Financial Statements That Omit Substantially All Disclosures Required by an Applicable Financial Reporting Framework After Issuing a Report on Financial Statements for the Same Reporting Period That Include Substantially All Disclosures Required by the Same Financial Reporting Framework

Inquiry—May an accountant accept a compilation engagement on financial statements that omit substantially all disclosures required by an applicable financial reporting framework, if he or she previously issued an audit, review, or compilation report on financial statements for the same reporting period with substantially all disclosures required by the same financial reporting framework presented?

Reply—Yes. The financial statements that omit substantially all disclosures are separate and distinct from the financial statements that include substantially all disclosures. Paragraph .24 of AR-C section 80 states that an accountant should not issue an accountant's compilation report on financial statements that omit substantially all disclosures required by the applicable financial reporting framework unless the omission of substantially all disclosures is not, to the accountant's knowledge, undertaken with the intention of misleading those who might reasonably be expected to use such financial statements.

[Revised, June 2009, to reflect conforming changes necessary due to the issuance of recent authoritative literature; Revised, December 2010, to reflect conforming changes necessary due to the issuance of SSARS No. 19; Revised, March 2016, to reflect conforming changes necessary due to the issuance of SSARS No. 21.]

[.25] Reserved

[.26] Reserved

[.27] Reserved

[.28] Reserved

.29 Effects on Compilation and Review Engagements When Management Does Not Assess Whether the Reporting Entity Is the Primary Beneficiary of a Variable Interest Entity and Instructs the Accountant to Not Perform the Assessment

Inquiry—FASB ASC 810-10-25-38A requires a reporting entity with a variable interest in a variable interest entity (VIE) to assess whether the reporting entity has a controlling financial interest in the VIE and, thus, is the VIE's primary beneficiary. If management of the enterprise with a variable interest in a VIE does not perform the required assessment and instructs the accountant engaged to perform the compilation or review of the reporting entity's financial statements to not perform the assessment, is the accountant required, in accordance with paragraph .16*a* of AR-C section 80, to withdraw from the compilation engagement because the accountant is unable to complete the engagement because management has failed to provide records, documents, explanations, or other information, including significant judgments, as requested or, in accordance with paragraph .08 of AR-C section 90, to not accept the review engagement because management imposition of a limitation on the scope of the accountant's work in terms of a proposed review engagement such that the accountant believes the limitation will result in the accountant being unable to perform review procedures to provide an adequate basis for issuing a review report?

Reply—No. Because management is required to perform the assessment in accordance with accounting principles generally accepted in the United States of America (GAAP), the failure to perform such an assessment and management's instructions to the accountant to not perform the assessment are a departure from GAAP, not a refusal to provide information or a scope limitation. In accordance with paragraph .27 of AR-C section 80 (for compilations) or paragraph .56 of AR-C section 90 (for reviews), as applicable, the accountant should consider whether modification of the standard report is adequate to disclose the departure.

If the accountant concludes that modification of the standard report is appropriate, the accountant may modify the accountant's compilation report as follows (assuming there are no other known departures from GAAP):

Management is responsible for the accompanying financial statements of XYZ Company, which comprise the balance sheet as of December 31, 20X1 and the related statements of income, changes in stockholders' equity, and cash flows for the year then ended, and the related notes to the financial statements in accordance with accounting principles generally accepted in the United States of America. I (We) have performed a compilation engagement in accordance with Statements on Standards for Accounting and Review Services promulgated by the Accounting and Review Services Committee of the AICPA. I (We) did not audit or review the financial statements nor was (were) I (we) required to perform any procedures to verify the accuracy or completeness of the information provided by management. Accordingly, I (we) do not express an opinion, a conclusion, nor provide any form of assurance on these financial statements.

Accounting principles generally accepted in the United States of America require management to assess whether the company has a controlling interest in any entities in which the company has a variable interest in order to determine if those entities should be consolidated. Management has not performed the required assessment and therefore, if there are variable interest entities for which the company is the primary beneficiary, has not consolidated those entities. Although the effects on the financial statements of the failure to perform the required assessment have not been determined, many elements in the financial statements would have been materially affected had management determined that the company is the primary beneficiary of any variable interest entities.

[*Signature of accounting firm or accountant, as appropriate*]

[*Accountant's city and state*]

[*Date of the accountant's compilation report*]

If the accountant concludes that modification of the standard report is appropriate, the accountant may modify the accountant's review report on as follows (assuming there are no other known departures from GAAP):

Independent Accountant's Review Report

[*Appropriate Addressee*]

I (We) have reviewed the accompanying financial statements of XYZ Company, which comprise the balance sheet as of December 31, 20XX, and the related statements of income, retained earnings, and cash flows for the year then ended, and the related notes to the financial statements. A review includes primarily applying analytical procedures to management's (owners') financial data and making inquiries of company management (owners). A review is substantially less in scope than an audit, the objective of which is the expression of an opinion regarding the financial statements as a whole. Accordingly, I (we) do not express such an opinion.

Management's Responsibility for the Financial Statements

Management (Owners) is (are) responsible for the preparation and fair presentation of these financial statements in accordance with accounting principles generally accepted in the United States of America; this includes the design, implementation, and maintenance of internal control relevant to the preparation and fair presentation of financial statements that are free from material misstatement whether due to fraud or error.

Accountant's Responsibility

My (our) responsibility is to conduct the review engagement in accordance with Statements on Standards for Accounting and Review Services promulgated by the Accounting and Review Services Committee of the AICPA. Those standards require me (us) to perform procedures to obtain limited assurance as a basis for reporting whether I am (we are) aware of any material modifications that should be made to the financial statements for them to be in accordance with accounting principles generally accepted in the United States of America. I (We) believe that the results of my (our) procedures provide a reasonable basis for my (our) conclusion.

Accountant's Conclusion

Based on my (our) review, except for the issue noted in the Known Departure From Accounting Principles Generally Accepted in the United States of America paragraph, I am (we are) not aware of any material modifications that should be made to the accompanying financial statements in order for them to be in accordance with accounting principles generally accepted in the United States.

Known Departure From Accounting Principles Generally Accepted in the United States of America

As disclosed in Note X to these financial statements, accounting principles generally accepted in the United States of America require management to assess whether the company has a controlling interest in any entities in which the company has a variable interest in order to determine if those entities should be consolidated. Management has not performed the required assessment and therefore, if there are variable interest entities for which the company is the primary beneficiary, has not consolidated those entities. Although the effects on the financial statements of the failure to perform the required assessment have not been determined, many elements in the financial statements would have been materially affected had management determined that the company is the primary beneficiary of any variable interest entities.

[*Signature of accounting firm or accountant, as appropriate*]

[*Accountant's city and state*]

[*Date of the accountant's review report*]

If the accountant believes that modification of the standard report is not adequate to indicate the deficiencies in the financial statements as a whole, in accordance with paragraph .30 of AR-C section 80 (for compilations) or paragraph .59 of AR-C section 90 (for reviews), as applicable, the accountant is required to withdraw from the compilation or review engagement. The accountant may wish to consult with his or her legal counsel in those circumstances.

[Issue Date: April 2012; Revised, March 2016, to reflect conforming changes necessary due to the issuance of SSARS No. 21.]

.30 Disclosure of Independence Impairment in the Accountant's Compilation Report on Comparative Financial Statements When the Accountant's Independence Is Impaired in Only One Period

Inquiry—When the accountant is not independent with respect to the entity, in accordance with paragraph .22 of AR-C section 80, the accountant is required to indicate that accountant's lack of independence in a final paragraph of the accountant's compilation report. How may an accountant modify the accountant's compilation report on comparative financial statements for an entity with respect to which the accountant was not independent as of and for the earlier period ended, but such impairment was subsequently cured?

Reply—The accountant may indicate the independence impairment as of and for the earlier period ended that was subsequently cured by including language such as the following as the final paragraph of the accountant's compilation report: "As of and for the year ended December 31, 20X1, I was not independent with respect to XYZ Company."

The accountant is not precluded from disclosing a description about the reason(s) that the accountant's independence is impaired. However, pursuant to paragraph .23 of AR-C section 80, if the accountant elects to disclose a description about the reasons the accountant's independence is impaired, the accountant is required to include all such reasons in the description.

Although the accountant is not required to disclose that his or her independence impairment was subsequently cured, the accountant may elect to make such a disclosure. An illustration of the final paragraph in an accountant's compilation report if the accountant elects to make such a disclosure is as follows: "As of and for the year ended December 31, 20X1, I was not independent with respect to XYZ Company. I am currently independent with respect to XYZ Company."

As noted previously, the accountant is not precluded from disclosing a description about the reason(s) for the impairment and how the impairment was subsequently cured.

[Issue Date: May 2012; Revised, March 2016, to reflect conforming changes necessary due to the issuance of SSARS No. 21.]

[.31] Reserved

.32 Modification to the Accountant's Compilation or Review Report When a Client Adopts a Private Company Council Accounting Alternative

Inquiry—A private company client has adopted one or more of the Private Company Council (PCC) accounting alternatives in the current year and disclosed the change in accounting principle, which is material to the financial statements. Is the accountant required to add a separate paragraph to the compilation or review report for this change in accounting principle?

Reply—No, there is no requirement in the SSARSs for an accountant to add a separate paragraph to a compilation or review report to disclose a change in accounting principle. Though there is no requirement for an accountant to add a separate paragraph to a compilation or review report, the SSARSs do not preclude the accountant from voluntarily including such a paragraph regarding the change in accounting principle.

[Issue Date: March 2014; Revised, March 2016, to reflect conforming changes necessary due to the issuance of SSARS No. 21.]

.33 Compilation or Review Report in Which Management Does Not Include Disclosure Related to Adoption of a PCC Accounting Alternative

Inquiry—When management has adopted one or more of the PCC accounting alternatives but does not disclose this change in accounting principle, which is material to the financial statements, how should the accountant's compilation or review report be modified?

Reply—If the accountant has determined that the change in accounting principle has a material effect on the financial statements and management does not disclose this change in the financial statements, the accountant is required to address the known departure from GAAP

- modifying the compilation report (assuming management has not elected to omit substantially all disclosures) in accordance with paragraphs .27–.31 of AR-C section 80, or
- modifying the review report in accordance with paragraphs .56–.60 of AR-C section 90.

[Issue Date: March 2014; Revised, March 2016, to reflect conforming changes necessary due to the issuance of SSARS No. 21.]

[.34] Reserved

Q&A Section 9160

Other Reporting Issues

[.01] Reserved

[.02] Reserved

.03 Dates on Cover for Financial Statements

Inquiry—Paragraph .57 of AU-C section 700A, *Forming an Opinion and Reporting on Financial Statements* (AICPA, *Professional Standards*), specifies that an auditor's report disclose that prior year financial statements presented for comparative purposes are unaudited. Is it appropriate to include the dates of both the current year and prior year financial statements on the cover of the financial statements?

Reply—Both years may be included on the cover if the financial statements for the prior year are referred to as unaudited.

[Revised, December 2012, to reflect conforming changes necessary due to the issuance of SAS Nos. 122–126.]

[.04] Reserved

[.05] Reserved

[.06] Reserved

.07 Financial Statements Cover Period Longer Than Twelve Months

Inquiry—Is it acceptable for an auditor to express an opinion on financial statements covering a period longer than 12 months?

Reply—It is acceptable provided the title of the financial statements is descriptive of the period covered and the auditor's report clearly indicates the period covered by the financial statements.

.08 Title of Auditors' Report

Inquiry—Does the auditor's report require a title?

Reply—Paragraph .23 of AU-C section 700 states "The auditor's report should have a title that includes the word *independent* to clearly indicate that it is the report of an independent auditor." Paragraph .16 of AU-C section 705, *Modifications to the Opinion in the Independent Auditor's Report* (AICPA, *Professional Standards*), states, in part, "When the auditor is not independent but is required by law or regulation to report on the financial statements, the auditor should disclaim an opinion and specifically state that the auditor is not independent." Therefore, if the auditor is not independent, the auditor's report should not have a title that includes the word *independent*.

[Revised, December 2012, to reflect conforming changes necessary due to the issuance of SAS Nos. 122–126.]

[.09] Reserved

.10 Distinction Between Internal and General Use of Financial Statements

Inquiry—Are financial statements differentiated between internal and general use in the professional reporting literature?

Reply—Internal use by management and general use of financial statements are not differentiated with respect to audit, review, or compilation reports on historical financial statements. However, the distinction between general and internal use is relevant with respect to examinations, agreed-upon procedures, and compilation reports with respect to financial forecasts and projections.

[Revised January 2015.]

[.11] Reserved

[.12] Reserved

[.13] Reserved

.14 Part of Audit Performed by Another Independent Auditor Who Has Ceased Operations

Inquiry—If an auditor who has ceased operations audited the financial statements of one or more components included in an entity's group financial statements, may the group engagement partner make reference in the auditor's report on the group financial statements to the audit of that auditor or assume responsibility for that auditor's work in accordance with AU-C section 600, *Special Considerations—Audits of Group Financial Statements (Including the Work of Component Auditors)* (AICPA, *Professional Standards*)?

Reply—The group engagement partner may make reference to the audit of a component auditor, or assume responsibility for that auditor's work, only if the component auditor has issued an audit report and the group engagement team has completed the procedures required by AU-C section 600 regarding the component auditor prior to the time that the other auditor ceased operations. The procedures described in AU-C section 600 cannot be appropriately performed after the other auditor has ceased operations. In situations in which the group engagement team cannot use the work of the component auditor in accordance with AU-C section 600, the group engagement team should perform audit procedures sufficient to afford a reasonable basis for an opinion on the financial statements under audit. However, review of the component auditor's working papers may have an effect on the nature, timing, and extent of those procedures.

[Revised, December 2012, to reflect conforming changes necessary due to the issuance of SAS Nos. 122–126.]

[.15] Reserved

[.16] Reserved

[.17] Reserved

[.18] Reserved

[.19] Reserved

[.20] Reserved

.21 Fiscal Years for Tax and Financial Reporting Purposes Differ

Inquiry—Can an entity have different fiscal years for tax and reporting purposes?

Reply—There is no requirement in the accounting literature for the tax and the financial reporting year-end to be the same. However, having different fiscal years complicates further any interperiod tax allocation the entity may have.

[.22] Reserved

[.23] Reserved

.24 Required Presentation of the Statement of Stockholders' Equity

Inquiry—Is the statement of stockholders' equity required when financial position and results of operations are presented?

Reply—Disclosure of changes in capital accounts and retained earnings is required. According to Financial Accounting Standards Board (FASB) *Accounting Standards Codification* (ASC) 505-10-50-2, "if both financial position and results of operations are presented, disclosure of changes in the separate accounts comprising stockholders' equity (in addition to retained earnings) . . . is required to make the financial statements sufficiently informative. Disclosure of such changes may take the form of separate statements or may be made in the basic financial statements or notes thereto."

[Revised, June 2009, to reflect conforming changes necessary due to the issuance of FASB ASC.]

.25 Use of Singular v. Plural Terminology for Accountants and Auditors

Inquiry—In reporting on financial statements subjected to an audit, review, or compilation engagement, should accountants use singular or plural terminology when referring to themselves?

Reply—Use of plural or singular terminology is not addressed in the professional standards. Illustrative auditors' reports in Statements on Auditing Standards use plural terminology, while the accountants' compilation and review reports in Statements on Standards for Accounting and Review Services use both singular and plural.

In practice, sole practitioners often use singular terms; firms that have one partner with professional staff use both singular and plural; and firms that have more than one partner most often use plural. However, the use of singular or plural references to the accountant or auditor is purely discretionary. Firm may recognize efficiencies in report preparation by being consistent in their use of singular or plural in all reports.

[Revised January 2015.]

[.26] Reserved

.27 Providing Opinion on a Schedule of Expenditures of Federal Awards in Relation to an Entity's Financial Statements as a Whole When the Schedule of Expenditures of Federal Awards Is on a Different Basis of Accounting Than the Financial Statements

Inquiry—An entity subject to Office of Management and Budget Circular A-133, *Audits of States, Local Governments and Non-Profit Organizations* (Circular A-133), prepares its Schedule of Expenditures of Federal Awards (SEFA) on the cash basis of accounting while preparing its basic financial statements in accordance with GAAP. Paragraph .05*a* of AU-C section 725, *Supplementary Information in Relation to the Financial Statements as a Whole* (AICPA, *Professional Standards*), requires the auditor to determine that the supplementary information was derived from, and relates directly to, the underlying accounting and other records used to prepare the financial statements. If the SEFA is prepared on a different basis of accounting than that of the financial statements, but the SEFA can be reconciled to the underlying accounting and other records used in preparing the financial statements or to the financial statements themselves, may the auditor provide an opinion on whether the SEFA is presented fairly, in all material respects, in relation to the entity's financial statements as a whole?

Reply—As discussed in chapter 7 of the AICPA Audit Guide Government Auditing Standards *and Circular A-133 Audits*, Circular A-133 requires the auditor to determine and provide an opinion on whether the SEFA is presented fairly in all material respects in relation to the financial statements as a whole (often referred to as providing an in-relation-to opinion). Further, Circular A-133 does not specifically prescribe the basis of accounting to be used by the entity to prepare the SEFA. Therefore, some SEFAs may be presented on a basis of accounting that differs from that used to prepare the financial statements. Nevertheless, the entity is required to disclose the basis of accounting and the significant accounting policies used in preparing the SEFA.

As noted in paragraph 7.03 of the guide, the auditee should be able to reconcile amounts presented in the financial statements to related amounts in the SEFA. Further, paragraph .07*d* of AU-C section 725 would require the auditor to compare and reconcile the SEFA to the underlying accounting and other records used in preparing the financial statements or to the financial statements themselves.

Therefore, as long as the cash basis SEFA can be reconciled back to the underlying accounting and other records used in preparing the financial statements or to the financial statements themselves, the conditions set forth in paragraph .05*a* of AU-C section 725 are considered met, and, as long as the other conditions and requirements of AU-C section 725 are met, the auditor may provide an in-relation-to opinion on the SEFA.

[Issue Date: June 2011; Revised, December 2012, to reflect conforming changes necessary due to the issuance of SAS Nos. 122–126.]

.28 Combining a Going Concern Emphasis-of-Matter Paragraph With Another Emphasis-of-Matter Paragraph

Inquiry—In certain circumstances, generally accepted auditing standards (GAAS) requires the auditor to include an emphasis-of-matter paragraph in the auditor's report.[1] For example, paragraph .15 of AU-C section 570A, *The Auditor's Consideration of An Entity's Ability to Continue as a Going Concern* (AICPA, *Professional Standards*), states that if, after considering identified conditions or events and management's plans, the auditor concludes that substantial doubt about the entity's ability to continue as a going concern for a reasonable period of time remains, the auditor should include an emphasis-of-matter paragraph in the auditor's report to reflect that conclusion.

In addition to certain paragraphs in GAAS that require the auditor to include an emphasis-of-matter paragraph in the auditor's report, an emphasis-of-matter paragraph may also be included in the auditor's report, at the auditor's

---

[1] Exhibit B, "List of AU-C Sections Containing Requirements for Emphasis-of-Matter Paragraphs" of AU-C section 706, *Emphasis-of-Matter Paragraphs and Other-Matter Paragraphs in the Independent Auditor's Report* (AICPA, *Professional Standards*).

discretion, to draw users' attention to a matter appropriately presented or disclosed in the financial statements that, in the auditor's professional judgment, is of such importance that it is fundamental to users' understanding of the financial statements, in accordance with paragraph .06 of AU-C section 706, *Emphasis-of-Matter Paragraphs and Other-Matter Paragraphs in the Independent Auditor's Report* (AICPA, *Professional Standards*).

May an auditor combine a going concern emphasis-of-matter paragraph with another emphasis-of-matter paragraph, such as an emphasis-of-matter paragraph highlighting the significance of related-party transactions?

Reply—AU-C section 706 does not preclude the auditor from combining matters in an emphasis-of-matter paragraph that are either required to be included in the auditor's report or included at the auditor's discretion, recognizing that the requirements in paragraph .07 of AU-C section 706 should be followed for each matter identified. Whether the auditor decides to combine more than one matter in the same paragraph is a matter of professional judgment. However, it may be prudent to emphasize each matter separately in separate paragraphs to make it clear that you have more than one matter of emphasis in your report.

Regardless whether the matters are combined or separated, the auditor should (*a*) include the emphasis-of-matter paragraph(s) immediately after the opinion paragraph, (*b*) use the heading "Emphasis of Matter" or other appropriate heading, (*c*) include in the paragraph(s) a clear reference to the matters being emphasized and to where relevant disclosures that fully describe the matters can be found in the financial statements, and (*d*) indicate that the auditor's opinion is not modified with respect to the matters emphasized.

With regard to (*b*) preceding, another heading may be used if it adequately describes the nature of the matter being disclosed or communicated. When more than one matter is being emphasized, it may be appropriate to be more descriptive in the use of the headings.

[Issue Date: May 2012; Revised, December 2012, to reflect conforming changes necessary due to the issuance of SAS Nos. 122–126.]

.29 Modification to the Auditor's Report When a Client Adopts a PCC Accounting Alternative

Inquiry—A private company audit client has adopted one or more of the PCC accounting alternatives in the current year and disclosed the change in accounting principle, which is material to the financial statements. Is the auditor required to add an emphasis-of-matter (EOM) paragraph to the auditor's report for this change in accounting principle?

Reply—Yes. According to paragraphs .07–.12 of AU-C section 708, *Consistency of Financial Statements* (AICPA, *Professional Standards*), if an entity has adopted a change in accounting principle and that change has a material effect on the financial statements, the auditor should include, in the auditor's report, an EOM paragraph in the period of the change and in subsequent periods until the new accounting principle is applied in all periods presented. If the change in accounting principle is accounted for by retrospective application to the financial statements of all prior periods presented, the EOM paragraph is needed only in the period of such change.

The auditor's EOM paragraph should describe the change in accounting principle and provide a reference to the entity's note disclosure. Following is an illustration of this paragraph when a private company has elected to adopt a change in accounting for goodwill in its December 31, 2014 financial statements (and that change is material and has been disclosed in the financial statements):

> ***Change in Accounting Principle***
>
> As discussed in Note X to the financial statements, the Company has elected to change its method of accounting for goodwill in 2014. Our opinion is not modified with respect to this matter.

[Issue Date: March 2014.]

.30 Modification to the Auditor's Report When a Client Adopts a PCC Accounting Alternative That Results in a Change to a Previously Issued Report

Inquiry—A private company client has adopted the guidance in FASB Accounting Standards Update (ASU) No. 2014-07, *Consolidation (Topic 810): Applying Variable Interest Entities (VIE) Guidance to Common Control Leasing Arrangements*, in the current year. In the prior year, the private company elected not to consolidate a material variable interest entity (VIE) and, therefore, the auditor's report was modified in order to note a material departure from GAAP. The private company is now presenting comparative financial statements, and this accounting change (which is required to be applied retrospectively) no longer requires the material VIE to be consolidated. Accordingly, the prior year auditor's report on those statements would no longer need to be modified. Is the auditor required to add an EOM paragraph to the current year's report?

Reply—Yes. According to paragraph .53 of AU-C section 700A when reporting on prior period financial statements in connection with an audit of the current period, the auditor should disclose the following matters in an EOM paragraph in accordance with AU-C section 706 if the auditor's opinion on such prior period financial statements differs from the opinion the auditor previously expressed:

1. The date of the auditor's previous report
2. The type of opinion previously expressed
3. The substantive reasons for the different opinion
4. That the auditor's opinion on the amended financial statements is different from the auditor's previous opinion

Following is an illustration of an EOM paragraph when a private company has elected to adopt ASU No. 2014-07 for a VIE when there is a common control leasing arrangement and that VIE was material in 2013 and 2012:

> ***Emphasis of Matter—Variable Interest Entity***
>
> In our report dated March 1, 2013, we expressed an opinion that the 2012 financial statements did not fairly present the financial position, results of operations, and cash flows of ABC Company in accordance with accounting principles generally accepted in the United States of America because ABC Company excluded a variable interest entity from the accompanying financial statement that, in our opinion, should have been consolidated. As described in Note X, in March 2014 the Financial Accounting Standards Board issued Accounting Standards Update No. 2014-07, *Consolidation (Topic 810): Applying Variable Interest Entities Guidance to Common Control Leasing Arrangements*, which makes changes to the FASB guidance and no longer

requires nonpublic companies to apply variable interest entity guidance to certain common control leasing arrangements. This guidance required retrospective application. Accordingly, our present opinion on the 2012 financial statements, as presented herein, is different from that expressed in our previous report. Our opinion on the 2013 financial statements is not modified with respect to this matter.

[Issue Date: April 2014; Revised: September 2014.]

Q&A Section 9170

Supplementary Information

.01 Consolidating Information Presented on the Face of the Financial Statements

Inquiry—An entity wants to present consolidating information in order to present the separate financial statements of the components of the consolidated group. Does the auditor's reporting responsibility change depending on whether the consolidating information is presented on the face of the financial statements in separate columns or whether the consolidating information is shown outside the basic consolidated financial statements?

Reply—An entity may present consolidating information either on the face of the statements or outside the basic financial statements.

When the auditor is engaged to express an opinion only on the consolidated financial statements, and consolidating information is included on the face of the financial statements, such consolidating information would be considered supplementary information, the same as if the information was presented outside the basic financial statements, as long as such information is clearly differentiated from the financial statements because of its nature and how it is presented. For example, when the consolidated financial statements include columns of information about the components of the consolidated group, the balance sheets might be titled "Consolidated Balance Sheet—December 31, 20X1, With Consolidating Information," and the columns including the consolidating information, might be marked "Consolidating Information." When the consolidating information is presented outside the basic financial statements, the consolidating information might be titled "Consolidating Balance Sheets, December 31, 20X1." If the other information is clearly differentiated from the basic financial statements, such information may be identified as *unaudited* or as *not covered by the auditor's report*.

When the consolidated financial statements include consolidating information that has not been separately audited, and the auditor is engaged to report on the consolidating information in relation to the basic consolidated financial statements as a whole, the auditor's report on the consolidating information might read as follows:

> Our audit was conducted for the purpose of forming an opinion on the consolidated financial statements as a whole. The consolidating information is presented for purposes of additional analysis rather than to present the financial position, results of operations, and cash flows of the individual companies and is not a required part of the consolidated financial statements. Such information is the responsibility of management and was derived from, and relates directly to, the underlying accounting and other records used to prepare the consolidated financial statements. The information has been subjected to the auditing procedures applied in the audit of the consolidated financial statements and certain additional procedures, including comparing and reconciling such information directly to the underlying accounting and other records used to prepare the consolidated financial statements or to the consolidated financial statements themselves, and other additional procedures, in accordance with auditing standards generally accepted in the United States of America. In our opinion, the information

is fairly stated in all material respects in relation to the consolidated financial statements as a whole.

When the auditor is engaged to express an opinion on both the consolidated financial statements and the separate financial statements of the components presented in consolidating financial statements, the auditor's reporting responsibilities with respect to the separate financial statements are the same as his or her responsibilities with respect to the consolidated financial statements. In such cases, the consolidating financial statements and accompanying notes should include all the disclosures that would be necessary for presentation in accordance with generally accepted accounting principles of separate financial statements of each component.

[Issue Date: September 2011; Revised, December 2012, to reflect conforming changes necessary due to the issuance of SAS Nos. 122–126.]

.02 Supplementary Information That Accompanies Interim Financial Information

Inquiry—When performing an interim review in accordance with AU-C section 930, *Interim Financial Information* (AICPA, *Professional Standards*), is the auditor required to report on supplementary information when a client presents supplementary information along with interim financial statements?

Reply—No; however, nothing precludes the auditor from reporting on the supplementary information. If the auditor decides to report on the supplementary information, the auditor may disclaim on the supplementary information or issue a report based on the limited procedures performed as part of the interim review. An example of a report based on the limited procedures applied in the review follows:

> Our review was made primarily for the purpose of obtaining a basis for reporting whether we are aware of any material modifications that should be made to the interim financial statements in order for them to be in conformity with accounting principles generally accepted in the United States of America through performing limited procedures. The accompanying supplementary information is presented for purposes of additional analysis and is not a required part of the interim financial statements. The supplementary information has been subjected to the limited procedures applied in the review of the interim financial statements, and we did not become aware of any material modifications that should be made to such information.

[Issue Date: October 2012; Revised, December 2012, to reflect conforming changes necessary due to the issuance of SAS Nos. 122–126.]

Q&A Section 9180

Required Supplementary Information

.01 Required Supplementary Information in Historical Prior Periods and Auditor Independence of the Entity

Inquiry—AU-C section 730, *Required Supplementary Information* (AICPA, *Professional Standards*), defines required supplementary information (RSI) and requires the auditor of an entity's basic financial statements to perform specified procedures on such RSI and report in accordance with that section.

If the RSI extends back to any historical prior period (back periods) in which the auditor did not perform an engagement that required independence, is the auditor required, for purposes of complying with AU-C section 730, to be independent of the entity in those back periods?

Reply—Generally accepted auditing standards require the auditor to be independent for any period being audited and covered by the auditor's opinion. In the absence of any separate requirement in the particular circumstances of the engagement, the auditor's opinion on the basic financial statements does not cover RSI. In accordance with AU-C section 730, RSI is not part of the basic financial statements. Furthermore, the specified procedures required to be performed on RSI are limited and do not provide the auditor with sufficient appropriate audit evidence to express an opinion or provide any assurance on the RSI.

Because of the characteristics of RSI and the limited nature of the specified procedures, the auditor is not required, for purposes of complying with AU-C section 730, to be independent of the entity in those back periods as long as the auditor's opinion does not cover RSI.

[Issue Date: August 2015.]

Q&A Section 9500

ATTESTATION ENGAGEMENTS

TABLE OF CONTENTS

Section

Section

Section

Q&A Section 9510

Attestation Reports

.01 Testing Prospective Financial Information as Part of Performing Auditing Procedures

Inquiry—Generally accepted accounting principles require that certain accounts be carried at or adjusted to fair value. Many fair value models are based on the present value of future cash flows or earnings. In making those fair value calculations, management may seek the auditor's assistance in developing what may be considered either a full or partial financial forecast. In testing an entity's fair value calculation, an auditor might test management's assumptions including, for example future cash flows for the next five years. Similarly, the auditor may make an independent estimate of fair value, for example, by using a cash flow model developed and prepared by the auditor.

Does the auditor's assistance in developing or preparing prospective cash flows require the auditor to examine or compile such information in accordance with Statements on Standards for Attest Engagements (SSAEs)?

Reply—No. Paragraph .01 of AT section 101, *Attest Engagements* (AICPA, *Professional Standards*), states that the attest standards apply when a practitioner is "engaged to issue or does issue an examination…." Accordingly, the auditor would not be required to follow the SSAEs unless the auditor has also been engaged to examine, compile, assemble or apply agreed upon procedures to prospective financial information or the auditor issues an examination, compilation, assembly or agreed upon report on prospective financial information.

.02 Availability of Criteria for a Fee

Inquiry—A practitioner may perform an attestation engagement only if he or she has reason to believe that the subject matter is capable of evaluation against criteria that are suitable and available to users. Paragraph .33 of AT section 101 states in part that criteria should be available to users in one or more of a number of ways, including available publicly. Paragraph .34 of AT section 101 goes on to say "If criteria are only available to specified parties, the practitioner's report should be restricted to those parties who have access to the criteria as described in paragraphs .78 and .80 [of AT section 101]." If criteria is only available for a fee, is it considered available publicly for the purpose of paragraphs .33–.34 of AT section 101?

Reply—Yes, as long as the criteria is available to any person in the normal course of business, it is considered available publicly. This would include certain industry associations and other organizations that make criteria available free of charge to their members but charge a fee to nonmembers.

.03 Reporting on New York State Medicaid Cost Reports

On June 27, 2006, the New York State Department of Health ("DOH") issued a prescribed "Opinion of Independent Accountant" (the "Cost Report Opinion") that is required to be utilized by CPAs reporting on audits and attestation engagements associated with a nursing home's filing of its Annual Report of Residential Health Care Facility (RHCF-4). The purpose of this Technical Question and Answer ("TQA") is to provide clarity to CPAs performing these engagements. This TQA also may be useful to a CPA performing audits and attestation engagements for the purpose of reporting on an Annual Institutional Cost Report of Hospitals and Hospital Healthcare Complexes and other cost reports filed with the New York State Department of Health or other New York State agencies.

The Cost Report Opinion as prescribed by the DOH references certain data in the facility's RHCF-4 cost report (the "supplemental data"). The Cost Report Opinion includes three separate opinions:

1. An opinion on the facility's financial statements (displayed as schedules within the cost report) based on an audit conducted in accordance with generally accepted auditing standards.
2. An opinion as to whether the supplemental data is stated fairly in all material respects in relation to the financial statements as a whole.
3. An opinion under the attestation standards (the "attestation opinion") on the supplemental data's conformity with the DOH cost report instructions.

The required format of the Cost Report Opinion, as prescribed by the DOH, is attached as Exhibit A. The AICPA staff understands that all DOH Cost Reports, including the Annual Institutional Cost Report of Hospitals and Hospital Healthcare Complexes, within New York State will include similar language.

The Cost Report Opinion contains certain terminology that differs from the language found in AICPA professional standards and therefore may be unclear to practitioners. AICPA staff held conversations with the DOH for the purpose of better understanding their views about these wording differences and their expectations about the procedures a CPA would perform to issue the Cost Report Opinion. The following responses are those of AICPA staff based on their understanding of the requirements and expectations of the DOH.

Four issues are addressed in this Technical Question and Answer:

1. The CPA's consideration of materiality in completing the attestation engagement.
2. The meaning of the term "certification" in the Cost Report Opinion, and its impact on the CPA's procedures.
3. The Independence Standards that the CPA is expected to adhere to in the performance of the engagement.
4. Dating the CPA's report.

Inquiry—The attestation opinion contained in the Cost Report Opinion reads as follows:

> In our opinion, the above supplemental data are in all material respects in conformity with the applicable instructions relating to the preparation of the RHCF-4 as furnished by the New York State Department of Health for the year ended Month XX, 20XX.

With respect to the attestation opinion's phrase, "in all material respects," may a CPA utilize materiality applied at the financial statement level to plan the scope of the attestation procedures, or in the evaluation of misstatements, if any, that are identified through the attestation procedures?

Reply—No. The AICPA staff understands that the DOH believes that the use of materiality applied at the financial statement level would not be appropriate for planning or performing attestation procedures related to cost report instructions, or for evaluating any misstatements identified related to conformity with cost report instructions. Rather, the AICPA staff's understanding is that materiality should be determined and applied at the individual schedule level. Accordingly, the DOH expects the CPA to perform procedures on line items, columns, and totals in the specific schedules covered by the CPA's attestation opinion to be able to opine that the financial and statistical data presented on each schedule has been prepared in conformity, in all material respects as determined at the individual schedule level, with the applicable instructions. As a result, the CPA ordinarily will perform procedures beyond those performed in the audit of the financial statements with respect to certain amounts included in the supplemental data. These additional procedures result from the application of a lower materiality level for procedures performed on information included in the individual schedules as compared to the materiality level applied in the financial statement audit.

The CPA may consider attestation risk and materiality in applying his or her professional judgment in determining the nature, timing and extent of attestation procedures for testing the financial and statistical data. The CPA's risk assessment should give consideration to the effects of whether amounts in a particular schedule are either understated or overstated. The quantity of attestation evidence needed is affected by the risk of misstatement (items presenting greater risk likely will require evaluation of attestation evidence beyond that deemed necessary for purposes of the financial statement audit) and by the quality of such attestation evidence. In determining the nature, timing and extent of attest procedures to perform, the CPA may give consideration to:

1. His or her assessment of the facility's policies and procedures related to the preparation of the cost report in accordance with the applicable instructions and,
2. Deficiencies related to internal control over the preparation of the cost report (which may differ from internal control over financial reporting evaluated for purposes of the financial statement audit).

In addition to the above considerations, the CPA may focus his or her testing on those amounts, line items, or schedules that impact the facility's reimbursement or rate setting most significantly.

The purpose of testing the supplemental data is to obtain sufficient appropriate attestation evidence to provide a reasonable basis for the CPA's opinion on whether the financial and statistical data in the schedules is in conformity, in all material respects as determined at the individual schedule level, with the applicable instructions. The CPA will have performed audit procedures directed toward evaluating certain amounts included in the supplemental data in connection with the audit of the facility's financial statements. The CPA may consider the results of those procedures in determining the nature, timing and extent of additional work necessary because of a lower materiality level for individual schedules compared to the materiality level for the financial statements.

The CPA ordinarily would select individual amounts from the supplemental data to examine based on the risk of misstatement or departure from the cost report instructions or by applying sampling. A combination of both selection techniques as described below may be necessary to provide the CPA with sufficient appropriate attestation evidence relative to the supplemental data.

The CPA may select amounts to test based on the risk of material misstatement associated with the reimbursement or rate-setting impact of a particular amount, line item, or schedule. For example, the costs associated with non-moveable equipment may have a greater impact on rate setting when compared with major moveable equipment. Accordingly, the CPA may determine that it is necessary to obtain more attestation evidence related to costs for non-moveable equipment. Factors influencing the CPA's assessment of risk might include the facility's history of misstatements in the cost report, the complexity associated with the preparation of a schedule and the effectiveness of management's internal control over the preparation of the applicable cost report schedules.

The CPA may select amounts to test utilizing sampling. The CPA uses his or her professional judgment to determine when it may be appropriate to use sampling and the sample size.

The CPA's procedures ordinarily will include agreeing individual supplemental data amounts, as appropriate, to related audit documentation or the audited financial statements, or to the general ledger, sub-ledgers, or client analyses prepared in support of the cost report schedules. In addition, the CPA's procedures ordinarily will include substantive procedures applied to selected supplemental data amounts, which are designed to identify material misstatements at the individual schedule level. Substantive procedures include tests of details and substantive analytical procedures. For example, the CPA might select supplemental data amounts and compare them to vendor's invoices or analytically compare the relationship of amounts and current year expectations.

As a result of procedures performed, the CPA may identify departures from the cost report instructions. In that case, the CPA would need to re-consider his or her initial risk assessment and determine whether additional procedures need to be performed. If departures from the cost report instructions are not corrected by facility management, the CPA would consider whether such departures result in the CPA opining that there is a material departure from the cost report instructions.

Inquiry—The Cost Report Opinion includes the following paragraph:

> The undersigned hereby certifies this opinion and that I/we have disclosed any and all material facts known to me/us, disclosure of which is necessary to make this opinion, the basic financial statements and the supplemental data not misleading. The undersigned hereby further certifies that I/we will disclose any material fact discovered by me/us subsequent to this certification which existed at the time of this certification and was not disclosed in the basic financial statements or the supplemental data, the disclosure of which is necessary to make the basic financial statements or the supplemental data not misleading and will disclose any material misstatement in said financial statements or supplemental data.

Given that the terms "certifies" and "certification" are not defined in AICPA professional standards, should the CPA perform additional procedures beyond those contemplated by Statements on Auditing Standards (SASs) and Statements on Standards for Attestation Engagements (SSAEs) in order to provide a "certification"? Additionally, since the financial statements and supplemental schedules are the responsibility of management, what is the CPA's responsibility with respect to information discovered subsequent to the certification's report date?

Reply—New York State Public Heath Law Section 2808-b states in part "All financial statements or financial information…shall be certified in their entirety by an independent public accountant…." Although the phrase "certifies this opinion" does not appear in AICPA professional standards, there is nothing in the concept of a certification that would be in conflict with or contrary to those standards. The CPA may consider the phrase "certifies this opinion" to be the equivalent of rendering or expressing an opinion. However, it is the responsibility of the CPA to determine, and take any and all steps that are necessary and proper, in order to be able to appropriately sign the Cost Report Opinion.

Public Health Law 2808-b further states that "Subsequent to such certification (the CPA should disclose) any material fact discovered by him which existed at the time of such certification …which is necessary to make the financial statements or financial information not misleading …." If the CPA becomes aware of information, which relates to the audited financial statements or supplemental schedules previously reported on by him or her, but which was not known to the CPA prior to the release date of the Cost Report Opinion, and such subsequently discovered facts are deemed to be necessary to make the basic financial statements not misleading, the CPA should ensure that such subsequently discovered information is communicated to the DOH, including that the audited financial statements are not to be relied upon. Paragraph .17*b* of AU-C section 560, *Subsequent Events and Subsequently Discovered Facts* (AICPA, *Professional Standards*), provides that the CPA should assess whether the steps taken by the client are timely and appropriate to ensure that the DOH is informed of the situation. However, the CPA retains the responsibility to ensure that such information is communicated to the DOH—whether by the client or the CPA. In fulfilling this responsibility, if the client refuses to make such communication the CPA should notify the DOH of the information and that the Cost Report Opinion should no longer be relied upon.

Inquiry—The Cost Report Opinion is titled "Opinion of Independent Accountant" and includes the following paragraph:

> During the period of this professional engagement, at the time of expressing this opinion, and during the period covered by the financial statements I/we did not have nor were committed to acquire, any direct financial interest or material indirect financial interest in the ownership or operation of the facility and I/we were not connected in any way with the ownership, financing or operation of the facility as a director, officer or employee, or in any capacity other than as an independent certified public accountant or independent public accountant.

What independence requirements are expected to be followed in conducting the engagements contemplated by the Cost Report Opinion?

Reply—The CPA should follow Independence Standards as issued by the AICPA and that are codified in the AICPA *Code of Professional Conduct* as well as any independence standards issued by the N.Y. Board of Accountancy.

Inquiry—The engagements underlying the Cost Report Opinion may have been completed on different dates. For example, the audits of the financial statements and the supplemental data in relation to the basic financial statements taken as a whole may have been completed (and the CPA's opinions thereon rendered) before the CPA completes the work related to the attestation opinion. In those situations, may the Cost Report Opinion be dual-dated?

Reply—Yes. Although dual-dating is not required, the Cost Report Opinion may be dual dated for the attestation opinion as follows:

> **[Date]**, except for our examination of the conformity of specified data with the instructions for the year ended December 31, 20XX, as to which the date is **[Date]**.

Exhibit

FORM RHCF-4 DOH 490 (06/07/06)

PLEASE COMPLETE ALL OF THE FOLLOWING INFORMATION

____

NAME OF FACILITY

____

OPERATING CERTIFICATE NUMBER

____

NAME OF ADMINISTRATOR

____

NAME OF CONTROLLER OR CHIEF FISCAL OFFICER

Opinion of Independent Accountant

We have audited the balance sheet of __________________________ as of December 31, 2004 and the related statements of operations, changes in net assets or equity and cash flows for the year then ended included as Exhibits A through E (the basic financial statements), except for lines 041, 042 and 043 of Exhibit E of Part IV of the accompanying Annual Report of Residential Health Care Facility (RHCF-4) identified by Declaration Control Number _______. These financial statements are the responsibility of the facility management. Our responsibility is to express an opinion on these financial statements based on our audit.

We conducted our audit in accordance with auditing standards generally accepted in the United States of America. Those standards require that we plan and perform the audit to obtain reasonable assurance about whether the financial statements are free of material misstatement. An audit includes examining, on a test basis, evidence supporting the amounts and disclosures in the financial statements. An audit also includes assessing the accounting principles used and significant estimates made by management as well as evaluating the overall financial statement presentation. We believe that our audit provides a reasonable basis for our opinion.

In our opinion, the aforementioned financial statements present fairly, in all material respects, the financial position of __________________ as of December 31, 2004 and the results of its operations, changes in net assets or equity and its cash flows for the year then ended, in conformity with accounting principles generally accepted in the United States of America.

Our audit was conducted for the purpose of forming an opinion on the basic financial statements taken as whole. The following supplemental data, which are the responsibility of the facility management, are presented for the purpose of additional analysis and are not required as part of the basic financial statements identified by Declaration Control Number ________.

PART I—STATISTICAL DATA
Bed Capacity—Patient Days, Line 017
PART II—CROSSWALK
Schedule 7, Column 0161
Schedules 8 through 11, except for Schedule 8C, Lines 010 through 035
PART IV—UNIFORM REPORT
Exhibit H, except Columns 0034–0044, Lines 054–057, 060–069 and 090
Exhibit I
Schedule 4, except Columns 0114–0122, Lines 054–057, 060–069 and 090
Schedule 6

The above supplemental data have been subjected to the auditing procedures applied in the audit of the basic financial statements and, in our opinion, are stated fairly in all material respects when considered in conjunction with the basic financial statements included as Exhibits A through E of the RHCF-4, taken as a whole.

Our procedures were not intended to determine compliance with, and therefore would not necessarily disclose deviations from, reporting requirements contained in the New York State Residential Health Care Facility Accounting and Reporting Manual.

The other information included on Parts I, II, III and IV of the Annual Report of Residential Health Care Facility (RHCF-4) identified by Declaration Control Number ________, (not detailed in the preceding paragraphs), was not audited by us and, accordingly, we express no opinion thereon.

We have examined the above supplemental data for the year ended December 31, 2004. [Facility name] ______________ management is responsible for the preparation of the supplemental data in conformity with the applicable instructions relating to the preparation of the RHCF-4 as furnished by the New York State Department of Health for the year ended December 31, 2004. Our responsibility is to express an opinion on the supplemental data's conformity with those instructions based upon our examination.

Our examination was conducted in accordance with attestation standards established by the American Institute of Certified Public Accountants and, accordingly, included examining, on a test basis, evidence supporting the supplemental data's conformity with the applicable instructions and performing such other procedures as we considered necessary in the circumstances. We believe that our examination provides a reasonable basis for our opinion.

In our opinion, the above supplemental data are in all material respects in conformity with the applicable instructions relating to the preparation of the RHCF-4 as furnished by the New York State Department of Health for the year ended December 31, 2004.

This RHCF-4 report, including this accountant's opinion, is intended solely for the information and use of the management and ownership of the facility and the officers and agencies of the State of New York, and is not intended to be and should not be used by anyone other than these specified parties.

The undersigned hereby certifies this opinion and that I/we have disclosed any and all material facts known to me/us, disclosure of which is necessary to make this opinion, the basic financial statements and the supplemental data not misleading. The undersigned hereby further certifies that I/we will disclose any material fact discovered by me/us subsequent to this certification which existed at the time of this certification and was not disclosed in the basic financial statements or the supplemental data, the disclosure of which is necessary to make the basic financial statements or the supplemental data not misleading and will disclose any material misstatement in said financial statements or supplemental data.

During the period of this professional engagement, at the time of expressing this opinion, and during the period covered by the financial statements I/we did not have nor were committed to acquire, any direct financial interest or material indirect financial interest in the ownership or operation of the facility and I/we were not connected in any way with the ownership, financing or operation of the facility as a director, officer or employee, or in any capacity other than as an independent certified public accountant or independent public accountant.

____

Signature of Accounting Firm

____

Name of Accounting Firm

By: ____________________

Signature of CPA Partner-in-Charge

____

Name of CPA

____

CPA License Number

____

Date of CPA Signature

____

Address

____

City/State/ZIP

____

Telephone

DOH 490

[Revised, December 2010 and April 2017.]

Q&A Section 9520

Statement on Standards for Attestation Engagements No. 16, Reporting on Controls at a Service Organization

[.01] Reserved

[.02] Reserved

[.03] Reserved

.04 Definition of *Service Organization* and *User Entity*

Inquiry—Statement on Standards for Attestation Engagements (SSAE) No. 16, *Reporting on Controls at a Service Organization* (AICPA, *Professional Standards*, AT sec. 801),[1] uses the terms *service organization* and *user entity*. What do these terms mean?

Reply—AT section 801 defines a *service organization* as an organization or segment of an organization that provides services to user entities, which are likely to be relevant to user entities' internal control over financial reporting (ICFR). A service organization performs a function or task for the user entities that results in data or other information that the user entities incorporate in their financial statements. Some examples of service organizations are custodians for investment companies, mortgage servicers that service loans for others, and claims processors that process medical claims for self-insured entities. AT section 801 defines a *user entity* as an entity that uses a service organization.

[Issue Date: June 2011; Revised, November 2011.]

[.05] Reserved

[.06] Reserved

.07 Types of Reports Under AT Section 801

Inquiry—Are there type 1 and type 2 reports under AT section 801?

Reply—Yes, AT section 801 enables practitioners to provide two types of service auditor's reports. In both reports the service organization must prepare a description of its system that includes, among other things, the nature of the service provided, how the service is performed, and the service organization's controls and related control objectives as they relate to the service provided. In a type 1 report, the service auditor expresses an opinion on whether the description is fairly presented (that is, does it describe what actually exists) and whether the controls included in the description are suitability designed. Controls that are suitably designed are able to achieve the related control objectives if they operate effectively. In a type 2 report, the service auditor's report contains the same opinions that are included in a type 1 report and also includes

---

[1] For service auditors' reports for periods ending on or after June 15, 2011, Statement on Standards for Attestation Engagements (SSAE) No. 16, *Reporting on Controls at a Service Organization* (AICPA, *Professional Standards*, AT sec. 801), supersedes the guidance for service auditors that previously was contained in Statement on Auditing Standards (SAS) No. 70, *Service Organizations*, as amended (now superseded). For audits of financial statements for periods ending on or after December 15, 2012, AU-C section 402, *Audit Considerations Relating to an Entity Using a Service Organization* (AICPA, *Professional Standards*), supersedes the guidance for user auditors that previously was contained in SAS No. 70, as amended (now superseded). [Footnote added, December 2012, to reflect conforming changes necessary due to the issuance of SAS Nos. 122–126.]

an opinion on whether the controls were operating effectively. Controls that operate effectively do achieve the control objectives they were intended to achieve. Both reports are examination reports, which means the practitioner obtains a high level of assurance.

[Issue Date: June 2011; Revised, November 2011.]

.08 Changes Introduced by AT Section 801

Inquiry—Does the implementation of AT section 801 result in significant changes to a service auditor's engagement?

Reply—The following are the three major changes introduced by AT section 801:

1. Management of the service organization is required to provide the service auditor with a written assertion about the fairness of the presentation of management's description of the service organization's system, the suitability of the design of the controls included in the description and, in a type 2 engagement, the operating effectiveness of those controls. That assertion is either attached to or included in the service organization's description of its system.
2. In a type 2 engagement, the description of the service organization's system and the service auditor's opinion on the description covers a period (the same period as the period covered by the service auditor's tests of the operating effectiveness of controls). In Statement on Auditing Standards (SAS) No. 70, *Service Organizations*, as amended (now superseded), the description of the service organization's system in a type 2 report was as of a specified date, rather than for a period.
3. The service auditor is required to identify, in the description of tests of controls, any tests of controls performed by the internal audit function (other than those performed in a direct assistance capacity) and the service auditor's procedures with respect to that work. Tests of controls are procedures designed to evaluate the operating effectiveness of controls in achieving the control objectives stated in management's description of the service organization's system.

The following are other differences introduced by AT section 801:

- Suitable criteria are used by management to measure and present the subject matter and by the service auditor to evaluate the subject matter. Paragraphs .14–.16 of AT section 801 provide suitable criteria for the fairness of the presentation of a service organization's description of its system and the suitability of the design and operating effectiveness of its controls. Criteria are the standards or benchmarks used to measure and present the subject matter and against which the service auditor evaluates the subject matter.
- The service auditor's examination report contains the report elements identified in paragraph .85 of AT section 101, *Attest Engagements* (AICPA, *Professional Standards*). Paragraphs .52–.53 of AT section 801 tailor these report elements to a service auditor's engagement.
- The service auditor may not use evidence obtained in prior engagements about the satisfactory operation of controls in prior periods to provide a basis for a reduction in testing in the current

period, even if it is supplemented with evidence obtained during the current period.

- AT section 801 specifically states that it is not applicable when the service auditor is reporting on controls at a service organization relevant to subject matter other than user entities' ICFR (such as controls related to regulatory compliance or privacy).

[Issue Date: June 2011; Revised, November 2011; Revised, December 2012, to reflect conforming changes necessary due to the issuance of SAS Nos. 122–126.]

.09 Implementation Guidance for Reporting on Controls at a Service Organization Under AT Section 801

Inquiry—Has the AICPA Guide *Service Organizations: Applying SAS No. 70, as Amended* (commonly known as the SAS 70 guide)[2] been rewritten to reflect AT section 801?

Reply—Yes. AICPA Guide *Service Organizations: Applying SAS No. 70, as Amended* was rewritten to reflect the requirements and guidance in AT section 801 and is available as AICPA Guide *Service Organizations, Applying SSAE No. 16*, Reporting on Controls at a Service Organization *(SOC 1)* (SOC 1[3] guide).

[Issue Date: June 2011; Revised, November 2011.]

.10 Illustrative Assertion for Management of Service Organization in an SSAE No. 16 Engagement

Inquiry—Where can I find an illustrative management assertion for an SSAE No. 16 engagement?

Reply—Exhibit A, "Illustrative Assertions by Management of a Service Organization," of AT section 801 contains illustrative management assertions for type 1 and type 2 engagements. In addition, appendix B, "Illustrative Service Auditor's Reports," of the SOC 1 guide contains illustrative type 2 reports that include management assertions.

[Issue Date: June 2011; Revised, November 2011.]

.11 Illustrative Assertion for Management of Subservice Organization in an SSAE No. 16 Engagement

Inquiry—AT section 801 requires management of a subservice organization to provide a written assertion when the inclusive method is used. AT section 801 contains illustrative management assertions for management of a service organization. Is an illustrative assertion for management of a subservice organization available?

---

[2] Prior to the issuance of SSAE No. 16, the guidance for service auditors reporting on controls at a service organization and for user auditors auditing the financial statements of a user entity was contained in SAS No. 70, as amended (now superseded). For that reason, reports on controls at a service organization were frequently referred to as "SAS 70 reports," and the related AICPA Guide *Service Organizations, Applying SAS No. 70, as Amended* was referred to as the "SAS 70 guide." [Footnote renumbered and revised, December 2012, to reflect conforming changes necessary due to the issuance of SAS Nos. 122–126.]

[3] The AICPA has introduced the service organization controls (SOC) series of reports, which are further explained in section 9530.02, "Service Organization Controls Reports." Engagements performed under AT section 801 are designated as SOC 1 engagements. AICPA Guide *Service Organizations, Applying SSAE No. 16*, Reporting on Controls at a Service Organization *(SOC 1)* is referred to as the SOC 1 guide. [Footnote renumbered, December 2012, to reflect conforming changes necessary due to the issuance of SAS Nos. 122–126.]

Reply—Yes. Example 2 of appendix B of the SOC 1 guide contains an illustrative assertion for an inclusive engagement.

[Issue Date: June 2011; Revised, November 2011.]

.12 Another CPA Firm Acts as the Accounting Department for Your Client—Auditor Responsibility

Inquiry—An auditor is in the process of planning an audit for a client and determines that significant accounting and financial reporting processes and controls are performed by an outside CPA firm. What is the auditor's responsibility with respect to the functions performed by the other CPA firm?

Reply—Paragraph .01 of AU-C section 315, *Understanding the Entity and Its Environment and Assessing the Risks of Material Misstatement* (AICPA, *Professional Standards*), addresses the auditor's responsibility to identify and assess the risks of material misstatements in the financial statements through understanding the entity and its environment, including the entity's internal control. Paragraph .13 of AU-C section 315 states that the auditor should obtain an understanding of internal control relevant to the audit. Therefore, the auditor's responsibility is the same regardless of whether the client designs and operates its own accounting processes and controls or whether those processes and controls are outsourced to a third party.

Assuming that the other CPA firm has not undergone a type 1 or type 2 service auditor's examination and, therefore, cannot provide user entities with such a report, the auditor may obtain the necessary understanding by visiting the other CPA firm's office where the information is processed to understand how the processes and controls have been designed and whether those controls have been implemented.

If the auditor intends to rely on any of the controls performed by the other CPA firm, then those controls would need to be tested to determine if they are operating effectively, just as they would if the controls had been implemented by the client.

[Issue Date: November 2011; Revised, December 2012, to reflect conforming changes necessary due to the issuance of SAS Nos. 122–126.]

.13 Placement of Management's Assertion in an SSAE No. 16 Engagement

Inquiry—Does AT section 801 require that management's assertion accompany the service organization's description of its system?

Reply—Yes. Paragraph .09*c*(vii) of AT section 801 states that one of the conditions for engagement acceptance or continuance is that management provide a written assertion that will be included in or attached to management's description of the service organization's system.

[Issue Date: November 2011.]

.14 Type 2 Reports That Cover Less Than a Six-Month Period

Inquiry—Does AT section 801 require that a type 2 report cover a minimum period?

Reply—AT section 801 discourages the service auditor from performing a type 2 engagement that covers a period of less than six months. Paragraph .A42 of AT section 801 indicates that a type 2 report that covers a period that is less than six months is unlikely to be useful to user entities and their auditors. However, there are certain limited circumstances, such as the following, in which a type 2 report covering less than six months may be considered:

- The service auditor was engaged close to the date by which the report on controls is to be issued, precluding the service auditor from testing the operating effectiveness of controls for a six month period.
- The service organization or a particular system or application has been in operation for less than six months.
- Significant changes have been made to the controls, and it is not practicable either to wait six months before issuing a report or to issue a report covering the system both before and after the changes.

[Issue Date: November 2011; Revised, December 2012, to reflect conforming changes necessary due to the issuance of SAS Nos. 122–126.]

.15 Information About Relevant IT Control Objectives and Related Controls in Description of Service Organization's System

Inquiry—Does AT section 801 require that management's description of the service organization's system include a description of the service organization's IT control objectives and related controls? If so, does the SOC 1 guide address which IT control objectives and controls would usually be relevant to a user entity's ICFR?

Reply—The definition of *service organization's system* in paragraph .07 of AT section 801 indicates that the description of the service organization's system includes the policies and procedures designed, implemented, and documented by management of the service organization to provide user entities with the services covered by the service auditor's report. Paragraph .A11 of AT section 801 further clarifies that sentence: "The policies and procedures referred to in the definition of service organization's system refer to the guidelines and activities for providing transaction processing and other services to user entities and include the infrastructure, software, people, and data that support the policies and procedures." Paragraph 3.65 of the SOC 1 guide indicates that if the control objectives in a service organization's description of its system only address application controls, and the proper functioning of general computer controls is necessary for the application controls to operate effectively, the service organization would be expected to include the relevant general computer controls in its description of the system as they relate to the specified control objectives. Appendix D, "Illustrative Control Objectives for Various Types of Service Organizations," of the SOC 1 guide includes illustrative control objectives related to general computer controls.

[Issue Date: November 2011.]

.16 Identification of Risks in the Description of the Service Organization's System

Inquiry—Does the service organization's description of its system need to identify the risks that could prevent the service organization's controls relevant to user entities' ICFR from achieving the related control objectives?

Reply—AT section 801 does not require that management identify, in its description of the service organization's system, the risks related to each control objective included in the description. However, the service auditor would probably expect management to be able to discuss its consideration of risks in designing the controls to achieve the related control objectives.

[Issue Date: November 2011.]

.17 Information About the Risk Assessment Process to Be Included in the Description

Inquiry—Paragraph .14 of AT section 801 indicates that management's description of a service organization's system should include aspects of the service organization's risk assessment process. What information should be included in describing the risk assessment process?

Reply—The content of the description of the risk assessment process will vary depending on the complexity of the service organization's process. Paragraph .A18 of AT section 801 indicates that management may have a formal or informal process for identifying relevant risks. A formal process may include estimating the significance of identified risks, assessing the likelihood of their occurrence, and deciding about actions to address them. In those circumstances, nothing precludes management from including the details of its process in the description. However, because control objectives relate to the risks that controls seek to mitigate, paragraph .A18 of AT section 801 indicates that thoughtful identification by management of the control objectives when designing, implementing, and documenting the service organization's system may itself comprise an informal process for identifying relevant risks.

[Issue Date: November 2011.]

.18 Purpose of SSAE No. 16 Reports

Inquiry—Will entities now become "SSAE 16 certified"?

Reply—No. A popular misconception about SAS No. 70, as amended (now superseded), was that a service organization became "certified" as SAS No. 70 compliant after undergoing a type 1 or type 2 service auditor's engagement. No such certification existed under SAS No. 70, as amended (now superseded), nor does it exist under AT section 801. An SSAE No. 16 report (as was the case for a SAS No. 70 report) is primarily an auditor-to-auditor communication, the purpose of which is to provide user auditors with information about controls at a service organization that are relevant to the user entities' ICFR.

[Issue Date: November 2011; Revised, December 2012, to reflect conforming changes necessary due to the issuance of SAS Nos. 122–126.]

.19 Providing a Service Organization With a Bridge Letter

Inquiry—May a service auditor provide a service organization with a *bridge letter* under AT section 801 (a letter from a service auditor stating that nothing has changed since the last type 1 or type 2 report)?

Reply—No. AT section 801 does not address such letters or reports. A service organization may choose to issue a letter that describes updates or changes in its controls since the previous type 1 or type 2 report. However, there are no provisions in AT section 801 for service auditors to report on such a letter. Service auditors and user auditors are cautioned against providing assurance on or inferring assurance from such letters, respectively.

[Issue Date: November 2011; Revised, December 2012, to reflect conforming changes necessary due to the issuance of SAS Nos. 122–126.]

.20 Format of Type 1 and Type 2 SSAE No. 16 Reports

Inquiry—Other than the addition of management's assertion and changes to the auditor's report, is the format of the SSAE No. 16 report package the same as it was under SAS No. 70, as amended (now superseded)?

Reply—Except for the addition of management's assertion, AT section 801 has the same report package as it did under SAS No. 70, as amended (now superseded). That package consists of the following components:

- Section 1: The service auditor's report, that is, the letter from the service auditor
- Section 2: Management of the service organization's written assertion
- Section 3: Management's description of the service organization's system
- Section 4: The service auditor's description of tests of the operating effectiveness of controls and results of those tests (type 2 reports only)
- Section 5: Optional other information provided by management of the service organization

[Issue Date: November 2011; Revised, December 2012, to reflect conforming changes necessary due to the issuance of SAS Nos. 122–126.]

.21 Understanding Internal Control in Audit of a Service Organization's Financial Statements When Also Reporting on Service Organization's Controls Under AT Section 801

Inquiry—If an auditor performs an SSAE No. 16 engagement for a service organization and also audits that service organization's financial statements, when auditing the service organization's financial statements, does the auditor still need to obtain a sufficient understanding of the service organization and its environment, including its internal control, sufficient to assess the risk of material misstatement and design audit procedures?

Reply—Yes. In an SSAE No. 16 engagement, the service auditor focuses on controls at the service organization that are relevant to the *user entities'* ICFR, rather than controls at the service organization that are relevant to the *service organization's* ICFR. Some of the controls included in the service organization's description of its system may be relevant to the service organization's ICFR, but because controls evaluated and tested for the purposes of an SSAE No. 16 engagement are not necessarily controls that affect the service organization's financial reporting, the auditor of the service organization's financial statements would still need to obtain an understanding of the service organization's internal control for the purpose of the audit.

[Issue Date: November 2011.]

.22 Determining Control Objectives and Controls in an SSAE No. 16 Engagement

Inquiry—Does AT section 801 define or suggest specific control objectives for service organizations that provide services that are likely to be relevant to user entities' ICFR or does the service organization define its own control objectives and controls?

Reply—AT section 801 does not define or suggest specific control objectives for service organizations that provide services that are likely to be relevant to user entities' ICFR. In an SSAE No. 16 engagement, the service auditor evaluates whether the service organization's controls were suitably designed or operating effectively by determining whether the control objectives specified by management of the service organization were achieved. AT section 801 requires that the control objectives be reasonable in the circumstances. Although most service organizations that provide similar services will have similar control objectives, in order for control objectives to be reasonable in the circumstances, they should reflect features of the particular service organization, such as the nature of the services provided, the industry in which the user entity operates, and the needs of the user entities. Accordingly, in SSAE No. 16 engagements, not all service organizations will have the same control objectives. However, certain control objectives are typical for certain types of service organizations. To assist service auditors, appendix D of the SOC 1 guide contains illustrative control objectives for various types of service organizations, including application service providers, claims processors, credit card payment processors, investment managers, payroll processors, and transfer agents. The appendix also includes illustrative general control objectives that may be applicable to any service organization.

[Issue Date: November 2011; Revised, December 2012, to reflect conforming changes necessary due to the issuance of SAS Nos. 122–126.]

.23 Reporting Under International Standard on Assurance Engagements 3402, *Assurance Reports on Controls at a Service Organization*

Inquiry—AT section 801 is based on International Standard on Assurance Engagements (ISAE) 3402, *Assurance Reports on Controls at a Service Organization*, issued by the International Auditing and Assurance Standards Board (IAASB). May a U.S. CPA perform and report on a service auditor's engagement under ISAE 3402?

Reply—Unless they also meet the international requirements, a U.S. CPA could not issue a stand-alone ISAE 3402 report. However, a U.S. CPA could issue a report indicating the examination was performed in accordance with AICPA and IAASB standards, assuming that the requirements of both standards have been met.

[Issue Date: November 2011.]

.24 Engagements Performed Under AICPA and IAASB Standards

Inquiry—Under what circumstances would a service organization request that the service auditor report under both AICPA and IAASB standards?

Reply—Engagements performed under AT section 801 and ISAE 3402 are very similar. (Exhibit B, "Comparison of Requirements of Section 801, *Reporting on Controls at a Service Organization*, With Requirements of International Standard on Assurance Engagements 3402, *Assurance Reports on Controls at a Service Organization*," of AT section 801 identifies differences between AT section 801 and ISAE 3402.) For service organizations with international operations or international clients, there may be a benefit to obtaining a report indicating that the examination was performed in accordance with AICPA and IAASB standards. An engagement that is performed in accordance with both sets of standards would not be expected to involve a substantially different examination scope or approach than an individual SSAE No. 16 engagement would.

[Issue Date: November 2011.]

.25 Applying AT Section 801 Internationally

Inquiry—If a service organization in the United States provides services to a user entity in Europe, may the practitioner perform the examination under AT section 801 or should it be performed under ISAE 3402?

Reply—The applicability of AT section 801 is not limited to user entities located in the United States. Accordingly, a user entity in Europe could be a recipient of an SSAE No. 16 report.

[Issue Date: November 2011.]

.26 Reporting on Controls at a Service Organization Relevant to Subject Matter Other Than User Entities' ICFR

Inquiry—May AT section 801 be used for reporting on a service organization's controls relevant to subject matter other than user entities' ICFR?

Reply—No. AT section 801 does not apply to examinations of controls over subject matter other than user entities' ICFR. In the past, some CPAs used SAS No. 70, as amended (now superseded) to report on controls at a service organization relevant to subject matter other than user entities' ICFR. However, SAS No. 70, as amended (now superseded) was never intended for such reporting, and neither is AT section 801. Paragraph .A2 of AT section 801 clarifies this point, and paragraph .02*a* of AT section 801 indicates that AT section 801 may be helpful to practitioners in developing and performing such engagements under AT section 101. AT section 101 provides a framework that enables practitioners to develop engagements and report on subject matter other than financial statements. For example, an entity may be required by law or regulation to maintain the privacy of the information it collects from its customers. Such information may be passed on to a service organization that performs certain tasks for the user entity. Even though certain controls over the privacy of the information are implemented by the service organization, management of the user entity is not relieved of its responsibility for effective internal control over the privacy of the information it processes for the user entity. In this situation, management of the service organization may engage a CPA to report on the effectiveness of its controls over privacy that are relevant to the user entities, and it may provide that report to the user entities and other specified parties identified in the report. Such an examination would be performed under AT section 101, not AT section 801. The increasing use of *cloud computing* companies (that provide user entities with on-demand network access to a shared pool of computing resources, such as networks, servers, storage, applications, and services) has created an increasing demand for CPAs to report on a cloud computing service organization's controls relevant to subject matter other than user entities' ICFR.

[Issue Date: November 2011; Revised, December 2012, to reflect conforming changes necessary due to the issuance of SAS Nos. 122–126.]

Q&A Section 9530
Service Organization Controls Reports

.01 Reporting on Controls at a Service Organization Relevant to Subject Matter Other Than User Entities' Internal Control Over Financial Reporting

Inquiry—Is authoritative guidance available for reporting under AT section 101, *Attest Engagements* (AICPA, *Professional Standards*), on a service organization's controls relevant to subject matter other than user entities' internal control over financial reporting (ICFR)?

Reply—Yes. The AICPA Guide *Reporting on Controls at a Service Organization Relevant to Security, Availability, Processing Integrity, Confidentiality, or Privacy (SOC 2)* (SOC 2 guide) is designed to assist practitioners in reporting under AT section 101 on an examination of controls at a service organization relevant to the security, availability, or processing integrity of a system or the confidentiality, or privacy of the information processed by the system.

[Issue Date: November 2011.]

.02 Service Organization Controls Reports

Inquiry—What does the acronym "SOC" stand for?

Reply—The acronym SOC stands for service organization controls, as in "service organization controls reports." The AICPA introduced this term to make practitioners aware of the various professional standards and guides available to them for examining and reporting on controls at a service organization relevant to user entities and to help practitioners select the appropriate standard or guide for a particular engagement. The following are the designations for the three engagements included in the SOC report series and the source of the guidance for performing and reporting on them:

- SOC 1: Statement on Standards for Attestation Engagements (SSAE) No. 16, *Reporting on Controls at a Service Organization* (AICPA, *Professional Standards*, AT sec. 801), and AICPA Guide *Service Organizations: Applying SSAE No. 16*, Reporting on Controls at a Service Organization *(SOC 1)*
- SOC 2: AICPA Guide *Reporting on Controls at a Service Organization Relevant to Security, Availability, Processing Integrity, Confidentiality, or Privacy (SOC 2)* and AT section 101
- SOC 3: TSP section 100, *Trust Services Principles, Criteria, and Illustrations for Security, Availability, Processing Integrity, Confidentiality, and Privacy* (AICPA, *Trust Services Principles and Criteria*), and AT section 101

[Issue Date: November 2011.]

.03 Authority of SOC 1 and SOC 2 Guides

Inquiry—What is the authority of the SOC 1 and SOC 2 guides?

Reply—The SOC 1 and SOC 2 guides have been cleared by the AICPA's Auditing Standards Board. AT section 50, *SSAE Hierarchy* (AICPA, *Professional Standards*), classifies attestation guidance included in an AICPA guide as an interpretive publication and indicates that a practitioner should be aware of and consider interpretive publications applicable to his or her examination. If a practitioner does not apply the attestation guidance included in an applicable interpretive publication, the practitioner should be prepared to explain how he or she complied with the SSAE provisions addressed by such attestation guidance.

[Issue Date: November 2011.]

.04 SOC 3 Engagements

Inquiry—What is a SOC 3 engagement?

Reply—A SOC 3 engagement is similar to a SOC 2 engagement in that the practitioner reports on whether an entity (any entity, not necessarily a service organization) has maintained effective controls over its system with respect to security, availability, processing integrity, confidentiality, or privacy. Like a SOC 2 engagement, a SOC 3 engagement uses the criteria in TSP section 100. Unlike a SOC 2 engagement, a SOC 3 report (1) does not contain a description of the practitioner's tests of controls and results of those tests and (2) is a general-use report rather than a restricted use report. (The term *general use* refers to reports for which use is not restricted to specified parties.)

[Issue Date: November 2011.]

.05 Types of Reports for SOC 2 Engagements

Inquiry—Are there type 1 and type 2 reports for SOC 2 engagements?

Reply—Yes. In a SOC 2 engagement, like a SOC 1 engagement, the practitioner has the option of providing either a *type 1* or a *type 2 report*. In both reports, management of the service organization prepares a description of its system. In a type 1 report, the service auditor expresses an opinion on whether the description is fairly presented (that is, does it describe what actually exists) and whether the controls included in the description are suitability designed. Controls that are suitably designed *are able* to achieve the related control objectives or criteria if they operate effectively. In a type 2 report, the service auditor's report contains the same opinions that are included in a type 1 report, and also includes an opinion on whether the controls were operating effectively. Controls that operate effectively *do* achieve the control objectives or criteria they were intended to achieve. Both SOC 1 and SOC 2 reports are examination reports, which means the practitioner obtains a high level of assurance.

[Issue Date: November 2011.]

.06 Minimum Period of Coverage for SOC 2 Reports

Inquiry—Does the SOC 2 guide require that a type 2 report cover a minimum period?

Reply—The SOC 2 guide does not prescribe a minimum period of coverage for a SOC 2 report, however, paragraph 2.09 of the SOC 2 guide states that one of the relevant factors to consider when determining whether to accept or continue a SOC 2 engagement is the period covered by the report. The guide presents an example of a service organization that wishes to engage a service auditor to perform a type 2 engagement for a period of less than two months. The guide states that in those circumstances, the service auditor should consider whether a report covering that period will be useful to users of the report, particularly if many of the controls related to the applicable trust services criteria are performed on a monthly or quarterly basis. A practitioner would use professional judgment in determining whether the report covers a sufficient period.

[Issue Date: November 2011.]

.07 Placement of Management's Assertion in a SOC 2 Report

Inquiry—In a SOC 2 engagement, does management's assertion need to accompany the service organization's description of its system?

Reply—Paragraph 2.13*b* of the SOC 2 guide states, in part, that a service auditor ordinarily should accept or continue an engagement to report on controls at a service organization only if management of the service organization acknowledges and accepts responsibility for "providing a written assertion that will be attached to management's description of the service organization's system and provided to users." The recommendation in the SOC 2 guide is that the assertion be attached to the description rather than included in the description to avoid the impression that the practitioner is reporting on the assertion rather than on the subject matter.

[Issue Date: November 2011.]

.08 Illustrative Assertion for Management of a Service Organization in a SOC 2 Engagement

Inquiry—Where can I find an illustrative management assertion for a SOC 2 engagement?

Reply—Appendix C, "Illustrative Management Assertions and Related Service Auditor's Reports on Controls at a Service Organization Relevant to Security, Availability, Processing Integrity, Confidentiality, and Privacy," and appendix D, "Illustrative Type 2 Service Organization Controls Report," of the SOC 2 guide contain illustrative assertions by management of a service organization for type 2 SOC 2 engagements.

[Issue Date: November 2011.]

.09 Illustrative Assertion for Management of a Subservice Organization in a SOC 2 Engagement

Inquiry—The SOC 2 guide contains illustrative management assertions for management of a service organization. Is an illustrative assertion for management of a subservice organization available in the SOC 2 guide?

Reply—No. However, the illustrative assertions in appendix C or appendix D of the SOC 2 guide can be used to construct the subservice organization's assertion. Paragraphs 2.13–.15 of the SOC 2 guide address the requirement for an assertion by management of a subservice organization when the inclusive method is used.

[Issue Date: November 2011.]

.10 Management of a Subservice Organization Refuses to Provide a Written Assertion in a SOC 1 or SOC 2 Engagement

Inquiry—When using the inclusive method, if management of a subservice organization will not provide a written assertion, what should the service auditor do?

Reply—Paragraph .A8 of AT section 801 indicates that the subservice organization's refusal to provide the service auditor with a written assertion precludes the service auditor from using the inclusive method. However, the service auditor may instead use the carve-out method. Paragraph 2.15 of the SOC 2 guide contains similar guidance for SOC 2 engagements.

[Issue Date: November 2011.]

.11 Determining Whether Management of a Service Organization Has a Reasonable Basis for Its Assertion (SOC 1 and SOC 2 Engagements)

Inquiry—Paragraph .09*c*(ii) of AT section 801 states that one of the requirements for a service auditor to accept or continue a type 1 or type 2 engagement is that management acknowledge and accept responsibility for having a reasonable basis for its assertion. Paragraph .A17 of AT section 801 indicates that the service auditor's report on controls is not a substitute for the service organization's own processes to provide a reasonable basis for its assertion. How does the service auditor determine whether management has a reasonable basis for its assertion?

Reply—AT section 801 indirectly describes how the service auditor makes this determination. First, paragraph .14*a*(vii) of AT section 801 indicates, in part, that the service organization's description of its system should include the service organization's monitoring activities. Because a service auditor is required to determine whether the description is fairly stated, in doing so the service auditor would determine whether the section of the description that describes monitoring controls is fairly stated. Second, paragraph .A17 of AT section 801, shown subsequently, defines the term *monitoring of controls* and indicates that management's monitoring activities may provide evidence of the design and operating effectiveness of controls in support of management's assertion. Similar guidance for SOC 2 engagements is included in appendix A, "Information for Management of a Subservice Organization," of the SOC 2 guide, in the section titled "Providing a Written Assertion."

[Issue Date: November 2011.]

.12 Reasonable Basis for Management of a Subservice Organization's Assertion (SOC 1 and SOC 2 Engagements)

Inquiry—In an inclusive SOC 1 engagement, is the service auditor required to determine whether management of the subservice organization has a reasonable basis for its assertion?

Reply—Paragraph .09*c*(ii) of AT section 801 states that one of the requirements for a service auditor to accept or continue a type 1 or type 2 engagement is that management acknowledge and accept responsibility for having a reasonable basis for its assertion. Paragraph .A7 of AT section 801 states that when the inclusive method is used, the requirements of AT section 801 also apply to the services provided by the subservice organization, including the requirement to acknowledge and accept responsibility for the matters in paragraph .09*c*(i)–(vii) of AT section 801 as they relate to the subservice organization. Paragraph .09*c*(vii) requires a service organization to provide a written assertion; therefore, a subservice organization would also be required to provide a written assertion and have a reasonable basis for its assertion.

In determining whether a subservice organization has a reasonable basis for its assertion, the service auditor would analogize the requirements and guidance in AT section 801 to the subservice organization. Paragraph .14*a*(vii) of AT section 801 would require that the subservice organization's description of its system include the subservice organization's monitoring activities. Because a service auditor is required to determine whether the subservice organization's description is fairly stated, in doing so the service auditor would determine whether the section of the description that describes monitoring controls is fairly stated. Paragraph .A17 of AT section 801 defines the term *monitoring of controls* and indicates that management's monitoring activities may provide evidence of the design and operating effectiveness of controls in support of management's assertion. Similar guidance on this topic for a SOC 2 engagement is included in paragraphs 2.13*b*–*c* and 2.15 of the SOC 2 guide.

[Issue Date: November 2011.]

.13 Point in a SOC 1 or SOC 2 Engagement When Management Should Provide Its Written Assertion

Inquiry—At what point in a SOC 1 or SOC 2 engagement should management provide the service auditor with its written assertion?

Reply—Management may provide its written assertion to the service auditor at any time after the end of the period covered by the service auditor's type 2 report and, for a type 1 report, at any time after the as of date of the type 1 report. The date of the service auditor's report should be no earlier than the date on which management provides its written assertion.

[Issue Date: November 2011.]

.14 Implementing Controls Included in Management's Description of the Service Organization's System (SOC 1 and SOC 2 Engagements)

Inquiry—In a type 1 report for a SOC 1 or SOC 2 engagement, do the controls included in management's description of the service organization's system need to be implemented?

Reply—Yes. In order for the description of the service organization's system to be fairly presented, the controls included in the description would have to be placed in operation (implemented). See paragraph 4.01*b* of the SOC 1 guide and paragraph 3.13 of the SOC 2 guide.

[Issue Date: November 2011.]

.15 Responsibility for Determining Whether a SOC 1, SOC 2, or SOC 3 Engagement Should Be Performed

Inquiry—Who determines whether a SOC 1, SOC 2, or SOC 3 engagement should be performed—the service auditor or management of the service organization?

Reply—SOC 1 engagements address a service organization's controls relevant to user entities' ICFR, whereas SOC 2 and SOC 3 engagements address a service organization's controls relevant to the security, availability, or processing integrity of a system or the confidentiality or privacy of the information the system processes. In SOC 2 and SOC 3 engagements, the service auditor uses the criteria in TSP section 100 for evaluating and reporting on controls relevant to the security, availability, or processing integrity of a system, or the confidentiality or privacy of the information processed by the system. In TSP section 100, these five attributes of a system are known as *principles.* A service auditor may be engaged to report on a description of a service organization's system and the suitability of the design and operating effectiveness of controls relevant to one or more of the trust services principles The criteria in TSP section 100 that are applicable to the principle(s) being reported on are known as the *applicable trust services criteria*.

If management of the service organization is not knowledgeable about the differences among these three engagements, the service auditor may assist management in obtaining that understanding and selecting the appropriate engagement. Determining which engagement is appropriate depends on the subject matter addressed by the controls and the risk management and governance needs of the user entities, and it often involves discussion with the user entities regarding their needs.

[Issue Date: November 2011.]

.16 Criteria for SOC 2 and SOC 3 Engagements

Inquiry—Are there a prescribed set of control objectives for SOC 2 and SOC 3 engagements?

Reply—In SOC 1 engagements, the service auditor determines whether controls achieve specified control objectives. In SOC 2 and SOC 3 engagements, the service auditor determines whether controls meet the applicable trust services criteria. Although the terminology is different in these engagements (control objectives versus criteria), the control objectives in a SOC 1 engagement serve as criteria for evaluating the design and, in a type 2 report, the operating effectiveness of controls. Unlike SOC 1 engagements, in which management of the service organization determines the service organization's control objectives based on the nature of the service provided and how the service is performed, in all SOC 2 and SOC 3 engagements, the service organization's controls must meet all of the criteria in TSP section 100 that are applicable to the principle(s) being reported on. The applicable trust services criteria serve as a prescribed set of criteria.

[Issue Date: November 2011.]

.17 Using Existing Set of Controls for a New SOC 2 or SOC 3 Engagement

Inquiry—In the past, many IT service organizations provided their user entities with reports issued under Statement on Auditing Standards (SAS) No. 70, *Service Organizations*, as amended (now superseded), covering their IT services. If a service organization plans to undergo a SOC 2 or SOC 3 examination for the first time and has a fully defined set of controls and control objectives related to its IT services, does the service organization need to adopt a new set of controls to meet the applicable trust services criteria?

Reply—The SOC 2 guide and appendix C of TSP section 100 require the service organization to establish controls that meet all of the applicable trust services criteria. A service organization that is planning to undergo a SOC 2 or SOC 3 engagement for the first time may have controls in place that address all of the applicable trust services criteria. However, the service organization will need to determine whether its existing control objectives align with the applicable trust services criteria and whether its controls address all of the applicable trust services criteria. If not, it will need to implement or revise certain controls to meet all of the applicable trust services criteria.

[Issue Date: November 2011; Revised, December 2012, to reflect conforming changes necessary due to the issuance of SAS Nos. 122–126.]

.18 Reporting on Compliance With Other Standards or Requirements in SOC 2 or SOC 3 Engagements

Inquiry—May a SOC 2 or SOC 3 report cover compliance with other standards or authoritative requirements that are substantially similar to the applicable trust services criteria, for example, requirements in Special Publication 800-53, *Recommended Security Controls for Federal Information Systems*, issued by the National Institute of Standards and Technology or in Payment Card Industry (PCI) Security Standards issued by the PCI Security Counsel?

Reply—Yes. A service organization may request that a SOC 2 or SOC 3 report address additional subject matter that is not specifically covered by the applicable trust services criteria. An example of such subject matter is the service organization's compliance with certain criteria established by a regulator, for example, security requirements under the Health Insurance Portability and Accountability Act of 1996 or compliance with performance criteria established in a service-level agreement. Paragraph 1.39 of the SOC 2 guide states that in order for a service auditor to report on such additional subject matter, the service organization provides the following:

- An appropriate supplemental description of the subject matter
- A description of the criteria used to measure and present the subject matter
- If the criteria are related to controls, a description of the controls intended to meet the control-related criteria
- An assertion by management regarding the additional subject matter

Paragraph 1.40 of the guide states

> The service auditor should perform appropriate procedures related to the additional subject matter, in accordance with AT section 101 and the relevant guidance in this guide. The service auditor's description of the scope of the work and related opinion on the subject matter should be presented in separate paragraphs of the service auditor's report. In addition, based on the agreement with the service organization, the service auditor may include additional tests performed and detailed results of those tests in a separate attachment to the report.

[Issue Date: November 2011.]

.19 Issuing Separate Reports When Performing Both a SOC 1 and SOC 2 Engagement for a Service Organization

Inquiry—Does a service organization that wishes to have a practitioner report on controls relevant to user entities' ICFR along with controls that are not relevant to user entities' ICFR need to request two separate reports—SOC 1 and SOC 2?

Reply—Yes. Service organizations need to request two separate SOC reports if the service organization would like to address controls relevant to user entities' ICFR and controls that are not relevant to user entities' ICFR. See paragraph 1.24 of the SOC 2 guide.

[Issue Date: November 2011.]

.20 Deviations in the Subject Matter (SOC 1 and SOC 2 Engagements)

Inquiry—In a SOC 1 or SOC 2 engagement, if the service auditor identifies deviations in the subject matter (that is, the fairness of the presentation of the description, the suitability of the design of the controls, and the operating effectiveness of the controls) and qualifies the report because of these deviations, does management need to revise its assertion to reflect these deviations?

Reply—If management of the service organization agrees with the service auditor's findings regarding the deviations, management would be expected to revise its assertion to reflect the deviations identified in the service auditor's report. If management does not revise its assertion, the service auditor should add an explanatory paragraph to the report indicating that the deficiencies identified in the service auditor's report have not been identified in management's assertion. Similar guidance for a SOC 2 engagement is included in paragraph 3.105 of the SOC 2 guide.

[Issue Date: November 2011.]

.21 Use of a Seal on a Service Organization's Website

Inquiry—Is there a SOC seal that can be displayed on a service organization's website indicating that the service organization has undergone a SOC 1, SOC 2, or SOC 3 engagement?

Reply—A seal is available only for SOC 3 engagements. A SOC 3 SysTrust for Service Organization Seal (seal) may be issued and displayed on a service organization's website. All practitioners who wish to provide this registered seal must obtain a license to provide the seal from by the Canadian Institute of Chartered Accountants (CICA). Typically the seal is linked to the report issued by the practitioner. For more information on licensure, go to www.webtrust.org. It is important to note that a practitioner can perform a SOC 3 engagement and issue a SOC 3 report without issuing a SOC 3 seal. In such cases the practitioner does not need to be licensed by the CICA. The license is only for the issuance of a seal.

In addition, SOC logos are available for use by (*a*) CPAs for marketing and promoting SOC services and (*b*) service organizations that have undergone a SOC 1, SOC 2, or SOC 3 engagement within the prior 12 months. These logos are designed to make the public aware of these SOC services and do not offer or represent assurance that an organization obtained an unqualified (or clean) opinion. For additional information about logos, go to www.aicpa.org/interestareas/frc/assuranceadvisoryservices/pages/soclogosinfo.aspx.

[Issue Date: November 2011.]

.22 Attestation Standards and Interpretive Guidance for Reporting on a Service Organization's Controls Relevant to User Entities and for Reporting on an Entity's Internal Control

Inquiry—AICPA professional literature includes a variety of attestation standards and interpretive guidance for reporting on a service organization's controls relevant to user entities and for reporting on an entity's internal control. How does a practitioner determine the applicable attestation standard and interpretive guidance for these engagements?

Reply—The following table identifies a variety of attestation engagements that involve reporting on a service organization's controls relevant to user entities, or reporting on an entity's internal control. The table also identifies the appropriate attestation standard or interpretive guidance to be used in the circumstances.

Engagement	*Professional Standard or Other Guidance*	*Restrictions on the Use of the Report*
***Reporting on Controls at a Service Organization Relevant to User Entities' Internal Control Over Financial Reporting:* Controls were not designed by the service organization; management of the service organization will not provide an assertion regarding the suitability of the design of the controls, and the practitioner is reporting on**		
• the fairness of the presentation of management's description of the service organization's system and	Report on the fairness of the presentation of the description under AT section 101, *Attest Engagements* (AICPA, *Professional Standards*), using the description criteria in paragraph .14 of AT section 801, *Reporting on Controls at a Service Organization* (AICPA, *Professional Standards*), and adapting the relevant requirements and guidance therein	Management of the service organization, user entities, and the auditors of the user entities' financial statements

(continued)

Engagement	***Professional Standard or Other Guidance***	***Restrictions on the Use of the Report***
• the operating effectiveness of the service organization's controls relevant to user entities internal control over financial reporting. Such a report may include a description of tests of the operating effectiveness of the controls and the results of the tests.	Report on the operating effectiveness of controls under AT section 101 or AT section 201, *Agreed-Upon Procedures Engagements* (AICPA, *Professional Standards*)	The specified parties that agreed upon the sufficiency of the procedures for their purposes
***Reporting on Controls at a Service Organization Relevant to User Entities' Internal Control Over Financial Reporting:* Controls were not designed by the service organization; management of the service organization provides an assertion regarding the suitability of design of controls**	AT section 801	Management of the service organization, user entities, and the auditors of the user entities' financial statements
***Reporting on Controls at a Service Organization Relevant to Security Availability, Processing Integrity, Confidentiality, or Privacy*: Includes Description of Tests and Results**		

Engagement	***Professional Standard or Other Guidance***	***Restrictions on the Use of the Report***
Reporting on the fairness of the presentation of management's description of a service organization's system; the suitability of the design of controls at a service organization relevant to security, availability, processing integrity, confidentiality, or privacy; and in a type 2 report, the operating effectiveness of those controls A type 2 report includes a description of tests of the operating effectiveness of controls performed by the service auditor and the results of those tests.	AT section 101 AICPA Guide *Reporting on Controls at a Service Organization Relevant to Security, Availability, Processing Integrity, Confidentiality, or Privacy (SOC 2)*	Parties that are knowledgeable about • the nature of the service provided by the service organization • how the service organization's system interacts with user entities, subservice organizations, and other parties • internal control and its limitations • the criteria and how controls address those criteria • complementary user entity controls and how they interact with related controls at the service organization
***Reporting on Controls at a Service Organization Relevant to Security Availability, Processing Integrity, Confidentiality, or Privacy:* No Description of Tests and Results**		

(continued)

Engagement	*Professional Standard or Other Guidance*	*Restrictions on the Use of the Report*
Reporting on whether an entity has maintained effective controls over its system with respect to security, availability, processing integrity, confidentiality, or privacy If the report addresses the privacy principle, the report also contains an opinion on the service organization's compliance with the commitments in its privacy notice. This report does not contain a description of the service auditor's tests performed and the results of those tests.	AT section 101 AICPA/Canadian Institute of Chartered Accountants Trust Services Principles, Criteria, and Illustrations (TSP section 100, *Trust Services Principles, Criteria, and Illustrations for Security, Availability, Processing Integrity, Confidentiality, and Privacy* [AICPA, *Trust Services Principles and Criteria*])	This is a general-use report.[1]
Reporting on a Service Provider's Controls to Achieve Compliance Control Objectives Relevant to SEC Rules 38a-1 and 206(4)-7		
Reporting on the suitability of the design and operating effectiveness of a service provider's controls over compliance that may affect user entities' compliance This report does not contain a description of the practitioner's tests performed and the results of those tests.	AT section 101 Statement of Position (SOP) 07-2, *Attestation Engagements That Address Specified Compliance Control Objectives and Related Controls at Entities that Provide Services to Investment Companies, Investment Advisers, or Other Service Providers* (AICPA, *Professional Standards*, AUD sec. 40)	Chief compliance officers, management, boards of directors, and independent auditors of the service provider and of the entities that use the services of the service provider

[1] The term *general use* refers to reports for which use is not restricted to specified parties.

Engagement	Professional Standard or Other Guidance	Restrictions on the Use of the Report
Performing the Agreed-Upon Procedures Referred to in Paragraph .03 of AT section 801		
Performing and reporting on the results of agreed-upon procedures related to the controls of a service organization or to transactions or balances of a user entity maintained by a service organization This report contains a description of the procedures performed by the practitioner and the results of those procedures.	AT section 201	The specified parties that agreed upon the sufficiency of the procedures for their purposes
Reporting on Controls Over Compliance With Laws and Regulations		
Reporting on the effectiveness of an entity's internal control over compliance with the requirements of specified laws, regulations, rules, contracts, or grants	AT section 601, *Compliance Attestation* (AICPA, *Professional Standards*)	Use is restricted if the criteria are • appropriate for only a limited number of parties who established the criteria or can be presumed to understand the criteria. • available only to specified parties.
Reporting on Internal Control in an Integrated Audit		

(continued)

Engagement	***Professional Standard or Other Guidance***	***Restrictions on the Use of the Report***
Reporting on the design and operating effectiveness of an entity's internal control over financial reporting that is integrated with an audit of financial statements	AU-C section 940, *An Audit of Internal Control Over Financial Reporting That Is Integrated With an Audit of Financial Statements* (AICPA, *Professional Standards*)	This is a general-use report.

[Issue Date: November 2011; Revised, December 2016, to reflect conforming changes necessary to reflect the issuance of SAS No. 130.]

Q&A Section 9540

Attest Engagement: American Land Title Association Best Practices Framework

.01 Types of Engagements

Inquiry—The American Land Title Association (ALTA) seeks to guide its membership on best practices to protect consumers, promote quality service, provide for ongoing employee training, and meet legal and market requirements. These policies, procedures, controls, and practices (collectively referred to as *practices* for purposes of this section) are voluntary and designed to help members illustrate to consumers and clients the industry professionalism and best practices to help ensure a positive and compliant real estate settlement practice. These practices are not intended to encompass all aspects of title or settlement company activity.

The ALTA Best Practices Framework[1] (the framework) has been developed to assist lenders in satisfying their responsibility to manage third party vendors. The framework comprises the following documents a company needs when electing to implement such a program:

- *Title Insurance and Settlement Company Best Practices*
- *Assessment Procedures*
- *Certification Package*, which includes the following three parts:
  - "Agency Letter" (part 1)
  - "Best Practices Certificate" (part 2)
  - "Declarations Page" (part 3)

What types of engagements may a practitioner perform for a title insurance and settlement company (the company) in order to assist management and third parties about whether the company has implemented the framework?

Reply—A practitioner may perform an engagement that the company would consider best suited to its circumstances. Such engagements may include attestation engagements (such as an examination, review, or an agreed-upon procedures engagement) or an engagement under CS section 100, *Consulting Services: Definitions and Standards* (AICPA, *Professional Standards*).

[Issue Date: April 2015.]

.02 Applicability to an Attest Engagement

Inquiry—The company may request its independent public accountant (practitioner) to examine or review its title insurance and settlement practices for the purpose of expressing an opinion or a conclusion about whether those practices comply with the framework's best practices as of a point in time or for a period of time. Would such an engagement be an attest engagement under AT section 101, *Attest Engagements* (AICPA, *Professional Standards*)?

Reply—Yes. AT section 101 states that the attestation standards apply when a CPA in public practice is engaged to issue or does issue an examination,

[1] Information regarding the American Land Title Association (ALTA) Best Practices Framework is available at ALTA's website at www.alta.org/bestpractices/index.cfm.

a review, or an agreed-upon procedures report on subject matter, or an assertion about the subject matter that is the responsibility of another party. When a practitioner is engaged by a company to provide an examination or a review report on the company's practices, such an engagement involves subject matter that is the responsibility of the company. Consequently, AT section 101 applies to such engagements.

[Issue Date: April 2015.]

.03 Suitability of Criteria

Inquiry—Paragraph .23 of AT section 101 specifies that "the practitioner must have reason to believe that the subject matter is capable of evaluation against criteria that are suitable and available to users." What are the criteria against which such subject matter is to be evaluated and are such criteria suitable and available?

Reply—The criteria for evaluating whether the company's practices have been implemented to comply with the framework's best practices are set forth in the framework. The suitability of those criteria should be evaluated by assessing whether the criteria meet the characteristics discussed in paragraph .24 of AT section 101. AICPA staff believe that the criteria set forth in the framework will, when properly followed, be suitable and, because the framework is available on ATLA's website, the criteria are generally available.

[Issue Date: April 2015.]

.04 Nature of Examination or Review Procedures

Inquiry—What is the nature of the examination or review procedures that should be applied to the company's best practices?

Reply—The objective of the procedures performed in either an examination or a review engagement is to accumulate evidence, sufficient in the circumstances, about whether the company has implemented practices in a manner that supports the company's assessment recap provided in the framework questionnaire, *Assessment Procedures*, and to provide an opinion or a conclusion based on that evidence. The objective does not include providing assurance about whether the company's best practices operated effectively to ensure compliance with federal and state consumer financial laws. In an examination, the evidence should be sufficient to limit attestation risk to a level that is appropriately low for the high degree of assurance imparted by an examination report. In a review, this evidence should be sufficient to limit attestation risk to a moderate level.

Examination procedures include obtaining evidence by reading relevant policies and programs, making inquiries of appropriate company personnel, inspecting documents and records, confirming company assertions with its employees or others, and observing activities. In an examination, it will be necessary for a practitioner's procedures to go beyond simply reading relevant policies and programs and making inquiries of appropriate company personnel. Alternatively, review procedures are generally limited to reading relevant policies and procedures, and making inquiries of appropriate company personnel. When applying examination or review procedures, the practitioner should assess the appropriateness (including the comprehensiveness) of the company's practices supporting the company's assessment recap.

A particular company's practices may vary from those of other companies. As a result, the sufficiency of evidence obtained from the practitioner's procedures performed cannot be evaluated solely on a quantitative basis.

Consequently, it is not practicable to establish only quantitative guidelines for determining the nature or extent of the evidence that is necessary to obtain the assurance required in either an examination or a review. The qualitative aspects should also be considered.

In determining the nature, timing, and extent of examination or review procedures, the practitioner should consider information obtained in the performance of other services for the company, for example, the audit of the company's financial statements. For multi-location companies, whether practices were designed and placed in operation as of the assessment date should be evaluated for both the company's headquarters and selected locations. The practitioner may consider using the work of the company's internal auditors. AU-C section 610, *Using the Work of Internal Auditors* (AICPA, *Professional Standards*), may be useful in that consideration.

Examination procedures and (in some instances) review procedures may require access to information involving specific instances of actual or alleged noncompliance with laws. An inability to obtain access to such information because of restrictions imposed by a company (for example, to protect attorney-client privilege) may constitute a scope limitation. Paragraphs .73–.75 of AT section 101 provide guidance in such situations. The practitioner should assess the effect of the inability to obtain access to such information on the practitioner's ability to form a conclusion about whether the related policies and programs operated during the period. If the company's reasons for not permitting access to the information are reasonable (for example, the information is the subject of litigation or a governmental investigation) and have been approved by an executive officer of the company, the occurrences of restricted access to information are few in number, and the practitioner has access to other information about that specific instance or about other instances that is sufficient to permit a conclusion to be formed about whether the related best practice operated during the period, the practitioner ordinarily would conclude that it is not necessary to disclaim assurance.

If the practitioner's scope of work has been restricted with respect to one or more matters, the practitioner should consider the implications of that restriction on the practitioner's ability to form a conclusion about other matters. In addition, as the nature or number of matters on which the company has imposed scope limitations increases in significance, the practitioner should consider whether to withdraw from the engagement.

[Issue Date: April 2015.]

.05 Form and Content of Report

Inquiry—What is the form of report that should be issued to meet the requirements of AT section 101?

Reply—The standards of reporting in AT section 101 provide guidance about report content and wording, and the circumstances that may require report modification. Example 1, "Illustrative ALTA Best Practices Program Assertions and Examination Reports," and example 2, "Illustrative Review Report Review Report," of this section are illustrative reports appropriate for various circumstances. Paragraph .66 of AT section 101 permits the practitioner to report directly on the subject matter or on management's assertion. In either case, the practitioner should ordinarily obtain a written assertion. An illustrative company assertion is also presented in examples 1 and 2.

The engagements addressed in this section do not include providing assurance about whether the company's procedures operated effectively to ensure compliance with federal and state consumer financial laws or to evaluate the extent to which the company or its employees have complied with federal or state laws. The practitioner's report should explicitly disclaim an opinion on the extent of such compliance.

When scope limitations have precluded the practitioner from forming an opinion, the practitioner's report should describe all such scope restrictions. If the company imposed such a scope limitation after the practitioner had begun performing procedures, that fact should be stated in the report.

A company may request the practitioner to communicate to management or the board of directors or one of its committees, either orally or in writing, matters noted that do not constitute significant findings about the company's best practices. Agreed-upon arrangements between the practitioner and the company to communicate findings noted may include, for example, the reporting of findings of less significance than those contemplated by the criteria, the existence of findings specified by the company, the results of further investigation of findings noted to identify underlying causes, or suggestions for improvements in various best practices. Under these arrangements, the practitioner may be requested to visit specific locations, assess the effectiveness of specific policies or programs, or undertake specific procedures not otherwise planned. In addition, the practitioner is not precluded from communicating findings believed to be of value, even if no specific request has been made.

Example 1—Illustrative ALTA Best Practices Program Assertions and Examination Reports

Illustration 1—Unqualified Opinion; General-Use Report; Criteria Attached to the Presentation

Company Assertion

The responses in the accompanying *Assessment Procedures* portion of the American Land Title Association (ALTA) Best Practices Framework are based on company practices as of [*date, for example July 15, 20XX*]. Based on the results of our assessment procedures as set forth in the *Assessment Procedures* and our responses indicated in the "Assessment Recap" column, we believe our title insurance and settlement practices as of [*date, for example July 15, 20XX*], comply, in all material respects, with ALTA best practices based on the ALTA criteria.

Examination Report

<u>Independent Accountant's Report</u>

To the Board of Directors of the XYZ Company

We have examined XYZ Company's (Company) title insurance and settlement practices and the Company's responses in the accompanying *Assessment Procedures* document from American Land Title Association (ALTA) Best Practices Framework as of July 15, 20XX. XYZ Company's management is responsible for its practices and for its responses to its assessment procedures. Our responsibility is to express an opinion based on our examination.

Our examination was conducted in accordance with attestation standards established by the American Institute of Certified Public Accountants and, accordingly, included examining, on a test basis, evidence as to whether the Company's practices support the responses indicated in the Assessment Recap column of the *Assessment Procedures* and performing such other procedures as we considered necessary in the circumstances. We believe that our examination provides a reasonable basis for our opinion. Our examination procedures were not designed, however, to evaluate whether the aforementioned practices operated effectively to ensure compliance with the Federal and State Consumer Financial Laws or to evaluate the extent to which the Company or its employees have complied with federal or state laws, and we do not express an opinion or any other form of assurance thereon.

In our opinion, the Company's title insurance and settlement practices, as of July 15, 20XX, comply, in all material respects, with the ALTA best practices based on the ALTA criteria.

Illustration 2—Unqualified Opinion; General-Use Report, Management's Assertion

Examination Report

Independent Accountant's Report

To the Board of Directors of the XYZ Company

We have examined management's assertion that XYZ Company's (Company) title insurance and settlement practices, as of July 15, 20XX, comply, in all material respects, with the American Land Title Association (ALTA) best practices. XYZ Company's management is responsible for its practices and for its responses to its assessment procedures. Our responsibility is to express an opinion based on our examination.

Our examination was conducted in accordance with attestation standards established by the American Institute of Certified Public Accountants and, accordingly, included examining, on a test basis, evidence as to whether the Company's practices support the responses indicated in the "Assessment Recap" column of the *Assessment Procedures* and performing such other procedures as we considered necessary in the circumstances. We believe that our examination provides a reasonable basis for our opinion. Our examination procedures were not designed, however, to evaluate whether the aforementioned practices operated effectively to ensure compliance with federal and state consumer financial laws or to evaluate the extent to which the Company or its employees have complied with federal or state laws, and we do not express an opinion or any other form of assurance thereon.

In our opinion, management's assertion referred to above is fairly stated, in all material respects, based on the ALTA criteria.

Example 2—Illustrative Review Report

Company Assertion

The responses in the accompanying *Assessment Procedures* portion of American Land Title Association (ALTA) Best Practices Framework are based on Company practices as of [*date, for example July 15, 20XX*]. Based on the results of our assessment procedures as set forth in the *Assessment Procedures* and our responses indicated in the "Assessment Recap" column, we believe our title insurance and settlement practices as of [*date, for example July 15, 20XX*], comply, in all material respects, with the ALTA Best Practices based on the ALTA criteria.

Independent Accountant's Report

To the Board of Directors of the XYZ Company

We have reviewed XYZ Company's (Company) title insurance and settlement practices and the Company's responses in the accompanying *Assessment Procedures* portion of the American Land Title Association (ALTA) Best Practices Framework as of July 15, 20XX. XYZ Company's management is responsible for its practices and for its responses to its assessment procedures.

Our review was conducted in accordance with attestation standards established by the American Institute of Certified Public Accountants. A review is substantially less in scope than an examination, the objective of which is the expression of an opinion on the Company's practices. Accordingly, we do not express such an opinion. Additionally, our review was not designed to evaluate whether the aforementioned practices operated effectively to ensure compliance with federal and state consumer financial laws or to evaluate the extent to which the Company or its employees have complied with federal or state laws and we do not express an opinion or any other form of assurance thereon.

Based on our review, nothing came to our attention that caused us to believe that the Company's title insurance and settlement practices, as of July 15, 20XX did not comply, in all material respects, with the American Land Title Association (ALTA) best practices based on the ALTA criteria.

[Issue Date: April 2015.]

Q&A TOPICAL INDEX
TECHNICAL QUESTIONS AND ANSWERS

References are to section numbers.

A

B

E

H

S